Cultural Diversity

A Primer for the Human Services

SIXTH EDITION

Jerry V. Diller

With contributions by:

Julius A. Austin, Ph.D., PLPC
University of Louisiana at Monroe

Jude T. Austin II, Ph.D., NCC, LPC-R(VA)
University of Mary Hardin-Baylor

 CENGAGE

Australia • Brazil • Canada • Mexico • Singapore • United Kingdom • United States

Cultural Diversity: A Primer for the Human Services, **Sixth edition**
Jerry V. Diller

Product Director: Marta Lee-Perriard

Product Manager: Julie Martinez

Project Manager: Julie Dierig

Content Developer: Matt Gervais, Lumina Datamatics

Product Assistant: Allison Balchunas

Digital Delivery Lead: Bonnie Yee

Marketing Manager: Zina Craft

Text Researcher: Lumina Datamatics

Senior Designer: Marissa Falco

Internal and Cover Designer: Cheryl Carrington

Cover Image: cienpies/Getty Images

For product information and technology assistance, contact us at
Cengage Customer & Sales Support, 1-800-354-9706 or **support.cengage.com.**

For permission to use material from this text or product, submit all requests online at **www.cengage.com/permissions.**

Library of Congress Control Number: 2018946250

Student Edition:
ISBN: 978-1-337-56338-3

Loose-leaf Edition:
ISBN: 978-1-337-56339-0

Cengage
200 Pier 4 Boulevard
Boston, MA 02210
USA

Cengage is a leading provider of customized learning solutions with employees residing in nearly 40 different countries and sales in more than 125 countries around the world. Find your local representative at **www.cengage.com.**

To learn more about Cengage platforms and services, register or access your online learning solution, or purchase materials for your course, visit **www.cengage.com.**

Printed at CLDPC, USA, 10-23

Contents

Preface   **xi**

CHAPTER 1
Introduction   **1**

CHAPTER 2
What It Means to Be Culturally Competent   **11**
Demographics   12
   Reactions to Changing Demographics   12
Why Become Culturally Competent?   13
   The Fear and Pain Associated with Moving Toward
     Cultural Competence   14
   Speaking Personally About Cultural Competence   17
   A Model of Cultural Competence   18
   Assessing Agency Cultural Competence   19
Individual Cultural Competence Skill Areas   21
Defining Professional Standards   25
   Training Programs and Ethical Standards   29
   Enforcing Professional Standards   30
Summary   34
Activities   35

CHAPTER 3
Working with Culturally Diverse Clients   **37**
How Is Cross-Cultural Helping Different?   38
   Conceptualizing Cross-Cultural Work   39
   Understanding Differences   41
Understanding Power   41
   Understanding Therapeutic Presence   42
Hays's Addressing Framework   43
   Preparing for Cross-Cultural Work   44
   Assessing Culturally Diverse Clients   46
Making Culturally Sensitive DSM-5 Diagnoses   49
   Establishing Rapport and the First Session   49
Talking About Race and Ethnicity with Clients   53

Summary 55
Activities 56

CHAPTER 4
Understanding Racism, Prejudice, and White Privilege 58
Defining and Contextualizing Racism 59
  Individual Racism and Prejudice 61
  Traits and Tendencies Supporting Racism and Prejudice 61
Modern Prejudice 62
  Microaggressions and Implicit Bias 64
  Implications for Providers 65
Institutional Racism 66
  Determining Institutional Racism 67
  Consciousness, Intent, and Denial 68
  Implications for Providers 75
  Cultural Racism 76
  Implications for Providers 77
Racial Consciousness Among Whites
  and White Privilege 78
White Racial Attitude Types 80
  A Model of White Racial Identity Development 82
  Identity Development in the Classroom 84
Becoming a Cultural Ally 85
  Doing the White Thing 86
  But I'm Not Racist 87
  Becoming White 88
  Finding Sangha 89
  Ways I Avoid Dealing with Racism (and Piss Off People
    of Color in My Life) 90
Summary 91
Activities 92

CHAPTER 5
Understanding Culture and Cultural Differences 94
What Is Culture? 95
  Culture vs. Race in the Definition of Group Differences 96
The Dimensions of Culture 98
  Comparing Cultural Paradigms in America 100
  Nature and the Environment 101
  Time Orientation 101
  People Relations 102

Work and Activity   102
Human Nature   103
Are Theories of Helping Culture-Bound?   106
Key Aspects of the Helping Process   107
Verbal Expressiveness and Self-Disclosure   107
Setting Long-Term Goals   108
Changing the Client vs. Changing the Environment   108
Definitions of Mental Health   109
Collective Personality: The Example of Arabs/Muslims   111
Collective vs. Individual Treatment Models   112
Conflicting Cross-Cultural Service Models   113
Adapting Generic Models vs. Evolving Culturally
Sensitive Models   116
Summary   117
Activities   118

CHAPTER 6
Working with Culturally Diverse Parents and Families   120
Open Letter to Barack Obama   121
Community Psychology   122
Two Scenarios   127
Parenting   128
Creating a Buffer Zone   128
Parenting for Self-Esteem   130
Preparing the Child Emotionally for Racism   131
Preparing the Child Cognitively for Racism   132
Bicultural Children and Families   134
Bicultural Couples   135
Patterns of Bicultural Relationships   137
Bicultural Children   138
Bicultural Adopted Children   140
Therapy with Bicultural Families   141
Summary   142
Activities   143

CHAPTER 7
Culturally Sensitive Treatment with children   146
Child Development   148
Temperament at Birth   149
Development of Racial Awareness   149
Racial Awareness and Self-Esteem   150
Clarifying the Question   151

Adolescent Racial Identity   153
   Academic Performance and Learning Styles   155
Some Basic Notions of Child Treatment   157
   Contemporary Examples of Culturally Sensitive Treatment:
      Working with Complex Trauma in Children and Adolescents   159
Narrative Collective Practice: The Tree of Life Exercise   165
School-Based Social Justice Intervention Program   167
Summary   171
Activities   172

CHAPTER 8

Bias in Service Delivery   174

The Impact of Social, Political, and Racial Attitudes   177
Who Are the Providers? Under-representation
   in the Professions   179
   Dissatisfaction Among Providers of Color   180
   The Use of Paraprofessionals   182
The Use of Traditional Healers   182
Cultural Aspects of Mental Health Service Delivery   184
Bias in Conceptualizing Ethnic Populations   185
   Bias in Assessment   188
   Bias in Diagnosis   191
Cultural Variations in Psychopathology   191
   Cultural Attitudes Toward Mental Health   192
   Cultural Differences in Symptoms, Disorders, and Pathology   193
   The Globalization of Treatment Modalities   194
   The Case of Suicide   195
   Racial Microaggressions and the Therapeutic Relationship   198
Summary   202
Activities   203

CHAPTER 9

Mental Health Issues   204

Racial Identity and Group Belonging   206
   The Inner Dynamics of Ethnic Identity   206
   Models of Racial Identity Development   208
Racial Identity Development and the Helping
   Process   212
Assimilation and Acculturation   214
Views of Acculturation   215

Immigration and Acculturation   217
Acculturation and Community Breakdown   218
Stress   219
Psychological Trauma   221
Drug and Alcohol Use   224
Comparing Latinos and Asian Americans   228
The Cultural Meaning of Recovery   230
Summary   231
Activities   232

CHAPTER 10
Treating Victims of Ethnic Conflict, Genocide, and Mass Violence   233

An Alternative View of the Trauma Experience and Its Treatment   236
Historic Trauma and Unresolved Grief Among Native Americans   239
Brave Heart's Cultural Intervention   240
PTSD in Native American Males   241
South Africa and Its Truth and Reconciliation Commission   **242**
Impact on Victims   244
Impact on Bystanders   245
Impact on Perpetrators   246
Institute for the Healing of Memories   247
Forgiveness   248
Reparations   249
Holocaust Survivors, Nazis, Their Children, and
Reconciliation   251
Seeking Justice   253
Treating Traumatized Refugee and Immigrant Populations   257
Refugees   257
Immigrants   259
Center for Empowering Refugees and Immigrants (CERI)   261
History of Cambodian Refugees   262
Adult Clinical Services   263
Clinical Counseling   264
Medical Management   264
Body Work, Homeopathy, and Acupuncture   264
Youth Services Program   265
Innovations in Trauma Treatment   267
Summary   269
Activities   270
The Interviews   272

CHAPTER 11

Working with Latino/a Clients: An Interview with Roberto Almanzan   274

Demographics   275

Family and Cultural Values   276

Our Interviewee   278

   The Interview   278

Summary   292

Activity   293

CHAPTER 12

Working with Native American Clients: An Interview with Jack Lawson   294

Demographics   295

Family and Cultural Values   296

   Sharing and Cooperation   296

   Noninterference   296

   Time Orientation   297

   Extended Families   297

   Harmony with Nature   298

Our Interviewee.   299

   The Interview   299

Summary   313

Activity   314

CHAPTER 13

Working with African American Clients: An Interview with Veronique Thompson   315

Demographics   316

Family and Cultural Values   316

   Kinship Bonds   317

   Role Flexibility   318

   Religion   319

Our Interviewee   321

   The Interview   321

Summary   335

Activity   335

CHAPTER 14

Working with Asian American Clients: An Interview with Dan Hocoy   336

Demographics   337

Family and Cultural Values   339
Our Interviewee   341
   The Interview   341
Summary   357
Activity   357

CHAPTER 15
**Working with Arab and Muslim American Clients:
An Interview with Marwan Dwairy   358**
Demographics   359
Family and Cultural Values   360
Our Interviewee   363
   The Interview   363
Summary   376
Activity   376

CHAPTER 16
**Working with South Asian American Clients:
An Interview with Sumana Kaipa   377**
Demographics   378
Acculturation   380
   Family Organization and Values   380
Our Interviewee   383
   The Interview   383
Summary   400
Activity   401

CHAPTER 17
**Working with White Ethnic Clients:
An Interview with the Author   402**
Demographics and Cultural Similarities   403
Cultural Similarities   404
Our Interviewee   405
   The Interview   406
Summary   418
Activity   418

CHAPTER 18
**Working with American Male Clients:
An Interview with Jon Davies   419**
Demographics   420

Historical Background   421
    Family and Cultural Values   422
    Male Socialization and Role Expectations   422
    Gender Role Conflict and/or Gender Role Strain   423
Our Interviewee   424
    The Interview   425
Summary   432
Activity   432

CHAPTER 19
Working with Deaf Clients: An Interview with Valentino Vasquez and Johanna Larson   433
Our Interviewees   434
    The Interview   434
Summary   439
Activity   439

CHAPTER 20
Closing Thoughts   440
Gaining More Knowledge   442
    Learning About Client Cultures   446
    Finding Support for Cross-Cultural Work   446
Summary   447
Activities   447

Glossary   448
References   459
Index   482

Preface

The previous editions of *Cultural Diversity: A Primer for the Human Services* were well received by students and faculty alike. In them, I tried to speak honestly and directly to the reader about the kinds of knowledge, awareness, and skills necessary for effectively working with culturally diverse clients. The book's accessibility, personal style, anecdotal and clinical examples, and broad range of topics make it a popular introductory text for both students in training and professionals in the field. Especially popular were the interviews with providers from various ethnic groups about how to work with clients from their respective communities. The honest sharing of personal experiences, cultural knowledge, and clinical suggestions seemed to engage the reader and make the topic of becoming culturally competent come alive.

This text has evolved over the years. Statistical demographics of communities of color are continually updated for each edition. There are also new and innovative suggestions and activities to encourage and support readers' continued cultural competence. As the world changed, so did this text; new information has been added through the editions regarding trauma, genocide, and mass violence. In addition, more in-depth conceptual analysis of cross-cultural therapeutic work was added to each edition.

In this sixth edition, there are two new chapters: Chapter 18, "Working with American Male Clients: An Interview with Jon Davies"; and Chapter 19, "Working with Deaf Clients: An Interview with Valentino Vasquez and Johanna Larson." "Some Closing Thoughts," previously Chapter 18, is now Chapter 20. New learning objectives in each chapter have been added as well, and content has been updated or added in many chapters.

Substantively, the following new or updated material and topics have been introduced:

▶ Chapter 1

- ▶ Offered new information on sociocultural and social media issues such as LGBTQI+ rights and laws, women's rights, gun laws, the #MeToo movement, the #TimesUp movement, and #BlackLivesMatter
- ▶ Discussed how the election of Donald Trump has influenced minorities

▶ Chapter 2

- ▶ Updated demographic information
- ▶ Provided updated information on cultural competencies, ethnocentric individuals, self-awareness, and the ACA Code of Ethics

▸ Created a table outlining the cultural standards for social workers, counselors, marriage and family therapists, and human services providers

▶ Chapter 3

▸ Added updated information regarding cross-cultural helping and understanding differences and power
▸ Added a section on understanding the therapeutic presence
▸ Updated references on preparing for cross-cultural work, as well as assessing and diagnosing culturally diverse clients

▶ Chapter 4

▸ Updated information on defining and contextualizing racism, modern prejudice, microaggressions and implicit bias, institutional racism, cultural racism, and white racial attitude types

▶ Chapter 5

▸ Updated literature on the definition of culture; the dimensions of culture, comparing cultural paradigms in the United States; verbal expressiveness and self-disclosure; and generic verses evolving models
▸ Provided information on understanding the difference between culture and race
▸ Added a section on how theories of helping are culture-bound

▶ Chapter 6

▸ Added information on community psychology; preparing children emotionally for racism, bicultural couples and children, and adopted children
▸ Updated information on buffer zones

▶ Chapter 7

▸ Updated information about culturally sensitive treatment of children, temperament at birth, development of racial awareness and racial identity, and some basic notions of child treatment

▶ Chapter 8

▸ Updated literature on ethnic groupings of helpers, dissatisfaction among providers of color, cultural aspects of mental health service delivery, bias in assessment and diagnosis, and cultural attitudes toward mental health

▶ Chapter 9

- ▶ Updated literature on perceived discrimination, model of racial identity development, views of acculturation, immigration and acculturation, community breakdown, stress, psychological trauma, and comparing Latinos and Asian Americans

▶ Chapter 10

- ▶ Updated literature on alternative view of trauma, truth and reconciliation commission, and seeking justice

▶ Chapters 11–20

- ▶ There are new learning objectives at the beginning of each of these chapters.
- ▶ There is a new summary and activities at the end of each of these chapters.
- ▶ As previously noted, Chapter 18, "Working with American Male Clients: An Interview with Jon Davies," is new to this edition.
- ▶ As previously noted, Chapter 19, "Working with Deaf Clients: An Interview with Valentino Vasquez and Johanna Larson," is new to this edition.

▶ A WORD ABOUT DIVERSITY

Human beings are diverse in a variety of ways: race, ethnicity, language, culture, gender, socioeconomic class, age, sexual orientation, religion, ableism and disability, and more. Each must be fully appreciated and accounted for in order to understand the complexity of human behavior. This is no small task, however, because each affects the individual differently and operates by a unique set of rules and dynamics. No single text can adequately and comprehensively cover all forms of diversity. The present book focuses on working with clients from diverse racial and ethnic groups. Diversity within these groups is discussed throughout the book. The decision to highlight only race and ethnicity in this text is pragmatic and in no way minimizes the import of gender, class, age, sexual preference, and other characteristics. Rather, it underlines the fact that each deserves its own text to do it justice. There are even those who argue that covering too many forms of diversity in a single treatment tends to be superficial and minimize the importance of each. For those who would like to read further on other forms of diversity, I have included a selected bibliography arranged by areas of diversity.

▶ ACKNOWLEDGMENTS

A book like this is not written in a vacuum. I would first like to thank my daughters, the lights of my life, Becca and Rachel, whose support kept me going and whose encouragement allowed me to complete the dream of writing this book. And to Carole Diller, for her help in supporting my escape to Berkeley, where this book was written.

A number of indispensable people made writing this book possible. Stuart W. Cook, Tom Vernon, Harrie Hess, Gil Davis, Zalman Schachter-Shalomi, Ed Diller, and Nevitt Sanford were early teachers who taught me about race, ethnicity, and my own Jewish tradition. More recent teachers include Bob Cohen, Manny Foreman, Martin Acker, Reuben Cota, Jack Lawson, and Guadalupe Quinn. In particular, Leland Robison shared with me the richness of his Rom tradition. Saul Siegel, Myrna Holden, Deb Johnson, and Carol Stone provided helpful feedback on early drafts of the work. And most recently, I would like to acknowledge the following people who made contributions to the sixth edition: Jon Davies, Johanna Larson, Shoshana Kerewsky, Valentino Vasquez, and Lucy Zammarelli. In addition, a special thank-you to Jude Austin and Julius Austin, who made significant contributions to this text. They worked together to create learning objectives, add more updated written content and references, and create summaries, key terms, and class activities to the interview chapters.

At Cengage, I am thankful for the help of the staff, who offered useful support, creative ideas, and enormous help in taking care of a variety of details and small but necessary tasks. Special thanks to the following people, who served as readers and reviewers of the text:

Shann Hwa Hwang, Texas Woman's University
Trevor Hyde, Cardinal Stritch University
Maureen Kenny, Florida International University

Introduction

LEARNING OBJECTIVES

1-1 Recognize developments in the field of cultural diversity over the years.

Much has happened in the world since *Cultural Diversity: A Primer for the Human Services* first appeared in print. Ethnic populations in the United States have continued to grow at an astounding rate. There has been a significant move toward conservatism in politics and heightened racial tensions; both have contributed to a backlash against immigration as well as efforts to promote equity and social justice. Sociocultural issues such as LGBTQI+ rights and laws, women's rights, gun laws, the #MeToo Movement, #TimesUp movement, and #BlackLivesMatter have been highlighted since the last edition of this text.

With the past election of Barack Obama, a biracial man of African descent, as the 44th U.S. president, many in the United States dared to hope this event would mark the beginning of a new and more positive era of race relations. Although the deeply rooted effects of institutional and cultural racism are the most resistant to change, there were clearly discernable differences in the climate for ethnic identity formation and pride. The image of a black man in the White House and the increasing number of individuals of color in powerful political positions, as well as the role models these all offered, could not help but reinforce and strengthen the self-concept, ethnic identity, aspirations, and pride of children of color and other diverse populations. The reaction of white America was mixed. For many, it shattered old stereotypes and normalized their perceptions of individuals of color in positions of power; for others, however, it only intensified their hatred.

The recent election of Donald Trump has frightened many minorities who are unsure of what his presidency means for them. It seems as though the United States. has grown increasingly racially polarized since President Trump took office. The Southern Poverty Law Center (SPLC) reported 437 incidents of intimidation, targeting blacks and other people of color, Muslims, immigrants, members of the LGBT community, and women between the election on November 8 and November 14. For many minorities, the world has become much more precarious since November 8, 2016. There is a dynamic tension between members of the dominant culture and minorities who both feel as though their values are threatened. In a sense, it feels like America is fragmented and both cultures are fighting for survival.

This process makes culture a polemical and confusing word. In 2014, Merriam-Webster announced the word "culture" was their 2014 Word of the Year because of the spike in look-ups on their website. Although Merriam-Webster offers six definitions of it, many people are still desperate to know what it means. Culture is complex and the world becomes increasingly more diverse every day.

In addition to ethnic and racial changes, today, human service providers will work in a world changed by powerful movements and hashtag activism. Some are:

▶ #BlackLivesMatter: Created by Alicia Garza, Patrisse Cullors, and Opal Tometi in response to the acquittal of Trayvon Martin's murderer, George

Zimmerman. According to blacklivesmatter.com, the hashtag and no member-led global network is "an ideological and political intervention in a world where black lives are systematically and intentionally targeted for demise. It is an affirmation of black folks' humanity, our contributions to this society, and our resilience in the face of deadly oppression."

▶ #MeToo: Emerged after stories of the Hollywood producer Harvey Weinstein's abuse of women he employed. It has now become a vehicle for women to share their abuse stories and they are being believed.

These are two of the many movements our clients may be connected to today. These movements are a part of popular culture and define their stories. To work effectively with diverse clients, understanding the roles popular culture plays in their culture is essential.

In the present, sometimes confusing climate of race relations in the United States today, with its population growth and regression by way of disproportionate economic harm to minority populations and fear of greater immigration numbers, the importance of training culturally competent *human service providers* is all the more critical. This is the goal of *Cultural Diversity: A Primer for the Human Services.* I have called this book a *primer*; according to Webster, a primer is a book of elementary or basic principles. This book's intention is to provide you with basic principles, sensitivities, and knowledge that will lay a foundation for becoming a culturally competent professional. While reading this book, I hope you can expand your understanding of what culture and diversity means for yourself and your clients.

I once worked at a university counseling center baffled by the fact very few members of the university's rather sizable Asian student population ever sought treatment. In the hope of remedying the situation, the center invited Asian student leaders to visit the counseling center to learn about available services. After a very polite but unproductive meeting, I overheard one of the students commenting to another: "This place looks like a hospital. Why would anyone want to come here? This is where people come to die." No one on the staff had ever considered the remodeled health center, with its hospital-like rooms, might deter clients (students) from seeking help, or that in some cultures, hospitals are places people go to die and are thus to be avoided.

Contained in this simple scenario is the crux of a serious problem currently facing human service providers. How can one hope to offer competent services cross-culturally when one lacks basic knowledge about the people one hopes to serve? Ethical guidelines of all human services professions expressly forbid discriminating against clients on the basis of race and ethnicity. However, although increasing efforts are being made in this direction, only now have professional organizations begun to define specifically what culturally competent and ethical sensitive services might look like, as well as develop bases for censuring those who provide services without the requisite skills. The reality is most service providers regularly, although unknowingly, discriminate against culturally diverse clients by lacking the awareness, skills, and knowledge necessary to serve them competently.

This fact is reflected in research that consistently shows community facilities and services are underutilized by culturally diverse clients, especially those of color. The following are a number of reasons for this:

- Mainstream agencies may inadvertently make clients feel uncomfortable or unwelcome, as in the abovementioned scenario.
- Clients may not trust the motives or abilities of providers because of past experiences they have had with the system.
- Clients may believe they will not be understood culturally or will not have their needs met in a helpful manner.
- Clients may be unfamiliar with the kinds of services available or come from a culture in which such services are perceived very differently.

Each of these possibilities is sufficient to deter culturally diverse clients, who as a group tend to have especially high mental health needs, from seeking treatment or help.

The purpose of this book is to sensitize providers and those learning to be providers to the complex issues involved in *cross-cultural service delivery*. Only when culturally sensitive services are routinely available will the utilization rates of public facilities among culturally diverse clients begin to approach those of mainstream white groups. As professionals, providers are expected to demonstrate expertise and competence in the services they offer. Cross-cultural service delivery should be no less an area to master. Only by gaining the requisite awareness, knowledge, and skills necessary to be "culturally competent" can human service providers hope to actualize their professional commitment to nondiscrimination and equal access for all clients.

Discrimination in this context involves more than merely refusing to offer services to those who are racially or ethnically diverse. It also includes the following:

- Being unaware of one's own prejudices and how they may be communicated inadvertently to clients
- Being unaware of differences in cultural style, interactive patterns, and values, and realizing how these can lead to miscommunication
- Being unaware that many of the theories taught during training are culture-bound
- Being unaware of differences in cultural definitions of health and illness, as well as the existence of traditional cultural healing methods
- Being unaware of the necessity of matching treatment modalities to the cultural style of clients or of adapting practices to the specific cultural needs of clients

Of equal importance to effective cross-cultural service delivery is developing empathy and an appreciation for the life experiences of those who are culturally diverse in the United States. Why do so many culturally diverse clients harbor fears and mistrust of providers and others who represent the system? Why are so many of them angry and frustrated? Why do many culturally diverse people tend to feel tenuous and conflicted about their traditional identities? Why is parenting such a major challenge for these clients? What is the source of the enormous stress that is an ongoing experience of many culturally diverse clients? And why do they so often feel that majority group members have very little awareness of or concern for the often-harsh realities of their daily lives? Without keen insight into the complex answers to these questions, well-meaning professionals cannot hope to serve their clients sensitively.

Through training, providers are familiar with the inner workings of the system and thus able to gain access to it on behalf of clients. However, special care must be taken in this regard. First, there is the danger that culturally diverse clients may—as a result of interacting with providers and the system—be unintentionally socialized into the ways of the dominant culture. For example, in working with women from traditional cultures, it is important for them to understand that becoming more independent and assertive—a frequent outcome of counseling with mainstream women—can prove highly problematic when they re-enter the traditional world. Culturally competent providers educate their clients as to the service alternatives available—as well as the possible consequences—and then allow them to make informed choices. Such providers also consult and collaborate with traditional indigenous healers when such interaction is useful or supportive to the client.

A second danger is dependence. Culturally diverse clients are especially susceptible, given their more limited knowledge of mainstream culture. As the conduit to the system, providers may unknowingly perpetuate dependence rather than help these clients learn to function independently. Often, for example, it is easier and more expedient to make referrals for clients than to teach them how to arrange them for themselves. Helping is most useful, however, when it facilitates clients' interactions with the system on their own terms and in light of their cultural values and needs. In the literature, this is called *empowerment*, and it involves supporting and encouraging clients to become their own advocates.

Providers and clients from culturally diverse backgrounds do not come together in a vacuum. Rather, each brings a certain amount of baggage about the ethnicity of the other. Clients, for example, may initially feel mistrust, anger, fear, suspicion, or deference in the presence of the provider. In turn, providers may respond with feelings of superiority, condescension, discomfort, fear, or inadequacy. Each may also perceive the other in terms of cultural stereotypes; such reactions may be subtle or covered up, but one can be sure they will be there and, for a time at least, they will get in the way of forming a working alliance. Projections such as these fade with time as client and provider come to know each other as individuals instead of stereotypes. The least helpful thing that a provider can do at this point, however, is to take these reactions personally and respond defensively. A much better strategy is to acknowledge their existence and raise them as a topic for discussion. Research shows that clients of all backgrounds are most comfortable with professionals from their own culture. Unfortunately, there is a serious shortage of non-white providers, and clients of color find themselves working with dominant group professionals. This is where cultural competence comes in. It is my belief and experience that basic trust can develop cross-culturally, but it is not easy. It requires the right skills, a sincere desire to help, a willingness to openly acknowledge and discuss racial and ethnic differences, and a healthy tolerance for being tested.

This book focuses on working with clients from diverse cultures; its principles, however, are applicable in a variety of facilitating situations where provider and client come from qualitatively diverse backgrounds. This is even true for members of the same cultural group. Differences in class, gender, age, geography, social and political leanings, and ableism can lead to such diverse life experiences that members of the same group may feel they have little in common.

For example, a middle-class white provider, having grown up in a major Eastern city, may experience difficulties similar to those just described when working with poor whites from the rural South. Likewise, providers and clients from diverse cultural backgrounds who share similar demographics of class, gender, geography, and other elements may feel that they have much in common upon which they can build a working relationship.

I consciously use a number of different terms in referring to culturally diverse clients. Anyone familiar with this field is aware of the power of such terms. First of all, they possess subtle connotations and, at times, implicit value judgments. They have often been used as a means of oppressing and demeaning devalued groups, but they can also serve as powerful sources of empowerment and pride. It is not surprising that members of ethnic groups pay very serious attention to the ways in which they label themselves and are labeled by others. Finding out what term is preferable is a matter of respect, and if providers are in doubt, they should just ask clients what name they prefer; I have never seen anyone offended by that question. I have, however, repeatedly watched providers unintentionally alienate clients through their use of outdated and demeaning terms like "Orientals" or insensitive general references such as "you people."

Consider the following terms used in this text:

▶ *Cultural diversity* refers to the array of differences among groups of people with definable and unique cultural backgrounds.
▶ *Culturally diverse* implies that the client and provider come from different cultures. It suggests no value judgment as to the superiority of one culture over the other—only that the two have been socialized in very different ways and may likely find communication problematic.

- *Culture* is viewed as a lens through which life is perceived. Each culture, through its differences (in language, values, personality and family patterns, worldview, sense of time and space, and rules of interaction), generates a phenomenologically different experience of reality. Thus, the same situation (e.g., an initial counseling session at a community mental health center) may be experienced and interpreted very differently depending on the cultural background of individual clients and providers.

- *Ethnic group* refers to any distinguishable people whose members share a common culture and see themselves as separate and different from the majority culture. The observable differences—whether physical, racial, cultural, or geographic—frequently serve as a basis for discrimination and unequal treatment of a minority ethnic group within the larger society.

- A *racial group*, or *race*, is a biologically isolated, inbreeding population with a distinctive genetic heritage. Socially, the concept of race has created many difficulties. In general, I avoid the concept of race as a definer of group differences (with the exception of talking about the development of racial awareness and consciousness in people of color). The distinction between race as a social and biological category is discussed in Chapter 4.

- *People of color* and *clients of color* refer to non-white clients.

- *Communities of color* are collectives of non-whites who share certain physical (racial), cultural, language, or geographic origins/features. In naming specific communities of color, I try to use the term or referent that is most current and acceptable to members of that group (although there is always some debate within communities about what names are most acceptable). In relation to clients and communities of color, the following terms are generally used: African Americans, Latinos/as, Native Americans or Native Peoples, and Asian Americans or Asians. In quotes and references to research, terms are used as they appear in the original text.

- *Whites* refer to members of the dominant or majority group whose origins are Northern European.

- *White ethnics* refer to dominant or majority group members whose origins are not Northern European.

This book is written from a perspective that assumes there are certain psychological characteristics and experiences that all ethnically and culturally diverse clients share. First is the experience of belonging to a group that is socially stigmatized and the object of regular discrimination and derision. Second is the stress and harm that this causes to the psyche and the resulting adaptations—some healthy and empowering and others unhealthy and dysfunctional—that ethnic individuals and families must make in order to survive. Third is the stress and harm that result from problems regularly associated with prejudice and racism (e.g., poverty, insufficient health care, crime, and drug abuse). Not all cultures or individuals within cultures, however, experience these factors with equal intensity. Each society, in its inner workings, designates certain groups as primary scapegoats and others as secondary. In the United States, for example, people of color have traditionally been the primary objects of derision. In Europe, on the other hand, it has been Jews and the Rom (Gypsies); there, religion rather than race defined primary minority status. Fourth is the fact that problems in *ethnic* or *racial identification* are often evident in non-white and white ethnic clients. Ethnic and racial identification involves two related processes. First is the attachment that individuals feel toward their cultural group of origin. Second is the awareness or consciousness that individuals have of the impact that race or ethnicity has had on their lives. In one form or another, most clients from ethnic minorities exhibit some modicum of these four factors and thus share their dynamics.

It is also important that providers be aware of the diversity existing both across and within ethnic groups. First of all, each group has a unique history in the United States. As a result, somewhat different problems have emerged for each around its status as a culturally diverse group. People of color, for example, are set apart primarily by the color of their skin and differences in racial features. As a consequence, they may struggle with concerns over body image and the possibility of "passing" for white. Many Latinos/as and Asians have immigrated from traditional homelands and face ongoing dilemmas regarding assimilation, bilingualism, and the destruction of traditional family roles and values. Native Americans, as victims of *colonization* of their own land, have experienced the destruction of their traditional ways and identities and struggle to come to grips with these losses. African Americans have faced a similar psychological dislocation because of slavery. Whites in minority ethnic groups, in turn, find themselves suspended between worlds. They are culturally diverse yet perceived—and often wish to be perceived—as part of the majority.

These ethnically specific circumstances shape and determine the kinds of problems for which clients seek help. Differences among clients in the same ethnic group (be it class, age, gender, ableism, language, etc.) can also be extensive. The surest indicator of cultural insensitivity is the belief that all members of a particular group share all characteristics and circumstances. A recently arrived migrant worker from central Mexico, poor and barely able to speak English, faces very different life challenges from those of a similarly aged married man from a wealthy Chilean family, born in the United States, well-educated, and working as a banker.

The first task of any cross-cultural worker is to carefully assess the client's demographic and cultural situation. Some of the following information may be critical in determining the situation and needs of a culturally diverse client: place of birth, number of generations in the United States, family roles and structure, language spoken at home, English fluency, economic situation and status, amount and type of education, amount of acculturation, traditions practiced in the home, familiarity and comfort with the Northern European lifestyle, religious affiliation, and community and friendship patterns. In order to address such *cultural myopia*, I have introduced in Chapter 3 the ADDRESSING Framework, a tool developed by Pamela Hays in 2008 to help counselors and therapists track the cultural influences or identity dimensions at work within each client as well as within each therapist.

The culturally competent provider not only seeks such information, but also is aware of its possible meaning. The migrant worker just described may be in need of financial help, unfamiliar with the system, homesick, fearful of authorities, traditional, and macho in his attitudes. His Chilean counterpart is more likely to be concerned with issues of cultural rather than economic survival—how ethnicity is affecting him in the workplace, parental concern over his acculturation, changing roles with his wife and children, balancing success with retaining traditional ways.

I bring to this text both my own perspective on ethnicity and my experience as an American Jew and white ethnic. The autobiographical material I share in Chapter 15 should make it quite clear that these are not merely academic issues for me. Like so many other racial and ethnic group members, I have struggled personally with conflicts over group belonging and identity.

This has taught me both the complexity of the issues that are the focus of this book and the fact that becoming culturally competent is indeed a lifelong process that needs constant monitoring. It is important for you to know, as someone beginning to learn about this field, that even those of us who have gained some competence in working cross-culturally never stop struggling with these issues. It is just part and parcel of the process of becoming culturally competent.

I have worked in intergroup relations for more than thirty years: teaching courses on multicultural issues in counseling, consulting with various public and private agencies and institutions, and doing clinical work with a wide range of ethnic populations. Yet, I still grow uneasy when I am put in the position of speaking about those who are culturally different from me. To this end, I have written the chapters dealing with the broader conceptual issues by drawing on both research and examples from my experience and have invited experts from various minority and culturally diverse communities in the United States to discuss working with clients from their respective groups. I am still learning about my own culture and heritage, so how can I presume to speak authoritatively about the culture of others?

The chapters that follow explore different aspects of cultural diversity:

▸ Chapter 2, "What It Means to Be Culturally Competent," discusses the need for cultural competence, why one should become culturally competent, the skill areas involved in doing so, and the kind of benefits gained by providers who choose to pursue it.
▸ Chapter 3, "Working with Culturally Diverse Clients," directs attention to the actual process of beginning to work with culturally diverse clients and

provides a conceptualization of cross-cultural work, as well as guidelines and specific hands-on information for beginning to do so.

‣ Chapter 4, "Understanding Racism, Prejudice, and White Privilege," describes the dynamics of racism and prejudice as they operate at individual, institutional, and cultural levels, and how they may impinge on the helping relationship. It also highlights the notion of white privilege, as well as ways in which whites structure and protect their racial attitudes.

‣ Chapter 5, "Understanding Culture and Cultural Differences," focuses on the elusive concept of *culture*—its various dimensions, how to make sense of and deal with cultural differences, and the meaning of multiculturalism.

‣ Chapter 6, "Working with Culturally Diverse Parents and Families," is the first of five chapters that focus on the psychological experience of people of color and other diverse populations—or what has been called *ethnic psychology*. Chapter 6 explores the concept of Community Psychology and its relevance for ethnic children and parenting, the challenges of being an ethnic parent (creating a buffer zone, parenting for self-esteem, and preparing the child for racism), and issues related to biracial or bicultural families.

‣ Chapter 7, "Culturally Sensitive Treatment with Children," discusses developmental issues peculiar to children from oppressed racial and ethnic backgrounds, working therapeutically with diverse children, and presents in-depth examples of clinical work with children suffering from *complex trauma*, two approaches to narrative treatment with children, and a school-based, social justice intervention program.

‣ Chapter 8, "Bias in Service Delivery," examines various sources of bias in cross-cultural service delivery, as well as ways of adapting human service delivery to the specific cultural needs of clients.

‣ Chapter 9, "Mental Health Issues," deals with various mental health factors that have particular relevance for culturally diverse clients. Included are discussions of racial and ethnic identity development in adults, acculturation, stress, trauma, and substance abuse.

‣ Chapter 10, "Treating Victims of Ethnic Conflict, Genocide, and Mass Violence," looks at the extreme consequences of ethnic and racial hatred, as well as models for healing both the traumatized victim/survivor and the society in which such violence occurs. Included are sections on historic trauma and unresolved grief among Native Americans; South Africa and its Truth and Reconciliation Commission; Holocaust survivors and Nazis; and the treatment of traumatized Cambodian immigrants and refugees.

‣ Chapters 11–19 provide culturally specific information on minority communities in the United States.

What It Means to Be Culturally Competent

LEARNING OBJECTIVES

2-1 Explain the shifts in the current cultural demographics of the United States.

2-2 Discuss reasons to become culturally competent.

2-3 Analyze cultural competence skill areas in therapeutic relationships.

2-4 Define professional and ethical standards related to cultural competency.

▶ Demographics   2-1

The demographics of the United States have been changing dramatically, and central to these changes is a significant increase in the non-White populations. Atkinson (2004) refers to this trend that began in the 1980s as the "diversification" of America. The statistics speak for themselves; according to the National Center for Education Statistics (2016), White school-age children in the United States decreased from 62 percent in 2000 to 53 percent in 2013. In contrast, school-age children of other racial/ethnic groups increased. For example, children who identified as Hispanic increased from 16 to 24 percent. These percentages represent not only a sizable increase in the actual numbers of people of color in the United States, but also a significant decline in the relative percentage of Whites. Colby and Ortman (2015) expressed that Hispanic, Asian, Native Hawaiian, Black, American Indian, and Alaska Native populations are expected to make significantly more growth by the year 2060.

By 2042, barely a generation from now, racial minorities will make up a majority of the U.S. population. By 2050, non-Hispanic Whites, today 66 percent of the population, will reduce to 46 percent of the population. Hispanics, the fastest-growing minority, will triple in number from 15 percent of the U.S. population to 30 percent; Asians will grow from 5 percent of the population to 9 percent; African Americans from 13 percent to 15 percent; and Native Americans from 1.6 percent to 2.0 percent. The Native Hawaiian and Pacific Islander population will double, and the number of self-identified biracial people will triple. And the increases are even more dramatic among the young. By 2023, minority children under 18 years of age will become a majority, and by 2030, for example, half of all elementary school-age children in the United States will be children of color. By 2039, the majority of working-age Americans will be of color.

Two factors—immigration and birthrates—are particularly responsible for these dramatic changes. The last thirty years of the twentieth century saw an unprecedented wave of immigration to the United States, with yearly numbers rising to 1 million. Unlike earlier immigration patterns, however, the new arrivals were primarily non-European: approximately one-third from Asia and one-third from Central and South America. Colby and Ortman (2015) expressed that between 2014 and 2060, the U.S. population will increase from 319 million to 417 million. Furthermore, Colby and Ortman (2015) explained that by 2044, more than half of the U.S. population will belong to a minority group.

Reactions to Changing Demographics

What has been the reaction to this growing diversification? First, White America has clearly felt threatened by these changes. The sheer increase in non-White numbers has stimulated a widespread political backlash. Most prominent has been a rise in anti-immigrant sentiment and legislation and a strong push to repeal affirmative action practices, which were instituted over the last several decades to level the economic and social playing fields for people of color.

As economic times have worsened for White working and middle classes, frustration has increasingly been directed at non-White newcomers who are blamed for "taking our jobs" and told to "go back to where you came from if you're not willing to speak English." In a similar vein, White supremacists, militias, and anti-government groups, playing on racial hatred and a return to "traditional values" and "law and order," have attracted growing numbers. The result has been a society even further polarized along color lines. People of color, in turn, have sensed their growing numbers as an ultimatum to White America: "Soon, you won't even have the numerical majority. How can you possibly continue to justify the enormous injustice and disparity against us?"

For those in the helping professions, a major implication of these new demographics is a radically different client base. More and more, providers will be called on to serve clients from diverse cultures. Job announcements increasingly state: "Bilingual and bicultural professionals preferred" and "Cross-cultural experience and sensitivity a requirement." At the same time, there is a growing awareness that it is insufficient to merely channel these new clients into the same old structures and programs or to hire a few token professionals of color. Rather, a radical reconceptualization of effective helping vis-à-vis those who are culturally diverse and how it occurs is needed. At the center of such a renewed vision is the notion of *cultural competence*.

▶ Why Become Culturally Competent?   `2-2`

In the past, gaining what is now called *cultural competence* was an ethical decision undertaken by practitioners with a particularly strong moral sense of what was right and fair. Usually, such individuals sought training with the express purpose of working with specific cultural groups, and they gravitated toward minority agencies. Mainstream providers, with their predominantly White client base, had little reason to pursue cultural competence. Although today, the picture is quite different. All agencies are seeing more culturally diverse clients walk through their doors and it may not be long before cultural competence becomes a professional imperative. Jones, Kawena Begay, Nakagawa, Cevasco, and Sit (2016) suggest that clinicians integrate cultural competencies into evidence-based treatment modalities when treating diverse populations. In time, cultural competence may be a routine requirement for all jobs, not just those in the helping professions.

Whether it is a matter of working under a superior who is a person of color, supervising others from diverse backgrounds, or retaining good relations with colleagues who are culturally diverse, being skilled in cross-cultural communication will increasingly be an asset. Given the dramatic diversification currently under way in the United

States, gaining cultural competence may someday reach a status comparable to that of computer literacy. Twenty-five years ago, computer skills were an isolated novelty, but today it is difficult to compete successfully in any job market without them. The same may eventually become true of cultural competence.

The Fear and Pain Associated with Moving Toward Cultural Competence

It is my experience most people are apprehensive of learning about race and ethnicity; thus they approach the topic with some reluctance, even dread. The same may be true for you. When I start a new class, the tension in the room is palpable; students do not know what to expect. Race is a dangerous subject for everyone, and even cause people to become unglued in relation to it. White students wonder if they will be attacked, called racists, and made to feel guilty. Students of color wonder if the class is "going to be for real" or just another "exercise in political correctness." Everyone wonders whether they will really be able to speak their minds, whether things might get out of control, and, if so, whether I will be able to handle it. Their concerns are understandable.

What is more familiar in such discussions are accusations and attacks, name-calling, and long, endless diatribes about racial profiling, affirmative action, anti-immigrant legislation, and differing perspectives on terrorism.

What one does not hear about or talk about, and what must become a focus of attention if there is ever going to be any positive change in this arena, is the psychological pain and suffering caused by racism and the ways in which everyone is touched by it. I cannot help but think of these past students and their stories:

- The young White woman who was traumatized as a young child when her mother found her innocently touching the face of their African American maid and freaked out.
- The Latina girl who was never the same after being accused of stealing the new bike that her parents had scrimped and saved to buy for her.
- The Jewish man who discovered, at the age of 25, that his parents had been hiding from him the fact that they were Jews.
- The Asian woman, adopted at birth by White parents, who could not talk to them about how difficult it was for her living in an a predominantly White world.
- The White woman consumed by guilt because of what she felt to be an irrational fear of African American and Latino men.

There is clearly as much fear and nervousness about letting out such feelings as there is about the unknowns of working with clients from other cultures.

I try to alleviate the anxiety by reviewing the ground rules and assumptions that define how we will interact in class. My intention is to create a safety zone where students can talk about race in ways that cannot be talked about in normal daily life. The following guidelines are clearly spelled out at the beginning of the course:

▶ There will be no name-calling, labeling, or blaming one another. There are no heroes or villains in this drama; no good people or bad. Each of us harbors negative reactions toward those who are different; it is impossible to grow up in a society and not take on its prejudices. So, it is not a matter of whether one is a racist or not—we all are. Rather, it is a question of what negative racial attitudes one has learned so far and, from this moment on, what one is willing to do about them.

▶ Everything that is said and divulged in this classroom is confidential, and it is not to be talked about with anyone outside of here. Students often censure, measure their words, and are less than honest in what they say out of fear of either looking bad or having their personal disclosures treated insensitively or as gossip.

▶ As much as possible, everyone will personalize his or her discussion and talk about personal experiences. There is much denial around racism that serves as a mechanism for avoiding responsibility. Only by personalizing the subject and speaking in the first person, rather than the third, can this be avoided.

▶ You can say whatever you believe. This may, in turn, lead to conflict with others. That is OK. But you must be willing to look at what you say, take responsibility for your words, and learn from what ensues. Anything that happens during class is a learning opportunity. It can and may be analyzed as part of the process. The class is a microcosm of the outer racial world with all its problems, and as such, honest interaction in class can shed valuable light on the dynamics of intergroup conflict.

Most students have serious questions about race and ethnicity that need to be answered, or experiences in relation to these elements that must be processed and better understood. Significant learning about race and ethnicity cannot proceed without this happening. Opportunities to do so are rare, but only through such occasions can growth and healing begin. Once a degree of safety has been established, the floodgates open, and students become emboldened by the frank comments of others to share what is really on their minds. These are the kind of concerns that emerge:

▶ Why do so many immigrants to the United States refuse to learn English? If they want to live here and reap the benefits, the least they should be willing to do is learn our language.

▶ My parents came over from Italy. They were dirt poor but made successful lives for themselves. They didn't have all this help.

- I really don't understand why it should be any different for people of color.

- This is all really new to me. I grew up in a small town in rural Oregon. There was one Black family, but they stayed to themselves mostly. It's confusing, and to be perfectly honest, it's also pretty scary. There's just so much anger. If I had a client of color, I'm not sure I would know what to say or do.

- My biggest issues are with Black men. I try to be supportive of them and understand the difficulties they face. But when I see them always with White women, overlooking me and my sisters and all we have to offer, I get really angry.

- To be perfectly honest, I hate being White. I feel extremely guilty about what we have done to people of color and don't know how to make up for it. I don't feel I have any culture of my own. We used to joke about being "Heinz 57–variety" Americans. And I envy people of color for all their culture and togetherness. We tried practicing some Native American ways, but that didn't seem exactly right, and besides, we were never made to feel very welcome.

- I've come to realize how much racial hatred there was in my family while I was growing up, and this disturbs me greatly. I find it very hard to see my parents in this negative light and don't know what to do with all of this.

- It's gotten pretty hard being a White male these days. You've always got to watch what you say, and as far as getting a job—forget it. There's a whole line of women and minorities and disabled [people] in front of you. I guess I sort of understand the idea of affirmative action, but just because I'm White doesn't mean I have it made. I find it very difficult just getting by financially. I don't see where all this privilege is.

- I just can't buy all this cultural stuff. People are just people and I treat everyone the same. I grew up in an integrated neighborhood. I always had a lot of Black and Latino friends and never saw them as different. Frankly, I think all this focus on differences is creating the problem.

- I'm Jewish but am finding it hard to discover where I fit in all of this. I don't feel White, but everyone treats me and classifies Jews as White. I was very involved in the Civil Rights Movement a number of years ago; even worked down in the South for a summer registering voters. But that seems so far away, and now Blacks hate Jews. What did we do?

- I'm in this class because I have to be. I don't need to take a class on racism. I've lived it all my life. White people don't get it. They just don't want to see, and no class is going to open their eyes. What I'm not willing to do is be a token person of color in here.

Moving toward cultural competence is hard, emotional work. Personal issues such as those just described have to be given voice and worked through. Students need good answers to their questions and support in finding solutions to personal conflicts with the material. It is as if a whole new dimension of reality—that of culture—has been introduced into a student's phenomenological world. Old beliefs about oneself, others, and what one does and does not have in common must be examined and adjusted where necessary. There are, in addition, vast amounts of information to learn and new cultural worlds to explore. Perhaps most exciting, however, are the ways in which one's mind has to stretch and grow to incorporate the implications of culture. Students who have progressed in their learning about cultural matters often speak of a transformation that occurs in the ways they think about themselves and the world.

Bennett (1993) has tried to describe these cognitive changes. Of particular interest is the qualitative shift that occurs in a person's frame of reference—what Bennett describes as movement from *ethnocentrism* to *ethnorelativism*. In typical ethnocentric thinking, culturally diverse behavior is assessed in relation to one's own cultural standards; it is good or bad in terms of its similarity to how things are done in one's own culture. In ethnorelative thinking, "cultures can only be understood relative to one another and . . . particular behavior can only be understood within a cultural context, . . . cultural difference is neither good nor bad, it is just different . . ." (p. 26). Mayer (2012) added that individuals who are ethnocentric deny the existence of other frames of reference and those whom are ethnorelative accept the existence of other frames of reference. People who make this shift increase their empathic ability and experience greater ease in adopting a process orientation toward living. When the actions of others are not assessed or judged but are just allowed to exist, it is far easier to enter into their felt experience and thereby empathize with them. Similarly, realizing that behavior, values, and identity itself are not absolute, but rather are constructed by culture, frees one to appreciate more fully the ongoing process of living life as opposed to focusing entirely on its content or where one is going or has been. These skills not only transform how people think, but also prepare them for working more effectively with culturally diverse clients.

Speaking Personally About Cultural Competence

An old adage states: "You get as much out of something as you put into it." The same is true for pursuing cultural competence and using this book as a beginning. There is much useful information in the pages that follow that cannot help but contribute to your growth as a provider of cross-cultural services, which is certainly worth the "price of admission." Furthermore, it can be the start of a journey that can change you in deep and unpredictable ways. As suggested earlier, engaging in the serious pursuit of cultural competence can be transformational, not so much in a religious sense as a perceptual one.

Black-and-white thinking will eventually be replaced by relational and process thinking. In time, you will think very differently than you do now. I can also guarantee that if you pursue a deeper understanding of culture, you will at times find yourself disturbed and disoriented, feeling very lost and alone. I can remember the first time I experienced cultural relativity and realized that what I had taken for my entire life as absolute reality—the underpinnings of my world—was actually relative. It came from reading the books of Alan Watts on Zen Buddhism and beginning to explore meditation. What I found so disturbing and unsettling was the realization that there was more than one way to understand reality. I was never quite the same again, as if the center of my consciousness had shifted somewhat and everything looked a little different. It is an unhinging aspect of the journey that will often be repeated in miniature as one continues to delve into cultural material.

Two qualities will make a difference in how you relate to this book, and ultimately in your pursuit of cultural competence. The first is self-honesty. There is an aspect of ethnocentrism that is self-delusional; it seeks to hide the fact that human experience can be relative and that there might be "another show in town." As will become evident in Chapter 3, we all have a strong tendency to deny and hide from consciousness the negative feelings that we hold about race, ethnicity, and cultural differences. Together, these tendencies conspire to keep us in the dark. Only by pushing oneself to engage the concepts and material of this book critically and to discover precisely how they have played themselves out in the confines of one's life can the power of cultural competence be truly appreciated.

The second quality is a sustained commitment. The kind of learning that leads to cultural competence takes place over the long term. It consists as much of process as content, tends to be cumulative in nature, and is highly developmental. This means that you may go through various predictable stages of growth, emotion, and change. This book is only a beginning. What happens next—what additional cultural learning experiences you seek and the extent to which you seriously engage in providing services cross-culturally—is up to you.

A Model of Cultural Competence

In its broadest context, cultural competence is "typically distinguished from a therapist's general competence to provide quality care and is operationalized as the therapist's effectiveness in treating racial/ethnic minority clients" (Imel, Baldwin, Atkins, Owen, Baardseth, & Wampold, 2011). The work of Cross et al. (1989) on cultural competence offers a good example of such an evolving model. Cross is the executive director of the National Indian Child Welfare Association in Portland, Oregon. For many years he and his associates have attempted to articulate an effective, reality-based, and comprehensive approach to cross-cultural service delivery.

Cross et al. (1989) believed that a culturally competent care system must rest on a set of unifying values—or what might be called *assumptions*—about how services are best delivered to people of color. These values share the notions that being different is positive, that services must be responsive to specific cultural needs, and that they must be delivered in a way that empowers the client. According to Cross et al., a culturally competent care system respects the unique, culturally defined needs of various client populations, acknowledges culture as a predominant force in shaping behaviors, values, and institutions, and functions with the awareness that the dignity of the person is not guaranteed unless the dignity of his or her people is preserved. Culturally competent care systems also respect the family as indispensable to understanding the individual because the family provides the context within which the person functions and is the primary support network of its members. Lastly, a culturally competent care system recognizes that the thought patterns of non-Western peoples, though different, are equally valid and influence how clients view problems and solutions.

Taken together, these assumptions provide the psychological underpinnings of a truly cross-cultural model of service delivery. First, they are based on the experience of people of color and those who have worked intimately with them. Second, they take seriously notions that are not typically included in dominant culture service models. These notions include the impact of cultural differences on mental health, the family and community as a beginning point for treatment, agency accountability to its constituent community, and biculturalism as an ongoing life experience for people of color. Third, they provide a yardstick against which existing agencies can measure their own treatment philosophies and assumptions.

Chu, Leino, Pflum, and Sue (2016) explained that based on the past research from Cross et al. (1989), cultural competency can have positive outcomes in treatment. However, recent research has established several reasons why cultural competency actually works. In explaining essential principles of cultural competency, Chu et al. (2016) established that cultural competency works because it creates "(a) a contextual match with clients' external realities; (b) an experiential match in the microsystem of the therapeutic relationship or framework; and (c) an intrapersonal feeling of being understood and empowered within the client" (p. 18).

Assessing Agency Cultural Competence

Though created almost 30 years ago, the developmental continuum agencies of Cross et al. (1989), which differ and can be assessed, are still relevant today. This continuum assesses agencies according to their ability to deal effectively with cultural differences in their clients. Table 2-1 offers a summary of the six levels of this continuum. At one extreme are agencies they describe as exhibiting cultural destructiveness; included are those whose policies and practices are actively destructive to cultures and their members. Although it is difficult to find examples of such blatant practices today, it

TABLE 2-1

Continuum of Cultural Competence in Agencies

Level of Cultural Competence	Typical Characteristics
Cultural destructiveness	Policies and practices are actively destructive of communities and individuals of color.
Cultural incapacity	Policies and practices unintentionally promote cultural and racial bias; discriminate in hiring; do not welcome, devalue, and hold lower expectations for clients of color.
Cultural blindness	Attempt to avoid bias by ignoring racial and cultural differences (i.e., all clients are treated the same), yet adopt a mainstream approach to service delivery. Ignore cultural strengths of clients, encourage assimilation, and participate in victim blame.
Cultural pre-competence	Have failed at attempts toward greater cultural competence due to limited vision of what is necessary. Either hold false sense of accomplishment or overwhelmed by failure. Tend to depend on tokenism and overestimate impact of isolated staff of color.
Basic cultural competence	Incorporate five basic skill areas into ongoing process of agency. Work to hire unbiased staff, consult with communities of color, and actively assess who they can realistically serve.
Cultural proficiency	Exhibit basic cultural competence, advocate for multiculturalism throughout the health care system, carry out original research on how to better serve clients of color, and disseminate findings.

Source: Adapted from *Towards a Culturally Competent System of Care* by Cross et al., 1989. Washington, DC: Georgetown University Child Development Center.

is important to realize that "historically, some agencies have been actively involved in services that have denied people of color access to their natural helpers and healers, removed children of color from their families on the basis of race, or purposely risked the well-being of minority individuals in social and medical experiments without their knowledge or consent" (Cross et al., 1989, p. 14).

Cultural incapacity is the designation given to the next set of agencies along the continuum. These providers, although not intentionally destructive, lack the capacity to help people of color and their communities. In the process of doing their work, they routinely perpetuate societal biases, beliefs in racial inferiority, and paternalism. In addition, they tend to discriminate in hiring practices, send messages that people of color are not valued or welcomed, and usually have lower expectations for these clients.

Agencies exhibiting cultural blindness, the third group of providers, try to be unbiased in their approach, but they do so by asserting that race and culture make no difference in how they provide services and then proceed to apply a dominant cultural approach to all clients. They routinely ignore the cultural strengths and uniqueness of people of color, encourage assimilation, and tend to blame victims rather than society for their problems.

More to the positive end of the continuum, providers move into a phase that Cross et al. call *cultural pre-competence*. Such agencies are sincere in their efforts to become more multicultural but have had difficulty in making progress. They realize that they have problems in serving minority ethnic group clients and have discovered this fact through ineffectual efforts at serving a single ethnic population. They tend to lack a realistic picture of what is involved in becoming culturally competent and often succumb to either a false sense of accomplishment or a particularly difficult and discouraging failure. In addition, they tend to fall prey to tokenism and put unrealistic hopes in the hiring of one or two professionals of color, whose cultural competence they tend to overestimate. It is probably fair to say that the majority of human service agencies today are culturally pre-competent, with some still functioning at the level of cultural incapacity.

The last two points on the continuum, which are still probably more hypothetical than real in today's service world, represent increasing levels of cultural competence. Agencies that possess basic cultural competence are well-versed in the five skill areas believed to be essential to competent cross-cultural service delivery (to be described shortly). Such agencies also "work to hire unbiased employees, seek advice and consultation from the minority community, and actively decide what they are and are not capable of providing minority clients" (Cross et al., 1989, p. 17). Finally, cultural proficiency, the positive endpoint of the continuum, refers to providers who, in addition to those qualities exhibited in basic cultural competence, advocate more broadly for multiculturalism within the general health care system and are engaged in original research on how to serve culturally diverse clients better and its dissemination.

Having defined this continuum, Cross et al. are quick to point out that movement from one stage to the next takes significant effort. It requires a determined reshuffling of agency attitudes, policies, and practices; the implementation of skill development for all staff; and the serious involvement of all agency personnel: board members, policymakers, administrators, practitioners, and consumers alike. You may find it useful to consider where agencies with which you are familiar might be placed on this continuum and why.

▶ Individual Cultural Competence Skill Areas   2-3

Turning their attention to the development of cultural competence in individual practitioners, Barden, Sherrell, and Matthews (2017) explained that "Professional counselors need to be knowledgeable of cultural values, aware of their own cultural background and personal biases, and able to integrate culturally relevant and appropriate interventions in their work with all clients" (p. 203). Cross et al. (1989) define five basic skill areas necessary for effective cross-cultural service delivery. Each can be assessed on its own continuum, although growth in one tends to support positive movement in the

TABLE 2-2
Summary of Individual Cultural

Skill Area	Definition
Awareness and acceptance	Culturally competent providers are aware of the existence of cultural differences, accept their reality and value, and actively and creatively use them in the service of helping.
Self-awareness	Culturally competent providers appreciate the impact of their own ethnicity and racial attitudes on potential clients and actively work to limit the impact of such factors.
Dynamics of difference	Culturally competent providers are aware of likely areas of potential cross-cultural miscommunication, misinterpretation, and misjudgment; anticipate their occurrence; and have the skills to set them right.
Knowledge of client's culture	Culturally competent providers actively educate themselves with regard to a client's culture in order to understand behavior in its cultural context. They also actively seek consultation with indigenous experts when necessary.
Adaptation of skills	Culturally competent providers adapt and adjust generic helping practices to accommodate cultural differences to meet the needs and goals of culturally different clients better.

Source: Adapted from *Towards a Culturally Competent System of Care* by Cross et al., 1989. Washington, DC: Georgetown University Child Development Center.

others. It is believed that these skills must infuse not only the provider's work, but also the general climate of agencies and the health care system as a whole. These five individual skill areas are summarized in Table 2-2.

These skill areas must be taught, supported, and, even more basically, introduced as underlying dimensions of everyday functioning within agencies. The first skill area, for example, involves being aware of and accepting differences. For providers, this means respecting differences in their clients. At an agency level, however, a similar commitment to accepting and valuing diversity must also be evident in the clinical practices that are adopted, in the philosophy that is shared, and in the relationship between colleagues and with associates from other parts of the care system.

Awareness and Acceptance of Differences. A first step toward cultural competence involves developing an awareness of the ways in which cultures differ and realizing that these differences affect the helping process. While all people strive to meet the same basic psychological needs, they differ greatly in how they have learned to do so. Cultural differences exist in values, styles of communication, perception of time, how health is defined, community, and so on. In attuning one's efforts to work with clients from other cultures, acknowledging and looking at differences are as important as highlighting similarities. The discovery of exactly what dimensions of living vary with culture is an ever-evolving drama. Each individual begins life with a singular experience of culture that is taken for reality itself. Only with exposure to additional and differing cultural realities does one begin to develop an appreciation for the diversity in human behavior.

Equally critical to becoming aware of differences is accepting them. The most difficult things to accept are cultural ways and values at odds with our own. For instance, as a success-oriented, hyper-punctual client of Northern European ancestry, I might find it very difficult to accept the perpetual lateness of individuals who belong to cultures where time is viewed as flexible and inexact. What eventually emerges in providers who are moving toward cultural competence, however, is a broadening of perspective that acknowledges the simultaneous existence of differing realities that requires neither comparison nor judgment. All exist in their own right and are different. Further along the continuum is a position where differences are not merely accepted, but are truly valued for the richness, perspective, and complexity that they offer. A culturally competent practitioner actively and creatively uses these differences in the service of the helping process.

Self-Awareness. It is impossible to appreciate the impact of culture on the lives of others, particularly clients, if one is out of touch with his or her own cultural background. Culture is a mold that gives shape to life experience, promoting certain values and experiences as optimal and defining what is possible. As a skill area, self-awareness involves understanding the myriad ways that culture affects human behavior. Bell, Limberg, Jacobson, and Super (2014) explained that "counselor self-awareness refers to the counselor's ability to remain transparent, referring to the counselor's level of awareness about how they experience their client and the therapeutic relationship" (p. 401).

In addition, the skill of self-awareness requires sufficient self-knowledge to anticipate when one's own cultural limits are likely to be pushed, foreseeing potential areas of tension and conflict with specific client groups and accommodating them. If my day is tightly scheduled, as is the case in most agencies, and it is in the nature of my clients' culture to be late, I must find a strategy for meeting with them that allows me to remain true to my cultural values and concurrently allows them to do the same. Cultural self-awareness is an especially difficult task for many White providers, who grew up in households where intact cultural pasts have been lost. What remains instead are bits and pieces of cultural identity and personal history that were long ago cut loose from the extended family, traditions, and community and, as a result, lack meaning. Without such a felt sense of the role of culture in the lives of people of color, certain areas of client experience become difficult to empathize with and understand.

Dynamics of Difference. Related to self-awareness is what Cross et al. (1989) call the "dynamics of difference." When client and provider come from different cultures, there is a strong likelihood that sooner or later, they will miscommunicate by misinterpreting or misjudging the other's behavior. An awareness of the dynamics of difference involves knowing what can go wrong in cross-cultural communication and knowing how to set it right. Bell et al. (2014) suggest self-reflection as an appropriate method to explore cultural miscommunication within the therapeutic relationship. Cultural miscommunication has two general sources: experiences either the client or practitioner has had with members of the other's group and the nature of current political relations between groups. Mexican immigrants, for example, tend to be hypervigilant in relation to anyone who is perceived as either White or authoritative. Or, given tensions between African Americans and Jews in the United States that emerged in the 1960s and 1970s, a helping relationship between an African American provider and a Jewish client (or vice versa) might initially prove problematic.

Dynamics of difference also involve differences in cultural style. If a teacher from a culture that interprets direct eye contact as a sign of respect works with a student who has been taught culturally to avert eye contact as a sign of deference, there is a good chance that the teacher will come away from the interaction with erroneous impressions of the student. If providers are prepared for the possibility of such cross-cultural miscommunication, they are better able to diagnose a problem immediately and more quickly set things back on track.

Knowledge of the Client's Culture. Regarding the client's culture, the American Code of Ethics states, "Counselors communicate information in ways that are both developmentally and culturally appropriate" (Section A.2.c.). Many serious mistakes can be avoided if only the provider would preface each attempt at analyzing client motivation or behavior by considering what it might mean within the context of the client's cultural group. Similarly, other kinds of cultural information can be clinically useful. "Workers must know what symbols are meaningful, how health is defined, and how primary support networks are configured" (Cross, 1988, p. 4). Interpreting the behavior of someone who is culturally diverse without considering cultural context or ethnocentricity (i.e., from one's own cultural perspective) is fraught with danger, as the following anecdote amply demonstrates.

Several years ago, during a period of particularly heavy immigration from Southeast Asia, Children's Protective Services received a rash of abuse reports on Vietnamese parents whose children had come to school with red marks all over their bodies. A bit of cultural detective work quickly turned up the fact that the children had been given an ancient remedy for colds called *cupping*, which involves placing heated glass cups on the skin, leaving harmless red marks for about a day. The resulting fallout was a group of irate Vietnamese parents, always hyperattentive to the needs of their children, being deeply insulted by accusations of bad parenting, and several workers feeling rather foolish about their cultural ignorance. Given the variety of populations that must be served and the diversity that exists within each of them, it is not reasonable to expect any single provider to be conversant in the ways of all cultures and subcultures. However, it is possible to learn to identify the kind of information that is required to understand what is going on in the helping situation and have available the use of cultural experts with whom one can consult.

Adaptation of Skills. The fifth skill area involves adapting and adjusting generic helping practices (that in reality, as we shall see, have their roots in the dominant cultural paradigm) to accommodate cultural differences. Such adaptations can take a variety of forms. Treatment goals can be altered to fit cultural values better. For example, a Chinese family may not feel comfortable working toward an outcome that involves greater assertiveness in their children. The style of interaction in which the helping process is carried out can be adjusted to something more familiar to the client. In many cultures, for instance, healing practices are highly authoritative and directive, with advice freely given by experts. Some clients respond to healers only by showing deference.

The definition of who is a family member—and thus should be included in treatment—can also vary greatly from culture to culture. Family therapy with African Americans, for instance, usually involves the inclusion of multiple generations as well as non-biological family members, such as good friends and neighbors. The time and place of meetings can be modified to fit the needs of those who could not ordinarily be available during traditional hours or would find it difficult or threatening to come to a professional office far from their community. Finally, treatment topics can be expanded to include issues that are unique to culturally diverse clients. Dealing with racism, resolving conflicts around assimilation and acculturation, and clarifying issues of ethnic identity are three examples.

▶ Defining Professional Standards   2-4

What currently exists vis-à-vis standards of cultural competence in professional codes, such as that of the American Counseling Association (2014), are general prescriptions of "Multicultural/Diversity Considerations (Section B.1.a.). However, without specific guidelines as to what cultural competence specifically looks like, how is one to achieve, assess, or enforce it? According to Sue, Arredondo, and McDavis (1992), this problem "represents one of the major shortcomings of our profession" (p. 481).

The framework that the two groups have developed defines three areas of characteristics of culturally skilled counselors, borrowed from Sue and Sue (1999). First, such counselors "understand their own worldviews, how they are the product of their cultural conditioning, and how it may be reflected in their counseling and work with racial and ethnic minorities" (p. 481). Second, they "understand and share the worldviews of their culturally diverse clients with respect and appreciation" (p. 481). Third, they "use modalities and define goals consistent with the life experiences and cultural values of clients" (p. 481). Next, each of these three general characteristics— counselor awareness of his or her own assumptions, values, and biases; understanding

TABLE 2-3
Professional Multicultural Competencies I

Counselor Awareness of Own Cultural Values and Biases

Beliefs and Attitudes

Culturally skilled counselors believe cultural awareness and sensitivity to one's own cultural heritage is essential.

Culturally skilled counselors are aware of how their own cultural background and experiences, attitudes, and values and biases influence psychological processes.

Culturally skilled counselors are able to recognize the limits of their multicultural competency and expertise.

Culturally skilled counselors recognize their sources of discomfort with differences that exist between themselves and clients in terms of race, ethnicity, and culture.

Knowledge

Culturally skilled counselors have specific knowledge about their own racial and cultural heritage and how it personally and professionally affects their definitions and biases of normality-abnormality and the process of counseling.

Culturally skilled counselors possess knowledge and understanding about how oppression, racism, discrimination, and stereotyping affect them personally and in their work. This allows individuals to acknowledge their own racist attitudes, beliefs, and feelings. Although this standard applies to all groups, for White counselors, it may mean they understand how they may have directly or indirectly benefited from individual, institutional, and cultural racism as outlined in White identity development models.

Culturally skilled counselors possess knowledge about their social impact upon others. They are knowledgeable about communication style differences, how their style may clash or foster the counseling process with persons of color or others different from themselves, and how to anticipate the impact that all this may have on others.

Skills

Culturally skilled counselors seek out educational, consultative, and training experiences to improve their understanding and effectiveness in working with culturally different populations. Being able to recognize the limits of their competencies, they (a) seek consultation, (b) seek further training or education, (c) refer cases to more qualified individuals or resources, or (d) engage in a combination of these strategies.

Culturally skilled counselors are constantly seeking to understand themselves as racial and cultural beings and are actively seeking a nonracist identity.

the worldview of the culturally diverse client; and developing appropriate intervention strategies and techniques—is broken down into three dimensions that underlie them: attitudes and beliefs, knowledge, and skills. Nine competence areas (three characteristics by three dimensions) are thus defined as basic to a culturally skilled counselor or helper. The specific characteristics of the three dimensions of professional standards are presented in Tables 2-3, 2-4, and 2-5.

TABLE 2-4
Professional Multicultural Competencies II

Counselor Awareness of Client's Worldview
Attitudes and Beliefs
Culturally skilled counselors are aware of their negative and positive emotional reactions toward other racial and ethnic groups that may prove detrimental to the counseling relationship. They are willing to contrast their own beliefs and attitudes with those of their culturally different clients in a nonjudgmental fashion.
Culturally skilled counselors are aware of the stereotypes and preconceived notions that they may hold toward other racial and ethnic minority groups.
Knowledge
Culturally skilled counselors possess specific knowledge and information about the particular group with which they are working. They are aware of the life experiences, cultural heritage, and historical background of their culturally different clients. This particular competency is strongly linked to the minority identity development models available in the literature.
Culturally skilled counselors understand how race, culture, ethnicity, and other background elements may affect personality formation, vocational choices, manifestation of psychological disorders, help-seeking behavior, and the appropriateness or inappropriateness of counseling approaches.
Culturally skilled counselors understand and have knowledge about sociopolitical influences that impinge upon the life of racial and ethnic minorities.
Culturally skilled counselors understand how immigration issues, poverty, racism, stereotyping, and powerlessness may affect self-esteem and self-concept in the counseling process.
Skills
Culturally skilled counselors should familiarize themselves with relevant research and the latest findings regarding mental health and mental disorders that affect various ethnic and racial groups. They should actively seek out educational experiences that enrich their knowledge, understanding, and cross-cultural skills for more effective counseling behavior.
Culturally skilled counselors become actively involved with minority individuals outside the counseling setting (e.g., community events, social and political functions, celebrations, friendships, neighborhood groups) so their perspective of minorities is more than an academic or helping exercise.

Midgett and Doumas (2016) expressed several professional standards that may help foster cultural competence at the educational level. They suggest that educational programs must prepare students to adequately work with individuals of diverse backgrounds. In doing so, programs can implement culturally focused assignments or classroom activities, have students engage with culturally diverse populations in the community, and also allow students to gain real world experiences with cultural immersion/exchange programs.

TABLE 2-5
Professional Multicultural Competencies III

Culturally Appropriate Intervention Strategies

Attitudes and Beliefs

Culturally skilled counselors respect clients' religious and/or spiritual beliefs and values, including attributions and taboos, because these affect worldview, psychosocial functioning, and expressions of distress.

Culturally skilled counselors respect indigenous helping practices and respect help-giving networks among communities of color.

Culturally skilled counselors value bilingualism and do not view another language as an impediment to counseling (monolingualism may be the culprit here).

Knowledge

Culturally skilled counselors have a clear and explicit knowledge and understanding of the generic characteristics of counseling and therapy (culture-bound, class-bound, and monolingual) and how they may clash with the cultural values of various cultural groups.

Culturally skilled counselors are aware of institutional barriers that prevent minorities from using mental health services.

Culturally skilled counselors have knowledge of the potential bias in assessment instruments and use procedures and interpret findings in a way that recognizes the cultural and linguistic characteristics of the clients.

Culturally skilled counselors have knowledge of family structures, hierarchies, values, and beliefs from various cultural perspectives. They are knowledgeable about the community where a particular cultural group may reside and the resources in the community.

Culturally skilled counselors should be aware of relevant discriminatory practices at the social and community level that may be affecting the psychological welfare of the population being served.

Skills

Culturally skilled counselors are able to engage in a variety of verbal and non-verbal helping responses. They are able to send and receive both verbal and non-verbal messages accurately and appropriately. They are not tied down to only one method or approach to helping, but rather recognize that helping styles and approaches may be culture-bound. When they sense that their helping style is limited and potentially inappropriate, they can anticipate and modify it.

Culturally skilled counselors are able to exercise institutional skills on behalf of their clients. They can help clients determine whether a "problem" stems from racism or bias in others (the concept of healthy paranoia) so clients do not inappropriately personalize problems.

Culturally skilled counselors are not averse to seeking consultation with traditional healers or religious and spiritual leaders and practitioners in the treatment of culturally different clients when appropriate.

Culturally skilled counselors take responsibility for interacting in the language requested by the client and, if not feasible, make appropriate referrals. A serious problem arises when the linguistic skills of the counselor do not match the language of the client. This being the case, counselors should (a) seek a translator with cultural knowledge and appropriate professional background or (b) refer to a knowledgeable and competent bilingual counselor.

Culturally skilled counselors have training and expertise in the use of traditional assessment and testing instruments. They not only understand the technical aspects of the instruments, but also are aware of the cultural limitations. This allows them to use test instruments for the welfare of the culturally different clients.

Culturally skilled counselors should attend to as well as work to eliminate biases, prejudices, and discriminatory contexts in conducting evaluations and providing interventions and should develop sensitivity to issues of oppression, sexism, heterosexism, elitism, and racism.

Culturally skilled counselors take responsibility for educating their clients to the processes of psychological intervention, such as goals, expectations, legal rights, and the counselor's orientation.

Source: Based on from *Operationalization of the Multicultural Counseling Competencies* by P. Arredondo, R. Toporek, S. P. Brown, J. Jones, D. C. Locke, J. Sanchez, and H. Stadler, *Journal of Multicultural Counseling and Development,* 3, January 1996, 42–78. Copyright 1996.

Training Programs and Ethical Standards

It is also important to acknowledge that, in addition to Human Services, professional organizations monitoring the cultural competence of their members, Human Services training programs play an important role in teaching and sensitizing their students about diversity, culture, and cultural competence. Although such programs generally do not have stand-alone policies regarding diversity education, such requirements more typically are folded into the training guidelines and standards of educational monitoring groups. For example, take the Council for Standards in Human Service Education (CSHSE). In its National Standards for Master's Degree in Human Services (October 2009), cultural competency requirements are folded into three of their standards as follows:

- ▶ STANDARD 10: The curriculum shall include knowledge and theory of the interaction of human systems including: individual, interpersonal, group, family, organizational, community, and societal... Demonstrate broad conceptual mastery of the philosophical and theoretical underpinnings of the profession through... Emphasis on context and the role of diversity (including, but not limited to ethnicity, culture, gender, sexual orientation, age, learning style, ability, and socioeconomic status) in determining and meeting human needs.
- ▶ STANDARD 17: The curriculum shall incorporate human service values and attitudes and promote understanding of human services ethnics and their application in practice... Demonstrate broad conceptual mastery of the philosophical and theoretical underpinnings of the profession through... Recognition of the worth and uniqueness of the individual including ethnicity, culture, gender, sexual orientation, age, learning style, ability, and socioeconomic status.

▶ **STANDARD 18:** The program shall provide experiences and support to enable students to develop awareness of their own values, personalities, reaction patterns, interpersonal styles, and limitations ... Demonstrate broad conceptual mastery of the philosophical and theoretical underpinnings of the profession through ... Awareness of diversity.

Enforcing Professional Standards

In the 2017 revision of its Ethics Code, the American Psychological Association (APA; American Psychological Association, 2017) has moved even further in its efforts to monitor and police the profession vis-à-vis culture. This has occurred in several different ways. First, in its Standards on Competence, the APA specifically includes a section requiring the following acquisition of knowledge related to issues of diversity. It reads as follows:

2.01 Boundaries of Competence: (b) Where scientific or professional knowledge in the discipline of psychology establishes that an understanding of factors associated with age, gender, gender identity, race, ethnicity, culture, national origin, religion, sexual orientation, disability, language, or socioeconomic status is essential for effective implementation of their services or research, psychologists have to obtain the training, experience, consultation, or supervision necessary to ensure competence of their services or they make appropriate referrals.

Similarly, in its *Guidelines on Multicultural Education, Training, Research, and Organizational Change for Psychologists* (American Psychological Association, 2003), the APA defined a broad range of professional activities for careful scrutiny regarding issues of diversity and culture. The following guidelines provide a sense of the breadth of coverage:

▶ "Psychologists are encouraged to recognize that, as cultural beings, they may hold attitudes and beliefs that can detrimentally influence their perceptions of and interactions with individuals who are ethnically and racially different from themselves.

▶ "Psychologists are encouraged to recognize the importance of multicultural sensitivity/responsiveness, knowledge, and understanding about ethnically and racially different individuals.

▶ "As educators, psychologists are encouraged to employ the constructs of multiculturalism and diversity in psychological education.

▶ "Culturally sensitive psychological researchers are encouraged to recognize the importance of conducting culture-centered and ethical psychological research among persons from ethnic, linguistic, and racial minority backgrounds.

▶ "Psychologists strive to apply culturally appropriate skills in clinical and other applied psychological practices.

▶ "Psychologists are encouraged to use organizational change processes to support culturally informed organizational (policy) development and practices."

Even more specific and far-reaching is Celia Fisher's (2009) definition and enumeration of "multicultural ethical competence." Fisher, who is the director of the Fordham University Center for Ethics Education, chaired the APA Ethics Code Task Force that created the 2002 revision. According to her, multicultural ethical competence is comprised of three related processes: multicultural ethical commitment, multicultural ethical awareness, and goodness-of-fit ethics and multicultural ethical decision making. *Multicultural ethical commitment* implies the desire to understand how culture interacts with the resolution of ethnical problems and "moves psychologists to explore cultural differences and creatively apply the APA Ethics Code to each cultural context." It also implies a recognition of the harmful effects that practitioners can unknowingly create for culturally diverse individuals and groups "by invalidating their life experiences, defining their cultural values or differences as deviant, and imposing the values of Dominant culture upon them." *Multicultural ethical awareness* implies that commitment itself is not enough but must be accompanied by the requisite knowledge "about cultural differences and how they may affect the expression of and solution of ethical problems." Finally, *goodness-of-fit ethics and multicultural ethical decision making* implies that culturally-based ethical challenges are always new and unique. Variables such as the particular culture involved, "the salience of the culture for a particular individual in a particular context, other within-culture individual differences, the environment in which the psychological activity occurs, and the goals of that activity" generate such complexity that each new ethical challenge requires a somewhat different ethical decision-making process adjusted to both the cultural context and the practitioner's work setting and goals, thereby requiring "a process of co-learning that ensures this fit." In Table 2-6, the specific content areas of each of these three aspects of multicultural ethical competence are defined more fully.

A comparison of the models of Cross et al. (1989), Arredondo et al. (1996), and the American Psychological Association (2017) shows considerable overlap in the kinds of development and learning that each model sees as essential for those who hope to move toward cultural competence. You may find it valuable to consider the specific categories of these different models and assess where you might currently fall. Of late, there has been a significant increase in the availability of good training programs and courses designed to develop such skill areas. These learning experiences use a variety of process and interactive techniques, including self-exploratory and self-assessment exercises (such as those included in the "Activities" sections of each chapter of this book), immersion in alternative cultural environments, and observation and on-the-job training in culturally competent agencies.

TABLE 2-6
Multicultural Ethical Competence

Ethical decision making in diverse cultural venues must be sensitive to cultural attitudes toward individual autonomy and communal responsibility, historical and contemporary discrimination within society and psychology as a discipline, sociopolitical factors influencing definitions of race and ethnicity, and variations in immigration history, acculturation, cultural/ethnic identity, language, and mixed race/ ethnic heritage (Ponterotto et al., 2001; Sue and Sue, 2003; Trimble and Fisher, 2006). Multicultural responsibility requires "a fusion of personal and professional commitments to consider culture during ethical encounters" (Ridley et al., 2001, p. 176).

Multicultural Ethical Commitment

Multicultural ethical commitment requires a strong desire to understand how culture is relevant to the identification and resolution of ethical problems. It demands a moral disposition and emotional responsiveness that moves psychologists to explore cultural differences and creatively apply the APA Ethics Code to each cultural context. Cultivation of these competencies thus includes motivation to consider the influence of culture in psychologists' work conscientiously, prudently, and with caring discernment.

The desire to ensure cultural sensitivity is integrated into ethical decision making requires a willingness to reflect on how one's own cultural values and cultural identity influence the way one conceives of ethics as a psychologist (Arredondo, 1999; Helms, 1993). Furthermore, multicultural ethical competence entails recognition of harms that psychology can exert on culturally diverse groups by invalidating their life experiences, defining their cultural values or differences as deviant, and imposing the values of dominant culture upon them (Fisher, 1999; Fisher et al, 2002; Fowers and Davidov, 2006; Prilleltensky, 1997; Trimble and Fisher, 2006).

In psychological research and practice, multicultural ethical commitment involves motivation to:

- Critically examine the moral premises in the discipline that may largely reflect Eurocentric conceptions of the good

- Question "deficit" and "ethnic group comparative" approaches to understanding cultural differences

- Address the reality and impact of racial discrimination in the lives of cultural minorities

- Recognize that socially constructed racial labels can strip participants of their personal identity by responding to them only in terms of racial or ethnic categorizations

- Avoid conceptually grouping members of ethnic minority groups into categories that may not reflect how individuals see themselves

- Engage in self-examination of how institutional racism may have influenced each psychologist's own role, status, and motivation to develop professional identities that are free of these influences

- Develop the flexibility required to respond to rapid cultural diversification and fluid definitions of culture, ethnicity, and race

Multicultural Ethical Awareness

Multicultural ethical commitment is just the first step toward multicultural ethical competence. Good intentions are insufficient if psychologists fail to acquire relevant knowledge about cultural differences and how they may affect the expression of and solutions for ethical problems. Psychologists must be familiar with research, theory, and practice guidelines that are relevant to their work with diverse populations. This may include an understanding of the following:

- The history of ethical abuses of cultural minorities in the United States and how this may exacerbate disparities in mental health care, employment, criminal justice, and involvement in psychological research

- The impact on mental health of historical and contemporary discrimination in employment, education, housing, and other areas

- Cultural and contextual factors that may facilitate or interfere with psychological well-being or responsiveness to treatment

- Scientific, social, and political factors influencing the definitions of race, ethnicity, and culture and how these may serve as barriers to conducting psychological activities that protect individuals' rights and welfare

- Within-group as well as between-group differences that may be obscured by cultural stereotypes in society and within the discipline of psychology

- Knowledge and skills in constructing and implementing culturally valid and language-appropriate assessments, treatments, research procedures, teaching strategies, and consulting and organizational evaluation techniques

- Knowledge of relevant ethical standards in the APA Ethics Code and organizational guidelines relevant to multicultural ethical competence in research and practice

- Knowledge of federal and state antidiscrimination laws that are relevant to the contexts in which psychologists work

Goodness-of-Fit Ethics and Multicultural Ethical Decision Making

Multicultural ethical commitment and ethical awareness are essential but insufficient to ensure ethical resolution of multicultural challenges. Given the dynamic nature of individual, institutional, and sociopolitical concepts of race, culture, and ethnicity, ethical decision making across different cultural contexts can be informed but may not be resolved by previous approaches to ethical problems. Many multicultural ethical challenges are unique to the culture, the salience of the culture for a particular individual in a particular context, other within-culture individual differences, the environment in which the psychological activity occurs, and the goals of that activity. In applying the steps for ethical decision-making described in Chapter 3, multicultural ethical decision-making includes (a) creating a goodness of fit between the cultural context and the psychologist's work setting and goals; and (b) engaging in a process of co-learning that ensures this fit (Fisher and Ragsdale, 2006).

- Address the reality and impact of racial discrimination in the lives of cultural minorities

- Recognize that socially constructed racial labels can strip participants of their personal identity by responding to them only in terms of racial or ethnic categorizations

- Avoid conceptually grouping members of ethnic minority groups into categories that may not reflect how individuals see themselves

- Engage in self-examination of how institutional racism may have influenced each psychologist's own role, status, and motivation to develop professional identities free from these influences

- Develop the flexibility required to respond to rapid cultural diversification and fluid definitions of culture, ethnicity, and race

Source: From C. B. Fisher (2009), *Decoding the ethics code: A practical guide for psychologists.* Thousand Oaks, CA: Sage Publishing (pp. 87–89). Reprinted with permission.

SUMMARY

We are currently experiencing a diversification of American society. This includes both a sizable increase in the actual numbers of people of color in the United States and a decline in the relative percentage of Whites. Projections suggest that these trends will only increase. By 2060, for example, non-Hispanic Whites will represent less than 50 percent of the population. Two factors are primarily responsible for these changes in demographics: immigration rates and birthrates. The implications for our human services and mental health systems are staggering. Increasingly, we will be asked to provide services to individuals from non-majority cultures, those born outside the United States, and those for whom English is not the primary language. Adequately serving these populations requires more than merely color-coding or applying bandages to a system designed for a monocultural White population. In its place, we must establish a new vision of service delivery based on the notion of cultural competence.

Moving toward cultural competence is an emotionally demanding process that does not occur overnight or with a single course or workshop. There are few places in which it is safe to speak openly and honestly about ethnicity and race. Everyone has been personally hurt by prejudice and racism—Whites as well as people of color. Developing cultural competence requires looking at the pain and suffering that racism has caused, as well as examining one's own attitudes and beliefs. Gaining cultural competence can also provide enormous personal growth in the form of increased self-awareness, cultural sensitivity, non-judgmental thinking, and broadened consciousness.

Cultural competence is the ability to provide effective helping services cross-culturally. It can reside in individual practitioners, in agencies, and in a system of care. It is generally defined by an integrated series of awarenesses and attitudes, knowledge areas, and skills. Cross et al. (1989) offer a comprehensive model of effective cross-cultural service delivery. They define the underlying assumptions of such a model, levels of agency competence, and individual practitioner competence skill areas. The latter includes awareness and acceptance of difference, self-awareness, understanding the dynamics of difference, knowledge of the individual's culture, and ability to adapt the provider's skills to changing cultural needs and demands. Arredondo et al. (1996) define a series of professional multicultural competencies revolving around three themes: counselor awareness of his or her own cultural values and biases, counselor awareness of the client's worldview, and culturally appropriate intervention strategies. Human Services training programs and their educational monitoring groups such as the CSHSE also play an important role in teaching and sensitizing students to issues of diversity, culture, and cultural competence by referring to them in the National Standards for Training. The American Psychological Association (2017) offers a set of comprehensive guidelines for multicultural practice among psychologists, and Fisher (2009) defines and enumerates specific "multicultural ethical competencies."

Becoming culturally competent is increasingly a professional imperative and will eventually become a basis for hiring. Increasingly, human service practitioners will find themselves working with clients and colleagues who are culturally diverse.

ACTIVITIES

This and subsequent chapters of this book end with various activities that will help you understand the chapter's material in deeper and more personal ways. Some of these are self-assessment exercises and activities. A theme that reverberates through the beginning chapters of this book is the critical nature of self-awareness. Again, it is not a question of whether you hold racist attitudes and stereotypes or if you are involved with practices of institutional or cultural racism. We all are and do. Rather, the issue is discovering in what ways your thinking as a provider is slanted racially, how this affects your role as helper, and what you can do to change it. The exercises in this book are meant to stimulate increased self-awareness. They are useful in counteracting natural tendencies toward denial, avoidance, and rationalization in matters of race and ethnicity. They will be productive to the extent that you take them seriously, give sufficient time to process and complete each thoroughly, and approach them with honesty and candor.

1. *Keep a cultural journal.* As you study about race, culture, and ethnicity, you will begin to notice these issues more broadly in school, at work, and in your personal life. It is a matter of becoming aware of what has always been there. One method of optimizing such learning is to keep a journal of your observations throughout the term or semester and regularly review past entries. Also, you probably will notice how observations stimulate questions. Make note of these as well and consider how you will go about answering these questions.

2. *Observe and analyze an organization's cultural competence.* This exercise will help you identify the dynamics and aspects of racism and cultural insensitivity in organizations and agencies. Choose an agency or organization with which you are familiar; it may be one in which you are currently working or volunteering or one you are familiar with from the past. Answer the following questions, some of which may require you to do research or seek additional information.

    a. How many people of color or other minority ethnic group members work in this organization, and what kind of jobs do they have?

    b. How are people hired or brought into the organization? Is there anything about this process or what might be required that may affect people of color or other ethnic group members differentially?

    c. Does the organization promote cultural diversity? Do any mission statements, plans, or projections in this area exist? Can you discern any unwritten feelings or attitudes that prevail around race and ethnicity within the organization? Has it done anything specific to promote greater diversity?

d. How would you describe the organizational culture? Do you feel that members of various communities of color would be comfortable entering and being a part of it? Specify your answers by ethnic group and explain in detail. How do you think your coworkers or fellow volunteers would react to the entry of a person of color?

e. How is the organization run? Who has the power? Who makes decisions? Is there anything about the organization's structure that makes it accessible or inaccessible to people of color, ethnicities, or ableism?

f. What does it feel like working or volunteering in this organization? Are there unique or unusual rules, policies, and styles of working? Would you say that the organization's culture is predominantly Euro-American? Explain.

g. If it is a service organization or agency, who are its clients? Are there any efforts being made (or have any efforts ever been made) to broaden the racial and ethnic composition of the clientele?

You may find it particularly informative to have coworkers or fellow volunteers answer these questions and then compare answers or use the questions as stimuli for discussing the cultural competence of the organization.

Working with Culturally Diverse Clients

LEARNING OBJECTIVES

3-1 Distinguish between cross-cultural helping and working with same-culture clients.

3-2 Apply the ADDRESSING Framework as a clinical tool.

3-3 Formulate culturally sensitive DSM-5 diagnosis.

3-4 Plan ways to discuss race and ethnicity with clients.

In subsequent chapters of this text, you will be introduced to a variety of conceptual issues intimately related to working with culturally diverse clients. We will explore the meanings of prejudice, racism, and white privilege—especially as these relate to and affect clients and providers—and come to understand culture, cultural differences, and worldview, as well as the cultural limits of the helping models that have shaped most providers' thinking. In addition, you will learn about a number of psychological factors and aspects of service delivery that are unique to the experience of ethnically diverse clients and critical to an understanding of their behavior. These will include aspects of child development and parenting, differences in family structure and biracial or bicultural families, and various areas of psychological difficulty and disturbance that especially challenge clients of color. Material to be covered will include conflicts in identity development, problems with assimilation and acculturation, and higher levels of stress, traumatic experience, and use and abuse of alcohol and drugs. There will also be chapters that discuss bias in service delivery and working with collective trauma.

At this point, however, I would like to provide readers—especially those who are or will be enrolled in practicum settings where they will be beginning to do hands-on counseling work—some basic ideas and tools that will be helpful (as well as anxiety-reducing) in getting started. We will begin this chapter by exploring how the service provider's therapeutic presence influences multicultural work. We will then discuss how cross-cultural service delivery differs from monocultural work and then proceed to develop an understanding of the psychological dynamics that play themselves out in situations where the therapist and client are ethnically different. Next, you will learn how to assess and diagnose culturally diverse individuals, receive tips on establishing rapport, learn how to maximize productivity in your initial contacts with culturally different clients, and finally learn how to sensitively raise and talk about the issues of race and ethnicity with clients. At the end of this chapter, you will be given an opportunity to analyze two case studies of hypothetical clients of color as a means of beginning to assess your cross-cultural knowledge and skills.

▶ How Is Cross-Cultural Helping Different?   `3-1`

There is a general agreement among practitioners that cross-cultural helping is more demanding, challenging, and energy-draining than work with same-culture clients. According to Pedersen et al. (2015), for example, it tends to be more experiential, malleable, and collaborative.

> ▶ Cross-cultural helping is more likely to affect the provider directly and emotionally. It is akin to culture shock, where providers are immersed in a foreign culture in which familiar patterns of behavior are no longer useful and new means of acting and relating must be discovered. It has also been described as more labor-intensive and more likely to result in fatigue.

- The term *malleable* refers to the fact the helping process must be continually adapted to the specific cultural needs of differing clients. As suggested earlier, the only constant is the shared humanity. Standard approaches are overwhelmingly culture-bound and northern European in nature, and even efforts to catalog cultural similarities among racially related ethnic groups must be tentative and ever-mindful of enormous intragroup diversity. The authors suggest:
  - Be prepared to adapt your techniques (e.g., general activity level, mode of verbal intervention, content of remarks, tone of voice) to the cultural background of the client; communicate acceptance of and respect for the client in terms that make sense within his or her cultural frame of reference; and be open to the possibility of more direct intervention in the life of the client than the traditional ethos of the counseling profession would dictate or permit.
- Finally, the very nature of cross-cultural work is collaborative because the provider is more dependent on the client for help in defining the process itself. For example, although it is common practice for providers to collaborate with clients in setting treatment goals, doing this is even more imperative in cross-cultural work. Providers need direct and continuing client input on what is culturally valued so goals are culturally appropriate and useful and minimize ethnocentric projection. Since provider and client begin at very different cultural places, it is reasonable to expect some mutual movement in each other's direction. Culturally competent professionals adapt and adjust their efforts to the cultural milieu of the client. At the same time, by entering the helping process, culturally diverse clients cannot help but gain some knowledge and insight into the workings of mainstream culture and its worldview.

Conceptualizing Cross-Cultural Work

Cross-cultural work is challenging in yet another respect, which has to do with the complexity of emotional and psychological dynamics at work in the lives of ethnic individuals. As pointed out earlier, for example, ethnic children must negotiate not only the same developmental challenges that all other children face, but also a series of issues resulting from race, ethnicity, and minority status. Keeping track of these various psychological phenomena, sorting them out, and addressing them is our job as human services providers. One might say that this is yet another aspect of cultural competence.

There are four different systems of psychological dynamics that influence cross-cultural work and the relationship between client and practitioner: difference, ethnicity, race, and power. The task of the practitioner is to not only understand how these systems shape the behavior and experience of the client, but also see how they play themselves out in the way the practitioner perceives and relates to the culturally diverse client. As stressed throughout this text, self-awareness is a critical aspect of cultural competence.

Ethnicity is connected to processes, both conscious and unconscious, that satisfy a fundamental need for historical connection and security. Thus, it embraces notions of both the group and the self that are, in turn, influenced by the value society places on

TABLE 3-1

The Therapist's Cultural Self-Assessment: Example of Olivia

Cultural influences	Olivia's self-assessment
*Age and generational influences	52 years old; third-generation U.S. American; member of politically active generation of Chicanos and Chicanas in California; first generation affected by post–civil rights academic and employment opportunities in the 1970s.
*Developmental disability	No developmental disability.
Disability acquired later in life	Chronic knee problems since early adulthood, including multiple surgeries; sometimes I use crutches to walk.
*Religion and spiritual orientation	Mother is a practicing Catholic, father nonpracticing Presbyterian; my current beliefs are a mixture of Catholic and secular; I do not attend mass.
Ethnic and racial identity	Mother and father both of mixed Mexican (Spanish and Indian) heritage, both born in the United States; my own identity is Chicana; I speak Spanish, but my primary language is English.
*Socioeconomic status	Parents urban, working, lower-middle-class members of an ethnic minority culture; however, my identity is as a university-educated Chicana; I identify with working-class people, although my occupation and income are middle class.
*Sexual orientation	Heterosexual; I have one friend who is lesbian.
*Indigenous heritage	My maternal grandmother was Indian and immigrated to the United States from Mexico with my grandfather when they were young adults; what I know about this part of my heritage came from her, but she died when I was 10 years old.
*National origin	United States, but deep understanding of the immigration experience from my grandparents.
Gender	Woman, Chicana, divorced, mother of two children.

*Connotes dominant cultural identity.
Source: Hays, P. A. (2008). *Addressing cultural complexities in practice: Assessment, diagnosis, and therapy.* 2d ed. Washington, D.C.: American Psychological Association.

the group. Societal definition and assigned value, among other factors, help determine whether ethnic meaning for a given group or individual becomes positive or negative, which then has great significance for how they behave (p. 39).

Race, in turn, refers to an acquired social meaning in which biological differences, via the mechanism of stereotyping, have become markers for status assignment within the social system. The status assignment based on skin color identity has evolved into complex social structures that promote a power differential between whites and various people of color. These power-assigning social structures, in the form of institutional racism, affect the life opportunities, lifestyles, and quality of life for both whites and people of color. In so doing, they compound, exaggerate, and distort biological and behavioral differences and reinforce misconceptions, myths, and distortions on the part of both groups about one another and themselves (p. 71).

Pinderhughes's (1989) descriptions of race and ethnicity align with more recent descriptions by Robinson-Wood (2016). The psychologies of difference and power deserve additional attention.

Understanding Differences

According to Robinson-Wood (2016), how the provider responds to being different and what it means to him or her are issues that are rarely attended to in preparing people for culturally diverse work. Feelings generated by the experience of being different tend to be negative and can include the reactions of confusion, hurt, pain, anger, and fear, as well as envy, guilt, pity, sympathy, and privilege. Interpersonally, these reactions can lead to a sense of distance from others, loneliness, isolation, rejection, and abandonment. All these reactions influence the helping situation.

▶ Understanding Power   3-2

According to Baruth and Manning (2016), *power* is having control and authority or influence over others; *powerlessness*, in turn, is the inability to influence others. The helping relationship is by nature a power imbalance in favor of the practitioner; therefore, the client is in a potentially vulnerable situation in which practitioners may seek to use their power to meet personal needs. This dynamic is a natural part of therapy, according to Totton (2016), who said clients come into counseling giving their counselor power. They expect and hope that the counselor will use skills, attitudes, and knowledge to help. Without awareness of how power influences the therapeutic process, counselors can grab this power through their structuring of the therapy session. Responses to clients early in the therapeutic relationship may seem appropriate to a trained professional but mystical and humiliating to clients. These interactions can socially dislocate the clients—throwing them off balance (Smail, 2002).

This is especially likely when the helper is unaware of or uncomfortable with his or her ethnic or racial identity or unaware of or uncomfortable with those aspects of the cross-cultural client. Helpers must strive to develop greater awareness of how power impacts their clients' lives and relationships. The therapeutic relationship is impacted by helpers' own cultural definition of power and the influence of power in their lives (Brammer, 2012).

Powerlessness can be an unpleasant and painful psychological experience, and people respond to it by trying to end their pain and regain a sense of power. Such responses can be very positive and productive, as in the case of those who gain power through self-development, achievement, and personal mastery. Alternatively, a false sense of power can be gained by putting down others, inspiring fear, and/or manipulating them. Even accommodation and dependency can be seen as strategies for overcoming powerlessness. Often, such maladaptive practices are related to problems in clients' lives and exploring them in treatment and developing alternative behavioral reactions can be very freeing and empowering.

Clinicians can also take the one-down position to equalize or reverse the power relationship between a practitioner and a culturally diverse client. For example, the client may take on the role of cultural expert, teaching the practitioner, who is ignorant in the ways of the client's culture. Through such strategies, clients can learn to become more comfortable in this new role and empowered by the acquisition of new behaviors in relation to it.

Understanding Therapeutic Presence

An additional aspect of cross-cultural work is the service provider's ability to be therapeutically present with his or her clients (Geller, 2017). Without being therapeutically present, a practitioner's understanding of differences, ethnicity, race, and power would be less effective in cross-cultural work. According to Erskine (2015), when being therapeutically present, the service provider behaves and communicates in a way that respects and enhances the worth of the client. Also, the service provider's empathic attunement allows him or her to be impacted by the client's experience in the world. According to Erskine, "it is more than communication, it is communion—full interpersonal contact" (p. 192). Being therapeutically present is a developmental process (Austin and Austin, 2018). Early in a student's development, therapeutic presence can be defined as a student's ability to be aware of him or herself, the client, and the therapeutic relationship and using that awareness to act (behave and communicate) in a way that is therapeutic. Increased practice of being with clients in this way in session, with intentional attention to systems of psychological dynamics of differences, ethnicity, race, and power, can strengthen a student's ability to have the whole self in the encounter with a client by being completely in the moment on a multiplicity of levels—physically, emotionally, cognitively, and spiritually (Geller and Greenberg, 2012). Additionally, when clients experience their service providers as being therapeutically present with them, it influences that polyvagal system, causing them to feel safer within the therapeutic relationship. The polyvagal system is a social engagement system that helps us navigate relationships. Therapists can trigger this system using their presence, making the client feel safe and more willing to share their experiences. A client's feelings of safety in cross-cultural work is pivotal to positive treatment outcomes (Geller, Greenberg, and Watson, 2010; Geller and Porges, 2014).

▶ Hays's Addressing Framework `3-3`

Acknowledging the inner diversity of individual clients helps us to avoid oversimplifying, overcategorizing, or stereotyping them. Too often, we tend to underemphasize the variety of cultural influences that affect any given individual that makes him or her a unique person. For example, by identifying an individual by race or ethnicity alone—because it seems most salient or central to them or to us—we unintentionally turn them into stereotypes and one-dimensional beings, losing the full complexity of their cultural experiences and limiting our understanding of them as complex individuals. In so doing, we not only privilege a particular aspect of their cultural identity over others, but also unwittingly set various aspects of identity in opposition to each other.

To overcome this pitfall, Pamela Hays (2008, 2012) has created what she calls the ADDRESSING framework, a list of cultural influences or identity dimensions that human services providers need to address in their work as therapists. The framework includes the following:

- ▶ Age and generational influence
- ▶ Developmental disabilities
- ▶ Disabilities acquired later in life
- ▶ Religion and spiritual orientation
- ▶ Ethnic and racial identity
- ▶ Socioeconomic status
- ▶ Sexual orientation
- ▶ Indigenous heritage
- ▶ National origin
- ▶ Gender

According to Hays, she uses the first letter of each of these influences to create an acronym and as a starting point for what I call the ADDRESSING framework, a practitioner-oriented approach that conceptualizes cross-cultural work in two broad categories (Table 3-2). The first category, Personal Work, involves the therapist's introspection, self-exploration, and an understanding of the influences of culture on one's own belief

TABLE 3-2
Addressing Clients' Cultural Influences and Identities: The Case of Jean

Cultural influences	Jean's influences, as noted by Marie
Age and generational influences	46 years old; born in 1972 and grew up under the oppressive Duvalier government (1957–1986)
Developmental disability	None reported or apparent.
Disability acquired later in life	None reported or apparent.
Religion and spiritual orientation	Self-identifies as Catholic; I did not ask about, and he did not mention, any voodoo beliefs or practices.
Ethnic and racial identity	Haitian; reports he "does not feel Canadian," although he has landed immigrant status (i.e., permanent residency).
Socioeconomic status	Middle-class parents, has a university education, underemployed, probably as a result of discrimination; speaks French fluently (a class-related ability).
Sexual orientation	Probably heterosexual.
Indigenous heritage	None.
National origin	Haitian; speaks Haitian Creole and French fluently; immigrated to Quebec, Montreal, Canada in 1985.
Gender	Male, single (divorced), father of one son; also a brother and uncle.

Source: Hays, P. A. (2008). *Addressing cultural complexities in practice: Assessment, diagnosis, and therapy.* 2d ed. Washington, D.C.: American Psychological Association.

system and worldview. The second category, Interpersonal Work, focuses on the therapist's learning about and from other cultures, which usually involves interpersonal experiences. The importance of both the personal and interpersonal aspects of cross-cultural learning has been emphasized throughout multicultural literature (pp. 4–5).

Preparing for Cross-Cultural Work

To be perfectly honest, no amount of preparation can totally allay the anxiety typical of providers-in-training when they first contemplate working with culturally diverse clients. Students regularly ask: "But what do I do when I find myself sitting across the desk from someone who is culturally different from me? I'm afraid I'll panic or draw a blank and not know what to say." This anxiety and hesitancy reflects a basic discomfort with cultural differences and the fact that most providers have grown up in a racist society separated from those who are different from them. They are afraid—because of their ignorance about a client's culture—that they will make a cultural faux pas or miss something very obvious. They are, in addition, often anxious and uncomfortable because of feelings of guilt over the existence of racism or embarrassed because of past indifference, the racist behavior of family and friends, or feelings of personal privilege or entitlement. It feels like very dangerous territory, and after you have read chapter after chapter about the complexity of issues in working with diversity and how easily cross-cultural communication can break down, the prospect of facing people from diverse cultures and providing them with useful help can be rather daunting. Recently, Dillon et al. (2016) found that, on average, clients who generally perceived their counselors as multiculturally competent reported no improvement to their psychological well-being after four sessions. These findings could suggest that cross-cultural work may take more than four sessions to impact a client's well-being. Rather than focusing on doing *it* right or wrong, counselors should focus on being patient and trusting the process of cross-cultural work. At moments of doubt, it is important to remember several things:

- First, as a provider, one is already—or is in the process of becoming—a skilled professional. Becoming culturally competent does not mean starting from scratch or learning everything anew. Rather, it means honing skills that one already has, broadening clinical concepts that are too narrow in their application in the first place, and gaining new cultural knowledge about clients with whom one will be working. Culturally competent providers are, in general, more competent professionals because they must remain more conscious about what they are doing to be vigilant as to the cultural appropriateness of tasks, methods, and perspectives that others may routinely overlook. In a certain sense, one might say that every client carries his or her own unique culture, and it is the professional helper's task to discover how to gain entry into that culture respectfully and offer services that are sensitive to its rules and inner dynamics.
- Second, the clients with whom one will be working are, above all, human beings, and this is the ultimate basis for connection. They are also anxious about meeting with a new, unfamiliar person, especially if that person is culturally different. More than likely, they have had experiences that make them mistrust the kind of system in which the provider works. The initial task, then, is to set clients at ease in a manner that has meaning for them. Helping is, above all, a human process; it is bound to fail, however (with all clients, not just culturally diverse ones), when this awareness is lost.
- Third, unfortunately in the process of teaching people about cultural differences, there is a tendency to objectify and stereotype clients by seeing them only in terms of their differences; this must always be guarded

against. By attending to differences too fully, one can easily lose sight of the entire person sitting across from the provider.

▶ Fourth, focusing too heavily on differences and thereby overlooking basic human similarities (e.g., with Asian Americans, you must do this, be aware of this, assume this, and so forth) can turn cross-cultural work into a mechanical process. This is exactly the wrong approach. Cross-cultural interaction must be based on the shared humanity that exists between client and provider—it is the one place where both are similar and can most easily join. Kroeber (1948), an early anthropologist, pointed out three kinds of human characteristics: those that one shares with all other human beings, those that one shares with some other human beings, and those that are unique to each individual. It is in relation to the first kind that cross-cultural communication and helping are made possible. A sensitivity to the second and third kinds of characteristics allows for the defining of human differences and uniqueness once a basic connection has formed. Again, it is through the very human capacities of caring, having sympathy and empathy for others, and identifying with the basic joys and predicaments of being human that differences can be best bridged.

To prepare for cross-cultural work, service providers should be aware of critical race theory (CRT) and how it can influence their work with diverse clients. According to Delgado and Stefancic (2017), CRT is a "collection of activists and scholars engaged in studying and transforming the relationship among race, racism, and power" (p. 3). Critical race theorists believe that racism is ordinary, the usual way society works, and the common daily experience of most people of color in America. Critical race theorists also believe that racism serves a purpose for the dominant culture. These beliefs mean that racism is hard to address because it is not always acknowledged and, because it serves a purpose for the dominant culture, it is difficult to eradicate. To work from this theoretical framework, service providers will need to increase their awareness of how racism influences the daily lives and mental well-being of their clients of color.

Assessing Culturally Diverse Clients

A good, culturally sensitive assessment provides valuable information about how to proceed with treatment. It can give insight into the problem as conceived by clients and a sense of barriers that might stand in the way of seeking and providing help. It can suggest what clients expect to receive from the helping process and their notions of what the process will involve. It can also provide a sense of how acculturated clients are, how comfortable they would be with a more mainstream approach, how much the process needs to be adjusted, and whether any special preparation of clients is necessary prior to treatment. On the basis of answers to these questions and impressions gained during early contact, reasonable and informed decisions about how to proceed can be made. Collecting data about the client's cultural history and lifestyle is an excellent place to start. The following list of specific items can serve as a starting point:

- Place of birth
- Number of generations in the United States
- Family roles and structure
- Language spoken at home
- English fluency
- Economic situation and status
- Amount and type of education
- Amount of acculturation
- Traditions still practiced in the home
- Familiarity and comfort with the Northern European lifestyle
- Religious affiliation
- Community and friendship patterns

Together, these items provide a good initial basis for understanding the client ethnically and culturally.

Grieger and Ponterotto (1995) suggest six additional areas of assessment that should be useful in deciding how the helping process must be adjusted in relation to the cultural needs of the client. These include:

- Client's level of psychological mindedness
- Family's level of psychological mindedness
- Client's and the family's attitudes toward helping
- Client's level of acculturation
- Family's level of acculturation
- Family's attitude toward acculturation

If a client's or family's worldview precludes "conceptualizing one's problems from a psychological point of view and having the construct of emotional disturbance as a part of one's interpretive lens" (Grieger and Ponterotto, 1995, p. 363) and their levels of acculturation are low, several alternatives to insight approaches are possible. One is to work with the problem as defined by the client (regardless of whether the provider sees underlying psychological issues). Pinderhughes (1989) offers the following series of questions that further pinpoint and define the cultural dimensions of the problem being presented. All are worth exploring in depth:

- To what extent is the problem related to issues of transition, such as migration and immigration?
- To what extent is the client's understanding of the problem based on a cultural explanation; for example, "evil curse," "mal ojo," and so forth?

> Is the behavior that is a problem considered normal within the culture or is it considered dysfunctional?
> To what extent is the problem a manifestation of an environmental lack of access to resources and supports?
> To what extent is the problem related to culture conflict in identity, values, or relationships?
> To what extent is the behavior a consequence of psychological conflict or characterological problems?
> What are the cultural strengths and assets available to the client, such as cultural values and practices, social networks, and support systems? (p. 149)

Even today, combining all three sources of information—namely, the basic demographics and the more specific questions raised by Grieger and Ponterotto (1995) and Pinderhughes (1989)—provides a good beginning for understanding the life situation and presenting the problem of the culturally diverse client.

Paniagua (2013) provides general guidelines for the assessment and diagnosis of culturally diverse clients. He suggests service providers first develop a strong therapeutic relationship on three different levels: conceptual, behavioral, and cultural. The conceptual level "includes such issues as the client's and therapist's perception of sincerity, openness, honesty, motivation, empathy, sensitivity, inquiring concerns, and credibility in their relationship" (p. 8). The behavioral level includes the client's perception of the therapist's expertise in the specific issue that the client is experiencing. The cultural level includes the cultural compatibility hypotheses and the universalistic argument. The cultural compatibility hypotheses suggest that service providers are more effective when working with individuals of their own ethnic/racial background, while the universalistic argument states that service providers can be effective with different racial/ethnic backgrounds regardless of their own racial/ethnic backgrounds.

In addition to building strong therapeutic relationships, Paniagua (2013) encourages service providers to consider acculturation when assessing and diagnosing diverse clients. Acculturation can be defined as the degree to which individuals integrate new cultural patterns into their original patterns. This process can be negative or positive from different clients.

Additionally, when assessing clients, Paniagua (2013) encouraged service providers to use translators when therapeutically necessary, to select translated psychological tests, to be mindful of overdiagnosing some multicultural groups, to consider the role extended family members play in clients' lives and involving extended family members in the therapeutic process, to consider the modality of therapy, and to remember that many different cultures have a different idea of what a therapist is and does.

▶ Making Culturally Sensitive DSM-5 Diagnoses   `3-4`

DSM diagnoses are made with consideration of normal and abnormal behaviors. Sue et al. (2015) state these behaviors originate from an individual's culture. Cultural backgrounds can greatly influence behaviors and perceptions of mental illness. Sue et al. (2015) explained that many DSM-5 diagnoses "have symptoms that are very similar across cultures . . . however, there are cultural differences in the definition, descriptions, and understandings of mental illness."

The DSM-5 (American Psychiatric Association, 2013) is the most widely used clinical diagnostic tool in the United States. It has, however, been repeatedly criticized for its ethnocentrism and insensitivity to issues of culture and ethnicity. There have been various efforts to adapt it for use with culturally diverse clients.

One example is the "Outline for Cultural Formulation," which can be found in the Appendix of DSM-5. Based on the work of Lu, Lim, and Mazzich (1995), the outline was developed to help clinicians identify cultural factors in individual cases that may dictate special attention or alternative approaches or conceptions to diagnosis and treatment. The Outline has five general components: the cultural identity of the individual (aspects of self-definition); cultural conceptualizations of distress (a description of the illness from within the individual's culture); psychosocial stressors and cultural features of vulnerability and resilience (stresses and supports related to the psychosocial environment and levels of functioning); cultural features of the relationship between the individual and the clinician; and the overall assessment (how cultural considerations specifically affect diagnosis and treatment activities and interpretations). The construction of the Outline was an attempt to address some of the diagnostic and treatment biases described in Chapter 5. Lewis-Fernández et al. (2017) conducted a mixed-methods study, collecting data from 318 clients and 75 helpers, which found the Cultural Formulation Interview feasible, acceptable, and useful. A more detailed version of the Outline appears in Table 3-3.

Establishing Rapport and the First Session

In working with culturally diverse clients, the first session is especially critical. Research has shown that clients of color underutilize mental health services (Villatoro, 2017). When clients of color do seek services, past research shows that up to 50 percent of these clients do not return for a second session (Sue and McKinney, 1975; Sue et al., 1974). Some common barriers include "poverty, inadequate insurance coverage, access to transportation, access to childcare, cultural mistrust of mental health professionals and medical establishments, insufficient understanding of the mental health profession, institutional racism, discrimination, and stigma associated with

TABLE 3-3
DSM-5 Outline for Cultural Formulation

A. **Cultural Identity of the Individual**
- Ethnic or cultural reference group
- Degree of involvement with both culture of origin and host culture
- Language ability, use, and preference
- Other aspects of identity: age, gender, sexual orientation, religion or spirituality, disability, class, etc.

B. **Cultural Conceptualizations of Distress**
- Predominant idioms of distress
- Meaning and perceived severity of the individual's symptoms in relation to the norms of their cultural reference group
- Local illness categories used by the individual's family and community to identify the condition
- Perceived cause or explanatory models
- Current preferences for and past experiences with professional and popular sources of care

C. **Psychosocial Stressors and Cultural Features of Vulnerability and Resilience**
- Culturally relevant interpretations of social stressors, available social support, levels of functioning and disability
- Stressors in the social environment
- Role of religion and kin networks

D. **Cultural Features of the Relationship Between the Individual and the Clinician**
- Differences in culture and social status between the individual and the clinician
- Problems their differences might cause in diagnosis and treatment
- Negotiating an appropriate level of intimacy
- Rapport
- Respect
- Communication (verbal and nonverbal)
- Using interpreters

E. **Overall Cultural Assessment for Diagnosis and Care**
- Differential diagnosis and treatment
- Effects on treatment planning: biological outcomes, psychotherapy outcomes, social cultural outcomes, spiritual outcomes

Source: Adapted from Cultural Formulation, pp. 749–759. In *Diagnostic and Statistical Manual of Mental Disorders, Fifth Edition - DSM-5* by American Psychiatric Association, 2013. Washington, D.C.: American Psychiatric Association. Copyright © by American Psychiatric Association

mental illness" (Obasi and Leong, 2009, p. 228). Culturally diverse clients must come away from early sessions with a sense that their problems are understood from their own perspective and that they will receive concrete benefits from their work with the provider. Thus, goals for the first session should include:

- Establishing good rapport
- Gaining an understanding of the client's problem

- Gaining an understanding of what he or she expects from the helping relationship
- Communicating clearly what the provider can reasonably offer
- Providing the client with the experience of being heard and understood and (if possible and appropriate) hope that the process into which he or she has entered can offer some immediate help

The following general suggestions will contribute to approaching these goals:

- Be warm, sincere, and respectful in your manner. Introduce yourself by the title and name you wish the client to use. Mutual introductions are very important. Northern European American culture is unusual in its desire to "get down to business." Other cultures are more personal in their approach, preceding business matters with introductions and inquiries as to health, family, and the like. Refer to adult clients as Mr., Miss, or Mrs. initially. (It is usually most appropriate to address the oldest family member present if it is a family session.) Be sure to inquire as to whether you are pronouncing their name correctly and how they wish to be addressed. Also, ask by what name or names they wish you to refer to their ethnic group. If you are comfortable doing so, share with them some personal information (e.g., family data, where you reside) along with your professional credentials. Most cultures do not view others in terms of their social roles to the extent that European Americans do with regard to professional behavior.
- If you are anxious about your lack of knowledge about your client's culture, do something about it by researching it prior to meeting with him or her. At the same time, it is unrealistic to expect that you can become an expert on their culture and all its diverse aspects; exhibiting such a position about another person's culture is, in fact, likely to be taken very negatively—as haughty, presumptuous, or even demeaning. It is far better to be open about one's lack of knowledge and ask questions. For example: "I have not worked with many clients from your community and feel I do not know as much about your culture as I would like. I would appreciate your help in explaining certain things I may not understand as you refer to them." Your sincere openness and desire to learn is not a hindrance, but rather a matter of respect for the client and the client's culture. At the same time, it is necessary to point out that many people of color (e.g., African Americans) may react negatively to being expected to educate whites about their culture, which they may express in statements such as "If you want to learn about me, read a book." Anger at such expectations reflects a historical experience of people of color, which involves

both an attitude on the part of whites that it is the responsibility of people of color to deal with racism and injustice and the feeling that the desire to "learn about us" is not really sincere. I would suggest asking the client if he or she is comfortable playing such a role.

▶ Give a brief and nontechnical description of the helping process, its purpose, and the specifics of how often you would like to meet, for how long, when, where, and so forth, as well as any other relevant information, such as where and how to contact you. Describe what is expected of him or her and what can be expected from you. Be sure to discuss confidentiality and what happens to the information shared with you. Remember that this may be the client's first experience with a professional helper, and such roles may not exist formally in their culture.

▶ Have clients describe in their own words the problem(s) for which they are seeking help. Feel free to ask questions and get as much clarification as necessary. Then, summarize for them what you heard and ask if your summary is accurate. It is critical that you truly understand what they are communicating and similarly, that they are aware you understand. Also, ask what kind of help they need most immediately, how other family members view them and the problem, and whether family members or significant others are willing to participate in future sessions. Throughout this phase of the process, try to determine what the client expects vis-à-vis gaining help with the problem.

▶ On the basis of the information you now have, share with them what you believe can be accomplished in terms of both more immediate and long-range needs. It is important to describe possible goals in collaborative terms (but at the same time, do so in a manner that continues to emphasize your skills and knowledge) and indicate that if they choose to proceed, the specific goal setting will be done jointly. Also, discuss what might be some of the changes associated with achieving the goals.

▶ Ask clients if there are any aspects of the helping process, as it has been described and experienced so far, that may be difficult for them. Similarly, if you notice anything that already seems problematic, it would be good to raise your concerns at this point.

▶ The session should end with a formal goodbye and concrete plans for what will transpire next: another appointment, a referral, or a call to the client with some additional information, at which time you will discuss continuing.

Remember that these general suggestions must be altered and adjusted in relation to the individual circumstances and personal characteristics of each client.

▶ Talking About Race and Ethnicity with Clients   3-5

By far, the most challenging task facing beginning practitioners in cross-cultural work is introducing the topic of race and ethnicity into the therapeutic discussion. This fact is not all that surprising, however, given the enormous difficulty and emotionally charged nature of such discussions in our society in general.

The following section on talking about race and ethnicity with clients was contributed by Deborah Ronay Psy.D., a clinical psychologist in private practice and graduate of The Wright Institute in Berkeley. Deborah has had extensive experience working with the Latino community.

We are all racial and ethnic beings. To not invite and include this aspect into the therapeutic treatment is a missed opportunity for both therapist and client. There are many ways to bring the client's ethnicity into the treatment. There are active invitations, which are spoken and tangible actions on the therapist's part, as well as more passive invitations, which can be unspoken and mainly consist of the therapist holding in mind the importance of the client's ethnicity and how it factors into their psychological strengths and challenges.

In order to actively bring the client's race or ethnicity into therapy, it is important to consider timing, the therapeutic relationship, and the client's presenting problem. Furthermore, it is essential to bring our own ethnicity into the treatment as therapists if we want to be able to invite the client's ethnic self into it also. Like sharks in the water, clients can sense the therapist's reticence in talking about race and racism. This is especially true for clients of color. In general, as therapists we need to be willing to go to the psychological places our clients take us while helping them further explore what remains uncharted.

Race and ethnicity are very often uncharted places, often left unexamined by clients and untouched by most therapists. The responsibility is on the therapist to keep bringing up issues of race and ethnicity. It takes persistence and courage. This is mostly because as therapists we aren't trained to talk about it, and because as a society we are extremely well trained to avoid talking about it. This is especially true if you are a white client working with a white therapist or if you are a person of color working with a white therapist. These therapeutic dyads need to work especially hard to discuss issues of race and ethnicity.

The common denominator here is white therapists, the largest group of service providers practicing in the United States. It is especially challenging for white therapists to talk about issues of race and ethnicity with clients, both of minority and of majority status. White therapists have the least amount of practice talking about these issues and may have spent the majority of their lives unconsciously disavowing their own white ethnic identity. The importance of this is that it is not only crucial that the therapist understands how racial identity affects clients, but also that they understand how their own racial identity is a variable that influences counseling dynamics.

Within the helping professions, the concept of cultural sensitivity is applied almost exclusively to cross-racial therapeutic dyads. The literature vastly underestimates the importance of white therapists and white clients consistently working on racial issues together. Responsibility and expertise in cross-cultural psychological services tend to be deferred to professionals of color because the assumption is made that they are the exclusive experts on these issues and on treating minority clients. This is unfortunate in that it places an unfair burden on minority professionals and further disavows race as located only within the "other," that is, within the professional and client of color. The recent push for multiculturalism in the field has increased the visibility of clients of color and their needs, yet has left issues of whiteness unacknowledged. Therefore, the importance of white therapists developing their racial identity in order to become culturally sensitive clinicians remains largely unaddressed.

There is, however, a small but growing body of literature that speaks of white therapists becoming *anti-racist*; of challenging whiteness, white privilege, and racism as part of both their personal lives and professional work as therapists. The journey is often characterized as painful, yet rewarding and lifelong. It is often mentioned within the literature that leaning into discomfort, taking risks, and making mistakes are integral parts of giving in to this process.

It is reasonable to be nervous about discussing issues of race and racism as therapists given society's general reluctance to speak about these issues. Yet holding in mind a sense of curiosity, openness, and courage is most of what it takes to foster this invitation. Any attempt to address race and racism within treatment should aim to first and foremost preserve the therapeutic relationship. In order to preserve the therapeutic relationship, it is suggested that therapists retain a straightforward, yet not confrontational stance to keep the client connected to the therapist, limit the amount of client defensiveness, and prevent the client from feeling rejected or judged by the therapist. It is highly important that there is a balance between the therapist addressing race and racism and using the safety and security of the therapeutic relationship to buffer those delicate conversations. Therefore, the therapist must find a way to gently push while holding the client. Of course, the same is true for the therapist as they address their client's race and racism, in that they, too, have to take risks and push themselves while remaining grounded.

There are concrete ways to address race and racism within therapy. A white therapist working with a white client might explicitly ask as part of the initial assessment what the client's cultural background is, what he identifies as racially/ethnically, what is the racial makeup of his friends, family, and workplace, and how this may contribute to or buffer the presenting problem. By asking these questions, the therapist takes the initiative of introducing race into the conversation and models for the client that ethnicity is a valuable part of identity, thereby diminishing the invisibility of whiteness. Therapists must think about race and ethnicity in a conscious, overt manner and be able to engage in what Laszloffy and Hardy (2000) call the "language of race." This includes being able to introduce the topic of race overtly or metaphorically, as well as being able to decode indirect and metaphorical racial comments made by clients.

It is important to mention the therapist should expect some resistance from the client in talking about these themes. After all, it should be expected that the client will not have much practice in reflecting on their racial identity. Clients may refuse to discuss these themes and at that point, it is recommended that the therapist normalize their reaction—be it discomfort, shame, guilt, or pain—and that the therapist self-discloses that it was difficult for them as well in the past to reflect on these themes, while stressing the importance of knowing these important aspects of the client's identity. The therapist can also state that they ask these questions of all clients and can explain that they want to know more about this because it may be connected to the presenting problem.

As suggested in the beginning, there are many ways to bring race and ethnicity into the treatment and whether a more overt, purposeful exploration is fostered or the therapist chooses to hold the issue in mind depends on many factors. Timing and the therapeutic relationship are two that may especially influence the decision to more explicitly address race and ethnicity with a client. Most important is the therapist's intention in relation to addressing issues of race and ethnicity. If it is one of openness, curiosity, courage, willingness to take risks, and self-awareness, then their ability to promote a similar attitude in their clients will be greatly enhanced. Setting this intention as therapists in our work with clients is the beginning of a lifelong process of acknowledging and strengthening our own and our client's racial and ethnic identities.

SUMMARY

This chapter speaks more specifically about concrete issues in working with culturally diverse clients. There is general agreement among practitioners that cross-cultural helping is more demanding, challenging, and energy-draining than work with same-culture clients. It can be more experiential, freewheeling, and bilateral. It is also more complex conceptually in that it involves an understanding of the dynamics of race, ethnicity, difference, and power. It is critical for practitioners to understand these concepts as they both operate in the lives of clients and within themselves as they work with culturally diverse clients. Cross-cultural helping can represent a particularly imbalanced power situation. The traditional therapeutic dyad represents a power imbalance in favor of the practitioner; in cross-cultural helping, this differential is tipped even further by differences in respective cultural group identities and connections. Therapeutically, power is important because (1) powerlessness often forces individuals to adopt behaviors that allow them to feel more powerful—these strategies are often counterproductive and need to be addressed in treatment; and (2) empowerment may be best dealt with in the therapeutic situation by the practitioner consciously choosing to take a one-down position. Hays (2008, 2014) offers an excellent tool for conceptualizing the diverse social identities that define each individual: the ADDRESSING framework. Hays suggests that information on each of these identity statuses be collected and updated as new information is forthcoming for each client or patient that we see.

Various suggestions are offered by way of allaying some of the anxiety that is a natural part of beginning to do cross-cultural work. For example, it is useful to focus on human similarities as well as differences and begin by just trying to make human contact with the client. A good cultural assessment is critical in defining the kinds of help a culturally diverse client needs as well as how the client may be viewing the problem from his or her cultural perspective. Several strategies for collecting such information are described, including the DSM-5's "Cultural Outline for Case Formulation," a guide developed to sensitize users of the DSM-5 to cultural issues in clients. In addition to the collection of ADDRESSING information for all clients, Hays also suggests a strategy for optimizing the use of the DSM-5 diagnosis with culturally diverse clients.

Next, guidelines for developing rapport with culturally diverse clients during the first and early sessions are offered. For example, clients should come away from the first session feeling that they have been understood from their own perspective and they have received something concrete from their work with the provider.

ACTIVITIES

1. *Construct an ADDRESSING framework of your own cultural identities or influences.* Carry out this task individually in as much detail as you are able, and then, in a pair or small group, share your information. Also discuss in which identities you are a majority member and in which a minority member, and what are the implications and experiences of these distinctions.

2. *Explore power in the therapeutic relationship.* Pair off with a partner or gather in a small group and take turns answering and discussing the following questions:

   ▶ Do you believe that there is a significant power difference between the helper and the client? Why or why not?

- Do you experience yourself as having more power and control in the helping relationship than those with whom you are working? How so? Describe your emotional reactions to that experience.
- Are there things you do or might do in session to change the power balance in the room? If so, describe them.
- Have you ever worked with someone and felt that you were not in control or in charge? Describe the situation and how you felt in it and handled it.
- What might you envision to be some of the differences and difficulties that white therapists and therapists of color face vis-à-vis their reactions to power in their role as helpers?

Understanding Racism, Prejudice, and White Privilege

LEARNING OBJECTIVES

4-1 Differentiate between different types of racism and between racism and prejudice.

4-2 Differentiate between the psychological theories of prejudice.

4-3 Analyze institutional and cultural racism.

4-4 Recognize specific stages of white racial identity development and aspects of white privilege.

4-5 Explain the methods for becoming a cultural ally.

Ron Takaki (1993) begins his book *A Different Mirror* by recounting a simple but powerful incident. While riding in a taxi from an airport to a hotel in a large Eastern city for a conference on multiculturalism, Takaki and the cab driver engaged in casual conversation. After the usual discussion of weather and tourism, the driver asked, "How long have you been in this country?" Takaki winced and then answered: "All my life . . . I was born in the United States . . . My grandfather came here from Japan in the 1880s. My family has been here, in America, for over a hundred years." The cab driver, obviously feeling uncomfortable, explained, "I was wondering because your English is excellent!" (p. 1).

Encapsulated in this incident are the basic feelings that fuel racial tensions in the United States. The cab driver was giving voice to a belief shared by the majority of white Americans: that this country is European in ancestry and white in identity, and that only those who share these characteristics truly belong. All others, no matter how long they have resided here, are viewed and treated with suspicion and relegated to the status of outsider. Takaki's wince tells the other side of the story. People of color who also call the United States home are deeply disturbed by their second-class citizenry. Being reminded of their unequal and unwanted status is a daily occurrence. This country, they argue, has grown rich on the labor of successive generations of immigrants and refugees, and their reward should be the same as whites—full citizenship and equal access to resources as guaranteed in the Constitution. The situation is only exacerbated by white America's seemingly indifference to the enormous injustice that exists in the system. Cross-cultural service delivery is most usefully viewed against this backdrop.

The helping relationship is, after all, a microcosm of broader society, and as such is susceptible to the same racial tensions and dynamics. It was suggested in Chapter 2 that cultural competence depends on self-awareness, and this includes, above all, an awareness of the attitudes and prejudices that providers bring to their work. Neither provider nor client exists in a vacuum. Rather, each carries into the helping situation prejudices and stereotypes about the other's ethnicity; if unaddressed, these biases cannot help but interfere with communication. In this chapter, you will learn about the dynamics of racism: its structure and meaning, the functions it serves for the individual and for society, how it operates psychologically, and why it is so resistant to change. The chapter ends with a self-assessment tool: a series of exercises intended to help you explore personal prejudices, stereotypes, and attitudes toward specific ethnic groups.

▶ Defining and Contextualizing Racism   `4-1`

Hoyt Jr. (2012) defines racism as "a particular form of prejudice defined by preconceived erroneous beliefs about race and members of racial groups." It is supported simultaneously by individuals, the institutional practices of society, and dominant cultural values and norms. Racism is a universal phenomenon that exists across cultures and tends to emerge wherever ethnic diversity and perceived or real differences in group characteristics become part of a struggle for social power. In the case of the United States, African Americans, Latinos/as, Native Americans, and Asian Americans—groups that we have been referring to as people of color—have been systematically subordinated by the white majority.

There are four important points to be made initially about racism:

> Prejudice and racism are not the same thing. Prejudice is a negative, inaccurate, rigid, and unfair way of thinking about members of another group. All human beings hold prejudices. This is true for people of color, as well as for majority group members. But there is a crucial difference between the prejudices held by whites and those held by people of color. whites have more power to enact their prejudices and therefore negatively impact the lives of people of color than vice versa. The term *racism* is used in relation to the racial attitudes and behavior of majority group members. Similar attitudes and behaviors on the part of people of color are referred to as *prejudice* and *discrimination* (a term commonly used to mean actions taken on the basis of one's prejudices). Another way of describing this relationship is that prejudice plus power equals racism.

> Racism is a broad and all-pervasive social phenomenon that is mutually reinforced at all levels of society.
>> *Institutional racism* involves the manipulation of societal institutions to give preferences and advantages to whites and at the same time restrict the choices, rights, mobility, and access of people of color.
>> *Cultural racism* is the belief that the cultural ways of one group are superior to those of another. Cultural racism can be found both in individuals and in institutions. In the former, it is often referred to as ethnocentrism. Jones (2000) mentioned that historical insults, societal norms, unearned privilege, and structural barriers are all aspects of institutional racism.

> People tend to deny, rationalize, and avoid discussing their feelings and beliefs about race and ethnicity. Often, these feelings remain unconscious and are brought to awareness only with great difficulty.

> When young children hear the stories of people of color, they tend to feel deeply and sincerely with the storyteller. "I'm really sorry that you had to go through that" is the most common reaction of a child. By the time one reaches adulthood, however, the empathy is often gone. Instead, reactions tend to involve minimizing, justifying, rationalizing, or other forms of emotional blocking. Human service providers are no less susceptible to such defensive behavior, but they must force themselves to look inward if they are sincere in their commitment to work effectively cross-culturally. For this reason, this chapter concludes with a set of activities and exercises aimed at stimulating self-awareness.

Individual Racism and Prejudice

The burning question that arises when one tries to understand the dynamics of individual racism is: Why is it so easy for individuals to develop and retain racial prejudices? As suggested earlier, racism seems to be a universal phenomenon that transcends geography and culture. Human groups have always exhibited it, and, if human history is any lesson, they always will. The answer lies within the fact that people tend to feel most comfortable with those who are like them and are suspicious of those who are different. They tend to think categorically, to generalize, and to oversimplify their views of others. They tend to develop beliefs that support their values and basic feelings and avoid those that contradict or challenge them. Also, they tend to scapegoat those who are most vulnerable and subsequently rationalize their racist behavior. In short, it is out of these simple human traits and tendencies that racism grows.

Traits and Tendencies Supporting Racism and Prejudice

The idea of in-group and out-group behavior is a good place to begin any discussion of racism. There seems to be a natural tendency among all human beings to stick to their own kind and to separate themselves from those who are different. One need not attribute this fact to any nefarious motives; it is just easier and more comfortable to do so. Ironically, inherent in this tendency to love and be most comfortable with one's own are the very seeds of racial hatred. Thus, what is different can always be and often is perceived as a threat. The tendency to separate oneself from those who are different only intensifies the threat because separation limits communication and thus heightens the possibility of misunderstanding. With separation, knowledge of the other also grows vague. This vagueness seems to invite distortion, the creation of myths about members of other groups, and the attribution of negative characteristics and intentions to the other.

Prejudice is also stimulated by the human proclivity for categorical thinking. It is a basic and necessary part of the way people think to organize perceptions into cognitive categories and to experience life through these categories. As one grows and matures, certain categories become very detailed and complex; others remain simplistic. Some become charged with emotion; others remain factual. Individuals and groups of people are also sorted into categories. These "people" categories can become charged with emotion and vary greatly in complexity and accuracy. On the basis of these categories, human beings make decisions about how they will act toward others.

For example, I have the category "Mexican." As a child, I remember seeing brown-skinned people in an old car at a stoplight and being curious about who and what they were. As we drove by, my father mumbled, "Dirty, lazy Mexicans," and my mother rolled up the window and locked her door. This and a variety of subsequent experiences, both direct and indirect (e.g., comments by others, the media, what I read), are filed away as part of my "Mexican" category and shape the way I think about, feel, and act toward Mexicans.

But it is even more complicated than this because categorical thinking, by its very nature, leads to oversimplification and prejudgment. Once a person has been identified as a member of an ethnic group, he or she is experienced as possessing all the categorical traits and emotions internally associated with that group. I may believe, for instance, that Asian Americans are very good at mathematics and that I hate them because of it. If I meet individuals whom I identify as Asian American, I will both assume that they are good at mathematics and find myself feeling negative toward them.

The concept of stereotype is related. Weinstein and Mellen (1997) define *stereotype* as "an undifferentiated, simplistic attribution that involves a judgment of habits, traits, abilities, or expectations ... assigned as a characteristic of all members of a group" (p. 175). For instance, Jews are short, smart, and money-hungry; Native Americans are stoic and violent and abuse alcohol. Implied in these stereotypes is that all Jews are the same and all Native Americans are the same (i.e., share all characteristics). Ethnic stereotypes are learned as part of normal socialization and are amazingly consistent in their content. As a classroom exercise, I ask students to list the traits they associate with a given ethnic group. Consistently, the lists that they generate contain the same characteristics, down to minute details, and are overwhelmingly negative. One cannot help but marvel at society's ability to transmit the subtlety and detail of these distorted ethnic caricatures. Not only does stereotyping lead to oversimplification in thinking about ethnic group members, but it also provides justification for the exploitation and ill treatment of those who are racially and culturally diverse. Because of their negative traits, they deserve what they get. Because they are seen as less than human, it is easy to rationalize ill treatment of them. Categorical thinking and stereotyping also tend to be inflexible, self-perpetuating, and highly resistant to change. Human beings go to great lengths to avoid new evidence that is contrary to existing beliefs and prejudices.

▶ Modern Prejudice   `4-2`

Psychologists, such as Gordon Allport, suggest that the factors just discussed—in-group and out-group behavior, categorical thinking and stereotyping, avoidance, and selective perception—together set the stage for the emergence of racism. But without the existence of some form of internal motivation, an individual's potential for racism remains largely dormant. Perry, Murphy, and Dovidio (2015) suggested that the awareness of one's biases is a major factor in the reduction of prejudice.

Various theories have been offered regarding the psychological motivation behind prejudice and racism. In reality, there does not seem to be a single theory that can explain the impetus toward racism adequately in all individuals. More likely, there is some truth in all the theories that follow, and in the case of any given individual, one or more of them may be at work. (The summary of theories that follows derives largely from Allport, 1954; Rutland, Killen, & Abrams, 2010; Melamed & North, 2010; Poteat & Anderson, 2012; Carr, Dweck, & Pauker, 2012; Perry, Murphy & Dovidio, 2015.)

- *Self-regulation of prejudice*: When a low-prejudiced person has a negative implicit evaluation of an outgroup member (of which he or she may or may not be aware), this evaluation leads to the recognition of a discrepancy between his or her egalitarian goals and his or her negative behavior toward the outgroup.
- *Frustration-aggression-displacement hypothesis*: This theory holds that as people move through life, they do not always get what they want or need, and as a result, experience varying amounts of frustration. Frustration, in turn, creates aggression and hostility, which can be alternately directed at the original cause of frustration, directed inward at the self, or displaced onto a more accessible target. Thus, if my boss reprimands me, I go home and take it out on my wife, who, in turn, yells at the kids, who then kick the dog. Such displacement, according to the theory, is the source of racism.
- *Authoritarian personality*: This theory holds that prejudice is part of a broader, global personality type. The classical example is the work of Adorno, Frenkel-Brunswik, Levinson, and Sanford (1950). Adorno and his colleagues postulated the existence of a global bigoted personality type manifesting a variety of traits revolving around personal insecurity and a basic fear of everything and everyone different. Such individuals are believed to be highly repressed and insecure and to experience low self-esteem and high alienation. In addition, they tend to be highly moralistic, nationalistic, and authoritarian; to think in terms of black and white; to have a high need for order and structure; to view problems as external rather than psychological; and to feel anger and resentment against members of all ethnic groups.
- *Tajfel's Social Identity Theory*: This maintains that individuals have a natural propensity to strive toward a positive self-image, and social identity is enhanced by categorizing people into in-groups and out-groups.
- *Rankism*, offered by Fuller (2003), is the persistent abuse and discrimination based on power differences in rank or hierarchy. The experience

of being ranked above or below others, which Fuller refers to as being a somebody or a nobody, exists throughout our social system and persists "in the presence of an underlying difference of rank signifying power." Somebodies receive recognition and experience self-satisfaction and pride in themselves; on the other hand, nobodies face derision and experience indignity and humiliation. Somebodies use the power associated with their rank to improve or secure their situation to the disadvantage of the nobodies below them. Fuller argues that a person's self-esteem and identity are based on the recognition and appreciation that he or she receives and that a lack of recognition can have serious mental health consequences.

All these theories share the idea that through racist beliefs and actions, individuals meet important psychological and emotional needs; to the extent that this process is successful, their hatred remains energized and reinforced. Within such a model, the reduction of prejudice and racism can occur only when alternative ways of meeting emotional needs are found.

Microaggressions and Implicit Bias

In more recent studies, researchers have increasingly argued that overt racist acts and hate crimes do not do as much damage to people of color as subtler microaggressions and implicit biases that tend to be unconscious, invisible, and thus more insidious forms of attack (Constantine and Sue, 2007). *Racial microaggressions* "are brief and commonplace daily verbal, behavioral, and environmental indignities . . . that communicate hostile, derogatory, or negative racial slights and insults to the target person or group" (Sue et al., 2007, p. 273). Jones (2008) summarizes an emerging picture of *implicit bias*; that is, negative, cognitive racial attributions held unconsciously, interacting with brain activity at the core of white racism:

> The implicit measures of racial attitudes have proven to be powerful detectors of racial biases. Moreover, we have utilized social neuroscience to show that racial biases are often "hard-wired." For example, we have learned that the amygdala region of the brain, commonly associated with fear responses, is activated when the faces of out-group members are detected. Implicit measures of racial attitude such as the Implicit Association Test (IAT) have demonstrated strong connections between positive concepts (heaven, ice cream) and negative concepts (devil, death) and Blacks. (p. XXVIII)

Thus, it seems that the small and repetitive racial slights, misconceptions, and diminutions routinely experienced by people of color are no less destructive and, in many ways, more debilitating than more overt forms of racism. Microaggressions were discussed in Chapter 3 in relation to their traumatizing impact on people of color and will be discussed further in Chapter 8 in regard to unconscious racial slights and biases within therapy.

Implications for Providers

What does all this information about individual racism have to do with human service providers? Put most directly, it is the source or at least a contributing factor to many problems for which culturally diverse clients seek help. Some clients present problems that revolve around dealing with racism directly; they live with it on a daily basis. Relating to the racism that they encounter in a healthy and non-self-destructive manner, therefore, is a major challenge. To be the continual object of someone else's hatred, as well as that of an entire social system, is a source of enormous stress, and such stress takes its psychological toll. It is no accident, for example, that African American men suffer from and are at particularly high risk for stress-related physical illnesses.

Other clients present with problems that are more indirect consequences of racism. A disproportionate number of people of color find themselves poor and with limited resources and skills for competing in a white-dominated marketplace. The stress caused by poverty places people at high psychological risk. More affluent people of color are no less susceptible to the far-reaching consequences of racism. Life's goals and aspirations are likely blocked (or at least made more difficult) because of the color of their skin. There is a saying among professionals of color that one has to be twice as good as one's white counterpart to make it. This is also a source of inner tension, as are the doubts that a professional of color may have as to whether he or she received a job or promotion because of his or her ability, or because of skin color.

It is critical that providers become aware of the prejudices that they hold as individuals. (Exercises at the end of this chapter, if undertaken with honesty and seriousness, can provide valuable insight into your feelings and beliefs about other racial and ethnic groups.) Without such awareness, it is all too easy for providers to confound their work with their prejudices. For example, if I think stereotypically about clients of color, it is very likely that I will define their potential too narrowly, miss important aspects of their individuality, and even unwittingly guide them in the direction of taking on the very stereotyped characteristics I hold about them. My own narrowness of thought will limit the success that I can have working with culturally diverse clients. It is critical to remember that prejudice often works at an unconscious level and that professionals are susceptible to its dynamics. It is also critical to be aware that, after a lifetime of experience in a racist world, clients of color are highly sensitized to the nuances of prejudice and racism and can identify it very quickly. Finally, it is important to re-emphasize that professional codes of conduct consider it unethical to work with a client with whom one has a serious value conflict. Prejudice and racism are such value conflicts.

▶ Institutional Racism   4-3

Consider the following statistics from various sources about African Americans in the United States:

- ▶ Of the prisoners in the United States in 2014, 34 percent are African Americans (NAACP).
- ▶ In 2015, the U.S. Census Bureau reported that 25.4 percent of African Americans, in comparison to 10.4 percent of non-Hispanic whites, were living at the poverty level (U.S. Department of Health and Human Services, Office of Minority Health).
- ▶ The death rate for African Americans was generally higher than whites for heart diseases, stroke, cancer, asthma, influenza and pneumonia, diabetes, HIV/AIDS, and homicide (U.S. Department of Health and Human Services, Office of Minority Health).
- ▶ According to a 2015 Census Bureau report, the average African American household median income was $36,515 in comparison to $61,394 for non-Hispanic white households (U.S. Department of Health and Human Services, Office of Minority Health).
- ▶ In 2015, the unemployment rate for African Americans was twice that for non-Hispanic whites (11.4 percent and 5.0 percent, respectively). This finding was consistent for both men and women (U.S. Department of Health and Human Services, Office of Minority Health).
- ▶ African Americans are overrepresented in low-pay service occupations (e.g., nursing aides and orderlies, 30.7 percent) and underrepresented among professionals (e.g., architects, 0.9 percent) (Hacker, 1992).
- ▶ In 2015, as compared to non-Hispanic whites 25 years and over, a lower percentage of African Americans had earned at least a high school diploma (84.8 percent and 92.3 percent, respectively); 20.2 percent of African Americans have a bachelor's degree or higher, as compared with 34.2 percent of non-Hispanic whites (U.S. Department of Health and Human Services, Office of Minority Health).

These are the consequences of institutional racism: the manipulation of societal institutions to give preferences and advantages to whites and at the same time restrict the choices, rights, mobility, and access of people of color. In each of these varied instances, African Americans are seen at a decided disadvantage or at greater risk compared to whites. The term *institution* refers to "established societal networks that covertly or overtly control the allocation of resources to individuals and social groups" (Wijeyesinghe, Griffin, and Love, 1997, p. 93). Included are the media, the police, courts and jails, banks, schools, organizations that deal with employment and education, the health system, and religious, family, civil, and governmental organizations. Something within the fabric of these institutions causes discrepancies, such as those just listed, to occur on a regular and systematic basis. Jones (2000) explained that institutional racism can manifest in two conditions: material and access to power. The author added that examples of material conditions include housing, employment, education, and appropriate medical facilities. Example of access to power include access to information, presence in government, and financial resources.

In many ways, institutional racism is far more insidious than individual racism because it is embedded in bylaws, rules, practices, procedures, and organizational culture. Thus, it appears to have a life of its own and seems easier for those involved in the daily running of institutions to disavow any responsibility for it.

Determining Institutional Racism

How does one go about determining the existence of institutional racism? The most obvious manner is through the reports of victims themselves—those who regularly feel its effects, encounter differential treatment, and are given only limited access to resources. But such firsthand reports are often held suspect and are too easily countered by explanations of "sour grapes" or "they just need to pull themselves up by their own bootstraps" by those who may not, for a variety of reasons, want to look too closely at the workings of racism.

A more objective strategy is to compare the frequency or incidence of a phenomenon within a group to the frequency within the general population. One would expect, for example, that a group that comprises 10 percent of this country's population would provide 10 percent of its doctors or be responsible for 10 percent of its crimes. When there is a sizable disparity between these two numbers (i.e., when the expected percentages do not line up, especially when they are very discrepant), it is likely that some broader social force, such as institutional racism, is intervening.

One might alternatively argue that something about members of the group itself is responsible for the statistical discrepancy, rather than institutional racism. Such explanations, however—with the one exception of cultural differences (to be described later in this chapter)—must be assessed very carefully because they are frequently based on prejudicial and stereotypical thinking. For instance, members of Group X consistently score lower on intelligence tests than do dominant group members. One explanation may be that members of Group X are intellectually inferior. However, there has long been debate over the scientific merit of taking such a position that has yet to prove anything more than the fact that proponents who argue on the side of racial inferiority in intelligence tend to enjoy the publicity they inevitably receive. An alternative and more scientifically compelling explanation is that intelligence tests themselves are culturally biased and, in addition, favor individuals whose first language is English.

There are indeed aspects of a group's collective experience that predispose its members to behave or exhibit characteristics in a manner different from what would be expected statistically. For instance, because of ritualistic practices, Jews tend to experience relatively low rates of alcoholism. Therefore, it is not surprising to find that the percentage of Jews suffering from alcohol abuse is disproportionately lower than their representation in the general population.

Such differences, however, tend to be cultural rather than biological.

Consciousness, Intent, and Denial

Institutional racist practices can be conscious or unconscious and intended or unintended. "Conscious or unconscious" refers to the fact that people working in a system may or may not be aware of the practices' existence and impact. "Intended or unintended" means the practices may or may not have been purposely created, but they nevertheless exist and substantially affect the lives of people of color. A similar distinction was made early in the Civil Rights Movement between de jure and de facto segregation. The former term refers to segregation that was legally sanctioned and the existence of actual laws dictating racial separation. De jure segregation was, thus, both conscious and intended. De facto segregation, on the other hand, implies separation that exists in actuality or after the fact, but may not have been created consciously for racial or other purposes.

It is important to distinguish among consciousness, intent, and accountability. I may have been unaware that telling an ethnic joke could be hurtful, and I might not have intended any harm; however, I am still responsible for the consequences of my actions and the hurt that may result. Similarly, someone I know works in an organization that unknowingly excludes people of color from receiving services, and it was never his or her intention to do so. But, again, intention does not justify consequences, and as an employee of that institution, he or she should be aware of its actions. Thus, lack of intent or awareness should never be regarded as justification for the existence of or compliance with institutional or individual racism.

Although denial is an essential part of all forms of racism, it seems especially difficult for individuals to take personal responsibility for institutional racism, for the following reasons:

> ▶ First, institutional practices tend to have a history of their own that may precede the individual's tenure in the organization. To challenge or question such practices may be presumptuous and beyond one's power or status. Alternatively, one might feel that he or she is merely following the prescribed employee practices or a superior's dictates and, thus, cannot fairly be held responsible for them. Similar logic is offered in discussions of slavery and white responsibility:

"I never owned slaves; neither did my ancestors. That happened 150 years ago. Why should I be expected to make sacrifices in my life for injustices that happened long ago and were not of my making?"

▶ Second, people tend to feel powerless in relation to large organizations and institutions. Sentiments such as "You can't fight City Hall" and "What can one person do?" seem to prevail. The distribution of tasks and power and the perception that decisions come down "from above" contribute further to feelings of powerlessness and alienation.

▶ Third, institutions are by nature conservative and oriented toward keeping the status quo. Change requires far more energy and is generally considered only during times of serious crisis and challenge. Specific procedures for effecting change are seldom spelled out, and important practices tend to be subtly yet powerfully protected.

▶ Fourth, the practices of an institution that supports institutional racism (i.e., that keeps people of color out) are multiple, complicated, mutually reinforcing, and, therefore, all the more insidious. Even if one were to undertake sincere efforts to change, it is often difficult to know exactly where to begin.

To provide a better sense of the complexity with which institutional racism asserts itself, I would like to share three very different case studies.

CASE STUDY 1

The first case is an excerpt from a cultural evaluation of Agency X focusing on staffing patterns. The purpose of the project was to assess the organization's ability to provide culturally sensitive services to its clients and to make recommendations as to how it might become more culturally competent. Although the report does not point directly to instances of institutional racism in staffing practices, they become obvious as one reads through the text and its recommendations.

Currently, People of Color are underrepresented on the staff of Agency X. In the units under study, only two workers are of Color: a Latino and an African American male. Neither are supervisors. In the entire office, only seven staff members are of Color: two Latino/as, one African American, and three Asian Americans. Two of the Asian Americans are supervisors. There are no People of Color in higher levels of management. An often-cited problem is the fact that there are few minority candidates on the state list from which hiring is done. To compensate requires special and proactive recruitment efforts to get People of Color on the lists, as well as the creation of special positions and other strategies for circumventing such lists. At a systems level, attention must be given to screening practices that may inadvertently and unfairly reject qualified minority candidates. While parity in numbers of Staff of Color to population demographics should be an important goal, holding to strict quotas misses the point of cultural competence. The idea is to strive for making the entire organization, all management and staff, more culturally competent, that is, able to work effectively with those clients who are culturally different. Nor is it reasonable to assume that all Staff of Color will be culturally competent. While attempting to add

continued

CASE STUDY 1   *continued*

more Staff of Color, it is highly useful to fill the vacuum through the use of community resources and professionals hired specifically to provide cultural expertise.

In general, the staff interviewed were found to be in need of cultural competence training. This would include awareness of broader issues of culture and cross-cultural communication, history and cultural patterns of specific minority cultures, and implications of cultural differences for the provision of client services. Especially relevant was knowledge of normal vs. dysfunctional family patterns within different cultural groups so that culturally sensitive and accurate assessments might be carried out. In moving toward a family support model within the agency, as was indicated by several staff members during our interviews, it is critical to understand family dynamics of a given family from the perspective of its culture of origin as opposed to a singular, monocultural Euro-American perspective. Also evident was a basic conflict within the organization between treatment and corrections models of providing services. Staff adhering to the latter tended to devalue the importance of cultural differences in working with Clients of Color and tended to see Youth of Color as using racism and cultural differences as an excuse for not taking responsibility for their own behavior.

White staff members report the following needs and concerns in regard to working with Children of Color: need help in identifying culturally appropriate resources and placements; discomfort in dealing with issues of race; don't know the right questions to ask; families often unwilling to discuss or acknowledge race as an issue; the need for more and better training; lack of knowledge about biracial children; and the need for a better understanding of the role of culture in the service model they use.

Staff of Color did not report any experiences of overt discrimination and felt respected by their colleagues. They believed that Agency X was, in fact, trying to deal with the problem of cultural diversity, but that this interest was of rather recent vintage and motivated primarily by political and legal concerns. They also suggested that the liberal climate of the organization did much to justify a pervasive attitude that "we treat everyone the same" and "I know good service provision and can deal with anyone." Together, such attitudes often served as an excuse for not dealing directly with cultural differences in clients. They also stated that cultural diversity was experienced by some coworkers as an extra burden, requiring extra work from them. As in most work situations, the Staff of Color did experience some distance from coworkers. The onus of keeping up good relations was often felt to be on the Person of Color to put their White coworkers at ease. Staff of Color we interviewed were subject to especially high burnout potential and needed their own resources and support outside the organization. We found both Staff of Color in the units under investigation to be especially strong and competent individuals who were particularly stretched thin between their regular duties and their roles within the organization as cultural experts.

The recent hiring of a Latino professional by Agency X, as a means of dealing with a growing Spanish-speaking population, deserves some comment. The need to provide services to this population has been well documented by the demand that has already arisen for his services. We are concerned, however, that the way in which the position was created will eventually lead to burnout and failure and that much more support for the position must be consciously and systematically provided. We perceive an expectation from within and from outside the organization that this individual will be able to "do it all"—help organize an advisory board and provide services to it, do outreach to the Latino/a community, be an in-house cultural expert, be an advocate with other agencies and a referral source for all Latino/a members of the community, and carry a full caseload of Latino/a and non-Latino/a families. The work demands are already cutting into personal time, and as he deals with other agencies and realizes the lack of culturally relevant services available elsewhere, he becomes even further burdened.

Providing culturally competent services to the Latino/a community, as Agency X is now trying to do, will merely open the floodgates of additional demands for services. The current position holder suggested: "The agency doesn't realize that this is only the tip of the iceberg." It is likely that Agency X will soon be faced with adding bicultural, bilingual staff to meet the growing need. In this regard, two caveats should be offered. First, culturally sensitive workers and those assigned caseloads of individuals from non-Euro-American cultures tend to work most effectively and creatively when they are allowed maximum flexibility, leeway, and discretion in how they carry out their duties. Rules and policies established in the context of serving Euro-American clients may be of little help and possibly obstructive to working with culturally different groups. Second, the existence of a defined cultural expert in an organization should not be viewed in any way as a justification for not actively pursuing the cultural competence of the agency in general and its staff.

CASE STUDY 2

The second case study, drawn from the work of Oakland psychiatrist Terry A. Kupers, deals with prisons, mental health, and institutional racism. Kupers (1999) argues that a disproportionate number of mentally ill individuals reside in prison, receive limited or no treatment, and decompensate as a result of the trauma and stress of life behind bars. These same conditions cause previously normal inmates to regularly experience "disabling psychiatric symptoms as well" (p. xvii). Especially dramatic is the impact of these conditions on Prisoners of Color.

According to Kupers (1999), "Racism permeates the criminal justice system" (p. 94). People of Color are more likely than Whites to be stopped, searched, arrested, represented by public defenders, and receive harsh sentences. Incarceration rates are badly distorted, as 50 percent of the current prison population is African American, 15 percent is Latino/a, and Native Americans are dramatically overrepresented in relation to their numbers in the general population. It is estimated that by the year 2020, one third of African Americans and one quarter of Hispanics aged 18 to 34 years will be in the criminal justice system. The numbers grow even more disproportionate as the level of incarceration becomes more severe. For example, minimum security units are primarily White, "whereas the super-maximum-security units contain up to 90 or 95% blacks and Latinos" (Kupers, 1999, p. 95).

The prisons themselves are replete with racial tension, and "racial lines are drawn sharply" within the institutions (p. 93). For their own protection, prisoners self-segregate along racial lines and gangs dominate the political landscape. When tensions rise in the prison yard, inmates "quickly join the largest group of their own race they can reach" (p. 96). Some analysts suggest that racial tensions are kept alive within the system as a means of social control, and that there are many little things that keep Blacks and Whites angry at each other. The bottom line, according to Kupers, is that "race matters very much, to everyone" (p. 96).

Located primarily in rural settings, a majority of prison staff is White, as are those who sit on hearing and appeals panels. In general, they lack experience and knowledge of People of Color and tend to view racially different prisoners in stereotypical ways. Complaints of racial discrimination among guards are rampant. Jobs, supervisory positions, and training tend to be doled out along racial lines, with the more prestigious and better paying ones going to White inmates. At times, practices are just plain cruel. Kupers tells the story of an African American inmate who was "confined in a cell covered with racist graffiti" (p. 98). Although there are "good" guards, inmates complain that codes "among correctional officers" make it difficult "to interfere when a 'bad cop' is harassing or brutalizing a prisoner" (pp. 98–99). There are even accusations of guards inciting interracial and gang violence.

continued

CASE STUDY 2   *continued*

Prison life cannot help but remind Prisoners of Color of the injustices and discriminations they have experienced in the outside world. Kupers feels that there is good reason for Prisoners of Color to fear being abused because of race behind bars and that such fear "creates psychiatric symptoms" (p. 103). Stable prisoners are traumatized, and those with histories of mental illness tend to deteriorate and become self-destructive. When victimized by racism, the former report feeling frustrated and full of rage, despair, and powerless. If they cannot hold on to sanity by remaining in contact with family and community or planning for release, the result is often lethargy and/or acting out in fits of defiance. Kupers reports observing significant "anxiety, depression, panic attacks, phobias, nightmares, flashbacks, and uncontrollable rage reactions" in these prisoners (pp. 104–105). The plight of less stable Prisoners of Color is even more precarious.

In the face of persistent and significant racism, they decompensate. Especially frequent are two patterns of emotional breakdown, depending on the prisoner's mental history. Some are driven to clinical depression due to increasing cycles of hopelessness and despair. Others, in the grip of ever-increasing rage, move toward ego disintegration and psychosis. In both cases, the breakdown tends to be progressive as the correctional staff responds to the increasingly symptomatic behavior with more oppressive measures. Finally, in relation to treatment, Prisoners of Color are more likely to be labeled "paranoid" and "disruptive," punished by being sent to "lockup" rather than treated, and medicated as opposed to receiving psychotherapy or admittance to prison mental health programs. Kupers summarizes his findings vis-à-vis institutional racism in prison as follows: "Prisoners of Color are doubly affected by racial discrimination behind bars. Racism plays a big part in the evolution and exacerbation of their psychiatric symptomology, and they are more likely than whites to be denied adequate mental health services" (p. 111).

CASE STUDY 3

The third case study is drawn from observations made by the author about issues of race, mental health, and psychology training in South Africa during a two-month stay in Cape Town. During that time, he served as a visiting faculty member in the psychology department of Stellenbosch University, as well as a facilitator for the Institute for Healing of Memories, Cape Town (see Chapter 10).

Stellenbosch is a small university town in the beautiful wine-growing region of the Western Cape known as the Garden Route, an hour's drive from Cape Town. Beneath its seemingly sleepy exterior, however, lies a most interesting—and at times—chilling history. It is a traditional area of Afrikaner culture, and Afrikaans is still the language in which most undergraduate courses are taught. I would learn that during the World War II era, several members of the psychology department had been among the intellectual architects of the apartheid. In fact, the building in which the psychology department is located was named after a social scientist who had carried out many studies of racial differences in intelligence between Blacks and Whites. It was nothing short of ironic, then, that I would find, housed in that building, by far the most racially balanced and integrated, culturally sensitive, and community-oriented psychology program I had ever come across. Once I had come to know several of the faculty members, I would kid them about the "amount of karma they still had to work off." In time, I realized just how true that was—how South Africa's history of colonialism, apartheid, and the pursuit of social justice permeated all aspects of life, including its psychology world.

The lingering symptoms of the past were obvious in many of the community counseling programs I visited. At my first "Healing of Memories" workshop, I watched in amazement as a White facilitator—a very kindly person whom I had previously met—lead a group of almost exclusively Black and Colored participants in a very authoritarian and at times even belittling manner. When asked about the style, I was told that that was all that seemed to work. During visits to several innovative high school "life skills" classrooms, I found similar "tough love" to be the rule rather than the exception. When asked about the use of psychotherapy and individual counseling, I was told that they found it necessary to stay away from that kind of individual work. "Too likely to open these kids up," I was told. American students in South Africa whom I had supervised also reported being discouraged from and steered away from any kind of dynamic work. They too were cautioned that "we need to keep a lid on these kids' emotions."

I am also aware that in the Youth Program at the Institute for Healing of Memories, their work focuses on teaching children South African history rather than direct psychological intervention. Like many second-generation survivors of historic trauma, these children know nothing of what their parents faced during apartheid and the revolution because of their parents' traumatic silence. I also learned about internalized oppression, South African style. I was introduced to the work of Steven Biko, who was hounded and eventually killed by the apartheid government for his preaching of "black consciousness," and the importance of psychological liberation from self-hatred and the internalization of colonialism. There was certainly no lack of insight and knowledge about their country's psychological past. In fact, I found high school and undergraduate students to be far more culturally and racially sophisticated than their American counterparts. The problem is lack of psychological resources. I learned that there was one psychologist for every 100,000 people in South Africa.

In my travels and the various institutions I visited, I was particularly struck by the openness and candor with which South Africans—Black, White, and Colored—spoke about racism and apartheid. In a guided visit to one of the townships, the young Black man who was our guide brought us into the home of his granny, a respected elder of her clan, who, sitting regally in her best finery in an overstuffed chair, proceeded to tell us about her life in intimate detail and the coming of apartheid, the forced migrations, the identity cards, and the death of her husband. There was no hesitation or concern for personal boundaries. I also spent three days sharing a house with two other Healing of Memories facilitators on the grounds of a maximum-security prison, where we did a workshop for high-risk prisoners. Both were colored, experienced educators and shared freely about their families and experiences growing up in South Africa. Especially powerful was watching a TV documentary about the forced relocation of a community under apartheid with the commentary of one of my housemates who had lived through that actual experience. The stories he told were chilling. The Whites I met were equally forthcoming. I particularly remember conversations with South Africans, both of Afrikaans descent, who served as guide and bus driver on a trip through Namibia. The driver had been a career soldier and spoke at length with open candor over a couple of beers about fighting in the war with Angola, South Africa's protectorate of Namibia, his theories of race superiority, and the uselessness of the Truth and Reconciliation Committee. He was extremely prideful of his past and the history of Afrikaners in South Africa and in no way apologetic about the excesses of the past. "We did what we had to do," he kept repeating. Our guide, a woman in her forties with a grown family, spoke most openly about the impact—mostly negative—that the democratization of South Africa had had on her world. She complained about how "things," meaning public services, were not running as well as they had when they were run by Whites. She also talked about how her children in their mid- to late-twenties could not find employment in South Africa and were considering leaving the country to find work. She said that such jobs were going to Blacks and Colored young people. She hesitated for a moment and then added: "I guess that is the way it should be, but it sure has been hard on us. But we are a Christian country, and the changeover probably needed to happen, and we need to just forgive and look for the best in it all." And, finally, I am reminded of the Healing of Memories workshop that we did for the students in psychology at Stellenbosch, mostly of Afrikaans descent, who shared very honestly about the problems that the apartheid and the political changeover had created

continued

CASE STUDY 3   *continued*

in their families. More liberal and well-educated than their parents, they tended to hold very different ideas about apartheid, race relations, and the past. This had caused much tension at home, and they spoke of this sadly and with great pain. They also spoke of their feelings of pride about being Afrikaners—but of trying to forge a new identity, not based on race relations. In hearing them, I was reminded of the German youth and their anger at their parents' generation over World War II and what Germany had done.

Each time, I listened to the frank and straightforward manner in which South Africans openly spoke about racial politics and the specifics of the apartheid years. I could not help but compare it to the difficulty with which we engage our own racial history in the United States. We speak of it only haltingly, if at all, and almost exclusively in our racially separate communities. We teach a course called "Multicultural Awareness" at The Wright Institute, in which we help students explore their own attitudes toward diversity and multiculturalism, and every year, there is widespread and palpable anxiety among the students who are required to take this course. I believe the differences lie in the nature of race relations in the two countries. Apartheid—no doubt one of the most heinous forms of racism ever conceived—did not hide or conceal itself. Actually, it was openly celebrated. It was acknowledged as a legal reality. It was not hidden from view but was proudly acknowledged by the perpetrators, who saw it as "God's Way." The beliefs in racial differences and inequality were built into the social structure and openly celebrated by most Whites and mourned as well as challenged with increasing ferocity by those they repressed. South Africa was not a democracy and in no way pretended its values were egalitarian. Apartheid was the law and structured into the legal system of the country. And, eventually, South Africa fought a bloody revolution for change, and once democracy had been introduced, it undertook a process of public healing—the Truth and Reconciliation Committee—that sought to acknowledge what had occurred under apartheid and the bloody war for independence and to create together an honest and objective narrative and make what reparations were possible to its victims so the country might go on in peace. In the United States, quite the opposite has occurred. Race and race relations have always remained mystified and hidden. As a nation, we have neither acknowledged nor sought to make amends for the destructive acts or the various forms of individual, institutional, or cultural racism we have visited on our minorities throughout our history. Its White majority are largely unaware of their privilege and the hidden forms of institutional racism that exists systemically. Its minorities, which will in less than forty years become a majority, are mystified and enraged by the lack of willingness to acknowledge what they know to be an ever-present reality within their daily lives. The psychic consequences of these two alternative approaches to racism is very different, especially in the way that anger is managed and processed within the psyches of the respective victim populations.

Finally, I would like to speak about the psychology department at Stellenbosch. What I encountered there—much to my surprise—was a very different kind of psychology than typically practiced here in the United States. I found it to be communal rather than individualistic, and self-critical and self-reflective rather than organized around themes of managed care and the medicalization of treatment. What they called "critical psychology" was a central theme in their orientation and work, and by this, they meant addressing the social problems their society now faced—postapartheid and a bloody revolution. According to Painter and Blanche (2004), it represents efforts to address the manner in which mainstream psychology "has positioned itself vis-à-vis neo-colonialism, racism, capitalist exploitation, and neo-liberal market ideologies"; that is, perpetuated the dehumanizing tenets of the broader society in general. I was amazed by the number of research projects being carried out by the faculty in the townships of the Cape Town area. These interventions actively addressed the dysfunctions and healing of a population traumatized by a long history of racism and war. Much of the work was focused on children and youth—their hope for the future. I was also struck by their emphasis on communal themes. Although students (and I worked primarily with their Honors students) were exposed to a broad range of individualistic psychological theories and interventions, these were never isolated from either their community or cultural contexts. I had repeatedly found the word "community" reverberating through my previous visits to South Africa.

During my first visit, I especially remember being taken for a tour of a township and the reaction of several women on our tour who did not want to participate for fear of being depressed by the squalid living conditions they had seen running for miles along the road from the airport. My reaction was something quite different. Even though we were tourists, the residents that showed us around and welcomed us into their homes did so with great sincerity and pride in showing off their community, humble though it was in physical terms. I was also aware of a sense of inner peace and joy—of people being comfortable in one's own skin—that I've seldom seen in the more "developed" world. South Africa has myriad and staggering social problems, and the trauma they have experienced has certainly left its mark. But who one was did not seem to be defined exclusively by the lack of affluence and possessions, but also—and perhaps more centrally— by a palpable sense of one's community and connection. The psychology department was itself a similar community. I was especially struck by the kindly and thoughtful manner in which I was welcomed into their midst and how so many extended themselves to make sure that I was made to feel comfortable. It was also clear that they sincerely cared about each other and were friends as well as colleagues. In many ways, it reminded me of how I envisioned university life in the United States fifty years ago. Faculty socialized with each other, knew of each other's lives intimately, gathered regularly to discuss and argue ideas (including every morning over tea and coffee), and presented colloquia on their research for the broader university. And I was invited to do the same. In the United States, we speak of community but live primarily fragmented and individualized lives. I found something very different—to which I was very drawn—in South Africa.

Implications for Providers

What, then, are the implications of institutional racism for human service providers? First and foremost, the vast majority of providers work in agencies and organizations that may suffer in varying degrees from institutional racism, to the extent that the general structure, practices, and climate of an agency make it impossible for clients of color to receive culturally competent services, the efforts of individual providers, no matter how skilled, are drastically compromised.

It is just not possible to divorce what happens between a provider and clients from the larger context of the agency. Culturally diverse clients may avoid seeking services from a discriminatory agency once they are familiar with its practices. (Such information travels very quickly within a community.) If they must go there, their willingness to trust and enter a working relationship with the individual provider to whom they are assigned is seriously diminished.

Again, their work with individual staff members is affected by how clients perceive and experience the agency as a whole. In their eyes, the provider is always a part of the agency and perceived as responsible for what it does. Finally, the ability to do what is necessary to meet the needs of a culturally diverse clientele may be limited by the rules and atmosphere of the workplace. Are there support, resources, and knowledgeable supervision for working with culturally diverse clients? Is the provider afforded enough flexibility to adapt services to the cultural demands of clients from various cultural groups? If the answer to either of these questions is no, then the provider must be willing to try to initiate changes in how the organization functions—its structure, practices, climate—so it can be supportive of efforts to provide more culturally competent services.

Cultural Racism

Closely associated with institutional racism is *cultural racism*—the belief that the cultural ways of one group are superior to those of another. Whenever I think of cultural racism, I remember a Latino student once telling a class about painful early experiences in predominantly white schools:

> One day, a teacher was giving us a lesson on nutrition. She asked us to tell the class what we had eaten for dinner the night before. When it was my turn, I proudly listed beans, rice, tortillas. Her response was that my dinner had not included all of the four major food groups and, therefore, was not sufficiently nutritious. The students giggled. How could she say that? Those foods were nutritious to me.

Institutions, like ethnic groups, have their own cultures: languages, ways of doing things, values, attitudes toward time, standards of appropriate behavior, and so on. As participants in institutions, people are expected to adopt, share, and exhibit these cultural patterns. If they do not or cannot, they are likely to be censured and made to feel uncomfortable in a variety of ways. In the United States, the cultural form that has been adopted by and dominates all social institutions is white Northern European culture. The established norms and ways of doing things in this country are dictated by the various dimensions of this dominant culture. Behavior outside its parameters is judged as bad, inappropriate, different, or abnormal. Thus, the eating habits with which my student was raised in his Latino home—in that they differed from what white culture considers nutritious—were judged unhealthy, and he was made to feel bad and ashamed because of it. Herein lies the real insidiousness of cultural racism—those who are culturally diverse must either give up their own ways, and thus a part of themselves, and take on the ways of majority culture or remain perpetual outsiders. (Some people believe that it is possible to be bicultural—that is, to learn the majority culture's ways and also to function comfortably in two very different cultures. This idea is discussed in Chapter 7.) Institutional and cultural racism are thus two sides of the same coin. Institutional racism keeps people of color on the outside of society's institutions by structurally limiting their access. Cultural racism makes them uncomfortable if they do manage to gain entry. Its ways are foreign to them, and they know that their own cultural traits are judged harshly.

Wijeyesinghe, Griffin, and Love (1997) offer the following examples of cultural racism:

- **Holidays and celebrations**: Thanksgiving and Christmas are acknowledged officially on calendars. "Traditional" holiday meals, usually comprising foods that represent the dominant culture, have become the norm for everyone. Holidays associated with non-European cultures are given little attention in American culture.
- **Personal traits**: Characteristics such as independence, assertiveness, and modesty are valued differently in different cultures.
- **Language**: "Standard English" usage is expected in most institutions in the United States. Other languages are sometimes expressly prohibited or tacitly disapproved of.
- **Standards of dress**: If a student or faculty member dresses in clothing or hairstyles unique to his or her culture, he or she is described as "being ethnic," whereas the clothing or hairstyles of Europeans are viewed as "normal."
- **Standards of beauty**: The prevailing ideals of eye color, hair color, hair texture, body size, and shape in the United States exclude most people of color. For instance, black women who have won the Miss America beauty pageant have closely approximated white European looks.
- **Cultural icons**: Jesus, Mary, Santa Claus, and other cultural figures are portrayed as white. The devil and Judas Iscariot, however, are often portrayed as black (p. 94).

Implications for Providers

Cultural racism has relevance for human service providers in several ways. First, it is important that providers be aware of the cultural values that they, as professionals, bring to the counseling session and acknowledge that these values may be different from, and even at odds with, those of their clients. This is especially true for white providers working with clients of color. It is not unusual for clients of color to react to white professionals as symbols of the dominant culture and to initially act out their frustrations with a society that so systematically negates their cultural ways.

Second, all helping across cultures must involve some degree of negotiation around the values that define the helping relationship. Most importantly, therapeutic goals and the general style of interaction must make sense to the client. Yet, at the same time, they must fall within the broad parameters of what the provider conceives as therapeutic. Most likely, the provider will have to make significant adaptations to standard methods of helping to fit the needs of the culturally diverse client.

Third is the realization that traditional training as helping professionals and the models that inform this training are themselves culture-bound and have their roots in dominant Northern European culture. As such, what exactly are the values and cultural imperatives that providers bring to the helping relationship? And what relevance do these have for clients whose cultural worldview might be very different? Cultures differ greatly in how they view healing and how they conceive of the helping process. The notion of seeking professional help from strangers makes little sense in many cultures. Similarly, questions of what healthy behavior is and how one treats dysfunction vary greatly across cultures. Given all this cultural variation and the ethnocentricity of traditional helping models and methods, helping professionals must answer for themselves a number of very knotty questions. Is it possible, for example, to expand culture-bound models so they can become universally applicable (i.e., appropriately applied multiculturally)? If so, what would such a model look like? Or is there, perhaps, some truth to the contention of many minority professionals that something in the Northern European dominant paradigm is inherently destructive to traditional culture and that radically different approaches to helping must be forged for each ethnic population? These questions are addressed in Chapter 5.

▶ Racial Consciousness Among Whites and White Privilege 4-4

In a very heated classroom discussion of diversity a few years ago, several white male students complained bitterly: "It has gotten to a point where there's no place we can just be ourselves and not have to watch what we say or do all the time." The rest of the class—women and ethnic minorities—responded in unison: "Hey, welcome to the world. The rest of us have been doing that kind of self-monitoring all of our lives." What these men were feeling was a threat to their privilege as men and as whites, and they did not like it one bit. Put simply, *white privilege* encompasses the benefits that are automatically accrued to European Americans just on the basis of their skin color. Most insidious is that to most whites, it is all but invisible. For them, it is so much a basic part of daily experience and existence and so available to everyone in their "world" that it is never acknowledged or even given a second thought. Or at least it seems that way.

If one digs a little deeper, however, there is a strong element of defensiveness and denial. Whites tend to see themselves as individuals, just "regular people," part of the human race but not members of any particular racial group. They are, in fact, shocked when others relate to them racially (i.e., as "white"). In a society that gives serious lip service to ideas of equality and equal access to resources ("With enough hard work, anyone can succeed in America" or "Any child can nurture the dream of someday being president"), it is difficult to acknowledge one's "unearned power," to borrow the description from McIntosh (1989).

It is also easier to deny one's white racial heritage and see oneself as colorless than to allow oneself to experience the full brunt of what has been done to people of color in this country in the name of white superiority. Such awareness demands some kind of personal responsibility. If I am white and truly understand what white privilege means socially, economically, and politically, then I cannot help but bear some of the guilt for what has happened historically and what continues to occur. If I were to truly "get it," then I would have no choice but to give up my complacency, try to do something about rectifying racial disparity, and ultimately find myself with the same kind of discomfort and feelings as the men in my class did. No one gives up power and privilege without a struggle.

It is easy, as whites, to feel relatively powerless in relation to others who garner more power than they do because of gender, class, age, and so forth, and thereby deny that they hold any privilege. As Kendall (2002) points out, one need only look at statistics regarding managers in American industry to find out otherwise. While white males constitute 43 percent of the workforce, they hold 95 percent of senior management jobs. White women hold 40 percent of middle management positions compared to black women and men, who hold 5 percent and 4 percent, respectively. Having said all this, it is equally important to acknowledge that as invisible as white privilege is to most European Americans, that is how clearly visible it is to people of color. To them, we are white, clearly racial beings, and we obviously possess privilege in this society. The idea that we do not realize this obvious fact is, in fact, mind-boggling to most people of color because to them, race and racial inequity are ever-present realities. To deny them must seem either deeply cunning or bordering on the verge of psychosis.

At a broader level, white privilege is infused into the very fabric of American society, and even if they wish to do so, whites cannot really give it up. Kendall (2002) enumerates some reasons for this:

- It is "an institutional (rather than personal) set of benefits."
- It belongs to "all of us, who are white, by race."
- It bears no relationship to whether we are "good people" or not.
- It tends to be both "intentional" and "malicious."
- It is "bestowed prenatally."
- It allows us to believe "that we do not have to take the issues of racism seriously."
- It involves the "ability to make decisions that affect everyone without taking others into account."
- It allows us to overlook race in ourselves and to be angry at those who do not.
- It lets me "decide whether I am going to listen or hear others or neither" (pp. 1–5).

What can be done about white privilege? Mainly, individuals can become aware of its existence and the role that it plays in their lives. It cannot be given away. Denying its reality or refusing to identify as white, according to Kendall (2002), merely leaves us "all the more blind to our silencing of people of color" (p. 6). By remaining self-aware and challenging its insidiousness within oneself, in others, and in societal institutions, it is possible to begin to address the denial and invisibility that comprise its most powerful foundation. Like becoming culturally competent, fighting racism and white privilege—both internally and externally—is a lifelong developmental task.

▶ White Racial Attitude Types   4-5

Rowe, Behrens, and Leach (1995) offer a framework for understanding how white European Americans think about race and racial differences. Their research has generated seven attitude structures or types that whites can adopt vis-à-vis race and people of color.

The authors describe the first three types (avoidant, dependent, dissonant) as unachieved and the remaining four (dominative, conflictive, integrative, reactive) as achieved. The distinction between unachieved and achieved refers to the extent to which racial attitude is "securely integrated" into the person's general belief structure—in other words, how firmly it is held versus how easily it can be changed.

- ▶ **Avoidant types**: Tend to ignore, minimize, or deny the importance of race in relation to both their own ethnicity and that of non-whites. Whether out of fear or just convenience, they merely avoid the topic.
- ▶ **Dependent types**: Hold a position but merely have adopted it from significant others (often from as far back as childhood). Therefore, it remains unreflected, superficial, and easily changeable.
- ▶ **Dissonant type**: Held by individuals who are uncertain about what they believe. They lack commitment to their position and are, in fact, open to new information, even if it is dissonant. Their position may result from a lack of experience or knowledge, may indicate incongruity between new information and a previously held position, or may reflect a transition between positions.

Rowe, Behrens, and Leach (1995) next define four types of racial attitudes that they consider as having reached an achieved status (i.e., sufficiently explored, committed to, and integrated into the individual's general belief system).

- ▶ **Dominative attitudes**: Involve the belief that majority group members should be allowed to dominate those who are culturally diverse. They tend to be held by people who are ethnocentric, use European American culture as a standard for judging the rightness of others' behavior, and devalue and feel uncomfortable with non-whites, especially in closer personal relationships.

▶ **Conflictive attitude**: Held by individuals who, although they would not support outright racism or discrimination, oppose efforts to ameliorate the effects of discrimination, such as affirmative action. They are conflicted around the competing values of fairness, which requires significant change, and retaining the status quo, which says, "I am very content with the way things are."

▶ **Integrative attitudes**: Tend to be pragmatic in their approach to race relations. They have a sense of their own identity as whites and at the same time favor interracial contact and harmony. They further believe racism can be eradicated through goodwill and rationality.

▶ **Reactive attitudes**: Involves a rather militant stand against racism. Such individuals tend to identify with people of color, may feel guilty about being white, and may romanticize the racial drama. They are, in addition, very sensitive to situations involving discrimination and react strongly to the inequities that exist in society.

According to the authors, these are the most frequently observed forms of white attitudes toward race and race relations. The unachieved types are most changeable; by definition, they have not been truly integrated into the person's worldview. The four achieved forms are more difficult to change, but under sufficient contrary information or experience, they can be altered. When that does occur, it usually involves a process of change during which the individual looks a lot like those who are in the dissonant mode. A summary of Rowe, Behrens, and Leach (1995) can be found in Table 4-1.

TABLE 4-1
Racial Attitude Types and Statuses

Types	Status	Summary
Avoidant	Unachieved	Ignore, minimize, or deny race
Dependent	Unachieved	Adopt positions of significant others
Dissonant	Unachieved	Lack commitment and change position easily
Dominative	Achieved	Adopt classic bigotry
Conflictive	Achieved	Oppose efforts at social justice
Integrative	Achieved	Open to change through goodwill and rationality
Reactive	Achieved	Stand militantly against racism

Source: Adapted from "Racial/Ethnic Identity and Social Consciousness: Looking Back and Looking, Forward," by W. Rowe, J. T. Behrens, and M. M. Leach, 1995, in *Handbook of Multicultural Counseling* (pp. 218–235), edited by J. P. Ponterotto, J. M. Casas, L. A. Suzuki, and C. M. Alexander, Thousand Oaks, CA: Sage Publications, Inc.

A Model of White Racial Identity Development

Helms (1995) offers a somewhat different approach to understanding how whites experience and relate to race in the United States through her model of white racial identity development. Rather than suggest a series of independent attitude statuses, as do Rowe, Behrens, and Leach (1995), she envisions a developmental process (defined by a series of stages or statuses) through which whites can move to recognize and abandon their privilege. According to Helms, each status or stage is supported by a unique pattern of psychological defense and means of processing racial experience. A statement typical of someone at that developmental level follows the description of each stage.

The first stage, contact status, begins with the individual's internalization of the majority culture's view of people of color, as well as the advantages of privilege. Whites at this level of awareness have developed a defense that Helms calls "obliviousness" to keep the issue of race out of consciousness. Bollin and Finkel (1995) describe contact status as the "naive belief that race does not really make a difference" (p. 25).

> I'm a White woman. When my grandfather came to this country, he was discriminated against, too. But he didn't blame Black people for his misfortune. He educated himself and got a job; that's what Blacks ought to do. (Helms, 1995, p. 185)

The second stage, disintegration status, involves "disorientation and anxiety provoked by unresolved racial moral dilemmas that force one to choose between own-group loyalty and humanism" (Helms, 1995, p. 185). It is supported by the defenses of suppression and ambivalence. At this stage, the person has encountered information or has had experiences that led him or her to realize that race in fact does make a difference. The result is a growing awareness of and discomfort with white privilege.

> I myself tried to set a nonracist example (for other Whites) by speaking up when someone said something blatantly prejudiced—how to do this without alienating people so that they would no longer take me seriously was always tricky—and by my friendships with Mexicans and Blacks who were actually the people with whom I felt most comfortable. (Helms, 1995, p. 185)

Reintegration status, the third stage, is defined by an idealization of one's racial group and a concurrent rejection and intolerance for other groups. It depends on the defenses of selective perception and negative out-group distortion for its evolution.

Here, the white individual attempts to deal with the discomfort by emphasizing the superiority of white culture and the natural deficits in cultures of color.

> So what if my great-grandfather owned slaves. He didn't mistreat them, and besides, I wasn't even here then. I never owned slaves. So, I don't know why Blacks expect me to feel guilty for something that happened before I was born.

Nowadays, reverse racism hurts Whites more than slavery hurts Blacks. At least they got three square (meals) a day. But my brother can't even get a job with the police department because they have to hire less qualified Blacks. That (expletive) happens to Whites all the time. (Helms, 1995, p. 185)

The fourth stage, pseudoindependence status, involves an "intellectualized commitment to one's own socioracial group and deceptive tolerance of other groups" (Helms, 1995, p. 185). It is grounded in the processes of reshaping reality and selective perception. The individual has, at this point, developed an intellectual acceptance of racial differences and espouses a liberal ideology of social justice but has not truly integrated either emotionally.

Was I the only person left in America who believed that the sexual mingling of the races was a good thing, that it would erase cultural barriers and leave us all a lovely shade of tan? . . . Racial blending is inevitable. At least, it may be the only solution to our dilemmas of race. (Helms, 1995, p. 185)

A person functioning in the immersion/emersion status, fifth along the continuum, is searching for a personal understanding of racism, as well as insight into how he or she benefits from it. As a part of this process, which has as its psychological base hypervigilance and reshaping, there is an effort to redefine one's whiteness. Entry into this stage may have been precipitated by being rejected by individuals of color and often includes isolation within one's own group in order to work through the powerful feelings that have been stimulated.

It's true that I personally did not participate in the horror of slavery, and I don't even know whether my ancestors owned slaves. But I know that because I am White, I continue to benefit from a racist system which stems from the slavery era. I believe that if White people are ever going to understand our role in perpetuating racism, then we must begin to ask ourselves some hard questions and be willing to consider our role in maintaining a hurtful system. Then, we must try to do something to change it. (Helms, 1995, p. 185)

The final stage, autonomy status, involves "informed positive socioracial-group commitment, use of internal standards for self-definition, and capacity to relinquish the privileges of racism" (Helms, 1995, p. 185). It is supported by the psychological processes of flexibility and complexity. Here, the person has come to peace with his or her whiteness, separating it from a sense of privilege, and is able to approach those who are culturally diverse without prejudice.

I live in an integrated (Black-White) neighborhood and I read Black literature and popular magazines. So, I understand that the media presents a very stereotypical view of Black culture. I believe that if more of us White people made more than a superficial effort to obtain accurate information about racial groups other than our own, then we could help make this country a better place for all people. (Helms, 1995, p. 185)

Helms's model of white identity development parallels models of racial identity development for people of color that are introduced in Chapter 6. Both involve consciousness raising; that is, becoming aware of and working through unconscious feelings and beliefs about one's connection to race and ethnicity. However, the goal of identity development in each group is different.

For people of color, it involves a cumulative process of "surmounting internalized racism in its various manifestations," while for whites, it has to do with the "abandonment of entitlement" (Helms, 1995, p. 184). What the two models share is a process wherein the person (whether of color or white) sheds internalized racial attitudes and social conditioning and replaces them with greater openness and appreciation for racial and cultural identity, as well as cultural differences.

Identity Development in the Classroom

Ponterotto (1988), drawing parallels with the earlier work of both Helms (1985) and Cross (1971), describes "the racial identity and consciousness development process" of white participants in a multicultural learning environment, an educational setting that may well be similar to that in which you may find yourself. Ponterotto identifies four stages through which students proceed:

- Pre-exposure
- Exposure
- Zealot-defensive
- Integration

In the pre-exposure stage, the student "has given little thought to multicultural issues or to his or her role as a white person in a racist and oppressive society" (p. 151). In the exposure stage, students are routinely confronted with minority individuals and issues. They are exposed to the realities of racism and the mistreatment of people of color, examine their own cultural values and how they pervade society, and discover that the "mistreatment extends into the counseling process" and "the counseling profession is ethnocentrically biased and subtly racist" (p. 152). These realizations tend to stimulate both anger and guilt—anger because they had been taught that counseling was "value free and truly fair and objective" and guilt because holding such assumptions had probably led them to perpetuate this subtle racism themselves.

In the zealot-defensive stage, students tend to react in one of two ways—either overidentifying with ethnic minorities and the issues they are studying or distancing themselves from them. The former tend to develop a strong "pro-minority perspective" (p. 152) and through it are able to manage and resolve some of the guilty feelings. The latter, on the other hand, tend to take the criticism very personally and withdraw from the topic as a defense mechanism, becoming "passive recipients" (p. 153) of multicultural information. In the real world, such a reaction leads to avoidance of interracial contact and escape into same-race associations. In classes, however, where students are a "captive audience," there is greater likelihood that the defensive feelings will be processed and worked through as the class proceeds.

In the final stage, integration, the extreme reactions of the previous stage tend to decrease in intensity. Zealous reactions subside, and those students become more balanced in their views. Defensiveness is slowly transformed, and students tend to acquire a "renewed interest, respect, and appreciation for cultural differences" (p. 153). Ponterotto, however, is quick to point out that there is no guarantee that all students will pass through all four stages, and some can remain stuck in any of the stages.

▶ Becoming a Cultural Ally   `4-6`

After participating in a class or workshop on cultural diversity, white students often ask how they can support people of color in addressing racism and moving toward greater social justice. Relevant here is the concept of becoming a *cultural ally*. Bell (1997) suggests that whites "have an important role to play in challenging oppression and creating alternatives. Throughout our history, there have always been people from dominant groups who use their power to actively fight against systems of oppression . . . Dominants can expose the social, moral, and personal costs of maintaining privilege so as to develop an investment in changing the system by which they benefit, but for which they also pay a price" (p. 13). Wijeyesinghe, Griffin, and Love (1997) define an ally as a white person who actively works to eliminate racism. Melton (2018) expresses a more general definition of allyship as "a person, group, or nation that is associated with another or others for some common cause or purpose" (p. 2). "This person may be motivated by self-interest in ending racism, a sense of moral obligation, or a commitment to foster social justice, as opposed to a patronizing agenda of 'wanting to help those poor People of Color'" (p. 98). Melton goes on to describe four steps to best address the role of becoming an ally: (1) awareness of oneself as a cultural being, (2) choose a plan and act, (3) take professional and personal responsibility for our actions and decisions, and (4) self-care. These authors, along with Thompson (2005), describe a more detailed list of the characteristics of a cultural ally. This person:

- ▶ Acknowledges the privilege that he or she receives as a member of the culturally dominant group
- ▶ Listens and believes the experiences of marginalized group members without diminishing, dismissing, normalizing, or making their experience invisible

- ▶ Is willing to take risks, try new behaviors, and act in spite of his or her own fear and resistance from other agents
- ▶ Is humble and does not act as an expert in the marginalized group culture
- ▶ Is willing to be confronted about his or her own behavior and attitudes and consider change
- ▶ Takes a stand against oppression even when no marginalized-group person is present
- ▶ Believes he or she can make a difference by acting and speaking out against social injustice
- ▶ Knows how to cultivate support from other allies
- ▶ Works to understand his or her own privilege and does not burden the marginalized group to provide continual education

Doing the White Thing

I would like to end this section on white privilege, identity, and consciousness with a firsthand account of one woman's personal journey of discovery into her own whiteness and its meaning.

The author, Swan Keyes, is a psychotherapist, consultant, writer, and racial justice educator dedicated to dismantling white supremacy and other forms of oppression. She delivers trainings, lectures, and workshops specializing in helping white people investigate their racial conditioning to become more effective at interrupting oppression, building healthy communities, and advocating for social change.

As we pull into our driveway, I notice a young Black man walking down the sidewalk toward us, a brown paper bag full of flowers in his hands. I can see that he wants to engage and I am tired and don't want to deal with anyone.

I step out of the car to hear him say hello. He extends his hand and introduces himself. Mustering up all the friendliness I can, I offer a weak smile and ask him if he is selling flowers.

"Uh, no," he says, looking surprised. "I'm here to see Alicia." Alicia is my neighbor of many years.

Ah. Now I notice that this young man is wearing a nice suit. I realize that instead of seeing him, I just projected an image of one of the many Black men who approach me downtown selling the local homeless newspaper or asking for change for the bus. Considering that I've never actually met a homeless person selling newspapers in my neighborhood up in the Oakland foothills, I wonder, how is it that instead of seeing this sharply dressed young man bringing flowers for his date, I am seeing some kind of salesman or beggar?

I start to backpedal, fast, hoping he has no idea what has just passed through my mind.

"Oh, I was hoping for some flowers," I stammer.

He looks embarrassed (probably for me) and asks if I want some from his bag.

"Oh, no, no, give them to Alicia. Thank you so much. It's really great to meet you." We shake hands and quickly part.

My friend Kenji, who has witnessed the interaction, says hi to the man, and we walk into our house.

"Damn!" is all I can say.

"Yeah," Kenji says, shaking his head, clearly displeased with what he has just observed.

Such a vivid illustration of how my mind has been trained to see a stereotype, rather than a person. Does this young man see how quickly I projected the image of a homeless person onto him? If so, is he hurt or angry, or just laughing it off? Is he used to this kind of projection?

I want to pretend this incident has no impact and could have happened to anyone.

I didn't mean any harm, and perhaps he had no idea what was going on for me. But if it's no big deal, why is my stomach in knots? I feel like a jerk, anxious and ashamed. I want to purge the image of the beggar from my mind, eliminate the part of me that can see this young man in that way—the entwined racial and class training embedded in my psyche.

But I know that my white conditioning isn't just going to evaporate due to my good intentions. So disappointing. I wish intention was everything. Unfortunately, my actions can have harmful effects even when my intentions are great. And in this case, there was another person impacted by the interaction. My friend, Kenji, who witnessed the interaction, is a man of Asian American descent, and daily faces a multitude of stereotypes projected on him from white people and others.

So my practice is to try to put positive intentions into action to learn as much as possible about the origins and impacts of stereotypes and racial conditioning and how they affect people of whiteness and people of color. Although I may not eliminate the mental conditioning that paints a young Black man as a nuisance, I can develop awareness of it and eventually learn to respond in better ways and hopefully work to shift the power imbalance that maintains these stereotypes (the same system that holds Black people on the whole in economic bondage, on the bottom of the social ladder, even in a country that can elect a Black man president).

But I'm Not Racist

I like to think of myself as a very open person, dedicated to social justice. Yet I see that when that incident occurred with my neighbor's date, there were very few African Americans in my life. I had plenty of acquaintances of color whom I proudly called friends, but very few truly intimate relationships. Living in one of the most diverse regions in the country, I socialized mostly with white people—at work, at home, at school, at my meditation center, at parties. At all of these places I can expect the majority of people to look like me.

My lack of close relationships with people of color meant that I rarely had to confront my racial conditioning. This is one of the privileges of being white in U.S. society. For the most part, I can choose whether and when to acknowledge or address racism. I choose not to think about race a good deal of the time. I enjoy films, books, and other media that focus almost entirely on white characters without having to think of this as a racial experience. I go to restaurants, night clubs, and beaches that are predominantly white without thinking about why it is that some spots remain so exclusive. I can just see myself and other white people as the norm (as "human") and see race only when it comes to people outside of that norm. And I can live in a way where I rarely have to engage the "other."

So what is this white racial conditioning, or training, and how does it work in the U.S. today? White training is how people are taught to be what we call white. People of all different European ethnicities come to the U.S. and through a process of assimilation, accrue unearned benefits due to light skin color and other features that allow them to be considered "white." People often give up their ethnic identities to blend in to the mainstream white culture. To be successful requires one to blend in and seek economic privilege and independence within the system. This white training tells us what it means to be "civilized," professional, beautiful, intelligent, responsible, successful, and such. The training tells us who is outside of this norm and bombards us daily with images of the Other, as strange, deviant, criminal, etc. The stereotypes are often negative and sometimes positive as well (soulful, spiritual, musical, etc.), but always a projection of the parts not recognized within the norm of the dominant culture.

Becoming White

As a child when my hippie father took me to visit his working-class family, descendants of English Protestant early colonial settlers, I knew I did not fit in. Growing up on a commune with a Jewish mother, I was embarrassed at not knowing the social customs of this "normal" family. I knew my father had stepped outside of the bounds of conventional whiteness (though I didn't yet think of it in racial terms), both in his counterculture lifestyle and in marrying my mother, who was too loud, too emotional, too intellectual, too opinionated, too expressive, too sexual, too much for a white Christian family to have any idea what to do with.

I learned that to fit in (to become like them—culturally white) meant to make myself very small. So, I became a very nice girl. I spoke softly, observed their table manners, didn't talk about politics, religion, or sex, and generally left most of myself at the door in order to gain entrance to this world that I saw on TV, the world I craved so much to be part of.

Along with the benefits of light skin, there are also many hidden costs to white conditioning. Just as I have learned that to be Jewish is to be "too much" for many other light-skinned people to deal with, I have also taken on a feeling that there is some inadequacy in me because I am white. I used to feel terribly insecure in racially mixed groups, always afraid of doing or saying the wrong thing, or else wanting to say something radical to prove my worth.

I have been immobilized at times, feeling so much shame at the legacy of racism that I couldn't stand up against racism when I should have. I felt too small, too weak, too incompetent, which is what happens when we are not taught to see our racial conditioning and understand our place in the racial hierarchy. So, I let racist comments go by. I remember once as a teenager meeting an elderly African American man coming out of the health food store in the rural town of Shelburne Falls, Massachusetts, where I grew up. I saw that the man was upset and asked if he was okay. He told me he had just been informed by another customer that Blacks weren't welcome here. I felt so bad all I could do was tell him how sorry I was. In retrospect, I wish I had confronted the customer or the owner of the store, rather than sink into a sense of helplessness. At the time, I had no idea what to say or do, so I did what I had learned to do: nothing. And the cost was guilt, fear, and alienation. I had connected to this man in my grief and sense of injustice, but the connection ended in my feeling stuck and ashamed, and I wonder if there might have been a reluctance on my part to engage with African Americans afterward, wanting to avoid that feeling of inadequacy I experienced.

The legacy of assimilation has also cost me a sense of connection to my cultural and spiritual roots, so that I have looked to the traditions of others— Native Americans, Africans, Asians, South Americans—for spirituality and culture, wanting to take on something of theirs to fill the void in myself. (I believe this is a major part of why "tribal" tattoos, jewelry, and clothing are so popular in the U.S. today, why we can so easily become culture vultures.)

Finding Sangha

When I finally decided that I wanted to learn about racism and racial conditioning, I had no idea where to begin. I wanted a place where I could speak honestly and ask some really basic questions. I had already seen that in mixed-race groups, it wasn't always a good idea for me to speak my mind, partly because I was coming from a preschool level of understanding of race (like most white people) and required people of color in the group to be continually teaching and speaking to my level—exhausting and often quite unpleasant for them (not that all people of color have awareness of these issues, but I do believe that all are targeted by racism and stereotyping to varying degrees, with varying results). I wanted to sit down with some other white people and lay my questions and stereotypes on the table.

Such a group is extraordinarily hard to come by. Yet as soon as I put out this intention, Kenji found a flyer from a local library advertising the "UNtraining," a program for white people to explore what it means to be white and how we unconsciously participate in a system that keeps white people in positions of power. I called and talked for hours with the founder, Robert Horton.

Robert's work was founded on the approach of Rita Shimmin, a woman of African American and Filipina descent who he met at a weeklong international Process Work seminar with Arnold Mindell in the early 90s. People of color at the seminar repeatedly requested that the white folks in the room get together and look at whiteness, rather than asking people of color to teach them about racism. At one point, Robert asked, "Why don't white people get together and do this?" to which Rita replied, "Why don't you?" Fortunately for him, she was willing to mentor him while he formed such a group, and remains his teacher to this day, due to his demonstrated commitment to the work.

In the UNtraining, we work with the parts of ourselves we most want to disown, including the areas where we see our racial training. Just as we learn in meditation to observe our thoughts, feelings, and physical states as they rise and pass, so too we can become familiar with how our racial training works. It takes study, long-term commitment, and community, as we learn to overcome the individualistic white training that tells us that we can "fix it" all on our own.

Ways I Avoid Dealing with Racism (and Piss Off People of Color in My Life)

One of the things I discovered early on in the work was the way I was thinking about racism held me back from doing any real work around it. I thought there were two separate kinds of people: good people and racists. I didn't feel hatred toward people of color, so I didn't consider myself racist. I was one of those people who might innocently (and not altogether truthfully) state, "Some of my best friends are Black."

As Robert Horton pointed out, this fallacy that there are two types of people—the racist and the nonracist—is counterproductive. By acknowledging that all people (including so-called people of color) have racial conditioning, and no one chooses it, we stop trying to prove that we are the "right" type of person and we free up energy to develop nonblaming awareness of the stereotypes, fears, and unconscious prejudices we have learned. Also, we begin to see that racism is more than just unconscious attitudes and prejudices, which anyone can have, but it is also a system that holds some people in a position of structural power over others (when one group dominates a society's economic, government, education, health, and other systems of power, then psychological conditioning is important to understand not just to shift attitudes, but to shift structural imbalance and increase justice and connection between groups).

I also had to give up any attempts at colorblindness. Growing up in a hippie commune where we considered ourselves all one on a spiritual level, I had learned to use spiritual bypass to avoid dealing with social issues. We believed that just because we were caring people, we were somehow immune to social conditioning. We thought that our love was enough to free us from any accountability for the ills of society. Unfortunately, ignorance of issues doesn't make them go away.

Over the years, examining racism, sexism, heterosexism, class oppression, and other -isms that keep people apart, alliance building became my primary spiritual practice. As with my meditation practice, the ability to develop compassionate awareness became a great source of liberation. Today, it is such a relief when I can see my racial conditioning and not hit myself over the head with it, but instead take the opportunity to go a little deeper in inquiry and make more conscious choices about how to respond to it.

SUMMARY

Racism is "the systematic subordination of members of targeted racial groups who have relatively little social power ... by members of the agent racial group who have relatively more social power" (Wijeyesinghe, Griffin, and Love, 1997). Prejudice is a negative, inaccurate, rigid, and unfair way of thinking about members of another group. Racism equals prejudice plus power and exists on three levels: individual, institutional, and cultural. In general, people deny, rationalize, and avoid discussing feelings and beliefs about race and ethnicity.

Individual racism emerges out of the normal and natural tendencies of how people think, feel, and process information. In-group and out-group behavior, categorical thinking and stereotyping, avoidance, and selective perception set the stage for the emergence of racism. There are a variety of theories about the psychological motivation behind racist behavior. The frustration-aggression-displacement hypothesis and the authoritarian or global personality type are two of the most popular. The impact of microaggression and implicit bias is also discussed. *Institutional racism* involves the manipulation of societal institutions to give preferences and advantages to white people and at the same time restrict the choices, rights, mobility, and access of people of color. One method of identifying institutional racism involves comparing the frequency or incidence of a characteristic within a group to the group's general frequency within the population. Lack of intent or consciousness should never be regarded as justification for institutional racism. Although denial is typically at work in all forms of racism, it is especially difficult for individuals to take responsibility for institutional racism. Three cases of institutional racism are presented.

Cultural racism is the belief that the cultural ways of one group are superior to those of another. In most institutions in the United States, white Northern European culture has been adopted and dominates. Behavior outside its parameters is judged as bad or inappropriate. To succeed, people of color must give up their own ways—and, thus, a part of themselves—and take on the ways of majority culture or remain perpetual outsiders.

White privilege refers to the benefits that are accrued automatically to European Americans merely on the basis of skin color. What is most insidious and surprising about such privilege is that it is largely invisible to the people who hold it. Most whites tend to see themselves not as racial beings or members of a racial grouping, but as individuals. As such, they tend to deny or play down the import of race and ethnicity as social forces. One reason may be that it is difficult to acknowledge "unearned power" in a society that gives such powerful lip service to equality and equal access to resources. A second reason is that acknowledging the import of race and the obvious racial inequity in our society would lead to strong feelings of guilt and responsibility and a need to make amends. It is also easy for many European Americans to experience themselves as powerless in relation to class, gender, age, and so on, thereby downplaying the power that they have accrued in relation to their whiteness.

Rowe, Behrens, and Leach (1995) offer a model of racial attitude types to describe the ways that European Americans think about and relate to race and racial differences. Helms (1995) offers a model of white racial-identity development that assumes the existence of five stages of a white individual's progress toward self-awareness and the abandonment of privilege. Based on teaching diversity in the college classroom, Ponterotto (1988) identified a progression of four stages that most students pass through as they become more culturally sensitive and competent. White individuals interested in supporting people of color and reducing racism and promoting greater social justice might consider becoming a cultural ally. The chapter ends with Swan Keyes' firsthand account of her personal journey of exploration into the meaning of her own whiteness.

ACTIVITIES

1. *Explore personal experiences around race and ethnicity.* The following questions concern your experiences with ethnicity and cultural difference. Several ask you to identify a time or event in the past. Allow yourself to relax and visualize the time or event you have identified. Try to re-experience it as much as possible. When you are finished, describe the experience in writing or to a partner. Include how you felt at the time, how you feel about it now, how it affects you today, and any other associations, images, or strong feelings that may come up. Use as much time and detail as you find valuable.

   ▸ When did you first become aware that people were different racially or ethnically?
   ▸ When did you first become aware of yourself as a member of a racial or ethnic group?
   ▸ When were you first made aware of people being treated differently because of their race or ethnicity?

- When did you first become aware of being treated differently yourself because of your race or ethnicity?
- When were you proudest being a member of the group to which you belong?
- When were you *least* proud of being a member of the group to which you belong?
- How do you identify yourself racially/ethnically? Culturally? How has your sense of race/ethnicity or culture changed over time?
- How would you describe the extent of your contact with people who are racially/ethnically different from you? How has this changed over time? If your contact is limited, why do you think it is that way? You can increase the intensity and learning value of these exercises by sharing your answers with someone else. After you have shared each answer, use it as a spring-board for further soul-searching and personal discussions of each topic.

2. *Identify your attitudes toward members of diverse racial and ethnic groups.* This exercise gives you an opportunity to verbalize and identify your experiences with, attitudes toward, and beliefs about members of diverse racial and ethnic groups. Answer the questions or carry out the activity in relation to each of the following groups toward which you feel an affinity or dislike:

(a) African Americans, (b) Latinos/as, (c) Asian Americans, (d) Native Americans, (e) white Northern Europeans, (f) white ethnic groups (Jews, Irish, Italians, etc.).

- Describe in detail experiences that you have had with members of this group.
- At present, how do you feel about members of this group (describe your reactions in detail and, if possible, relate them to specific experiences), and how has that changed over time?
- Are there characteristics, traits, or other things about members of this group that make it difficult for you to approach them?
- Without censoring yourself, generate a list of characteristics—one-word adjectives—that describe your beliefs and perceptions about members of this group.
- What reactions, feelings, thoughts, or concerns come to mind when you think about working professionally with members of this group?
- What kinds of answers, information, learning experiences, contact, and so forth do you need to become more comfortable with members of this group?

5

Understanding Culture and Cultural Differences

LEARNING OBJECTIVES

5-1 Define culture and identify cultural differences among populations.

5-2 Distinguish between the different dimensions of culture.

5-3 Examine the key aspects of the helping profession as they relate to multicultural counseling.

5-4 Recall definitions of mental health.

5-5 Compare conflicting cross-cultural service models.

5-6 Contrast adapting generic models and evolving culturally sensitive models.

5-7 Identify cross-cultural treatment models.

When culture is alive and vibrant, it provides the kind of inner programming that keeps the millipede walking along. It is always there—and much of the time it is lying beyond our awareness. It gives life structure and meaning. When it becomes fragmented, however, a central part of what it is and what it can offer gets lost. This chapter discusses a number of issues related to culture. What exactly is it, and how does it function in the life of a person? Why are social scientists finding it preferable to describe group differences in terms of culture rather than race? Along what cultural dimensions do groups differ, and in what ways do the cultures of Euro-Americans and people of color clash? What happened to white culture? Are the theories that inform professionals helping the culture-bound, as some practitioners have suggested? And, finally, is there such a thing as multicultural counseling (i.e., a single approach that can adjust itself to the needs of many cultural groups)? Answers to these questions provide a better understanding of the ways in which culture affects service delivery.

▶ What Is Culture?   5-1

Culture is a difficult concept to grasp because it is so basic to human societies and so intertwined with our very natures that its workings are seldom acknowledged or thought about by those who have internalized it. It is all encompassing, like water for a fish, so it remains largely preconscious and is obvious only when it is gone or has been seriously disturbed. Anthropological definitions point to certain aspects of it. Culture comprises traditional ideas and related values, it is learned, shared, and transmitted from one generation to the next, and it organizes life and helps individuals interpret their existence. In an interview for Live Science website, Cristina De Rossi, and anthropologist at Barnet and Southgate College in London said, "Culture encompasses religion, food, what we wear, how we wear it, our language, marriage, music, what we believe is right or wrong, how we sit at the table, how we greet visitors, how we behave with loved ones, and a million other things" (Zimmermann, 2015). De Rossi went on to explain that culture is fluid and constantly in motion, which makes it difficult for culture to be defined just one way.

I like the notion of culture as the ways that a people have learned to respond to life's problems. For instance, all human groups must deal with death, but the rituals and practices that have developed around it vary greatly from culture to culture. However, all these definitions lack something that would be particularly helpful for the present purpose—a more strongly felt sense of how culture functions within the individual. To get at this, the concept of paradigm is very useful. A paradigm is a set of shared assumptions and beliefs about how the world works. It describes the cognitive worldview through which human beings perceive and relate to their world. Their paradigms, without people being very aware of them, tell us how human existence works—what is possible and impossible, what the rules are, and how things are done.

In short, paradigms shape an individual's experience of reality. Culture is the stuff of which human paradigms are made. It provides them content—their identity, beliefs, values, and behavior. It is learned as part of the natural process of growing up in a family and community and from participating in societal institutions. These are the purveyors of culture.

One's culture becomes one's paradigm, defining what is real and right. Diverse cultures, in turn, generate different paradigms of reality, and each is protected and defended as if a threat to it were a threat to a member's very existence. From this perspective, it is easy to understand why the imposition of a Northern European cultural paradigm onto the lives of people of color—who possess and live by very different cultural paradigms—is experienced so negatively.

Culture vs. Race in the Definition of Group Differences

Before you learn about the various dimensions along which cultures differ, it is useful to take a short digression to discuss difficulties with the concept of race. Increasingly of late, social scientists have chosen to distinguish between human groups on the basis of culture rather than race. For example, when they refer to tribal subgroups within the broader racial category of Native Americans as separate ethnic groups, they are emphasizing cultural differences as opposed to biological or physical ones. I have followed a similar practice here by using terms such as *ethnic group* and *culturally diverse clients* to describe human diversity. The term *ethnic group* was defined in Chapter 1 as any distinguishable people whose members share a culture and see themselves as separate and different from the cultural majority.

The emphasis is on shared cultural material as a basis for identification. It is not likely that the concept of race and its usual breakdown into five distinct human groups will ever disappear. It is just too deeply ingrained in the fabric of American society. Rather, its importance as a social—as opposed to a biological—concept will increasingly be emphasized.

There are many serious problems with the concept of race:

▸ Physical anthropologists have shown quite conclusively that what has always been assumed to be clear and distinct differences among the races are not very clear or distinct at all. In fact, it appears that there is as much variability in physical characteristics within racial groups as there is among groups. For example, it is not uncommon to see a wide array of skin colors and physical features among individuals who are all considered members of one racial group. It is believed that there has been so much racial mixing throughout history that, today, groups that may have once been genetically distinct are no longer distinguishable.

▸ The term *race* has become so emotionally charged and politicized that it can no longer serve a useful role in scientific discussion.

▶ Racial categories have been used throughout U.S. history to simultaneously oppress people of color, justify white privilege, and confuse racial
politics. For example, U.S. Census classifications of race have changed
regularly every decade from 1889 to the present. In 1890, for example,
they included "White, Black, Mulatto, Quadroon, Octoroon, Chinese,
Japanese, and Indian." The 2000 Census tracked the following racial
groups: "White, Black, American Indian or Alaskan Native, Asian Indian,
Chinese, Filipino, Japanese, Korean, Vietnamese, Native Hawaiian, and
Guamanian or Chamorro." In addition, Hispanic/Latino group membership has become a separate racial category, as has the acknowledgment of
more than one racial background. Of particular interest in regard to such
redefinitions is the fact that they seem to parallel changes in immigration
restrictions passed by Congress. An increased demand for entry into the
United States from groups who are perceived as threats by the white establishment results in reduced immigration quotas.

▶ Defining race biologically and genetically opens the door for pseudosci-
entific arguments about intellectual and other types of inferiority among
people of color.

▶ The social reality of race in the United States does not conform to the
existence of five distinct groups. Rather, only two bear any real social
meaning: "white" and "of color." The notion of the great melting pot,
for instance, was actually only about melting white ethnics. The myth
was never intended to apply to people of color. For white ethnics, upper
mobility involved discovering and asserting their group's whiteness as a
means of setting themselves apart from and above the groups of color who
perpetually resided at the bottom of the social hierarchy of the United
States. When they first arrived, various white ethnic groups were met with
prejudice and scorned and were merely tolerated because they represented
a source of much-needed cheap labor. In time, however, as they acculturated into the system, they discovered that they could progress most
quickly by identifying themselves as white and by taking on the prejudices
against people of color that were an intrinsic part of white culture.

For all these reasons, it has become increasingly compelling to set aside the term
race as a distinguishing feature among groups and to turn to cultural differences as a
more useful and less controversial yardstick.

However, according to Desmond and Emirbayer (2016), this is easier said than
done. The election of Donald Trump, for most, ended the post-racial myth that the
past election of Obama created for some Americans. Although there are serious
problems with the concept of race, there are reasons for its existence. As the previous

statements explain and Desmond and Emirbayer (2016) expand upon, these reasons are not always in the best interest of all individuals. It is important for helpers to understand the reality faced by clients who are living in a world where race, more than culture, still heavily influences how individuals relate to each other.

▶ The Dimensions of Culture   5-2

Cultures differ depending on their *worldview* or particular philosophy of life or conception of the world; the content and specifics of each vary from culture to culture. These differences and our natural tendency toward *ethnocentrism*, the assumption that everyone else views the world in the same way as we do, are the reasons that cross-cultural misunderstanding occurs. Brown and Landrum-Brown (1995) enumerate the following dimensions of culture:

- ▶ *Psychobehavioral modality* refers to the mode of activity most preferred within a culture. Do individuals actively engage their world (doing), more passively experience it as a process (being), or experience it with the intention of evolving (becoming)?
- ▶ *Axiology* involves the interpersonal values that a culture teaches. Do they compete or cooperate (competition vs. cooperation)? Are emotions freely expressed or held back and controlled (emotional restraint vs. emotional expressiveness)? Is verbal expression direct or indirect (direct verbal expression vs. indirect verbal expression)? Do group members seek help from others or do they keep problems hidden so as not to shame their families (help seeking vs. "saving face")?
- ▶ *Ethos* refers to widely held beliefs within a cultural group that guide social interactions. Are people viewed as independent beings or as interdependent (independence vs. interdependence)? Is one's first allegiance to oneself or to one's family (individual rights vs. honor and family protection)? Are all individual group members seen as equal, or is there an acknowledged hierarchy of status or power (egalitarianism vs. authoritarianism)? Are harmony, respect, and deference toward others valued over controlling and dominating them (control and dominance vs. harmony and deference)?
- ▶ *Epistemology* summarizes the preferred ways of gaining knowledge and learning about the world. Do people rely more on their intellectual abilities (cognitive processes), their emotions and intuition (affective processes, vibes, intuition), or a combination of both (cognitive and affective)?
- ▶ *Logic* involves the kind of reasoning process that group members adopt. Are issues seen as being either one way or the other (either-or thinking)?

Can multiple possibilities be considered at the same time (both-and thinking)? Or is thinking organized around inner consistency (circular)?

▸ *Ontology* refers to how a culture views the nature of reality. Is what is real only what can be seen and touched (objective material)? Is there a level of reality that exists beyond the material senses (subjective spiritual)? Or are both levels of reality experienced (spiritual and material)?

▸ *Concept of Time* involves how time is experienced within a culture. Is it clock-determined and linear (clock-based), defined in relation to specific events (event-based), or experienced as repetitive (cyclical)?

▸ *Concept of Self* refers to whether group members experience themselves as separate beings (individual self) or as part of a greater collective (extended self).

In relation to these dimensions of worldview or culture, each society evolves a set of cultural forms—ritual practices, behavioral prescriptions, and symbols—that support them. For example, a given culture stresses the doing mode on the first dimension. Certain kinds of child-rearing techniques tend to encourage directed activity. Parents differentially reinforce activity over passivity; they also model such behavior. Cultural myths portray figures high on this trait, and moral teachings stress its importance. The group's language likely favors active voice over passive voice. What makes a culture unique, then, is the particular profile of where it stands on each of these dimensions combined with the specific cultural forms it has evolved.

As will become apparent shortly, the dimensions of culture are not totally independent. Rather, some tend to cluster. In relation to ethos, for instance, beliefs concerning independence, individual rights, egalitarianism, and control and dominance tend to occur together in the belief system of a culture, as do interdependence, honor and family protection, authoritarianism, and harmony and deference. Such clusters tend to be mutually reinforcing. It will become clear that certain cultures share a number of dimensions; for example, the cultures of color in the United States have many dimensional similarities and, as a group, differ considerably from Northern European cultures.

Finally, it is important to note that each culture generates a unique *felt experience of living*. The quality of life differs in tone, mood, and intensity. The same is true of the kind of mental health issues that members must face, as well as the emotional strengths that they develop. A very dramatic example of this occurred many years ago. I was a graduate student running a personal growth group for students at a multicultural weekend retreat. The students who showed up for my group were all white, with the exception of one young Latino man, who was really there to spend more time with one of the young women in the group. Such groups seldom attracted non-white participants because it was the belief of most students of color that it was a "white thing" and something that "whites really needed." "As for us, we don't have any trouble relating

TABLE 5-1
Summary of Worldview Positions

Worldview Dimensions	Sample Worldview Positions
Psychobehavioral modality	Doing vs. being vs. becoming
Axiology (values)	Competition vs. cooperation Emotional restraint vs. emotional expressiveness Direct verbal expression vs. indirect verbal expression Seeking help vs. "saving face"
Ethos (guiding beliefs)	Independence vs. interdependence Individual rights vs. honor and family protection Egalitarianism vs. authoritarianism Control and dominance vs. harmony and deference
Epistemology (how one knows)	Cognitive processes vs. affective processes (vibes) Intuition vs. cognitive and affective
Logic (reasoning process)	Either-or thinking vs. both-and thinking vs. circular
Ontology (nature of reality)	Objective material vs. subjective vs. spiritual and material
Concept of Time	Clock-based vs. event-based vs. cyclical
Concept of Self	Individual self vs. extended self

Source: From Brown, M. T., & Landrum-Brown, J. (1995). Counselor supervision: Cross-cultural perspectives. In J. P. Ponterroto, J. M. Casas, L. A. Suzuki, & C. M. Alexander (Eds.), *Handbook of Multicultural Counseling* (pp. 263–287). Thousand Oaks, CA: Sage.

to other people." The group was quite successful, and it did not take long until people were sharing deeply and talking about feelings of disconnection from parents, isolation, and loneliness. At a certain point, the young Latino man could contain himself no longer and said, "I don't understand what you are all talking about. I am part of a big extended family; there is always someone around. I can't imagine feeling alone or isolated." Only after that did I realize that what I had thought to be the "universal malaise" of loneliness and isolation was, in fact, a cultural experience and an artifact of the Northern European lifestyle.

Comparing Cultural Paradigms in America

Ho, Rasheed, and Rasheed (2003) compare the cultural paradigm of white European Americans to those of the four cultures of color on five dimensions, which overlap extensively with those of Brown and Landrum-Brown (1995). It is worth reviewing these in some detail to appreciate the breadth of difference that does exist. It should be remembered, however, that these comparisons speak in generalities and may not fit or apply to individual group members, especially those who have acculturated. In addition, each of the five "racial" groups described is actually made up of numerous subgroups whose cultural content can differ widely. In the United States, for example, Manson and Trimble (1982) identified 512 federally recognized Native "entities" and an additional 365 state-recognized Indian tribes, each with its cultural uniqueness.

Nature and the Environment

Ho et al. classify the four cultures of color—Asian Americans, Native Americans, African Americans, and Latin Americans—as living in "harmony with" nature and the environment, whereas European Americans prefer "mastery over" them. For the former, the relationship is one of respecting and coexisting with nature. Human beings are seen as part of a natural order and, as such, must live respectfully and non-intrusively with other aspects of nature. To destroy a fellow creature is to destroy a part of oneself. On the other hand, European American culture views human beings as superior to the physical environment and entitled to manipulate it for their own benefit. The world is a resource to be used and plundered. In contrast, cultures of color see the component parts of nature as alive and invested with spirit—which must be related to respectfully and responsibly. Great value is placed on being ever-attentive to what nature has to offer and teach. Out of such a perspective come notions such as the Native American idea of Turtle Island, a myth that views the nonhuman inhabitants of the continent as an interconnected system of animal spirits and archetypal characters. A "mastery" mentality results in environmental practices such as runaway logging, strip mining, and oil drilling, as well as the impetus for institutions such as human slavery, which exploits "inferior" human beings for material gain.

Time Orientation

There is great diversity among the five cultural groups with regard to how they perceive and experience time. European Americans are dominated by an orientation toward the future. Planning, producing, and controlling what will happen are all artifacts of a future-time orientation. What was and what is are always a bit vague and subordinated to what is anticipated. At the same time, European Americans view time as compartmentalized and incremental, and as such, being on time and being efficient with one's time are positive values.

Asian and Latino/a cultures are described as past or present-oriented. For both, history is a living entity. Ancestors and past events are felt to be alive and influencing present reality. The past flows imperceptibly into and defines the present. Both Native Americans and African Americans, in turn, are characterized as present-oriented. Focus is directed toward current experience of the here and now, with less attention to what led up to this moment or what will become of it. As a group, and distinct from European American culture, cultures of color share a view of time as an infinite continuum and find it difficult to relate to the white "obsession" with being on time. Interestingly, each of these groups has evolved a term to describe its "looser" sense of time: "Colored people's time," "Indian time," "Asian time," and "Latin time." Invariably, time becomes an issue when non-whites enter institutions where European American cultural values predominate. Lateness is often mistakenly interpreted by whites as indifference, provocative, or symptomatic of a lack of basic work skills.

People Relations

Ho et al. (2003) distinguish European Americans as having an "individual" social focus compared to a "collateral" one for the four cultures of color. Individual behavior refers to actions undertaken to actualize the self; collateral behavior involves doing things not for oneself, but in light of what they may contribute to the survival and betterment of family and community. These differences, in turn, become a basis for attributing value to different and opposing styles of interaction. For example, European Americans are taught and encouraged to compete, to seek individual success, and to feel pride in and make public their accomplishments. Native Americans and Latino/a Americans, in particular, place a high value on cooperation and strive to suppress individual accomplishment, boasting, and self-aggrandizement. Having pointed out this shared collateral focus, it is equally important to understand that the four communities of color differ significantly in their communication styles and the meaning of related symbols. Native Americans place high value on brevity in speech, while for African Americans, the ability to "rap" is treated as an art form. It is considered impolite in certain Asian American subgroups to say "no" or refuse to comply with a request from a superior. Among Latino/a Americans, deferential behavior and the communication of proper respect depend on perceived authority, age, gender, and class. And the same handshake can be given in one culture to communicate respect and deference and in another to show authority and power.

Work and Activity

On the dimension of work and activity (similar to Brown and Landrum-Brown's Psychobehavioral Modality), European Americans, Asian Americans, and African Americans are described as "doing-oriented" compared to Native Americans and Latin Americans, who are characterized as "being-becoming." Doing is an active mode; it involves initiating activity in pursuit of a given goal. It tends to be associated with societies where rewards and status are given on the basis of productivity and accomplishment. But even here, there are differences in motivation. European Americans' work and activity are premised on the idea of "meritocracy"—that hard work and serious effort ultimately bring a person financial and social success. Asian Americans, on the other hand, pursue activity in terms of its ability to confer honor on one's family and, concurrently, to avoid shaming them or losing face. African Americans fall somewhere between these two extremes. Being-becoming, in turn, is more passive, process-oriented, and focused on the here and now. It involves allowing the world to present opportunities for activity and work rather than seeking them out or creating them. It is a mode of activity that can easily be misinterpreted from a doing perspective as "lazy" or "lacking motivation." On a recent trip to the Sinai in Egypt, one of my traveling companions was a hardworking lawyer from New York City, clearly high on the *doing* dimension. After spending several hours visiting a Bedouin village, he could barely contain his shock at how the men just sat around all day. Our guide, himself a Bedouin, suggested that they were not merely sitting but were thinking and planning. He explained, "There is a lot to think about: where to find water, missing goats, perhaps a new wife, maybe a little smuggling." This did not satisfy the lawyer, however, who said, "I don't understand how they can get anything done without meetings. Give me six months, and I'd have this whole desert covered with condos."

One last point: activity and work, whether of the doing or becoming variety, must occur in the context of other cultural values. For example, in many cultures, work does not begin until there has been sufficient time to greet and properly inquire about the welfare of one's family. To do otherwise is considered rude and insensitive. In white European American business culture, such activity would be seen as lazy, wasteful, and maybe even the shirking of one's responsibilities.

Human Nature

This dimension of culture deals with how groups view the essence of being human. Are people inherently good, bad, both, or somewhere in between? According to Ho et al. (2003), African Americans and European Americans see human nature as both good and bad and as possessing the potential for both. But, for each, the meanings of *good* and *bad* are quite different. In African American culture, where all behavior involves a collateral focus—or what Nobles (1972) calls "experiential communality"—*good* and *bad* are defined in relation to the community. It is good if it benefits the community and bad if it does not. Thus, human nature is seen as existing in the interaction between the person and the group.

European American culture, on the other hand, sees good and bad as residing in the individual. Freud's view of human nature is an excellent example. The instinctive urges of the id are seen as a negative force that must be controlled. The ego and the superego are assigned this task and, as such, play a positive role in containing baser drives. In addition, Freud hypothesized a life instinct that is balanced by a death instinct. Thus, the two sides of human nature—the good and bad—are seen in constant opposition and conflict.

Ho et al. describe Asian Americans, Native Americans, and Latin Americans as sharing a view of human nature as good. This tendency to attribute positive motives to others has, at times, proved less than helpful in interaction with members of the dominant culture. Early treaty negotiations between Native American tribes and the U.S. government are a case in point. Tribal representatives entered these negotiations under the assumption that they were dealing with honest and honorable men and that whatever agreements were struck would be honored. By the time sufficient experience forced them to reevaluate their assumptions, it was too late and their lands had been stolen. Similarly, in the workplace, when members of such groups exhibit helpfulness, generosity, and caring for their fellow workers (behavior that follows from an assumption that others are basically good), they are frequently viewed as naïve, gullible, and in need of "smartening up."

CASE STUDY 1

A Case of Cross-Cultural Miscommunication

Sue and Sue (1990) offer the following example of cross-cultural miscommunication:

Several years ago, a female school counselor sought the senior author's advice about a Hispanic family she had recently seen. She seemed quite concerned about the identified client, Elena Martinez, a 13-year-old student who was referred for alleged peddling of drugs on the school premises. The counselor had thought that the parents "did not care for their daughter," "were uncooperative," and "were attempting to avoid responsibility for dealing with Elena's delinquency." When pressed for how she arrived at these impressions, the counselor provided the following information.

Elena Martinez is the second-oldest of four other siblings, ages 15, 12, 10, and 7. The father is an immigrant from Mexico and the mother a natural citizen. The family resides in a blue-collar neighborhood in San Jose, California. Elena had been reported as having minor problems in school prior to the "drug-selling incident." For example, she had "talked back to teachers," refused to do homework assignments, and had "fought" with other students. Her involvement with a group of Hispanic students (suspected of being responsible for disruptive schoolyard pranks) had gotten her into trouble.

Elena was well known to the counseling staff at the school. Her teacher last year reported that she was unable to "get through" to Elena. Because of the seriousness of the drug accusation, the counselor felt that something had to be done, and that the parents needed to be informed immediately.

The counselor reported calling the parents in order to set up an interview with them. When Mrs. Martinez answered the telephone, the counselor had explained how Elena had been caught on school grounds selling marijuana by a police officer. Rather than arrest her, the officer turned the student over to the vice principal, who luckily was present at the time of the incident. After the explanation, the counselor had asked that the parents make arrangements for an appointment as soon as possible. The meeting would be aimed at informing the parents about Elena's difficulties in school and coming to some decision about what could be done.

During the phone conversation, Mrs. Martinez seemed hesitant about choosing a time to come in and, when pressed by the counselor, excused herself from the telephone. The counselor reported overhearing some whispering on the other end, and then the voice of Mr. Martinez. He immediately asked the counselor how his daughter was and expressed his consternation over the entire situation. At that point, the counselor stated that she understood his feelings, but it would be best to set up an appointment for tomorrow and talk about it then. Several times the counselor asked Mr. Martinez about a convenient time for the meeting, but each time he seemed to avoid the answer and to give excuses. He had to work the rest of the day and could not make the appointment. The counselor stressed strongly how important the meeting was for the daughter's welfare and that the several hours of missed work [were] not important in light of the situation. The father stated that he would be able to make an evening session, but the counselor informed him that school policy prohibited evening meetings. When the counselor suggested that the mother could initially come alone, further hesitations seemed present. Finally, the father agreed to attend.

The very next day, Mr. and Mrs. Martinez and a brother-in-law (Elena's godfather) showed up together in her office. The counselor reported being upset at the presence of the brother-in-law when it became obvious he planned to sit in on the session. At that point, she explained that a third-party present would only make the session more complex and the outcome counterproductive. She wanted to see only the family.

The counselor reported that the session went poorly, with minimal cooperation from the parents. She reported, "It was like pulling teeth," trying to get the Martinezes to say anything at all.

Source: From *Counseling the Culturally Different*, 2e, by S. W. Sue & D. Sue, pp. 118–119. Copyright © 1990 John Wiley & Sons, Inc. Reprinted with permission.

Before proceeding with an analysis of this case, I encourage you to first try your hand at identifying areas of cultural insensitivity in the reactions and behavior of the counselor.

The following are some of my thoughts on the matter. This is a clear case of misunderstanding cultural differences. The counselor proceeds with her normal *modus operandi*, regardless of the very obvious cultural differences that exist between her and the Martinez family. She misreads their reactions and intentions and draws erroneous and insulting conclusions about them as parents. She communicates these to the Martinezes, who immediately withdraw and become nonreactive. What are some of the assumptions that she made and cultural artifacts that she missed?

▸ It is very possible that because of her ethnicity and her involvement with a group of other Hispanic students, Elena was being carefully watched as a potential troublemaker.

▸ The counselor appears unaware that in a traditional Mexican family, the wife would not make a decision without first consulting her husband, which she did by "whispering on the other end [of the phone line]." Similarly, it is the husband who represents and talks for the family in a formal situation such as this.

▸ The counselor assumes that Mr. Martinez is indifferent about his daughter because he seemed reluctant to miss work on her behalf. She has no idea of what his work situation is or what the consequences of missing work might be for him and his family. But she assumes that he, like any middle-class professional, can make himself available during the day and even presumes to moralize at him—something he is probably not used to from a woman—about several hours of missed work being more important than his daughter. But at the same time, she is unwilling to accommodate herself to the family's need for an evening session and hides behind bureaucratic rules to avoid doing so.

▶ The counselor thinks too narrowly about what constitutes a family, is used to dealing with nuclear families as opposed to extended families, and has no idea of the appropriateness of the brother-in-law's presence. Godfathers, in Latin culture, are responsible for the spiritual life of their godchildren and are expected to fill in for the father when the necessity arises. Elena was possibly in the midst of serious spiritual difficulties.

Are Theories of Helping Culture-Bound?

In Chapter 4, cultural racism was defined as the belief that the cultural ways of one group are superior to those of another. It can exist within the mind of an individual, as in the case of Elena's counselor, who seems largely unaware that she is imposing her cultural values on the Martinez family. Cultural racism can also assert itself through the workings of institutions—such as the agencies in which most health care providers work—and through the theories and practices they hold. Many researchers strongly believe that the assumptions and practices of mainstream service delivery are based on Northern European cultural values (Draguns, 1981; Huey, Tilley, Jones, and Smith, 2014; Kim and Berry, 1993; Sue and Sue, 1990). Because of this, serious questions exist as to whether practitioners trained in such a model can serve culturally diverse clients adequately.

Anthropologists draw a distinction between emic and etic approaches to working cross-culturally. *Emic* refers to looking at a culture through its indigenous concepts and theories. For example, making traditional healers available to Native American clients is an emic approach to service delivery. *Etic* means viewing a culture through "glasses" that are external to it. This is the strategy that the helping professions have adopted. It has been assumed that their approach has relevance for all people, regardless of their cultural backgrounds, but this may not be true. Some critics argue that since the helping profession has its origins and roots in Northern European ideas, values, and sensibilities, it cannot appropriately be applied to individuals who hold diverse cultural values and assumptions (Duran and Duran, 1995). They further contend that such models are at best "pseudoetic" (Draguns, 1981), which means that they naïvely misjudge the universality of their approach and that what really has been created are "emic approaches to counseling that are designed by and for middle-class European Americans" (Atkinson, Morten, and Sue, 1993, p. 54).

▶ Key Aspects of the Helping Process   5-3

If one looks carefully at the assumptions and practices that are central to the helping professions as they currently exist, it becomes immediately clear that much is in conflict with the general worldview of non-white clients. Four key aspects of the helping process can be identified as especially problematic:

- ▶ Importance of verbal expressiveness and self-disclosure
- ▶ Setting long-term goals
- ▶ Relative importance placed on changing the client vs. changing the environment
- ▶ Definition of what is mentally healthy

Verbal Expressiveness and Self-Disclosure

Most practitioners believe that verbal expressiveness and self-disclosure by clients are critical aspects of the helping process. In fact, Henretty, Currier, Berman, and Levitt (2014) found that counselors who self-disclose had a more positive impact on clients. Their clients had a more favorable perception of disclosing counselors and were more likely to disclose to their counselors. Clients prefer when counselors share similarities they have with the client, express uncomfortable thoughts or emotions for the client, or share extra therapeutic experiences with the client. Additionally, Levitt et al. (2016) found that clients experienced less post-session clinical symptoms and interpersonal problems when the counselor's disclosures humanized them.

However, the cultures of color do not share this value or feel comfortable talking about themselves or disclosing personal material to relative strangers. Asian Americans, for example, learn emotional restraint at an early age and are expected to exhibit modesty in the face of authority as well as subtleness in dealing with personal problems (Atkinson, Whitely, and Gin, 1990; Ho, 1994; Pedersen et al., 2015). To reveal intimate details of one's life to strangers is seen as bringing shame on the family and is experienced as "losing face." Similarly, it has been shown that Native Americans and Latino/a Americans also feel threatened with the demand for such disclosure (Fleming, 1992; Pedersen et al., 2015; Vontress, 1981). For both, intimate sharing is done only with friends of long standing. Only European Americans seem comfortable revealing intimate details of their life to relative strangers. Foreign travelers to the United States are often shocked by the amount of personal information revealed to them by the Americans they encounter.

African Americans, in turn, tend to be suspicious of requests by white providers for intimate life details (Gordon, 1964; Pedersen et al., 2015; Sue and Sue, 1990). The African American community considers it dangerous and potentially self-destructive to reveal one's feelings to whites before their trustworthiness can be assured. I am reminded of a very bizarre but sad incident when minority youth leaders, mostly African American, from a major urban area were taken to an isolated part of the Grand Canyon for a sensitivity training experience by a group of white professionals. Communication between the two groups broke down very quickly, and only when it was learned that the African American youths had come to believe that they had been taken there to be assassinated was it possible to defuse the situation. Helping professionals obviously need to be aware of how culturally diverse clients view their efforts at helping, as well as being careful in drawing conclusions about a client's reluctance to self-disclose. Such behavior is normative in many cultural groups and should not be interpreted as defensiveness or as reflecting depression, shyness, or passivity.

Setting Long-Term Goals

Psychodynamic approaches to counseling and other forms of helping place importance on long-term treatment planning. Helping is envisioned as a long-term, ongoing process where therapist and client interact in a rather unstructured situation with the aim of making significant changes in the client's inner psychology. Clients of color, on the other hand, tend to be more action-oriented and desirous of concrete advice and immediate solutions to the problems for which they seek help (Sue and Sue, 1990). They seem to find directive approaches, as opposed to nondirective approaches, most helpful and often express confusion or frustration around the idea of abstract, long-term goal-setting (Chao and Zhang, 2017). The differences may result from differing time orientations, a belief that the individual's purpose is to serve the collective (rather than the self), or the fact that "sitting around and talking" is a luxury they just cannot afford or cannot see as potentially helpful. Again, the helper must avoid the temptation to interpret their "reluctance" to go along with long-term goal-planning as resistance.

Changing the Client vs. Changing the Environment

Practitioner and client can differ greatly in how they conceive and think about the change process: Is it important to change the client to fit his or her circumstances or vice versa? These orientations are referred to technically as *autoplastic* and *alloplastic* solutions. Helping clients cope with a difficult life situation by accommodating or adapting to it (i.e., changing themselves in that direction) is autoplastic; encouraging or teaching clients to impose changes on the external environment so that it better fits their needs is alloplastic.

Cultures of color differ widely on this question. Asian American culture tends to stress a passive acceptance of reality and a transcendence of conflict by adjusting one's perceptions so harmony can be achieved with the environment (Han and Pong, 2015; Ho, 1994). African Americans, on the other hand, tend to point to a racist environment as the cause of many of their distresses and advocate changing it as opposed to themselves (Hook et al., 2016; Kunjufu, 1984). To this end, in the late 1960s, African

American psychologists in the state of California called for and obtained a moratorium on testing minority children in the public schools (Bay Area Association of Black Psychologists, 1972). They argued that culturally biased psychological assessment was being used to funnel culturally diverse children into special education classes by white teachers and administrators who were not comfortable with their non-white ways. In a similar vein, Braginsky and Braginsky (1974) and others (Pedersen et al., 2015) have called the helping profession to task for serving as a "handmaiden to the status quo" by encouraging culturally diverse clients to adapt their behavior to the demands of white institutions as opposed to encouraging their clients to pursue societal change. Northern European culture, for its part, tends to encourage the confrontation of obstacles in the environment that restrict one's freedom.

What seems most influential in determining the stance a provider assumes is the general theoretical perspective that he or she follows. Psychodynamic approaches, for example, locate problems and conflicts within the individual and dictate inner changes as the exclusive solution. More behaviorally and cognitively oriented theories do the opposite; they advocate changing the environment to change behavior.

Sue and Sue (2015) offer an interesting perspective on this question. They suggest that much client behavior can be understood as resulting from their beliefs about locus of control and locus of responsibility. *Locus of control* refers to whether individuals feel that they are in control of their own fate (internal control) or that they are being controlled externally (external control) and, therefore, whether their actions can change the external world. *Locus of responsibility* refers to whether individuals believe that they are responsible for their own fate (internal responsibility) or that they cannot be held responsible because there are more powerful forces at work (external responsibility). Sue and Sue propose four "worldviews" based on combining these two dimensions and argue that people of color may exhibit any of the four. Generally, Northern European American helpers believe in internal control and internal responsibility—that clients are in control of their own fate, their actions do affect their outcomes, and success or failure in life is related to their personal characteristics and abilities. If this does not match a client's perception of how the world works, there are likely to be serious differences regarding treatment goals and just what constitutes helping.

▶ Definitions of Mental Health   5-4

The human service professions have tended to adopt Northern European cultural definitions of what constitutes healthy and normal functioning. Self-reliance, autonomy, self-actualization, self-assertion, insight, and resistance to stress are seen as hallmarks of healthy adjustment and functioning (Saeki and Borow, 1985; Sue and Sue, 2015). These are the characteristics toward which clients are encouraged to strive. They are not, however, the same personal qualities that are valued in all cultures. For example, Asian American cultures value interdependence, inner enlightenment, negation of self, transcendence of conflict, and passive acceptance of reality (Han and Pong, 2015; Ho, 1994). This view is largely antithetical to that of mainstream Western thought. What Asian American culture shares with the other three cultures of color—and what sets them apart from Northern European culture—is the diminished importance of individual autonomy and self-assertion. A similar idea is expressed in the way Native American culture views health and illness (Duran and Duran, 1995; Wilson, 2003). Illnesses, both mental and physical, are thought to result from disharmony of the individual, family, or tribe from the ways of nature and the natural order. Healing can occur only when harmony is restored. This is the goal of traditional healing practices.

Another way to describe this important difference is the distinction between the individual and the *extended self* (Brown and Landrum-Brown, 1995). The individual self is characteristic of Northern European culture. It exists autonomously, is fragmented from its social context, and has personal survival and betterment as its goal. The self develops very differently in cultures that limit its narcissism and free expression. The term *extended self* is used to describe ego development in group members who conceive of themselves not as individuals but as part of a broader collective. All behavior occurs with an awareness of what its impact will be not on the self but, more important, on the larger social group of which the person is a part. Referring back to the axiology and ethos dimensions suggested by Brown and Landrum-Brown, the sub-values of competition, emotional restraint, direct verbal expression, and help seeking and the sub-beliefs of independence, individual rights, egalitarianism, and control and dominance (all typical of the Northern European cultural paradigm) represent ideas that support the existence of an individual self.

Similarly, their opposites (the sub-values of cooperation, emotional expressiveness, indirect verbal expression, and "saving face" and the sub-beliefs of interdependence, honor and family protection, authoritarianism, and harmony and deference), most typical of the worldview of the communities of color, are related to an extended self. Independence, for example, allows for greater self-assertion; interdependence allows for greater intergroup harmony. In speaking of the extended self, I am reminded of a former graduate student of color who, when introduced to a model of identity development in people of color that described the final stage of growth as "transcending specific group identities," reacted: "This can't be right. How can they see this as optimal growth? The person is no longer a part of the community." Thus, practitioners must be aware of incongruence between their notion of what is healthy and where treatment should be leading and that of the client. Where differences exist, they must be respected, and great care must be taken not to project one's values onto the helping process and not to unintentionally judge a client's behaviors that vary from one's own standards as inferior and deficient.

Collective Personality: The Example of Arabs/Muslims

Marwan Dwairy (2006), who contributed a chapter for this edition entitled "Working with Arab/Muslim American Clients" (Chapter 15), offers yet another powerful example of why traditional Western approaches to helping may not always be appropriate for culturally diverse clients. He makes a most useful distinction between the personality structure of people who live in collective social systems and that of those who live in individualistic social systems. Earlier in this chapter, this distinction was referred to as the individual vs. the extended self. In response to our previous question (Are theories of helping culture-bound?), Dwairy would suggest that the vast majority of our theories of personality and psychotherapy are individualistically based and thus inadequate to "explain and predict the behavior of people who possess a collective, non-individualistic personality." He is talking about a qualitatively different structuring of personality development. As a metaphor, Dwairy suggests that "an encounter with a traditional Arab/Muslim individual is an encounter with a group of people that live inside her or him and still play a major role in directing their behavior." And, similarly, all aspects of the person's psychology and inner structuring are organized around their membership in the family, tribe, etc. In this regard, Dwairy describes collective people as motivated by group rather than personal goals, situationally and contextually rather than dispositionally oriented, prioritizing interpersonal responsibilities over issues of personal justice or individual rights, and other-focused emotionally rather than ego-focused. He goes on to make the following important distinctions regarding the structure of the collective personality as they differ from the individualistic personality in Western psychology:

- Conflict within the person tends to be intrafamilial rather than intrapsychic. Behavior tends to be directed by external pressures, not internal ones, whereby inner needs are set against familial pressures and expectations. Most typically, the latter hold sway.
- The family is the source of threat, esteem, and joy, and enormous personal energy is directed toward avoiding familial rejection and seeking its approval.
- The inner psyche is structured around social rather than unconscious mechanisms. As opposed to dependence on Freudian mechanisms of defense, Arabs/ Muslims internalize and act upon mechanisms such as *Mosayara* (getting along), which involves hiding real feelings and instead reacting in socially acceptable ways, and *Istighaba,* which involves expressing authentic feelings away from family and social observation.

▸ Rather than being highly differentiated internally in regard to separation of constructs such as thoughts, emotions, and attitudes, the inner world of the collective individual tends to be much less differentiated and more indistinct and fused. Rather, the primary inner distinction is between a "social layer" and a "private layer."

▸ Consistency of behavior tends to exist within each of these layers rather than between them, and individual differences in public life among Arabs/Muslims tend to be minor rather than extensive and related to the amount of individuation within each person as well as their social status.

Not surprisingly, according to Dwairy, these differences lead to very different manifestations of psychopathology as well as major differences in the goals and processes of psychotherapy with collective peoples. Rather than exhibiting itself in the form of intrapsychic disorders, psychopathology tends to be more indistinct and more pervasive across interpersonal, intrapsychic, and somatic levels. Problems arise when the system of give and take within family interaction and between social and private layers becomes imbalanced, as well as when cohesion within the family and familial support of the individual is disrupted. Psychotherapy must also be conceived very differently. According to Dwairy: "For Arab/Muslim people, psychotherapy should aim to find new order within the psycho-social-somatic system. Joining the family authority, revising the efficiency of the client's social coping mechanisms, and implementing indirect metaphoric interventions are basic directives for working with Arab/Muslim clients."

Collective vs. Individual Treatment Models

While Dwairy's clinical work is adapted for use in a collective society, his basic approach is decidedly individualistic or one-to-one, with the exception of bringing in authoritative family members in order to reify family structures and power relationships. *Collective treatment models*, such as the Tree of Life exercise developed by Ncube and Denborough (2009) of the Dulwiche Center, Australia, and Father Michael Lapsley's Healing of Memories workshop developed in South Africa—which you will be learning about in Chapters 7 and 10, respectively—actively depend on interactions with other group members for therapeutic outcomes. Such approaches, especially when they are coupled with narrative therapy techniques of inviting group members to "tell their stories" in the presence of witnesses, are especially useful in working with collective trauma. According to Tabak (2011),

> "A principal task, then, in working with traumatized populations is to assist people in constructing stories or narratives that help to contain and organize their traumatic experiences, which will then help them to better cope with their suffering (Graybill, 1999; Wigren, 1994). Tuval-Mashiach et al. (2004) believed

that sharing one's trauma experience or story with another helps the survivor to construct a detailed, coherent, and chronologically accurate trauma story. Once the construction of the narrative is completed, the survivor begins to make meaning and regain control over his or her trauma and can then start incorporating it into the larger autobiographical story."

After reviewing Herman's (1997) emphasis on group work as critical to the treatment of trauma, Tabak continues: "The group environment offers members the solace of being in the presence of supportive others who have been through similar experiences and serves to metaphorically welcome victims of trauma back into the world of humanity. With a particular focus on strengths, group members are encouraged to draw upon the resources and strengths of other group members and in doing so, the group as a whole, begins the process of grieving past losses, integrating traumatic experiences, and refocusing their lives in the present."

Drawing upon the work of the author in Diller (2011), Tabak completes her discussion of collective treatment models by pointing to the reasons they tend to be preferable to one-to-one and individualistic methods in the treatment of trauma:

- ▸ They are more common and culturally syntonic to non-Western family and tribally based cultures that view physical and mental dysfunction or disease as communal issues rather than problems that are unique to the individual.
- ▸ They require active involvement of all tribal members in a communal setting and the merging of individual identities to form a collective whole, a process that strongly encourages the emergence of new behaviors.
- ▸ They tend to encourage the use of a broader range of interventions such as expressive arts, rituals, rites of passage, and celebrations to bond communities together and facilitate healing.
- ▸ Because they tend to be more intensive and short-term, they can provide treatment to a greater number of individuals in a shorter period of time.
- ▸ They are able to better facilitate individual healing through multiple witnessing in a manner that one-to-one treatment cannot.

▸ Conflicting Cross-Cultural Service Models   `5-5`

Recall from Chapter 2 that one of the central skills associated with cultural competence is the ability to adapt mainstream practices to the needs of culturally diverse groups. For example, it does not seem unreasonable or impossible to expect providers to alter their expectations (especially in the early stages of working together) regarding self-disclosure, verbal openness, or fluency. The provider should also be able to adjust the type of interaction that occurs and, when helpful, move into a less ambiguous and more directive problem-solving mode. Similarly, it should be possible to adapt the provider's view of where change should take place (changing the individual vs. changing the environment) to align with the client's cultural tendencies and to rethink treatment goals and outcomes in light of the client's cultural beliefs.

Sue and Zane (1987) suggest two additional strategies for improving provider credibility. First is to ensure the client feels that his or her problem or reason for seeking help is understood by the provider in terms of the client's own cultural viewpoint. This involves both appreciating the client's worldview in terms of the intricacies of his or her cultural background and being able to communicate that awareness to the client. Second is to ensure that the client receives some immediate benefit or reinforcement as a result of the helping process. This may involve advocating for the client with another agency, teaching the client some skill or practice that might help him or her navigate the system, or even directly intervening in a situation on the client's behalf. Although such interventions push the boundaries of what is considered appropriate behavior for mainstream providers, it should be remembered that such helping practices were developed primarily for working with dominant-culture clients. Such therapeutic guidelines just may not make cultural sense in relation to working with clients of color.

Certain critics, however, suggest that merely making adjustments to a predominantly Northern European model of helping is insufficient. Approaching the problem of cross-cultural service delivery from such a limited perspective seems like something akin to "rearranging the deck chairs on the *Titanic*." They argue that merely making cosmetic changes to a process that is, by its very nature, highly destructive to traditional people and their cultures does little to get at the real heart of the problem. Duran and Duran (1995), for example, believe that Northern European culture and its application through Western psychology has been instrumental in fragmenting Native American culture and lifestyle. They further contend that inherent in the Northern European worldview is an inability to tolerate the existence of alternative ways of knowing and experiencing the world.

> The critical factor in cross-cultural psychology is a fundamentally different way of being in the world. In no way does Western thinking address any system of cognition other than its own. Given that Judeo-Christian belief systems include notions of the Creator putting human beings in charge of all creations, it is easy to understand why this group of people assumes that it also possesses the ultimate way of describing psychological phenomena for all of humanity. In reality, the thought that what is right comes from one worldview produces a narcissistic worldview that desecrates and destroys much of what is known as culture and cosmological perspective. (p. 17)

Diamond's (2017) work on "primitive" vs. "civilized" societies offers a useful metaphor through which to compare the nature of traditional cultures (which include the cultures of color in the United States) with that of postmodern Northern Europe. Like Duran and Duran, Diamond contends that there is something fundamentally skewed within "civilized" culture—that something essential has been lost. Only through a careful analysis of the dimensions of traditional culture can one discern what those elements might be. Diamond summarizes eight characteristics of "primitive" culture that have been lost through the civilizing process:

- Good psychological nurturance of the individual
- Multiple and engaging relationships throughout the life cycle
- Various forms of institutionalized deviance
- Celebration and fusion of the sacred—within nature, society, and the individual—through ritual
- Direct engagement with nature and natural processes
- Direct and active participation in cultural forms
- Equating goodness, beauty, and the natural environment
- Socioeconomic support as a natural inheritance

One consequence of the breakdown of traditional culture vis-à-vis the civilizing process, according to Diamond (1987), was a radical increase in stress, dysfunction, and mental illness. The author, in Diller (1991), documents a similar destructive tendency in contemporary Western culture. Specifically, he looks at Jewish emancipation in nineteenth-century Europe and describes how it psychologically altered and transformed traditional Jewish culture. The result was widespread fragmentation and the destruction of traditional Jewish values, ways, community, and identity. Such concerns have led some researchers in cross-cultural service delivery to suggest alternative models that go beyond mere adaptation and adjustment of the Northern European paradigm. Three trends of this sort can be identified:

- Some theorists call for the creation of individual ethnic-specific (emic) models, or "psychologies," each developed by providers and researchers from a given ethnic community. The aim is to define a unique and unbiased understanding of the mental health and treatment issues of each community. In arguing for the wisdom of a "black psychology," for example, White (1972) contends that "principles and theories developed by white psychologists to explain the behavior of white people simply do not have sufficient explanatory power to account for the behavior of blacks" (p. 2). In a similar vein, Clark (1972) suggests the need for "creating an alternative framework within which black behavior may be differently described, explained, and interpreted" (p. 1).

According to Jones (1972), Mosby "makes the case for qualitative differences in the life experiences of blacks which lead to differences in developmental, social, personal, intellectual, educational, and family functioning. Black Psychology would account for the differences" (p. 2). Each evolving model would dictate a unique and culturally sensitive approach specific to providing helping services to members of that community.

- A second approach, such as that suggested by Duran and Duran (1995), advocates for a return to traditional healing practices from the client's culture. Over time, each community of color has developed its own conceptions of health and illness, as well as unique indigenous healing practices. First of all, availing oneself of such services guarantees that the help being received has not been compromised by dominant cultural ways. Second, it provides an avenue for strengthening ethnic identity and cultural ties. Finally, offering such services is especially useful to clients who remain steeped in traditional cultural ways and values and for whom dominant U.S. culture has little relevance or feels unsafe.

- There is also a logical compromise that involves including traditional healers and healing practices as part of a broad range of helping services within a community. Such a strategy, above all, provides a strong statement about the value of cultural diversity in the area of human services. Most culturally diverse clients, however, have experienced some level of acculturation or—to put it differently—are in varying degrees of biculturalism. For these individuals, a full return to traditional, cultural ways is probably neither possible nor desirable. More relevant to their situation is the use of models of helping that have been sensitively and extensively adapted to the cultural needs of their group by practitioners, either indigenous or culturally diverse, that are truly culturally competent.

▶ Adapting Generic Models vs. Evolving Culturally Sensitive Models   `5-6`

Much of the previous discussion regarding conflicting models is more visionary and theoretical than reflective of our current state of the art of cross-cultural counseling. According to Baruth and Manning (2016), to be culturally sensitive counselors have to be aware that cultural similarities and differences exist, but they should avoid placing a value on that existence. It is the judgment of these differences and similarities that causes harm to clients. At present, I would suggest that there exist two general approaches to cultural sensitivity in service delivery. The first is to adapt generic models of psychopathology, counseling, and psychotherapy to the situation of culturally diverse clients. Much of what currently exists in this regard can be found in Chapter 3, especially the exemplary efforts of Pamela Hays (2008), with her ADDRESSING framework and thoughts about how to approach DSM diagnosis in the most culturally sensitive manner.

The second type of model is one that has been designed specifically for working cross-culturally. These models tend to include culture of the client as a central issue, acknowledge social disparities, include social justice as an orienting principle, and is non-pathologizing, strength-based, and non-hierarchical in their structure. Examples of such work can be found in previous and subsequent chapters as follows:

- In the case study of the Just Therapy model as practiced by the Family Center in Wellington, New Zealand, described in Chapter 6
- In the case studies of narrative therapy with children of color, the Tree of Life exercise for working with child trauma victims, and the School-Based Social Justice Intervention Program—all of which appear in Chapter 7
- In the collective trauma work practiced by the Institute for Healing Memories, in Cape Town, South Africa, presented in Chapter 10
- In the work of Marwan Dwairy, introduced earlier in this chapter and in his interview that appears in Chapter 15

It is also important to acknowledge that as the demand for cross-cultural helping continues to grow and increasingly complex and effective strategies for serving culturally diverse clients are developed, it is just a matter of time before dominant forms of helping will begin to lose their decidedly Northern European perspective and become increasingly infused and informed by the wisdom and values of a variety of other cultural forms. In other words, it will become more multicultural.

SUMMARY

Culture is the conscious and unconscious content that a group learns, shares, and transmits from generation to generation that organizes life and helps interpret existence. A useful analogy for understanding culture is the concept of paradigm. A paradigm is a set of shared assumptions and beliefs about how the world works that structures an individual's perception and ideas about reality. Our paradigms, or worldviews, tell us what is possible and impossible, what the rules are, and how things are done. The culture into which a person is born and socialized defines the dimensions of his or her personal paradigm. Different cultures generate different paradigms and experiences of reality.

Increasingly, social scientists have chosen to distinguish among human groups on the basis of culture rather than race. For example, there seems to be as much variability in physical characteristics within traditional racial categories as among these various groups, and the social reality of race in the United States does not conform to the existence of five distinct racial groupings.

Brown and Landrum-Brown (1995) define eight dimensions along which cultures can vary. Each culture generates a unique profile along these various dimensions and, as a result, generates a unique experience of living and reality that is shared by members of the cultural group. Ho (1987) compares the five racial groups on various cultural dimensions, including views of nature and the environment, time orientation, human relations, work, and activity.

Contemporary theories of helping and counseling are themselves culture-bound, embodying the values and style of Northern European culture. Examples include an emphasis on verbal expression and self-disclosure, setting long-term goals, and changing the client rather than changing the environment, as well as using definitions of mental health that emphasize individuality and self-assertion. Dwairy (2006) distinguishes between collective and individualistic family and social systems and argues that the latter are also culture-bound and Euro-centric. Because of such concerns, serious questions exist as to whether practitioners trained in such a paradigm can serve culturally diverse clients adequately. Often such therapeutic objectives are in conflict with the cultural tendencies and values of the four communities of color. Tabak (2012) in turn argues for the use of collective treatment methodologies both in working with collective communities and, more broadly, in the treatment of trauma.

Various strategies for creating adequate cross-cultural service delivery models have been suggested. Some theorists believe that it is possible to adjust and adapt existing dominant-group-oriented paradigms, while others think that there is something inherently destructive to traditional peoples and cultures in the Northern European worldview and call for the creation of ethnic-specific psychologies. A third alternative is to use traditional healing practices from the client's culture. A reasonable compromise is the inclusion of traditional healers and healing practices as part of a broad range of helping services offered to a community; examples of each of these approaches are included in later chapters.

ACTIVITIES

1. *Explore your culture.* This exercise will help you become more aware of your cultural roots and identity. Answer the following questions (developed by Hardy and Laszloffy, 1995) in relation to each ethnic group that constitutes your culture of origin. You might need to seek additional information from parents or other relatives.

   a. What were the migration patterns of the group?
   b. If other than Native American, under what conditions did your family enter the United States (immigrants, political refugees, slaves, etc.)?
   c. What were or are the group's experiences with oppression? What were or are the markers of oppression?

    d. What issues divide members within the same group?

    e. Describe the relationship between the group's identity and your national ancestry. (If the group is defined in terms of nationality, skip this question.)

    f. What significance do race, skin color, and hair play within the group?

    g. What is or are the dominant religion(s) of the group? What role does religion and spirituality play in the everyday lives of members of the group?

    h. What role does region and geography play in the group?

    i. How are gender roles defined within the group? How is sexual orientation regarded?

      1. What prejudices or stereotypes does this group have about itself?

      2. What prejudices or stereotypes do other groups have about this group?

      3. What prejudices or stereotypes does this group have about other groups?

    j. What role (if any) do names play in the group? Are there rules, mores, or rituals governing the assignment of names?

    k. How is social class defined in the group?

    l. What occupational roles are valued and devalued by the group?

    m. What is the relationship between age and values of the group?

    n. How does the group define family?

    o. How does this group view outsiders, in general, and mental health professionals, specifically?

    p. How have the organizing principles of this group shaped your family and its members? What effect have they had on you? (Organizing principles are "fundamental constructs which shape the perceptions, beliefs, and behaviors of members of the group." For example, for Jews, an organizing principle is "fear of persecution.")

    q. What are the ways in which pride or shame issues of the group are manifested in your family system? (Pride or shame issues are "aspects of a culture that are sanctioned as distinctively negative or positive." For example, for Jews, a pride or shame issue is "educational achievement.")

    r. What impact will these pride or shame issues have on your work with clients from both similar and dissimilar cultural backgrounds?

    s. If more than one group comprises your culture of origin, how are the differences negotiated in your family? What are the intergenerational consequences? How has this impacted you personally and as a therapist?

2. *Take a cultural self-inventory.* Review Brown and Landrum-Brown's (1995) dimensions of culture. Ask yourself where you fit on each dimension and from where in your cultural past this characteristic is likely to have derived. Are there ways that you have personally changed on any of these dimensions as you have grown and matured? How and why?

6

Working with Culturally Diverse Parents and Families

LEARNING OBJECTIVES

6-1 Recognize and define the meaning of community psychology.

6-2 Identify and evaluate parenting styles within culturally diverse families.

6-3 Prepare children emotionally and cognitively for racism.

6-4 Support bicultural children and families.

6-5 Build and assess the therapeutic relationship with bicultural families.

The following "open" letter from African American writer Alice Walker was sent to Barack Obama when he was inaugurated to his first term as President of the United States.

Open Letter to Barack Obama

Dear Brother Obama,

You have no idea, really, of how profound this moment is for us. Us being the black people of the Southern United States. . . . seeing you deliver the torch so many others before you carried, . . . only to be struck down before igniting the flame of justice and of law, is almost more than the heart can bear. And yet, this observation is not intended to burden you, for you are of a different time, and, . . . North America is a different place. It is really only to say: Well done. We knew, through all the generations, that you were with us, in us, the best of the spirit of Africa and of the Americas. Knowing this, that you would actually appear, someday, was part of our strength. Seeing you take your rightful place, based solely on your wisdom, stamina, and character, is a balm for the weary warriors of hope, previously only sung about.

. . . you did not create the disaster that the world is experiencing, and you alone are not responsible for bringing the world back to balance. A primary responsibility that you do have, however, is to cultivate happiness in your own life. . . .

I would further advise you not to take on other people's enemies. Most damage that others do to us is out of fear, humiliation, and pain. Those feelings occur in all of us, not just in those of us who profess a certain religious or racial devotion. . . . It is understood by all that you are commander in chief of the United States and are sworn to protect our beloved country; this we understand, completely. However, . . . There must be no more crushing of whole communities, no more torture, no more dehumanizing as a means of ruling a people's spirit. This has already happened to people of color, poor people, women, children. We see where this leads, where it has led.

Finally, it is the soul that must be preserved, if one is to remain a credible leader. All else might be lost; but when the soul dies, the connection to earth . . . also dies. . . .

We are the ones we have been waiting for.

In Peace and Joy, Alice Walker

Source: Excerpted from Walker, Alice (November 7, 2008). "An open letter to Barack Obama." https://www.theroot.com/an-open-letter-to-barack-obama-1790900340.

In these words of Alice Walker, one senses the emotion of a proud parent passing on the hard-won wisdom and cautions of a generation that has doggedly fought racism and institutional inequity. Its hope has always been to provide its children access to the "American Dream." Although Walker is almost left speechless at the profundity of what this moment of Obama's election represents, she feels it necessary to give voice to the values of those in the black community upon whose work Obama's victory stands. These values include the importance of self-empowerment and pride, of resiliency and self-care, of retaining a sense of spirit and hope, and, above all, an awareness of the multi-layered web of societal practices and institutions that serve to dehumanize and break the spirit of communities, families, and children of color and other diverse populations.

▶ Community Psychology   6-1

As Walker indicates, Barack Obama was well aware of these dynamics. Though the Obama presidency ended, there are certain tenets residing in the administration's tenure that are still relevant to working with culturally diverse parents and families. Walker's letter sheds light on the fact that social problems represent systemic problems and to bring about social change, interventions must be initiated at all levels of the system: in relation to individual lives, across social networks, support systems, and communities, and within society as a whole. In the world of mental health, this approach is called *community psychology*. It is, however, not a perspective that dominates the field today. More typically, as Nelson and Prilleltensky (2005) suggest:

> Along their journeys, many disadvantaged people have encountered psychologists. Sometimes the response of psychology has been to further perpetuate oppression. Today, the more typical response of psychology is to offer "help," but the help is typically in the form of some type of therapy or intervention that strives to change the disadvantaged individuals so that they can better adjust to unjust social conditions. We believe that the response of [Community Psychology] should be one that recognizes the injustices that disadvantaged people have experienced and that involves a partnership to work in solidarity with disadvantaged people towards social change. (p. 27)

Community Psychology also involves:

- ▶ A focus on correcting issues of social injustice
- ▶ Promoting well-being
- ▶ A cessation of oppression for disadvantaged people
- ▶ Prevention and mental health promotion, as opposed to merely treating symptoms
- ▶ Acknowledging and addressing power differentials in society
- ▶ Community development and empowerment
- ▶ Social commitment and accountability as professionals

While Community Psychology, with its systemic approach to mental health care, is no longer normative in the United States, it can still be found alive and well and in extensive use in several "down-under" countries, including Australia, New Zealand, and South Africa. For a fuller understanding of the values and principles of Community Psychology, see Case Study 1 for a description of the "Just Therapy" approach to mental health treatment, as developed and implemented by the Family Center in Wellington, New Zealand.

 CASE STUDY 1

Just Therapy
by Charles Waldegrave

Therapy can be a vehicle for addressing some of the injustices that occur in a society. It could be argued that in choosing not to address these issues in therapy, therapists may be inadvertently replicating, maintaining, and even furthering, existing injustices. A "Just Therapy" is one that takes into account the gender, cultural, social, and economic context of the persons seeking help. It is our view that therapists have a responsibility to find appropriate ways of addressing these issues and developing approaches that are centrally concerned with the often-forgotten issues of fairness and equity. Such therapy reflects themes of liberation that lead to self-determining outcomes of resolution and hope.

Introduction: The New Zealand and Agency Context

In all our therapeutic work we have endeavoured to relate to, and incorporate, the current issues that make up the New Zealand social and economic context. These include: the struggles to address the injustices to the indigenous Maori of New Zealand, and initiate an equitable partnership based on the Treaty of Waitangi; the emerging consciousness and implications of New Zealand colonisation and consequent responsibilities to Pacific people; the marginalisation and increasing poverty of people and families. On low incomes, as a result of deregulated economic and labour markets and the attempts to address the inequities that persist between men and women as the rigidities of patriarchal webs of meaning are loosened.

Our agency structure has developed over the years to reflect our response to these issues. There are Maori, Samoan, and European (white) therapists who work, each from their own self-determining sections. The workers in these sections carry out family therapy and community development work in the fields of poverty, unemployment, housing, sexism, and racism.

This approach emerged ten years ago after we realised, during one of our six monthly reflective retreats, that many families were approaching our agency for therapy with problems which were not intrinsic to the family but imposed by broader social structures. These included: families where members were unemployed; those living in inadequate housing conditions; the victim survivors of abuse; or cultures that were marginalised by the dominant culture.

Our retreats involve five days together in a large house beside a beautiful lake. We analyse and reflect on our work over the past six months and set our goals for the following six months. At this particular retreat, about ten years ago, we realised that the problems these families were bringing to us were not the symptoms of family dysfunction, but the symptoms of broader structural issues like poverty, patriarchy, and racism. We, like most other therapists, were treating their symptomatic behaviour as though it were a family problem, and then sending them back into the

continued

CASE STUDY 1   *continued*

structures that created their problems in the first place. We recognised that we were unwittingly adjusting people to poverty or the other forms of injustice by addressing their symptoms, without affecting the broader social and structural causes.

This realisation led us to set aside resources and initiate a community development base to our work. Over time we slowly and sensitively became involved with Maori and Pacific Island communities in our area. We then employed members of these communities in our agency who focused on the issues facing their own people, adopting welfare thought to social policy initiatives. They also worked with the family therapists and developed culturally appropriate ways of bringing the resources of therapy to their own people.

The co-operative work between the cultural sections has led to a number of interesting organisational processes. For example, all the workers in the agency, including those who type and receive people, take home the same salary. All work that involves someone from the Maori or Pacific Island communities is accountable directly to that cultural section. Likewise, gender work, including that carried out in men's groups, is directly accountable to the women in the agency. This is to ensure that a therapy is judged as just, primarily by the group that has been treated unjustly. Various ways of doing things that are uncommon to European culture, but central to Maori or Pacific Island cultures, are adopted. For example, we eat communally, make decisions consensually, receive and farewell guests formally and traditionally, and we share and express different forms of spirituality.

We are a small agency with eleven staff. Each cultural section has male and female workers so that we can appropriately address cultural and gender issues in ways that do justice to both. Because staff work in both the community development and family therapy fields, experiences from one inform the other. A family therapist may, for example, work on emergency housing, community organising, and housing policy projects in their community development work. This experience broadens their understanding and responses to people coming for therapy who are inade-quately housed. Likewise, the feelings of self-blame and helplessness often expressed by unemployed people when a community worker is involved in a project with unemployed people, are able to be addressed by a worker who is experienced and knowledgeable in therapeutic work.

As a group, a number of underlying assumptions to our work have emerged over the years. They are reflected in all the work that we do and are, therefore, worthy of note in this introduction. They can be summarised under three headings:

Spirituality, Justice, and Simplicity

Since spirituality informs every aspect of life in Maori and Pacific Island cultures, it naturally plays an important role in a great deal of our work. Instead of the traditional European dualistic world view that separates physical and spiritual values, we have learned to respect the sacredness of all life. Spirituality for us is not centred on organised religion, but on the essential quality of relationships, and refers to the relationship between people and their environment, people and other people, people and their heritage, and people and the numinous.

We view the process of therapy as sacred. People come, often in a very vulnerable state, and share some of their deepest and most painful experiences. For us, these stories are gifts that are worthy of honour. The therapists honour them by listening respectfully for their meaning, and offering new meanings which enable resolution, hope and self-determination. This process necessitates a high view of humanity and relationships, and as such is sacred.

Justice highlights equity in relationships between people: it involves naming the structures, and the actions that oppress and destroy equality in relationships. This is reflected in families at the micro level, and beyond that to the social structures at the macro level. Just therapy must always take both into account. Unfortunately, the resources of therapy have been largely utilised by one group of people. In most Western societies, it is the middle-class groups, and they get most of the other resources as well. A just therapy ensures that those most in need, like those on low incomes and those cultures that are oppressed, receive the resources of therapy in a manner that addresses their daily experiences of inequity.

Effective therapy, in our view, should reflect simplicity! It does not of necessity involve complex knowledges or processes, otherwise most societies before the advent of modem science would not have been able to resolve their families' problems. In essence, the therapy we offer finds its expression in the movement in meaning from problem-centred patterns to new possibilities of resolution and hope. Therapists listen for the meanings as people articulate their problems and the way they understand them. Therapists then offer alternative and liberating meanings of those same events.

It is this essentially simple exchange that determines the nature and gives quality to the therapy. It follows from this that people from particular cultures have expertise in the meanings associated with their culture, just as women have particular expertise to understand women's stories. This expert knowledge is at least as important as expertise in the body of Western psychological knowledge.

What Is Just Therapy?

"Just Therapy" is a reflective approach to therapy developed with colleagues over eleven years at The Family Centre in New Zealand. It is termed 'Just' for a number of reasons: firstly, it indicates a "just" approach within the therapy to the client group, one which takes into account their gender as well as the cultural, social, and economic context. Secondly, the approach attempts to demystify therapy (and therapists) so that it can be practised by a wider range of people including those with skills and community experience or cultural knowledge. These people may lack an academic background, but nevertheless have an essential ability to effect significant change. It is just (or simply) therapy, devoid of the commonly accepted excesses and limitations of some professional approaches and Western cultural bias.

The term "Just Therapy" could suggest a dilution of therapeutic knowledge and competence and could imply a general counselling framework for non specialised therapeutic work—a sort of social therapy that may improve our ability to address racism and poverty, rather than psychotic illnesses and the more serious psychosomatics, for example. We believe that this 'professional' reflex, not uncommon in clinical circles, may have helped create mythical boundaries around therapy, which have restricted its practice, clientele and effectiveness.

Far from being a dilution, "Just Therapy" attempts a distillation of therapeutic practices. Though it encourages novel and more effective ways of working with poor families, for example, its techniques also offer improved approaches to working with those who are socio-economically comfortable. Likewise, the significance given to cultural processes and patterns of communication not only enables therapy to be more accessible and effective with black, Hispanic, or Polynesian groups, for example, but also highlights, by contrast, the significance of socio-cultural experience in therapy for white middle-class groups.

"Just Therapy" attempts to extract the essence of therapy, which relates to the manner in which people give meaning to experience and create their "reality." Both therapists and clients weave webs of meaning around the problems presented in therapy. This therapy, in essence, concerns the movement from problem-centred stories of pain, to stories of resolution and hope; new meaning is given to experience, by the skillful weaving of new patterns.

This therapy is equally valuable for people who have psychotic problems, for example, as it is for those people broken as a result of being unemployed. In both

continued

CASE STUDY 1   *continued*

examples the meaning ascribed to the problem has to be addressed, and new meanings that encourage creative change responses developed. However, the focus for the psychotic case will probably be more on intra-psychic and family communication than for the unemployed case. While these emphases would certainly have their place with the unemployed, the social, community, and political meanings would also be very significant: high levels of unemployment trace their origins to economic and political policies rather than individual motivation.

Thus "Just Therapy" rejects the commonly accepted boundaries around therapy whereby practice is limited to intra-psychic, individual, couple, family or group work. As we have noted, broader contextual approaches to therapy are absolutely essential. Take, for example, a seriously depressed adult whose work and general expectations of happiness have been truncated as a result of restructuring and subsequent redundancy in the workplace. The significance given to work in the society, and the implications of increasing free market policies in Western economies are as important to healing as the intra-psychic work. This does not suggest that one is more important than the other. 'Just Therapy' simply complements modem approaches to therapy with information and method that is usually considered outside the parameters of clinical practice. These include social, gender, cultural, and political data as it is appropriate. Thus, any work with a family where the problem centres around a father's violent abuse will, of necessity, include qualitative information on the nature and development of patriarchy. The abuse will be addressed in relation to its immediate effects on family members, but also its association with the control men exercise over so many aspects of society and the violence implicated within sexist structures.

"Just Therapy" is essentially concerned with the often-forgotten issues of justice in therapy, but it also attempts to effect the change in people's lives which characterises therapy. These two aspects complement each other. In our view, broader social and political change, like therapeutic change, is essentially about giving new meaning to the world of experience.

The reason that I chose to introduce these ideas from Community Psychology at the beginning of this chapter is because children and families, especially those of color, are most vulnerable to the injustices of society. They tend to be among its most powerless members and have historically been the primary recipients of mental health treatment and other human services. In our delivery of these services—rather than implicating the more general root causes of "their problems," such as social exclusion, racism, and economic disenfranchisement—we tend to focus our attention on the symptoms of their dysfunction. In so doing, we unwittingly pathologize them, blame the victim, and at the same time overlook the "bigger picture" that is of interest to the Community Psychologist. It is in this spirit that I encourage you, the reader, to hold this caution in mind as we review the literature on culture and child development, parenting, and biculturalism that follows.

We will begin with two clinical scenarios drawn from real therapeutic situations that highlight the kinds of demands and challenges that face diverse parents and their children. Most striking is the complexity of dynamics that affect these families and their members and to which they must respond and adapt. As suggested above, forces in the broader environment affect them in negative ways. In turn, we as providers are challenged to intervene creatively and sensitively, so as to allow normal and healthy development to proceed. Culturally competent interventions involve helping family members learn to draw upon their unique cultural strengths and attributes to solve life problems creatively through empowerment and the development of self-worth and resiliency. Consider the following case scenarios regarding ethnic parenting.

Two Scenarios

Scenario 1. Ho (1992) describes family therapy for a Native American boy who had grown increasingly withdrawn and exhibited acting-out behavior, primarily in the form of glue sniffing. The boy's mother, who was Cherokee, blamed her son's behavior on marital discord and the unwillingness of the father, a Hopi, to discipline their son. She reported that the father had always been "apathetic" toward his child-rearing responsibilities, especially with regard to discipline. The father, a "kind, soft-spoken, mild-mannered man," explained that in Hopi culture, the male moves in with the wife's family, and it is she and her family who retain primary responsibility for raising the children. He, in turn, is responsible for overseeing the rearing of her sister's children (if any), especially the boys. Having acted upon this cultural prescription, he saw nothing amiss in his actions. With the father's permission, the therapist consulted an elder of the father's tribe, who privately met with the father and advised him that "the taboo of shared parental responsibility" held only in marriages within the tribe, and that he was free to take on a bigger parenting role with his son in this situation (pp. 154–155).

Scenario 2. As part of his private practice, the author once saw an interracial couple for marital problems. The husband, of Chinese American descent and the wife, Irish American, disagreed bitterly about the role that his mother should play in their lives. He said that it was normal in his culture for the mother of the family to give advice and guidance to the daughter-in-law and that even though it might at times be a little "heavy-handed," it was done out of love and caring. He further believed that his wife should be more tolerant out of respect for his culture. She, in turn, responded that she had spent the last 10 years trying to recover from an abusive home situation and refused to subject herself to any further abuse from the mother-in-law, no matter how pure her intentions or how normal such behavior might be in Chinese culture. "I married you, not your family, and don't feel it is fair or very loving to ask me to continue to subject myself to your mother's intrusive and abusive ways." The husband just lowered his eyes, as if embarrassed by what his wife was saying. With help, the couple came to see that their conflicting perceptions were as much cultural as personal, and thereby less threatening and more amenable to change.

Ho, M. K. (1992). Minority children and adolescents in therapy. Newbury Park, CA: Sage.

▶ Parenting   6-2

Margaret Burroughs captures the dilemma that faces all parents of color in the opening lines of this poem:*

> What shall I tell my children who are black
> Of what it means to be a captive in this dark skin?
> Of how beautiful they are when everywhere they turn
> They are faced with abhorrence of everything that is black . . .

All parents face a similar task—that of creating a safe environment in which their child can move without harm through the various developmental tasks and stages that are part of growing up. In the case of mainstream white parents, threats to the child's health or safety, when they do exist, are random and unpredictable. Children of color, however, are born into an environment in which they are systematically subjected to the harmful effects of racism. Parents of color, having grown up under similar conditions, are aware of what awaits their children and of the fact that there is only so much they can do to protect them. What can parents of color do? First, they can create a buffer zone in which the child is protected from the negative attitudes and stereotypes of the broader society. Such a safety zone can increase the likelihood of instilling ethnic pride and a positive sense of self in the child. Second, parents of color can teach their children how to deal constructively with the emotions that are stimulated by the experience of racism. Third, they can prepare their children cognitively for what they will encounter in the world outside the buffer zone.

Creating a Buffer Zone

Mainstream theories in social psychology hold that society's negative views and stereotypes of people of color are directly reflected onto the psyches of children of color and internalized into their sense of self and identity. Other theorists—Norton (1983), for example—argue that messages sent by the child's immediate environment of home, significant others, and community can mitigate those of the broader society and provide a basis for the internalization of positive ethnic identity and self-worth. DeVoe and Ross (2012) added that children are most protected when caregivers fulfill their roles and use appropriate support systems. For white children, there is generally little difference between the messages received from their immediate environment and those from society in general. For children of color, however, the situation may be very different, with the two systems offering conflicting messages. The family, in turn, can act as a buffer between children and society's negative evaluations of them,

---

*Excerpt from poem "What Shall I Tell My Children Who Are Black?" by Margaret Burroughs. (Reprinted with permission of the author.)

thus becoming the primary sculptor of feelings about self and a source of healthy self-esteem. In this regard, Norton raises a number of questions: "What happens in the interaction between black parents and their children in those stable nurturing families from any educational or socioeconomic level who manage to rear children with a strong sense of self? How and with what patterns do these families defy the 'mark of oppression'? How can we determine the strengths and healthy coping mechanisms in the interaction between black parents and their children?" (p. 188).

The idea of creating a buffer zone in which the child can develop without harmful intrusions from the outside is the essence of all good parenting. Young children need protection and nurturance until they are able to venture into the outside world with sufficient skills and abilities to protect themselves. Children of color, being generally at risk, are in special need of good psychological grounding in a positive sense of self with which to go out into the world.

Research, for example, has correlated positive self-concept with effective social functioning, higher levels of cognitive development, and greater emotional health and stability (Curry and Johnson, 1990). The creation of a buffer zone (against racism and negative racial messages) can provide a place and time for such optimal personal growth. Psychological theories about the development of the self speak of mirroring and reflection and imply that children take in and make a part of themselves the reflected views of others (Wylie, 1961). If they are loved, they will love themselves; if they are demeaned or devalued, that is how they will come to feel about themselves. Sharma and Sharma (2010) suggest that "each culture specifies permissible forms of self and serves as a major force shaping the way people conceptualize self" (p. 119). In this regard, Clark (1963) writes: "Children who are consistently rejected understandably begin to question and doubt whether they, their family, and their group really deserve no more respect from the larger society that they receive" (pp. 63–64). This is why the buffer zone is so critical. When parents of color can substitute the reflection of loving parents and significant others for that of a hostile environment that routinely negates the value of children because of their ethnicity, their children are likely to develop a positive sense of self.

Norton (1983) describes the ingredients for optimal (i.e., esteem-producing) parent-child interaction as follows: "Early consistent, loving, nurturing interaction is the ideal process of interaction leading to a good sense of self. The child who is loved, accepted, and supported in appropriate reality-oriented functioning in relationship to others comes to love himself and to respect himself as someone worthy of love" (p. 185). Menashe and Atzaba-Poria (2016) explained that "the relationship between the parent and the child is shaped, not only by the child's direct experience of parental care, but also by the secondary representations of experience, mediated by language" (p. 519). The idea of a buffer zone, however, should not be limited merely to parents and family. The entire ethnic community, with its various institutions, can function in a similar way to protect its children. The African adage "It takes a village to raise a child" is relevant here. The idea of ethnic separatism, such as that practiced by black Muslims, is predicated on such a notion of creating a safe, supportive, and economically viable system that does not depend on whites and, in fact, limits interaction with them and their institutions.

Parenting for Self-Esteem

Wright (1998) offers an interesting but controversial perspective on the relationships among parenting, race, and the nurturing of self-esteem. She believes that there are three crucial ways in which parents, especially African American parents, can support or negate their child's developing sense of self-worth:

> ▶ **Disciplinary style:** According to Wright, "many parents in the black community hold a ... strong belief in the value of corporal punishment." Regardless of the reason for it—whether to follow the biblical injunction not to "spare the rod" because it is "cultural" for African Americans to use physical pain in disciplining their children and it "worked well for me"; or to "toughen" children in order to prepare them for life in a hostile world because of the belief that African American children "need more severe discipline than the children of other races" and it is the only thing that works with them—physical punishment may erode self-esteem. Wright suggests that children learn less about internal control and self-regulation and more about fear and hostility from physical punishment. Most important, Wright believes that when black children are spanked, for whatever reason, they may learn at the hands of their own caretakers a message that mimics "the same message that white society ... has traditionally sent to blacks" (p. 131). Gentler discipline, on the other hand, may foster greater emotional health by sending a very different message—that the child is worthy of such treatment and respect. It is important to point out that many black parents may take exception to Wright's views on corporal punishment.
>
> ▶ **Parental closeness or distance:** To the extent that parents can be present and emotionally involved in the daily lives of their children, there is greater likelihood for the development of positive self-worth. At times, this has been a challenge for many in the African American community. The absence of fathers because of the cycle of poverty and racism; single mothers torn between having to earn a living and being away from their children, often without the traditional African American extended support system; and, especially of late, the ravages of addictions on family life all threaten the emotional health of children who encounter them. It is important to realize that when a parent is unavailable, for whatever

reason, children tend to blame themselves for the absence, often interpreting it as evidence of their own worthlessness. Such factors are highly related to socioeconomics.

▶ **Parents' attitude toward race and life in general:** Wright (1998) describes working with children who seem "unusually vulnerable to perceived and actual racism. Some of them obviously have to deal with an unusually heavy share of discrimination, but more often these children come from families who habitually blame their child's problems on race and who bring their children up to believe that they are victims because they are black" (p. 6). Premature sensitization to racism before children are developmentally ready may take an enormous toll on their future ability to cope. Similarly, Wright raises concerns about the parents' basic attitude toward life, distinguishing between attitudinal "impoverishment" and "enrichment." Seeing the glass as half empty or half full, in spite of one's level of disadvantage, is a perceptual habit that parents pass on to their children that can play a major role in how the children feel about themselves and their futures. This concern, like others raised by Wright, could be considered controversial, and some even view it as "blaming the victim."

▶ Preparing the Child Emotionally for Racism   6-3

Speaking to the situation of African American parents, children should not be allowed to feel alone in their struggles. They must not only feel the support of their parents, peers, and teachers, but also understand that they are part of a long history of individuals who have similarly struggled against racism. Parents should model active intervention and mastery over the environment as well as help their children develop competence and the ability to achieve personal goals. Allen (2016) explained that black fathers play an important role in helping children to "engage in positive racial socializing practices, sending their children messages of racial pride, preparing them to navigate potential racial barriers, and emphasizing racial resiliency and self-determination" (p. 1834). Allen (2016) also mentioned the importance of preparing children to deal with anger as a result of perceived or real racism. Poussaint (1972) points out the importance of helping children learn to manage the righteous anger that they will feel as objects of racial hatred. Suppressing anger eventually leads to feelings of self-loathing and low self-esteem. Overgeneralized anger is counterproductive, leading nowhere and consuming a vast amount of undirected energy. Rather, a more balanced approach seems optimal: teaching children to assert themselves sufficiently, to display their anger appropriately, and to sublimate and channel much of it into constructive energy for actively dealing with the world. "Our job," Poussaint writes, "is to help our children develop that delicate balance between appropriate control and appropriate display of anger and aggression, love and hate" (p. 110). He summarizes as follows: "As parents, we must try to raise men and women who are emotionally healthy in a society that is basically racist. If our history is a lesson, we will continue to survive. Many black children will grow up to be strong, productive adults. But too many others will succumb under the pressures of a racist environment. Salvaging these youngsters is our responsibility as parents" (p. 111).

Thomas and Blackmon (2014) offer some good insights into how to help children deal emotionally with the negative racial experiences they encounter. Speaking to the situation of African American parents, names like Trayvon Martin, Freddy Gray, Christian Taylor, Michael Brown, and Tamir Rice profoundly impact our culture and our emotional preparation for racism. Thomas and Blackmon (2014) emphasize that children of color are racially socialized by learning their parents' experiences with bias and discrimination. Parents should directly teach their children how to handle discrimination. Additionally, children should learn racial pride through familial customs, celebrations, and history.

Preparing the Child Cognitively for Racism

Equally important to creating a strong emotional base in children is helping them to understand racism. While many researchers have written on this topic, the early work of Lewin (1948) still offers the most compelling advice to parents vis-à-vis preparing their children to cope cognitively with the experiences of prejudice and discrimination:

> ▶ According to Lewin, never deny a child's ethnicity or underestimate
> the impact it will have on his or her life. Some parents feel that it is
> best to put off discussions of racism as long as possible, thereby keep-
> ing the child naïve until the subject can no longer be avoided. There
> are real problems with this approach. It models, first of all, a kind of
> denial of reality that not only confuses children, but also sets them on
> a life course of passively dealing with their ethnic identity. Parents who
> choose to avoid discussions of race also tend to underestimate the level
> of a child's knowledge and thus avoid issues that have already become
> real and problematic.
> ▶ Lewin also points out, using the analogy of adoption, that "learning the
> truth" can be much more damaging and hurtful the older the child is.
> In other words, the longer one lives with a given picture of reality, the
> more devastating it can be to have that reality shattered. Parents should
> answer questions as simply as possible and not overwhelm children
> with more knowledge than they currently need. As they encounter

racism in the real world, it should be discussed and processed, and as they mature, information and explanations should grow in depth and comprehensiveness.

▶ It is vital to help children develop strong and positive ethnic identities based on values inherent in group membership to counteract internally the negative experiences of being an object of prejudice. A statement of such a positive identity is: "I am Latino/a and come from a rich cultural tradition of which I am very proud. Sure, I experience a lot of racism, but that's just the way it is, although, at times, I get very angry. But I would never trade it for being white or anything else, even if it meant life would be a lot easier." An ethnic identity based solely on negative experiences is a very fragile thing that disappears as soon as the person can be rid of it. If children are made to feel bad because of their differences, it is psychologically crucial that they possess positive feelings about who they are as people and as members of a group.

▶ Racial hatred should always be presented as a social problem, not an individual or personal one. For example: "Why did Tommy call me that bad name?

I didn't do anything to him." A good answer to that might well be: "Of course you didn't. Sometimes, when people get angry or unhappy, they take it out on others who are different from them. There's something wrong with people when they do that." It is vital that children not come to believe, consciously or unconsciously, that something they did brought on the discriminatory behavior. Parents should never assume that a child has not personalized a negative racial experience. They must check it out openly.

▶ Children must learn that group membership is based not only on obvious physical or cultural features, but also on an "interdependence of fate." Members of ethnic groups often share experiences of mistreatment by society. Although this can serve to heighten intragroup solidarity, it is also possible for children to learn to vent their frustration on subgroups within their community, blaming them for the bad treatment that all group members experience. Such internalized racism can become a tyranny of its own and can lead to destructive intragroup wrangling and bickering. There does exist, within some communities of color, powerful caste systems based on lightness and darkness of skin color.

▶ Children must not learn to fear multiple group allegiances. If children are unnecessarily made to choose between alternative roles and group memberships, they will grow resentful and eventually find ways to get even with parents, often through the rejection of ethnicity. Some parents, for instance, are very critical of their children's attempts at being bicultural (i.e., trying to become competent in the ways of the dominant culture as well as their own). Fearful that their children will lose touch with traditional ways and values, they force them to choose. The result is usually severe family strife. The reverse may also occur—forcing children to acculturate into the mainstream culture can engender eventual resentment and yearning for identity.

▸ Parents must realize that a child's feelings about ethnicity and group belonging are most likely to model their own attitudes. If they themselves are in some way confused or conflicted about who they are ethnically, those feelings are likely to be passed on. Poussaint (1972) made a similar point in relation to compensatory mechanisms, as discussed in the previous section. If cycles of dysfunction are to be broken, they must be interrupted by parental awareness and healing.

▸ Bicultural Children and Families   6-4

In the final section of this chapter, we look at an increasingly important, yet generally underserved ethnic family system: that of bicultural families. We will learn about the dynamics of bicultural couples and their relationships, the unique developmental issues that face bicultural children in discovering who they are ethnically and where they fit socially, and some suggestions for working therapeutically with bicultural families and couples.

Bicultural families represent a little-understood yet increasingly important subgroup in American society. Witness, for example, the fact that bicultural or *multiracial* (the U.S. Census term of choice) individuals were not counted officially within the U.S. Census until the year 2000. In the latest census briefs from 2010, individuals who identified as *multiracial* grew from 6.8 million to 9 million, or 2.9 percent of the population chose more than one race, an increase of about 32 percent since 2000. In spite of these dramatic increases, a number of myths and distorted beliefs about bicultural children remain. This is not surprising given the fact that in 1967, when they were found unconstitutional, there were still laws against interracial marriages in 16 states.

Kerwin and Ponterotto (1995) describe three of the most prevalent of these myths:

▸ Bicultural children turn out to be very tragic and marginal individuals.
▸ Bicultural children must choose to identify with only one of their parents' cultural groups.
▸ Bicultural children are very uncomfortable discussing their ethnic identity with others.

According to these authors, however, each of these myths is a distortion of the psychological reality, as follows:

- Bicultural children are quite capable of developing healthy ethnic identities and finding a stable social place for themselves.
- Contrary to being forced to choose one parent's ethnic affiliation over the other, healthy identity development in bicultural children involves an integration of both cultural backgrounds into a unitary sense of self that is an amalgam of both and yet uniquely different than either.
- Bicultural children welcome the opportunity to discuss and explore who they are ethnically.

Such myths are most likely sustained by individuals who are uncomfortable with the idea of bicultural relationships and who project their own discomfort onto the children.

There are two general forms of bicultural families: ones in which parents come from two or more diverse cultures and ones in which parents come from the same culture with a child adopted from another cultural group. Our exploration begins with a discussion of bicultural parental relationships and ends with a consideration of the unique dynamics related to cross-cultural adoption.

Bicultural Couples

Clinical work with bicultural spouses yields a very informative psychological profile. First, bicultural couples tend to approximate extremes in healthy functioning. Some are very high functioning and bring to the relationship advanced communication skills, good cultural understanding of each other, and a strong motivation toward openness and working through difficulties. Others enter the relationship with a culturally different partner for reasons of which they are largely unaware and bring to the relationship very poor interpersonal skills and little insight.

Jacobs (1977) carried out extensive interviews with African American and European American bicultural couples and their children, which is still supported by more current research (Allen, Garriott, Reyes, and Hsieh, 2013; Perry, 2014; Powell, Hamilton, Manago, and Cheng, 2016). Because of sampling methods, parents in the study tended to be higher functioning. All reported personal attraction as opposed to race as the motivation for entering a bicultural relationship. Jacobs found that several spouses acknowledged a drive toward asserting autonomy as a secondary motive. For white spouses, this tended to be autonomy from rigid and overcontrolling families, and for the African American spouses, it represented "overcoming limits placed on them by racism." None of the fourteen spouses felt any guilt over their relationships. Jacobs's couples were assessed as well differentiated from each other and, because of this, were able to allow their children to separate and individuate. The parents did suggest that it was easier to give their children autonomy because each child was experienced as "being different" and not exactly like either of them.

Only two of the seven white spouses reported acceptance by parents of their intention to intermarry. In contrast, all the black spouses reported families of origin as accepting of their partner choice. This data parallels previous research findings that communities of color tend to be more accepting of bicultural relationships and marriages than whites. A notable exception to this tendency can be found among Asian American subgroups. White spouses reported an interesting sequence of reactions to parental rejection. After a period of initial anger that lasted anywhere from several months to several years, they were able to develop some empathy and understanding for the rejecting parents and moved toward reestablishment of contact and attachment. Spouses who exhibited unhealthy attachment patterns found it impossible to make such movements and efforts at reconciliation. They tended to be flooded with guilt over their marriages, were heavily preoccupied with race (the healthier couples were less preoccupied), harbored serious prejudices of their own, and continued to act out behaviorally the same conflict that had drawn them into the interracial relationships in the first place.

Jacobs's bicultural couples also reported frequent focus on issues of race and ethnicity. Being in close and intimate interaction with someone who is culturally diverse cannot help but elicit racial material from both partners. Such issues must be discussed honestly and worked through if the marriage is to function. What, in effect, exists is a microcosm of race relations in the home, with numerous opportunities to explore resolving cross-cultural problems. For example, Memmi (1966) suggests that during arguments between bicultural couples, racial prejudices and stereotypes often surface in the heat of battle. Because of the hurtful nature of such attacks, resolution must be achieved in these situations. Jacobs (1977) also found that interracial couples were more open to discussing topics of race and ethnicity than were either African American or white monocultural couples.

Bicultural couples tended to be rather isolated as a unit, often experiencing social rejection and preferring social contact with other bicultural couples, who can more easily understand what they face in daily living. As a result, they often developed patterns of strong interdependence between them, which included an unwillingness to acknowledge problems or seek help as a unit. On the positive side, interdependence and isolation caused them to try harder to resolve conflicts on their own; on the negative, airing of problems could be experienced as a particular threat.

Finally, bicultural couples faced another challenge that monocultural couples were generally spared. They have to face not only personality differences and conflicts, but also the complex and difficult terrain of cultural differences. Interfaith couples—for example, Jewish and Christian—must agree on shared practices in the home and religious education. Bicultural couples of color, in turn, face stylistic, value, priority, and expectation differences that are cultural in origin. Northern Europeans, for instance, become quiet and distant during interpersonal conflicts and tend to move away from the partner, while individuals from more traditional cultures tend to become more verbal and emotional and move toward their partner in an effort to resolve conflicts. If problems are ever to be resolved by such bicultural couples, they must learn to accommodate their differences in style.

Patterns of Bicultural Relationships

Bicultural children are psychologically privy not only to reflections of conflicts and tensions within the broader society, but also to those that originate within the family. Difficulties in bicultural marriages represent a microcosm of the kinds of conflicts that bicultural children face in their lives. Falicov (1986), for example, believes that cross-cultural marriages demand from each partner a kind of cultural transition. According to her, the couple must "arrive at an adaptive and flexible view of cultural differences that make it possible to maintain some individuated values, to negotiate conflictual areas, and even to develop a new cultural code that integrates parts of both cultural streams" (p. 431).

Falicov identifies the following three patterns of cultural tension, with bicultural families as most frequent:

- First is what she calls "conflicts in cultural code." This involves cultural differences in how marriages are conceived and structured. Particularly important are differences in rules related to the inclusion and exclusion of others (especially extended family members) and the relative power and authority between spouses. In the hope of mutually adapting to each other's style, partners often minimize or maximize cultural differences. In either case, they tend to have only limited knowledge of the other's culture and are generally unable to carry out what Falicov sees as a necessary developmental task for the marriage—that of negotiating together a new cultural code that implies the melding of their different ways. She also points out that errors in this arena often stem from "ethnocentric or stereotyped views of the other." As a result of such limited knowledge, cultural differences may be "mistaken for negative personality traits" of the other.
- A second type of problem involves "cultural differences and permission to marry." Here, Falicov includes difficulties related to parental disapproval of the relationship and cultural style issues, such as the tendency toward enmeshment, which makes separating from family of origin a more conflictual task. She identifies two differing patterns of adaptation in couples who have not received emotional permission to marry. In the first, partners "maximize their differences and do not blend, integrate, or negotiate their values and life styles. They lead parallel lives, each holding on to their culture and/or family of origin. Often, the counterpoint of the marital distance is an excessive involvement of one or both parties with the

family of origin. There may also be unresolved longings for the past ethnic or religious affiliations, even if these were of little importance previously." This pattern is often accompanied by expectations and pressures for children to choose between parents and their respective families. A second pattern involves the opposite: a minimizing and denying of differences, which may take the form of either adopting a third and alternative culture style or cutting ties with culture and family altogether. One often sees in such couples an attitude of "us against them" (meaning the world) or "we only have each other." Structurally, rigid boundaries are constructed externally (especially with families of origin) and unclear boundaries internally. The child often internalizes the resulting isolation.

▸ Falicov's third problem area in cross-cultural marriages is "cultural stereotyping and severe stress." In such situations, impending stress (e.g., the death of a parent) initiates a maximizing of cultural differences and stereotyping between partners. Falicov suggests that in this case, cultural material that was previously dealt with constructively is now used as a defense against looking at other noncultural problems and that the resulting stress wears down the couple's ability to cope. Children in families reacting to stress in this manner may need extra help negotiating the pull of competing cultures. Teachers alerted to impending stress within bicultural families may need to be prepared to offer more than the usual care and empathy for such children. As we shall see next, the three patterns of cultural tension in marriage identified by Falicov exacerbate the kind of developmental tasks that the bicultural child must navigate.

Bicultural Children

Monocultural children of color will eventually face the realities of a hostile social environment, but bicultural children must also come to grips with their parents' interracial drama and the perpetually repeated question "What are you?" Kich (1992) suggests that the interracial child not only represents the parents' racial differences, but also is a unique individual who must work through very personal identity issues related to their differences. Evans and Ramsay (2015) proposed that "racial identity is fluid and unique to the individual. Thus, a multiracial person might identify his or her racial background differently based on the environment and pressure received from monoracial groups" (p. 264). Kerwin and Ponterotto (1995) summarize the development of racial identity in biracial children. In many ways, the process parallels that of monocultural children of color, but with the added task of simultaneously exploring two (or more) ethnic heritages rather than a single one and then integrating them into a unique whole. Perhaps the most salient point to remember in working with bicultural and multicultural children is that, psychologically, they are not merely reflections of their two or more sides but unique integrations of them.

Bicultural children, on average, develop awareness of race and racial differences even earlier than monocultural children of color, usually by age 3 or 4 years. This is because they are exposed to such differences from birth in the confines of their own families. It is also likely that their parents are more attuned to these differences because of their interracial relationship. Upon entry into school, bicultural children are immediately confronted with questions that serve as major stimuli for their internal processing of "What are you?" Concurrently, they begin to experiment with labels for themselves. Children may create self-descriptions based on perceptions of their skin color (e.g., coffee with cream) or adopt parental terms (e.g., interracial).

In general, bicultural children are most successful moving through the identity formation process when race is openly discussed at home and parents are available to help sort out various issues of self-definition. Rate of development also depends on the amount of integration in their classrooms and the availability in school of role models from both cultural sides. During pre-adolescence, children begin to regularly use racial or cultural descriptions as opposed to physical descriptions of themselves. They are becoming increasingly aware of group differences other than skin color (physical appearance, language, etc.) and of the fact that their parents belong to distinct ethnic groups. Exposure to "racial incidents" and first-time entry into either integrated or segregated school settings also accelerate learning.

Adolescence is particularly problematic for bicultural children. It is a time of marked intolerance of differences for both these children and their peers. There are likely to be strong pressures on bicultural adolescents to identify with one parent's ethnicity over the other—usually with the parent of color, if one parent is white. Peers of color push the adolescent to identify with them, and increasingly, whites perceive and treat the bicultural adolescent as a person of color. Jacobs (1992) believes that vacillation between identification with one ethnicity and the simultaneous rejection of the other, followed by its opposite, is a natural part of identity formation in bicultural youth. Perhaps only by internalizing one aspect of the self at a time, and even vacillating between the two over the duration of adolescence and young adulthood, can there be any real integration of both identities. Dating begins in adolescence, and this fact accentuates race as a central life issue. It is not unusual for bicultural youth to experience rejection because of their color or ethnicity, and such experiences are likely to have a great impact on their emerging sense of identity. The heightened sexuality of adolescence also stimulates questions such as "If I become pregnant or make someone pregnant, what will the baby look like?" Bicultural women have a particularly difficult task meshing their body images with either of their bicultural physical types. Young black women often opt out of mainstream society's "beauty contests" because of an inability to match mainstream standards. Ironically, this may lead to the establishment of a more realistic and healthy body image. Bicultural women may be torn between the media image on one hand and her body image identity with her mother (if of color) on the other.

Interactions between bicultural children and their parents are at times complex and conflictual. As children grow more mature and aware, they are increasingly confronted with and confused by the experience of being different. Some have described it as akin to "going crazy" or having no way of making sense of how the world is reacting to them. Bicultural parents often have a difficult time understanding exactly what the child is going through. At the root of this misunderstanding is each parent's tendency to see the child as an extension of himself or herself rather than as an amalgam of the couple. The realization by parents that their child sees him or herself as something different from them can be quite anxiety-provoking.

In family situations where one of the parents has detached from his or her group of origin, bicultural children tend to feel particularly protective of that parent. Similarly, where one of the parents is white, they may overly empathize with the parent of color when he or she is feeling bad or rejected because of racism. Divorce in such marriages can be especially traumatic because it represents a severing of the two sides of a child's identity. Because of this, a child may feel a real need to keep the warring parents together at any cost. Such dynamics are especially exacerbated if parents use race against each other. Nor is it uncommon for the child to take on the prejudices of individual parents during divorce. In single-parent families, difficulties can arise when the lone parent, usually the mother, feels great hostility toward the father for abandoning them and unconsciously turns her resentment toward the child as a visible reminder of the union. Similarly, parental and child resentment may emerge as subtle racism toward the missing parent.

Bicultural Adopted Children

Samuels (2010) expressed that "adoption seeks to provide children with what has historically been one of the most fundamental characteristics of the human experience and the context in which cultural identities are first acquired—a family" (p. 26). Bicultural adoption is a second source of bicultural families. Communities of color have taken very strong stances against adoption and foster care across racial lines. Their feeling is that white parents are not capable of providing children of color with either adequate exposure and connection with their cultures of birth or training in how to deal with the racism they will eventually experience. Serious efforts have been made to sensitize and train adoptive parents in cultural competence, as well as to encourage them to keep their child connected to his or her community of origin. There are, however, real questions as to whether such efforts can overcome cultural gaps, let alone a racially hostile social environment. Samuels (2010) also mentioned that current adoption research states that because race and culture have not been central to evaluating successful adoption outcomes, some scholars refute the linkage between bicultural adoption and challenges adoptees face in identity formation.

White adoptive parents seldom understand the enormity of difference that their children face as people of color. In addition, they often unconsciously deny differences that exist between themselves and their children. This puts children in a very difficult psychological position. They feel isolated in dealing with the very complex issues of race and ethnicity. There is, for example, the aforementioned sense of "going crazy," fostered by the enormous gulf between how they are being reacted to in the external social world and at home. Finally, it can become confusing for adopted children of color when their adopted parents simultaneously represent nurturance or emotional support on one side and oppression on the other. A process somewhat akin to the identity vacillation suggested by Jacobs (1992) may also occur for these bicultural children.

▶ Therapy with Bicultural Families   6-5

Laszloffy (2008), by way of summarizing much of the above, points to three dynamics within bicultural or mixed-race families that tend to "undermine or compromise" a child's racial identity development in such families. The first has to do with messages sent about race in the family:

> Of particular importance is children's exposure to negative or devaluing messages about any of the groups that they have membership in, because this compromises their ability to embrace and successfully integrate these aspects of themselves into their self-concept. Even more challenging . . . is receiving mixed messages about race . . . Contradictory messages are confusing because it is unclear which messages they should follow. (p. 277)

Second is the creation of perceptions that "sides must be taken" when parents are in conflict, wherein children become "trapped in loyalty binds" between parents. The third problem area has to do with external racism. Both bicultural and monocultural families of color must prepare children adequately for the racism that they will inevitably be confronted with outside the home:

> One factor that tends to compromise how well parents are able to prepare their children . . . is one of the parents being white. This is especially likely to be the case if parents are no longer a couple and the white parent has primary custody . . . Because white parents are less likely to know how to offer support and guidance with racism, they are less likely to know how to offer support and guidance to their children . . .
>
> A common assumption is that a white person who is or was in an interracial relationship and has mixed-race children will automatically possess racial awareness, and sensitivity . . . This is often not the case . . . Such children suffer the loss that comes from not having a parent who can truly validate their race-related experiences and offer useful guidance and direction. (pp. 279–280)

Laszloffy suggests the following intervention strategies:

▶ **Confronting devaluing or mixed racial messages.** The therapist must be attuned to the existence of such messages and call the parents' attention to these whenever they occur in therapy. In certain cases, parents need to be educated as to why certain things that they say can be construed as insensitive or offensive. An alternative approach to direct confrontation is to invite the client to become "curious" about the nature of the messages about race that they are sending to their children.

▶ **Freeing children from racialized loyalty binds.** Therapists must bring the existence of such loyalty binds to the awareness of parents. "Once parents are aware of how their children have been triangulated . . . therapists should coach parents until they are able to communicate clear, explicit messages . . . that acknowledge the loyalty binds and give kids explicit permission to have their own relationships with each parent and with all parts of their racial identity" (p. 282). When parents believe that creating such binds are in the best interest of the child, the therapist should "align" with the parent devotion and commitment but at the same time educate them about the emotional damage that such pressures can cause.

▶ **Fostering strategies for resisting racism.** Therapists most often must teach families how to have open and direct talks about race. As such conversations become easier, families can begin to help children determine when a situation is race-based, how it might make them feel, and how they might respond in such offensive situations. As suggested above, special attention may have to be focused on racial awareness and sensitivity on the part of a white parent as part of this process.

SUMMARY

This chapter begins with African American writer Alice Walker's open letter to President Obama. In it, she reminds him of the struggle against racism and inequality that previous generations of African American parents endured in order to gain access for their children to the American Dream. In this regard, the concept of Community Psychology is introduced to remind us, as human service providers, to pay attention to the "big picture" and to not overlook the realities of social exclusion, racism, and economic disenfranchisement in understanding the lives and problems of the children and families with which we work. By way of example, the Just Therapy approach to mental health treatment, developed and implemented by the Family Center in Wellington, New Zealand, is introduced and described in some detail. The chapter continues with two short case studies that reflect two major themes of the chapter: parenting in culturally diverse families and biracial and bicultural children and families.

Parents of color face the difficult task of creating safe environments for children who are systematically subjected to the harmful effects of racism. Creating buffer zones in homes and communities where children are protected from the negative attitudes and stereotypes of racism represents one strategy of helping. Developing ethnic pride is a second one. Poussaint (1972) warned against "compensatory mechanisms" that parents may adopt to prepare their children for racism. Wright (1998) warned against the use of corporal punishment, emotional distancing, and blaming family problems exclusively on racism. Parents can prepare their children both cognitively and emotionally for what they will encounter outside the buffer zone.

Families of color tend to exhibit more diversity in their form and structure than do mainstream white families. It is critical to avoid interpreting cultural differences in family structure as cultural deficits. The example of the "black matriarchy" is presented, with an emphasis on interpreting differences in family patterns as indicative of creative and adaptive development rather than as pathology.

Bicultural couples and families represent a growing and special subset of ethnic families. A number of myths about bicultural children are shown to be unfounded. Bicultural couples tend to exhibit either very healthy or extremely dysfunctional relationship patterns. The work of Jacobs (1977) is reviewed. Falicov (1986) pointed to three typical problems in bicultural martial discord: conflicts in cultural codes, difficulties in separating from families of origin, and cultural stereotyping of partners during times of crisis and stress. Laszloffy (2008) points out that couples therapy with bicultural couples often focuses on three tasks in relation to their bicultural children: confronting devaluing or mixed racial messages, freeing children from racialized loyalty binds, and fostering strategies for resisting racism.

Bicultural children face not only prejudice and racism, but also the task of integrating two cultural identities; are aware of race and ethnicity earlier than mono-ethnic children; do best in environments where ethnicity is discussed openly; and receive help from parents in sorting out issues of self-definition. Adolescence is particularly difficult for bicultural children. Communities of color have opposed the adoption of ethnic children across racial lines. This may be because adopted children of color often find themselves isolated and on their own when dealing with issues of race and ethnicity.

ACTIVITIES

1. *Explore racial attitudes of your family of origin.* Divide into dyads or small groups. First, take turns sharing memories of the first time that you became aware of racially or ethnically diverse people. Describe the experience and what it taught you about such differences. Next, talk about the racial attitudes of members of your family. What messages did your family communicate to you about race and ethnicity, prejudice, people who are culturally diverse, and so on?

Finally, discuss differences in how such material was dealt with in your respective families and how these have affected you.

2. **Analyze race-related scenarios.** Read the following three scenarios and, drawing on the ideas and material presented in this chapter, analyze the diversity issues they pose and then answer the questions at the end of each. You can do this exercise individually or in dyads or small groups.

   a. You are a clinical social worker seeing children and families in an agency located in a primarily African American neighborhood. One of your clients, an eight-year-old African American girl, accidentally disclosed to you that her parents used spankings to discipline her and her siblings. Once she realized what she had said, she quickly tried to retract it, clearly anxious about her statement, and then asked you to not say anything to her parents about it. When asked why, she said that her parents had told her there were certain things that she should not talk about with the white social worker. As a mandated reporter, you know that you have a duty to report certain kinds of punishment to Children's Protective Services (CPS). You are also aware from reading the present chapter and previous experience in the agency that African American families (for a variety of good reasons) tend to be mistrustful of CPS and other social services agencies, that there is a debate within their community about the use of physical punishment, and that many see it as an acceptable cultural practice. You are also aware that making the report, or even talking with the parents, might lead them to terminate treatment (and you have been making significant progress), as well as possibly putting their daughter at risk for further punishment. How might you proceed sensitively to protect the child, respect the cultural attitudes of the parents, and maximize the likelihood that the therapy would continue? Explain your reasoning and choices.

   b. I was once awakened early in the morning to attend an emergency meeting of a Jewish religious school's board of directors. During the previous night, someone had broken into the school, made a mess of the place, scrawled anti-Semitic graffiti all over the walls, and destroyed and defaced religious articles and artwork. A night janitor discovered the break-in, and board members were meeting to decide how to handle the situation. In the very heated and emotional discussion, some argued that the school should not be reopened the next morning; it remained closed until all signs of the vandalism were removed. They felt that it would be too traumatic for the children, ages 5 through 12, to witness because they were not old enough to understand what had happened. One parent summarized this position as follows: "There will be plenty of time in their future for the children to learn about this kind of hatred." Others felt it was "never too early," and suggested that students be shown the school now and be given ample opportunity to talk about what had happened. Yet others favored exposing only the older children to what had happened or letting the choice be up to individual parents. Given the material presented in this chapter, how would you suggest they proceed, and what issues do you see at stake in this hard decision?

c. You are a cultural consultant to a local adoption agency. Recently, the agency has been the object of lobbying and protests of their policy of open adoption by a local group made up of ethnic parents and professionals who oppose cross-racial adoption. The agency has always prided itself on its color blindness and commitment to find the best parents for every child, regardless of race and ethnicity. You have been asked to advise the board, explain to them the position of the protestors, and take a position on which course would be in the best interest of these children of color. Also, if the board decides to continue cross-racial adoption, what guidelines for parent training might you suggest?

Culturally Sensitive Treatment with children

LEARNING OBJECTIVES

7-1 Explain culturally sensitive treatment with children.

7-2 Distinguish the development of racial identity in children and see its effects on self-esteem.

7-3 Explain adolescent racial identity.

7-4 Discuss contemporary culturally sensitive treatments for children.

7-5 Apply the Tree of Life exercise with diverse child populations.

7-6 Examine school-based social justice intervention programs.

Gil and Drewes (2015) explained that developing cultural sensitivity when working with children, counselors must develop three distinct levels of response that build upon one another: building sensitivity, obtaining knowledge responsibly, and developing active competence. Building sensitivity involves reflection and attunement to the interactions between the counselor and client. Obtaining knowledge responsibly requires counselors to not only gain the tools required to help, but to also do so in a way that holds them accountable for their insights and behaviors. Developing active competence involves a combination of the previous levels. The counselor's introspection builds sensitivity and awareness, which elicits the counselor's desire to learn and apply the knowledge and skills responsibly.

Psychologist Kenneth Clark (1963) summarizes the findings of his seminal exploration of racial identity among African Americans by describing the case of a 7-year-old African American child referred to therapy because of severe racial identity confusion. According to Clark, this was not atypical. Black psychiatric patients frequently had delusions involving the denial of their skin color and ancestry. He goes on to suggest, speaking of racism in general, that "the measure of a social injustice is its consequences in the lives of human beings . . . racial prejudices place unnecessary burdens upon human beings, sometimes even distorting and damaging the individual personality" (p. 58).

Few social scientists have or are afforded the opportunity to change national policy and law in the service of social justice through the force of their research and expertise. Clark, Chein, and Cook (2004) and twenty-nine other eminent psychologists did just that in 1952 when they contributed their collective knowledge and prestige to the "Social Science Statement" on the effects of segregation and the consequences of desegregation submitted in the case of *Brown v. Board of Education of Topeka* before the Supreme Court of the United States. The issue in question was whether state laws that enforced racial segregation within public schools were unconstitutional. The gist of their report stated that school segregation was psychologically harmful for both minority and majority group children. For a flavor of what they argued, consider the following excerpts from the Social Science Statement on the psychological impact of school segregation:

> ". . . minority children learn the inferior status to which they are assigned—as they observe the fact that they are almost always segregated and kept apart from others who are treated with more respect by the society as a whole—they often react with feelings of inferiority and a sense of personal humiliation. Many of them become confused about their own personal worth. On the one hand, like all other human beings, they require a sense of personal dignity; on the other hand, almost nowhere in the larger society do they find their own dignity as human beings respected by others. Under these conditions, the minority group child is thrown into a conflict with regard to his feelings about himself and his group.

He wonders whether his group and he himself are worthy of no more respect than they receive. This conflict and confusion leads to self-hatred and rejection of his own group." (p. 496)

"With reference to the impact of segregation and its concomitants on children of the majority group . . . the effects are somewhat more obscure. Those children who learn the prejudices of our society are also being taught to gain personal status in an unrealistic and non-adaptive way. When comparing themselves to members of the minority group, they are not required to evaluate themselves in terms of the more basic standards of actual person ability and achievement. The culture permits and, at times, encourages them to direct their feelings of hostility and aggression against whole groups of people, the members of which are perceived as weaker than themselves. They often develop patterns of guilt feelings, rationalizations, and other mechanisms which they must use in an attempt to protect themselves from recognizing the essential injustice of their unrealistic fears and hatreds of minority groups." (p. 496)

The Supreme Court voted unanimously (9–0) that "separate educational facilities are inherently unequal," and as a result, de jure racial segregation was ruled unconstitutional. This decision led the way to the subsequent integration of public schools and helped launch the Civil Rights Movement. It was clear from the Court's wording of its opinion that the Social Science Statement had played a significant role in their deliberations.

In this chapter, we begin our exploration of culturally sensitive treatment for children by first focusing on issues of child development that have special relevance for minority children, and then move on to review some basic notions of working clinically with children of color, and finally present four examples of contemporary child treatment approaches with in-depth case examples. These include the treatment of *complex trauma* in children and adolescents, a narrative approach to individual psychotherapy, a collective (group) narrative approach called the Tree of Life Exercise for at-risk youth, and a school-based Social Justice Intervention program.

▶ Child Development   7-1

We will begin our exploration of developmental issues related to mental health and treatment needs of children of color and other diverse populations by learning about how differences in cultural temperament are identifiable from birth and form the basis for personality development. We will subsequently explore the development of racial identity in children and see its effects on self-esteem, then learn about cultural and racial issues related to adolescent identity formation, and finally explore differences in cultural learning styles and their impact on academic performance.

Temperament at Birth

It is important to realize that cultural differences appear very early in life, provide a basis for the development of cultural uniqueness, and are highly responsive to cultural differences in parenting practices. The emotional characteristics of children from diverse ethnic and cultural groups, for example, vary greatly from birth (Trawick-Smith, 2013). It is easy to discern dramatic differences in temperament and activity levels of newborns and infants. Freedman (2003) offers the following examples: white babies of Northern European background cry more easily and are harder to console than Chinese babies, who tend to adapt to any position in which they are placed; Navajo babies show even more calmness and adaptability than the Chinese, as they calmly accept being placed on a cradleboard, while white babies cry and struggle to get out of the strapped confinement. Japanese children, in turn, are far more irritable than either the Chinese or the Navajo. Australian aboriginal babies react strongly, like whites, to being disturbed but are more easily calmed.

Differences are also found in the ways mothers and infants interact (Seifer et al., 1994). There is far less verbal interaction between a Navajo mother and baby than between a white mother and baby. The Navajo mother is actually rather silent and gets her baby's attention via eye contact. White mothers talk to their children constantly, and their children respond with great activity. The mothers are equally adept, however, at gaining their children's attention. According to Freedman, the differences result from the continual interplay of inherited genetic predispositions and patterns of cultural conditioning through child-parent interaction. Thus, children's genetic temperamental tendencies are reinforced by cultural learning about the proper way to respond emotionally, and the result is children who increasingly take on the temperamental style of their culture (Garcia Coll, 1990; Scarr, 1993).

Development of Racial Awareness

Children of color face the same developmental tasks as any other children. They are, however, at more risk for experiencing instances of racism and prejudice, which can powerfully impact fragile, developing psyches. As a result, they may exhibit problems navigating certain developmental tasks of childhood because of the preponderance of negative messages that they receive about themselves from the white world. Of particular importance are potential difficulties in developing unconflicted racial identities and internalizing positive self-esteem.

Children of color are aware of racial differences (i.e., differences in skin color and facial and body features) as early as age 3 or 4, and by age 7, one can begin to discern the rudiments of a racial awareness (Aboud, 1988; Grant and Haynes, 1995; Pauker, Apfelbaum, and Spitzer, 2015). Majority-group children, in comparison, are generally slower to develop a consciousness of the fact that they are white because race is not as central to their families' lives as it is to people of color (York, 2016). Although children are aware of racial differences, Weisman, Johnson, and Shutts (2015) explained that gender is a more important social distinction than race in early development. They went on to explain that young children see gender as a more natural and stable category compared to race. They went on to propose that this is a result of humans being born with capability to track gender, not race.

Racial identity evolves in relation to the sequential acquisition of three learning processes. The first is *racial classification ability* (Aboud, 1987; Syed and McLean, 2018; Williams and Morland, 1976) and involves the child's learning to apply ethnic labels accurately to members of diverse groups. For example, in the classic doll studies designed by Clark and Clark (1947) to measure racial identity in African American children, the child is told: "Show me the black doll" or "Show me the white doll" when presented with dolls of different skin tones. The child who can accurately perform such labeling on a regular basis is ready to move on to the next stage of forming a racial identification (Aboud and Doyle, 1993). Simply put, *racial identification* involves a child's learning to apply the newly gained concept of race to himself or herself. According to Proshansky and Newton (1968), this process requires a kind of inner dialogue through which children learn that because of their skin color, they are members of a certain group (i.e., that the child is black or yellow or brown) and, as such, visibly different from others. Thus, racial identification results from an interaction between children's comparisons of their skin color with those of parents, siblings, and others and what they are told about who they are racially. The final stage, which Proshansky and Newton (1968) called *racial evaluation,* involves the creation of an internal evaluation of one's own ethnicity. Racial evaluation develops as a child internalizes the various messages regarding his or her ethnicity received from significant others and society in general. By age 7, most ethnic children are aware of the negative evaluation that society places on members of their group (Syed and McLean, 2018).

▶ Racial Awareness and Self-Esteem 7-2

Early studies of racial awareness by Clark and Clark (1947), Kardiner and Ovesey (1951), and Goodman (1952) found that African American children had difficulty successfully completing the last two stages just described. These children would either deny the fact that their skin was black (as in Scenario 1), devalue people with black skin and black culture in general, or both. In addition, it was found that these same African American children often exhibited negative self-concepts. The authors concluded that such outcomes were inevitable for children of color. By living in a white-dominated society, they could not help but internalize the negative attitudes and messages that bombarded them daily, and the resulting negative self-judgments would inevitably translate into a diminished self-image.

As the ethnic pride movements of the 1960s gained momentum, however, the inevitability of such conclusions was vehemently challenged. Some referred to this early work as the "myth of self-hatred" (Trawick-Smith and Lisi, 1994). Earlier studies were criticized as being methodologically weak or as reflecting an earlier psychological reality that was no longer accurate. New studies showed no differences in self-esteem between African American and white children (Powell, 1973; Rosenberg, 1979). In racially homogeneous settings, in fact, African American children scored higher than their white counterparts (Spenser and Markstrom-Adams, 1990). The more extensive their interaction with whites and the white world, however, the lower their self-concept scores. The accuracy of these newer findings, in turn, was challenged as too conveniently fitting the researchers' political agenda.

Clarifying the Question

In order to bring some clarity to this controversy, Williams and Morland (1976) carried out an empirically sound, longitudinal study of racial identity formation in African American (which they called *Afro*) and white (which they called *Euro*) children over a period of 12 years. The implications of this study are still very much relevant today. Racial identity was assessed in the same cohort by four different measures administered at four different times during the 12-year period: during preschool, third grade, sixth grade, and junior high school. They published the following findings:

▶ With regard to racial classification ability (i.e., accurately applying racial labels to diverse racial groups), Williams and Morland found no differences between Euro and Afro students. Both began regularly classifying race by ages 4 and 5, with high accuracy by 6 years old.

▶ Racial identification (i.e., the ability to apply racial labels accurately to parents and self) was measured by asking children which of the various colored dolls (light- or dark-skinned) looked like them or a parent. Preschool Euro children chose the light-skinned figure 80 percent of the time and the dark-skinned figure 20 percent, whereas Afro preschoolers distributed their choices between the dark- and light-skinned dolls evenly, 50/50. By the third grade, however, the Afro children were also choosing the dark-skinned figures 80 percent of the time, paralleling the differential responses of the same-aged Euro children. By junior high school, both groups were almost 100 percent accurate in their respective choices.

▶ Racial evaluation (i.e., assigning positive evaluation to one's own racial group) was assessed by asking the young subjects to choose a figure (light- or dark-skinned) in response to a description that included a positive or negative adjective (e.g., choose the good parent). Both Euro and Afro preschoolers overwhelmingly assigned the positive features to the light-skinned figures (pro-Euro response) at a rate of 90 percent and 80 percent, respectively. These patterns repeated for both groups through late elementary school. In junior high school, however, the Afro students' responses changed dramatically to pro-Afro (i.e., positive adjectives assigned to dark-skinned figures), ending with a rate equal to that of Euro junior high students.

▶ Racial acceptance (a second measure of racial evaluation) was measured by showing the subjects photos of dark- and light-skinned individuals and asking if they would like to play with this person. Euro preschoolers were significantly less accepting of Afro photos than Afro preschoolers were of Euro photos. In fact, Afro preschoolers accepted Euro pictures slightly more frequently than they did Afro photos. By elementary school and beyond, both Afro and Euro students grew increasingly less accepting of photos of the other group, with Afros always a bit more accepting than Euros.

By way of summary, Williams and Morland (1976) found that by third grade, African American children were appropriately aware of their racial identity, accepted it, and preferred playmates from their own group. They did find African American preschoolers regularly making pro-Euro responses on all measures, which could be interpreted as indicating early identity confusion. The authors, however, attribute this to response bias rather than any underlying pathology, and their interpretation seems to be borne out by the fact that with further socialization, all except one of the measures showed group-appropriate responses by the third grade. Regarding racial evaluation, however, there does seem to be lingering pro-white attitudes among black youth until junior high school, when there is a dramatic reversal to predominantly pro-Afro responses. From these data, it seems likely that African American children do internalize to some extent the attitudes of society at large. But it is not clear from this study whether their pro-Euro preferences can be interpreted as indicative of negative feelings toward themselves or their own group. In any case, the effects are not lasting, and there does not seem to be any concurrent difficulty in racial identification itself. It is probably fair to say, however, that this is a critical period in the developmental life of children of color and may be problematic for the development of self-esteem as long as pro-Euro attitudes linger. A more recent study by Spenser and Markstrom-Adams (1990) supports these conclusions. See Table 7-1 for a summary of Williams and Morland's research. The implications of this study are still very much relevant today. Such studies clearly show that children of color regularly exhibit positive self-esteem and unconflicted racial identities. But this does not mean that racism poses any less risk for them. Additionally, Richardson et al. (2015) found that adolescent African Americans who experience discrimination are at a higher risk for internalizing these experiences if they receive fewer parental supports for negotiating and coping with this discrimination.

TABLE 7-1
Racial Identity Formation in African American and White Children

Measure of Racial Identity	Summary of Findings
Racial classification ability (ability to apply labels accurately to different racial groups)	Develops in both Euro and Afro children by ages 4–5. High accuracy in all children in both groups by age 6.
Racial identification (ability to accurately apply racial labels to parents and self)	In preschool, Euro children exhibit 80 percent Euro response, and Afro children exhibit 50 percent Euro response. By third grade, Euros had 90 percent Euro response and Afros had 80 percent Afro response. By adolescence, both Euros and Afros had 100 percent group-appropriate choices.
Racial evaluation (ability to assign positive evaluation to one's own racial group)	In preschool, Euros exhibit 90 percent pro-Euro responses, and Afros exhibit 80 percent pro-Euro responses. Percentages remain the same until adolescence, when Afro students reverse their preferences to 90 percent pro-Afro.
Racial acceptance (acceptance of playmates of different race)	In preschool, Euros exhibit 50 percent acceptance of Afro playmates, and Afros exhibit 60 percent acceptance of Euro playmates. By third grade, both Euros and Afros show 80 percent preference for own race playmates.

Source: Adapted from *Race, Color, and the Young Child*, by J. E. Williams and J. K. Morland, 1976, Chapel Hill, NC: University of North Carolina Press.

A final perspective on the impact of racism on self-esteem can be gleaned from interviews with people of color who came to the United States as adults after growing up in countries where they were in the racial majority. Only after they had arrived in this country did they have their first personal experiences with prejudice and racism. How did they respond? Their first reported reaction was shock and disbelief. Once they had sufficient time to process what had happened and to label it as a "racial attack," they were able to put up sufficient ego defenses to protect themselves emotionally as well as physically. They quickly learned to identify such situations before or as they happened and to deal with them quickly and effectively. They uniformly believed that it was only because of their own strong sense of self and well-developed ego defenses as adults that they were able to come out of these experiences relatively unharmed. When asked how they might have felt as children facing such experiences, they all indicated that they would have been overwhelmed and likely scarred in some essential way.

▶ Adolescent Racial Identity   `7-3`

In her book *Why Are All the Black Kids Sitting Together in the Cafeteria? And Other Conversations About Race,* Tatum (2017) points out that race and racial identity issues become particularly salient when children of color enter adolescence. Changes in school groupings, dating, and broader participation in the social environment highlight the existence of racism and the need to understand "what it means for *me* to be a Black [person]." With adolescence, there is a greater likelihood of encountering "experiences that may trigger an examination of their racial identity." Boy-girl events and interaction become much less racially diverse, and white peers seem less likely to understand or be able to provide support for the emerging black identities. As a result, adolescents of color gravitate naturally to like-race peers and often adopt an "oppositional stance or identity," absorbing stereotyped images of being of color and rejecting characteristics and behaviors that they see as white. "The anger and resentment that adolescents feel in response to their growing awareness of the systematic exclusion of black people from full participation in U.S. society leads to the development of an oppositional social identity. This... both protects one's identity from the psychological assault of racism and keeps the dominant group at a distance" (p. 60). Tatum sees this attachment to the peer group as a "positive coping strategy" in the face of stress. It is not without its difficulties, however. Images of blackness tend to be highly stereotyped, and academic success is often discounted as white. As we shall see in Chapter 9, this stage of racial identity development entails a turning toward one's own group, and a rejection of the majority and its values is followed by the emergence of greater individualization and diversification of racial identity.

Earlier studies have also found different patterns of personal identity formation across ethnic groups. Hauser and Kasendorf (1983), for example, compared working-class urban African American and white adolescent boys in relation to the development of self-image. Building on the work of Erikson (1968), they explored the manner in which adolescents integrate various images of themselves into a coherent sense of self. For Erikson, adolescence is a time of self-exploration during which one tries to find a comfortable synthesis of past experience, sense of family, current questions and concerns, and hopes and plans for the future.

Hauser and Kasendorf found that African American adolescents formed a stable integration of self-images much earlier than did their white counterparts, who seemed to experience higher levels of confusion, disequilibrium, and personal exploration. In fact, it took the white youth all four years of high school to reach the same level of identity stability as the African American sample accomplished after one or two years. Compared to whites, who exhibited greater variability and flexibility in content, African American adolescents showed a striking sameness in how they saw themselves. According to Erikson's model, the white youth were experiencing "identity progression and moratorium" (i.e., slow but steady movement toward a coherent definition of self, with extensive confusion and time out for exploration). African American adolescents, on the other hand, were exhibiting "identity foreclosure" (i.e., stabilizing identities early, with a premature closing off of possibilities in terms of content).

For many African American youth, rigid and fixed expectations were found in relation to images of themselves as future parents, fantasies of future accomplishment, and availability of positive role models. At the same time, Hauser and Kasendorf (1983) found that, on a daily basis, African American adolescents exhibited great capacity for coping with life. Current images of self-reflected levels of negativity and hopelessness that differed little from those of their white counterparts. Times have changed, and there is clearly greater access across racial and ethnic groups to the financial and social resources that can translate into more positive future expectations for the self. More recent studies continue to demonstrate the detrimental effects that poverty and racism can have on the hopes and possibilities of youth.

A word of caution should also be voiced about cultural differences in models of adolescent development. Erikson's (1968) model has its origins in Northern European culture and reflects a view of adolescence that may not be accurate or appropriate for all groups. Some anthropologists believe that the prolonged period of confusion and moratorium that typifies Western European adolescence is, in fact, a symptom of the loss of relevant rites of passage that are necessary for a firm sense of grounding and future role stability.

Academic Performance and Learning Styles

A final aspect of child development that has special relevance for children of color relates to academic performance in school. Research clearly demonstrates that children of color perform academically at a lower level than their white counterparts in the public school system (Tatum, 2004). Obgu (1978) attributes such differences to institutional racism. He distinguishes three types of ethnic minorities that differ in relation to success in academic performance. "Autonomous" groups, such as Jews, Amish, and Mormons, tend to be small in number and experience prejudice but not widespread oppression. They tend to possess distinctive cultural traits related to academic success, have many successful role models, and do well in academic performance. "Immigrant" groups, such as Koreans and Chinese, come to the United States voluntarily in order to improve their lives, and although the majority culture may view them negatively, they do not hold those views of themselves. Living conditions in the United States are a marked improvement over what they experienced in their countries of origin, and if they were to grow dissatisfied here, they can always return home. In spite of cultural differences, their children perform well in school and on academic tests. The third group, which includes what Obgu calls "caste-like" minorities, includes African Americans, Latinos/as, and Native Americans, and jointly experience disproportionate amounts of school failure. They are the objects of systematic racism and disadvantage both within and outside the schools, and according to Obgu, often view school success not as a path to advancement, but rather as "acting white" or "Uncle Tom" behavior.

A related factor in poor school performance is cultural differences in *learning styles.* Each culture has its characteristic manner of learning, and as children grow, they internalize a given learning style and become progressively more comfortable and proficient in its use. There is much evidence to show that poor school performance among ethnic-group children is related to conflicts in learning style (i.e., the U.S. school system as an institution is based on and rewards a mode of learning that is characteristic of Northern European culture). See, for example, Anderson and Adams (1992) who state those who are unable to adapt or to become comfortable interacting educationally in this mode are clearly at a disadvantage and likely to fail over time. When efforts have been made to adjust classroom interaction to the cultural needs of diverse groups, the results have shown dramatic increases in performance and school success (Wolkind and Rutter, 1985).

Cultural learning styles develop pragmatically. Native Americans, for example, developed a keen sense of visual observation out of necessity and in relation to the environment that was their home. Their survival depended on "learning the signs of nature," and thus observation became a central mode of learning: "watching and listening, trial and error" (Fleming, 1992). In addition, oral tradition is a primary mode of teaching values and traditional attitudes, and such storytelling was often stylized through the use of symbols, anthropomorphizing, and metaphor, a particularly powerful way of teaching complex concepts. Today, according to Fleming, "modern Indian children still demonstrate strengths in their ability to memorize visual patterns, visualize spatial concepts, and produce descriptions that are rich in visual detail and the use of graphic metaphor" (pp. 161–162).

Contrast this with the very different learning paradigm that is emphasized in white schools: auditory learning, conceptualization of the abstract, and a heavy emphasis on language skills. Similarly, African Americans (Hale-Benson, 1986), Hawaiians (Gallimore, Boggs, and Jordan, 1974), and Mexican Americans (Kagen and Madsen, 1972) exhibit learning styles that have a heavy relational component as opposed to the Northern European style, which emphasizes individualism and competition. Mexican American children, for example, are less willing than white students to enter rivalries or competitions or to internalize a drive to perform well to meet teachers' expectations. Similarly, Hawaiian children are not interested in forsaking their strong need to affiliate with peers for a more individualistic modality that reinforces goal-oriented behavior. Although children from these cultures might be able learn to process information in a manner consonant with majority culture, it is counter to their preferred mode of interacting. Simply put, it just feels foreign and unnatural; rather than adapt, most students of color choose to shut down in a variety of ways and thereby exit the formal U.S. education system. The real task of education in a multicultural society is to broaden the dimensions of the classroom in order to make room for the learning styles of all students (Collett and Serrano, 1992). Similarly, human service providers should be aware of optimal learning styles so clients can maximize learning during the helping process.

▶ Some Basic Notions of Child Treatment 7-4

According to Swan, Schottelkorb, and Lancaster (2015), the therapeutic relationship is essential to bridging the cultural gap between the child client and adult counselor. The therapeutic relationship is critically important in multicultural counseling (Sue and Sue, 2012). Swan et. al (2015) went on to claim that because minority children often do not feel empowered, counselors should conduct interventions that allows for these clients to feel in control and experience power. Before exploring some newer and innovative approaches to culturally sensitive child treatment, it may be useful to review certain basic notions about culture and families that have proven useful in clinical work with this population.

Cultural competence in clinical interventions with children of color requires simultaneous attention to a number of variables. Especially important are (1) an expanded definition of family, (2) use of a non-deficit definition of family structure and process, (3) resiliency as a therapeutic goal, (4) the reality of biculturalism in the life experience of most children and families of color:

- A key to understanding and working with families of color is an appreciation for their extreme diversity (especially in relation to mainstream white families). Their form varies from culture to culture. Each culture has different ways of understanding suitable family organization, values, communication, and behavior. For example, Mexican American families share certain general cultural forms. They tend to be hierarchical and male-dominated, religious, traditionally sex-typed, and often bilingual, with deep extended family roots. But to push such generalizations too far is to enter the realm of stereotyping. No two families are ever culturally the same, each internalizes aspects of the group's cultural norms in its own way. Some become very important; others are disregarded. There are a variety of ways ethnic patterns surface in families, including acculturation, class, education, ethnic identity, reason for migration to the United States, language status, geographic location, and stage in the family life cycle when they migrated.
- It is vitally important that cultural differences in family structure and process not be interpreted as cultural deficits.
- In a similar vein, resiliency has become an increasingly important meta-goal in clinical work with children and families of color. Promoting resiliency involves strengthening personal characteristics in the child that will permit better coping in stressful situations. One of the goals of counseling with African American children and youth is to promote coping strategies under unique circumstances. Therefore, one should avoid using

methods that encourage clients to accept their negative environmental circumstances and adapt to such an environment. Methods providing information that promote the effective use of underutilized resources and resources that are typically unattainable within their community should be sought. Help-seeking strategies and greater social mobility will enable them to survive in their environment.

▶ All treatment planning by providers working with children of color should incorporate resiliency-inducing strategies, as well as other forms of empowerment. A further meta-goal that providers should strive to incorporate in work with children of color is comfort and success in dealing with culture conflict and biculturality.

▶ It is valuable to teach children of color to negotiate this duality—that inconsistencies between home and school, for example, are likely to be ongoing realities of the bicultural child's world and that he or she must learn to negotiate them. Rather than unintentionally create a conflict, providers must monitor their own value judgments and treatment goals regularly so as not to undermine the children's ability to tolerate the inconsistency between home and school.

▶ There are a number of specific intervention skills that are particularly useful in working cross-culturally such as:

 ▶ Understanding the child's ethnicity, race, language, social class, and differences in minority status, such as refugees, immigrants, and native born; and making use of the worker's own culture or ethnicity and professional culture.

 ▶ Discussing openly racial or ethnic differences and issues and responding to culturally based cues; and adapting to the child's interactive style and language, conveying that the worker understands, values, and validates his or her life strategies.

 ▶ Identifying the ecosystemic sources (racism, poverty, prejudice) of a minority child's problems; and considering the implications of what is being suggested in about each child's cultural reality (unique dispositions, life strategy, and experiences).

 ▶ Reaffirming the child's life skills and coping strategies within a bicultural environment; and applying new strategies that are consistent with the child's needs and problem, degree of acculturation, motivation for change, and comfort in responding to the worker's directives.

 ▶ Assessing the accomplishment of therapeutic goals according to the child's collectivist culture; and assisting the child to incorporate the new changes into the child's original life strategy independent of the worker's interaction.

Contemporary Examples of Culturally Sensitive Treatment: Working with Complex Trauma in Children and Adolescents

The following section on trauma treatment for children and adolescents was contributed by Tracy Smith, Psy.D. Tracy is a graduate of The Wright Institute, Berkeley, CA, in clinical psychology and now serves as Program Coordinator of The Wright's School-Based Collaboration (SBC) with the Oakland Unified School District (OUSD). The SBC's mission is to foster academic and life success in children who concurrently suffer from discrimination, violence, racism, and poverty, as well as disproportionate levels of complex trauma. Tracy begins her presentation with a description of the psychology and dynamics of complex trauma in children and adolescents and then demonstrates how these issues play out in the real life of a child by presenting a case study of Malani, an 8-year-old Samoan American girl who suffers from complex trauma.

Traumatic experience can best be described as extreme stress that involves intense fear, feelings of helplessness, and a sense of being overpowered and out of control. It is experienced by the client as overwhelming, overstimulating, extremely painful, and terrifying, and such trauma results in a felt sense of internal threat of severe injury to self or others, profound loss, and even death. The more severe and prolonged the trauma, the more severe and disruptive its symptoms. In addition, its unpredictability and the sufferer's loss of inner control leave the client feeling intensely fearful, alone, and unable to escape. In addition, the client experiences guilt and shame, a loss of trust in others, and a decreased sense of personal safety. Finally, and especially in children and adolescents, there is a breakdown in the capacity to regulate internal states and meet developmental tasks integral to their growth (Cohen, Mannarino, and Deblinger, 2006; Cook et al., 2005; van der Kolk, 2003; van der Kolk, van der Hart, and Marmar, 1996; van der Kolk et al., 1996).

Some acute traumatic experiences result from singular events that are limited in time and place, such as serious accidents or natural disasters. For purposes of this section, however, we will be speaking more specifically about complex trauma, which occurs over long periods of time. Complex trauma is defined as the dual problem of exposure to traumatic events and the impact of this exposure on immediate and long-term outcomes (Cook et al., 2017). It involves the repeated exposure (internal and external) to traumatic stress and is also conceived as a series of many traumatic events that happen within the caregiving system, which is the source of safety and stability in a child's life (Cook et al., 2017).

Such trauma may occur in the contexts of home, school, community, and the world at large, and the many causes include (a) emotional, sexual, and physical abuse; (b) neglect; (c) the witnessing of domestic violence; (d) traumatic loss; (e) physical and sexual assault or rape; (f) sexual maltreatment; (g) community violence; (h) prolonged or severe medical illness; and (i) the ravages of war, terrorism, political violence, and historical trauma (e.g., genocide, racism, discrimination). However, in addition to what we traditionally conceive of as traumatic events in the lives of children and adolescents, complex trauma's chronic and often interpersonal nature tends to intensify the constant worry, vulnerability, and felt stress experienced by its young victims.

The impact of complex trauma extends beyond the narrower definition of PTSD (avoidance, re-experiencing, hyperarousal) and can result in revictimization and cumulative traumas. Moreover, its symptoms in the lives of children and adolescents tend to impact a broader range of functioning, much of which may not be readily traceable to the trauma itself. For children and adolescents, trauma occurs within the context of ongoing development. As a result, much of the behavior resulting from trauma can be subsumed, misunderstood, or ignored because it is viewed as a part of childhood. Because as adults and clinicians we are often primed to focus on behavior—and more specifically, negative behavior in children and adolescents—we may overlook the traumatic root causes of the behavior, especially if we do not perceive it as a typical response to trauma. For example, take a child who laughs when he or she experiences physical pain or is hurt or when someone else is in pain or has been hurt; it may register to an adult that this kind of response is inappropriate to the situation, but it may not register in the adult's mind that this child may be a victim of ongoing physical abuse and that, in fact, showing signs of pain, hurt, or weakness would result in further victimization for that child. In addition, with no one around to protect or sooth this child or adolescent, he or she has had to learn that feeling sad, hurt, or angry is futile and possibly more dangerous to the child's survival while laughing and pretending to be "okay" reduces feelings of intense fear and vulnerability. This way of responding might also have the added "benefit" of encouraging others around them to laugh (at their expense) or stop hurting them. In recent studies, for example, children and adolescents in crisis situations have reported that they feel deep inner pain that registers in similar ways in the brain as physical pain (Cohen, Mannarino, and Deblinger, 2006). The pain resulting from complex trauma is quite palpable, both internally and externally, even if we as observers do not see it or hear about it.

In children experiencing complex trauma, much of the suffering goes unnoticed and is eclipsed by the behavioral manifestations. This is particularly true in schools and in clinical settings where diagnoses such as the following are routinely given to these children: depressions, ADHD, ODD, Conduct Disorder, Generalized Anxiety Disorder, Separation Anxiety Disorder, and Reactive Attachment Disorder (Cook et al., 2017). In working clinically with traumatized children, their behavior becomes more salient. It is easier for them to express and communicate what is going on internally through behavior and often the only way children have of letting us know that they are distressed. However, the behavior, when looked at through the lens of trauma, is quite off task when compared with a child who has not experienced trauma.

In this way, it makes sense that we focus on behavior, but it also means that we sometimes miss what is going on internally, especially in those children or adolescents who are "internalizers." With this in mind, NCTSN suggested that the above-listed disorders are, in fact, valid descriptions of various aspects of a child's experience (of the child's environment and relationships), although not the child's entire presentation.

I would also add that our ability as clinicians to focus on the experience of trauma (e.g., anxiety, depression, problems with attachment and regulation, low self-esteem, acting-out behaviors, and reduced ability to attend), rather than the diagnosis of the responses to trauma is critical. Unfortunately, this focus can be negatively impacted by a number of sources, including pressures from insurance reimbursements, parental agendas, and the teacher's or clinician's own experience of trauma or personal biases and beliefs about children's development.

What research on childhood trauma does tell us about working with these children—in the classroom or in therapy—is that they experience certain significant areas of impairment in functioning, which are most important to look at. These include the general domains of self-regulation (the ability to identify, modulate, and appropriately express emotion), attachment (the ability to form and maintain positive and purposeful relationships), competency (the ability to experience success and self-esteem), and the following areas of impairment: (a) difficulty with emotional self-regulation, (b) difficulty knowing and describing feelings and internal experiences and states, (c) difficulty communicating wishes and desires, (d) poor modulation of impulses, (e) self-destructive behavior, (f) difficult attachment patterns, (g) behavioral regression, and (h) an increase in risky behaviors. The following behaviors may also be observed in traumatized children and adolescents and should be important areas of focus: (a) aggression, (b) disturbances in sleep, (c) poor self-soothing behaviors (e.g., head banging), (d) difficulties in attention and regulation, (e) indiscriminate affections, (f) problems with executive functioning, (g) learning difficulties, (h) low self-esteem, (i) somatic problems, (j) non-age-appropriate behavior, (k) sexualized behaviors, (l) overwhelming feelings of shame and guilt, (m) depression, (n) hopelessness, (o) anxiety, (p) fear, (q) insecurity—and more so in older youth, (r) eating disorders and (s) substance abuse (Kinniburgh et al., 2017).

In addition, what makes complex trauma particularly detrimental for children and adolescents is that it occurs within the context of their ongoing development. Children are endowed with certain strengths and limitations, and these are in turn shaped by their experiences and environment. It is possible that an entirely different developmental trajectory can result from the events of complex trauma; that is, it can literally change a child or adolescent's life. A major concern in this regard is possible disruptions in development that the child might experience: for example, acting younger or older than the child's biological age. Second, these disruptions compound over time as long as the trauma and its symptoms continue to go unrecognized and untreated.

That is, with each year the trauma is not dealt with, the child's developmental skills fall further behind, and the child must work overtime just to "catch up" in response to both the traumatic experience and the tasks appropriate to the child's age group. The loss or impairment of developmental skills means that the child or adolescent may well miss out on a significant amount of age-appropriate learning, especially in the realms of academics and learning about relationships and appropriate behavior for different settings. This working "overtime" often causes frustration, and with this added stressor, the child may learn inappropriate responses to many situations, whether social, interpersonal, academic, or emotional. Thus, a lack of success in such situations is continually reinforced. Over time, these developmental skills are, at best, only partially mastered. This in turn leaves the developing child or adolescent ill-equipped to manage life's circumstances and relationships, as well his or her ongoing intrusive trauma symptoms.

Another component of complex trauma—which causes it to become increasingly epidemic in the lives of children and adolescents—is the fact that many parents continue to suffer from their own traumatic experiences. As a result, they are often unable to provide, or have difficulty providing, safe and consistent environments for their child. Further, they lack insight and understanding of the child's traumatic experience and how to deal with it. Also, the parents themselves may be the perpetrators of the child's trauma. Research has shown that "the family plays a crucial role in determining how the child adapts to experiencing trauma" (Cook et al., 2016, p. 16). Without the presence of a caring and functional adult to help the child or adolescent understand and contextualize his or her traumatic experiences—as well as model healthy interactions— there can be little hope for growth and healing. In Bowlby's (1951, 1969, 1980) early research on attachment, he found that children learn to regulate their behavior by the interactions (call and response) and patterns established between them and their caregivers. This call-and-response pattern between children and their caregivers allows them to feel safe, learn to trust what they feel, have confidence in themselves and others, and it also impacts how the child understands the outside world.

As we reflect further on complex trauma and the disruptions it can cause in the developing child and adolescent, it quickly becomes apparent that such experiences may weigh especially heavily and translate differently for children of color and children living in poverty. For these children, the cost of these impairments or deficits in cognition, language, and motor and social skills is compounded by a lack of resources in other areas. Further, it has the potential to have an avalanche effect on poor and minority children and adolescents. For example, in the realm of biology, the effects of early malnutrition as a result of poverty may become compounded by health, behavioral, and academic difficulties. This level of "being overwhelmed" in turn further exacerbates any existing parental or family stress. The potential for lifelong distress in such situations is very high.

In the arena of cognition, one is reminded that our brain first deals with information important to survival, placing less emphasis on tasks higher up the needs hierarchy. Thus, for a child who is in a constant state of pursuing survival, focusing in the classroom can be difficult. Further, excessive or prolonged activation of the stress response systems in the body (e.g., producing high levels of cortisol), particularly in the brain, has deleterious effects on learning, behavior, and health across the lifespan.

It is also difficult to speak about complex trauma without thinking about resilience. What we once thought of as an elusive combination on "luck and will" is present in us all. Brendtro and Longhurst (2005) noted that "the term *resilient* comes from physics. A resilient object is one that bends under stress but then springs back rather than breaks" (p. 52). Researchers who have studied resilience also believe that stressed objects become even stronger; they also suggest that at the core of resilience are feelings of accomplishment that result from dealing with difficult and challenging life experiences. For some children, however, such experiences come too early and too often, and we are well aware that such "resilience" comes at a cost. However, a support system made up of both internal and external resources when available can do much to alleviate some of the cost. The development of resilience is intimately tied to the role of family, community, and school support. Positive attachments in a child's life can help alleviate the overwhelming and damaging effects of complex trauma, and such attachments do not always have to occur in the parental relationship. Such positive and healing connections can be made with other emotionally supportive, caring, consistent, and competent adults in the family and in the community, including teachers and therapists. Finally, when thinking about treatment and support for traumatized individuals, as adults, we want to ensure safety in their environment, development of skills in emotional regulation, development of positive and meaningful interpersonal relationships, enhanced resiliency, and the ability to make meaning of past traumatic events (Cohen, Mannarino, and Deblinger, 2006). These, ultimately, are the goals of our program. We accomplish this by providing general support, respect, and care for these traumatized individuals, as well as providing structure and predictability. And we also accomplish this by listening and accepting their feelings, allowing for a range of emotions and expression, and by helping them cope with their difficult daily realities and circumstances. The following case study of Malani is illustrative of a child who has experienced complex trauma.

Case of Malani. Malani is an 8-year-old Samoan American girl who lives in a small, cramped apartment with her biological mother, Ajola, her mother's boyfriend and sister (Malani's aunt), and two younger cousins. Malani was born in the United States, and although some of her relatives live in the U.S., most still live in Samoa. Ajola became pregnant with Malani at a very young age, and as result, was disowned by her family and Malani's biological father. The pregnancy and subsequent refusal of Malani's father to acknowledge the pregnancy brought shame to Ajola and her family. For this reason, Ajola found a way to immigrate to the U.S. with the hope of beginning a new life.

However, during the immigration process, Ajola experienced a series of severe traumas, and she likely experienced trauma while still in Samoa. Consequently, Ajola became clinically depressed. Malani was born preterm at eight months and remained in the hospital for six weeks. During this time, Ajola suffered from postpartum depression, and because she found it difficult to care for and bond with her new baby, she seldom visited Malani. Thus, Malani spent most of her first weeks of life with the hospital staff rather than with her mother. Ajola's postpartum depression persisted such that she continued to have difficulty feeding and providing basic care for Malani. Further, Ajola resisted reaching out to her family in the U.S., so she struggled to procure basic needs (e.g., food) and support in her new role as a mother.

After a few months, the extended family living in the U.S. found out about Ajola's child and the difficulties she was having, and they provided some support to Ajola, both financially and practically by helping Ajola take care of the baby. This provided much relief to Malani and Ajola. However, when Malani reached toddlerhood, their living situation changed dramatically. At this time, because of financial hardships, their only option was to move in with an aunt (Ajola's sister) and her two young children. Further complicating the situation, Ajola's sister was involved in a volatile relationship that often turned violent, and both she and her boyfriend used drugs intermittently, often in Malani's presence. It was also reported that, while intoxicated, a friend of the couple might have inappropriately touched Malani. Ajola felt powerless to help herself or Malani, and her depression recurred.

In second grade, Malani was recommended for counseling at her elementary school, and it was at this time that much of this information was learned from Ajola. Until this time, neither mother nor daughter had been in treatment. The school made its recommendation based on Malani's behaviors, which included yelling, screaming, throwing furniture, and hitting peers when she became upset. In these moments, Malani was difficult to deal with—if not impossible to calm down—and she would continue to lash out at whoever was attempting to help her. As a result, Malani missed valuable classroom instruction time because she had to be removed from the class for her own safety and the safety of her peers. In addition, she felt isolated in the classroom as her peers were unable to connect with her. Ajola attended many meetings at the school in an attempt to help solve these persistent problems. Malani's level of dysregulation was deeply concerning to all involved. At home, Ajola reported similar behaviors from Malani but with less frequency and intensity, and she was somewhat perplexed by the intensity of Malani's behavior at school.

Malani was provided individual therapy for the school year, and her degree of acting-out behaviors significantly decreased over the course of the year. It also became clear during this treatment that Malani struggled most during periods of transition, such as returning to school after the weekend and afterschool breaks.

Malani was referred for a second year of individual counseling, which was provided in conjunction with family therapy (consisting of Malani, Ajola, and Ajola's boyfriend). At first, Ajola was open to the idea of family therapy, but it became increasingly difficult for her once the therapist began to focus on the difficulties in her own early life. It also became apparent during this second year that Malani had experienced a significant amount of neglect and stress due to her mother's postpartum depression and her exposure to domestic violence and drug use, which caused her to feel unsafe. In addition, the inconsistencies in the adult relationships at home led to her own difficulties obtaining the support she needed to learn to manage her interactions with other adults and peers at school. Moreover, Malani's inability to look to her mother for guidance and support in managing her own difficult feelings as a result of her stressors (at home and school) made reaching out to and trusting other adults almost impossible. Her ability to self-regulate and also rely on her mother to help her in these situations was also compromised. These skills of self-regulation and learning to rely on and trust others, which are essential to children as they mature, are generally learned early on from caregivers. These skills help children stay on task, learn to love, develop empathy and trust, as well as foster self-esteem to flourish in life. These skills also help children function at home, at school, and most of all, in their relationships. Ajola's own trauma had made it difficult for her to seek out support from others, which she needed to provide an appropriate level of parenting, support, and modeling for Malani.

This case example illustrates the impact of trauma on the family unit, which directly and often intensely impacts the children in the household. It also illustrates the many areas of a child or adolescent's life that can be impacted: relationships, home life, academics, and classroom behavior. In Malani's case, further areas would likely have been impacted without intervention. However, positive outcomes were obtained by the combined efforts of mother, stepfather, classroom teacher, and family liaison to address Malani's academic and behavior issues.

▶ Narrative Collective Practice: The Tree of Life Exercise   7-5

The narrative approach has also been adapted for use with children in group and collective settings. Ncazelo Ncube and David Denborough (2006), for example, developed the Tree of Life exercise in response to the experience of vulnerable children in Southern Africa. The Tree of Life is a group experience that "enables vulnerable children to speak about their lives in ways that make them stronger. It also enables them to collectively speak about difficulties they are experiencing and share skills and knowledge in ways of dealing with these." It embraces narrative practices to help generate a "second story" that is more hopeful, sustaining, and empowering by focusing on individual strengths and skills and less pathologizing and self-blaming by stressing resources, the full picture of their lives, and collectivizing their experiences.

The Tree of Life is divided into four parts: the Tree of Life, the Forest of Life, the Storms of Life, and Celebration: Certificates and Song. It optimally takes place over several days, held in a setting away from the children's home environment and can accommodate twelve to twenty children. Each stage is facilitated by a leader trained in the method, and involves a series of exercises, followed by a processing by the whole group of what had just been done.

Stage One: The Tree of Life. The children are asked to think of their lives as a tree and its various parts: its roots, the ground, its trunk, its leaves, and its fruit. Each part represents the following aspect of their lives. *Roots* are comprised of where they come from, family history, ancestry, extended family, who taught them about life. The *ground* represents where they are currently living and the activities they engage in each day. The *trunk* represents the skills and abilities that they possess, including both work (such as cooking and sewing) and social (sharing, acts of kindness, and self-care). *Branches* are their hopes, dreams, wishes, and the direction they want their lives to go in. *Leaves* represent important people in their lives and whom they love and value— both alive and dead. *Fruit* is the gifts that one has received from people: support, love, etc. The children are given a sheet of paper with an outline of "this tree" and are asked to fill in all the above information on their Tree of Life, and in so doing, begin to rewrite their individual stories.

Stage Two: The Forest of Life. Children are next asked to put their trees on the walls of the room where everyone can see them and then asked one by one to tell the entire group about their tree stories. When this is done, they are next asked to go up to other children's trees and write words of encouragement and support for those whose stories they had just heard, especially as they relate personally to those stories. At this point, the children are asked how it felt to have others make such supporting and encouraging comments about their stories. In this and subsequent discussions, it is critical that the facilitator move to a mode of discussion that takes the focus away from individual lives and problems and instead speak of issues in the "third person," allowing for greater perspective on each child's life issues and processes. At the same time, as stressing life problems as collective rather than individual, strengths and abilities are increasingly the object of focus.

Stage Three: The Storms of Life. The next phase in the metaphor involves looking at the bad things that can happen to the tree stories in life, but within the broader, more balanced perspective that has been developed. Just as trees in the forest are not free from danger, disease, or hazards, neither are the lives of children. A number of questions are raised for group discussion in this regard. What kind of difficult and "bad" things happen to children that you know? What strengths and resources do children have to bring to bear in such difficult times? What sustains "you" and others you know at these difficult times of life? A final question and revisioning have to do with just how much of one's life is focused on these difficult periods exclusively. In looking back across your lives, are things always bad all the time or just sometimes? What about the good and peaceful times in your life? Again, a broader, more balanced perspective is encouraged in restoring wholeness in these children's lives.

Stage Four: Celebration: Certificates and Song. The Tree of Life exercise ends with a celebration of what has been accomplished by these young people, as well as a variety of efforts to reinforce the learning and re-storying that has occurred and prepare them for going back home. As part of their final discussion, they are asked to brainstorm about what it will be like for them returning to their home community and ways to keep their learning and excitement alive. As part of the final process, they are given certificates of accomplishment, asked to write letters home to their families to be read to them upon returning from the workshop, and to choose and sing a group song that captures the feelings and sentiments that they experienced in the Tree of Life exercise.

Each child's certificate is customized to his or her own issues and situation. Throughout the process of the Tree of Life exercise, staff takes notes about each child's life experiences, strengths and abilities, and hopes and dreams in order to individualize the certificates. For many of the children, this will be the first certificate of accomplishment they have ever received. To inform and bring loved ones and family members into the process that the children have been experiencing, letters are written summarizing what the children have learned about themselves and what they hope to become. These are to be read to the family upon returning home. Finally, the group song and the discussion around what song to choose to encapsulate and capture what happened to them during the Tree of Life exercise provide yet another opportunity to talk about what has happened, as well as a transitional object for the children to take home with them.

Again, throughout these closing exercises, reminders and tools for transferring the learning from the training site to the child's home environment are introduced. Follow-up activities and reunions are also possible ways to reinforce learning and connection between the group of young people who have shared the experience.

▶ School-Based Social Justice Intervention Program   7-6

The following section on school-based intervention programs, adapted from Waterman and Walker (2009) with an integrated social justice approach to working with youth of color, was contributed by Mahtab Moaveni, a second-year student in clinical psychology at The Wright Institute, Berkeley, with a strong interest and experience in working with youth from marginalized communities.

The school-based group therapy program I will be describing was aimed at working with youth at risk for academic, behavioral, and emotional difficulties. It encouraged greater achievement and social-emotional growth by helping students build on personal strengths and potential rather than merely addressing external challenges they faced. The program was based on an integration of cognitive behavioral psychoeducational models aimed at building and promoting competence, growth, and change through the development of insight and specific skills. Topics addressed included interpersonal conflict resolution, effective communication skills, peer pressure and gang resistance, and academic achievement. It also addressed ethnic identity and discrimination as well as psychological and emotional processing of trauma, including chronic exposure to community violence and family stress. Consistent with the multi-dimensionality of the program, it also integrated aspects of social justice theory in working with at-risk, historically marginalized populations. When working with disenfranchised communities, it is crucial to name and acknowledge the oppression and injustices that impact the lives of these children and their families on a daily basis. For example, I remember a group discussion in which one student talked about the shooting and murder of an older sibling. In particular, she commented on how long it took for the police to get to the scene, and once there—after labeling it as gang-related—[the police] did nothing to pursue the perpetrators. For this young student, unsolved cases of young men of color senselessly murdered and never followed up on was a common experience. As one listens to these kinds of stories, it is imperative to pay attention to and recognize the existence of the various layers of power, privilege, injustice, and oppression at work in the lives of these young people. The ability to consider, integrate, and exercise cultural sensitivity—both conceptually and practically—is essential when working with culturally disenfranchised communities.

As a group co-facilitator, my role was to help create a safe place where these kids could feel comfortable disclosing stressful events that were occurring in their lives. Through various activities and discussions, group members were encouraged to share experiences and feelings and find support from other members who could relate to what they were saying. In other words, my role was to mentor this group of kids— to help them process the various traumatic experiences that they were dealing with and provide them the emotional support that was often missing in their environment. When necessary, I provided individual counseling to students that was supportive and strength-based in nature. There were certain issues that students did not want to bring up in the group for fear of being stigmatized, retaliated against, or simply because they may be too intimidated or embarrassed to speak of them in front of others.

I also supported students by doing collateral work with their parents, families, and teachers. Collateral work with teachers involved teaching them different strategies for relating to the students. For example, during group sessions, I was able to identify each child's particular strengths and abilities and reinforced these. When I met with their teacher, I pointed these out and encouraged them to also play to their strengths in the classroom. This allowed the child to develop a more positive sense of self by having their strengths and abilities acknowledged by different adults in different settings. A final aspect of my job was to advocate for and empower students and their families both within the school and the broader community. This included explaining parents their rights, providing them with information and resources, and referring them to community services as needed. Examples of resources include food banks, daycare services, housing, immigration assistance, and ESL classes. Hopefully, these efforts served to empower families to take action and improve their current situations as well as provide—along with the teachers— the kinds of ongoing support and attention I had been modeling for them on a long-term basis for their children.

One final thought before going on to the case of Raul. In order to build rapport with these students from the beginning, it was very helpful to actually introduce myself and the program to the children and invite them by asking if they were interested in participating rather, than telling them they must join. The idea behind this was to give these youth agency in the process. I liked to tell them from the beginning that they were not in trouble but rather that their teacher and I believed that they would make strong candidates for group work and would really benefit from being a part of this group because we would be talking about issues that particularly concerned and affected them.

Case of Raul. Raul, a seventh-grade student of Latino descent, was referred to therapy by his teacher. She reported that he refused to work in class, had low grades, did not turn in homework, was easily angered, and exhibited frequent outbursts that disturbed class and caused other students to lose focus. His mother was very concerned about him and his tendency to lash out and become violent at home. Raul was also conflicted about his behavior and occasionally expressed remorse after acting out. He described himself as suffering from anger management problems and openly acknowledged his mother's fear of and inability to control him.

During our first session, Raul would not make eye contact and remained slouched in his chair. My strategy in working with him was to remain calm and relaxed, show deep interest in what he was saying, and invite him to talk about the realities of his world, his daily experiences, and his culture. This provided me with an opportunity to gain a deeper understanding of his world and allowed him the opportunity to teach another who was genuinely interested in learning from him. Over time, Raul became more and more comfortable with me. I felt it important to show him that he was capable of forming a positive relationship with another adult who treated him with dignity and respect. Even when he was unable to attend individual therapy during periods of suspension (which occurred several times over the course of the year), I conducted weekly phone sessions with him for consistency.

A major goal in working with Raul was to help him learn to deal with his anger in a constructive manner. We spent time identifying triggers for the anger, typical modes of dealing with it, consequences, and alternatives behaviors. We role-played triggering situations with peers and teachers to practice alternative, non-confrontational, and positive ways of expressing his feelings. I also paraphrased his typical language back to him by way of highlighting it for him. Raul was especially responsive to this technique. I also worked with him to change the language and word choice he used to describe himself. Often, disenfranchised youth are constantly told that they are "bad," "violent," "angry," "stupid," "a problem child," etc. These labels become internalized to the point that they become self-fulfilling prophecies. Raul had been told from an early age that he had "anger management problems" and came to act it out and use it as a descriptor of self. I would interrupt him whenever he spoke of himself in this manner and suggest that he reframe it more positively, such as "I have a lot of energy that is not being expressed in the best way." In so doing, I hoped he would begin to view himself more positively. Raul also showed an interest in sports, so I actively encouraged him to join such activities to channel energy in more constructive ways. He eventually did so.

At the same time, I worked closely with his teacher to reinforce positive rather than negative behavior in the classroom. At first, the only attention he got was when he was acting out, which, in turn, merely served to negatively reinforce that sort of behavior. I therefore encouraged her to notice, praise, and reinforce any and all positive contribution that Raul made in the class, no matter how small.

I met regularly with Raul's parents, scheduling meetings at their convenience since both worked several jobs in order to provide for the family. We were joined by a Latina female staff member as translator. Although both parents understood basic English, it was imperative that they fully understand our work with Raul and the purposes of us meeting with them, the psychoeducation materials I presented, and any referral we would make for additional services in our role as advocates for the patients and their family.

I began each meeting by telling Raul's parents how much I enjoyed working with their son and described in detail the strengths I noticed in him beginning family meetings on a positive note is extremely important when working with marginalized youth because many times their parents are so used to receiving negative comments about their child and their academic performance that positive feedback really gets their attention and provides them with an important sense of hope and optimism. I let them know we will all be working as a team to give Raul the support he needs in changing his behavior. I began to work with them on setting limits, following through with consequences when rule-breaking occurs, and especially reinforcing positive instead of negative behavior to be consistent with what he is learning in individual therapy. An equally important goal was to empower Raul's parents. I explained to them that they had the right to inquire about what is happening to their son at school without fearing negative consequences and also that it would not jeopardize his situation if they ask about alternatives to suspension or different ways to discipline Raul when he misbehaves. I worked as a liaison between the school principal and Raul's family to open and increase communication. In time, his parents expressed interest in getting additional mental health services for the family. I researched and made appropriate referrals to an affordable community mental health clinic.

A final goal of the school-based group therapy project was to help students set higher educational aspirations as well as address barriers to academic success. Too often, postsecondary education seems far out of reach for disenfranchised youth. The following incident shows just how powerful a supportive experience and a little extra effort can be in working with these young people. A field trip to a local university was planned for students in Raul's class, but he was unable to attend. I decided to organize a separate trip to the campus for Raul and his older brother. We were accompanied by a Latino male who was a student at the university. This trip turned out to be a very powerful experience for both Raul and his older brother because the Latino student was able to relate to them in ways that I never could. He told them about the kinds of support and financial aid that existed for students of color on campus, their right to a public higher education, about his own struggles and pressures with being a male of color, and the injustices that he had encountered on campus. In addition, he offered support, information, and guidance and even directly connected Raul's older brother for help with the application process. As we walked around campus, Raul's brother, clearly moved by the student's encouragement, shared that he had at times considered college but was not really sure that he belonged there, but he was now much more motivated to apply. He was especially amazed by the services and clubs and organizations available to people "from his background," information that was clearly surprising and new to him.

Raul, for his part, has continued to improve his behavior because of all the structures that have been put in place to help him. I believe this case shows the importance of working across systems, including the individual child, the family, the school, and various community organizations, rather than treating the child in isolation. The more comprehensive the approach, the better the student will be supported. An integral part of the therapy and advocacy also involved honoring and validating Raul's story, his family's story, their cultural context, and the realization and understanding that a child like Raul needs an entire community to support his efforts.

SUMMARY

The chapter begins with a review of the 1952 U.S. Supreme Court case of *Brown vs. Board of Education of Topeka* in which the Court found that racial segregation of children in public schools was unconstitutional and needed to cease. A major aspect of the case was the presentation of what has become known as the "Social Science Statement," a statement by Clark, Chein, and Cook (2004) and twenty-nine eminent psychologists to the deleterious psychological impact of school segregation on both minority and majority children. It is believed that the Social Science Statement played a significant role in the Court's deliberation. This decision led to the subsequent integration of public schools, helped launch the Civil Rights Movement, and represents a significant national contribution to the mental health of children of color in U.S. history.

We next turned to a review of various issues of child development that appear especially influential in the lives of children of color. From birth, characteristics and development of children vary greatly across ethnic groups. Differences in reactivity, temperament, and mother-child interactions are most prominent. Children of color are aware of racial differences as early as age 3; majority-group children are slower to develop awareness of their whiteness. Early studies suggested that children of color exhibited negative self-concepts and lower self-esteem (Clark and Clark, 1947). The "myth of self-hatred" has been challenged by subsequent researchers, such as Williams and Morland (1976). Studies of personal identity formation in adolescence show that African American youth formed stable integration of self-images much earlier than did white youth, although they also exhibited identity foreclosure, a sign of premature closing of the possibilities of who they could become. Children of color show higher achievement scores when they learn activities that are culturally relevant to their life experiences and when learning strategies fit cultural learning styles.

Cultural sensitivity in therapeutic interventions with children depends on the following: an expanded definition of family, use of a non-deficit definition of families and children, resiliency as a therapeutic goal, and acknowledgment of biculturality in the life experience of families and children of color. Four different approaches to ethnic child treatment are discussed and case examples provided, including the treatment of complex trauma in children and adolescents, a narrative approach to individual psychotherapy, the Tree of Life Exercise, and a school-based Social Justice Intervention program.

ACTIVITIES

1. *Explore the psychological experience of being different.* Although you can do this by yourself, it works well to pair off with a partner and take turns answering the following questions:

   ‣ What is your earliest memory of encountering someone who was different from you? See if you can briefly go back to it. Who was there? What was happening? What were you feeling? Stay with your recollection for a moment.
   ‣ What is your earliest memory of feeling yourself as different? See if you can briefly go back there. Who was there? What was happening? What were you feeling? Stay with your recollection for a moment.

- When growing up, in what ways did you feel different?
- In what ways do you feel different today?
- In what ways do you feel challenged as a helping professional by the racial or ethnic differences of a client, the personal experience of "being different" that clients report as part of their life experiences, or your clients' voicing feelings that they experience you as different from them?

2. *Compare and contrast the four child therapy approaches and related cases described in this chapter.* Individually, in pairs, or in small groups, take turns answering the following questions:

- What do you see as the strengths and weaknesses of the different approaches?
- To which approaches are you personally drawn, and which, if any, are you put off by? Why?
- With which, if any, of the case studies would you have identified as a child? Explain.

CHAPTER

8

Bias in Service Delivery

LEARNING OBJECTIVES

8-1 Recognize the impact of social, political, and racial attitudes in service delivery.

8-2 Understand and appraise the importance of cultural representation in the professions.

8-3 Explain the cultural significance of the usage of traditional healers.

8-4 Evaluate and support cultural aspects of mental health service delivery.

8-5 Identify bias in assessment and diagnosis.

8-6 Use the differences in suicide rates in ethnic groups to create support and awareness.

The following case study of a Navajo male who was diagnosed psychotic, first described by Jewell (1965), is a classic example of cross-cultural misunderstanding and bias in the delivery of mental health services.

CASE STUDY 1

Bill was a 26-year-old Navajo man who had been hospitalized as psychotic in a California state mental hospital for 18 months. Little was known about him on admission. He had been jailed for bothering a woman dressed in white (he had mistaken her for a nurse) on a street corner in Barstow. He was taken for Mexican and placed in the jail's psychopathic ward when he did not respond to the questions of a Spanish-speaking interpreter. He appeared "anguished," kept repeating the phrase "Me sick," was diagnosed as a schizophrenic, catatonic type by the medical examiner, and was eventually sent to the state hospital. There, he was taken to be Filipino, but he did not respond to questions in that language either. He appeared "confused, dull, and preoccupied," kept repeating the phrase "I don't know," seemed anguished, and was believed to be hallucinating. He was again diagnosed as schizophrenic, this time the hebephrenic type, which was altered back to catatonic two months later when a psychiatrist tested him and found *cerea flexibilitas*. He was very quiet, appeared withdrawn and sleepy (there is no mention of the medication that was probably administered), and would rouse himself only for eating and personal care.

He would periodically approach staff in broken English and, pointing at his chest repeat: "Me, no good in here." He would also at regular intervals ask: "Can I go home?" Eight months after admission, D. P. Jewell, a psychology intern at the hospital who had been testing Bill, managed to discover his true ethnicity and was able to find a professional Navajo interpreter. Bill talked freely with the interpreter and expressed appreciation for being able to converse in his native tongue.

His answers to questions indicated that he was experiencing no hallucinations, delusions, or other manifestations of schizophrenic thinking, and according to the interpreter, who had extensive experience interviewing young Navajos in strange environments, "Bill's behavior and attitudes were not unusual under the circumstances." He was subsequently released to a Native American boarding school, where he adjusted well and later returned to the reservation.

The life journey that ultimately brought Bill to the hospital was not atypical for a young Navajo. He was born in a remote, very traditional, poverty-stricken area of the Arizona reservation. He was born during an eclipse, which spiritually destined him to take part, at different points in his life, in a ceremony that he described as the "Breath of Life" sing. He had participated in it as an infant and at age 6 and was supposed to engage in it once again during the time of his hospitalization. At age 6, he went to live with and assist his grandfather as a sheepherder. He worked for him until the old man's death, when Bill was 17. He reported that his grandfather never talked to him.

Bill then got a job with the railroad, which was interrupted by an eight-month hospital stay for tuberculosis. He returned to his previous employment, which took him to several states. He was always part of a Navajo crew and, thus, never exposed to acculturative influences. After saving a good bit of money and a brief return home to his family, Bill traveled on his own to California in search of additional work. A White man offered to find him a job and, in the process, swindled him out of his savings. Bill returned home, sold some jewelry, borrowed money, and returned to California in search of the man who had tricked him out of his money. He ended up in jail for vagrancy. He traveled with some Navajos whom he met in jail in search of employment and picked up a few odd jobs, but his money quickly ran out, and eventually he decided to return home again. He thought that if he could get to a hospital, they would send him back to the reservation. That was why he had approached the woman whom he had mistaken for a nurse.

What is most striking about Bill's misdiagnosis is the fact that it was made on the basis of external observation alone. The doctors had never talked with him and, until Jewell took an interest in Bill, did not even know his ethnic origin. He had, in fact, been twice misidentified: first as Mexican, and then as Filipino. The doctors first assumed the existence of serious pathology (i.e., if he is here in a mental hospital, he must be crazy) and then proceeded to find evidence for their assumption in Bill's observable behavior. Evidently, they had never felt the need to actually talk with him to make a diagnosis. Equally disturbing was their total disregard of culture and the possibility that cultural differences might have played a role in understanding Bill's behavior. I am reminded of research by Rosenhan (1975), who had himself and colleagues, all mentally fit (though perhaps that goes without saying), checked into a private mental hospital where they merely observed what happened to them and others and took careful notes. Their copious note-taking received extensive comment in their respective clinical files: "Patient exhibits excessive writing behavior."

From the perspective of Navajo culture, Bill's behavior made perfect sense and was anything but indicative of the deep mental and emotional pathology that the label "schizophrenia, catatonic type" implies. Consider the various symptoms on which Bill's diagnosis rested. His "apathetic and withdrawn behavior" was characteristic of the way Navajos respond to situations of stress and crisis. Inactivity is their chosen mode of psychological defense. He must have been traumatized by his experiences with the mental health system—not to mention culture shock—and he was also being forced to reside in a hospital, which is a symbol of death in Navajo culture. His unwillingness to talk and his repeated statement: "Me no good in this place" (pointing to his chest) relate to his need to perform the "Breath of Life" ceremony and the belief that he must conserve vocal energy until the ritual is completed. This statement may also have referred to his earlier bout with tuberculosis. The *cerea flexibilitas* (muscular rigidity and lack of movement characteristic of catatonia) that Bill was exhibiting was demystified when Jewell learned from the interpreter that Bill held these grotesque positions because he thought that it was expected of him. The most significant symptom of schizophrenia—lack of contact with reality and massive ego disintegration—was never really assessed because that requires talking with the patient.

Bill's experience with the mental health system, although perhaps extreme in its absurdity, is not atypical. In a variety of ways, mental health professionals have repeatedly introduced bias and cultural insensitivity into their work with culturally diverse clients. Ethnic patients, in turn, have responded by avoiding such services whenever possible and resisting them when they are not voluntary. The result has been the systematic underuse of services by clients of color.

This chapter focuses on various sources of bias in cross-cultural helping. You will begin by looking at ways in which attitudes of the provider can shape treatment values and decisions, as well as who the providers are and the kind of skills and preparation they bring with them to their work with cross-cultural clients. Next, you will learn about the helping process itself and the cultural relevance of its various practices and the concepts that support it and their applicability to culturally diverse populations. A number of important questions will emerge. Do ideas such as "helping" and "mental health," especially as they have been traditionally conceived, make sense in all cultures? Has racism or stereotyping played any role in how helping professionals have conceptualized work with clients of color? Have standard methods of assessment and diagnosis been culture-free, or has their use tended to differentially affect clients of color? Are the various forms of mental disorder, as defined by DSM-5, found in all cultures, and are their symptom patterns and etiology (i.e., how they develop) the same cross-culturally? For example, do all cultural groups experience emotional states similar to what Western psychology calls "clinical depression," and if so, do they manifest symptoms in the same way?

▶ The Impact of Social, Political, and Racial Attitudes   8-1

There is a vast body of research in social psychology that shows how attitudes can unconsciously affect behavior. Some examples include the following:

▶ Rosenthal and Jacobson (1968) looked at the relationship between teacher expectations and student performance. Teachers were told at the beginning of the school year that half the students in their class were high performers and the other half were low. In actuality, there were no differences among the students. By the end of the year, however, there were significant differences in how the two groups performed. Those who were expected to do well did so, and vice versa. In another experiment, Rosenthal (1976) assigned beginning psychology students rats to train. Some were told that their rats came from very bright strains; others were told that their rats were genetically low in intelligence. The rats were, in actuality, all from the same litter. By the end of the training period, each group of rats was performing in keeping with their "heredity." In these two experiments, what the teachers and the psychology students believed and expected were translated into differential behavior, which in turn, became what Rosenthal called a "self-fulfilling prophecy." In other words, what we believe (i.e., the attitudes that we hold) about people shapes our treatment of them. Freud called this phenomenon *countertransference* when it occurred in the clinical setting. The following types of similar dynamics have also been demonstrated in relation to helping professionals.

▶ In another classic study, Broverman et al. (1970) looked at gender stereotyping and definitions of mental health. They asked a group of psychiatrists, psychologists, and social workers to describe characteristics that they would attribute to healthy adult men, healthy adult women, and healthy adults with gender not specified. There was high agreement among subjects, and there were no differences between male and female clinicians. As a group, the clinicians enunciated very different standards of health for women and men; that is, a healthy woman was described in very different terms than was a healthy man. The concept of a healthy adult man and that of a healthy adult of unspecified sex did not differ significantly, whereas that of a healthy adult man and a healthy adult woman did. Compared to men, healthy adult women were seen as more submissive, less independent, less adventuresome, more easily influenced, less aggressive, less competitive, more excitable in minor crises, more easily hurt, more emotional, less objective, and more concerned with appearance. It is probably fair to say that such beliefs about gender differences cannot help but translate into the ways that these clinicians work with their male and female clients.

▶ In yet another study, researchers looked at the effect of political attitudes on the diagnosis of mental disorders (Wechsler, Solomon, and Kramer, 1970). Clinicians in the study were asked to rate clients on the severity of their symptoms based on videotaped interviews. All clinicians were shown the same videotapes, in which the clients described their symptoms. The only difference was what the clinicians were told about the political activities of the clients. Clients described as being more extreme politically were regularly rated as having more severe symptoms (i.e., as being "sicker" than those who were presented as more conservative). Similarly, when clinicians were told that some subjects advocated violent means of bringing about political change, they, too, were rated as having more severe symptoms, as were those who were described as having very critical attitudes toward the field of mental health. Again, it is a short step to suggesting that the political attitudes and prejudices of providers can color their perception and treatment of politically diverse clients.

▶ Although there is less empirical data on the effect of racial attitudes on provider behavior (probably because of the desire to appear "politically correct" and, therefore, the difficulty in accurately measuring and identifying racist attitudes), some exemplary studies do exist. Jones and Seagull (1983), for example, asked African American and White clinicians to evaluate the level of adjustment of African American therapy clients. He found that White clinicians tended to rate African American clients as more disturbed than did the African American therapists, especially in relation to how seriously they viewed external symptoms and their assessment of the quality of family relations. Other studies show that counselors and trainees tend to think in terms of stereotypes when working with culturally diverse clients (Atkinson, Casas, and Wampold, 1981; Wampold, Casas, and Atkinson, 1982).

▶ In addition, there is much research that shows dramatic differences in the kinds of services that White and non-White clients receive. For example, African Americans are more likely to receive custodial care and medications and are offered psychotherapy less often than are Whites (Hollingshead and Redlich, 1958). And even when they are offered psychotherapy, it tends to be short-term therapy or crisis intervention, as opposed to long-term therapy (Turner, 1985). Similarly, African Americans are overrepresented in public psychiatric hospitals (Kramer, Rosen, and Willis, 1972), and African Americans, Latinos/as, and Asian Americans are all more likely to receive supportive vs. intensive psychological treatment and to be discharged more rapidly than whites (Yamamoto, James, and Palley, 1968).

In short, there is no reason to believe that racial attitudes are any less likely to affect the perception and treatment of clients than social or political ones.

▶ Who Are the Providers? Under-representation in the Professions   8-2

It is well documented that clients prefer helpers from their own ethnic group (Cabral and Smith, 2011). The sense of familiarity and safety that this affords cannot be underestimated. However, present statistics do not bode well for potential clients of color; the reality is that people of color are sadly underrepresented among the ranks of helping professionals. This serious lack of non-white providers is often cited as one of the reasons for the underuse of mental health services by people of color.

A study of membership in the American Psychological Association (APA) in 1979, for example, showed that only 3 percent of the members were non-white (Russo et al., 1981). Of more than 4,000 practitioners who claimed their specialty to be in counseling psychology, fewer than 100 were of color. A more recent study showed little change, with members of color representing only 4 percent of the APA membership (Bernal and Castro, 1994).

Nor does the situation improve noticeably when one looks at enrollment figures for graduate training programs. As Atkinson et al. (1996) point out, "the key to achieving ethnic parity among practicing psychologists rests on the profession's ability to achieve equity in training programs" (p. 231). Statistics collected by Kohout and Wicherski (1993) show that African Americans make up only 5 percent, Latinos/as 5 percent, Asian Americans 4 percent, and Native Americans 1 percent of students enrolled in doctoral psychology programs. These figures represent a decrease for African American students and only a slight increase for the other three groups over the previous 25 years

(Kohout and Pion, 1990). Over the course of training, however, disproportionate dropout rates for students of color bring their number at graduation close to the 3 percent or 4 percent reported for APA membership. Recent research from the APA suggest that there was an increase in racial/ethnic minority students in psychology departments—the largest increases were seen by students who considered themselves multi-ethnic.

While much lip service is paid to the need for recruiting more students and faculty of color, the numbers say it all: they have remained consistently low over time. In addition to cost, a major deterrent keeping non-White students out of college (and contributing to their dropout rate when they do go) is the Northern European cultural climate that predominates in such settings. It is not only difficult for students of color (especially those who are not highly acculturated) to navigate the complex application and entry procedures that training programs typically require, but it is also hard to feel comfortable, safe, and welcome in a monocultural environment that is not their own.

An equally critical factor is the number of faculty of color within these programs. These statistics also continue to be quite low. Atkinson et al. (1996) note that within doctoral training programs in clinical, counseling, and school psychology, African Americans make up 5 percent of the faculty, Latinos/as 2 percent, and Asian Americans and Native Americans 1 percent each. These authors succinctly summarize the current situation as follows: "Although ethnic minorities make up approximately 25 percent of the current U.S. population, with dramatic increases ahead, they constitute less than 15 percent of the student enrollment and less than 9 percent of the full-time faculty in applied psychology programs" (p. 231).

Dissatisfaction Among Providers of Color

These numbers will not change until significant diversity is introduced in the helping professions, as well as in their training facilities. At present, both remain overwhelmingly White. Cabral and Smith (2011) expressed that "to improve mental health services for people of color, professionals have emphasized the need for cultural congruence between therapists and clients" (p. 3). D'Andrea (1992) documents this fact by pointing to "some of the ways in which individual and institutional racism imbues the profession." He offers the following seven examples:

- Less than 1 percent of the chairpersons of graduate counseling training programs in the United States come from non-White groups (89 percent of all chairpersons in counseling training programs are White males).
- No Hispanic American, Asian American, or Native American person has ever been elected president of either the American Counseling Association (ACA) or the APA.
- Only one African American person has been elected president of the APA; that was Kenneth Clark, in 1971.

- None of the five most commonly used textbooks in counselor training programs in the United States lists "racism" as an area of attention in its table of contents or index.
- A computerized literature review of journal articles found in social science periodicals over a 12-year period (1980–1992) indicated that only 6 of 308 articles published during this time period that examined the impact of racism on one's mental health and psychological development were published in the three leading professional counseling journals (*The Counseling Psychologist,* the *Journal of Counseling and Development,* and the *Journal of Counseling Psychology*).
- All the editors of the journals sponsored by the ACA and the APA (excluding one African American editor with the *Journal of Multicultural Counseling and Development*) are White.
- Despite more than 15 years of efforts invested in designing a comprehensive set of multicultural counseling competencies and standards, the organizational governing bodies of both the ACA and the APA have consistently refused to adopt them formally as guidelines for professional training and development.

It is not difficult to read between the lines of D'Andrea's examples and sense the enormous frustration of providers of color with the seeming slowness with which the professional counseling establishment has moved toward actively embracing and implementing its verbalized commitment to multiculturalism. D'Andrea and Daniels (1995) summarize these feelings as follows:

> Although persons from diverse racial/cultural/ethnic backgrounds must continue to lead the way in promoting the spirit and principles of multiculturalism in the profession, it is imperative that White counseling professionals take a more active stand in advocating for the removal of barriers that impede progress in this area. Together we can transform the profession, or together we will suffer the consequences of becoming an increasingly irrelevant entity in the national mental health care delivery system. (p. 32)

Similar sentiments are offered by Parham (1992):

> To make the types of changes that are necessary in order that the counseling profession will be able to meet the needs of an increasing number of clients from diverse cultural and racial backgrounds, the profession in general and its two national associations—the American Psychological Association and the American Counseling Association—in particular, will have to learn to share more of its power and resources with persons who have traditionally been excluded from policy-making and training opportunities. (pp. 22–23)

The Use of Paraprofessionals

One strategy that held great promise for dramatically increasing the number of providers of color was the use of indigenous paraprofessionals. Stimulated by a visionary book by Arthur Pearl and Frank Reisman (1965) entitled *New Careers for the Poor,* the National Institutes of Mental Health (NIH) committed extensive resources to educating mental health facilities in the use of ethnic paraprofessionals.

The idea was a rather simple one. Individuals who were natural leaders within ethnic communities were given training in the rudiments of service delivery (basic assessment, interviewing skills, knowledge of psychopathology) and then hired to act both as liaisons and outreach workers to the community and as adjunct providers working under the direction of professional staff. Often, special satellite centers were established in ethnic communities and staffed by these local paraprofessionals. The concept worked exceptionally well for over ten years. Community members were more willing to bring their problems to paraprofessionals who were already known, respected, and able to understand their culture and lifestyle.

Paraprofessional involvement in mainstream agencies, in turn, gave them a certain credibility that was not afforded when the staff was all White. The strategy also served to inject a large number of entry-level ethnic paraprofessionals into the system. Many, in fact, chose to return to school and became professionals. Ironically, this strategy was ultimately undermined by the development of a number of academic paraprofessional training programs. Viewing the paraprofessional role, not so much as a means of creating more indigenous providers but rather as a new entry point into mental health jobs, these programs attracted primarily White middle- to upper-middle-class students. Agencies, in turn, received increased pressure to hire these "professional nonprofessionals." The ultimate result was that indigenous providers were slowly but systematically replaced by trained paraprofessionals, and a very functional approach to infusing ethnic community members into the mental health delivery system was undermined.

▶ The Use of Traditional Healers   8-3

Another potentially useful strategy for overcoming the lack of ethnic helping professionals is the involvement of traditional healers—that is, indigenous practitioners from within traditional ethnic cultures—as part of a mental health organization's treatment team, either on staff or in a consultative role. This is not only a mark of cultural respect, but it is also an invitation to less acculturated community members who would not normally avail themselves of mainstream services to view mental health services (thus more broadly defined) as a resource for them as well. Barriers to including traditional healers usually come from Western professionals who see the use of shamanic healers as unscientific, superstitious, and regressive. Their hesitancies come from conflicting worldviews, although Torrey (1986), for one, has argued that Western mental health approaches work structurally in much the same way as do indigenous healing systems. Both, for example, are afforded high status and power and also depend on clients sharing the same worldview. Torrey suggests that both be incorporated under the broad multicultural rubric of healer.

Lee and Armstrong (1995), however, enumerate a number of content differences:

- Traditional healing views human capacities holistically, whereas Western providers typically distinguish among physical, spiritual, and mental well-being.
- Western healing stresses cause and effect; traditional approaches emphasize circularity and multidimensional sources in etiology.
- In Western psychology, helping occurs through cognitive and emotional change. In traditional healing, there is also a spiritual basis to health and well-being.
- In Western psychology, helpers tend to be passive in their interventions; indigenous healers are more active and take a major role and responsibility in the healing process itself.

In spite of such differences, the only reason for not pursuing cooperation and consultation is ethnocentrism. Such narrow thinking typically goes hand in hand with cultural insensitivity in Western providers because the very spirituality and religiosity of which they are generally critical play a central role in the worldview of most culturally diverse clients.

One last point needs to be made regarding increasing the number of ethnic helpers. Just because providers have certain racial or cultural roots does not guarantee their cultural competence or ability to work effectively with clients from their group of origin. Making an extra effort to hire providers of color sends an important social and political message. But to do so without careful consideration of a candidate's experience, skills, training, and cultural competence is merely racism in reverse. No agency would think of randomly selecting White candidates regardless of their credentials and assume that they will be competent to work successfully with a broad spectrum of White clients. However, on a much more frequent basis, agencies do assume that hiring a person of color will resolve problems of racism and cross-cultural service delivery automatically.

As has been continually stressed throughout this book, ethnic groups encompass enormous diversity, and it is dangerous to make assumptions about the characteristics that a given individual possesses merely on the basis of group membership. For example, an agency has within its service jurisdiction a small but growing Latino/a population and wishes to hire someone of Latino/a descent to help provide services. Some of the following questions may prove useful in making informed and culturally sensitive choices among possible candidates:

- Is the person bilingual and fluent in both English and Spanish, written and verbal?
- Is the person bicultural—that is, familiar with the traditional as well as the dominant culture?
- With what specific ethnic subgroups within the broad category of Latino/a culture is the candidate familiar and knowledgeable?
- What is this person's knowledge of class, gender, and regional differences in the Latino/a community?
- Where was the person born, and how acculturated was the family of origin?
- Does the candidate have firsthand experience with the migration process?
- What is the nature of his or her own ethnic identity?
- With what other ethnic populations has this person worked?
- How culturally competent is this person?

▶ Cultural Aspects of Mental Health Service Delivery   8-4

So far, this chapter has looked into sources of bias related to the provider. There are, in addition, aspects of the helping process per se that limit its relevance to clients of color. In general, these relate to the fact that current mental health theory and practice are defined in terms of dominant Northern European cultural values and norms and therefore limit the ability of providers to address and serve the needs of non-White populations adequately. Chapter 5 includes a description of four characteristics of the helping process (as it is currently constituted) that directly conflict with the worldview of communities of color.

Research has shown that African Americans, Hispanics, and Asian mental health is similar or better than whites. Hearld, Budhwani, and Chavez-Yenter (2015) explained that "even with a health advantage, some studies have found discrimination to negatively affect certain mental health outcomes" (p. 107). Here, we explore additional sources of this cultural mismatch, as well as describe ways in which the current helping model portrays clients of color in a negative light, highlights their "weaknesses," and assumes pathology even when it does not necessarily exist. An extreme example is the case study of Bill, a supposedly psychotic Navajo, with which this chapter opens. His behavior, when viewed through the lens of Navajo culture, looked quite normal, but from the perspective of Western psychology, it reflected a deep disturbance and psychopathology.

▶ Bias in Conceptualizing Ethnic Populations   8-5

There is a long history in Western science of portraying ethnic populations as biologically inferior. Highlights include the following:

- ▶ Beginning with the work of luminaries such as Charles Darwin, Sir Francis Galton, and G. Stanley Hall, one can trace what Sue and Sue (1990) call the "genetic deficiency model" of racial minorities into the present, continued by research psychologists such as Jensen (1972).
- ▶ Similarly, Jews have been vilified under the guise of psychological analysis. Jung (1934), for example, wrote the following comparison of Jewish and Aryan psychologies: "Jews have this peculiarity in common with women, being physically weaker, they have to aim at the chinks in the armor of their adversary, and thanks to this technique ... the Jews themselves are best protected where others are most vulnerable" (pp. 165–166). Jung, who also wrote disparagingly of the African American psyche, found his ideas on national and racial character warmly received by the Nazi regime.
- ▶ McDougall (1977), an early American psychologist, offers similar sentiments against Jews in his analysis of Freud's work: "It looks as though this theory which to me and to most men of my sort seems to be strange, bizarre and fantastic, may be approximately true of the Jewish race" (p. 127).

As biological theories of genetic inferiority lost intellectual credibility, they were quickly replaced in social science circles by notions of "cultural inferiority" or "deficit theories." While political correctness would not allow practitioners with negative racial attitudes to continue to embrace the idea of genetic inferiority, they could easily attach themselves to theories that assumed "that a community subject to poverty and oppression is a disorganized community, and this disorganization expresses itself in various forms of psychological deficit ranging from intellectual performance ... to personality functioning ... and psychopathology" (Jones and Korchin, 1982, p. 19). These new models took two forms: cultural deprivation and cultural disadvantage. In relation to the former, non-whites were seen as deprived (i.e., lacking substantive culture).

The word *disadvantaged*—a supposed improvement over the term *deprived*—implies that although ethnic group members do possess culture, it is a culture that has grown deficient and distorted by the ravages of racism. More recent and acceptable are the terms *culturally diverse* and *culturally distinct*. But as Atkinson, Morten, and Sue (1993) point out, even these can "carry negative connotations when they are used to imply that a person's culture is at variance (out of step) with the dominant (accepted) culture" (p. 9).

Psychological research on ethnic populations has also tended to be skewed in the direction of finding and focusing on deficits and shortcomings. This body of research, which Jones and Korchin (1982) refer to as part of a "psychology of race differences tradition," has been widely criticized for faulty methodology. Jones and Korchin explain: Studies typically involved the comparison of ethnic and white groups on measures standardized on white, middle-class samples, administered by examiners of like background, intended to assess variables conceptualized on the basic U.S. population (p. 19). Turner and Kramer (2016) further this point by stating "in mental health settings the use of diagnostic criteria that fail to take into account major cultural and social class differences between African American and whites lead to invalid conclusions" (p. 9). But even more insidious have been two additional tendencies:

- Researchers have chosen to study and compare whites and people of color based on characteristics that culturally favor dominant group members. Thus, intelligence is assessed by measuring verbal reasoning, or schoolchildren are compared on their ability to compete or take personal initiative. In other words, research variables portray white subjects in a more favorable light and simultaneously create a negative impression of the abilities and resources of minority ethnic subjects.

- Where differences have been found between whites and people of color, they tend to be interpreted as reflecting weaknesses or pathology in ethnic culture or character. Looking at such studies, various researchers have asked why alternative interpretations stressing the creative adaptiveness or strengths inherent in ethnic personality or culture might not just as easily have been sought. Turner and Kramer (2016) suggest that "one needs to emphasize the uniqueness of persons and evaluate psychological status from the individual's particular perspective" (p. 9). These negative portrayals and stereotypes of people of color serve to justify the status quo of oppression and unfair treatment, and thus they serve political as well as psychological purposes.

An interesting and provocative example of the psychological mystification of ethnic culture and cultural traits is offered by Tong (2005). Tong argues that the psychological representation of Chinese Americans as the model minority—that is, ingratiating and passive—is more a survival reaction to American racism than a true reflection of traditional Chinese character. He goes on to suggest that there is within traditional culture a "heroic tradition" that portrays the Chinese in a manner very different from the uncomplaining model minority: "Coexistent with the Conventional Tradition was the 'heroic,' which exalted a time-honored Cantonese sense of self: the fierce, arrogant, independent individual beholden to no one and loyal only to those deemed worthy of undying respect, on that individual's terms" (p. 15). Tong calls to task fellow Chinese American psychologists for perpetuating the myth through their research and writings, and thus for confusing psychopathology with culture:

> Timid and docile behavior *is* indicative of emotional disorder. If Chinese Americans seem to be that way by virtue of cultural "background," it is the case only to the extent that white racism, in combination with our heritage of Confusion [*sic*] repression, made it so. The early Chinamans [*sic*] consistently shaped themselves and justified their acts according to the fundamental vision of the Heroic Tradition. Their stupendous feats of daring and courage, however, remain buried beneath a gargantuan mound of white movies, popular fiction, newspaper cartoons, dissertations, political tracts, religious meeting minutes, and now psychological studies that teach us to look upon ourselves as perpetual aliens living only for white acceptance. (p. 20)

Tong calls this mystification of the Chinese American psyche "iatrogenic." *Iatrogenesis* is a medical term that means sickness or pathology that results from medical or psychological intervention and treatment.

A final difficulty with contemporary psychology's model of helping is its theoretical narrowness and inability to acknowledge different cultural ways of looking at and conceptualizing mental health as valid. I once worked as part of a team whose task was to create a mental health service delivery system for recent southeast Asian refugees. This is an at-risk population that has suffered serious emotional trauma as a result of war, migration, and rapid acculturation in the United States. The first problem that we encountered was that there was no concept within their culture for mental health per se, nor was there a distinction between physical and mental health. Problems were not dichotomized, and as we were to learn later, what we considered mental health problems generally presented in the form of physical symptoms.

In time, however, it was possible to discern certain patterns of physical complaints that seemed to indicate emotional difficulties, such as depression and post-traumatic stress disorder (PTSD). But the symptom patterns for these disorders within Southeast Asian populations looked very different from those presented in the DSM-5, which is "normed" primarily on Northern European clients. In addition, the Western concept of helping (i.e., seeking advice, help, or support from a professional stranger) made no sense to our Southeast Asian clients. In most Asian cultures, one does not go outside the family for help, let alone to strangers. The acknowledgment of emotional difficulties brings shame on the family. It is expected that individuals accept their conditions quietly. From a Western perspective, this is considered denial or avoidance.

As a general strategy for intervention, we decided to train paraprofessionals from the community to serve as outreach and referral workers. Not only did our paraprofessionals (who were young adults and among the most acculturated individuals in the community) have great difficulty grasping, understanding, and using the mental health concepts and simple diagnostic procedures we tried to teach them, but there was also a problem in their being accepted by older community members as legitimate health providers. This was largely because of age. So long as we approached the community from a Northern European perspective, we were destined to fail. We had pushed the model of training with which we were familiar as far as it could be stretched, and we were still unable to accommodate major aspects of Southeast Asian culture.

What does one do when the very concept of mental health makes little sense within a culture, or when the very notion of helping as conceived in Western terms is irrelevant because it is considered shameful to share one's problems with complete strangers? I came away from that experience realizing that if we were to continue, we would have to start from scratch and create a new helping model that was not merely an adaptation of mainstream helping practices, but rather was specifically tailored to the cultural needs of Southeast Asians. (You might want to review Chapter 5 and its discussion of conflicting strategies of cross-cultural service delivery.)

Bias in Assessment

In no other area of clinical work has there been more concern raised about the possibility of cultural bias than in relation to psychological assessment and testing. This is because people of color have for many years watched their children being placed in remedial classrooms or tracked as retarded on the basis of IQ testing and seen loved ones diagnosed as suffering from serious mental disorders because of their performance on various personality tests. Serious life decisions are regularly made on the basis of these tests, and it is reasonable to expect that they be "culture-free"; that is, they should be scored based on what is being measured and not differentially affected by the cultural background of the test taker. In reality, there probably is no such thing as a culture-free test, and it has been suggested—and supported by some research—that ethnic group members tend to be overpathologized by personality measures and have their abilities underestimated by intelligence tests (Snowden and Todman, 1982; Suzuki and Kugler, 1995).

Reynolds and Suzuki (2003) list several factors that can contribute to cultural bias in testing:

- Test items and procedures may reflect dominant cultural values.
- A test may not have been standardized on populations of color, only on middle-class whites.
- Language differences and unfamiliarity or discomfort with the client's culture can cause a tester to misjudge them or have difficulty establishing rapport.
- The experience of racism and oppression may lead to groupwide deficits in performance on tests that have nothing to do with native ability.
- A test may measure different characteristics when administered to members of diverse cultural groups.

- Culturally unfair criteria, such as level of education and grade point average, may be used to validate tests expected to predict differences between whites and people of color.
- Differences in experience taking tests may put non-White clients at a disadvantage in testing situations.

In short, it is very difficult to ensure fairness in psychological testing across cultures, and practitioners should exert real care in drawing conclusions based exclusively on test scores (Kim and Zabelina, 2015). As a matter of validation, they should gain as much non-testing collaborative data as possible, especially when the outcome of the assessment may have real-life consequences for the future of the client. They should also be willing not to test a client if it is believed that the procedure will not give useful and fair data.

Having raised all these cautions, the fact remains that a great deal of culturally questionable testing still takes place. Clinicians tend to be overly attached to psychological tests as a means of gaining client information. When they do try to take into account cultural differences, it is done not by creating new instruments, but rather by modifying existing ones—adjusting scores, rewriting items, or translating them into a second language. In general, this merely creates new problems in the place of old ones. The Minnesota Multiphasic Personality Inventory (MMPI) and Thematic Apperception Test (TAT), probably the two most widely used personality assessment techniques, provide excellent examples.

The MMPI is by far the most widely used instrument to measure psychopathology. Historically, it has been administered without reservation to racial and ethnic minorities:

- Concerns about cultural bias were raised for two reasons: first, because it had been normed (i.e., standardized as far as cutoff scores reflecting normal vs. psychopathological behavior) exclusively on White subjects; and second, because it was being used extensively to make decisions about hospitalizing patients, a disproportionate percentage of whom were people of color.
- Cultural differences and the possibility of bias are most evident in differential scoring patterns. African American test takers (from normal, psychiatric, and inmate populations alike), for example, consistently score higher than whites on three scales: F (a measure of validity), 8 (a measure of schizophrenia), and 9 (a measure of mania).
- In addition, 39 percent of the items are answered differently by African American subjects than by white subjects. Of these, a third are not clinical scale items, which implies that differences are related to culture as opposed to pathology.
- There is also evidence that MMPI items are neither conceptually nor functionally equivalent for African Americans and whites; this suggests that they neither mean the same thing nor fulfill a similar psychological purpose for the two groups.

As a means of dealing with these problems, Costello (1977) developed a Black-White Scale that adjusted African American scores so they might be interpreted similarly to white scores. But Snowden and Todman (1982) are critical of this procedure:

> The Black-White Scale may be useful in the short term for making interpretive adjustments to allow for known differences, however, must be seen as a stopgap measure. In the long run, it leaves unanswered all the pertinent questions raised by both cross-cultural and environmental psychologists alike . . . The Costello Black-White Scale does not ask these questions; it merely corrects for them. The logical extension of this scale could very well be the following: If one subtracts a factor of *x* from the score of a black male, his profile is then "as good" as if it were of a white. One can conclude with confidence that the MMPI has never established its validity as a diagnostic or assessment instrument with blacks. (pp. 210–211)

The MMPI-2, a revision of its predecessor, was tested initially on both African American and Native American sample populations. The resulting research has been so confusing, however, that Dana (1988) and Graham (1987) both conclude that it is best not to use the test with ethnic group members.

The TAT and the Rorschach are the most widely used projective tests for assessing personality and psychopathology. The TAT involves showing clients drawings of people in various situations and asking them to tell a story about the picture. Scoring involves both the kinds of themes that are generated and the style of responding:

▸ Questions about its use with non-White populations were raised early because the stimulus figures on the cards were White, and there was the obvious question of whether African American clients, for example, could identify with these figures or rather would inhibit self-disclosure because of them. To test this, Thompson (1949) developed the same cards redrawn with African American figures and used them with African American clients. Although he showed that his cards generated more responses than did the original White cards, all the questions about cultural comparability raised by Reynolds and Kaiser (1990) remain unanswered.

▸ TAT scoring generates impressions about unmet needs within the client. Who is to say that such needs or motivations are equivalent across cultural groups or that the stimulus pictures, regardless of the race of the figures, have equivalent cultural meanings?

▸ Finally, there is a question about the use of projection with non-White groups. Generally, it has been found that blacks are less responsive, less willing to self-disclose, and more guarded about their participation in the TAT testing than members of other groups. Snowden and Todman (1982) suggest that this guardedness may be culturally determined and the result of a long history of dealing with racist institutions.

In spite of all these questions about the cultural validity of the TAT, it continues to be used cross-culturally. There is, in fact, now a Latino/a version, as well as one specifically designed for children, which has cards showing animal characters instead of people.

Bias in Diagnosis

Culture shapes and affects the very essence of how clinical work is done (Neighbors, Trierweiler, Ford, and Muroff, 2003). According to Gaw (1993), it colors the following areas:

- How problems are reported and how help is sought
- The nature and configuration of symptoms
- How problems are traditionally solved
- How the origin of presenting problems is understood
- What appropriate interventions involve
- How the helping relationship is maintained over time

In short, each culture has its own paradigm of how these processes occur, and there is enormous variation. Difficulties emerge, however, when practitioners superimpose their cultural worldviews onto the life experience of culturally diverse clients and then make clinical assumptions or judgments from that perspective. This is where things stand today vis-à-vis Western mental health service delivery and the desire to serve other cultural groups. Ricci-Cabello, Ruiz-Pérez, Labry-Lima, and Márquez-Calderón (2010) stated "the relevance of inequalities in terms of health-care is especially evident among patients suffering from chronic or long-term illnesses" (p. 572). Most practitioners tend to be far too narrow and ethnocentric in their thinking to acknowledge and accept other versions of clinical reality. Rather than try to redesign the "puzzle" and broadening their perspective, providers keep trying to force the "round piece" into the "square hole," and the "hole" keeps objecting. This method could cause serious issues when helping culturally diverse individuals.

▶ Cultural Variations in Psychopathology   8-6

Nowhere is the limited thinking of Western psychology more challenged by cultural variation than around the question of what psychopathology is and how it is diagnosed. This is also where misdiagnosis of those who are culturally diverse most regularly occurs. Jones and Korchin (1982) summarize the issue as follows:

> Most mental health workers proceed on the assumption of the pancultural (i.e., etic) generality of categories, criteria, and theories of psychopathology originated in Western cultures. Minority clinicians have long objected that standard psychiatric nomenclature does not recognize cultural variation in symptomology.

This position is quite consistent with a growing view among cross-cultural psychologists that problems of identifying cases of psychopathology in clients from different cultures and comparing incidence and forms of psychopathology across cultures need to be reconsidered. (pp. 26–27)

Cultural Attitudes Toward Mental Health

Cultures differ dramatically in their orientation and attitude toward mental disorders, as well as in their understanding of personality dynamics, what is considered therapeutic, and how help is to be sought. Cultural responses to these issues are shaped by certain key themes that contribute a distinctive Gestalt to how each culture relates to the problem of mental illness. Jang, Chiriboga, Herrera, Martinez, Tyson, and Schonfeld (2011) expressed that there needs to be more research on mental health among ethnic and racial minorities. More research could identify misconceptions, personal beliefs, and cultural attitudes related toward mental health. Regarding past research on cultural attitudes toward mental health, I will summarize the early research of Lum (1982) on mental health attitudes among Chinese Americans, whose clinical worldview differs substantially from that of Western psychology. Within the Chinese American culture, mental health and mental illness are two sides of the same coin.

- According to Lum, individuals are considered mentally healthy if they possess the capacity for self-discipline and the willpower to resist conducting oneself or thinking in ways that are not socially or culturally sanctioned; a sense of security and self-assurance stemming from support and guidance from significant others; relative freedom from unpleasant, morbid thoughts, emotional conflicts, and personality disorders; and the absence of organic dysfunctions, such as epilepsy or other neurological disorders. Similarly, mental illness involves the opposite: a loss of discipline, preoccupation with morbid thoughts, insecurity because of the absence of social support, and distress stemming from external factors.
- Consistent with this, Chinese Americans tend to externalize blame for mental illness, thus setting the stage for avoidance of unwanted thoughts and feelings. Traditional Chinese wisdom sees value in learning to inhibit and control one's emotions. Defensively, according to Hsu (1949), Chinese tend to use suppression as opposed to repression, which is more common among European Americans. Suppression tends to have an obsessional quality because to use it effectively, one must rationalize, justify, or use other intellectual strategies to blunt the anxiety. Using it, in turn, tends to encourage obsessive-compulsive qualities,

including extreme conscientiousness, meticulousness, acquiescence, rigidity, and a preference for thinking over feeling.

▶ As patients, Chinese Americans prefer helpers who are authoritarian, directive, and fatherly in their approach. They expect, in turn, to be taught how to occupy their minds to avoid unwanted thoughts and feelings. Insight approaches tend to have limited meaning, and generally, therapy does not seem to affect Chinese Americans characterologically.

▶ Finally, help-seeking is limited because within the Chinese community, there is a stigma and shame around mental illness. Shame often leads to minimizing the seriousness and frequency of a problem. Patients often feel "ashamed and ambivalent about their illness" and are reluctant to tell others about their emotional difficulties. In sum, the threads that run through the Chinese American worldview of mental health and illness are the importance of controlling emotions and thoughts and their avoidance when they become too intrusive or distracting, the necessity of social support as a precondition for healthy mental functioning, the submerging of the self as a means of deferring to family and authority, and mental illness as a stigma that requires the individual to tolerate disturbing symptoms rather than bring shame on the family. These themes translate basic cultural values into behavioral prescriptions for living that, in turn, reinforce basic cultural values.

Cultural Differences in Symptoms, Disorders, and Pathology

Cultures also differ as to what disorders are most typically observed, how symptom pictures are construed, and even what is considered pathological:

▶ Some disorders (e.g., schizophrenia and substance abuse) appear to be universal, although the exact content is culture specific. Hallucinations, for example, tend to contain familiar cultural material, such as voices speaking to the person in his or her native language or visions infused with cultural symbols and motifs. Other disorders (e.g., depression) can be observed across cultures, but they vary dramatically in relation to specific symptoms. In Western clients, for example, depression is diagnosed on the basis of a combination of psychological and physical symptoms, whereas among southeast Asian clients, physical symptoms such as headaches and fatigue are more prevalent indicators.

▶ There are also culture-specific syndromes or disorders that appear only among members of a single cultural group. Jones and Korchin (1982) point to two—ataque, found only among Puerto Ricans, is a hysterical seizure reaction in which patients fall to the ground, scream, and flail their limbs. Largely unfamiliar to majority practitioners, it tends to be misdiagnosed as a more serious seizure disorder. A similar disorder, called "falling out" disease, is found only among rural southern African Americans and West Indian refugees and is regularly misdiagnosed as epilepsy or a transient psychotic episode.

‣ The same symptom can have very different meanings depending on the cultural context in which it appears. Mexican Americans, for instance, view hallucinations as far less pathological and more within the realm of everyday (normal) experience than do whites. Hearing voices, thus, is more culturally sanctioned and often associated with deep religious experiences. Meadow (1982) shows that hospitalized Mexican American patients report significantly more hallucinations, both visual and auditory, than do whites. These variations in experiencing raise the important question of exactly where culture ends and psychopathology begins. Meadow (1982) attempts to sort it out as follows:

> Some Mexican-American hallucinatory experiences may simply reflect a cultural belief and occur in persons completely free of psychopathology. In other cases, Mexican-American hallucinations may have the same significance as those reported by Anglo-American patients. There exists an intermediate group of Mexican-American patients in which the hallucination may be interpreted as a symbolic expression of a wish fulfillment or as a sign of a warded-off superego criticism. For these patients, the hallucination is a symptom of psychopathology, but it does not signify the serious break with reality that would be implied if it occurred in an Anglo-American case. (p. 333)

The Globalization of Treatment Modalities

Equally disturbing is the recent trend toward the globalization and exportation of Western conceptions of mental health and their associated treatment modalities, especially in relation to Third World cultures. In his recent book, *Crazy Like Us: The Globalization of the American Psyche,* Ethan Watters (2010) warns of the enormous and unintended cultural consequences of such practices among Western mental health providers:

> Over the past thirty years, we Americans have been industriously exporting our ideas of mental illness. Our definitions and treatments have become the international standards. Although this has often been done with the best of intentions, we've failed to foresee the full impact of these efforts. It turns out that how a people think about mental illness—how they categorize and prioritize the symptoms, attempt to heal them, and set expectations for their course and outcome—influences the diseases themselves. In teaching the rest of the world to think like us, we have been, for better or worse, homogenizing the way the world goes mad. (p. 2)

Watters goes on to warn that as a result of the exportation of Western training in mental health, the use of the DSM as a standard for diagnosis and definition of various categories of mental illness, the worldwide distribution of Western-oriented professional journals and training conferences, and the enormous funding of research and marketing of medication for mental illness, "the remarkable diversity once seen among different cultures' conceptions of madness is rapidly disappearing" (p. 3).

Underlying this standardization of Western ideas of the mind and mental health is an enormous sense of hubris and ethnocentrism, not to mention drug company profit motives, that totally disregards the importance and value of culture and cultural variation and its critical role in the expression and healing of mental illnesses. However:

> Cross-cultural researchers and anthropologists... have shown that the experience of mental illness cannot be separated from culture. We can become psychologically unhinged for many reasons... Whatever the cause, we invariably rely on cultural beliefs and stories to understand what is happening. Those stories, whether they tell of spirit possession or serotonin depletion, shape the experience of the illness in surprisingly dramatic and often counterintuitive ways. In the end, all mental illness, including such seemingly obvious categories such as depression, PTSD, and even schizophrenia, are every bit as shaped and influenced by cultural beliefs and expectation... as any other mental illness ever experienced in the history of human madness. The cultural influence on the mind of a mentally ill person is always a local and intimate phenomenon." (p. 6)

As an example, Watters offers four in-depth examples of the Westernization and importation of mental illness in four different cultures: the rise of anorexia in Hong Kong, the wave that brought PTSD to Sri Lanka, the shifting mask of schizophrenia in Zanzibar, and the mega-marketing of depression in Japan. Watters ends his critique of the exportation of our own mental health concepts with a telling question: "Given the level of contentment and psychological health our cultural beliefs about the mind have brought us, perhaps it's time that we rethink our generosity" (p. 255).

The Case of Suicide

The same mental health problem can be configured very differently in terms of both its sources (etiology) and its frequency (incidence) across cultures. A classic example is suicide. According to the Group for the Advancement of Psychiatry Committee on Cultural Psychiatry (1984), suicide rates differ substantially across ethnic groups in the United States, as follows:

▶ By far, the highest aggregate suicide rate (i.e., for all ages and genders combined) is found among Native Americans.
▶ The next highest is among European Americans, followed by Chinese Americans and Japanese Americans.
▶ The lowest aggregate rates are found among African Americans and Latinos/as.

Practitioners are often surprised by the relatively low rates of suicide among people of color. Why? Because, stereotypically, many equate non-whites with violence. It is also useful to note, as pointed out previously, that as ethnic groups assimilate, their relative position in the hierarchy increasingly comes to approximate that of European Americans. Thus, with acculturation, it is expected that African Americans, Latinos/as, and Asian Americans will increase their aggregate suicide rates.

Looking at peak rates across ethnic groups provides even further insights, especially because it is reasonable to assume that suicide rates reflect periods of optimal stress in a group's life cycle:

▶ For European Americans, suicides tend to occur three times as often for men as for women. In addition, peak rates tend to increase with age. For men, the highest rates are in those over 65, and for women, rates are highest in their early 50s.
▶ The picture is very different for communities of color. First, suicide occurs most frequently among young males in African American, Native American, and Latin cultures. Japanese Americans show a similar trend, but it is less pronounced. Chinese American young males are a notable exception (Group for Advancement, 1989). These high rates most likely result from the fact that young, non-White males are usually "the point men" for acculturative stress. They tend to be the ones who have the closest, most sustained contact and least positive interactions with White institutions, usually through school and then work. High rates of unemployment and underemployment are certainly contributing factors. Research has also shown that young men of color who have consolidated a positive ethnic identity and attachment to tradition are less likely to be at risk of suicide than those who have become marginalized from their culture. The same is true for other self-destructive behaviors, such as substance abuse and violence.
▶ A second major finding of the 1989 study is the extremely low suicide rates among African American, Native American, and Latina women when compared with ethnic males and majority group members combined. The one exception was Chinese American women, who showed a peak incidence of it in later life. There seem to be two reasons for these low rates. First, because of traditional sex roles, ethnic women

have less exposure to the stressful effects of acculturation. In addition, they tend to experience much lower rates of unemployment and under-employment and can also derive personal satisfaction from alternative roles in the home. The higher suicide rate among older Chinese women is probably because of the interaction of several factors. They tend to remain closer to their cultural tradition and, as such, are separatist in their orientation toward majority culture. As they lose their nurturing role in the family with age and as their children acculturate, they tend to grow even more isolated and lack support for their traditional orientation. In addition, many experience poverty without support from their family, and they are unable or unwilling to seek help from majority social agencies.

▸ Finally, there are especially low rates of suicide among older African Americans, Native Americans, and Latinos/as in comparison to younger ethnic group members and majority group members combined (Group for Advancement, 1989). It is likely that these individuals have learned to cope with the acculturative stress. They tend to be revered in their communities and supported by strong community institutions that they likely helped found. The fact that older Asian Americans were not included in this statistic may reflect the effects of greater acculturation, which would lead to greater isolation of the elderly, as is more common in mainstream culture.

Given such cultural relativity in defining mental health and psychopathology, an interesting question arises as to the appropriate criteria to be used in assessing psychopathology. From what cultural perspective should deviant behavior be judged? And within any particular cultural perspective, what makes a behavior deviant or psychopathological? The problem is made difficult by the fact that ethnic group cultures exist within a broader framework than is usually identified and is defined culturally as Northern European. From a clinical standpoint, individuals' behavior must be judged in accordance with the values and criteria of their own group's culture (Garlow, Purselle, and Heninger, 2005). Thus, "to justify an interpretation of behavior as an instance of psychopathology, it must be established that there is intersubjective agreement among members of the culture that the behavior in question represents an exaggeration or distortion of a culturally acceptable behavior or belief" (Jones and Korchin, 1982, p. 27). If one applies this maxim to Bill, the institutionalized Navajo whose case is discussed at the start of this chapter, it is clear that he was acting within the bounds of culturally acceptable Navajo behavior and that his diagnosis as catatonic, his assessment as psychopathological from a Western psychological perspective, and his institutionalization were all inappropriate.

Racial Microaggressions and the Therapeutic Relationship

Bias can also be unintentionally introduced into the therapeutic relationship through the unexamined attitudes of the human service provider. In Chapter 2, I introduced the notion that a central tenet of cultural competence is the self-awareness of one's racial attitudes and the negative impact they might have in forming a bond with culturally diverse clients. In Chapter 3, I briefly discussed the topic of implicit bias and racial microaggressions. Here, we will explore how these largely unconscious aspects of the therapist's worldview can be introduced into the helping relationship and also how they might be addressed and eliminated.

According to Sue et al. (2007), *microaggressions* are "unconsciously delivered in the form of subtle snubs or dismissive looks, gestures, and tones. These exchanges are so pervasive and automatic in daily conversations and interactions that they are often dismissed and glossed over as being innocent and innocuous" (p. 273). They further argue that they are counterproductive to therapeutic efforts because they can be "detrimental to persons of color because they impair performance in a multitude of settings by sapping the psychic and spiritual energy of recipients by creating inequalities." They are also not limited to human interactions but can reside within various environments that by their nature expose people of color to assaults against their racial identities, often by the lack of familiar racial content.

The authors define three forms of microaggressions. *Microassaults* are verbal and nonverbal attacks intended with varying degrees of conscious awareness to hurt a person of color through name-calling, avoidance, or other forms of discriminatory behavior and insensitivity. *Microinsults* are communications that "convey rudeness and demean a person's racial heritage or identity." *Microinvalidations* are communications that exclude, negate, or nullify psychological thoughts, feelings, or experiential reality of people of color. All three types, especially the latter two, can be observed frequently in the therapeutic interaction between therapist and client, particularly among White mental health practitioners. Sue et al. have identified nine categories of microaggression with distinct themes. Table 8-1 provides examples of racial microaggressions in therapeutic practice and their accompanying hidden assumptions and messages.

Microaggressions are particularly insidious because of their invisibility to the perpetrator and often the recipient as well. Most whites tend to view themselves as "good, moral, and decent" and find it difficult to see themselves as racially biased or engaging in discriminatory behavior. In addition, such acts can "usually be explained away by seemingly non-biased and valid reasons." For the recipient, on the other hand, there is always the "nagging question" of what really occurred. It has been reported that in such situations, people of color often experience a vague feeling of having been attacked, disrespected, or that something is just not right.

TABLE 8-1

Examples of Racial Microaggressions in Therapeutic Practice

Theme	Microaggression	Message
Alien in Own Land When Asian Americans and Latin Americans are assumed to be foreign-born	A White client does not want to work with an Asian American therapist because "she will not understand my problem." A White therapist tells an American-born Latino client that he should seek a Spanish-speaking therapist.	You are not American.
Ascription of Intelligence Assigning a degree of intelligence to a person of color on the basis of their race	A school counselor reacts with surprise when an Asian American student had trouble on the math portion of a standardized test. A career counselor asks a black or Latino/a student, "Do you think you're ready for college?"	All Asians are smart and good at math. It is unusual for people of color to succeed.
Color Blindness Statements that indicate that a White person does not want to acknowledge race	When a client of color attempts to discuss her feelings about being the only person of color at her job and feeling alienated and dismissed by her coworkers, a therapist says "I think you are being too paranoid. We should emphasize similarities, not people's differences." A client of color expresses concern in discussing racial issues with her therapist. Her therapist replies with, "When I see you, I don't see color."	Race and culture are not important variables that affect people's lives. Your racial experiences are not valid.
Criminality/Assumption of Criminal Status A person of color being presumed to be dangerous, criminal, or deviant on the basis of their race	When a black client shares that she was accused of stealing from work, the therapist encourages the client to explore how she might have contributed to her employer's mistrust of her. A therapist takes great care to ask all substance abuse questions in an intake with a Native American client and is suspicious when the client says he has no history with using substances.	You are a criminal. You are deviant.
Denial of Individual Racism A statement made when whites renounce their racial biases	A client of color asks his or her therapist about how race affects their working relationship. The therapist replies, "Race does not affect the way I treat you."	Your racial or ethnic experience is not important.
	A client of color expresses hesitancy in discussing racial issues with his White female therapist. She replies "I understand. As a woman, I face discrimination also."	Your racial oppression is no different than my gender oppression.

Myth of Meritocracy Statements that assert that race does not play a role in succeeding in career advancement or education	A school counselor tells a black student that "if you work hard, you can succeed like everyone else." A career counselor is working with a client of color who is concerned about not being promoted at work despite being qualified. The counselor suggests, "Maybe if you work harder, you can succeed like your peers."	People of color are lazy and/or incompetent and need to work harder. If you don't succeed, you have only yourself to blame (blaming the victim).
Pathologizing Cultural Values/ Communication Styles The notion that the values and communication styles of the dominant or white culture are ideal	A black client is loud, emotional, and confrontational in a counseling session; the therapist diagnoses her with borderline personality disorder. A client of Asian or Native American descent has trouble maintaining eye contact with his therapist; the therapist diagnoses him with a social anxiety disorder. Advising a client, "Do you really think your problem stems from racism?"	Assimilate to the dominant culture. Leave your cultural baggage outside.
Second-class Citizen Occurs when a white person is given preferential treatment as a consumer over a person of color	A counselor limits the amount of long-term therapy provided at a college counseling center; she chooses all white clients over clients of color. Clients of color are not welcomed or acknowledged by receptionists.	Whites are more valued than people of color. White clients are more valued than clients of color.
Environmental Microaggressions Macro-level microaggressions, which are more apparent on a systemic level	A waiting room office has pictures of American U.S. presidents. Every counselor at a mental health clinic is white.	You don't belong or only white people can succeed. You are an outsider. You don't exist.

Source: Based on Sue, D. W., Capodilupo, C. M., Torino, G. C., Bucceri, J. M., Holder, A. M. B., Nadal, K. L., and Esquilin, M. (2007). Racial microaggressions in everyday life: Implications for clinical practice. *American Psychologist*, Vol. 62, No. 4, 271–286.

Sue et al. further identity four psychological dilemmas that microaggressions pose for both white perpetrators and the people of color involved in such encounters. These include:

▸ A clash in racial realities in which whites tend to underestimate the existence and impact of racism and discrimination as well as their capacity for bias and racism, and people of color view whites as racially insensitive, superior, needing to be in control, and actively discriminatory.

▸ An invisibility of unintentional expressions of bias on the part of whites, who tend to be stunned by the accusation of bias, feel betrayed by what they perceive as their good intentions in the interaction, or are consciously unaware when they respond differentially on the basis of race or automatically because of cultural conditioning. In other words, how does one prove that a microaggression has occurred?

▸ A perception on the part of whites that minimal harm has resulted from the alleged microaggression, accompanied by a belief that the person of color "has overreacted and is being overly sensitive and/or petty."

▸ A Catch-22 for people of color as to how to respond when a microaggression occurs and the conflicting questions that it raises. Did a microaggression really occur? If so, what is the best way to respond? What are the consequences of deciding that responding will do no good, engaging in self-deception and denial, and getting angry when that likely will engender negative consequences? In other words: damned if you do, and damned if you don't.

In turning to the situation of counseling and psychotherapy, the authors suggest that "the therapeutic alliance is likely to be weakened or terminated when clients of color perceive white therapists as biased, prejudiced, or unlikely to understand them as racial/cultural beings" (p. 280). This, in turn, will lead to clients of color not receiving the help they need and, because of premature termination, possibly feeling worse than they did before seeking help. What, then, can be done to address the negative impact of unintentional, racial microaggressions in the therapeutic relationship? Sue et al. offer a number of suggestions, all having to do with therapist training and education about race in general and microaggressions in particular. These include:

▸ Overcoming trainee resistance to talk about race in the context of safe and productive learning environments

▸ Challenging trainees to explore their own racial identities, as well as their feelings about other racial groups, and to learn to tolerate the discomfort and vulnerability that doing so will likely produce

▸ White trainees addressing "what it means to be white," becoming aware of their own white racial identity development and how it may have a negative impact on clients of color

▸ Increasing trainees' skill in identifying microaggressions in general, but particularly in their own behavior

▸ Understanding how microaggressions, especially their own, negatively affect and alienate clients of color

▸ Learning to accept responsibility for becoming aware of and overcoming racial bias

Finally, it is important to point out that the negative impact of racial microaggressions is not limited to white therapists and clients of color only. Future research should include the existence of microaggressions between therapists of color and white clients, interethnic racial dyads, and microaggressions that occur in relation to other cultural identities and minorities, such as gender, sexual orientation, and disability.

SUMMARY

In various ways, mental health professionals have introduced bias and cultural insensitivity into their work with culturally diverse clients. Ethnic patients, in turn, have responded by avoiding such services in general whenever possible and resisting them when they were imposed involuntarily. The result has been systematic under-use of services by clients of color. This chapter focuses on sources of such bias in the field.

First, attitudes including prejudices and stereotypes can shape treatment values and decisions. Exemplary research shows that experimenter and teacher expectations affect the performance of subjects and students (an effect that has come to be known as a "self-fulfilling prophesy"); that social and political attitudes affect the assessment of clients' mental health by therapists; that clinicians differentially diagnose patients on the basis of race; and that white and non-white clients regularly receive different treatment options. In a similar vein, Watters (2010) points out that there has been a growing trend toward globalization and the exportation of Western conceptions of mental health and their associated treatment modalities, including psychotropic medications, especially in relation to Third World countries. What has been increasingly lost, however, is the unique and various relationships that have always existed between a culture and its unique expression of psychopathologies. To quote Watters: "In teaching the rest of the world to think like us, we have been, for better or worse, homogenizing the way the world goes mad" (p. 2).

Bias is also introduced because of who the providers are. People of color are sadly underrepresented among the ranks of helping professionals, and it has been shown regularly that clients prefer and feel most comfortable with therapists from their own ethnic background. People of color are underrepresented in professional group memberships, as students in training programs (and when they do take such a program, they drop out more frequently than white students), and as faculty in those training programs. Providers of color are frustrated by the slow pace in which the profession and its training facilities have moved toward addressing these numbers and committing themselves to multiculturalism. Neither the use of people of color as paraprofessionals in their communities nor the use of traditional healers has served to increase the number of available practitioners of color.

A third source of bias exists because of cultural differences and cultural insensitivity among providers. Ethnic populations have been regularly viewed pathologically and cultural differences interpreted so as to favor white "characteristics" and portray people of color in a less favorable manner. Because of culturally biased instruments and interview protocols, people of color have been harmed and had their opportunities limited through psychological assessment and diagnosis. The tracking of children of color in special education programs is a particularly disturbing example. Underutilization also has been attributed to cultural differences, for reasons such as negative or nonexistent attitudes toward the concepts of mental health and ignorance about cultural variation in symptomology, the characteristics that define a disorder, and what behaviors are considered pathological. The example of suicide shows how the etiology and frequency of psychological disorders can look very different across cultures. It has been found, for example, that people of color tend to have lower suicide rates than whites.

A final source of bias involves microaggressions—microassaults, microinsults, and microinvalidations—that occur, unconsciously or unintentionally, during the therapeutic encounter. The therapeutic alliance tends to be weakened or terminated when clients of color perceive white therapists as biased, prejudiced, or unlikely to understand them as racial/cultural beings. Suggestions for minimizing and correcting microaggressions in therapy are offered.

ACTIVITIES

1. *Rewrite Bill's case.* Re-familiarize yourself with the specifics of Bill's case at the beginning of this chapter and review our critique of it. Now try your hand at rewriting the case—but this time as it would unfold if Bill found his way into a mental hospital whose staff, procedures, and system were highly culturally competent—or as Cross et al. (1989) would have called it, "culturally proficient." Describe in detail this new scenario.

2. *Design a culturally sensitive mental health intervention strategy for assessing and serving a community of southeast Asian refugees living in a major U.S. city.* Earlier in the chapter, the author described such an effort in which he was a participant and enumerated a number of issues of "cultural disconnects" that occurred between the young paraprofessionals they hired to serve as intermediaries to the community and the mental health staff. Individually, in pairs, or in small groups review this material and then design an alternative intervention strategy that addresses the various disconnects with more cultural syntonic practices. After completing this exercise, the reader is directed to the final section of Chapter 10, in which the Center for the Empowerment of Refugees and Immigrants (CERI), an exemplary and highly culturally competent mental health center designed to work with Cambodian clients in Oakland, California, is described in depth. The reader is invited to use it as a yardstick to assess their success in the present activity.

Mental Health Issues

LEARNING OBJECTIVES

9-1 Identify models of racial identity development.

9-2 Understand intersection of the helping process and racial identity development.

9-3 Distinguish between acculturation and assimilation.

9-4 Understand the impact of psychological trauma.

9-5 Discuss the cultural meaning of recovery.

In an extraordinary book entitled *Black Rage*, psychiatrists William Grier and Price Cobbs (2000) explore the enormous anger lurking below the surface of the African American patients who seek their help. They begin by describing the life circumstances of three patients. (1) Roy was an overachieving painter who had become impotent and unable to work after a fall from scaffolding. He sought help because there was no physical basis for his malaise or reason for the way his life had fallen apart after the accident. (2) Bertha entered treatment because of severe depression. She was very dark-skinned, had grown up in the South, and had experienced a series of abusive relationships with working-class men who were far below her socially and intellectually. In treatment, she revealed deep feelings of self-hatred and self-deprecation and a self-image as black, ugly, ignorant, and dirty. Her depression had become clinical after a marriage to a fellow professional and the birth of a child. (3) John was a highly trained professional with a severe anger problem that had lost him a series of good jobs. He sought treatment after entering a very promising executive training program in which he was doing poorly because of his discomfort in supervising and competing with white coworkers.

The patterns that these patients presented were very typical of Grier and Cobbs' general African American clientele. All had been living reasonably functional lives until an emotional crisis knocked them down, and each had a difficult time recovering. Psychotherapy had revealed very negative self-perceptions that were deeply intertwined with their experiences as African Americans in the United States. According to the authors, because of their circumstances of having to live in, adapt to, and survive in a hostile and racist world, African Americans are at perpetual risk for developing serious physical and emotional disorders. Most survive, many even grow strong from it, but all pay an emotional price that may, with sufficient stress and personal difficulty, result in some type of psychological breakdown. For many, the ultimate consequence is depression and grief, which are understood by Grier and Cobbs (1992) to be nothing less than "hatred turned toward the self." But when these patients are helped to feel the depth of their sorrow, their grief begins to lift, and enormous anger is set free. According to the authors, African Americans stand at a precarious juncture, "delicately poised, not yet risen to the flash point, but rising rapidly nonetheless" (p. 213). As if looking into a crystal ball, they anticipated a growing violence that has increasingly become a part of race relations in the United States since the 1970s.

This chapter focuses attention on mental health issues that plague people of color. In it we will explore a number of factors, such as the racism described by Grier and Cobbs (1992), that put people of color at risk for mental and emotional difficulties. Chapters 6 and 7 discussed some of the psychological issues related to child development and parenting in communities of color. Chapter 8 explored various sources of bias in the delivery of mental health services to people of color and why, even when there is significant need, clients of color consistently avoid mental health services.

Together, these three chapters provide a clear picture of the kinds of psychological issues culturally diverse clients struggle with and that ultimately bring with them into the helping situation for treatment.

We begin this chapter by exploring problems related to racial identification and group belonging in adults of color and gain an understanding of the evolution of ethnic identity conflict, paying special attention to recent models of racial identity development that have proven particularly useful in making sense out of cross-cultural interactions in the helping situation. In subsequent sections, we will learn about the psychological impact of assimilation and acculturation, the role of stress as a mediator in the development of physical and emotional symptoms among people of color, the psychology of trauma, and, finally, drug and alcohol use and their relationship to ethnicity. These various problems are interrelated and mutually sustaining.

▶ Racial Identity and Group Belonging   9-1

The controversy over whether children of color regularly experience problems in group identification and low self-concept as a result of racism is discussed in some detail in Chapter 6. The conclusion, based on several sources of evidence, is that they did not necessarily, but without sufficient and appropriate family and community support, children of color were certainly at risk for such problems. There is also a certain hesitancy among researchers to underestimate the deleterious effects of racism and the negative views that society in general holds of ethnic group members. In this section, this picture will be expanded to include identity difficulties in ethnic adults.

The Inner Dynamics of Ethnic Identity

The general term *identity* refers to the existence of a stable inner sense of who a person is and is formed by the successful integration of various experiences of the self into a coherent self-image. *Ethnic identity*, in turn, refers to that part of personal identity that contributes to one's self-image as an ethnic group member. Thus, when one speaks of African American identity, Native American identity, or Jewish identity, what is being referred to is the individual's subjective experience of ethnicity. What does the person feel, consciously and unconsciously, about being a member of his or her ethnic group? What meaning do individuals attach to their ethnicity? What does their behavior reflect about the nature of their attachment to the group? Answers to these questions are subsumed under the notion of ethnic identity.

Ethnic identity formation, like personal identity formation, results from the integration of various personal experiences one has had, for example, as an African American, Native American, or Jew, combined with the messages that have been communicated and internalized about ethnicity by various family members and significant others.

In general, ethnic identity can be categorized as *positive ethnic identification*, *negative ethnic identification*, or *ambivalent ethnic identification* and individuals as positive, negative, and ambivalent identifiers (Klein, 1980). The latter two have also been referred to in the literature as internalized racism, internalized oppression, and racial self-hatred.

▶ As emphasized in the previous chapter, children of color, by the fact of being raised in a hostile and racist environment, are likely to have unpleasant experiences associated with their ethnicity. As these negative group-related experiences accumulate, it becomes increasingly difficult for the child—and, later, the adult—to integrate them into a coherent and positive sense of ethnic self. Instead, they are either actively rejected and disowned and thus relegated to the unconscious and experienced as "not me" (negative identification) or allowed to remain conscious but unintegrated. In time, they are likely to become a source of ambivalent feelings about the self as an ethnic group member (ambivalent identification). In this regard, Klein (1980) found that Jews with positive ethnic identities tend to be healthier psychologically and better adjusted than those with more conflicted feelings about their Jewishness. A similar logic would seem to hold for people of color. In fact, according to Brittian et. al (2015), African American and Latino/a students who experience perceived discrimination from their ethnic group experienced depressive symptoms. They went on to explain that while ethnic identity affirmations mediated the depressive symptoms for Latinos/as, it did not do the same for African Americans.

▶ Inner conflicts in ethnic identity, such as those just described, ultimately find expression in some form of overt behavior. In the case of negative identification (i.e., where aspects of the ethnic self are actively rejected or disowned), there is, first of all, a tendency in the individual to deny, avoid, or escape group membership in whatever ways possible. In communities of color, this is often referred to as "passing." It may include trying to change one's appearance so as not to look so typically ethnic, changing a name, moving to non-ethnic neighborhoods, dating and marrying outside the group, and taking on majority group habits, language, and affectations. Such behaviors are usually experienced as offensive within ethnic communities. In fact, specific derogatory terms have been created in each community of color to describe such individuals: "Oreos" among African Americans, "coconuts" among Latinos/as, "apples" among Native Americans, and "bananas" among Asian Americans. All refer to such individuals as being of color on the outside but white on the inside. As part of this rejection of ethnicity, one also finds the taking on of majority attitudes and habits, including the dominant culture's prejudices and stereotypes toward one's own group. For those who are unfamiliar with such patterns of "identity rejection and self-hatred," it is usually shocking to learn that some of the most virulent anti-Semites and racists can be Jews and blacks, respectively.

▸ In relation to ambivalent identification, where rejecting tendencies exist concurrently with positive feelings about group membership, there is either vacillation between love and hate (where individuals move back and forth, pulling away from feeling too identified if they get too close and moving back toward the group if they grow too distant) or the simultaneous expression of contradictory positive and negative attitudes and behaviors. One form of accommodation is to compartmentalize ethnic identity (i.e., retain certain aspects and reject others). For instance, a Latino/a might refuse to speak Spanish or identify as a Catholic or marry within the group but at the same time have strong preferences for native foods, prefer living in a barrio, and become involved in civil rights activities.

▸ However, psychological accommodations such as these tend to be precarious at best and often fall apart—or at least grow fragile—in relation to all forms of emotional upheaval and change. It is not uncommon, for example, for individuals to "rethink" their connection to ethnicity after the birth of a child, death of a parent or close relative, or a personal near-death experience. It is perhaps most accurate to conceive of ethnic identity formation as an ongoing and lifelong process. As such, it involves a series of internal psychological adaptations (that may eventually translate into changes in behavior) to an ever-changing complex of unfolding ethnic experiences. Generally, core conflicts around ethnicity that occur early in life continue to feed basic feelings of negativity or ambivalence and are difficult to resolve completely. But even here, there are instances when dramatic and significant changes toward positive identification do occur (Diller, 1991).

The three states of ethnic identification just described are summarized in Table 9-1.

Models of Racial Identity Development

A somewhat different approach to understanding the evolution of racial or cultural consciousness is offered by various researchers (Atkinson, Morten, and Sue, 1993; Cross, 1995; Hardiman and Jackson, 1992; Helms, 1990) who began in the 1970s to develop what has come to be called "models of racial identity development." These models, which were first developed in relation to the experience of African Americans, assume that there are strong similarities in the ways all ethnic individuals from diverse groups respond to the experience of oppression and racism. It is further believed that there is a series of predictable stages that people of color go

TABLE 9-1
Summary of Ethnic Identification States

Ethnic Identity State	Characteristic Reactions
Positive identification	Accepts and integrates ethnic-related experiences Ethnic-related reactions are conscious Accepts ethnic self Positive group attachment Retains and celebrates ethnic ways and attitudes
Negative identification	Rejects and disowns ethnic-related experiences Ethnic-related reactions remain unconscious Reject aspects of ethnic self Denies, avoids, or escapes group membership Takes on majority ways and attitudes
Ambivalent identification	Vacillates between the reactions described for both positive and negative identification and/or compartmentalizes areas of ethnic content

Source: Adapted from *Jewish Identity and Self-esteem: Healing Wounds Through Ethnotherapy*, by J. Klein, 1980, New York: Institute on Pluralism and Group Identity. Copyright 1980; and Freuds *Jewish Identity: A Case Study in the Impact of Ethnicity* by J. V. Diller, 1991, Cranbury, NJ: Fairleigh Dickinson University Press. Copyright 1991, held by Jerry V. Diller.

through as they struggle to make sense out of the relationship to their own cultural group as well as to the oppression of mainstream culture. Models of racial identity are still evolving (Robinson-Wood, 2016; Umaña-Taylor et al., 2014; Yip, 2014).

Cross (1995), whose work is exemplary, hypothesizes five such stages of development. It is assumed that each person of color can be located in one of the five stages depending on his or her level of racial awareness and identity:

- In Stage 1, called *Pre-encounter*, individuals are not consciously aware of the impact that race and ethnicity have had on their life experiences. They tend to assimilate, seek acceptance by whites, exhibit strong preferences for dominant cultural values, and even internalize negative stereotypes of their own group. By de-emphasizing race and distancing themselves from other group members, they are able to deny their actual vulnerability to racism and sustain—so long as they are able—the myth of meritocracy and the hope of achievement unencumbered by racial hatred.
- In Stage 2, *Encounter*, some event or experience shatters the individual's denial and sends him or her deep into confusion about his or her ethnicity. For the first time, the person must consciously deal with the fact of being different and what this difference means. At this stage, people of color often speak of "waking up" to reality, realizing that ethnicity is an aspect of self that must be dealt with and the enormity of what must be confronted out in the world.

- Stage 3, *Immersion-Emersion*, is characterized by two powerful feelings: first, a desire to immerse oneself in all things "ethnic"; for example, to celebrate all symbols of "blackness" and to simultaneously avoid all contact with whites, the white world, and symbols of that world. The result is at first an uncritical descent into blackness, where everything black is beautiful and everything white is abhorrent. During this more separatist period, people of color seek information about ethnic history and culture and surround themselves exclusively with "their own kind." The enormous anger that is generated during Stage 2 and lingers into Stage 3 slowly dissipates as the person grows increasingly focused on self-exploration, creating attachment within his or her ethnic world, and less in need of lashing out at the white world.
- *Internalization*, Stage 4 of the model, begins as the person of color becomes increasingly secure and positive in his or her sense of racial identity and less rigid in the attachment to group allegiances at the expense of personal autonomy. Pro-ethnic attitudes become more "expansive, open, and less defensive." Although the person feels securely connected to his or her ethnic community, there also emerges a greater willingness to relate to whites and members of other ethnic groups who are able to acknowledge and accept their ethnicity.
- Stage 5, *Internalization-Commitment*, represents a growing and maturing of the tendencies initiated in Stage 4. People of color at Stage 5 have found ways of translating their personal ethnic identities into an active sense of commitment to social justice and change. According to Tatum (1992), the Stage 5 person is "anchored in a positive sense of racial identity" and can "proactively perceive and transcend race." Race has become an instrument for reaching out into the world rather than an end in itself, as in Stage 3, or a social reality to be denied or avoided, as in Stage 1.

Separate racial identity models have been created in relation to each community of color. While some differences exist in the number of stages hypothesized, content of stages, and process of movement from one stage to the next, the general process of identity development and change is the same across groups.

Atkinson, Morten, and Sue (1993) and, later, Atkinson (2003) have reviewed these models and extrapolated four dimensions of change they believe occur universally as a person of color moves through the stages. Specifically, they see changes in attitudes toward:

- The self
- Others of the same ethnic group
- Members of different ethnic groups
- Dominant group members

In relation to attitudes toward the self, self-depreciating feelings are transformed into self-appreciation as one moves through the various stages. Attitudes toward one's own group change from group depreciating to group appreciating, with the disappearance of identity conflict and internalized oppression across stages. Attitudes toward other minorities move from discriminatory feelings to the eventual acceptance and appreciation of differences.

Attitudes toward dominant group members move from identifying with the majority through rejecting them to selective appreciation as the individual proceeds through the various stages. Atkinson, Morten, and Sue's progression of attitude changes across developmental stages is summarized in Table 9-2. It should be noted that they define five stages of development, as opposed to the six stages posited by Cross (1995). Also, the Cross model was later validated by Vandiver, Cross, Worrell, and Fhagen-Smith (2002).

TABLE 9-2
Minority Identity Development Model:
Attitude Changes Across Stages

Stage	Attitude Toward Self	Attitude Toward Others of Same Minority	Attitude Toward Others of Different Minority	Attitude Toward Dominant Group
1– Conformity	Self-depreciating	Group-depreciating	Discriminatory	Group-appreciating
2– Dissonance	Conflict between self-depreciating and self-appreciating	Conflict between group-depreciating and group-appreciating	Conflict between dominant-held views of minority hierarchy and feelings of shared experience	Conflict between group-appreciating and group-depreciating
3– Resistance and Immersion	Self-appreciating	Group-appreciating	Conflict between empathy for other minority experiences and culture centrism	Group-depreciating
4– Introspection	Concern with basis of self-appreciating	Concern with nature of unequivocal appreciation	Concern with ethnocentric basis for judging others	Concern with the basis of group depreciation
5– Synergetic	Self-appreciating	Group-appreciating	Group-appreciating	Selective appreciating

Source: Adapted from Counseling American Minorities, 4e (p. 34), by D. R. Atkinson, G. Morten, & D. W. Sue, 1999. Copyright 1993 by W. C. B. Brown & Benchmark. Reprinted with permission.

▶ **Racial Identity Development and the Helping Process** `9-2`

The value of these models of racial identity development to providers is twofold:

▶ They educate and sensitize providers to the importance of cultural identity in understanding the experiences of people of color.
▶ They suggest that individuals at different stages of development may exhibit very different needs and values and may feel differently about what is supportive or therapeutic in the helping situation.

Various authors have differentiated the counseling needs that clients of color exhibit as they move through the five stages of racial identity development (Atkinson, Morten, and Sue, 1993; Sue and Sue, 1999).

▶ Clients at Stage 1 tend to seek help for issues unrelated to ethnic identity and generally prefer working with white providers. According to Sue and Sue (1999), Stage 1 individuals are likely to feel threatened by direct explorations of race and ethnicity and tend to feel more comfortable with a "task-oriented, problem-solving approach." They also react differently to white and same-race providers. Stage 1 clients are likely to overidentify with and seek approval from the former and direct hostility toward the latter as a symbol of what he or she is trying to reject. Both types of therapist, however, have a similar task of bringing to consciousness the topic of race and culture.
▶ Clients at Stage 2 tend to be preoccupied with personal issues of race and identity but at the same time are torn between fading Stage 1 beliefs and an emerging awareness of race consciousness. They seek counselors knowledgeable about their cultural group and tend to do best with counseling modes that allow maximum self-exploration. Sue and Sue (1999), however, point out that the person may still be more comfortable with a white therapist, so long as he or she is culturally aware.
▶ Clients in Stage 3 are less likely to seek counseling. They tend to be absorbed in re-exploring and engaging in ethnic ways and see personal problems exclusively as the result of racism. If they must enter treatment, counselors of color are preferred. Sue and Sue (1999) offer the following suggestions in relation to Stage 3 clients: The therapist, whether white or of color, will inevitably be seen as a "symbol of the oppressive society" and thus challenged. The least helpful response for either is to become defensive and take any attacks personally. "White guilt and defensiveness" on the part of white therapists will especially exacerbate client anger. Therapists must realize that they will be continually tested and often find

that honest self-disclosure about matters of race is "a necessary requirement to establish credibility." Lastly, Sue and Sue (1999) suggest adopting
strategies that are more "action oriented" and "aimed at external change"
as well as group approaches when working with Stage 3 clients.

▶ Clients in Stage 4 are struggling to balance group and personal
perspectives and may seek counseling to help them sort out these issues.
They may still prefer a counselor from their own group, but they can begin
to conceive of receiving help from a culturally sensitive outsider. Sue and
Sue (1999) point out that those in Stage 4 appear in many ways similar to
those in Stage 1; they tend to experience conflict between identification
with their group and the need to "exercise greater personal freedom."
Unlike the Stage 1 person, however, reactions tend to be issue-specific and
do not challenge their positive attachment to the group. Approaches that
emphasize self-exploration are particularly helpful in integrating group
identity and personal concerns of the self.

▶ Clients who have reached Stage 5, according to Atkinson, Morten,
and Sue (1993), are again less in need of access to counseling.
They have developed good skills at balancing personal needs and
group obligations, have an openness to all cultures, and are able to deal
well with racism when it is encountered. Their preference for a counselor,
if needed, is most likely to be dictated by the personal qualities and
attitudes of the counselor rather than by group membership.

Recall that in Chapter 4, Helms's (1995) model of white identity development was
introduced. Her model, which parallels and evolved from the work just described, enumerates stages of racial consciousness development in whites and the eventual abandonment
of entitlement. Just as it is useful to be able to identify the stage of identity development
of individual clients of color, so too is it valuable to assess white helpers vis-à-vis Helms's
model in order to train them better and match them with appropriate clients of color.
According to Sue and Sue (2015), white providers will be most effective in cross-cultural
service delivery when they have successfully worked through their feelings about whiteness
and privilege. Such individuals, located in the highest stages of Helms's model, are able to
experience their own ethnicity "in a non-defensive and non-racist manner." They also warn
against mismatches, especially when the white therapist is at Stage 1 of Helms's model.

> A white therapist at the conformity level, for example, may cause great harm to
> culturally diverse clients . . . The therapist may . . . a) reinforce a conformity cli-
> ent's feelings of racial self-hatred, b) prevent or block a dissonance client from
> looking at inconsistent feelings/attitudes/beliefs, c) dismiss and negate resistance
> and immersion client's anger about racism . . . or d) perceive the integrative aware-
> ness individual as having a confused sense of self-identity. (p. 162)

▶ Assimilation and Acculturation   9-3

Ethnic group members differ widely in the extent of their *assimilation* and *acculturation*. Conceptually, ethnic assimilation is the coming together of two distinct cultures to create a new and unique third cultural form. This is the myth of the "great melting pot," taken from a play by the same name, written by Jewish playwright Israel Zangwill at the beginning of the twentieth century. It is referred to as a myth because it just never happened that way.

Gordon (1964) distinguishes several forms of assimilation:

- ▶ Acculturation involves taking on the cultural ways of another group, usually those of the mainstream culture.
- ▶ Structural assimilation means gaining entry into the institutions of a society. Gordon also refers to this as "integration."
- ▶ Marital assimilation implies large-scale intermarriage with majority group members.
- ▶ Identificational assimilation involves developing a sense of belonging and peoplehood with the host society.

It is probably most accurate to say that white ethnics—Irish, Italian, Jews, Armenians, and so forth—have assimilated into American society on all these dimensions, but only to the extent that they have been willing to give up their traditional ways and values. People of color, on the other hand, were never really considered part of the great melting pot and have remained structurally separate. They have, however, acculturated in varying degrees to the dominant Northern European culture. Thus, in the United States, assimilation has always been a one-way process that is perhaps, according to Healey (1995), better described as "Americanization" or "Anglo-conformity." Healey states:

> This kind of assimilation was designed to maintain the predominance of the British-type institutional patterns created during the early years of American society. Under Anglo-conformity there is relatively little sharing of cultural traits, and immigrants and minority groups are expected to adapt to Anglo-American culture as fast as possible. Historically, Americanization has been a precondition for access to better jobs, higher education, and other opportunities. (p. 40)

Acculturation, again, is the taking on of cultural patterns of another group—in this case, dominant white culture. In relation to working with culturally diverse populations, acculturation has importance in two ways:

- ▶ It is critical to be able to assess the amount of acculturation that has taken place within any individual or family and, simultaneously, to discover to what extent and in what specific areas traditional attitudes, values, and behavior still remain. Without such a "reading," it is impossible to know what form of helping process is most appropriate and most effective with culturally diverse clients. Just knowing that a client is Latino/a in origin tells us very little about who the person is or how he or she lives. To know where the individual falls on a continuum from traditional identification to complete acculturation offers more information. It is important, however, not to confuse group membership with the degree of acculturation that has occurred—or, as Sue and Zane (1987) warn, to "avoid confounding the cultural values of the client's ethnic group with those of the client" (p. 8).

▸ Acculturation can create serious emotional strain and difficulties for ethnic clients. A special term, *acculturative stress*, has been coined to refer to such situations. Take, for example, a newly arrived Vietnamese family. The children have learned English relatively quickly in comparison to their parents. As a result, they may end up translating for and becoming the spokespeople for the family. This is not a traditional role for Vietnamese children, who are trained to be very deferential to their elders; nor is it natural within their tradition for children to be in a position to wield so much power. As the children Americanize, they feel increasingly less bound by traditional ways. The result is enormous stress on the family unit, as is usually the case when traditional cultural ways are compromised or lost as a result of immigration and acculturation.

▸ Views of Acculturation 9-4

Researchers have long argued over how best to conceptualize the process of acculturation. Is it uni-dimensional or multi-dimensional? That is, does acculturation exist on a single continuum ranging from identification with the indigenous culture at one end to identification with the dominant culture at the other? Or does it make more sense to conceive of an individual's attachment to the two groups as independent of each other, with the possibility of simultaneously retaining an allegiance to one's traditional culture as well as to dominant American culture?

▸ The uni-dimensional view implies that as one moves toward dominant cultural patterns, there must be a simultaneous giving up of traditional ways. This approach has generated the notion of the "marginal" person, an ethnic group member who tries to acculturate into the majority but ends up in a perpetual limbo between the two cultures (Berry, 2017; Lewin, 1948; Stonequist, 1961). Such individuals have transformed themselves too much to return to traditional ways, but at the same time, they cannot gain any real acceptance in the majority culture because of their skin color. A variety of symptoms have been attributed to such marginality: feelings of inferiority, depression, hyper-self-consciousness, restlessness and anomie, and a heightened sense of race consciousness.

▶ Other writers see acculturation as bi- or multi-dimensional. Proponents of such biculturalism believe that it is possible to live and function effectively in two cultures (Berry, 2017; Cross, 1988; Oetting and Beauvais, 1990; Valentine, 1971). Unlike the marginal person who is suspended between cultures with little real connection to either, the bicultural individual feels connected to both and picks and chooses aspects of each to internalize. Thus, in this view, it is possible for an Asian American to remain deeply steeped in a traditional lifestyle while interacting comfortably in the white world, perhaps in relation to work, some socializing, and political activity outside the Asian American community. Problems with this notion arise when aspects of the two cultures are in clear conflict. For example, an immigrant Latina woman is forced to give up her traditional role and work outside the home and yet tries to remain true to traditional sex roles. Even if she is able to integrate the two, it will be very difficult for her children, not having been fully acculturated in traditional ways, to do the same (Casas and Pytluk, 1995). It should also be pointed out that biculturalism is not seen as a virtue in all ethnic communities. Some view those who have become proficient in majority ways with contempt—as "turncoats" who have rejected and turned away from their own kind.

▶ A third perspective, typified by the work of Marin (1992), suggests that the impact of acculturation can be best assessed by discovering the kinds of material that have been gained or lost through acculturation. Marin distinguishes three levels of acculturation. The superficial level involves learning and for getting facts that are part of a culture's history or tradition. The intermediate level has to do with gaining or losing more central aspects and behaviors of a person's social world (e.g., language preference and use, ethnicity of spouse, friends, neighbors, names given to children, and choice of media). The significant level of cultural material involves core values, beliefs, and norms that are essential to the very cultural paradigm or worldview of the person. For example, Marin (1992) points to the Latino culture's values of "encouraging positive interpersonal relationships and discouraging negative, competitive and assertive interactions," "familialism," and "collectivism" (p. 239). When cultural values of this magnitude are lost or become less central, acculturation has reached a significant point, and one might wonder what remains of an individual's cultural attachment. For many whites, traditional cultural ties progressively slipped away, generation by generation in America, according to Marin's model. The immigrant generation tended to trade more superficial cultural material. Their children, in turn, exchanged more intermediate and core cultural material as they increasingly acculturated.

Immigration and Acculturation

Acculturative stress is most pronounced during periods of transition, especially during and after significant migrations (e.g., to the United States) and the exposure and necessary adjustment to a new culture. Landau (1982) points to five factors that make the transition either easier or more difficult:

- The reasons for the migration and whether the original expectations and hopes were met
- The availability of community and extended family support systems
- The structure of the family and whether it was forced to assume a different form after migration (e.g., moving from extended family to exclusively nuclear)
- The degree to which the new culture is similar to the old (the greater the difference, the more substantial the stress)
- The family's general ability to be flexible and adaptive

According to Landau, and more recent writers McDowell, Knudson-Martin, and Bermudez (2017), when the stresses are severe, the support insufficient, and the family basically unhealthy, the family unit is likely to try to compensate in one of three ways, each leading to further stresses and a compounding of existing problems. The family may isolate itself and remain separate from its new environment. It may become enmeshed and close its boundaries to the outside world, rigidify its traditional ways, and become overly dependent on its members. Or the family may become disengaged, wherein individual family members become isolated from one another as they reject previous family values and lifestyles. Especially problematic is the situation in which family members acculturate at very different rates. Cobb et al. (2017) found that acculturation dimensions, such as ethnic identity of undocumented Latinos/as in the United States, were significantly related to experiences of everyday discrimination and increased depression. They went on to suggest that more research needs to be conducted, focused on the acculturation experiences of undocumented Latinos/as so that mental health professionals can offer more culture specific interventions (Cobb et al., 2017).

Perhaps the most common and problematic consequence of acculturation is the breakdown of traditional cultural and family norms. Among Latino/a immigrants, for instance, this may take the form of challenges to traditional beliefs about male authority and supremacy, role expectations for men, and standards of conduct for females. But such changes may not be limited to newer immigrants. Carrillo (1982) suggests that these same changing patterns are evident within the Latino/a community as a whole: "Clearly, Hispanics appear to be moving away from such strict concepts of role and authority within the family, and with this movement approaching new normative behavior for males and females" (p. 260). This suggestion aligns with current research by Allison and Bencomo (2015).

Carrillo (1982) goes on to warn helping professionals to exhibit caution in assessing pathology, appropriateness, and inappropriateness in relation to Latino/a sex-role behavior and provides the following example:

> An Hispanic man who prefers the company of other men and who behaves in an authoritative manner with his wife may be manifesting his "machismo" rather than indicating personal pathology. Such behavior among other cultural groups may imply "latent homosexuality," or an "inferiority complex," or that the woman is masochistic and prefers to be a "martyr." Such is not necessarily the case among Hispanic groups. (p. 261)

It is critical to be familiar with the norms of the group and subgroup of which the client is a member. This is not to say, however, that emotional problems do not develop as a result of cultural change; quite the contrary. Carrillo (1982), in fact, points out a number of problems that can emerge in relation to the individual's "inability to accept, conform to or adhere to sex-role defined standards of conduct" (p. 258). For males, symptoms can include difficulties in relation to authority, preoccupation and anxiety over sexual potency, conflict over the need for role consistency, and depression and isolation over having to feel invincible. For females, it tends to include feelings of failure and depression over not being able to live up to the strict sex-role requirements that are placed on them, as well as the somatization (development of bodily symptoms) of their frustration and rage.

Acculturation and Community Breakdown

A final dynamic worth exploring is the psychological consequences of the breakdown of communal support as a result of assimilation. As acculturation proceeds and individual group members feel less attached to traditional ways, they often choose to leave the community (or ghetto) in the hope of avoiding some of the hatred and animosity that are routinely directed toward the group. Lewin (1948), drawing on observations of highly assimilated German Jews prior to World War II, suggests a very different outcome than one would predict. Specifically, he found that by leaving the ghetto, acculturated individuals put themselves at greater risk of being the objects of prejudice and racial hatred than was true when they resided within the traditional community. Lewin writes:

> If we compare the position of the individual Jew in the Ghetto period . . . with his situation in modern times . . . we find that he now stands much more for and by himself.
>
> With the wider spread and scattering of the Jewish group, the family or the single individual becomes functionally much more separated . . . In the ghetto he felt the pressure to be essentially applied to the Jewish group as a whole . . . Now as a result of the disintegration of the group, he is much more exposed to pressure as an individual . . . Even when the pressure on the whole group from without was weakened, that on the individual Jew was relatively increased. (pp. 153–155)

A more recent example of this phenomenon is when a member of lower SES community is able to pull themselves up into a higher economic status. Throughout that process of growing, that individual may adjust themselves (i.e., change their accent, change appearance, change their clothes) to survive in a new environment. While that person chooses to sacrifice parts of their culture to survive in a new environment, he may still feel connected to their community. However, the changes cause their community to disown him, leaving that person feeling as if he does not belong in either world.

In other words, with acculturation and assimilation, the ability of the community to protect the individual is weakened, and efforts to avoid racial hatred by distancing oneself from group membership are likely to prove counterproductive.

In regard to acculturated individuals leaving the community, Lige, Peteet, and Brown (2017) studied the racial identity, self-esteem, and impostor phenomenon among African American students. For some of these students, going to college was not a part of their family's culture. In some cases, it took generations for African American families to be able to send an individual to college. These college students often experience the impostor phenomenon, which is a persistent perception of incompetence, despite contrary evidence (Lige et al., 2017). They went on to find that self-esteem mediates the relationship between racial identity and the impostor phenomenon.

Stress

A critical question that needs to be answered in order to understand the complex relationship between ethnicity and health is: How exactly does the negative impact of broad social factors, such as racism, acculturation, and poverty, get translated into the everyday physical and emotional distresses that disproportionately affect people of color?

According to Myers (1982), the mechanism is stress. Put most simply, being without resources and the perpetual object of discrimination makes life more stressful and, in turn, increases the risks of disease, instability, and breakdown. Myers begins his argument by suggesting that "for many blacks, particularly those who are poor, the critical antecedents appear to be the higher basal stress level and the state of high stress vigilance at which normative functioning often occurs" (p. 128). In other words, poor African Americans tend to live a "stress-primed" state of existence (Littleton, 2016).

Myers goes on to show how certain internal and external factors either increase or decrease (mediate) the subjective experience of stress and, as a result, the risk of stress-related diseases:

- Externally, current economic conditions set the stage for whether race- and social-class-related experiences will be sources of greater or lesser stress.
- Internally, individual temperament, problem-solving skills, a sense of internal control, and self-esteem reduce the likelihood that an event or situation is experienced as stressful.

With these factors as a baseline, two additional conditions seem to mediate the individual's response when a stressful situation is actually presented:

- The actual episodic stressful event that occurs
- The coping and adaptation of which the individual is capable

Myers (1982) contends that for poor African Americans, episodic crises are more frequent, and because of their higher basal stress levels, such crises are more likely to be damaging and disruptive.

> Thus, for example, the death of a spouse or relative or the loss of a job due to economic downturns is likely to be more psychologically and economically devastating to the person who is struggling to find enough money to eat, to pay the rent, and to support three or four children than it would to someone without those basic day to day concerns. (pp. 133–134)

Myers has identified substantial differences among group members in their ability to cope and in the type of coping strategies used. Street youth, for example, resort to engaging in less than legal activities as coping mechanisms for survival in the streets. For others, the "ability to remain calm, cool, and collected in the face of a crisis" is primary. Still others may turn to alcohol and drugs or religion as a means of gaming some distance. Myers believes that for African Americans as a group, stress-related illness risks are higher than for the general population. But he does point out that there are effective ways to reduce the risk:

> To the extent that ethnic cultural identity can be developed and stably integrated into the personality structure, to the extent that skills and competencies necessary to meet the varied demands can be obtained, to the extent that flexible,

contingent response strategies can be developed, and to the extent that support systems can be maintained and strengthened, then resistances can be developed that will enhance stress tolerance and reduce individual and collective risk for disorders and disabilities. (p. 138)

Daly et al. (1995) amplify on Myers's findings by describing specific coping mechanisms within the family, at the community level, and within organizations. Then, Utsey et al. (2000) continued this line of study, focusing on life satisfaction and self-esteem among African Americans. More recently, Myers et al. (2015) found that a lifetime of cumulative adversities such as experiences of discrimination, childhood family adversities, childhood sexual abuse, other childhood traumas, and chronic stress can have deleterious consequences on the mental health of African Americans and Latino/as.

▶ Psychological Trauma   9-5

Stress reactions, which Myers (1982) sees as having particular impact on people of color, serve to deplete psychic resources and ultimately lead to some kind of breakdown in functioning or illness. There are, however, stress experiences that are so extreme that they not only deplete personal resources but actually shut down an individual's basic psychic adaptation systems. Clinically, we call these traumas or traumatic events. Comas-Díaz (2016) defined racial trauma as "events of danger related to real or perceived experience of discrimination, threats of harm and injury, and humiliating and shaming events, in addition to witnessing harm to other ethnoracial individuals because of real or perceived racism" (p. 249). According to Herman (1997/2015), "traumatic events overwhelm the ordinary systems of care that give people a sense of control, connection, and meaning . . . Unlike commonplace misfortunes, traumatic events generally involve threats to life or bodily integrity, or a close encounter with violence and death" (p. 33). Intense trauma, which has been diagnostically labeled *post-traumatic stress disorder (PTSD)*, involves a loss of basic safety, intense fear, helplessness, loss of control, and threat of annihilation. Turner and Richardson (2016) explained that the impact of police shootings on African American communities has increased symptoms of depression, anxiety, fear, and low self-esteem. Herman (1997/2015) distinguishes four major symptom-groups associated with trauma:

- ▶ *Hyperarousal*, in which the internal biology of self-preservation goes on permanent alert.
- ▶ *Intrusion*, in which traumatized people relive the event as if it were recurring in the present.
- ▶ *Constriction and numbing*, which involve a psychic deadening or dissociation from reality.
- ▶ *Disconnection*, which involves a shattering of the self, its attachment to others, and the meaning of human experience.

Much of the research on trauma has involved victims of genocide, torture, ethnic conflict, and racism as well as women, children, and gay people. Too often, racial and ethnic animosities end in violence and hate crimes that target people of color and other minorities. It has been argued by certain authors (Brave Heart, 2004; Duran and Duran, 1995) that in some ethnic populations, PTSD is a derivative of racism and colonization. The topic of social trauma (and I refer to it and other forms of mass violence as social because it tends to involve identifiable ethnic populations and is fueled not only by personal, but also by social, cultural, and political motives) is more fully explored in Chapter 10.

There are a number of important points to be made in relation to psychological trauma.

▶ The source and type of trauma dictates its impact and magnitude. Trauma resulting from natural disasters, such as floods and earthquakes, tends to be less debilitating than that caused by other human beings. "Acts of God" tend to be less personally destructive and easier to recover from psychologically than those carried out in an interpersonal context. One possible explanation is that trauma caused by human hands is experienced as more personal and purposeful and, as a result, is more likely to destroy a victim's basic sense of attachment to others and safety in the world. Similarly, repeated and long-term abuse, as in the case of torture, captivity, and repeated child abuse, is generally more destructive and debilitating than single, isolated incidents.

▶ It is important to understand that, although the trauma experience happened in the past, it can best be understood, as Gobodo-Madikizela (2000) suggests, as "lived memory." The victim has been reliving it, over and over again, in great detail as if it is still happening. Gobodo-Madikizela relates the experience of listening to a South African mother describing the death of her 11-year-old son: The death was so vivid to me that it was as if it were happening in the moment. Her use of tense defied the rules of grammar as she crossed and recrossed the boundaries of past and present in an illustration of the timelessness of traumatic pain . . . "He *ran* out. He *is* still chewing his bread . . . *Now* I am dazed. I *ran* . . . " And the final moment when she recalled seeing her son's lifeless body: "Here *is* my son." With a gesture of her hand, she transformed the tragic scene from one that happened more than ten years earlier to one that we were witnessing right there on the floor of her front room (pp. 88–89).

▶ Various researchers (Duran and Duran, 1995; Epstein, 1998; Fogelman, 1991; Sangalang and Vang, 2017) have suggested that social trauma can be passed on or transmitted intergenerationally within ethnic families.

An individual growing up in such an environment internalizes the trauma of past generations and responds to present events and experiences in light of that traumatization. In fact, Brave Heart (2004) argues for the creation of a new diagnostic designation, *historic trauma*, that emphasizes the massive cumulative trauma that can occur across generations and reflects a broader range of social consequences and dysfunction than is referred to by the more limited and a historical diagnosis of PTSD. By way of evidence, Yehuda (1999) points to studies that show that children of Jewish Holocaust survivors are more vulnerable than others to the development of PTSD, including a greater degree of cumulative lifetime stress. Brave Heart (2004) explains: "This finding implies that there is a propensity among offspring to perceive or experience events as more traumatic and stressful; children of Holocaust survivors with a parent having chronic PTSD were more likely to develop PTSD in response to their own lifespan traumatic events. The traumatic symptoms of the parents, rather than the trauma exposure per se, are the critical risk factors for offspring manifesting their own trauma response" (p. 12). Historic trauma is also often associated with the destruction of traditional cultural and spiritual rituals that might have ameliorated the effect of the trauma in the first place.

▶ Substance abuse and dependence often occur with trauma. Physical pain and the disruption of healthy bodily functioning are regular occurrences in trauma. A first step in treatment involves regaining control of the body and often involves, as Herman (1997/2015) suggests, restoring biological rhythms of eating and sleep and reducing the symptoms of hyperarousal and intrusion. The psychic pain is less easily or quickly controlled, and patients regularly self-medicate in order to reduce the ongoing emotional pain.

▶ It is important to acknowledge that therapeutic work with trauma survivors is particularly challenging for a number of reasons. First, the clinical material that the trauma victim must share is not only painful for her or him to relive, but it is also very difficult for the therapist to hear and assimilate. There is in each of us a strong, unconscious tendency to avoid such disturbing material. Victims are often fearful that others, including the therapist, will not believe them. Second, it is also quite natural for the client to project feelings about the perpetrator onto the therapist. As McWilliams (2004) points out: "Because the transferences of clients with histories of traumatic abuse tend initially to be intense and relatively undiluted by observing capacities, it is hard for such individuals to take in the possibility that the therapist sincerely has their best interests at heart" (p. 253). It has been suggested that working with trauma survivors can be "traumatic" in its own right. Such trauma is referred to as *vicarious traumatization*. Third, trauma work is long term, highly emotional, and very draining, and it can involve frequent setbacks, re-traumatization, hospitalizations, and efforts at self-injury. Trauma in its most extreme form transforms one's physiology, sense of self and safety, attachment to others, and sense of meaning in life. As Herman (1997/2015) emphasizes: "Because trauma affects every aspect of human functioning, from the biological to the social, treatment must be comprehensive and stage-appropriate. A form of therapy that may be useful for a patient at one stage may be of little use or even harmful to the same patient at another stage" (p. 156).

▸ Root (1992) has introduced the idea of "insidious trauma"; that is, pervasive and ongoing attacks and slights associated with one's identity as a person of color or member of a targeted minority group devalued by the majority culture. Also related here are the concepts of racial microaggressions and implicit racism introduced in Chapter 4. Insidious trauma begins early when the child is particularly vulnerable to such emotional slights, is cumulative, and can eventually trigger full-blown complex trauma reactions that are experienced as life-threatening. Susceptibility to insidious trauma may also be exacerbated by a history of intergenerationally transmitted traumatic experience, as described earlier in this section.

▸ By way of assessment for trauma, Hays (2008) makes the following important suggestions: An assessment of trauma should be made only in light of each client's cultural life history and minority status. A client may not report a traumatic experience until trust has developed. If a client begins to decompensate while describing a traumatic event, back off and then proceed slowly and over time. Explore and validate clients strengthens by way of empowerment to balance the exploration of traumatic experiences. Be sure not to overpathologize the clients and emphasize growth and healing. With children, be very careful of re-traumatization with play therapy. Assess for trauma at the level of community experience as well as individual and personal.

▸ Additional, valuable material on the topic of trauma can be found in Tracy Smith's excellent article "Working with Complex Trauma in Children and Adolescents" in Chapter 7, as well as the entirety of Chapter 10.

Drug and Alcohol Use

There are three important points to be made about substance use and ethnicity:

▸ First, there are numerous myths about substance abuse among people of color. Rather than reflect anything akin to empirical reality, they are based on distorted stereotypes of excessive use and abuse by people of color, especially in comparison to beliefs about the consumption patterns of whites. "All Mexicans use and sell drugs" is a typical stereotype. Recently, for example, a report was issued regarding profiles of suspected drug traffickers to be routinely stopped and searched by the Oregon State Highway Patrol. Included among the characteristics that were sufficient to initiate a search was "being Hispanic." In reality, research shows that, with a few notable exceptions (to be discussed shortly), people of color tend to use drugs and alcohol much less frequently than do dominant-culture Americans.

▶ Second, there are real cultural differences in consumption patterns, in the meaning of drinking and substance use, and in what is socially acceptable across cultures. Like the interpretation of any cultural differences, it is dangerous to make clinical judgments about patterns of substance use by culturally diverse clients without knowledge of the norms that exist around drinking or drug use within their culture. The same consumption pattern in an Asian American male, for instance, may have very different meaning vis-à-vis possible excesses and pathology than it would for a similarly aged Native American male.

▶ Third, the meaning of recovery and abstinence is very different for people of color and dominant group members. Substance abuse among whites tends to be understood as a personal issue; for people of color, it is as much a social-cultural issue as a personal one.

A good place to begin is by citing research findings on substance use and abuse in youth of color. Drug research on youth is more plentiful than similar data on adults and, in general, tends to reflect similar patterns to those of adults within the same culture. The following data are drawn from and summarized in Bernard (1991) and Beker, Isralowitz, and Singer (2014):

▶ With the exception of Native American youth, other ethnic populations exhibit use patterns that are significantly less than young whites. This fact challenges common beliefs and stereotypes about runaway abuse and addiction among minority youth. As ethnic group members acculturate, however (and this is true for youth as well as adults), research shows that use levels increase and begin to approximate those of their white counterparts.

▶ The lower use rates among less acculturated African Americans, Latinos/as, and Asian Americans may reflect protective factors that exist in traditional ethnic cultures, including emphasis on cooperation, sharing, communality, group support, interdependence, and social responsibility. These values are believed to mitigate against social alienation, which has regularly been shown to be associated with high substance abuse. It is interesting to note that complementary values (i.e., competition, individualism, self-first, and non-sharing) are more closely aligned with Northern European dominant culture and are seen as risk factors implicated in the development of substance abuse problems.

▶ It has also been found that bicultural youth (i.e., those who can move effectively between the dominant culture and their culture of origin) tend to exhibit rather low levels of drug and alcohol use.

▶ Although youth of color generally show lower rates of substance use, their use tends to lead to more behavioral and health problems. This is because there is a cumulative effect of substance abuse with other risk factors, such as poverty, unemployment, discrimination, poor health care, and general depression, which correlate highly with ethnicity. It is believed that prevention is of little use unless these other risk factors are addressed.

More specific information on use and abuse patterns of youth of color by community is summarized in Tables 9-3 through 9-6.

TABLE 9-3
Key Findings from Prevention Research Update Number Three:
Substance Abuse Among Latino/a Youth

- Half of the Hispanic population is now under age 18, which makes them the largest, youngest, and fastest-growing of the nation's subgroups.
- Some researchers has found that Hispanics have more serious and chronic drug-related problems and multigenerational problems although, in general, they have no higher levels of use prevalence than whites or other ethnic groups.
- Hispanic youth consume higher quantities and experience more alcohol-related problems than do other adolescents.
- The value that the right to drink is a rite of passage is the result of the blending of drinking patterns of the donor cultures with those common among U.S. youth and reflect; this value leads to heavier use patterns beginning in late adolescence.
- Stress in family relationships and behavioral problems in immigrant children who may acculturate to the U.S. culture at a faster rate than their parents is known as differential acculturation
- Substance abuse prevention efforts must do three things: (a) encourage biculturalism and bilingualism, building on cultural strengths and pride while facilitating the development of skills necessary to succeed in U.S. society; (b) involve the community in community development efforts, especially the development of cultural arts centers; and (c) involve the community in public awareness campaigns to counter the efforts of the alcohol/ tobacco industry in Hispanic communities.

TABLE 9-4

Key Findings from Prevention Research Update Number Two: Substance Abuse Among Minority Youth: Asian Americans

- Asian Americans have low levels of use compared with other ethnic groups, with the exception of Native Hawaiians, whose drug and alcohol use is more similar to whites.
- Asian Americans suffer less from substance-related problems than other ethnic groups.
- Social norms condemning excessive use of alcohol govern drinking in Asian society and encourages moderation.
- Alcohol usage levels increase as acculturation increases in Asian males.
- Due to their "model minority" stereotype status and because they do not want to bring shame on their families, some researchers and practitioners are concerned that Asian American substance use problems are underreported.
- Substance abuse prevention efforts should focus on (a) encouraging biculturalism; (b) involving youth in community prevention; and (c) providing indigenously owned family counseling and support services.

Source: From *Moving toward a "just and vital culture": Multiculturalism in our schools*, by B. Bernard, April, 1991.
© 1991 Education Northwest, https://educationnorthwest.org/ Used with Permission. All Rights Reserved.

TABLE 9-5

Key Findings from Prevention Research Update Number Five: Substance Abuse Among Native American Youth

- The use of all drugs, but especially alcohol, marijuana, and inhalants, have been consistently higher among Native American youth than non-Indian youth.
- The rate of alcoholism is two to three times the national average for Native American youth.
- Heavy drinking is a contributing factor to one in two Native American students never finishing high school.
- Native American adolescents are profoundly isolated and depressed and experience high rates of lawbreaking, learning and behavior problems, and suicide.
- Deep sociocultural and economic exploitation has made Native Americans the most severely disadvantaged population in the United States.
- The foremost risk factors for Native American adolescent substance abuse are (a) cultural dislocation and lack of integration into either traditional Indian or modern American life; (b) community norms and peer-group supporting use; and (c) lack of hope for a bright future.
- Prevention efforts must emphasize (1) community involvement with youth playing a major role in community development efforts and (2) educational interventions that allow Native American youth to develop the skills necessary to be successful in the dominant culture while retaining their identification with and respect for traditional Native American values

Source: From *Moving toward a "just and vital culture": Multiculturalism in our schools*, by B. Bernard, April, 1991.
© 1991 Education Northwest, https://educationnorthwest.org/ Used with Permission. All Rights Reserved.

TABLE 9-6
Key Findings from Prevention Research Update Number Four:
Substance Abuse Among Black Youth

- Substance use is lower among black adolescents than among whites or any other ethnic group except Asian Americans.
- While blacks are more likely to be abstainers and to have lower levels of alcohol use than whites, they experience more drinking-related problems, especially binge drinking, health problems, symptoms of physical dependence, and symptoms of loss of control.
- Compared with whites, adult blacks are more likely to be victims of alcohol-related homicide, to be arrested for drunkenness, and to be sent to prison rather than to treatment for alcohol-related crimes.
- At even moderate levels of use, the adverse consequences of substance use are exacerbated by the conditions of poverty, unemployment, discrimination, poor health, and despair that many black youth face.
- Drug trafficking adversely affects the ability of the entire black community to function and deal with its other problems.
- Black communities are particularly exploited by the alcohol industry through excessive advertising and the number of sales outlets in these neighborhoods.
- Prevention efforts must (1) involve the community in community development efforts that include an active role for youth; (2) facilitate the development of racial consciousness and pride; (3) include public awareness campaigns that counter the alcohol/tobacco industry's advertising; (4) be broad-based (i.e., providing access to a range of social and economic services and opportunities); and (5) restructure schools to provide opportunities for academic success.

Source: From *Moving toward a "just and vital culture": Multiculturalism in our schools*, by B. Bernard, April, 1991.
© 1991 Education Northwest, https://educationnorthwest.org/ Used with Permission. All Rights Reserved.

Comparing Latinos and Asian Americans

Differences in patterns of use and social attitudes and behaviors associated with drinking and drugs vary dramatically across cultures. To appreciate the enormity of these differences, it is useful to juxtapose the characteristics of two groups—Latinos/as and Asian Americans—by way of comparison. It should be remembered, however, that with acculturation, these patterns move toward approximating dominant cultural norms or result in a kind of hybrid behavior.

For instance, the use of illicit drugs increases dramatically with acculturation among Latino/a youth. Drug use is much less prominent than alcohol use among more traditionally identified youth. Or by way of example of the interaction, Mexican men tend to drink less often, but more per occasion, than non–Mexican American males. After arrival in the United States, however, they tend to retain their heavier consumption patterns and also begin to drink more frequently. Gender differences in substance use among traditional Latino/a youth are far more pronounced than among whites. Traditional women have very low consumption rates. With acculturation, these rates increase dramatically, reducing the disparity between the genders. Young men's drinking patterns, on the other hand, do not change noticeably with acculturation because drinking is an acknowledged part of male role behavior within Latino culture; it is an aspect of male bonding. For women, American culture gives much more permission regarding drinking behavior than does Latina culture. In comparison to other communities of color, Latino/a youth are particularly susceptible to peer influence in drug and alcohol use. This is probably related to the high value placed on interpersonal relationships within the culture. In addition, consumption varies with the presence of parental and sibling role models of drinking in the home. The use of dangerous drugs by males also seems related to a need to both escape pain and present a macho image. Thus, cultural values such as *person-alismo* (an emphasis on interpersonal connections as opposed to personal accomplishments), *machismo* (male role characteristics), and *carnalismo* (an emphasis on ethnic pride) play a major role in shaping the way substances are used.

Among Asian Americans, on the other hand, use is more culturally controlled. First of all, there is evidence of innate biological reactions that discourage drinking. A "flushing" or reddening reaction, which is reported to be rather uncomfortable, is found among some Asian American subgroups. Similarly, there seems to be a physiologically based dislike for the taste of alcohol among some individuals. But these seem to discourage drinking only to the extent that traditional cultural prohibitions are still in place. According to Austin, Prendergast, and Lee (1989):

> In accordance with Asian cultural values, Asian drinking is social rather than solitary, occurs in prescribed situations, is usually accompanied by food, is used to enhance social interaction, and occurs within a context of modern drinking norms. Women drink little or no alcohol. Aggressive and noisy behavior when intoxicated is looked down upon. Even when drunk, Chinese and Japanese men are seldom loud or disorderly. Asian philosophies emphasize moderation, order, and social harmony and tend to discourage practices that compromise these values. Thus, for Asian Americans, alcohol consumption is culturally contained. It occurs as an essential part of religious ceremonies and festive occasions but only in moderation, and excesses are seen as an embarrassment to the individual and the family. (p. 8)

More information about these cultures' patterns of use and social attitudes and behaviors associated with drinking and drugs can be found in *Substance Abuse Counseling* (Lewis, Dana, and Blevins, 2018). Before discussing the cultural meaning of recovery, it is important to understand the cultural reasons some individuals have for not seeking help for alcohol or drug problems. Verissimo and Grella (2017) examined these reasons and found three barriers to seeking help—structural, attitudinal, and readiness for change, as stated:

▶ African Americans and Latinos/as were less likely than whites to endorse attitudinal barriers,

- Latinos/as were less likely than whites to endorse readiness for change as a barrier,
- African Americans were more likely to endorse structural barriers, and
- Among all ethnic groups, women endorsed attitudinal barriers of alcohol problems.

▶ The Cultural Meaning of Recovery   9-6

Substance abuse, although its addictive qualities make it a problem in its own right, is most usefully viewed as symptomatic of other underlying psychological and emotional conditions. From such a perspective, it is believed that individuals use substances to either medicate themselves or escape inner pain. For people of color, however, substance abuse and recovery also possess cultural and communal meanings. I will never forget a talk given by a Native American elder who had for many years worked as a substance abuse counselor and was himself a recovering addict. "My problem was not alcohol," he emphasized. "It was not knowing who I was and where I belonged. The alcohol was just the way I killed the pain."

In Chapter 10, you will learn more about unresolved historic grief and how its source can be located in a history of cumulative traumas, as well as the destruction of cultural methods of grieving. According to Duran and Duran (1995), before colonization, alcohol use (as well as the use of substances such as peyote) was strictly controlled by tribal tradition, and its consumption was primarily ceremonial. As Native American culture was systematically destroyed, these controls were eliminated, and with the widespread introduction of excessive drinking as a means of pacifying Native American males, heavy alcohol consumption itself became a tradition on the reservation.

Standard treatment methods, based on dominant cultural views of substance abuse, are totally ineffective with Native Americans because they do nothing to change the social and cultural roots of the problem. Only by retrieving what was culturally lost and simultaneously instilling a positive sense of ethnic identity is there any real hope for overcoming substance abuse among Native Peoples. As Duran and Duran pointed out earlier, to subject Native American clients to Western modes of treatment, substance abuse included, that have inherent in them the very processes that undermined Native American culture in the first place is merely to dig the hole deeper.

Duran and Duran (1995) argue for the adoption of indigenous views of alcohol abuse, coupled with traditional methods of healing. Traditionally, alcohol was viewed as a destructive spiritual entity that had to be addressed in the spiritual realm if healing was to occur. Healing, in turn, had to occur not only within the individual but also within the context of the community. More and more, even within the confines of some Western agencies, sweat lodge ceremonies and other spiritual rituals are being introduced as part of treatment.

At a more universal level, the idea is that true recovery for people of color must involve an acknowledgment of the impact of racism, as well as substantial clinical efforts to heal its destructive inner effects. In a group therapy session for older African American addicts, I once observed a clear consensus that getting "clean" was not enough. One could never get beyond the "inner prison of drinking or drugging" until the "spiritual ghosts" of racism had been laid to rest.

SUMMARY

This chapter focuses on mental health issues that plague people of color. We begin with a discussion of racial identification and group belonging in adults. (Similar issues related to the experience of children are explored in Chapter 7.) Ethnic identity refers to the individual's subjective experience of ethnicity and group belonging, including related meanings attached to ethnicity, conscious and unconscious feelings, and behavioral manifestations. Klein (1980) and Diller (1991) refer to three states of ethnic identity: positive identification, ambivalent identification, and negative identification. An alternative method of conceptualization—that of models of racial identity development, as proposed by Helms (1990), Cross (1995), and others— hypothesizes that people of color go through a series of predicable stages as they strug- gle to make sense of their relationship to their own cultural group, as well as to the oppression of mainstream white culture. Both approaches assume the possibility of difficulties in ethnic identification and suggest different implications for treatment.

Ethnic group members can differ greatly in the amount of assimilation and accul- turation that they have experienced. Both involve ethnic individuals taking on different cultural forms. Individual group members can vary from retaining intact traditional culture at one extreme to having totally acculturated into the mainstream at the other. One's location on this continuum is useful in determining the most appropriate mental health intervention.

Acculturation can also create serious emotional strain when contradictory cultural values have been internalized or vary within the family. Uni-dimensional, bicultural, and behavior-specific models of acculturation are contrasted. Acculturative stress is most pronounced during periods of transition, especially during migration and the adjustment to a new society.

Stress is suggested as the mechanism through which people of color are put at greater risk for physical and mental health; that is, how social factors such as racism, acculturation, identity issues, and poverty translate into physical and mental distress. Myers (1982) offers a broad-based model of the internal and external risk and coping factors related to stress in African Americans. For example, he contends that poor African Americans experience episodic crises more often, and because of higher basal stress levels, such crises are more likely to be damaging and disruptive. Positive ethnic identity is seen as an important resiliency factor.

Psychological trauma is an extreme and highly debilitating instance of stress, involves threats to life and body integrity or close contacts with violence and death, and causes a loss of basic safety, intense fear, helplessness, loss of control, and threats of annihilation. People of color and other minorities are at higher risk for social and insidious trauma. Trauma resulting from interpersonal and prolonged and repeated violations tends to be most debilitating. Trauma is best understood as lived and repetitious memory, can be transmitted from generation to generation, often coexists with substance abuse, is intimately related to minority status, and is particularly demanding to treat. Specific suggestions for assessing for trauma are presented.

Drug and alcohol abuse among people of color is explored. Various popular myths of excessive use by people of color are unfounded. Differences in consumption patterns and the meaning of substance use across cultures do exist, as well as avenues toward recovery.

ACTIVITIES

1. **Undertake a guided fantasy.** Seat yourself comfortably, close your eyes, take a few slow, deep breaths, and relax. Try to project yourself into the following situation (unrealistic as it may seem). You wake up one morning, get out of bed, see yourself in the mirror, and discover that you, normally a white person, have become African American. Or you, normally a person of color, have become a white person. Envision yourself as such. Now fantasize your way through a typical day as a person of color or as a white person. What happens, and how are your reactions, as well as the reactions of those around you, different? What kinds of emotions and feelings are building up within you? How has the world changed for you? Stay with it for as long as you can. This exercise can be done by yourself, in a dyad, or in a small group. In the latter configurations, take turns sharing your experiences and then discuss and compare them.

2. **Carry out a community needs assessment.** You have been recently hired as the director of a community mental health center located in a mixed-race, working-class neighborhood in a major urban area. You have become aware that in the community, there is a small group of South Asian Indian refugees who do not avail themselves of your center's services. You know from your course in cultural diversity that probably the most culturally sensitive way to approach them is a community needs assessment; that is, approaching the community and in various ways gaining information from them on what kind of mental health needs they may have and how you might best provide those services. Design a plan for carrying out such a needs assessment. Be specific.

Treating Victims of Ethnic Conflict, Genocide, and Mass Violence

LEARNING OBJECTIVES

10-1 Describe the historic trauma and unresolved grief among Native Americans.

10-2 Explain South Africa's Truth and Reconciliation Commission.

10-3 Explain the impact of the Holocaust on Holocaust survivors, Nazis, and their children.

10-4 Summarize treatment recommendations for traumatized refugee and immigrant populations.

In the following excerpt from a *New York Times* op-ed piece, psychologist Pumla Gobodo-Madikizela (2003) describes the complexity of healing in her native South Africa after apartheid.

In Chapter 9, you were introduced to the concept of trauma. A *trauma* is an extraordinary psychological experience—caused by threats to life and bodily safety or personal encounters with violence and death—that overwhelms ordinary human functioning. When the source of trauma is natural, such as a hurricane or flooding, we speak of disasters. When the traumatic event is caused by other human beings, it is referred to as an *a trocity*. In the pages that follow, you will learn about violence and atrocities caused by ethnic and racial hatred as well as efforts to heal the survivors of

CASE STUDY 1

The Roots of Afrikaner Rage

"There were places black people were forbidden to go," my mother says as we near the restaurant in an upmarket Cape Town shopping mall. "And now we can come to the same places as whites, walk into a cafe, and pay the same money—just like that."

For some white South Africans, mingling with blacks in urban malls is a welcome change from the racial isolation of the past. Some are simply resigned to this post-apartheid reality . . . But for others, the appearance of black faces in spaces that were previously reserved for whites is seen as an invasion of what belongs to them—things they worked so hard to build, their pride, their *vaderland*. This has evoked bitterness and unleashed their wrath and violent outrage.

Having been a child and an adult under apartheid, and having grown up in a family and community of dispossessed and disenfranchised adults, I can understand their anger. For the sake of the nation's future peace and unity, I hope that everyone concerned will consider its sources...

Some see the rising tide of discontent among Afrikaners as evidence of racist attitudes that won't go away. This may be so. But we also must consider the bitter memories that have been unleashed by the transfer of power to a black government. Most Afrikaners carry in their consciousness the spirit of survival; there is always an "other" from whom the *volk* must be protected. They suffered serious loss and humiliation in their war with the British, the Boer War. In that conflict . . . British troops destroyed thousands of Boer farms, blew up homesteads . . . Thousands of Afrikaner women, children, and elderly men were sent to internment camps . . . homeless and humiliated, the Afrikaners lost their fight against British domination.

After the British, there was another enemy. Mr. de Klerk apologized to South Africans who were oppressed by apartheid laws, "in the spirit of true repentance." Yet the ghosts of the past have yet been laid to rest . . . The dialogue that was begun by the truth and reconciliation commission must continue . . . Acknowledging the loss that Afrikaners feel would be a start."

The task of picking up the pieces of a society shattered by violence is not easy. My mother, who grew up in rural KwaZulu-Natal Provence, remembers the loss of her family's land and witnesses the humiliation of a father who had to seek work in the faraway place that black people call "Gauteng," "the place of gold": Johannesburg. She and my father were married in Cape Town in 1951, the year in which more than 70 oppressive laws were passed by the apartheid government.

She, like many black people I know, has every reason to remember with bitterness and to harbor a desire for revenge. But she prefers to live without that burden.

Note: From *New York Times,* January 10, 2003, p. A23.

such experiences. Herman (1997) describes a basic dilemma that confounds the treatment of such trauma.

> The ordinary response to atrocities is to banish them from consciousness. Certain violations of the social compact are too terrible to utter aloud: this is the meaning of the word *unspeakable*. Atrocities, however, refuse to be buried. Equally as powerful as the desire to deny atrocities is the conviction that denial does not work. Folk wisdom is filled with ghosts who refuse to rest in their graves until their stories are told . . . Remembering and telling the truth about terrible events are prerequisites both for the restoration of the social order and for the healing of individual victims. The conflict between the will to deny horrible events and the will to proclaim them aloud is the central dialectic of psychological trauma . . . When the truth is recognized, survivors can begin their recovery. But far too often secrecy prevails, and the story of the traumatic event surfaces not as a verbal narrative but as a symptom. (p. 1)

Violence and atrocities are typically directed toward the weak and the powerless. Victims of individual crimes of violence tend to be women, children, gays, the disabled, the poor, ethnic minorities, and the elderly. The same populations also tend to be the targets for mass violence: war, genocide, ethnic conflict, torture, enslavement, ethnic cleansing, colonialism, and racism. All are crimes of power and hatred. When the diagnosis of post-traumatic stress disorder (PTSD) was first introduced in 1980, it was described as "out of the range of usual human experience." Clinical, social, and historical reality has since shown just how naïve such an idea is. If one considers the actual frequency of rape and other sexual crimes, battery, child abuse, domestic violence, hate crimes, war, ethnic conflict, terrorism, what is "out of the range of usual human experience" is our tendencies to remain silent in the face of trauma, to not get involved, and to avoid actively responding in our roles both as ordinary human beings and as helping and healing professionals.

Herman (1997) points to an interesting parallel between the dilemma of silence and truth telling in treatment and the history of research on trauma. "The study of psychological trauma has a curious history—one of episodic amnesia. Periods of active investigation have alternated with periods of oblivion" (p. 7). She refers, for example, to Freud's early findings of sexual abuse in all children and his subsequent denial or recanting of it as fantasy, to research on shell-shock after World War I and PTSD after Vietnam and its subsequent suppression, and the emergence of concern over domestic violence in the 1960s stimulated by a new feminism and the continuing efforts to silence its voice. Once again, we find ourselves entering a new period of enlivened concern over trauma—this time in relation to mass ethnic violence. According to Minow (2000):

> The mass atrocities of the twentieth century, sadly, do not make it distinctive. More distinctive than the facts of genocides and regimes of torture marking this era are the search for and invention of collective forms of response . . . The

novel experiment of the Nuremberg and Tokyo tribunals following World War II reached for a vision of world order and international justice, characterizing mass violence as crimes of war and crimes against humanity. (p. 235)

In this chapter, we will identify some of the processes by which individuals and societies heal after the trauma of ethnic conflict, genocide, and mass violence and begin to provide answers to the following questions:

▸ What steps can be taken after mass violence to heal and restore its victims to ordinary living?
▸ Can societies—as well as individuals—heal from their own traumatic histories? In this regard, what is the distinction between retributive and restorative justice?
▸ Is it possible for enemies and perpetrators and victims to reconcile and have meaningful dialogue about what happened?
▸ What are the meanings and conditions of justice and forgiveness?

There is an important "given" fueling all trauma work, and that is the seemingly inconvertible evidence that if victims of violence are not healed, they will eventually perpetuate violence against others. We know this from research on child abuse, inter-generational trauma literature, and the clinical value of such theoretical notions as Freud's idea of identification with the aggressor and his prediction of the "return of the repressed." We also know that ethnic violence calls forth vengeance and some form of retribution unless there is some intervention and that history is bound to repeat itself if it is not remembered.

▸ An Alternative View of the Trauma Experience and Its Treatment `10-1`

Before exploring these four very different therapeutic approaches to social trauma, it is important to share with you an alternative view of the trauma experience itself that I believe holds enormous potential for rethinking both our clinical conception of what trauma is and how it is most successfully treated. In Chapter 9, I described in some detail the clinical and social manifestations of trauma. Within the realm of psychology and psychiatry, it is viewed as a mental illness and diagnostically referred to as *post-traumatic stress disorder (PTSD)*, a subset of the anxiety disorders. But, somehow, to those who have worked intimately with its survivors, this description does not do it justice nor does it fully capture the extent of its wounding. This is because in its extreme, trauma affects and involves the shutting down of all aspects of human psychological functioning. You may remember Herman's (1997) description of its impact on the person's basic physiology, sense of self and safety, attachment to others, and sense of meaning in life. In short, trauma compromises one's basic humanity. It is in this regard that Herman (1997), in speaking of group work as a final restorative context, writes the following: "Trauma dehumanizes the victim; the group restores her humanity" (p. 214). You will also read later in this chapter, in the section "South Africa and Its Truth and Reconciliation Commission," Pumla Gobodo-Madikizela's (2004) description of the relationship of the perpetrator and the victim: "When he committed the horrible deed, he denied not only the humanity of his victim . . . he denied his own humanity as well. His genuine apology is his way of reclaiming a humanity that was lost in a life of violence, and a crying out to be readmitted in the circle of humanity" (p. 19).

Harvey Peskin (2009) speaks of trauma in terms of "disorders of dehumanization." He writes the following:

> I think of Disorders of Dehumanization as reactions . . . to actual grim experiences or dark expectations that diminish us from feeling ourselves or others to be entirely human, to be like others belonging to the single species or genus called human. These disorders are not identified by any special set of symptoms but are more likely to be folded into established diagnoses . . . Hiddenness itself is at the core of disorders of dehumanization in which grim experiences have gone unwitnessed, unbelieved, or unverified and therefore take on an unutterable existence . . . Yet hiddenness also turns into habit, a place to hide in plain sight that is not easily penetrated—an inner refuge against acknowledging, believing or understanding one's own unspoken experience. (p. 3)

In this regard, Peskin suggests dehumanization and rehumanization as organizing principles in psychotherapy. Thus, as a result of traumatic experience, the self becomes disconnected from not only the reality and truth of her or his own victimization, but also "the discernments gleaned from communal witness that make a person feel credible to oneself and to others" (p. 3)—an essential part of feeling human. Doubt and disbelief in experiences that really happened are some of the most central and unyielding aspects of social trauma. The absence of witness is at the very center of dehumanization, for when self-experience goes unacknowledged, withheld, or betrayed, one is robbed of a basic sense of meaning and goodness. "Surviving unwitnessed trauma falls far short of achieving real freedom because confidence in self-witness is too fragile to overcome the abuser's remaining power over the survivor's mind. Deniers of genocide and crimes against humanity count on this fragility to rouse a survivor's festering abuser introject" (p. 7).

Peskin believes that in the treatment of trauma and other disorders of dehumanization, the therapist must take on the role of witness and help the patient come to discern the "selective inattention to his own dehumanization from lack of acknowledgment by its perpetrators," the first being the perpetrator him- or herself, "its community, and, ultimately by the patient himself" (p. 3). At the beginning of this chapter,

I quoted Herman (1997) about the "unspeakable" nature of traumatic violence. It is no easy task to be called upon to be a witness to the "unspeakable" in therapy. Being at the core human themselves, therapists are no less vulnerable to such silence. Without self-awareness and regular introspection upon what exactly we are doing with our clients, it is all too possible to slip into unconscious collusion with both the clients' and society's desire for silence (Staub, 2006). I particularly remember a Holocaust survivor telling me about her welcome to my hometown of Detroit, Michigan, at the end of World War II. She said that the Jewish social workers who had helped her in so many ways getting settled into her new home gave her a final bit of advice: "Just look ahead. Try not to think too much about the past. To tell you the truth, people don't really want to hear about all that stuff."

Peskin quotes Hans Loewald about the process of being a therapeutic witness. "If the analyst keeps his central focus on this emerging core he avoids molding the patient in the analyst's own image or imposing on the patient his own concept of what the patient should become." He goes on to suggest that the witness must be steadfast in his or her readiness to challenge the patient's "selective inattention to his own humanity that he cannot yet fathom, comprehend, or bring into his own." In other words, the patient's very sense of being rests on "being unconditionally seen" (p. 4). It is also important to acknowledge that the standard analytic pose of neutrality and interpretation, as taught in much of traditional therapeutic training—this is, working with and remaining primarily in the realm of psychic as opposed to external reality—is of little use in promoting therapeutic witness. There is an important lesson in this regard to be learned from the therapy given to Holocaust survivors after World War II. Much of this work, primarily traditionally psychoanalytic, has been viewed in retrospect as unproductive. Many of the major survivors who have given voice to their experience have, in fact in a variety of different ways, pointed to the absence of therapeutic witness in the help survivors were offered. And based on their parents as well as their own experiences in therapy, many children of survivors have been attracted to self-help groups for the healing they feel they still have to do. In this regard, Peskin offers the following by way of summing up the importance of therapeutic witnessing in trauma treatment.

> One comes away … realizing how much the sense of one's humanity—one's personal history, identity and aliveness—can hang by the thread of even a single witness, yet how absent are the witnesses, whether in their actual existence, in their unwillingness or unreadiness to come forward, or in their expulsion from psychic reality. In losing such witness, self-discovery gives way to self-invention, to life lived on the shifting sands of events and rapid identifications rather than on the truths that a witness helps recognize and understand. When the commonplace of witness in personality development no longer holds, as is the situation of Holocaust survivors

whose close relationships have vanished from their lives, an actual witness—or else a therapist as virtual witness—may redeem lost parts of the self and the self's internal objects in the unfolding process of rehumanization. (p. 9)

In the pages that follow, you will learn about four examples of efforts at healing and social restoration after the trauma of ethnic conflict, genocide, and mass violence. Specifically, we will discuss the plight of the Lakota Sioux in the United States and the efforts of Brave Heart (1995) to heal the historic trauma and unresolved grief in this Native American population; South Africa's national response to apartheid and its Truth and Reconciliation process; research on the treatment of Jewish Holocaust survivors, Nazis, and their children and efforts at reconciliation between the two groups; and lastly, treating traumatized refugee and immigrant populations through an in-depth presentation of an especially creative treatment center for Cambodians relocated in the United States—the Center for the Empowerment of Refugees and Immigrants (CERI) in Oakland, California.

Historic Trauma and Unresolved Grief Among Native Americans

The Lakota Sioux, like many Native American groups, are beset by serious and widespread social problems. Their rate of death by alcoholism is seven times the national average and 2.5 times that of other Native American people. Suicide rates are 3.2 times that of whites. Historically, they have been plagued by high rates of coronary heart disease and hypertension. Unemployment rates on the Lakota reservation average from 50 percent to 90 percent, and about 50 percent of the group live below the poverty level. Brave Heart (1995) contends that these depressing statistics are the result of generations of chronic historical trauma and unresolved grief, "a repercussion from the loss of lives, land, and aspects of culture rendered by the European conquest of the Americas" (p. 2). This unresolved grief has dual sources: massive trauma that has endured from generation to generation and the systematic destruction of traditional Lakota ways of grieving for both individuals and the community as a whole. In other words, not only have the Lakota been devastated by an ongoing series of traumatic events, but they have also been robbed of the traditional rituals that would have allowed them to adequately mourn and thereby resolve their grief. The result, according to Brave Heart, is frozen, unresolved grief, passed on across generations, which is the underlying cause of the community's out-of-control alcoholism and mental and physical health problems.

Legters (1988) believes that the treatment of Native Americans in the United States meets the definition of genocide by the United Nations (U.N.). Nowhere is this fact more evident than in the traumatic history of the Lakota Sioux. The mid-1800s saw the loss of traditional hunting grounds; the spread of smallpox and cholera; the killing, imprisonment, and relocation of hundreds of innocent tribal members; a bounty on Lakota scalps; and the death of hundreds by starvation and exposure.

In 1871, President Ulysses S. Grant asserted that the government would no longer consider Indians to be nations with whom treaties would be negotiated. Instead, they were wards of the state. This declaration set the stage for increased persecution and widespread invasion of Lakota territories. An army attack in 1868 on a peaceful encampment ultimately led to the Lakota victory at Little Big Horn.

This, however, only intensified government efforts to steal land and break the spirit of the People. In 1877, Lakota spiritual leader Crazy Horse was arrested and killed. The rise of Sitting Bull temporarily reunited and gave some encouragement to the People. By then, however, he alone remained a symbol of resistance to the white man and ensured the practice of traditional Native ways. His eventual assassination, the suppression of the spiritual Ghost Dance cult, and the massacre at Wounded Knee left the surviving Lakota totally traumatized.

A series of more recent experiences have only intensified the cumulative effect of the historic past. These include:

▶ The experience of Indian boarding schools with their forced separations of children from parents, physical and sexual abuses, and destruction of traditional cultural knowledge among the children
▶ Death by tuberculosis
▶ The introduction of widespread alcohol use
▶ Continued land loss, relocation, and government termination policies of Native rights

Paralleling this massive trauma and contributing to the difficulty in grieving was the systematic destruction of traditional beliefs, ceremonies, and rituals of grief. Boarding schools made many strangers to their own cultural heritage. Traditional ways were disenfranchised by government control of reservations, the prohibition of ceremonies, and the intrusion of white attitudes toward grieving. In other words, the massive trauma was accentuated by a lack of functional cultural methods of mourning the losses. The grief could not go away; it could only accumulate and be passed on from generation to generation.

Brave Heart's Cultural Intervention

To intervene in this process and see if it was possible to reintroduce traditional means of grieving to her people, Brave Heart designed an experimental healing intervention to be given first to a group of Lakota human service providers, healers, and community leaders. If successful, they, in turn, would take the experience back to their respective communities and lead similar workshops for community members. Brave Heart drew many of her ideas for treating trauma from research on Jewish Holocaust survivors and their children. She saw strong parallels in intergenerational transmission of grief and difficulties in accessing cultural and communal forms of grieving between the Lakota

People and the Jewish survivors who remained in Europe. Survivors who emigrated to Israel and the United States had significantly more opportunities for collective mourning than those who remained in Europe, living "among the perpetrators and murderers of their families" (Fogelman, 1991, p. 67) as did the Lakota Sioux. Similarly, both groups had also survived the loss of relatives to the anonymity of mass graves and had placed great import on collective grieving, community rituals, and memorials.

The Lakota intervention, spanning four days, entailed a series of experiential exercises and presentations of Lakota history, the process of trauma and grief, and traditional spiritual practices and ceremonies. It was designed for "stimulating mourning resolution of historical grief" among the provider participants, all of whom were Lakota. All were tested before and after the intervention on a variety of assessment instruments. Brave Heart (1995) found the following significant effects:

- Education about historical trauma led to an increased awareness of personal trauma and the experience of grief and related effects.
- Sharing grief and related effects within a traditional Lakota context led to a cathartic sense of relief.
- A grief resolution process was initiated, with an eventual reduction in grief-related effects.
- Positive group identification increased.
- Positive commitment to community healing increased (p. 126).

Subsequently, Brave Heart has expanded her work by creating a network of "survivors," who are carrying out trainings, therapy, and the creation of memorial ceremonies and grieving rituals in their respective Lakota communities.

PTSD in Native American Males

Duran and Duran (1995) argue similarly that the psychological consequences of communal traumatization and colonization have led to PTSD in Native American men (Ehlers, Gizer, Gilder, and Yehuda, 2013). "Once the warrior is defeated and his ability to protect the community destroyed, a deep psychological trauma of identity loss occurs" (p. 36). He will unconsciously turn against his loved ones and become abusive as his ego splits—one aspect in touch with the enormous pain and the other identifying with the aggressor. The rage that he feels and would like to turn on the destroyer of his culture is ultimately turned inward. The only way he can contain the rage and self-medicate the PTSD is through the use of alcohol. In discussing treatment, Duran and Duran (1995) warn against unintentionally retraumatizing the Native American patient:

> Without the awareness of some of these dynamics . . . most practitioners continue to invalidate the experience of trauma in Native American people, which in its own right becomes an ongoing infliction of trauma on the patient. The Native

American patient already feels decades of horrendous unresolved grief and rage, and the practitioner adds to this through the insensitivity of blaming the victim by pathologizing clients, as is so common in Western psychotherapy. Such iatrogenics perpetuate the suffering. (p. 42)

The work of Brave Heart and Duran and Duran on resolving historical grief and trauma holds relevance not only for Native Americans, but also for other ethnic groups with collective histories of trauma and oppression. Such wholesale loss and disenfranchisement have certainly been the experience of people of color in the United States: African Americans with the lingering effects of slavery and the ongoing trauma of racism; Latinos/as with the trauma of migration north, expatriation of lands in the Southwest, and, for some, escape from political genocide in Central and South Americas; and Asian Americans with their oppression as an immigrant labor force, internment of the Japanese during World War II, and the traumatic experiences of refugees from war in Southeast Asia. Similarly, there are groups within the United States (e.g., Jews, Irish, Armenians, and Gypsies [Rom]) with long histories as victims of political and social oppression in their native lands. It is possible that members of these various communities like the Lakota Sioux suffer from undiagnosed historic traumatic response and unresolved grief, and they might benefit from grief work, both individual and communal, similar to that developed by Brave Heart.

▶ South Africa and Its Truth and Reconciliation Commission 10-2

Hayner (2000) succinctly summarizes the history of South Africa that set the stage for the Truth and Reconciliation Commission (TRC):

> After 45 years of apartheid in South Africa, and thirty-odd years of some level of armed resistance against the apartheid state by the armed wing of the African National Congress (ANC) and others, the country had suffered massacres, killings, torture, lengthy imprisonment of activists, and severe economic and social discrimination against its majority black, coloured and Indian population. As the transition out of apartheid began to unfold in the early 1990s, many insisted that this horrific past must be addressed. (p. 10)

Nelson Mandela, then leader of the ANC, who became South Africa's first black president, favored a truth commission to make public all human rights abuses and atrocities committed on both sides during the years of the apartheid government. The ANC had already carried out its own internal inquiries into human rights abuses committed by its members during its military struggle against apartheid and hoped to do the same in relation to the activities of the outgoing apartheid government. Its intention was to send a strong message that things would be different in the new South

African regime, with strong human rights guarantees for all its citizens. The National Party (the outgoing government), not surprisingly, argued for a reconciliation process that would grant amnesty for all activities carried out in the name of the apartheid regime. A compromise of a conditional amnesty clause was struck and, on April 27, 1994, South Africa held its first-ever democratic elections.

The TRC was unique and unprecedented in world history. There had been truth commissions in other countries, but none had been so far-reaching nor had offered amnesty in exchange for telling the truth. The agreed-upon conditions for amnesty were that perpetrators had to apply in person and fully disclose the facts of their crimes, and those crimes had to be political rather than personal. The goal of the process was national reconciliation, not retribution. Never before had a nation so fully pursued the idea of restorative justice; that is, set a course toward healing rather than punishment (Gready, 2010). Restorative justice, according to Minow (1998),

> emphasizes the humanity of both offenders and victims. It seeks repair of social connections and peace rather than retribution against the offenders. Building connections and enhancing communication between perpetrators and those they victimize, and forging ties across the community, takes precedence over punishment or law enforcement. (p. 92)

Goals for the TRC were as follows:

▶ To document the human rights abuses that had taken place during apartheid
▶ To publicly acknowledge the experiences and fates of victims
▶ To restore their dignity, allowing them to bear witness to what had happened to them
▶ To grant reparations; that is, some type of compensation (although it must be understood that compensation can only be symbolic)
▶ To produce a final report that is a detailed and frank history of what took place over the half century of apartheid, a document that would become a shared, societal narrative

The essence of its philosophy was summarized by the then–Minister of Justice Dullah Omar (1996) as "the need for understanding, not vengeance; the need for reparation, not retaliation; and the need for *ubuntu* (fellowship and interconnection), not victimization."

The undertaking was enormous. The TRC comprised three committees: Human Rights Violations, Amnesty, and Reparations and Rehabilitation. The staff numbered 300; the budget amounted to $18 million per year; and four large offices located throughout South Africa coordinated activities. In four years, testimonies were taken from more than 23,000 witnesses and victims, 2,000 of whom appeared in public hearings throughout South Africa. All meetings were well attended. Coverage of the hearings by the media was extensive: newspapers, radio, and television—international and local. The overriding intent was to make the findings and testimonies public in the broadest possible ways and to write and disseminate a new narrative history.

Impact on Victims

Gillian Straker (1999), a white South African psychoanalyst, offers an insightful analysis of what happened psychologically as a result of the TRC. She divides her analysis into three parts: its impact on victims, bystanders, and actual perpetrators. In relation to the victims who gave testimony, Straker identified four important outcomes:

- Many victims described the experience of "*breaking the silence*" around their testimony as "amazingly liberating." To quote Straker: "What the TRC is doing is allowing the unspoken to be spoken, and in trying to locate perpetrators, it is both in a symbolic and in a real way putting a name to the nameless . . . and by affirming the reality of the victims and freeing them from the power of the secret, is serving a liberatory function" (p. 257). But it was a silence that had existed on many levels. Blacks in South Africa had to keep the daily horrors of apartheid contained within themselves for several reasons. First, there was the necessity of not "discomforting" whites and the white world around them with the truth of their existence (Gready, 2010). Also, for many active in the struggle for freedom, remaining silent was a matter of life and death. And, internally, what many people had experienced was so horrific that it was "almost impossible to conceptualize and . . . in the realm of the unthinkable and the unspeakable" (p. 257).

- The actual experience of "*telling one's story*" was enormously therapeutic as well as liberating. Increasingly, research on PTSD has shown that sharing the trauma narrative is a first step toward healing and a sign that healing has begun. Until then, the actual details of the story are frozen in time, locked away in "body and iconic memories," to use Cardinal's (1984) terminology, disconnected from both the narrative and the "words to say it." The TRC supported the process of giving voice to these words.

- "Telling the story in a public forum contributes to the documentation of history . . . it allows the victims to exercise an *altruistic function*" (p. 258). By their very acts, victims are reconstructing the past for others, creating a shared societal narrative, giving to others, and playing an active role in the healing of society. In a similar vein, Herman (1997) points to the importance of finding a "survivor mission"; that is, a personally meaningful source of social action in the world that is reparative and at the same time transcends their particular trauma situation as a further source of healing.

▶ Lastly, Straker emphasizes the importance of the TRC in *reconnecting the survivor* to his or her geographic and social community as well as humanity in general. Trauma at its most basic level involves disconnection from one's community and all that is human. It disrupts the "basic assumptions about one's own vulnerability and the notion of a just world. It interferes with the individual's internalized object relations and their containing functions" (p. 258).

One criticism of the TRC's healing function, as suggested by Straker, is that although giving testimony "stimulated catharsis and outpouring of emotion," it lacked a "forum for working these through" and for learning to contain such feelings upon returning to the ordinary demands of life. For example, some individuals who reported feelings of elation after testifying later experienced being overwhelmed by what they had revealed and needed support and ongoing help. This is a point where human services professionals can make significant contributions toward supporting processes such as the TRC by providing continuing services to survivors. Many South African mental health workers did involve themselves with the TRC by "preparing briefers and de-briefers who were assigned to individuals who spoke before the TRC and who followed them up after they had given evidence" (p. 259).

Impact on Bystanders

The impact of the TRC is less clear in relation to bystanders—that is, among whites, who had not been directly involved in perpetrating crimes but had remained silent and benefited from the apartheid regime—and active perpetrators. In relation to the former, the TRC seemed to have stimulated within many white South Africans an awareness, for the first time, of the scope of atrocities that had been carried out in their names as well as an appreciation of the need for giving reparations to those who had suffered. Many were deeply shocked and moved by the testimonies that were given. But what remains unclear is how so many were able to deny what was going on in the first place and to continue to not fully own their complicity in what happened. The majority of the white population had remained silent about the "evils of apartheid" and actively supported the Nationalist regime. Probably the best explanation of such behavior can be found in the idea of dissociation:

> The very existence of apartheid depended on the ability of white South Africans to dissociate and to compartmentalize aspects of the horror-filled reality of apartheid and racism to which they were exposed on a daily basis. Underpinning the ability to disassociate . . . is the mechanism of projective identification. It allows all good to be invested in one object . . . and all bad to be vested in another object. (p. 253)

This splitting is supported by another internal mechanism, projective identification, which allows bystanders to project their own unwanted, negative identifications onto out-group members and thereby justify their negative treatment of them. What this does psychologically is block the experiencing of empathy and concern in the bystander. Promoting empathy through TRC testimony may lessen the tendencies toward dissociation, splitting, and projective identification in bystanders and thus allow the creation of natural empathy. Klein (2002) sees such dynamics as being at the psychic roots of racism.

Impact on Perpetrators

"The impact of the TRC on perpetrators is probably most variable because testimony may be given solely for the reason of gaming amnesty rather than seeking forgiveness; that is, 'confession is not being solely made to obtain freedom from a sense of wrongdoing or from a sense of being chained to and haunted by the one whom one has wronged' " (p. 265). Sincere regret may be avoided in two ways: through shame and humiliation stimulated by feeling that one has been coerced into taking responsibility for a crime that one does not truly believe is wrong or by experiencing "superiority" or "triumph" by secretly retaining an "unshifting internal position" and denigrating the work of the TRC. Impact on perpetrators seems to be most likely to occur when they experience true remorse and when the victim feels that forgiveness is justified.

A final point that is quite important to understand is the profound, psychic interdependency of the victim and the perpetrator; each really holds the key to the other's healing process. Gobodo-Madikizela (2000) describes the reciprocity with a clarity that is worth quoting at length:

> People who come to the point of forgiveness have lived with and know pain . . . All these emotions connect them with their departed love ones . . . Paradoxically, these emotions also tie them to the one who caused the traumatic wounds. On the one hand, the perpetrator is the hated one responsible for the family's anguish; on the other hand, the family members . . . look to the perpetrator to get a glimpse of the final living moments of the loved one. The perpetrator is the bearer of the secrets, the only one who observed that important moment when the loved one breathed their last. (p. 19)

By providing loved ones with specific details, the perpetrator can allow them to finish their incomplete narrative and move on toward healing. Often, the unknown facts of how one's father or son or brother died freeze and interrupt the grieving process. Gobodo-Madikizela continues:

> When the perpetrator shows remorse, which is to say when that person knows the pain of the victim with a heartfelt "I'm sorry," the moment becomes his own turning point. When he committed the horrible deed, he denied not only the

humanity of his victim . . . he denied his own humanity as well. His genuine apology is his way of reclaiming a humanity that was lost in a life of violence, and a crying out to be readmitted in the circle of humanity. (p. 19)

Institute for the Healing of Memories

The healing work accomplished by the TRC was extensive, but it was only the beginning of a process of societal change. In addition to an ongoing reparations program, it was intended that those who had testified would receive follow-up therapy and support and that additional South Africans would also need to be brought into this process. The establishment of the Institute for the Healing of Memories is an example of the kind of organizations that have come forth to fill this void. The Institute's mission statement (2004) speaks directly to the importance of such continuity:

> At the time when the Truth and Reconciliation Commission was set up, it was obvious that only a minority of South Africans would have the opportunity to tell their story before the Truth Commission. It was argued that platforms needed to be provided for all South Africans to tell their stories, and it was in this context that the Healing of Memories workshops were developed as a parallel process to the forthcoming Truth Commission. (https://learningtoforgive.com/, History, p. 1)

The founder and director of the Institute, Father Michael Lapsley, is an Anglican priest and trauma specialist. He is an internationally known anti-apartheid activist and, although white, served as a chaplain and spiritual advisor to the ANC, the African party that formed South Africa's first black government. According to Nelson Mandela, "Michael Lapsley's life is part of the tapestry of the many long journeys and struggles of our people." Michael actively challenged the hierarchy of the church for its silence about apartheid, was exiled from South Africa because of his politics during the closing years of apartheid, and finally became a direct victim of the terror in April 1990, when he was the target of a letter bomb and lost both hands and one eye. His long and painful healing process served as inspiration for his trauma work with other victims around the world. In this regard, Lapsley speaks of the "journey" of healing as movement from being a victim, to a survivor, to "a victor over evil, hatred, and death." He argues that if an individual or a nation does not follow such a model of action and healing, the only alternative is for survivors, both individually and as a society, to become victims and then victimizers.

The Institute for Healing of Memories runs workshops, typically three days long, that bring together former enemies, victims, bystanders, and perpetrators in a context of mutual sharing and self-exploration:

> Emotional scars are often carried for very long, hindering the individual's emotional, psychological and spiritual development . . . The power of the workshops lie in their experiential, interactive nature, and their emphasis on the emotional

and spiritual, rather than intellectual, understanding and interpretation of the past. Through an exploration of their personal histories, participants find emotional release and as a group gain insight into and empathy for the experiences of others. These processes prepare the ground for forgiveness and reconciliation between people of diverse backgrounds, races, cultures and religions. (https://www.healing-memories.org/, Workshop)

The workshops are highly eclectic, based, to a large extent, on narrative therapy, the use of expressive arts and rituals, and group process. But their center is the sharing of personal narratives empowered by Lapsley's "journey" metaphor of healing. This idea is particularly well captured in the following excerpt from the Journey to Healing and Wholeness (2004) sponsored by the Institute and held on Robben Island, the site of Nelson Mandela's twenty-seven years of captivity and now a South African National Monument:

> At all times, the gathering was constructed around the metaphor of a journey. By constructing a process of "healing" as a journey, this implied movement, changes of territory, and attention to differences of experience over time. When people were interviewed in front of the group, the interviewers took care to ask about the differences in experiences of the past in comparison to the present. They also took care to elicit the different stages of a person's journey, including the most difficult periods as well as the passages of relief . . . In these ways we were all invited consider ourselves to be on a journey, one that would continue into our futures. This orientation captured participants' imagination and encouraged us to revisit territories we have passed through in our lives, the ground we are currently standing on, and the directions we wish to explore in the future. (p. 16)

Forgiveness

At this point, it is important to say something about the meaning of forgiveness within such models of healing as well as within the broader context of restorative justice. Forgiveness does not mean condoning or excusing what happened in the past. Nor does it mean forgetting, accepting the behavior of the other, reconciling with the other, suppressing feelings of hurt, or losing one's moral compass or outrage at injustice. Rather, it points to a process of healing within the victim, whereby he or she is able to disconnect from destructive defenses and reactions, such as anger and guilt, brought to bear intrapsychically in reaction to a traumatic experience and which keeps the person locked within its parameters (Gready, 2010). Luskin (2002) suggests a similar perspective for working with anyone who is self-destructively attached to grievances of the past. According to him, "Forgiveness is the feeling of peace that emerges as you take your hurt less personally, take responsibility for how you feel, and become a hero instead of a victim in the story you tell. Forgiveness is the experience of peacefulness in the present moment. Forgiveness does not change the past, but it changes the present" (pp. 68–69).

Luskin's (1999) cognitive-behavioral intervention strategy includes attention to all the following:

- Learning to view the offending event less personally
- Learning to take responsibility for one's own emotional experience rather than blaming the source of the frustration for those feelings
- Changing one's grievance story (the narrative about the event that supports a person's negative attachment to the grievance) to an alternative conception that focuses on a choice to grow and prosper instead of suffering
- Identifying and altering the "unenforceable rules" that underpin the grievance story; that is, internal rules that we have for our own and other people's behavior that one really has no control over (https://learningtoforgive.com/)

Reparations

The South African effort at implementing a system of restorative justice involved three components: truth-telling, public acknowledgment, and reparations. The final leg of the process—that is, the specifics of reparations—is being worked out by the South African government in consultation with various community groups (Gready, 2010). Minow (1998) speaks to the possible forms that reparation might take. "The TRC includes a committee devoted to proposing economic and symbolic acts of reparation for survivors and for devastated communities. Monetary payments to the victimized, health and social services, memorials, and other acts of symbolic commemoration would become governmental policies in an effort to restore victims and social relationships breached by violence and atrocity" (p. 91).

Reparations are, thus, acts of compensation offered to victims in an effort to restore what has been lost. They can include financial compensation, the offering of services, symbolic acts of acknowledgment, such as community art or the construction of memorials, or something as seemly small and individualistic as providing a mother who has lost a son with a copy of the death certificate. Two additional forms of reparation are restitution and apologies. *Restitution* is the return of property, things, and even human remains to their rightful owners. *Apologies* are formal statements of regret that include all the following:

- An acknowledgment of the facts of what occurred
- An acceptance of responsibility
- An expression of sincere regret
- A promise to not repeat the offense

Like compensations, each of these has its potential value but also its difficulties. Restoration, for example, is impossible in situations where innocent individuals are now living in the former residences of victims or entire communities have been totally destroyed. Or in relation to apologies, who is the appropriate person to give an apology and to whom should it be addressed? What good is an apology if no real changes have occurred in the material situation that created the atrocities in the first place?

As Joseph W. Singer so concisely suggests: "Compensation can never compensate." How can a dead child, a traumatized life, a lost past or a way of life be truly compensated for or restored? The bottom line is they cannot. Reparations can only be symbolic and, at their most, effectively communicate a society's formal and public acknowledgment of the violations that occurred within it and an acceptance of responsibility for trying to set things right, including a societal pledge of "never again." The ultimate value of reparations as restorative depends, according to Minow (1998), on several related factors:

▶ First, do reparations serve a role in the continued healing of the victim? Minow (1998) discusses such possibilities.

> The process of seeking reparations, and of building communities of support while spreading knowledge of the violations and their meaning in peoples' lives, may be more valuable than any specific . . . remedy. Being involved in a struggle for reparations may give survivors a chance to speak and to tell their stories. If heard and acknowledged, they may obtain a renewed sense of dignity. (p. 93)

▶ Second, how are reparations perceived by the victim and have the specifics of the reparative act been sensitively thought through? If not, such tokens may end up causing more harm than good. Minow gives the example of a Japanese offer of reparations to five hundred sex slaves exploited by the Imperial Army during World War II. Most refused the payments offered because they came from private funding sources rather than from the government. Many would have preferred some form of gesture of prosecution of specific perpetrators by the government, such as when the United States put sixteen Japanese individuals directly involved in enslaving them on a watch list that barred them from entry into the United States. Others suggest including treatment of their plight during the war in school textbooks as an act of reparation through memory. Similarly, many Jewish Holocaust survivors have refused reparation payments from Germany after the war because they found them demeaning and insulting.

▶ Third, are they offered with the implication, no matter how subtle, that accepting them in any way minimizes, undoes, or diminishes the harm that has occurred?

Minow speaks to this point as follows:

Nothing in this discussion should imply that money payments, returned property, restored religious sites, or apologies seal the wounds, make victims whole, or clean the slate. The aspiration of repair . . . will be defeated by any hint or hope that then it will be as if the violations never occurred. For that very suggestion defeats the required acknowledgement of the enormity of what was done. (p. 117)

There have been efforts within U.S. history to make reparations to groups that have been harmed by actions of the government. Most notable is the apology and payment of reparations to Japanese Americans for their internment in U.S. concentration camps during World War II. But it should be pointed out that this gesture of reparation did not issue forth on its own; rather, it was the result of forty-eight years of intense legal wrangling, politicizing, and lobbying by the Japanese American community. The eventual result was the signing of a letter of apology by President Ronald Reagan and checks in the amount of $20,000 sent to all survivors. Observers who have reflected on this lengthy process suggest that its most valuable consequence was the return of honor to members of the Japanese American community, which in fact grew more out of their own actions than any governmental perception or acknowledgment of culpability. Efforts for reparations have also been partially successful in relation to Native Hawaiians seeking redress for the overthrow of the Hawaiian monarchy by the U.S. government. Sadly, a variety of efforts by the African American community at seeking redress and reparations for slavery have failed, in spite of retired Michigan Congressman John Conyers's yearly introduction of a bill to establish a commission to determine if reparations for slavery are appropriate, which always lacked sufficient support from other congressmen to pass. In the few successful efforts at redress, the victims, not the government, were the driving force behind efforts to gain reparations. Similarly, none of these efforts were supported by processes of truth-telling or public acknowledgment of facts and responsibility, thus undermining their effectiveness as authentic gestures toward repair and healing. In fact, the opposite might be true. To once again quote Minow (1998): "Here and elsewhere, the process of seeking reparations and facing rejection can create new wounds for individuals affiliated with victimized groups" (p. 101).

▶ Holocaust Survivors, Nazis, Their Children, and Reconciliation   10-3

No event in history has generated more psychological research on the effects of trauma, its treatment, and its intergenerational impact than the Nazi Holocaust of Jews and other "undesirables."

> ▶ There is, first of all, an extensive literature regarding the psychological impact of the concentration camp experience on survivors. One sees in

these studies an array of serious reactions that would today be diagnosed as PTSD, including the full range of trauma reactions described by Herman (1997) as symptoms of hyperarousal, intrusion, constriction, and disconnection.

▸ In relation to the continuing effects transmitted to children—and children of children—terms such as *vicarious* and *secondary traumatization* are used. Research on the children points to high incidents of anxiety, depression, personality disorders, dependence, immaturity, and inability to cope, as well as emotional fragility, vulnerability to stress, fearfulness, and lack of trust.

▸ A second literature, although much more limited, involves the effects of the Holocaust on Nazi perpetrators and their offspring. Research on the Nazi generation itself focuses primarily on identifying internal psychological mechanisms that allowed individual perpetrators to carry out their heinous acts. Explanations of compartmentalization, splitting, dissociation, psychic numbing, and, most popularly, Lifton's (1986) concept of "doubling" have been offered. Doubling, for example, involves "the division of the self into functioning wholes, so that a part-self acts as an entire self" (p. 418). Thus, in a sense, two different autonomous sides of the individual are created, whereby a Nazi doctor could perform killings during the day and, without guilt or remorse, become the perfect, loving father and husband to his family in the evening. Studies such as those of Milgrim (1974) on conformity, the authoritarian personality complex of perpetrators (Adorno et al., 1950), and Arendt (1964) on the Eichmann trial have focused on processes of obedience to authority to explain the compliance of ordinary German citizens with orders to harm and kill others. Perhaps most shocking about such human possibility is Arendt's notion of the "banality of evil"; that is, the idea that what fueled the Holocaust and its killing of six million Jews was not a world gone insane or sadistic but rather the obedience and compliance of ordinary citizens to genocidal plans without protest (Meierhenrich, 2014).

▸ In turning to the literature on the children of Nazis and other Germans and their intergenerational psychic legacies, one can identify two general reactions: individuals who have split off negative feelings about their parents and the German past or those who are haunted by them. The latter tend to exhibit feelings of guilt, anger at their parents, an inability to mourn what happened and their parents' complicity, ambivalence about the past, and general emotional upset and turbulence.

Little is known, however, about the relationship that exists between children of survivors and children of Nazis and the possibility of reconciliation between the two groups or about each group's relationship with their own parents. The work of Mona Weissmark (2004) is exemplary in this regard. According to Weissmark (2004):

> Psychological studies have traditionally overlooked how stories about past injustices are transmitted from parent to child, how the offspring of both sides make sense of the stories, the way it influences their identities, and the way in which they rebalance an injustice in their lives. In short, there is practically no research relating to the actual experiences of offspring whose parents inflicted injustice or of those whose parents suffered injustice. There is little research on the quality of emotions or cognitive processes that follow perception of a past injustice. (p. 54)

Central to understanding the psychology of all survivors and their offspring is the difficulty experienced in letting go of perceived or real unjust harm done in the past. Such feelings, in spite of the emotional harm that carrying them causes to the self, are regularly passed on across generations, blocking and negating the possibility of returning to a more psychologically healthful state or of forgiving and reconciling with former enemies. Such dynamics can be regularly observed generations after the fact of the original trauma.

Seeking Justice

Thus, central to any discussion of healing after mass violence and reconciliation is the question of seeking justice (Meierhenrich, 2014). Most victims and children of victims continue to struggle with a desire for revenge and justice. When someone is harmed in what is perceived as an unjust manner, an inner process is set into motion, whereby there is a compulsion to even the score and gain some form of moral and psychic balance. Such balance may require:

- "An eye for an eye"; that is, some form of physical or psychic retribution
- A sense that the perpetrator has suffered for his or her acts
- A setting right of the moral wrong; that is, the perception that the perpetrator has learned a moral lesson and now repudiates the belief that once justified the harm that was done

According to Weissmark (2004), ethnic identity and the dynamics of interethnic conflict play a vital role in perpetuating this sense of injustice and the need for revenge and retribution. She points to five processes that exacerbate and fuel inter-ethnic hatred:

- Each side experiences past grievances, injustices, and harm as contemporary; that is, they have been passed down intergenerationally, internalized, and experienced as a current threat directed toward the self.
- The worldview of group members becomes one-dimensional; that is, narrows in perspective so that it becomes impossible for the wronged person to empathize with members of the enemy group or to adopt the other's perspective on his or her grievances.

- Only the crimes and injustices of the other side can be acknowledged: one's own acts of violence and harm cannot be judged in a morally balanced way; they are not perceived in a similar light.
- Each side sees itself as the legitimate victim. Weissmark calls this "double victimization."
- The "tunnel vision" just described is also supported by a need to protect one's own group and its values. To do otherwise is often experienced as "letting down one's people and ancestors" or as "being a traitor to the past."

Weissmark (2004) elaborates on these dynamics:

An individual's sense of justice is never simply a matter of rationality. It is first a matter of feelings in defense of one's self, one's group, and inherent in this is the unwillingness of both sides to face the others' passions and viewpoints . . . From one generation to the other, each is told stories of unjust acts perpetrated by others, and of the loyal acts in defense of one's own ethnic group and its honorable values . . . We can see that the experience of injustice leaves a powerful imprint upon both sides that continues to be transmitted through the generations. (p. 50)

In reference to the question of reconciliation, is it possible for members of longstanding ethnic conflicts to transcend such dynamics and change perceptions and stereotypes of the other as well as rid themselves of the desire for retribution and the sense of injustice? In her research, Weissmark (2004) addresses these questions directly by bringing together children of Jewish survivors of the Holocaust and children of Nazis. She first studied group members from each side individually, inquiring into four areas of information:

- Developmental histories with a focus on how they learned about the war, the Holocaust, and their parents' involvement
- Their reactions to this information and its influence on them
- Their ideas about justice
- Their views of descendants from the other side

Next, she brought the two groups together—twenty-two Jews and Germans—for four days of dialogue and discussion, facilitated by her husband, Daniel Giacomo, a psychiatrist who is ethnically neither Jewish nor German. It is important to acknowledge that in certain circles, the idea of bringing these two populations together is viewed as dangerous and as taboo. According to Weissmark: "Many people feared that my study would be interpreted as a justification of Nazism or as a challenge to the Holocaust's status as the symbol of absolute evil. Or as a voice of moral obtuseness" (p. 13). She responds to such charges as follows:

There is a difference between "understand" and "condone." Hearing the other side, seeing another view, only means we use thinking in an open manner, in contrast to a closed biased manner. It means we consider conflicting viewpoints . . . It does not mean we forgive or excuse, or approve their viewpoints or that "anything goes." (pp. 13–14)

Weissmark carefully observed the interaction of the two groups and identified six stages in the transformation of how the children of Holocaust survivors and the children of Nazis perceived and interacted with each other over the four-day period:

- *Stage 1: Generalizing.* Survivors' children saw Nazis' children not as individuals but as nonhuman stereotypes and symbols of anti-Semitic Germany. Nazis' children tried to explain and justify their parents' attitudes and behavior. Survivors' children refused to believe them and reacted with rage, indignation, and incredulity at the possibility that they would ever view the past in a different way. "What was the point of being here?" they asked.
- *Stage 2: Revealing.* The Nazis' children began to reveal personal views about what happened in Germany, condemned the perpetrators, and expressed negative feelings about their parents. The survivors' children in turn began to question some of their own anger at the Nazis' children present.
- *Stage 3: Distinguishing.* Survivors' children began to distinguish their desire to hurt and make Germans suffer from the emotions and reactions of their parents. They also began to experience the German participants as "good people" as opposed to their perception of the Nazis' children's parents. Both groups began to realize that they shared the experience of being imprisoned by their respective parents' pasts.
- *Stage 4: Discussing the here and now.* Both groups increasingly focused on themselves interacting in the present, in the "here and now," and explored the effects that the other group's words and actions have on them; for example, how it felt to be categorized and labeled by the other side.
- *Stage 5: Sharing of hurts.* Both groups talked in greater personal detail about the difficulties of growing up with their parents and how the experience of the Holocaust affected them. Both began to realize that what they shared was a sense of being victims of the past and that they have paid dearly for it emotionally.
- *Stage 6: Transformation.* As the group moved toward completion, both sides expressed how the group had affected them, the difference it could make in their lives, and how it had transformed their feelings, images, and attitudes toward the other. They also expressed hope about the possibility of working together in the future.

Although these results do not reflect the experience of all group members, they are substantial enough to reflect the possible value of such efforts at dialogue and reconciliation. By way of summing up her findings, Weissmark (2004) concludes:

> "These statements suggest that despite past injustices and the tendencies to revenge and one-dimensional views, when people experience a measure of compassion for one another person's well-being, a transformation occurs" (p. 162).

When one looks across such group experiences, one begins to discern certain critical dimensions that seem necessary for reconciliation between former enemies so each can move ahead emotionally:

▸ Members of ethnic groups in conflict are seldom given an opportunity to interact as equal individuals in safe settings. Segregation or isolation from the other breeds suspicion and creates distorted and dehumanizing perceptions of the other. Interactions that allow one to see the other as well-rounded human beings, not very different from themselves, is critical.

▸ Perceptions of the other tend to be based on stereotypes and distorted images that engender fear and a desire to avoid contact. Members of the other group, through real human interaction and sharing, can slowly be transformed into individual persons instead of faceless stereotypes.

▸ Intimate sharing of one's personal narrative allows for the humanization of the other as well as the development of mutual empathy, a critical ingredient necessary for mutual understanding and a hedge against psychic splitting of the world into good and bad.

▸ Learning to listen to the other is a very important process, as opposed to debating or arguing over the facts of the conflict, which actually serves as a defense against letting in contrary information about the other. By focusing on and expressing feelings instead of thoughts, the sharing of significant and impactful information is more likely.

▸ Safety and emotional comfort for all members of the group must be considered carefully and guaranteed. When individuals are threatened or feel unsafe in the group, they become defensive, cannot take in information, and may feel the need to blame and attack rather than remain open to the processes that are occurring.

▸ In the case of groups with offspring of victims and perpetrators, as in Weissmark's research, it is imperative that the group process serve to help children perceptually detach from their internalization of the parents' experience and attitude and learn to relate to the other as individuals rather than as sons and daughters of victims.

▸ It is, in addition, very useful to encourage members to speak in the here and now about their perceptions and reactions to others in the group.

- Finally, to the extent that members can develop perceptions of similarities between themselves and the other, empathy is more likely to occur.

Treating Traumatized Refugee and Immigrant Populations 10-4

In this final section of the chapter we will explore the complex mental health issues involved in working clinically with relocated and traumatized refugee and immigrant populations. In Chapter 9, you were introduced to some of the complex psychological dynamics often at work in such client populations, for example: issues of integrating ethnic, national, and self-identities, being traumatized, struggling with assimilating and acculturating to radically different cultures, and coping with enormous stress. In addition, members of these groups are often visited by a variety of social problems as a consequence of being relocated in their new homes in the United States and other western countries. These may include: racism, poverty, drug and alcohol abuse, intergenerational conflict, erosion of family and religious values. We will begin by reviewing some basic statistics, history, and dynamics associated with refugee and immigrant statuses and conclude with an in-depth example of a model treatment program in Oakland, California, that works primarily with Cambodian refugees with which the author is familiar—the Center for Empowering Refugees and Immigrants (CERI).

Refugees

According to Weiss (2018), there are currently 49 war and conflict zones around the globe. Such military actions not only kill and maim combatants, but also harm, both physically and psychologically, and displace large segments of the local populations. We use the term *refugee* to describe a person who "owing to well-founded fear of being persecuted for reasons of race, religion, nationality, membership of a particular social group or political opinion, is outside the country of his nationality . . ." (1951 Refugee Convention). A different term, *internally displaced people* or *IDPs,* is used to describe those who are displaced within their own country. A further distinction is made between "disaster IDPs" and "conflict IDPs." By way of example, villagers in Sudan's Darfur region who fled to camps in neighboring Chad were refugees, while those who fled to camps within Darfur were considered IDPs. A final distinction is made in relation to economic migrants and illegal immigrants. Neither is considered a refugee because both leave their home countries voluntarily, seeking a better life, at least in the case of economic migrants, those who choose to return are afforded protection by their government. Refugees are not.

Although refugees and IDPs leave their homes for similar reasons, there are great differences in how they are treated (Kirmayer, Narasiah, Munoz, Rashid, Ryder,

Guzder, and Pottie, 2011). According to the U.N. Refugee Agency (UNHCR), only when a refugee crosses an international border is she or he normally "protected by international laws and conventions" and also receives shelter, food, and a place of safety. "By contrast, IDPs have little, if any, of the protection and help that refugees get. The domestic government, which may view them as enemies of the state, retains control of their fate. They may also fall prey to rebels and militias operating inside or outside the camp."

As far as numbers, global refugee populations peaked in the early 1990s at 17.8 million, largely due to the breakup of Yugoslavia with numbers falling dramatically until the mass exodus due to the war in Iraq shot them back up. In 2010, UNHCR estimated the global refugee number at 15.4 million. As far as providing substantive help, UNHCR was responsible for 10.5 million refugees, while the U.N. Relief and Works Agency (UNRWA) for another 4.8 million Palestinian refugees in Jordan, Lebanon, Syria, Gaza, and the West Bank. Another 27.5 million IDPs were estimated to exist in their home countries due to violence and persecution. It should be noted that with more internal conflicts replacing interstate war, the number of IDPs has significantly risen in recent years. And these figures do not include individuals uprooted by disasters the may have numbered 42 million in 2010 (Internal Displacement Monitoring Center, 2012).

It is necessary to understand that arriving at a camp for refugees or IDPs does not ensure safety since violence can come from militias and rebels operating within and outside of the camps. A good example can be found in 1994 when Hutus in large numbers fled the Rwandan genocide by fleeing to the Democratic Republic of Congo. In time the aid organizations realized that Hutu militia leaders responsible for the massacre of Rwandan Tutsis virtually controlled the camps. Camps may also come under attack by troops targeting rebels they believe to be hiding inside, as well as being located in countries that are themselves far from being safe. In 2004, for example, armed rebels attacked a Congolese refugee camp in Burundi, setting huts on fire and killing 160 people, mostly women and children. Cross border attacks are another danger.

Refugee status is especially negatively impactful for women, children, and health. Consider the following concerns raised by UNHCR in regard to these three concerns.

Women. "Women face particular dangers when forced to flee their homes. They are at risk from sexual and physical violence both inside and outside camps . . . Often separated from their husbands, they may also be forced to take on the responsibility of providing for their families on top of their traditional roles . . . they may have to leave camps to forage for food . . . they may be forced to resort to prostitution to support their children. Often women refugees use all their savings just to get out of the country. They have no source of income and their bodies may be the only thing left they have to sell . . . Women may not even be safe within their families. There is strong evidence that domestic violence rises with displacement. Depression, unemployment and other stresses can lead men to take out their anger and frustration on women" (Kirmayer, Narasiah, Munoz, Rashid, Ryder, Guzder, and Pottie, 2011).

Children. "Displaced children also face many dangers, especially if they have become separated from their families. They risk abduction . . . Displaced children also miss out on education. Experts estimate that many of Colombia's displaced are school-age children and that most never return to the classroom . . . Malnutrition levels are often high among displaced children and healthcare limited or lacking altogether" (Kirmayer, Narasiah, Munoz, Rashid, Ryder, Guzder, and Pottie, 2011).

Health. "Poor nutrition, sanitary conditions, dirty water and lack of access to health services mean refugees and IDPs are prey to a host of diseases, most of them preventable. Common ones include diarrhea, acute respiratory infections, tuberculosis, malaria, cholera, measles and meningitis. Overcrowding in camps contributes to the spread of illness. Many people displaced by a conflict or disaster also suffer trauma-related problems. Children may be particularly affected. It is often forgotten that people fleeing war may have been tortured, raped or witnessed atrocities. Humanitarian agencies are increasingly recognising the importance of providing psycho-social help but support remains limited" (Kirmayer, Narasiah, Munoz, Rashid, Ryder, Guzder, and Pottie, 2011).

Finally, going home can present its own set of issues for returning refugees and IDPs. If the home country lacks capacity to absorb them, more problems can be created than are solved. If returnees find no house or job, it is believed that they might join perpetrator organization like the Taliban out of resentment or in order to survive or merely return to the camps from which they came. Going home is seldom straightforward. Returnees may find their land and homes taken over or destroyed. There may be nowhere to grow crops and there is often the danger of landmines. Healthcare, schools, roads, water supplies and sanitation may be limited or nonexistent. Returning may reignite ethnic hatred or land disputes. Some camps have been in existence so long that younger refugees have no knowledge or connection to their family's home territory, and others have grown so dependent on the camp's resources that they know no other way of life.

Immigrants

Martin and Midgley (2010) describe the changing landscape of *immigration* and *immigrants* in the United States since their original Population Bulletin article in 2006. They point to both some continuity and some change in relation to their earlier findings.

The continuity is reflected in the number of foreigners that arrive in the United States daily: 104,000 (3,000 with immigrant visas . . . but either violate their visas or do not depart. As far as the changing landscape, two developments "have rekindled the immigration reform debate. The recent recession, the worst since the Great Depression, exacerbated unemployment and reduced numbers of unauthorized foreigners entering the country" as well as the "stepped-up enforcement of immigration laws, especially after the failure of the U.S. Senate to approve a comprehensive immigration reform bill in 2007, including the proposal to require employers to fire employees whose names and social security data do not match." A second stimulus for renewed debate in 2010 was the increase in legal enactments by cities and states as measures to deal with unauthorized migration. Arizona was the first, with a law signed in April 2010 that made "unauthorized presence in the state a crime." Congress has debated immigration reform for ten years without coming up with comprehensive reform, and polls show citizen unhappiness with the "broken immigration system."

There has also been a "changing geographic makeup of immigrants over the past 50 years" according to Martin and Midgley (2010). As a result of average U.S. fertility falling (from 3.7 children per woman to 2.0) between the 1950s and 2010, immigration now makes up one-third of all U.S. population growth, and U.S.-born children and grandchildren of immigrants, immigration contributed to half of the U.S. population growth. Over the past several decades, immigrants have been largely Asian and Hispanic, and this is radically changing the U.S. population's composition.

Most immigrants enter the United States for economic reasons. Only about 100,000 per year (less than 10 percent) come as refugees, seeking asylum and fleeing persecution in their native countries. Today, the U.S. labor force is about equally divided between immigrants and native-born individuals, with a slightly higher number of foreign-born men and a slightly lower percentage of foreign-born women. In about half of immigrants and U.S.-born persons are in the U.S. labor force—a slightly higher share of foreign-born men and a slightly lower share of foreign-born women. In 2009, about 15 percent of U.S. workers were born outside the United States.

While the negative impact of foreign-born workers on labor markets has always been hotly debated—with the suggestion that it negatively impacts American born workers economically—no clear evidence has been presented. A related "hot button" issue involves the balance between immigrants paying taxes and consuming tax-supported services. Of the 12 million U.S. workers without high school diplomas, almost half are immigrants and most are low earners. While most taxes paid by the immigrant population go to the federal government in the form of Social Security and Medicare taxes, as a group they tend to consume education and other services provided by state and local governments. This dynamic has led the latter to refer to immigration as an "unfunded federal mandate," but efforts to recover such costs from the federal government have been generally unsuccessful.

Center for Empowering Refugees and Immigrants (CERI)

The Center for Empowering Refugees and Immigrants, better known as CERI, is "a grassroots, non-profit organization founded in 2005 by a small group of bilingual/bicultural mental health professionals" and paraprofessionals in Oakland, California. It is "dedicated to providing culturally competent mental health and other social services to refugee and immigrant families" that have experienced: "multiple layers of complex needs, exposure to violence and trauma in both their current environment and native countries, and weakening intergenerational relationships" in the United States (http://cerieastbay.org). Presently, the majority of its 200 clients are Cambodian refugees. CERI was established in December 2005, when 100 Cambodian clients, who had been receiving mental health services at another East Bay agency for three years, were abruptly informed that their program was closing due to lack of funding. These clients were all survivors of the Khmer Rouge genocide that took the lives of 1.7 million Cambodians between 1975 and 1979.

CERI is located on the second floor of an old Victorian mansion located in a mixed-ethnic, high-crime, and low-income section of Oakland, where many recent refugees and immigrants have created small enclaves. Mona Afary, CERI's director, tells the story of how her program was able to rent such prime office space. There was a rumor that a previous tenant had died on the second floor of the building, and because of ethnic superstition and the belief that the space was haunted, no one was interested in renting it. But Afary saw a golden opportunity. She rented it at a relatively low price, and then proceeded to invite Buddhist monks from the Cambodian community to come bless the area and ceremonially drive away the ghost. Such cultural creativity would become the hallmark of CERI and its director.

Entering CERI is itself a cross-cultural experience. On my first visit, I hesitated in front of the stately Victorian; *this could not be the right address*, I thought to myself—until I got close enough to identity a small group of Asian men congregated around the entrance, smoking and joking with each other. They made way for me to enter, nodding warmly as I passed into the foyer and the waiting area for the first-floor offices. Across the side of the stairs leading to the second floor was a sign stating: "CERI: Our mission is to improve the social, psychological & economic health of refugees affected by war, torture, genocide or other forms of extreme trauma." At the top of the stairs I found a very different world—much more like a bustling community center or an expansive private home than a set of sterile mental health offices. I was immediately struck by its warmth, hominess, and organized chaos; rows of shoes and sandals were lined up at the top of the stairs, removed out of respect by its Cambodian clients. Warm chatter filled every room, each with its own therapeutic activity in progress, yet the doors remained open as if there was nothing to hide. The strong smell of food cooking permeated everywhere. A young woman broke away from the animated discussion that she and a number of other women were having in Cambodian in the room closest to the stairs to come out and greet me.

"I have an appointment with Mona."

"Welcome, she is expecting you. Her office is at the end of the hall, to the right."

Mona greeted me warmly, offered me tea, and told me she was preparing lunch and hoped I would join her.

CERI is in its truest sense a therapeutic community where healing results from the human interconnectedness and caring of the clients, staff, and volunteers who are in so many ways indistinguishable. It also very much exemplifies the Community Psychology approach and principles that were introduced in Chapter 6. By way of reminder, Community Psychology, according to Burton, Boyle, Harris, and Kagan (2007), "is . . . concerned with how people feel, think, experience, and act as they work together, resisting oppression and struggling to create a better world" (p. 219).

Psychologist Mona Afary is the gentle and loving force behind CERI's enormous success. Mona is an amazingly warm person. Her actions and words exude sincerity, kindness, and caring. Her generous style and disposition draws people out, draws them to her, and makes them feel safe and comfortable. She is trusted and loved because she gives trust and love. This is no small feat given the mistrust and fear in the community, a community that Mona describes as "the most traumatized people that she has encountered in twenty years as a psychotherapist." As a cultural group, Cambodian Americans have learned to mistrust and fear, are too ashamed to ask for help, do not naturally respond to western mental health practices, and have been severely overlooked by the health field (Pottie, Greenaway, Feightner, Welch, Swinkels, Rashid, and Hassan, 2011).

Mona is herself an emigrant, an Iranian Jew, and her own personal experience as an outsider to America provides invaluable insight and empathy for her work with clients. Shavelson and Setterberg (2008) speak of this in a case study describing Mona's work with a Cambodian man:

> Mona let escape a small, wistful sigh. This sense of foreboding and loss—it was her story, too. For twenty-five hundred years, her own family had lived in Iran. In 1977, she moved to California to attend college. Two years later, from the safety of her new home, she received heartbreaking letters about the Islamic Revolution rapidly transforming Iran. Her friends were languishing in prison, enduring barbaric tortures, slated for the firing squads. Mona longed now to tell Lay and the other Cambodians about the tragedy of her own birthplace. Most of all, she wanted to convey that she, like them, still did not feel at home in America. (p. 104)

History of Cambodian Refugees

During the later years of the U.S. involvement in Vietnam, the American and South Vietnamese military sought to cut off community military supply routes which moved along the so-called Ho Chi Minh Trail through the forests of eastern Cambodia, a country which at that time proclaimed itself to be politically "neutral." Cambodia, however, was ineffective in defending its military neutrality. The United States and Vietnam supported the creation of an unpopular, anti-Communist military regime in Cambodia. When U.S. involvement in Southeast Asia waned and, in 1975, collapsed, a Communist force called the Khmer Rouge swept through the country and seized its government. Some 34,000 supporters of the old regime fled to the safety of Thailand at that time. Most of them were resettled in third countries such as the United States and France where many of them had personal ties.

The Khmer Rouge then imposed what became popularly known as the "killing fields," in which unspeakable brutality was carried out by the insurgents and their supporters against the Cambodian population. Their purpose was the restructuring of Cambodian society, and the destruction of all the features that characterized Khmer life and culture prior to their ascendancy. Through the most drastic of measures, the Khmer Rouge intended to create a supremely egalitarian agrarian society patterned after the most extreme strains of the Chinese Cultural Revolution. In the process, through starvation, disease, and murder, they killed 1.7 million Cambodians—or approximately one-eighth of the total population—between 1975 and 1979. So pervasive was their rule during those years that few Cambodians were able to escape.

In 1978 and 1979, after a series of minor conflicts and skirmishes, the Vietnamese invaded Cambodia and quickly captured the capital city of Phnom Penh, forcing the Khmer Rouge into the hinterlands, where they continued to wage guerilla warfare for several years. In the midst of the general confusion, hundreds of thousands of Cambodians moved westward toward the Thai border and into Thailand. In 1979, an international response led to the opening of several refugee camps within Thailand for some 160,000 refugees; another 350,000 lived in Thailand outside the camps, and some 100,000 fled to Vietnam, where the UNHCR provided them with assistance. Between 1978 and 1993, Cambodian refugees from the UNHCR camps were admitted to the United States, Australia, France, Canada, and several other countries. The U.S. admissions program for Cambodians largely concluded in 1985, and only small numbers have entered the country since then.

Adult Clinical Services

CERI offers a holistic array of culturally sensitive, bilingual services that support the mental health and well-being of refugee and immigrant clients who have multiple layers of complex needs. It integrates traditional services such as clinical mental health counseling and medication management with culturally or spiritually tailored intervention strategies such as a meditation group co-facilitated by a Buddhist monk.

Social Services and Advocacy. At CERI, building a trusting relationship with each client to meet his or her needs is a central principle. It offers direct services or links clients to appropriate agencies to help them overcome barriers and issues (housing, legal, citizenship, etc.) that impact their mental and physical health. By building these bonds of trust, it increases client participation in individual therapy, group therapy, and other services.

Support Groups. CERI offers a range of culturally-grounded support groups to its clients that emphasize self-expression, body awareness, and connecting to a peer support network that meet weekly. Currently, the majority of CERI's clients are enrolled in the following weekly or biweekly groups: Stress Reduction & Meditation Group, Movement Group, Yoga and Deep Relaxation Group, Men's Expressive Arts Group, and Women's Self-Expression Group (visualization and dream work, knitting and sewing, painting, jewelry making, and cooking).

Clinical Counseling

Therapy is conducted with the assistance of an interpreter to individual clients, couples and families. Therapy can be either short- or long-term, depending on the level of need.

Medical Management

For clients who require psychotropic medication, the agency offers a monthly psychiatric clinic that provides psychiatric evaluation and medication management on site. Interpreters are available at the monthly clinics.

Body Work, Homeopathy, and Acupuncture

Alternative medicine and healing bodywork are offered to clients by an experienced acupuncturist. In the future, they would like to expand their program and build relationships with homeopathic clinicians, massage therapy, chiropractic and physical therapy programs. Please refer to Case Study 2, "Keo's Story," for an example of adult treatment at CERI.

CASE STUDY 2: KEO'S STORY

Keo is a survivor of the Khmer Rouge genocide in Cambodia. Her husband was dragged out of their hut and murdered in front of her eyes. Afterwards, his body was hung with a sign behind his back, which said "War Slave."

Keo fled to Thailand in 1979. After five years, she was sent to the Philippines where she along with refugees from other parts of the world studied English prior to coming to the United States on asylum visas. It was here that she met her second husband, a Vietnamese man with a history of torture during the eleven years of his political imprisonment.

Keo and her husband were resettled in East Oakland. Not having any language skills, education, or job expertise, they were delighted to finally get a job—delivering

The San Francisco Examiner. Her husband's subsequent, massive heart attack paralyzed him and made him homebound. Keo continued the newspaper delivery for another ten years but had to quit because of episodes of passing out as a result of side effects from medication she was taking for diabetes. She was now living on disability.

When Keo came to CERI to get help for her citizenship application, she was asked about her psychological condition. She talked about her insomnia, flashbacks, and nightmares of the Khmer Rouge years, along with depression and panic attacks. She had no friends and her only social activity was going to the Cambodian grocery store and conversing with people while shopping. She welcomed the idea of attending a weekly therapy group where Cambodian women, all survivors of the Khmer Rouge genocide, would meet regularly to talk. She, like most of the clients at CERI, had never had the opportunity to talk about their psychological symptoms or share their life stories. Cambodians did not traditionally ask such personal questions of each other, and the non-Cambodian physician who treated her for diabetes either did not have an interpreter in the session or did not choose to ask about any psychological symptoms she might be experiencing. Keo had been referred to CERI for help her with her citizenship . . . she was also assessed clinically and was given treatment for her emotional and psychological symptoms. With the help of the psychiatrist and homeopathic clinician, her nightmares were reduced from nightly to once or twice a week, and her flashbacks reduced significantly. For the first time in more than 20 years, she was able to experience deep sleep at night. When she told her story to the group and experienced their deep sorrow and empathy, she felt relieved. "It was as if the ghosts had finally left me and I felt at peace."

Today, she came to her individual therapy session with a request from her husband. "He is skin and bones, and in and out of the hospital all the time. He wanted you to know that he and I have saved enough money for his cremation, but because we don't have family and neither of us knows anything about Cambodian system, he wants to know if CERI could help her with arranging his cremation ceremony upon his death."

Chanda, the bi-lingual Cambodian interpreter, and I looked at one another. I paused because of not knowing anything about Cambodian death ceremonies and rituals. Without verbally communicating this with Chanda, she read my mind and said, "Yes, we will take care of it." I nodded. Tears rolled down her eyes, and she said: "We both know that he is going to be gone soon, so I cook him a delicious meal every day. He is not able to eat much and has only a bite or two, but I enjoy looking at his face when the food is set in front of him. Today is going to be one of the happiest days of his life. He knows that he will be cremated respectfully and that his wife will not be left alone with all the women friends that she has made at CERI. So, I am going to Chinatown to buy him roast duck for dinner."

Note: From the Center for Empowering Refugees and Immigrants website. Copied with permission.

Youth Services Program

In 2008, CERI launched and established its Youth Services Program: Reviving Our Youths' Aspirations (ROYA), named in memory of Roya Forouzesh, who was a "close supporter of the clinic and a counselor who passionately worked with at-risk youth and their families." Launched in 2008 with the support of various Bay Area funders, ROYA is a holistic mental health intervention program designed specifically for Cambodian teens and young adults. ROYA's goal is "to prevent the involvement of this young and vulnerable population in crimes, gangs, underground sex trafficking, drug and alcohol abuse, and teen pregnancy" (http://cerieastbay.org). ROYA provides at-risk youth with individual and group counseling, case management, and other support services, in conjunction with family counseling and parenting education for parents or caregivers. Its ultimate goal is to help at-risk young people develop their potential and become leaders in their community. All services are provided free of charge.

ROYA is unique, not only because of the wide range of services it provides for Cambodian American youth, but also because it involves the parents of these children and youth in treatment. It can therefore make much more of an intergenerational change in the dynamics of the parent-child relationship, helping clients overcome communication issues and estrangement. In addition to clinical services, it takes an all-encompassing approach, providing home visits, workshops, support groups, parent education, and family counseling, helping to generate closeness, healing, compassion, and understanding among family members.

This is especially important since many of these young people have no idea about the extent of the violence and hardships that their parents experienced, and how they may have may have been traumatized. Most of the young people have either been sheltered from the truth by their parents, who are too traumatized to talk about the experience, or there are language barriers between the parents and their children (i.e., the parents speak Cambodian, the children speak English). Once they learn about their parents' experience, it opens them up to a new perspective about what they want to do with their lives and a new sense of cultural heritage and pride in their community is exhibited. The family can also begin a deeper level of healing.

Community partnerships are another important strategy employed by ROYA. CERI actively cultivates working relationships with other community-based social service, legal, and educational providers, as well law enforcement officials, in order to establish a network of support services for youth program clients. Current partners include The Wright Institute, the UC Berkeley Cambodian Students Association, Bay Area Legal Aid and Homeless Action Center (nonprofit legal aid organizations for low-income individuals), Banteay Srei (a program established in 2004 to address the increasing number of young Southeast Asian women engaged in underground sex trafficking), La Clinica's San Antonio Clinic (a community health clinic), among others. Please refer to Case Study 3, which includes both Derick's and Thavry's stories, for two first-hand accounts of examples of the impact of CERI's ROYA Youth Program.

⊂⊃ CASE STUDY 3: DERICK'S AND THAVRY'S STORIES

Derick's Story

"My mom had told me to come to CERI, but I thought CERI was bullshit. But I took a chance to go see what CERI was about."

Derick's parents, survivors of the Khmer Rouge genocide, referred Derick to CERI's Youth Program, ROYA, in March, 2008. Growing up in poor and high-crime neighborhoods of Oakland, Derick became involved in petty crime in his teen years. He was incarcerated for a year and a half and had been on probation for eight years when he came to CERI.

"For eight years, people would not give me a chance, . . . get on a positive track."

With CERI's help, Derick's probation was lifted. He now has a part-time job and is being trained to become a mentor for at-risk children at CERI.

Thavry's Story

Thavry's parents, also survivors of the Khmer Rouge genocide, have been CERI's clients since 2006. In January 2008, when they brought Thavry to family therapy, she was sixteen, had been in Juvenile Hall, had one child, and was pregnant with her second. Now a mother, she wanted to secure a better life for her children.

"If I didn't have my kids, I'd probably still be in the streets. I'd be an alcoholic, still smoking my head out. It happened a lot. I could have been in group homes and stuff."

In addition to family therapy, CERI offered Thavry individual therapy. Her hard work in therapy has brought new dynamics in her relationship with her parents.

"My parents are there for me now. They show a lot of love now. They are my support, my backbone; my kids, too."

A few months after coming to CERI, Thavry decided to help as a volunteer. It was her struggles and growth that inspired CERI to initiate its Youth Program, ROYA.

"CERI has been my backbone, has helped me a whole lot. I could have been on the streets, too. But I thought instead of being on the streets, I could be here instead of being caught up with something stupid. I could spend my time here wisely."

Now at eighteen Thavry is a student at Laney College, the office clerk at CERI, and is being trained to be a mentor for at-risk children.

Note: From the Center for Empowering Refugees and Immigrants website. Copied with permission.

Innovations in Trauma Treatment

Finally, I would like to acknowledge and provide an example of CERI and its director Mona Afary's enormous spirit of experimentation in pushing the boundaries of effective trauma treatment in relation to their Cambodian clients. According to Judith Herman (1997) in her classic work *Trauma and Recovery,* collective group experience is a critical aspect of later-stage trauma treatment, especially when it provides opportunity for the victim to find a "survivor's mission." According to Herman:

> Most survivors seek the resolution of their treatment experience within the confines of their personal lives. But a significant minority, as a result of the trauma, feel called upon to engage in a wider world. These survivors recognize a political or religious dimension in their misfortune and discover that they can transform the meaning of their personal tragedy by making it the basis for social action. While there is no way to compensate for an atrocity, there is a way to transcend it, by making it a gift to others. The trauma is redeemed only when it becomes the source of a survivor mission. (p. 207)

Please refer to Case Study 4, "A Spiritual Journey to the Homeland," as an example of CERI's clinical creativity in working with trauma.

CASE STUDY 4: A SPIRITUAL JOURNEY TO THE HOMELAND

In October of 2010, Clinical Director Mona Afary organized a trip to Cambodia with 13 clients, CERI's staff therapist, Hamid Shafiezadeh, and CERI's interpreter, Sandra Pech.

Most of the clients who travelled to Cambodia had not visited their homeland since they were forced to flee from Pol Pot's genocidal regime. For years since, they have struggled to acclimate to the wider Oakland community, facing not only cultural, linguistic, and social isolation, but also serious psychological symptoms. For five years, in weekly support groups at CERI, they had shared their fears, anger, and despair related to their horrific experiences under the Khmer Rouge. The compassionate space created over the years wove a strong bond among these men and women. With love as its foundation, at the scene of the genocide, this group was able to grieve their losses collectively, without drowning in their own sorrow.

Our group first visited Tuol Sleng [Genocide] Museum, also known as the S-21 Prison. Out of the 30,000 prisoners incarcerated here, seven survived. The Khmer Rouge General in charge of this prison, known as Duch, had compulsively kept detailed records: names and pictures of the prisoners, their alleged crimes, the tortures implemented to force confessions, and finally, how they were killed.

Our group of fifteen inspected it all. As we exited, a senior member of our CERI community whispered in my ear in her broken English: "I never know where my husband killed. I looked at every man's picture in Tuol Sleng. I so happy not find his picture. I know, he not killed here."

Next, we drove towards the Phnom Penh Killing Field where those who had not been killed at Tuol Sleng, were taken, beaten to death, and buried in mass graves. Amidst the magnificently beautiful countryside was a three-story-high memorial pagoda with piles upon piles of skulls stacked according to age and gender. At the entrance to the mass graves towered a large glass box with the clothes and shoes of the men, and women, and children who died there. As we left, we looked at our Cambodian clients wondering how they were going to cope, being witnesses to this memorial. Some silently cried on the ride back to the hotel; others looked lost in their thoughts. One man said in his broken English: "Mona, I never thought I could live anymore if I go Killing Fields. Talking to you, Chhom Chhuy, Hamid, Sandra, Jon, Dr. Gracer made me very strong. I happy to live and hope for future." I held him in my arms and we both cried.

The opportunity to return to Cambodia has proved to be a great source of healing and inspiration. It is greatly empowering for a survivor of torture to have the power to return to the site of trauma—to stand at the prison gates . . . to see them as historical fixtures, long non-operational, and devoid of all power.

The serious poverty and struggles facing those who remain in Cambodia provided a source of awakening as well. Our group returned to their homes in Oakland, grateful for having one another, their CERI family, and hope about their future. Many re-committed to take difficult yet positive steps to heal themselves and their families so that they would be better able to support loved ones living in horrible poverty in rural Cambodia. Subsequently, and motivated by what they saw and experienced in their return to Cambodia, the clients of CERI have undertaken their own "survivor mission." Each is donating $5 individually, and together about $350-$500 a month to support an orphanage that the group visited during their journey to the Homeland with needed food and medical expenses.

Note: From the Center for Empowering Refugees and Immigrants website. Copied with permission.

SUMMARY

Trauma is an extraordinary psychological experience that overwhelms ordinary human functioning. Herman points out that in working with trauma, there are always conflicting tendencies to seek the truth and to obliterate it. One sees this within the victim, within the helper, and within the history of trauma research and treatment. Violence and atrocities are typically directed toward the weak and the powerless, and victims will become perpetrators if no healing or intervention occurs. An alternative conceptualization to trauma as a category of mental illness and its treatment offered by Peskin (2009) is presented. It focuses on viewing trauma as a disorder of dehumanization and the necessity of the therapist playing the role of witness to the traumatized client's experience. Next, three examples of efforts to heal victims of mass violence are offered.

The Lakota Sioux are typical of Native Americans who are beset by serious and widespread social problems. Brave Heart contends that her people suffer from historical trauma and unresolved grief passed on from generation to generation. Its source is both massive trauma caused by violence against them by the U.S. government and the systematic destruction of traditional Lakota ways and rituals of grieving. Based on research on Jewish Holocaust survivors, Brave Heart created an intervention that included the education about Lakota history and personal trauma, the introduction and experiences of Lakota grieving rituals, and the development of positive group identification. The four-day workshops were given to professional helpers and community leaders who would then return to their communities and facilitate similar experiences with their members. Significant positive changes were found among workshop participants. Taking a similar perspective, Duran and Duran argue that Native American men routinely suffer PTSD as a result of their treatment by white society and that improper professional intervention can retraumatize this population.

The South African Truth and Reconciliation Commission (TRC) represents a unique and unprecedented effort at pubic healing through a process of restorative justice. Its goal was national reconciliation after fifty years of apartheid, not retribution. The TRC involved three processes: truth-telling, public acknowledgment, and reparations. In four years, testimonies were taken from more than 23,000 witnesses and victims, 2,000 of them in public hearings. Victims seemed to benefit from telling their stories publicly through a process of breaking the silence, sharing their narrative, experiencing its altruistic function, and reconnecting to others and the world. Mental health professionals aided victims in this process. The testimonies gave bystanders a new awareness of the atrocities that had occurred in South Africa in their names and with their support. Bystander behavior can be best understood as a result of internal mechanisms of disassociation, splitting, and projective identification. Perpetrators' behavior toward the TRC was variable. The intimate link between perpetrator and victim and their interdependency for healing is stressed. The work of the Institute for the Healing of Memories and its founder, Michael Lapsley, is an example of efforts to continue the work of the TRC. Forgiveness is viewed as an internal process of healing, whereby one disconnects from destructive defenses and reactions. The need for reparations, including restitution and apology, is discussed, and the relative merits and difficulties of each is described. Efforts at reparation in U.S. history are assessed.

No event has generated more research on the effects of trauma than the Nazi Holocaust, including its impact on victims, perpetrators, and the children of both. Little information, however, exists on the relationship between these parents and their children as well as how the children of each relate to each other. The role of the perception of justice in perpetuating mass violence is explored as well as its implications for reconciliation. Weissmark's study of the interaction of children of Jewish Holocaust survivors and children of Nazis in face-to-face encounters is summarized. Five stages in the interaction were noted, and suggestions for productive aspects of reconciliation efforts are given.

The fourth and final section of the chapter focuses on treatment issues related to refugee and immigrant populations. After reviewing the staggering numbers and plight of displaced refugee populations worldwide and then the status of immigration and immigrants to the United States, we look in depth at CERI, a treatment center located in Oakland, California, that works primarily with Cambodian immigrants that represent one of the most traumatized populations in the world. We review the specifics of their program and provide several case studies that exemplify their approach.

ACTIVITIES

1. **Explore a personal grievance.**   You can do this exercise individually, in a dyad, or in a small group. Think of a personal experience when you felt treated unfairly or unjustly by another person—one which you found particularly difficult to deal with. What exactly happened? Can you specify the aspects of the experience that were particularly painful for you? What specifically about the experience feels unjust and unfair to you? Were you ever able to forgive the other person or let go of your negative feelings about what had happened? If so, how did the resolution occur? If not, what is still in the way of moving on and what acts or changes would it take (perhaps from the person) for you to feel you could forgive?

2. **Explore personal experiences of trauma.**   Have you or anyone you know ever experienced or exhibited symptoms of trauma (such as PTSD)? Describe the precipitating situation. What happened? How did you or they react? What specific symptoms did you or the other person experience? Was there any treatment

for the symptoms or intervention to address what had happened? How did recovery and healing proceed, and are there still residues of the experience? How did it affect and change you or the other person?

INTRODUCTION TO CHAPTERS 11 THROUGH 17

Avoiding the Stereotyping of Individual Group Members

The chapters that follow are organized according to ethnicity—that is, each focuses on working with a diverse ethnic community. Chapters 11 through 16 deal with clients of color—Latinos/as, Native Americans, African Americans, Asian Americans, Arab and Muslim Americans, and South Asian Indian Americans—and Chapter 17 looks at white ethnics. Although adopting such a general "cookbook" approach (i.e., the enumeration of stock formulas or "recipes" for understanding and dealing with a certain group of people) is a convenient way of summarizing a good deal of culturally specific information, it does present certain pitfalls. To begin with, the division of America's non-white populations into four broad racial categories, although a common practice within majority culture, is artificial and serves to mask enormous diversity. For example, Americans who have emigrated from Asian countries do not generally identify as or call themselves Asian Americans. They may self-identify as Chinese Americans, Chinese, of Chinese descent, or even according to more regional or tribal groupings. Some may find being called Asian American offensive. The term is, in fact, bureaucratic in origin, developed by the U.S. Census Bureau. It is used here, as elsewhere, for convenience, but should not be assumed to imply sameness. In actuality, as Atkinson, Morten, and Sue (1993) point out, the term *Asian American* refers to "some twenty-nine distinct subgroups that differ in language, religion, and values" (p. 195). The important point here is that such broad categories subsume many ethnic groups, each with its unique culture, and to lump them together on the basis of certain common geographic, physical, or cultural features merely encourages an underestimation of their diversity and uniqueness.

Thinking about people of color through such categories also serves to encourage stereotyping. Such thinking tends to be most common among inexperienced providers who find the prospect of cross-cultural work, at least initially, anxiety-producing. Stereotyping, in turn, is an effective means of reducing what might be experienced as unpredictability in the behavior of culturally diverse clients. Thus, less experienced providers often project the same cultural characteristics onto all individuals they identify as belonging to a specific group. The thinking might be as follows: "If I can be sure that all clients will act similarly, I can more easily develop a general strategy of how to deal with them in session and, therefore, feel more in control. If I believe, for example, that all Native American clients are reticent, I can prepare myself to be more active in seeking information, or if I know that all Asian Americans are taught early to suppress emotions, I can be on the lookout for more subtle forms of emotionality in their presentation."

Similarly, descriptions of what approaches have been most successful with a given client population can be misread by those who wish to limit complexity as the only approaches to be adopted. In sum, then, taking the material that appears in the following chapters too literally (i.e., as some sort of gospel) limits provider creativity and adaptability and at the same time suppresses sensitivity to intragroup differences.

Instead of assuming unanimity among clients from the same group, a far better way to proceed is to treat all guesses about what is going on with a culturally diverse client as hypotheses to be verified clinically: "I may know, for example, that alcohol abuse is a very common problem in Native American communities. If I inquire about it and the client says he is not abusing alcohol, I must consider the possibility that his statement is true rather than suspect massive denial. Or in contemplating work with a recent immigrant Latina, I should not assume that she is experiencing serious conflict with her culture's traditional role for women, even though that often occurs. Perhaps she is, but then again, maybe she is not." It is clearly best to hold off making such judgments until one has carried out a thorough cultural assessment to check the hypotheses that the following chapters can help generate.

THE INTERVIEWS

These chapters contain six in-depth interviews—five focused on working with clients from one of the communities of color and the sixth on working with white ethnic clients, in particular American Jews. Each is written in conjunction with a member of that community who is a human service professional with extensive experience working with clients from his or her respective group. All were asked to answer the following general question: "What do you think is important or even critical for a culturally different provider to know in relation to working with a client from your community?" Their responses are presented according to a number of distinct topics that provide the structure for the interviews, including the following:

- ▶ Professional and ethnic autobiographical material
- ▶ Demographics and shared characteristics of their community
- ▶ Group names
- ▶ Group history and story in a nutshell
- ▶ Help-seeking behavior
- ▶ Family and community characteristics
- ▶ Cultural style, values, and worldview
- ▶ Common presenting problems
- ▶ Socioeconomic issues

- Important assessment questions
- Subpopulations at risk or experiencing transition
- Tips for developing rapport
- Optimal therapeutic styles
- A short case study

The text of each chapter was generated through an interview format in which the provider summarizes his or her thinking about the general characteristics that community members share. This is not an easy task given the fact that each racial category in essence represents an array of ethnic groups that are quite diverse. Each interviewee tried to speak broadly enough to fairly represent the cultural and psychological characteristics shared by the majority of the ethnic group he or she is representing. At the same time, they tried to make distinctions among subgroups where necessary. Because no single provider can claim expert knowledge or experience working with all the subgroups or divisions within any racial category, the interviewees were asked to specifically discuss and draw examples from subpopulations with which they are most familiar. Answers to the various questions in each interview have been left close to verbatim to retain their personal and cultural flavor.

11

Working with Latino/a Clients: An Interview with Roberto Almanzan

LEARNING OBJECTIVES

11-1 Interpret the implications of census data for Latinos/as in America.

11-2 Explain family and cultural values of Latinos/as.

11-3 Examine Mr. Almanzan's experience as a Mexican counselor, teacher, trainer, and consultant on diversity and multicultural issues.

▶ Demographics `11-1`

With the 2000 Census, Latinos/as became the largest racial minority in the United States, numbering 35,305,818, or 12.5 percent of the U.S. population. These figures increased in July 2016 when the U.S. Census Bureau reported Latinos/as at 17.8 percent of the U.S. population. Projections into the future suggest that by the year 2100, Latinos/as will make up one-third of the U.S. population. This dramatic growth is attributed to high birth and fertility rates, immigration patterns, and the average young age of the population. As a collective, Latinos/as are quite diverse, including individuals whose roots are in Mexico, Cuba, Puerto Rico, and Central and South Americas. Those of Mexican descent, now numbering 20 million, make up 64 percent of the Hispanic population, Puerto Ricans at 3.4 million and 10 percent, Cubans at 1.2 million and 4 percent, and South and Central Americans at 3.1 million and 10 percent. See Chapter 1 for more demographic information.

For the purpose of Census data, the government considers race and Hispanic origins as "two separate and distinct concepts." The term *Hispanic* is used to denote a common Spanish-speaking background. A notable exception, however, are Latinos/as of Brazilian descent whose native language is Portuguese. Racially, individuals of Mexican descent identify their roots as "*mestizo*" (i.e., a mixture of Spanish and Indian backgrounds). Puerto Ricans consider themselves of Spanish descent, Cubans of Spanish and black descent, and Latin Americans of having varying mixtures of Spanish, Japanese, Italian, and black heritage.

Geographically, Latino/a populations are largely urban and concentrated in the Southwest, Northeast, and in the state of Florida, according to country of origin: Mexican Americans in Texas, California, Arizona, New Mexico, and Illinois, where they make up a significant proportion of each state's population; Puerto Ricans in large northeastern urban areas; and Cubans in the Miami area.

The vast majority of Latinos/as are Spanish-speaking, are Roman Catholic, and share a set of cultural characteristics that are described later. One must be careful, however, to not underemphasize the differences among groups; there are as many differences as there are similarities. Compared to non-Hispanics (again, a Census term rather than an identity of choice among most group members), Latinos/as tend to be younger—on average younger than thirty years old and nine years younger than the average white American; poorer—40 percent of Hispanic children live below the poverty line; less educated—approximately 30 percent leave high school before graduation (the highest rate of all minorities); and more consistently unemployed or relegated to unskilled and semi-skilled jobs.

A unique set of factors related to their entry and circumstances in the United States puts Latinos/as at high risk for physical and psychological difficulties. Included are pressures around bilingualism, immigration and rapid acculturation, adjustment to American society, intergenerational and cultural conflict, poverty, racism, and the loss of cultural identity.

As our expert guest, Roberto Almanzan, indicates, a central factor in understanding the psychological situation of most Latino/a clients is their individual experience, as well as the experience of their family units in migrating to the United States.

▶ Family and Cultural Values 11-2

As a collective, Latino/a subgroups share a language, Spanish; a religion, Roman Catholicism; and a series of cultural values that define and structure group life. See Chapter 5 for more information on cultural values.

Carrasquillo (1991) lists the following shared values:

- ▶ Importance of the family, both nuclear and extended, or *familialismo*
- ▶ Emphasis on interdependence and cooperation, or *simpatico*
- ▶ Emphasis on the worth and dignity of the individual, or *personalismo*
- ▶ Valuing of the spiritual side of life
- ▶ Acceptance of life as it exists

Garcia-Preto (1996) offers an excellent description of the nature of Latino/a families:

Perhaps the most significant value they share is the importance placed on family unity, welfare and honor. The emphasis is on the group rather than on the individual. There is a deep sense of family commitment, obligation, and responsibility. The family guarantees protection and caretaking for life as long as the person stays in the system . . . The expectation is that when a person is having problems, others will help, especially those in stable positions. The family is usually an extended system that encompasses not only those related by blood and marriage, but also "compadres" (godparents) and "hijos de cnanza" (adopted children, whose adoption is not necessarily legal). "Compadrazco" (godparent-hood) is a system of ritual kinship with binding, mutual obligations for economic assistance, encouragement, and even personal correction. "Hijos de cnanza" refers to the practice of transferring children from one nuclear family to another within the extended family in times of crisis. The others assume responsibility, as if children were their own, and do not view the practice as neglectful. (p. 151)

Family roles and duties are highly structured and traditional, as are sex roles, which are referred to as *machismo* and *marianismo*. Males, the elderly, and parents are afforded special respect, and children are expected to be obedient and deferential, contribute to family finances, care for younger siblings, and act as parent surrogates. Males are expected to exhibit strength, virility, dominance, and provide for the family; females are expected to be nurturing, submit to the males, and self-sacrifice

(Sue and Sue, 1999). Both boys and girls are socialized into these roles early. Boys are given far more freedom—encouraged to be aggressive and act manly—and discouraged from playing with girls and engaging in female activities. Girls are trained early in household activities and are severely sheltered and restricted as they grow older.

The authoritative structure of the family also reflects a broader characteristic of Latino/a culture, which includes the valuing of conformity, obedience, deference to authority, and subservience to the autocratic attitudes of external organizations and institutions. Individuals from such high-powered and distancing cultures are most comfortable in hierarchical structures where there is an obvious power differential and expectations are clearly defined. Professionals and helpers who disrespect this power distance—by deemphasizing their authority, trying to make the interaction more democratic, communicating indirectly, or using subtle forms of control, such as sarcasm, and causing an individual to lose face—tend to confuse, alienate, and disrespect Latino/a clients. Respect for authority can also have its shadow side by forcing individuals from high power distant cultures to adapt to the status quo, as well as restraining them from asserting their rights. Garcia-Preto (1996) offers the example of illegal migrants whose cultural hesitancy is exacerbated only by the fear of being caught and sent back to more oppressive and dangerous circumstances.

Personalismo—an interpersonal attitude that acknowledges the basic worth and dignity of all individuals and attributes to them a sense of self-worth—serves as a powerful social lubricant in Latino/a culture. Unlike mainstream American culture, where respect is garnered through achievement, status, and wealth, the individual in Latino/a culture merits respect by the very fact of his or her humanity. *Simpatico*, or valuing of cooperation and interdependence, is a natural outgrowth of *personalismo*. Competing, undermining the efforts of another, asserting one's individuality, and working to inflate one's ego are all viewed negatively in Latino/a culture. In cultures where the needs of the individual are suppressed to serve the interests of the group—the dimension of culture that Brown and Landrum-Brown (1995) call "the individual vs. the extended self" (see Chapter 5)—the individual ego must be contained, and this is done through *simpatico*, which serves to promote cooperation, noncompetition, and the avoidance of conflict between individuals.

A final series of values in Latino/a culture relate to beliefs fostered by the Roman Catholic Church. These include:

- Focus on spirituality and the life of the spirit
- Fatalistic acceptance of life as it exists
- Time orientation toward the present

Latino/a culture places as much emphasis on non-rational experience as it does on the material world. Belief in visions, omens, spirits, and spiritual healers is commonplace, and such phenomena are viewed from within the culture as normative rather than pathological. Latinos/as are also willing to forgo and even sacrifice material comfort in the pursuit of spiritual goals. Yamamoto and Acosta (1982), for example, suggest that the Latino/a church emphasizes that sacrifice in this world promotes salvation, that one must be charitable, and that wrongs against the person should be endured. Sue and Sue (1999) assert that because of such beliefs, "many Hispanics have difficulty behaving assertively. They feel that problems or events are meant to be and cannot be changed" (p. 290). This relates in turn to a time orientation to the present that is shared by most Latinos/as. Focus tends to be on the here and now, not on what has happened in the past or what will happen in the future. Present-oriented cultures place special value on the nature and quality of interpersonal relationships as opposed to their history or functionality. Such an orientation is psychologically related to a kind of fatalism and particularly common in peoples who suffer economic deprivation and powerlessness and find themselves at the whim and mercy of those with more power. The family and cultural values identified in this section are still true in current literature (Adames and Chavez-Dueñas, 2016).

▶ Our Interviewee 11-3

Roberto Almanzan, M.S., is a counselor, teacher, trainer, and consultant on diversity and multicultural issues in the San Francisco Bay Area. He has worked with schools, corporations, mental health agencies, and various nonprofit organizations. He also teaches in the multicultural program at the Wright Institute, Berkeley. He has trained with Stirfry Seminars in Berkeley and was a key participant in the film *The Color of Fear*—produced in 1994 and probably the most widely used film in training and education on racism—and participated in the production of *The Color of Fear 2* and *The Color of Fear 3* as well as a number of other documentaries on racism, privilege, and social justice.

The Interview

Question: First, could you begin by talking about your ethnic background and how it has impacted your work?

Almanzan: I am Mexican, and this ethnic and cultural identity has been an influential factor in most facets of my life. It was my experiences as a Mexican American in a white-dominated society that really motivated me to do the kind of work that I do, much of which involves healing in the lives of people of color and in the relationships between them and with people of European descent. I'm the second generation born in the United States. My grandparents on my father's side migrated from Chihuahua in the north of Mexico to El Paso, Texas, on the border. My grandfather was a carpenter. He married my grandmother in Parral,

Chihuahua, and in the early 1900s in search of work, he went to El Paso, Texas, where he found employment. Shortly, he brought his wife and first child to El Paso. My father and other children were born there, and in gradual steps over ten years, the family moved to Los Angeles, where my father grew up.

My mother's family came from Sonora, a northern state on the western edge of Mexico and settled in Douglas, Arizona, another border town. I don't know much about my maternal grandparents. They both died before I was born. I do know that my mother's father was a successful businessman. My mother's family was large, like many Mexican families. My maternal grandfather owned a large general store and stables in Douglas. All the children, including my mother, were born in Douglas, so the family was settled there. My grandfather was able to send his eldest son, Jose, to Stanford University in 1915. However, when the United States entered World War I in 1917, my grandfather feared that his son was going to end up in the U.S. military fighting in the war. He did not want his son to go to war in Europe, so he pulled him out of the university and brought him home. He sold everything in Douglas, moved his family back to Mexico, and settled in Mexicali, a city on the border with California.

In the 1920s in Los Angeles, my father was the first of his family to graduate from high school. Some of his classmates from Polytechnic High School went to Stanford University. After hearing about Stanford from his friends, he set his mind on joining them. He was accepted at Stanford, and although he had to drop out for a while due to lack of finances, he graduated from Stanford as a civil engineer in 1933. Racism and the Depression made it very difficult for my father to land an engineering job. He finally ended up working for an American company that was doing some surveying in the agricultural area around Mexicali. My mother was living there with her eldest brother, Jose, and his family. By a miraculous coincidence, the kind that only happens in real life, my father was placed on a survey crew led by my mother's brother, Jose. It wasn't long before Jose introduced my father to his eligible sister, Bella. My father met my mother, courted her, and they married. I was their first child, born in Calexico, again on the border in California.

This was the history of my family, a border existence, back and forth, living on both sides. I grew up in Los Angeles but with family in Ensenada, Mexicali, and as far south as Mexico City. We visited our relatives in Ensenada and Mexicali often and occasionally our relatives in Mexico City. They visited us, sometimes staying for extended periods of time. I always thought of all of us as Mexicans. I was a Mexican that lived in the United States *(en este lado*—on this side) and they were Mexicans that lived in Mexico *(al otro lado*—on the other side). I was not aware of the differences between us and the privilege that I had growing up within the United States. So, I was shocked the first time my Mexican cousins called me a *pocho*, which is a derogatory term for Mexicans who have become Americanized by living in the United States. They could easily see and hear a difference in me and my life, but I couldn't, not for a long time. I thought I was Mexican. I didn't want to think of myself as different and therefore separate from them. But I was and am a *pocho*. I realized that I was culturally different from my relatives in Mexico.

I grew up in a Mexican barrio in East Los Angeles. We started out in Boyle Heights and moved eastward as I grew older. All the teachers, counselors, principals, police officers, anyone in authority in East Los Angeles then was white. Although there was racism present and a white power structure, I felt fairly protected and supported in my identity, as most of the people in my environment were Mexican, and I was enveloped in my extended family. It was a white world, but in some way, I did not really see that until I graduated from Garfield High School and, following my father's footsteps, went to Stanford University. That was fifty years ago. There was no diversity on the Stanford campus then. The need to include American students of color in universities or the benefits of a racially integrated student environment did not exist and were not known. The only ones I could see who were non-white on campus were the international students from Asia, Africa, and Latin America. I ended up hanging out at the International House because, in a way, I felt more at home there and more included.

Question: What led you to become a human service provider and involved in the kind of diversity training you do?

Almanzan: It's kind of a jagged history. When I graduated from Stanford with a degree in international relations, my first job was working for the State Department of Employment (now EDD) in one of its newly created Youth Opportunity Centers. There were at the time various efforts to locate satellite offices in minority communities in San Francisco and other cities and target youth of color for intensive counseling and support services in finding employment or vocational training. I worked in these programs for several years—at first excited by what seemed to be a shift in attitude and a desire to do more for people in minority communities. In time, however, I grew discouraged with things that were going on around me. Many of the people we had trained were coming back through for another vocational training program. It seemed like the programs were not working, and we were just going through the motions.

My disenchantment led me in another direction. It seemed to me that what we needed was to build our own economic institutions, engage in economic development for the community, start businesses and employ people from our communities, and train them in business practices and leadership. I started a business importing handcrafted sterling silver jewelry from Mexico and wholesaling to retailers. I managed to sell to retailers from the East Coast to Hawaii, but the business never became the multimillion-dollar enterprise that I had envisioned. I worked in this business for twenty years, and it supported me and my family, but in a way, it was not deeply fulfilling. Yet, I did not know what other work I could do or how I could transition.

In the mid-80s, I was drawn to the men's movement and attended several men's groups and conferences. I liked that men were encouraged to talk openly to each other about their inner lives in ways that men don't usually do. It was referred to as "men's work," although almost all of the men who participated were middle class, white, and heterosexual. I thought if we are really doing "men's work," where were the black men, the Latinos, the Asians, or the Native Americans? I met other men of color and gay men who wanted more diversity. Together, several of us went to the organizers of a large upcoming conference and challenged them to change it in ways that made it more accessible and attractive to men of color and gay men. After a bit of resistance, they agreed, and we created the most diverse men's conference I had ever seen.

My interest in these diversity issues led to a career change. I applied to CSU East Bay (Hayward) to enter their master's program in counseling. Shortly after, I was accepted, and before classes started, I was asked to participate in a documentary film about a racially diverse group of men talking about race and ethnicity. That documentary film was *The Color of Fear*. After earning my master's, I worked with immigrants, particularly Latinos, at The Center for New Americans in Contra Costa County. I kept getting requests to facilitate dialogue based on *The Color of Fear*, and these increased to the point that I had to make a choice between continuing my work with immigrants or to focus on dealing more directly with diversity issues. Although working with Latino immigrants and their families was very satisfying, I decided to focus on the diversity work because it connected me deeply with issues I had been dealing with all my life.

Question: Who are the Latinos and Latinas, and what characteristics do they share as a group?

Almanzan: *Latinos* refers to people whose ancestry lies in the nations to the south, who were originally conquered by Spain in the early sixteenth century, with the exception of Brazil, which was occupied by Portugal. Except for Brazil, where Portuguese is spoken, and a few other countries with historical connections to other European nations, all share Spanish as a common language. Although many Latinos in the United States today are immigrants or children of immigrants, some Latinos have lived in the United States for many generations. Some families have lived in the Southwestern part of the United States since before it was taken from Mexico in 1848 in the U.S.-Mexican War. Even though many of these Latinos have lost their Spanish-language skills, they still share many cultural traits with recent immigrants.

Latinos, first of all, share a deep belief in and connection to their extended families—a sense of family loyalty and honor that's very powerful. Often, extended family members live in close proximity to each other, and family members visit with each other often. When I was young, we visited my grandparents every weekend and sometimes during the week. Other members of our extended family would visit at the same time so that we spent a lot of time with our uncles, aunts, and cousins. This is different from what we see today in the dominant U.S. culture where the nuclear family and individualism are most valued. Among Latinos, the family is often more important than the individual. Extended family members often help each other in whatever way is needed. Sometimes, for economic or other reasons, children may live with an uncle and aunt for a while. In my family, we had different cousins and an aunt live with us at different times.

Latinos also share a sense of basic respect for the person—a sense that everyone merits respect and dignity whatever their status socially or economically. Elders especially merit respect and honor. Elders live within the family, are looked after and consulted, and treated with great dignity. My paternal grandmother, who survived my grandfather, was definitely the head of the family while she was alive. Interactions with Latinos need to convey a sense of respect in order to communicate effectively.

There is also a personal warmth that is expressed between people that often includes physical expression and connection. Latinos are much more likely to embrace, to touch, to kiss on the cheek, to connect with each other physically. There is also a certain generosity and willingness to share what one has with others. Often, this is expressed through food. When someone comes to the home, they are always offered something to eat, no matter who it is. In fact, if you are working with Latinos as a provider, it would not be unusual to be brought some kind of food during the relationship, and it has no meaning other than an act of kindness, gratitude, and respect.

Latino culture is hierarchical. Latinos hold authority and those with it in high esteem: doctors, priests, lawyers, therapists, counselors, and any other providers of services. Their authority is respected and listened to because it is assumed that they hold special knowledge that can be beneficial. They are likely to pay close attention to and follow the directions of such authority figures as long as those don't conflict with their values and traditions.

Latinos also tend to be religious—the majority of them Catholic. I remember that my mother always had an altar somewhere in the house where she lit candles and prayed, perhaps with an image of *la Virgen* (the Virgin Mary), a crucifix, and a rosary. Evangelical Christians are not uncommon, and one also sees in some areas elements of the Catholic religion with native Indian traditions, practices, and beliefs. In Cuba, Dominican Republic, Brazil, and elsewhere, Catholicism is mixed with African religions. Santeria is the most common and is a melding of Catholic and Yoruba beliefs.

Time also takes on a different flavor than in dominant white culture. Latinos tend to be more flexible about it and tend to experience the precision and narrowness of the white definition of time as overly rigid and often problematic. They don't think of time in such rigid concepts, and this can be a source of conflict. Latinos may not show up for appointments at the exact time specified. Punctuality does not have the same importance and value for Latinos or often for other people of color as it does for the dominant culture. Time does not take precedence over other matters, such as greeting others or attending to personal relationships.

A final difference has to do with gender roles and the concepts of *machismo* and *marianismo*. For men, the concept of machismo has been very much distorted and corrupted in the popular media in United States. In its purest form, it refers to the sense of responsibility the male feels to care for and protect his family and those around him. Especially in the United States, it has come to mean a sense of bravado, being loud, aggressive, and tough. This is really its shadow side. Latin America itself has been influenced by this distorted image through the media and has come to increasingly see machismo in this way. I remember growing up with this image of Mexican men from the movies I saw and was shocked when I asked my mother, and she told me this was not machismo. She said that machismo means that "you must make sure that your wife and children are safe and cared for and that you always show respect to your elders." Similarly, *marianismo*, the role of women in Latino culture, has come to be wrongly defined by its extremes. It is the tendency in women toward self-sacrifice and a focusing on the needs of others for the benefit of the family as well as to acquiesce to their husband's role as the head of the family.

Question: Could you now talk a bit more about the various names that different Latino and Latina subgroups use to describe and identify themselves?

Almanzan: The two most commonly used names today are Hispanics and Latinos/Latinas. *Hispanic* is a term that was adopted by the federal government in the early 70s for census and administrative purposes in order to create a single category for all the people whose origins are in Latin America. It seems to have been adopted more by people in Texas and on the East Coast. It is less popular in California. I prefer the term *Latino*. *Hispanic* doesn't acknowledge our indigenous past, and that's an important part of who I am. I identify more with the indigenous part than the Spanish. My family comes from Mexico, as do the majority of Latinos in the United States. I call myself Mexican American. Many people from Latin America are *mestizos*; that is, of mixed race that may include indigenous, African, Spanish, Portuguese, Jewish (Jews who converted to survive), Asians, and other Europeans. Identification as a mestizo is less common in parts of South America, where there is more of a tendency to identity with Spanish roots and with other Europeans. Some immigrants from these countries do not connect with the concept of being Latino or being a person of color.

A final term is *Chicano* or *Chicana*. Its origins probably go back to the 1920s and was developed by Mexican Americans who found themselves no longer from Mexico but also not clearly from the United States. It tended to be taken on by the young, coming out of the streets, and spoken with a sense of pride and assertiveness. I am Chicano. I am this hybrid. Those of the middle and upper classes tended to look down on them. They didn't want to be associated with being called Chicano. In the '60s and early '70s, there was a real sense of pride when Mexican Americans called themselves Chicanos. The term was associated with a struggle for civil rights and social justice. It is not widely used by Latinos whose origins are not in Mexico. The majority of Latinos today, if asked how they identify, would probably refer to their country of origin—I'm Mexican or Guatemalan or Peruvian or Colombian—or where their parents or ancestors came from. There is so much variety that one needs to ask a Latino or Latina how he or she identifies.

Question: Could you describe some of the shared history that Latinos and Latinas bring with them to the United States?

Almanzan: An important piece of our shared history is the fact that we were all colonized. We come from countries that were colonized and did not gain their independence until the nineteenth century. Historically, that's not very long ago. Along with this, there is a sense—that many immigrants carry with them—of having been bullied and oppressed by the United States. There is a long political history of the United States running roughshod over the interests and the peoples of Latin American. One-third of Mexico was in fact taken as a result of the War of 1848. This represents the whole of the U.S. Southwest: Texas, New Mexico, Arizona, California, Nevada, Utah, and parts of Colorado and Wyoming.

Even though this may seem like ancient history to many in the United States, it is still very much alive for Mexicans in Mexico. I remember growing up and being aware of a statue in one of the main parks in Mexico City of the cadets who were the last holdouts when the Americans invaded Mexico City. They all committed suicide, jumping from the highest tower of the national military institute—one wrapped in a Mexican flag—rather than surrender. This sense of pride in their history and connection to the past is something that is important to many. For some Latinos— those from Mexico, Guatemala, Honduras, and Peru—this sense of history stretches back thousands of years to indigenous civilizations that predated the invasions of the Europeans.

Many Central American immigrants—who have come more recently—share a history of war, repression, imprisonment, and torture at the hands of regimes that were supported by the United States. Many fled for their lives from their Central American countries and carry emotionally stressful memories of what happened to themselves, their families, or neighbors.

Another shared experience, which we will be talking about at greater length later, is the process of migration.

Question: Let's switch our focus and begin to look at issues related to providing services to the Latino community. Could you talk about factors that influence how Latinos and Latinas go about seeking help when they have problems?

Almanzan: First, it is important to keep in mind the great diversity within Latino culture. When I talk about aspects of service delivery—how members of the Latino community go about looking for help, for example—I will be making generalizations that cover many but not all Latinos. What I will be sharing are general guidelines, but these may vary from case to case.

The Latinos most likely to be looking for help or finding themselves with problems are recent immigrants and first-generation born in this country. Latinos will turn to their own extended families for help first. After that, they will usually go to their church for help. The church plays a powerful role in their lives, so when they encounter problems, it is often the first place they turn to outside the family. As much as possible, they will first try to solve their problems within the family. If there is a respected elder available, they might speak to him or her. If the problem revolves around issues of physical or mental health and the family believes in folk healers, they might consult a *curandera* or *curandero*. But, in general, they are more likely to first approach their priest or clergyman.

If they are willing to approach an agency, it is usually one that exists in their community and one with which someone they know and trust has had some experience. They have seen the agency and know of its existence in the community. They may know some of the people who work there or people who know people who work there. They may have family members, neighbors, or friends that have received services there. In some way, there needs to be a personal connection and credibility, often through word of mouth. They are less likely to seek services outside their community or speak to people who are strangers and not of their community. Referrals to unfamiliar agencies are most likely to be successful if they are made by someone familiar to the client's family.

In relation to mental health services, the less acculturated the individual or family, the less likely they are to look for mental health treatment. For many Latinos, mental health problems are manifested through physical symptoms.

More obvious emotional problems—anxiety, depression, paranoia—are understood as having had the evil eye put on them (*mal ojo*), been cursed by a witch (*bruja*), or a case of irritated nerves (*ataque de nervios, susto*). They don't usually look for therapy and to do so is often considered shameful.

I have sought therapeutic help at various times in my own life. My mother was scandalized when I told her that I had gone to see a therapist when I was at Stanford. She was perplexed and really outraged. "How can you do this? What are you talking to them about? You're going to talk to somebody outside the family? What do you think I'm here for? What do you think your father's here for?" It was scandalous and even offensive to conceive that someone outside the family would know about any problems within the family. In her declining years, before her death, my mother was living alone, having a hard time, but refusing to move. She would not leave her house, and we could only visit her every few days. We had a social worker come to see her once every week to listen, converse, and offer help. My mother wanted to believe that she was a friend coming by to talk, which meant she could then talk personally with her. My mother would put out coffee and some food and have a social visit with her. It took her about a year to realize that this was in fact counseling, and she immediately cut it off. Many Latinos—depending on class, education, and acculturation—are just not open to mental health approaches, especially nondirective therapy. If they do find themselves seeing a therapist or counselor, what they expect is good advice, not a free-flowing dialogue or therapeutic reflections. They want to be told what they need to do, what they should do, or where they can access resources.

Question: What are some of the common problems that Latino clients might bring to you as a counselor?

Almanzan: Many problems have to do with the process of immigration—coming to this country and not knowing how the system works. How do I do this? I got this letter from immigration—where do I go? Where can I get some legal assistance? What to do about food stamps. Very much related are the difficulties of learning and understanding English and, as a result, being taken advantage of, for example, by landlords. Being ripped off for their deposits or having their rent raised or given short notice to vacate. Not getting plumbing or roofs or other repairs taken care of. Then, there are problems related to dealing with the government and its bureaucracy: driver's licenses, taxes, Social Security, etc. All of these are issues that have to do with a lack of familiarity with American culture and how to operate within it. Also, employment and the fact that new immigrants can only get menial jobs that don't pay a lot and don't have benefits and that they often have to hold two or three jobs at once and require all family members to work in order to survive.

Many of the clients I have seen are here illegally and are incredibly fearful that they will be picked up and deported by Immigration and Naturalization Service (INS). But even those who are here legally can have continuing difficulties with INS. They get bureaucratic letters concerning actions they must take. Many of them can't read them, let alone understand them. Most of the time when they try to follow through by calling INS or going there, they can't get any resolution. The phone lines are always busy. The lines at the offices are blocks long. They can't afford to spend all day waiting. Most don't have leave of any kind. If they miss work, they don't get paid.

There are also social problems. With migration, children tend to acculturate more quickly than their parents. They are in school, exposed more extensively to an acculturated environment, learn English more rapidly, are attracted to the ways and values of the nonimmigrant children. This inevitably creates separation and conflicts with parents, especially when the values and behaviors that the children are adopting are in conflict with family values. And there are often relationship issues between husbands and wives due to changing gender roles and women having to work outside of the home and children getting involved in delinquent activities, antisocial behavior, maybe even gangs and drugs. All of these social and migration issues are translated into stress, culture shock, self-esteem issues, depression, anxiety, etc.

Question: How do socioeconomic and class issues affect the psychological lives of Latinos?

Almanzan: I have already talked about those who are poor and from lower socioeconomic classes. Often, Latinos who were professionals in their country of origin migrate to the United States but cannot work in their professions here. I have met lawyers and medical doctors who have menial jobs in the United States as janitors and warehousemen because they can't get anything else. For such middle-class people, the experience of such loss—of being reduced in status and income—can be very debilitating. They are more likely to seek help, including mental health treatment, because they tend to be more sophisticated about modern culture, having already acculturated in Latin America. They are also in a better position to assimilate because they tend to be more steeped in modern ways and knowledgeable about bureaucracies. Generally, with each generation here and the more education, economic stability, and acculturation they gain, Latinos tend to avail themselves of mental health services when they are needed.

Question: Could you talk about issues of identity and belonging in different generations of Latinos in America?

Almanzan: The majority of immigrants I have worked with say that they are here only temporarily and have come only to make some money and will then be returning permanently to Mexico or Guatemala or wherever. Often, several family members come together and send money back to the rest of the family. They truly believe they will be doing this for only a few years and then going back. But many of them never go back. I've talked to Latinos who have been living and working here eight, ten, twelve years and contend that they are not here permanently, but there's no evidence of any planning or intention to go back. One consequence of this dynamic is that it keeps them from putting down roots, really learning English, improving their education, and establishing a presence and identity here. For those who do not have the legal paperwork, it makes some sense; they could be deported at any time. For the others, it may have to do with a hesitancy to give up their cultural identities or acknowledge the emotional loss and separation that is involved. There are two things that can tip the scales. The first has to do with those who have children that are born here or have spent several formative years here. Their children do not want to go back. They were raised here, identify as Americans, and are used to the lifestyle. To propose a return to the country of origin creates an enormous conflict in the family. People who have been here for a while also get used to the higher standard of living and know that they will have to give this up if they return. Single men who have worked here for a long time often become attached to the new lifestyle and in time separate emotionally from their family back home. They may go home to visit but always seem to return. This conflict in going and coming—in never really separating or attaching—often is never resolved until the next generation.

Question: Next, let us talk about some of the factors that you see as important in assessing a Latino client. What kind of things would you look for? What kind of information do you need?

Almanzan: First, I'd notice if they spoke to me in Spanish or English. My Spanish is not completely fluent, but it's good enough to make myself understood. I would speak Spanish with them if they spoke Spanish. I'd try to find out whether they were born here or immigrated. Each represents a very different type of experience. I would assess their degree of acculturation.

What country did they come from? What is their immigration story? Did they come alone? If they joined family members that are already here, I would know that they are more secure and settled. If they are alone and their family is in Latin America, I would ask how long they have been away. If from Central America, I would try to ascertain if they immigrated because of the conflicts in their country. If they have fled a conflict, I would look for evidence of emotional distress.

If they are here with family and settled with children in school, I would expect that more acculturation has occurred. As the relationship develops, I can become more personal. I can find out what kind of home life they have, whether they observe more traditional relationships within the home between men and women, the value placed on education and who is to become educated. I also ask about religion. Are they religious? Most Latinos say they're Catholic, but do they actually go to church and follow the precepts of the church, and how big a role does it actually play in their daily lives? (See Chapter 3, page 45, for more information regarding ways to assess culturally diverse clients.)

Question: What suggestions might you have for providers about developing rapport with Latino clients?

Almanzan: When Latinos come to see a provider, they expect to see someone with authority—someone who is knowledgeable and appears professional. They want to see someone who is well dressed, not wearing casual clothes. A male provider should wear a dress shirt, tie, and jacket; for a woman, a dress or blouse and skirt. They want to be treated warmly, respectfully, greeted, and made to feel welcome. It would be good to inquire about the well-being of their family and to engage in social conversation before addressing the issues that bring them into the office. They don't want to be made to feel anonymous, or invisible, a nameless person in the system. They don't want to feel that they are being rushed. They want to see someone who will look them straight in the eyes, introduce themselves, shake hands, and make inquiries about their family. It helps if they feel listened to empathically. At the same time, they expect to be provided with some concrete assistance. It is very useful to develop a list of referrals and resources of services specifically tailored for Latinos, for instance, to help with legal and immigration issues, rent, even food. If you can provide some immediate concrete help with their situation, they are more likely to come back and trust that you will be able to help them next time. It is preferable if you can address them in Spanish—in a formal attitude but with warmth. At the end of the session, I would walk them to the door and offer regards and greetings to their family even though I hadn't met them.

I would be prepared for the person who is coming in with the problem to not come alone but to bring other relatives, a husband or a wife, an uncle, even children. Again, conveying warmth and genuine interest is critical. It is also helpful to self-disclose. I would say things about myself and my own experience with some of the issues being discussed, even though it may not be done traditionally in therapy. Two last points. If you aren't bilingual, use a translator—but someone who is truly familiar with Latino culture rather than a European American who has learned Spanish. Also, be very aware of appropriate sex role customs. And if you see a couple with a wife with the presenting problems, make sure you spend adequate time giving the husband a chance to speak and a place in the counseling if possible.

Question: Do you feel that there are any therapeutic approaches that are better matched with certain Latino subgroups?

Almanzan: I think that any approach can work well with someone who is acculturated. With more traditionally oriented people, I would use a more directive style and would take my lead from them. It is very important to be able to understand their problem from their own perspective, not that of the counselor, and communicate that understanding. Also, be very careful to not unintentionally pathologize them or their behavior. Try to get a sense of why it is problematic for them from their cultural perspective and normalize it.

When I first began therapy in my twenties at Stanford, I was still living at home with my parents. The counselor questioned my living situation, and his questioning made me feel that there was something wrong about that. I came to feel very bad about myself and that this reflected my thwarted development. In retrospect, I am aware that there was nothing wrong with the fact that I was living with my family at that time. It is a very normal behavior in my culture, and I had been pathologized because of his cultural ignorance.

Question: Are there any subgroups within the Latino/Latina community that are at particular risk for mental health problems?

Almanzan: Research has documented that the closer one is to the immigrant experience, the less mental health issues one has. The longer one has been living in the United States, the more likely that mental health issues will crop up. I find that very interesting. I have already talked about the stress of the immigration experience, but there is also the daily stress of living as a Latino, an immigrant, and a person of color in this country and experiencing the impact of racism and discrimination. Together, they wear on one's self-esteem and sense of who one is and what one's values are. But there is more. When people come from Latin America, they have coherent worldviews and coherent cultural values. Living here, these cultural identities and worldviews are taken apart, picked at, and strained. In time, they lose this coherent sense of who they are. They try to assimilate to improve their situation. They are pressured to adopt some of the cultural values and perspectives of the dominant culture, and this sets up a lot of conflicts within them and adds to their stress and internal confusion.

As far as specific groups at risk, I think first of the teenage children of immigrants. They are probably experiencing continuing language problems. They may well be doing poorly in school and getting a lot of negative feedback. They are prime candidates for getting involved in gang activity, drugs and alcohol, illegal behavior, and dropping out of school. The dropout rate among Mexican Americans is over 50%. One of every two young persons will not finish high school. Even fewer will go on to college. This is an incredibly high rate and a damning statistic when it is known that education is such a key to an individual succeeding in this culture.

Question: Last question. You've shared a lot of rich information with us. Could you finish by presenting a case that shows how it comes together in work with a client?

Almanzan: I would like to talk about a Latino woman I saw for depression whose husband eventually joined her in the treatment. I remember seeing this female client for depression, and it soon came out that there were serious relationship issues between her and her husband. At first, she came by herself for two afternoon sessions. She was in her mid-thirties, Mexican. They had been in the United States for less than ten years—probably around eight. They were lower socioeconomic class, with limited education, and had three children: one girl and two boys. The girl was sixteen; the boys twelve and ten. She came in complaining of depression, of hopelessness. Much of it revolved around surviving financially. She was desperately looking for work without success. Then, she found some work, and I didn't see her for a while.

After several weeks, she called and made an appointment to see me in the early evening because she was working in the day. Her husband came with her but sat in the waiting room as if he was only there to give her a ride in the evening. I was very conscious to attend to him with a sense of respect and to acknowledge that this was his wife that I was working with. There can be a lot of fear and jealousy in such a situation, and I wanted him to know that I respected him and his family.

She complained that her husband often spoke of going back to Mexico—that they were here just temporarily. Even after eight years in the United States, this was an ongoing conversation in the household. The children said they wouldn't go back. The girl, the oldest, had become rebellious and was staying out late and ignoring their rules. The daughter and what to do about her out-of-control behavior became a central issue in the parents' escalating conflict. The daughter worked at stimulating the conflict between her parents. The mother, though very worried about where her daughter's out-of-control behavior was heading, sided with her daughter because the husband was being increasingly violent with the kids.

She and I talked about what other resources that she might have available to her, about problems with her daughter, about speaking to school authorities about her two boys, and making sure they continued in school. Finally, she asked her husband to join us, and he did. He seemed quite scared initially, but he talked tough in the session. He said he was going to straighten out all of the kids and then was openly abusive toward his wife. I intervened, telling him that his behavior was not acceptable. I talked to him about his abusive behavior at home and how that was the source of many of the problems they were having. I tried to help him connect the abusive behavior with his own feelings about his work situation, which was sparse, and his inability to support his family. This was delicate because it was touching on his identity as a macho male who could provide for and protect his family. This was very hard for him to face. He didn't really want to go back to Mexico because there was nothing waiting for him, but he wasn't making it here for his family. I had him talk about the different perspectives on staying and leaving.

The process we went through helped them communicate a little better and lessened the tension in the household. But it did not totally change everything. He still had outbursts of violence, and she eventually decided to leave the relationship. I had given her information on an organization helping battered women earlier, and she had contacted them. She left him while he was at work and took the children with her. She spent some time in a battered women's shelter, then some transitional housing, before going on her own.

I saw him alone for two sessions afterwards, and we talked about what had happened, why she left, and how he was going to carry on. I can't say this therapy was totally successful. They were able to communicate better; she found the courage to move out and hopefully become helpful to her teenage daughter. I felt particularly proud that he was willing to meet with me and open to understanding why she had left, for it would have been very easy to blame others, me included, and not return. It was his style to externalize his anger, disappointment, and helplessness, all of which were made worse by his lack of work, the increasing loss of control at home, and his related migration experiences. I did feel he was able to relate his wife's leaving to his own behavior, and that was a big step in understanding what had happened. He left after the last two sessions, and I didn't hear from him again. I would have liked to see both of them longer, but in this kind of work, clients are often transitory, and it is important to appreciate the small successes and little victories in such difficult situations.

SUMMARY

In sum, Latinos/as are not the largest racial minority in the United States and growing. They face unique circumstances that put them at risk for experiencing physical and psychological difficulties: bilingualism, immigration, acculturation, adjustment, cultural conflict, poverty, and racism. Robert Almanzan explained that Latinos/as culture is collectivistic—the whole is more important than the individual. He continued to explain that they have a deep connection to their extended families and having a sense of honor and loyalty can be powerful. These elements should be respected in session. Robert suggested that clinicians seek to understand their Latino/a clients' unique experience and specific struggles. Clinicians should also expect family members to be a part of the therapeutic process. When working with Latino/a clients, counselors can increase their clinical effectiveness by using approaches that work best with the culture of their client.

ACTIVITY

This activity is designed to help students experience what it is like to be an immigrant. Students will be separated into two groups. Each group needs to be separated, out of hearing distance. Each group will co-create group rules of interactions. These rules should be limited to 3–5 interactive qualities such as, all members must cross legs when greeting one another, or only individuals wearing a certain color can speak aloud without permission, encourage students to keep these interactions simple and subtle. When both groups have identified 3–5 rules, they must then select 2–3 explorers. These explorers are tasked with going into the other groups and try to interact with the members. If the explorers break a rule, they will be sent back to their original group and given an opportunity to share what they have learned with their fellow explorers. Each group's explorers will try to identify the other group's rules.

RELATED KEY TERMS

Hispanic, 275	Hispanic, 283	Latinos, 281
personalismo, 277	mestizo, 275	Chicano/a, 284

12

Working with Native American Clients: An Interview with Jack Lawson

LEARNING OBJECTIVES

12-1 Interpret the implication of census data for Native Americans in America today.

12-2 Explain family and cultural values of Native Americans.

12-3 Examine Mr. Lawson's experience as a Native American counselor.

▶ Demographics `12-1`

The only word that adequately captures the horrors that befell the Native peoples of this continent at the hands of the white majority is *genocide*. According to Churchill (1994), the population of Native peoples in the United States fell from 12 million to 237,000 during the first 400 years of this country's history. During that period, the U.S. government expropriated (a fancy word for legal theft) 98 percent of Native lands. Today, 2.5 million people survive, but many are riddled by debilitating alcoholism, high suicide rates, unresolved historic grief, economic hardships, and loss of cultural ways. In Chapter 10, "Historic Trauma and Unresolved Grief Among Native Americans," it states the death rate by alcoholism is projected to be seven times greater than the national average and suicide rates are also greater than that of whites. They represent a true American tragedy. For more information regarding historic trauma of Native People, see Chapter 10.

According to the 2000 U.S. Census, American Indians and Alaska Natives (the U.S. Census category) number 2,475,956 individuals, or 0.9 percent of the population. If one includes those who identify themselves as multiracial with Native American as one of the components, the number increases by 1.6 million. Over the past four decades, the Native American population has been on the rise. Between 1960 and 1990, for example, their numbers increased 255 percent, and since the last census count (2000–2010), the population increased by 456,292, or another 18.4 percent. Adding multiracial individuals, the numbers leap to an increase of 2.2 million in the last 10 years, or 110 percent. Pollard and O'Hare (1999) offer a number of reasons for this upward trend:

▶ Census counting has improved.
▶ Birthrates are high.
▶ Mortality rates have gone down.
▶ Native American heritage and identity have been reclaimed by those who have been passing as white, black, or another race, as well as those with partial ancestry.

As a collective, Native Americans represent almost 500 tribes and 314 reservations. A total of 79 percent of the population report tribal enrollment. Tribes with the largest populations are the Cherokee (281,069), Navajo (269,202), and Latin American Indian (104,940), followed by the Choctaw, Sioux, and Chippewa. The largest Alaskan Native tribe is the Eskimo (45,919). Geographically, Native American populations cluster in certain regions: 49 percent live in the West, 31 percent in the South, 17 percent in the Midwest, and 9 percent in the Northeast. More than half the total population reside in nine states: California, Oklahoma, Arizona, Texas, New Mexico, Washington, North Carolina, Michigan, and Alaska. California has the largest total population with 627,562, followed by Oklahoma at 391,949. Alaska has the largest proportion of Native residents at 19 percent, followed by Oklahoma (11 percent) and New Mexico (10 percent). About half of the Native population is located in urban centers and half on rural reservations. There is, however, extensive mobility between the two locations: city dwellers returning to the reservation for ritual and family business; Indians traveling from the reservation to the cities for work, advanced education, and so forth.

▶ Family and Cultural Values   `12-2`

Sue and Sue (1999) identify five values that typify Native American cultures:

- ▶ Sharing and cooperation
- ▶ Noninterference
- ▶ A cyclical orientation to time
- ▶ The importance of extended families
- ▶ Harmony with nature

Sharing and Cooperation

Sutton and Broken Nose (1996) quote an Oglala Lakota elder regarding the Native American attitude toward sharing: "When I was little, I learned that what's yours is mine and what's mine is everybody's" (p. 40). Status and honor are earned not by accumulating wealth, but rather by sharing and giving it away. Gifts are profusely given, especially during life cycle events, as a means of thanking others and acknowledging their achievements. Material possessions are freely shared and expected to be shared. Similarly, great importance is placed on hospitality and caring for the needs of strangers. Working for wages is purely instrumental. A native person, for example, may stop working once enough money has been earned to meet immediate needs. Of course, such a selfless attitude toward material wealth and possessions may prove counterproductive in the mainstream economy. Sutton and Broken Nose (1996) describe the traditional owners of a restaurant on a Navajo reservation who were hard put financially because they felt obliged to serve free food to relatives, and most people on the reservation were relatives. Related to sharing is cooperation.

As in the Latino/a culture, competition and egotism are anathema to Native ways. The family and tribe take precedence over the individual, and it is expected that one will set aside personal activities and striving in order to help others. Interpersonal harmony is always sought and discord avoided.

Noninterference

It is considered inappropriate in Native American culture to intrude or interfere in the affairs of others. Boundaries and the natural order of things are to be respected.

Similarly, stoicism and nonreactivity are highly valued. With regard to communication, a premium is placed on listening. Sutton and Broken Nose (1996) suggest that "silence may connote respect, that the client is forming thoughts, or that the client is waiting for signs that it is the right time to speak" and that the "non-Indian therapist may treat silence, embellished metaphors, and indirectness as signs of resistance, when actually they represent forms of communication" (p. 37).

Time Orientation

"*Indian Time*" is cyclical, rhythmic, and imprecise. People are oriented toward the present—the here and now—not to future events and deadlines. Activities take as long as they take and have a natural logic and rhythm of their own. "Lateness" and defining time by external clocks and circumstances are Western concepts, the product of a linear time frame. Long-term goal-setting is viewed as egotism, and life events are experienced as processes that unfold in their own time and way. As Sutton and Broken Nose (1996) suggest: "The focus is placed on one's current place, knowing that the succeeding changes will inevitably come" (p. 39). Such a notion of time, which has a tendency to frustrate mainstream providers who work on a "tight schedule," interfaces perfectly with the previous value of noninterference in the natural order of things.

Extended Families

Although the specifics of power distribution, roles, and kinship definitions vary from tribe to tribe, the vast majority of Native peoples live in an extended family system that is conceptually different from the Western notion of family. Some tribes are matrilineal, which means that property and status are passed down through the women of the tribe. When a Hopi man marries, for example, he moves in with his wife's family, and it is the wife's brothers, not the father, who have primary responsibility for educating the sons. Family ties define existence, and the very definition of being a Navajo or a Sioux resides not within the individual's personality, but rather in the intricacies of family and tribal responsibilities. When strangers meet, they identify themselves not by occupation or residence, but by their relatives. Individual family members feel a close and binding connection with a broad network of relatives (often including some who are not related by blood) that can extend as far as second cousins. The very naming of relationships, in fact, reflects the unusual closeness that exists between relatives. The term *grandparent*, for instance, applies not only to the parents of one's biological parents, but also to their brothers and sisters. Similarly, the concept of "in-law" has no meaning within Native culture because after entry into the family system, no distinctions are made between natural and inducted individuals (Sutton and Broken Nose, 1996). Thus, the person one would call "mother-in-law" in mainstream culture is referred to simply as "mother" in Native culture. The responsibility for the parenting of children is communal and shared throughout the extended family. Sue and Sue (1999) point out that it is not unusual for children to live in various households of the extended family while growing up.

Harmony with Nature

Native American cultures emphasize the interconnectedness and harmony of all living things and natural objects. This spiritual holism affirms the value and interdependence of all life forms. Nature is held in reverence, and Native peoples believe that it is their responsibility to live in harmony and safeguard the valuable resources we have been given. Sutton and Broken Nose (1996) quote the following sentiment from Chief Seattle:

> My mother told me, every part of this earth is sacred to our people. Every pine needle. Every sandy shore. Every mist in the dark woods. Every meadow and humming insect. The Earth is our mother. (p. 40)

This message, which implies the importance of noninterference in the natural order and stewardship over the environment, stands in stark opposition to the mainstream value of mastering, controlling, and taking what we want from the earth. The idea of spiritual harmony with the natural order also underlies Native beliefs about health and illness. Illness, both physical and emotional, reflects disharmony between the person or the collective and the natural world. Only by bringing the system back into harmony with itself can healing be achieved.

Unlike other people of color, Native Americans have found it impossible to assimilate upward into American society. While the other communities of color struggle to increase their underrepresentation in the ranks of the middle class, in professional and white-collar job categories, in higher education, and so on, Native representation in these groups is all but nonexistent. Why these great disparities?

- First, if one were to construct a continuum of cultural differences with white Northern Europeans at one end and plot other cultural groups in America along that line, Native culture would most appropriately be placed at the far extreme. The radical differences between their ways and those of mainstream white culture set the stage for what was to occur. Their notions of stewardship of the land, fair play, honor, and dignity paled in comparison to mainstream values of capitalism and "might makes right" and made them easy victims in a clash of cultural systems.
- Second, so horrendous were the actions against Native peoples that the victims needed to be silenced. To accomplish this, Native peoples were turned into stereotypes: savages of the frontier, drunken Indians, Pocahontas, mascots for sports teams, and emblems for automobiles.

Regarding the latter, Kivel (1996) suggests various mechanisms of denial, such as minimizing estimates of the number of Native Americans who lived here, questioning the vitality and stability of their culture, picturing the genocide as a natural process with a life of its own, and attributing their demise to biological inferiority.

▸ Third, for generations, the government systematically destroyed Native culture and alienated individuals from their traditions and customs. Our guest expert, Jack Lawson, describes this loss of identity and disconnection from tradition as the source of all contemporary Native woes.

▸ Our Interviewee   12-3

Jack Lawson has worked in the field of alcohol and drug treatment, primarily with Native peoples, for over twenty-two years. Currently, he is the Native American Coordinator for the State of Oregon Youth Authority. In this position, he is responsible for establishing relations with the nine federally recognized tribes in Oregon, developing and implementing culturally relevant treatment services, and helping to oversee the Oregon Youth Authority's mission of implementing cultural competency and community development in juvenile crime prevention plans. He has also provided treatment services to Native inmates in the Oregon State Prison System, was lead trainer for the Oregon State Alcohol and Drug Office's cultural diversity training program, and worked as a counselor in a wilderness treatment program for the Siletz tribe in central Oregon. Ethnically, he is a member of the Creek Nation.

The Interview

Question: Could you first talk about your own ethnic background and how it has led to your work in alcohol and drug treatment?

Lawson: I am a Creek. My family is originally from Oklahoma. I was born in California and moved to Oklahoma when I was about six years old, and then moved back to California when I was ten years old, where we continued to live. While in Oklahoma, I remember attending ceremonies and gatherings. Feasts, singing, and dancing are part of my memories of that time. After returning to California, I lost contact with my relatives in Oklahoma. As a consequence of moving back to California, I was separated from my Native culture and traditions. I attended public schools all my life, and for the most part, the information I received about Native Americans has been negative and based on stereotypes. Most Western movies portrayed us as drunks, heathens, violent, and dirty, which supported the information I received in the schools. I knew I was a Native American, but I didn't have any way of accessing positive information about who I was racially and culturally. Growing up in a situation where I was not exposed to my own culture and traditions left me lost as to who I was and open to accepting what others said about Native people. One of the first signs of oppression is when you start believing other people's version of history about yourself. I seemed to have only numb feelings about my Native identity back then.

Both my mother and stepfather were alcohol-dependent. After their separation, my stepfather died in a fire. My mother remarried when I was about sixteen and had quit drinking. During high school, I developed an alcohol addiction. I took to alcohol like birds to flight. In retrospect, I realized what I was struggling with was issues of internalized racism and, as a result of it, a variety of self-destructive behaviors.

I received my first message about recovery from a couple of Native Americans who were active in Alcoholics Anonymous (AA) while serving in a military jail. After a couple of false attempts at sobriety, I was able to catch onto the program. My first two years of recovery were made possible by strict attendance at AA meetings. Several years later, I had the opportunity to attend my first sweat lodge ceremony. Experiencing it seemed to make all the difference in the world for me. It directed my recovery in a way that would not have been possible without access to my culture and identity as a Native person. It was through exposure to the traditions of my People that allowed me for the first time to develop long-term relationships with others and good connections with my community. As a result of this experience, I began to understand the influence of culture and identity in the recovery process and the influence of people who can teach these cultural ways and traditions to us. My own recovery experience taught me what has to happen for other Native People. It has been a real blessing to be exposed to people knowledgeable in the ways of our culture and traditions, who could and did teach me about myself, about who I am, and where I came from.

Having those mentors in my life, with their understanding of Native ways and identity issues, has allowed me to access areas of my life that otherwise would have remained invisible to me. I would have been left with a substantial void inside. Learning how I, as well as my People, reacted to being oppressed by oppressing others and losing ourselves in destructive behavior and thinking has made it possible for me to bring that understanding to the treatment process and to others who are still suffering from mental health and addiction problems so that they too can transcend those barriers for themselves.

Question: How would you define Native Americans or Native People as a group, and what characteristics do they share?

Lawson: Native People comprise over 350 different tribes and languages that are unique to this continent. We are both very different and very similar. There is not, for example, one monolithic religion that belongs to all Native People. We have many languages, cultures, and many religions. We understand these differences, as we always have. But, today, we are focusing more on our commonalities—on those things that pull us together. Paramount among these are historical experiences. As a group, we have all been systematically subjected to colonization, to the effects of losing our language and our culture, and to governmental policies that have been destructive to our People and eventually led us to a variety of social and health problems. These, in turn, have divided us in relation to ourselves and into differences in levels of acculturation. There are people that range from very traditional to fully assimilated and differ enormously in how they relate to their culture and identity.

Differences among Native Peoples are small in comparison to those things that set us apart from members of the dominant culture. I think we stand apart because of a value system that is qualitatively different and a set of historic experiences that cannot really be understood by dominant culture. When I take a look at the behavior of Native People, the first thing that strikes me is that we keep to ourselves—[we] are very insular and private, especially in comparison to members of the dominant culture. Some of this is certainly dictated by culture. But for Native Peoples, it is also a matter of self-protection. This is because of a shared sense of historical oppression and victimhood. The historical experiences of genocide and culturicide have left a deep mark upon our thinking and feelings, which is all the more tragic because our only "crime" was being on this land first. Everyone else that is in America today has come from somewhere else, but as Native People, this is the land from which we originated. We believe that we were created here. This is where our People have come from. It is an intricate part of who we are—how we define our communities and our mental health. When we view many of the problems that have arisen in our communities, we know they arise because of the loss of our land and our way of life that is so tied to the land. And of all the peoples in America today, we have been the least welcome.

The process of becoming an "American" for most citizens involved willingly giving up one's cultural heritage or identity in order to assimilate into the dominant culture and its values. This has been a very damaging process for Native People. We did not ask to be part of this process; it was forced upon us. Native People experienced enormous and longstanding traumas in their lives as a result of the assimilation process. And it is not an experience that many dominant culture people can really identify with: having your religion outlawed, having your language outlawed, and living in a world that has devalued your very existence. And that brings about feelings of justified anger that are present in our Native communities. Anger is everywhere, and it plays itself out in different ways as our People respond to both historical and ongoing oppression. It comes out in the form of self-destructive behavior, alcoholism and drug addiction, suicide, and homicide. We have become very different as a result of our historical experiences in "America," and these differences have to be paid attention to in the counseling setting. Our mental health issues involve the forced imposition of the dominant culture's value system over our indigenous value system and have resulted in vast conflicts and misunderstandings as well as much resentment and mistrust that exist in our community.

Culturally, Native People tend to be nonintrusive and nondirective. They let people make up their own minds. If people come and seek advice, it will be given but not offered. Life is experienced as an interconnected entity. Nature, the People, the community all intertwine and depend upon each other for meaning and existence. We also tend to be very spiritual in our orientation, and the underlying force of our spiritual beliefs comes from the geology of the area from which we come. That spirituality infuses the community and becomes its base. It is central to the identity of each person and gets expressed through various religious and cultural practices. The creation stories of each People, for example, are set in the geographic area from which they came. The Navajo and the Hopi believe that they came up through the center of the world, and that center is located in their sacred places. For the Modoc people of central Oregon, their creation story is built around the lava beds of northern California, and they believe that humanity enters the world through the creation center, which is located there. All things come from our ties to the land, and all Native People are joined in their commonality with the Turtle Island, as we refer to the continent.

Question: Could you describe some of the names that have been used historically to describe and identify Native Peoples and the general process of naming within the culture?

Lawson: In regard to names, there are the names that we call ourselves and then there are the names that other people have given us. Most familiar to dominant culture is the term *Indian*. It is actually a misnomer. It comes from the time that Europeans first landed on this continent. Christopher Columbus mistakenly believed he had landed on the coast of India, and, hence, we got tagged with the name *Indian*, which has over time taken on a pejorative meaning for us. In spite of the fact that the term has been prevalent in describing us, it carries no significance in our world. At some point, we as a People decided to take control of how we identify ourselves.

The process began with the term *Native American*, which signifies that we come from this continent. But, then, because we predate the naming of this continent and the Americas, we have begun to look at ourselves as the Indigenous People or First People of this land.

Outside of these more political distinctions, we also have names which we prefer to use and with which we more closely identify ourselves. There are tribal names and affiliations, such as Creeks, Choctaw, Crow, and so on. There are often clan names within the tribes and then there are individual names—how we identify ourselves personally. Many of us have a Christian name that was given to us. But we also have personal names that are received through ceremony—a spiritual name that is often kept secret and used only for special occasions. It is important to realize that Native Peoples vary greatly in which of the various terms they prefer, and to some extent, our choices say something about where we stand politically and culturally. Some of us still refer to ourselves as Native American, and others prefer Indigenous People. Sadly, there are still many who do not care or feel anything about who they are.

When first making contact with a Native client, it is perfectly appropriate to ask where they are from, what their tribal affiliation is, and how they prefer to identify themselves. I think we get into trouble when we don't do that and start making assumptions or just randomly use a term without being respectful enough to ask.

Asking about this information is probably a good way to begin contact. In mainstream America, people are identified primarily by what kind of work they do. We don't ask people what they do for a living. Instead, we ask each other: "Where are you from?" or "Who are your people?" This is because we come from a relationship-based culture, and our relationships are defined by our communities, our relatives, and our tribal affiliations. We socially locate ourselves by our human connections, not by our activities or jobs. Two last points. Spiritual names are sacred and private and used only during ceremonies. It is considered inappropriate to inquire about these names unless they are spontaneously offered. In addition to Christian names, nicknames are very commonly used in Native communities. One might go an entire lifetime calling someone by a nickname and never know their given name.

Question: We have already talked some about history. Could you give us a nutshell version of historical events of which a provider should be aware?

Lawson: Historically speaking, Native People have suffered greatly at the hands of governmental policies and the actions of various religious groups. The experience of colonization is not just historical but is still happening in our communities today. Loss of our culture, loss of religion, loss of community, and loss of family cohesion are contemporary realities. And these patterns, which are the consequences of oppression, continue to play themselves out emotionally and psychologically in the lives of our people. They are major issues that concern us deeply because they involve nothing less than the loss of our identities and integrity.

The boarding school experience is a particularly destructive example. Until the mid-1980s, many Native children were taken from their natural families and communities and forced to reside in boarding schools, where they were isolated from Native culture and ways and then immersed in the dominant culture and Christian values. In these institutions, children were punished for speaking their Native tongue or practicing traditional ways. The motto of the time was "Kill the Indian, but save the man," and its purpose was to eradicate all traces of Native culture and identity. Once accomplished, the child could be molded as desired, which meant shaping them into white Christians with mainstream values and attitudes. To make the task easier, the government outlawed our religion.

Perhaps most insidious about this practice was its effect on the Native family and its cohesion. When the children were taken out of their families, they were separated from their grandparents, parents, extended family, aunts, uncles, community, and so on. For generations, many Native American children were robbed of the nurturing of their families—deprived of the opportunity to learn parenting skills and other cultural lessons that would have enabled them to raise healthy families of their own. These children were forced to reside in institutions that were harsh and brutal. Some of our elders believe that our many social problems stem from the boarding school experience. Many of the children, as adults, remained isolated from families, no longer able to communicate because their language had been beaten out of them. They felt no comfort returning to their communities and were generally left alone to deal with the many internal issues that had been created as a result of growing up in the schools: low self-esteem, negative feelings about being Native, and a deep self-hatred. We can now see very clearly how generations of such experiences have impacted our communities and made them into what they are today.

We have begun to look at the consequences of the loss of our culture and realize that some Native People have come to internalize the stereotypes whites hold about them. As a result, they have become those stereotypes: the subtle ones and the not-so-subtle ones, the "drunken Indian," the "lazy Indian." How can all those negative stereotypes not affect us? I am thinking of one of my uncles. He once told me that during high school, he very much wanted to go on to college. He went to see a school counselor and was strongly discouraged from going on. "Native People tend to be better with their hands," he was told and encouraged to pursue a trade. And so, with that advice, he didn't go to college but went on to a trade school. He also went on to become alcoholic and drug-dependent and has since been in recovery. He attributes a lot of his problems to that stereotype and how believing in it changed his life. So, for some of us, it is all too easy to live down to the stereotypes and to begin thinking about ourselves in self-deprecating terms—that we are not very smart or that we are only good with our hands and that we are destined to become alcoholic. These issues—residual effects of the boarding schools and stereotypes—are still being played out in our present-day experience. But, fortunately, there has been a growing movement among many Native Peoples to regain our self-identity, to regain cultural pride, to regain our self-respect, and to learn about the traditions of our families, tribe, and People.

Question: Let us switch focus and begin to look at issues related to help giving and treatment. What factors influence how Native People go about seeking help?

Lawson: When Native People become involved in treatment programs, it's usually because of some external motivating force. That is, they are mandated either because of trouble with the law, family problems, child protective services, or the like. Generally speaking, that's how most people will come to be involved with outside agencies. Sometimes, the tremendous anger and mistrust that Native People feel prevent them from seeking help outside of their community. Sometimes, it is discrimination against them that serves as a barrier to accessing treatment. When you do find Native People coming into your agencies by themselves seeking help or assistance, they often are assimilated or bicultural—those who are more familiar and comfortable with white institutions and practices.

As a result of these patterns, there is a movement among various tribes to develop mental health and addiction services within our own communities so that people no longer have to choose between white services or no services at all. The hallmark of this trend is the creation of culturally relevant services. "Culturally relevant" means that the treatment process is infused with Native cultural values, that treatment goals make sense to Native sensibilities, that the need and value of developing positive ethnic identity are acknowledged, and that services are relevant to the lives and daily existence of the people being served. It also means that services are provided in a manner that is culturally comfortable to Native People. This trend is extremely important because the fact is that Native People usually experience less success in programs designed for mainstream white clients. Cultural barriers are a major obstacle to successful treatment in any program.

Question: Are there any other things you would like to say about the nature of family, community, and culture among Native People that have relevance for human service providers?

Lawson: Family structure in Native communities is very different from the nuclear family that predominates in dominant culture. Among Native Peoples, extended families are more typical, where an aunt may also act in the role of the mother or the grandparents raise the children or an uncle is the primary teacher for a youth or cousins are treated as brothers and sisters. Traditionally, responsibility for child care is communal. Also included in the family structure are clans, which are determined by kinship, and bands, which are people living in the same locale.

There are and have been many obstacles for the Native American family. As mentioned previously, the boarding school experience left many people devastated. Many of our social problems stem from them. Having been forced into these institutions, children were separated from an environment where they would have been socialized and reared culturally by parents, grandparents, aunts, and uncles and placed in an often-harsh environment which did not recognize Native American beliefs as having any value. Today, alcoholism is our number one health problem, with 100 percent of all Native Americans affected either directly or indirectly. In the age group of sixteen to twenty-one, we lead the nation per capita in suicides and higher than national rates of diabetes. Currently, our average life span is forty-five. These statistics attest to the problems faced in the Native American community and more privately by family members, and most of these are linked to the destruction of the cultural family.

Other disruptions for the family come from state children services agencies that routinely adopt our Native children out to non-Native homes. Often, in conjunction with religious organizations or acting on stereotypical beliefs about Native American families, these agencies disregard the critical importance of Native culture for these children. There are many horror stories from the past of white people coming into Native American communities and removing children. Fortunately, this is a practice that has been stopped by implementation of the Indian Child Welfare Act of 1978, which re-established tribal authority over the adoption of Native children. Even though our rights have been reinforced, we are constantly struggling with agencies who are working to undermine the law. By these few examples, it is obvious how there has been a basis for the development of mistrust of social service agencies—a feeling that continues today.

Oppression has had a significant effect on our family structure. Some Native People have decided not to teach their children about the culture, language, or traditions because they do not want their children to experience the same treatment of degradation and rejection from the outside world. Others have successfully made the transition into dominant society, taking on mainstream values and religious beliefs and living happily. There are also many who have managed to hang onto and practice cultural traditions and beliefs, learning from elders who have been able to share their wisdom with a younger generation. Some families mix traditional and dominant cultural ways. Clearly, we are a community in transition, adjusting to significant changes in social structure and identity, with much from the past to set right. But in spite of the historical and contemporary obstacles, our Native community is healing itself. We have weaknesses and strengths within the Native families. We have oppression and discrimination to overcome. We have social problems with addiction and abuse. But our People are making a comeback in pride and dignity by reclaiming indigenous family values and recovery.

Question: What are the kinds of problems with which a Native client might present?

Lawson: One hundred percent of Native People are affected either directly or indirectly by alcoholism. Underlying this are a host of complex problems related to the loss of culture, identity, and disruption of the family unit, all symptomatic of a long history of genocide and oppression. There are also a lot of anger and anger-related issues, depression and hopelessness, health problems, and unusually high rates of suicide and homicide, especially among the young. There has also been a serious increase in the diagnosis of HIV in our community, mostly related to IV drug use. Among Native People who are incarcerated, alcohol and drugs are a major contributor to their incarceration.

Question: Do class or other socioeconomic issues play any role in these various problems?

Lawson: Definitely. Unemployment rates can be astronomical on a reservation, and the same is true for Native Peoples living in urban areas. The Relocation Act of the 1940s was one in a series of efforts by the government to encourage Native Peoples to leave the reservation, move to cities where jobs are more plentiful, and become part of the American mainstream. That was the ultimate goal. However, the reality was not quite as simple as that. Although some did relocate successfully, many found the experience traumatic. In the move from reservation to city, many traditional ties were lost. Kinship ties weakened with distance, and some people became disassociated from their relatives and community. Many ended up living marginal existences in the skid row areas of cities, and those who followed them from the reservations would tend to migrate toward these same enclaves. What the logic of the Relocation Act did not envision was the reality that most of these people, familiar with a very different kind of existence, did not have the dominant cultural tools to survive successfully, let alone prosper in such a foreign environment where they were met with substantial discrimination and rejection.

The move to the city was also instrumental in cutting off many from traditional cultural ties to their People. In addition, certain patterns of connection between the reservation and urban settings began to emerge. First, it was not uncommon for individuals to move back and forth between the two, and for many, this became a lifelong pattern. Second, animosities and various conflicts developed between people from these increasingly divergent lifestyles, with each looking down on the other. In general, some people in the urban centers may tend to view those on the reservation as backward, their ways antiquated, rustic. Those on the reservation, in turn, tend to see the urban dwellers as having lost their way—as suffering from the same malaise as the white man. Today, increasing numbers of Native People are returning to their traditions and culture in both locations and striving for unity.

There is an important cultural point here as well. In mainstream culture, success is measured in economic terms, and socioeconomic success implies a certain lifestyle that depends on having sufficient monetary resources, accumulating wealth, regular employment, living according to a certain style, and so forth. Our traditional cultural values are very different from this. Our wealth is located in the richness of our culture, tradition, ceremonies, and in the richness of our lifestyle. Difficulties arise when a person tries to live by a cultural value system that is not based on material economic gain within a broader culture that is so absolutely dedicated to it. These are not value systems that are easily integrated. Such clashes set the stage for Native Peoples losing our lands and having our language and culture outlawed in the first place. Today, we struggle with a similar conflict around remaining attached to our traditional way of life that cares little about accumulating economic wealth. It comes down to the question of divergent value systems. Those who are bicultural know what they would need to do to be successful—and that would be to eliminate their culture and perform accordingly—but that would go against their beliefs, which are based in indigenous culture and tradition. The integration of two such diverse value systems is difficult, to say the least.

Question: In making an initial assessment, what kinds of information do you feel it is important to collect from a Native client?

Lawson: Before getting too specific, I want to say something about cultural perspective and worldview. During any assessment process, it is *vital*—I can't emphasize this enough—that counselors and other human service providers be aware of their own cultural values, biases, and barriers and understand clearly how they themselves have been influenced by culture. All behavior is derived from a cultural context, as are treatment programs. If one is going to assess a client whose worldview is culturally different from one's own, then it is likely that if the client displays culturally relevant behavior, it may well be labeled as "deviant" or "abnormal." For example, in dominant culture, a firm handshake is seen as a sign of honesty, sincerity, and straightforwardness, whereas if one encounters a person of traditional Native beliefs, a firm handshake is avoided because in our culture, it is sometimes seen as being intrusive, rude, overbearing, and impolite. However, someone assessing that behavior from a dominant cultural perspective might construe it as reflecting dishonesty, nonassertion, withdrawal, and evasiveness. When working with people from diverse cultures, it's always important to validate their experience and existence in terms of their own cultural perspective. In order to do this, we as service providers must be aware of our own culture and how that culture affects our lives.

Assessments must be carried out within the framework of the client's own culture. It is important, however, to not let the client be your only source of information about their culture. This information needs to be balanced with information from their community as well. It's necessary that you reach out to our communities and listen to the people. It has been my experience that the more you learn about another's culture, the more open they are to you. Learn as much as you can. You get that information from the community through developing relationships. Go to the communities and events and develop relationships. This doesn't mean that you have to give up your own cultural values or beliefs. It does mean that you should be able to understand and respect beliefs of others and evaluate their behavior from within their cultural context.

Perhaps the most important piece of information to gain about Native clients is where they fall on a continuum from assimilated to traditional. People that are assimilated will often feel uncomfortable around their own People, not knowing the behaviors and what is expected of them. They appear to be Native and possess all the physical features of being Native, but internally, they're different. They may feel uneasy because of their lack of knowledge of traditional ways and may feel unaccepted because of it. Assimilated individuals tend to act differently than those who live by traditional values and possess a traditional belief system. The assimilated person may appear more talkative and open, even though there might be distrust. They will be the ones who know the rules of the program and of society in general. In short, they will have learned what one needs to do within dominant culture to survive. Traditional Native People present themselves as more reserved and quiet. But rather than being indicative of withdrawal, it comes from a cultural value of respect, non-intrusiveness, and honor.

What kind of information should you seek from a client? There is all the standard assessment material. Who was a person raised by? Family structure? Religion? But with Native People, what is important is to interpret this information through the filter of how they see themselves culturally.

This would include identity development, involvement with the community, involvement with family, how family views its situation, whether or not traditional beliefs are practiced. Again, the distinction between assimilated and traditional is important because treatment methods may differ according to where a person falls on that continuum. By way of example, there was a doctor in Seattle who noticed that Native People weren't recovering as fast in the hospitals as he felt they should. They regularly spent longer periods in the hospital. One of the things he did was go to the elders of the Native community and started incorporating medicine people and traditional healers as part of the treatment process in the hospital. And recovery times shortened dramatically.

Question: Are there subgroups within the Native community that are particularly at risk?

Lawson: I believe that all Native People, especially children, are at risk for developing alcoholism or some other form of dependency. There are physiological issues—social, economic, and emotional ones as well. They have been passed down from generation to generation and together create a "lump sum" of a risk for us as Native People. At one time, it was prevalent in our communities to accept alcoholism as a way of life. That is how we tended to cope with oppression and the discrimination in our lives. It became part of our continual grieving process. Although in many places this is still the norm, there are many of us who are beginning to take more control over our lives and find recovery.

Question: What suggestions can you give regarding developing rapport with Native clients?

Lawson: I believe we have to be aware of our own prejudices and biases and the way we regard people who are culturally and racially different from us. It is not a matter of learning to say or do the right things. Instead, we have to be aware of ourselves and the underlying issues that affect our clients. It's not about having to learn all the ins and outs. We are dealing with a very diverse population. It's impossible for me to say, "Well, this is the one thing you will need to say or this is the one thing that you do in order to develop rapport." I would be merely creating a new stereotype.

We are all going to make mistakes, and mistakes are a common thing in working with diverse cultures. But if one really comes from a place of acceptance and respect as a care provider, then that is going to translate into developing rapport with clients. As helpers, we all have a goal in mind: helping to develop a therapeutic relationship so that clients can heal themselves. But there is more than one road we can travel to get to the same place.

In order to develop rapport with Native clients, one has to learn to not be afraid of their anger. You can be sure that there is going to be mistrust and anger that may very well be directed toward you personally as a white provider. But if you can tolerate it, not be frightened by it, and just allow it to be expressed as honest communication, you will be on the road to making a connection. There is the possibility the client will see you as part of the white establishment and, as such, unlikely to be of any real help. Remember: Historically, Native Peoples have had their feelings discounted, been patronized and demeaned, and chronically abused by the system. You may be witnessing justified anger running rampant. In short, you may be stereotyped and lumped into this category of the enemy. The only way to get beyond this is to acknowledge your whiteness and the feelings they are likely to project onto you as well as your general understanding of what they have experienced as a people. But be clear: The walls are not going to come down overnight but only with time and patience. In addition, becoming aware of the effects oppression has on a People will aid in understanding self-destructive behavior, such as addiction being systemic to oppression.

Question: What else is important to know about working therapeutically with Native clients?

Lawson: I have provided services to both white and Native clients, and there are clearly some important differences. In the white groups, traditional counseling methods are effective. I am more direct and confrontational here, and the clients tend to respond positively. I use a very different approach with Native clients. We sit in a talking circle, but it is the issues we talk about that are important. The issues have to do with Native culture, identity, how they see themselves as Native People, the effects of stereotyping, justified anger, positive identity development, and ceremony. And we use ritual objects and ceremonies as part of the process: eagle feathers and pipes, smudging, sweat lodges, and so on, introducing our culture into the treatment process and acknowledging what they are going through ritually and with ceremonies. Such a process fits naturally with our cultural understanding of health and sickness. We also discuss the effects of oppression while at the same time addressing the issues around denial, relapse prevention planning, and recovery maintenance.

As far as therapeutic styles with Native People, you will most likely be working with those who either know nothing of their culture or are bicultural. In both cases, I find that traditional counseling methods generally prove effective but with the incorporation of cultural material. My approach with Native Americans is to use culture as an avenue to recovery because loss of culture and identity is the most basic problem that Native People face. In this regard, I assist clients in identifying their culture, how it has influenced them, how they came to lose touch with it, and how they may become reconnected to their culture. I also have them identify where they stand along the continuum between traditional and assimilated. At times, I come across clients who hide their issues behind culture or try to use it to get something for themselves. They use it as a "front"—as a means of not dealing with treatment issues. The value of culture and community is not about what it can get you but who you can become because of it. The challenge for non-Native service providers is to know the difference between clients using culture as a defense and when the Native culture is genuine.

I provided culturally relevant treatment services for the Native Americans incarcerated within the Oregon Department of Corrections who are dealing with their addictions. As a part of those services, I conducted a weeklong alcohol and drug workshop and ongoing treatment groups that focus on Native American spirituality, ceremony, and recovery. As a part of the workshop, we utilized the talking circle, drumming and singing, sweat lodge ceremony, smudging with sweet grass or sage, use of eagle feathers and other sacred objects, and discussed issues that are relevant to their recovery. Through this service, many Native inmates have been given their first positive encounter with Native American culture and tradition. I believe this is an important thing to offer them—to be able to get in touch with their culture and to be able to have some experience with their traditions. Again, I see that as critical to recovery for Native American clients. But there are some diverse opinions about this within our communities. Some of our elders say: "They never sought out the culture while they were in the community. Why should we go to the institutions to provide them with anything cultural? When they get out of the institution, let them come to us." That's a valid point. But at the same time, I feel that it's important for a person's recovery to develop some cultural awareness. The issue of them learning it in the institutional setting is that, often, much of the learning comes from other inmates. So, information can get contaminated inside institutions.

Similar dynamics can occur in treatment in general, and that's why it's important for non-Native providers to have connections and resources in the Native community. It is clearly not productive for providers to exclusively learn about Native culture from their clients. Contact with the community will also give you a certain credibility. In working with our People on a regular basis, you just have to get out of your office and make contacts. We are a relationship-based culture.

Question: Finally, could you present a case that brings together the different issues and dynamics about which you have been talking?

Lawson: I am thinking of a client I'll call Joe. Joe came to a program where I once worked called Sweathouse Lodge. It was an inpatient alcohol and drug treatment program that focused heavily on traditional Native modes of healing. We used sweat lodges, brought in traditional people to speak, brought in medicine people, hosted spiritual gatherings, took clients to powwows, and did a lot of resocialization work. When Joe entered the program, he was twenty-five and very angry and mistrustful not only toward the system, but toward the program as well. He had developed a severe alcohol and drug problem by the age of seventeen. His family had a long history of alcoholism. His parents knew nothing about their culture and traditions, and although he had a grandfather who was very traditional, he had only limited contact with him. Joe was mandated to the program by court order and was initially very resistant to treatment. While in the program, he experienced his first sweat lodge ceremony. It was a very positive experience for him, and he reported that during the ceremony, he felt for the first time some connection with his Native heritage and the value it might have for him. This motivated him to seek out further information about his own culture and traditions. In group therapy, he revealed harboring prejudicial and destructive thoughts about being Native. As a result of growing up in an alcoholic home, he had learned to equate being Native with being drunk and violent, as these were the only role models he had.

Through continuing positive contact with Native culture, in the form of ceremonies and positive role models, he was able to begin to distinguish between what was truly cultural and what was internalized from negative stereotypes of Native People and culture. This, in turn, enabled him to develop a more positive cultural self-image, something which was totally lacking before coming to the program. He increasingly took pleasure in attending sweat lodge ceremonies, learned to drum and sing, learned more about Native values, and in time began to work at incorporating these values in his treatment plan. He became more open to attending Alcoholics Anonymous (AA) and Narcotics Anonymous (NA) meetings and eventually involved himself more and more in the Native community. As part of treatment, he received a lot of very direct feedback from other Native clients and staff. He found it very helpful to hear others who had gone down a similar path of alcoholism and dysfunction "call him" on his self-destructive behavior, attitudes, thinking patterns, and lifestyle.

The eventual result was better feelings about himself, an emerging ethnic identity, and a positive sense of belonging to the Native community. During group therapy, he was able to make the connection between his own self-destructive ways and the lack of culture and traditions in his life. In short, participation in the program forced him to experience a powerful identity crisis and reformation, and it gave him an outlet and place to experience feelings that he thought were unique to him. After completion of the program, Joe continued to seek out sweat lodges and remained actively involved in community events. He has begun to take on some communal leadership roles and actively strives to encourage others to find recovery through their culture and traditions.

SUMMARY

This chapter is comprised of an in-depth interview with Jack Lawson. He is a Native American Coordinator for the State of Oregon Youth Authority and a member of the Creek Nation. During the interview, Jack discussed several key points such as how he defines Native People and characteristics they share, the process of naming within Native culture, historical events that providers should know, and the factors that influence how Native People seek help. A highlight among these topics is the notion that contemporary Native culture focuses on the commonalities between the more than 350 different tribes while also acknowledging the uniqueness of each tribe. Another highlight was the mentioning of help seeking behavior in Native culture, which consists of tremendous anger and mistrust. Regarding human services providers, Jack mentioned that it is important to acknowledge the importance of family structure, the effects of colonialism on the culture, and the issues with alcoholism. Jack also expressed that it is of the utmost importance for human service providers to be aware of their own cultural values, biases, and barriers.

ACTIVITY

This chapter discusses several aspects of Native Peoples culture. Take a minute a think about aspects of your culture that define your values, sharing and cooperation, noninterference, "lateness," and how you define extended families. List five ways in which your definitions of the previously listed attributes are different or similar to Native People culture.

KEY TERMS

genocide, 295   Indian Time, 297   grandparent, 297

Working with African American Clients: An Interview with Veronique Thompson

LEARNING OBJECTIVES

13-1 Interpret the most recent census data for African Americans in America today.

13-2 Explain the family and cultural values of African Americans.

13-3 Examine Dr. Thompson's experience as an African American counselor, counselor educator, supervisor, and clinical director.

▶ Demographics `13-1`

Chapter 4 discussed the *African American* experience and how it was and still is affected by racism, prejudice, and white privilege. This chapter explores the African American experience more in-depth and provides suggestions on how the African American experience influences their work in counseling. The term *African American* subsumes a diverse array of peoples, including African Americans born in this country, Africa, and individuals from the West Indies and Central and South America. The 2000 Census numbered African Americans in the United States at 34,658,190, or 12.3 percent of the population. Since the time of slavery, they have been this country's largest minority—until the 2000 Census, when they were passed by Latinos/as, at 12.5 percent of the population. According to a 2016 Census report, African Americans increased to 13.3 percent of the population. They are the most widely dispersed ethnic group in the United States, both geographically and economically. Although most African Americans are descendants of families who have been in the United States since the time of slavery, immigration has been slowly increasing over the last two decades, leading to increasing levels of linguistic and cultural diversity. Immigrants from former British Caribbean colonies bring with them a mixture of African and British customs, and those from former Spanish, French, and Dutch colonies do the same. In 1980, only 3 percent were foreign-born. By 1998, the figure had risen to 5 percent, with most of the increase coming from immigration from the Caribbean. Previous immigration from Africa has primarily come from Nigeria, Ethiopia, Ghana, Kenya, and Morocco (Pollard and O'Hare, 1999). According to the Pew Research Center analysis of U.S. Census Bureau data, 2.1 million African immigrants were living in the United States in 2015. Such diversity leads Hines and Boyd-Franklin (1982) to warn providers against assuming the existence of a "typical" African American family.

▶ Family and Cultural Values `13-2`

Black (1996) points to four factors that have shaped African American experience and culture (see Chapter 4 for more information on African American cultural values):

- ▶ African legacy—rich in culture, customs, and achievements
- ▶ History of slavery and deliberate attempt to destroy the core and soul of the people
- ▶ Racism and discrimination and ongoing efforts to continue the psychological and economic subjugation started during slavery
- ▶ A victim system and process by which individuals and communities are denied access to the instruments of development and advancement (p. 59)

Black slaves brought with them a rich amalgam of cultures from West Africa and, according to Hilliard (1995), rather than eradicate African culture and consciousness, slavery actually served to preserve it. Aspects of an African worldview still infuse African American life: a deep religiosity and spirituality, cooperation and interdependence, and a oneness with nature. According to Marshall (2002), enslavement added a complex of core values and attitudes—emphases on resistance, freedom, self-determination, and education. African culture also contributed a tradition of strong family structure, in which extended families and close-knit kinship systems were the basis for larger tribal groupings.

According to researchers who have worked to adapt family therapy practices to the cultural realities of African American families, three strategies are critical:

▶ Understand the cultural context of the family.
▶ View differences in family dynamics as adaptive mechanisms and strengths.
▶ Develop practices that take into account the needs, cultural dynamics, and style of African American culture.

Furthermore, these researchers favor interventions that mobilize existing family structures, and they are opposed to creating new forms similar to those found in white families. Hill (1972, 2003) identifies the following three factors as positive strengths to be built upon.

Kinship Bonds

Most African American families are embedded in complex kinship networks of blood and nonrelated individuals. Stack (1975) found patterns of "co-residence, kinship-based exchange networks linking multiple domestic units, elastic household boundaries, and a lifelong bond to three-generation households" as typical (p. 124). White (1980) points to a series of "uncles, aunts, big mamas, boyfriends, older brothers and sisters, deacons, preachers, and others who operate in and out of the black home" (p. 45). Such extended patterns and the multiple resources that they provide must be acknowledged and worked with by family therapists as a legitimate locus of intervention. Key family members must be identified and included in the treatment planning, even if they do not fit traditional definitions of the family. It is critical that they play significant roles in the family system. One is reminded of Elena's godfather in the case study of the Martinez family in Chapter 4.

Hines and Boyd-Franklin (1982) and Boyd (1982) suggest the use of genograms or "family trees" to map out the roles of family actors and their relationships and conflicts. Caution, however, should be exercised in the collection of such data because African American families are often suspicious of "prying" professionals. These authors suggest delaying data collection until adequate trust has been developed and that information be sought in a natural way, as opposed to a forced manner. Extended *kinship bonds* also suggest the usefulness of working with subgroups of the extended family and including only those who are directly relevant to a particular issue. It may also be necessary to schedule family sessions in the home to include key figures who cannot or will not visit clinics. Again, entering the home, like seeking information, should be done with sensitivity, in light of past abuses of the welfare system against poor families.

Role Flexibility

Role flexibility within the African American family, like extended kinship bonds, is highly adaptive for coping with the stresses of oppression and socioeconomic ills. It is most evident in the greater role diversity found among African American men and women as well as in the existence of unique familial roles, such as the *parental child*. African American males have traditionally been seen by social scientists as "peripheral" to family functioning (Moynihan, 1965); Hill (1972), among others, has challenged this notion. He argues that the father's frequent absence from the home reflects a lack of neither parenting skill nor interest, but rather the time and energy required to provide basic necessities for the family. The father's precarious economic position, coupled with the need for African American females to work outside the home, often leads to extensive role reversals and flexibility in childrearing and household responsibilities. These circumstances have led researchers to suggest that, as a result, African American children may not learn as rigid distinctions between male and female roles as their white counterparts. In approaching therapy, Hines and Boyd-Franklin (1982) caution against routinely excluding the father, as has frequently been the case with those who subscribe to the myth of peripheralness. Instead, they suggest doing everything possible to include him, even if for only a single session. They encourage the therapist to regularly keep him abreast of events and developments in therapy when he is unable to attend. They also caution against assuming the absence of a male role model when the father has abandoned the family. Given the variety of extended family figures, someone often emerges to fill this role.

While the African American male has been viewed as peripheral, the African American female—often forced to assume responsibilities well beyond those typically taken on by white women—has frequently been mislabeled as overly dominant. African American couples are, in fact, often more egalitarian than their white counterparts. Scanzoni (1971), for example, found that more often than whites, black males and females grow up with the expectation that both men and women will work. Minuchin et al. (1967) offer some interesting insights into the dynamics between African American males and females. Discord tends to be dealt with indirectly rather than through direct confrontation. Solutions to long-term disharmony are typically informal, and long periods of separation may occur without the thought of divorce.

African American couples tend to remain together for life, often for the sake of the children, and typically seek therapy for child-focused issues rather than for marital dissatisfaction. In spite of ill treatment by the husband, African American women tend to resist the dissolution of a relationship. Hines and Boyd-Franklin (1982) suggest that this may result from three factors:

- Greater empathy for the husband's frustration in a racist society
- Awareness of the extent to which they outnumber black males
- Strong religious orientation that teaches tolerance for suffering

Economic demands and oppressive forces have, in addition, created unique roles in the African American family. Included are the *parental child*—which involves parental responsibilities allocated to an older child when there are many younger children to attend to or when both parents are absent from the home for considerable amounts of time—and the extended generational system of parenting, in which the parent role is shared and distributed across several generations living in the home. It is important to emphasize that such adaptive strategies within the African American family, while clearly a potential positive force, can in themselves become sources of problems that require intervention. This occurs when their intended function becomes distorted, overused, or rigidified. According to Pinderhughes (1982), "if the mother's role is over-emphasized . . . it can become the pathway for all interactions within the family. This requires children to relate primarily to her moods and wishes rather than to their own needs. The result is emotional fusion of the children with the mother . . ." (p. 113). Or parental children can be forced to take on responsibilities well beyond those of which they are capable and at the expense of necessary peer group interactions (Minuchin, 1974). Shared parenting in the multigenerational family can become highly chaotic or a source of open conflict and dispute. In each of these cases, the goal of therapy should not be to eliminate or "repair" the adaptive pattern (i.e., to move the family closer to white middle-class norms). Such patterns may, in fact, be necessary for family survival. Rather, the goal should be to set it back on its purposeful course so that it can once again function as intended.

Religion

Religion is an extremely important factor in the life of the African American community and provides a valuable source of social connection, as well as self-esteem and succor in times of stress. According to Boyd (1977), however, it is frequently overlooked by clinicians in therapy. Specifically, religious issues are seldom discussed; African American families seeking help from mental health agencies may be unconnected to church networks, and clients may dichotomize problems as appropriate for discussion either with ministers or with mental health professionals. For clients with elaborate church connections, such networks can represent valuable resources. This might include seeking necessary information from religious leaders, calling on the network for help and resources during times of crisis, or including ministers as "significant others" in therapy or as co-therapists. In addition, religiosity is not infrequently related to a family's presenting problem. For example, Larsen (1976) reports the case of a highly religious family dealing with the rejection of religion and traditional values by a rebellious pre-adolescent. An understanding of its impact on behavior (e.g., strict adherence to harsh physical punishment and discipline of children based on religious maxims such as "Spare the rod and spoil the child") is critical to any potentially successful therapeutic intervention.

The trauma of slavery and a long history of racism have shaped and defined the African American experience in the United States. It is impossible to understand the African American psyche without keeping these two events clearly in mind. Kivel (1996) states the facts of slavery quite succinctly: "From 1619 until slavery ended officially in 1865, 10–15 million Africans were brought here, and another 30–35 million died in transport" (p. 121). The magnitude is staggering and even difficult to conceive. But that is not even the full story; there was also the systematic destruction of African culture and identity by the slavers and slave masters, the tearing apart of families, the creation of myths of inferiority and subhuman status to justify what was being done, and an entire nation that benefited greatly—economically and socially—from this cruel institution.

Racism replaced slavery as a vehicle for the continued exploitation of African Americans, as well as a justification for continuing to deny them the equality guaranteed by the U.S. Constitution. As a people, they survived, grew strong, and fashioned a new culture in America, but they continue to this day to pay an awesome price for the color of their skin. Hacker (1992) argues that the United States is functionally "two nations"—black and white—and that there is an enormous disparity in the access that these two groups have to the resources and benefits of this rich nation. The long list of statistical inequities—from average salaries to unemployment, from incarceration figures to education levels, from teenage pregnancies to poverty statistics—is staggering. For example, poverty rates among African Americans is almost three times that of whites; life expectancy is six years shorter; and infant mortality rates are twice those of whites, Asians, and Latinos/as. African American households receive the lowest annual median income at $25,100, and African American men experience the highest rate of unemployment among ethnic minorities. African Americans have, in turn, been the "point men" for the struggle that has been waged against the inequality and social injustice that continues to exist in this country. Through the civil rights and various other social movements, they have been the voice of conscience in America, not allowing it to forget the grave injustices that are still very much alive. As Kivel (1996) suggests, they have been the "center of racial attention," and all other oppressed groups have learned from and modeled their fights after those of African Americans. But it is little wonder, as our guest expert Veronique Thompson points out, that

African Americans mistrust and avoid seeking help from established white agencies and institutions. Their motives and agendas—throughout history and into this day—have just not proved to be trustworthy.

▶ Our Interviewee   13-3

Veronique Thompson, Ph.D., received her training at Spelman College and the University of California, Berkeley, where she held several distinguished minority fellowships. She is a licensed clinical psychologist and a tenured faculty member at the Wright Institute in Berkeley. She is the director of clinical training at the Center for Family Counseling in East Oakland, where she conducts training for the counseling staff that provides family therapy and community-based prevention programs in the Oakland Public Schools. She also maintains a small private practice. Dr. Thompson has special expertise in narrative theory and social justice therapy and has received training at the Dulwich Center, Australia, and the Family Center, New Zealand.

The Interview

Question: Can you begin by talking about your own ethnic background and how it has impacted your work?

Thompson: I identify as African American, although I use the words *black* and *African American* interchangeably. My racial identity impacts and shapes my life—who I am—and has a heavy, heavy influence in my work. Racism, in fact, makes it impossible for me to forget about the color of my skin. In some ways, sexism does the same thing. Both are at the forefront of my thinking and so cannot help but affect me as a professional. African American culture focuses my attention on certain aspects of experience. It teaches me about what's important, like spirituality and respect, education, family relationships, political unity, and fighting for the oppressed, freedom fighting. My culture has me paying attention to these things, and it shows up in my practice. It forms the metaphors and language I use and shapes and defines the way I think about psychological problems. Take respect, for instance. Because I come from a group that's been very disrespected, respect is a real important thing to me and other African Americans. There's a slang term that the young people use called "dis"—to "dis" somebody—and it means to disrespect them. My style of therapy is very connected, intimate. The humor that I use is very cultural. My language, the intonations that I use, how I speak, all come from being African American.

Being African American has also sensitized me to spirituality. I didn't grow up in the black church the way a lot of people did and so am not terribly religious, though being in church is quite comfortable for me. Yet, I have a strong sense of spirituality that runs very deep and affects my work in terms of values such as humility, obligation, respect, being thankful, being grateful, not putting myself at the center of things. I also feel a strong sense of responsibility as an African American, both personally and in my work, to understand the African American perspective and what the psychological effects of living in this country and this culture are. What kind of problems does that pose for us and how the negative effects can be best treated. But it is important to not define these effects only as pathology, for I feel a responsibility to focus on the strength it brings out—to observe and promote these strengths.

The thing that really got me interested in psychology was a book called *I Never Promised You a Rose Garden* that I read as a teenager. It was about mental illness, and I was fascinated by the realization that everybody had different minds, different inner worlds, different personalities. I have a sibling who struggles with depression, and it made me curious about such differences. As African Americans, we also occupy a certain reality that is different than other peoples' reality. Things like sexism and racism are really up close and personal. They're not merely interesting intellectual constructs. As a result of the denigration and oppression, there is often rage and anger, and you have to do something with that. I use it to inform my work, turn it into something constructive. It fuels my commitment for working with my own people.

Lastly, I have a lot of passion and try to be creative with it in my work. That part of me feels very African American. My mother always mentions a paradox she sees in our culture—that there is so much joy among us in spite of all the hardship. There's really a lot of exuberance, joy, and zest for life that shows up in things like the arts and all the many ways that African American people contribute to American culture. It comes from a deep place of both spirituality and joy.

Question: How would you define African Americans as a comprehensive group? What characteristics do they share?

Thompson: The term *African American* refers to people of black, African descent, who can be distinguished from people of white African descent, as well as from black Africans who are currently immigrants to this country. There are Caribbean blacks who have a very similar history to African Americans but who reside or have resided in the Caribbean Islands, and black people from South America and other places in the larger African diaspora. African Americans have a particular common history of being the descendants of those people who survived the Middle Passage and went through post–Civil War Reconstruction, the period of Jim Crow law, the period of cultural revolution, really from the '30s up into the 1950s and '60s.

The characteristics that African American people share are residuals of African culture that have sometimes been reshaped and adapted because of our current circumstances in North America. I like the way James Jones talks about those cultural residuals. He calls them TRIOS, which stands for time, rhythm, improvisation, oral, and spiritual.

Time. Every group has their own time frame. We refer to ours as CP time—that is, Colored People time. African Americans tend to be more informal around social time. For example, when I have a party and am inviting both my African American and white friends, I often tell them . . . speaking well and having good verbal communication and persuasive skills are highly prized among African Americans. Look at rap music, the high value placed on people being ministers and preachers. In my generation, it was called "capping," a contest to see who could verbally outdo the other person. *Spirituality,* even if it's not religious, there's great respect there. You almost never see African American people, if they win some kind of award on TV, I don't care what it is, you know, the Academy Awards, the Tony Awards, the music awards, they thank God. That reverence is always there.

As African Americans, we also have a shared history here in America that has been organized around oppression and its consequences. Included are the experiences of economic disenfranchisement, second-class citizenship, racial discrimination, healthy paranoia, social vigilance. Not every African American person reacts to these factors in the same way, and some may be well off right now or second- or third-generation middle class, but at some point, economic disenfranchisement was a shared and common experience, even if it is not currently in a person's life. It remains a generation or two away from you. A last thing related to all of this is a shared concern for the importance of respect. Parents being respected by their children; men being respected in a certain way. Self-respect is shown in how we dress, grooming, the very fancy clothes. Dressing down— not wearing shoes or going barefoot—are not valued because such activities are associated with being poor and economically disenfranchised. I remember being at an agency picnic and noticing that all of my white colleagues were sitting on the ground to eat and my African American colleagues were all standing. They all agreed that if you have on your professional clothes, you just never sit on the ground.

Question: What names or terms do individuals within the African American community use to describe and identify themselves?

Thompson: I think the most current and contemporary term is *African American.* Whether one prefers black or African American seems to depend on the era in which one was raised. *Black* was more typical of the 1960s and '70s. What I think is interesting about the list of names we have called ourselves—Negro, colored, black, African American—is that the earlier names all focused on skin color. *Negro,* though non-derogatory in its meaning, comes from the Spanish word *negre,* which means "black." But it focused on skin color. *Colored* brought us further away from the word *black,* and it tends to be kinder and politer. My mother's generation referred to themselves as *colored. Black* was a reaction of pride and solidarity. "Let's not water it down anymore. Let's say black! 'Say it loud: I'm Black and I'm proud.' " That whole thing. It was an affirming of African identities in both skin color and hair style. The afro was really a fascinating thing. It was like we're going to take our hair and let it stand up on our heads very proudly. Though it was about pride, it was still about appearance and skin color.

The term *African American* is my preference. First, it focuses on culture—both our connection to Africa, where we came from, and America, where we reside now. It also distinguishes us from other peoples with black skin. East Indians can be very dark in their complexion. The aboriginals in Australia have very dark skin. But what makes us African American is having a cultural connection to Africa and to others who have come from there. It is also the only term that we've truly chosen for ourselves. It puts us on the same status as other groups in America. It describes the kind of American you are. Like, a person is an Italian American or Jewish American or African American. It both gives us status and places culture in a very salient position in defining who we are. Finally, it tends to be more inclusive. I have not found it useful to distinguish people who are recently mixed racially from African Americans, who have always been a mixed people. From the time we came to this country, there was extensive mixing with Whites and Native peoples. By "recently mixed," I mean a person who has a parent from another race and an African American parent. I see these children as part of the African American group. They are welcome within our community, and the term *African American* is more inclusive and makes room for them. Jane Lazar wrote a book entitled *Beyond the Whiteness of White: White Mother Raising Black Sons.* In it, she argues for the importance of giving her mixed-race sons a powerful and accurate identity as part of the African American community.

Question: What historical experiences should providers be aware of in relation to the African American community and African American clients?

Thompson: I would divide our history into four segments: pre-enslavement, the Middle Passage, enslavement, and post-enslavement. You'll notice I'm using the term *enslavement.* I do that because it is more socially responsible and accurate as far as providing a context for understanding. It focuses on what has been done to our people, as opposed to labeling them as just slaves, as if that is a part of their character and who they are.

I begin with the period of *pre-enslavement* because it is important for providers as well as African Americans themselves to be aware that we were not always slaves but rather descended from many different cultural groups across the continent of Africa. We existed prior to enslavement. The *Middle Passage* describes the ways in which African Americans were physically brought to America. It was the brutal transition from pre-enslavement to being enslaved; from being free and autonomous to becoming slaves. It was a journey by ships, human beings packed like sardines, during which more people died than were actually delivered to the United States. It is important to know about the brutality of the process as well as the fact that the enslaved Africans resisted from the very beginning, many choosing to jump ship, end their lives, rather than be enslaved.

The *enslavement* period—the institution of slavery—was about economics. Skin color, race, and supposed inferiority were all concepts used to justify slavery, which was at its core economic. The money that was made from slavery allowed this country to become what it is. Providers need to know that this person in front of them belonged to a group that was enslaved and helped create the wealth of this country. What is particularly ironic are the stereotypes that paint African American people as lazy. It's so crazy. Here's a group of people that worked for over 300 years for free, doing backbreaking and servile work, to be described as lazy. What an incredible reaction formation. But it is important to also realize that the institution of slavery challenged us with a lot of psychological residuals that still exist today. For example, Ken Hardy talks about silence and rage—how, during slavery, African Americans were going through a dehumanizing process in which they had to be silent and witness their own abuse and how this has turned into rage and then violence. There is a lot of anger in the African American community, and anger is always a reaction to something. It comes from injustice, brutality, and abuse. So, when you see a lot of violence in the African American community, and you might be tempted as a provider to say, "Why are these people so violent?" If you understood what the process of enslavement did to turn rage directed toward the self—directed toward one's community as violence—it would give you a different way of understanding.

How can one deal with that rage without pathologizing the person and making their anger the only issue to be addressed? I actually like to talk about turning rage into outrage. Typically, we say if a person is full of rage and anger, they need treatment. They have an "anger" problem, and we give them a diagnosis, medication, perhaps an anger management group. When a person is outraged, they're outraged for a reason, and the reason is injustice. So, the period of enslavement is important because it shows us where the anger came from. And there are a lot of residuals from our history having to do with anger, trust, suspicion, which really should be renamed healthy paranoia.

Post-enslavement. There was the whole post–Civil War Reconstruction period. It was quite short-lived, however. The period of Reconstruction was important because it showed our talents, our forgiving spirit, and our intelligence. The newly freed Africans were ready to pitch in and become part of American culture and to contribute with businesses and industry. Many black businesses and communities thrived after slavery. And, amazingly, there was not a strong spirit of retaliation. I think African American people have an incredibly forgiving spirit. It's something I try to draw upon in therapy. I think spirituality has a lot to do with forgiveness.

Here were a people ready to participate in healthy, positive, forgiving ways. Film director Spike Lee has named his film company 40 Acres and a Mule. With the end of slavery, each slave was promised forty acres and a mule, and as Lee suggests, he is still waiting for those forty acres and a mule. This broken promise was only the beginning of a process of re-enslavement through a system of legislation known as Jim Crow laws, segregation, and unequal treatment. The psychological residual of Reconstruction followed by Jim Crow for African Americans was a widespread mistrust of the governmental systems as well as of whites in general. The people I know and clients I see freely state that: "I don't trust white folks." The distrust is immediate and general, and whites must prove themselves as safe and okay. Until proven otherwise, they're not. So, it's important for practitioners to know that this is a group of people that were lied to in this country; if you see mistrust, that may be its roots.

Post-enslavement also includes a number of revolutions within the African American community, continuing the longstanding spirit of resistance within our history. There was a cultural revolution in the '30s with the Harlem Renaissance led by authors such as Langston Hughes and Zora Neale Hurston. It was the beginning of social commentary, of great creativity and intelligence, and, again, the forgiving spirit of African American people as expressed through the work of these writers. They fought with the pen rather than with arms. We all know the Civil Rights Movement of the late 1950s and '60s with Martin Luther King and Malcolm X. They all show how we have resisted our mistreatment. We've not been docile or turned over on our backs. It's really important for young people to know that—and practitioners as well. In growing up, I knew about slavery, but I didn't know about the uprisings. And having the opportunity to have black scholars focus our attention on resistance to slavery, the uprisings, and the incredibly creative ways that Africans tried to resist their inhumane treatment leads to a very different kind of self-understanding. But at the same time, it is necessary to realize that though resilient, creative, and strong, we are not indomitable. Many people fail to see the soft side of African Americans, the fragility, the need for human kindness and connection like anyone else. There are many negative statistics and problems in our communities that bear this out: poverty, drug addiction. We're not infallible, but we are strong. So, holding both of these ideas at the same time is critical for practitioners.

Question: Can you next discuss some of the factors that influence the ways African Americans seek mental health services?

Thompson: Trust, as I said before, is a very big influence. African Americans tend not to seek help from professionals. We have learned not to trust them, and our reasons are legitimate and sound, not a reflection of some sort of pathology. Really bad things have happened to us in the name of professional treatment, like the Tuskegee Syphilis Study. African American men participated in research without their knowledge and consent; they had treatment withheld so that the researchers could watch the course of development of syphilis. Psychological testing has been used against us, and many in our community just don't feel that psychology has much to offer us as a system of care. Cost and access are also factors. Many of the fees are just too high, and it is difficult to get to where therapists are located. There aren't tons of people with private practices located in East Oakland. Cultural competence is also a big issue. Will my life experience be understood and valued by the counselor? I would say that most practitioners are not culturally competent. I've also talked about respect. I think many African Americans expect that if they go to a practitioner, they will be blamed, misunderstood, and pathologized. We feel we're going to be seen as somebody who has a problem with anger, as opposed to somebody who's outraged at unjust treatment.

So, we don't go. Instead, we find other help-seeking opportunities, find other institutions for help. We rely heavily on the church, on black social organizations, and there are many of these. And we rely upon our leaders in the community and our ministers. We seek out people that we can relate to, identify with, who understand us. So, it's about how we relate, our accessibility, and how we enter the community. I recently spoke to a women's group that meets at a local church. I was asked to come and talk about psychotherapy: what it can offer, what I do. This group of African American women was incredibly receptive, and we had a wonderful time. But it came through the church. Someone that they trusted invited me, and this was a group of African American parishioners. Of course, my being African American helped—but not just because of my skin color. I think it was how I related to them that was key. Because for African American people, it's all about how you relate to them—how it feels, if they can identify with you, if there is respect and comfort. I could be African American and still put them off by a certain kind of professional distance or behavior that seems too "white," for instance. So, my being black is not the issue; it's how I relate. I use a more interactive and personal way of relating, and that was what allowed them to hear what I was saying. Most people wouldn't go or continue with therapy if they feel like they cannot relate to, identify with, or connect with their therapist. Nancy Boyd-Franklin talks about this when she describes the concept of "vibes."

Question: What do providers of service need to know about family and community issues among African Americans?

Thompson: As I have been saying all along, practitioners need to know the present-day ramifications of our history: to really understand what it is like for an African American client to live life in their community today, to focus on and appreciate the strengths and creativity that it takes to survive and live a full life, and to understand and acknowledge the privileges they hold in the world because they are white and how their African American client might feel about those privileges.

Let's begin with privilege. It is important to know that African Americans see white privilege as problematic for them as is racism. And I want to acknowledge that this is hard stuff for white providers to sit with. So, I appreciate that. But unless you understand this and bring it into the room with you, you are not going to be accepted and trusted. The fact is that not only are there the acts of direct discrimination and racial injustice that African Americans experience on a daily basis, but also, we see that white people are by and large still benefiting from a system that gives them advantage and at the same time treats us unfairly. We just want a fair and equitable system, and the privilege whites hold is a constant reminder of what we as African Americans don't have. When white practitioners are able to cop to the fact that white privilege exists—to acknowledge it and the effects of racism—they're more likely to be trusted and thus helpful.

Let me switch to what life experience is like for many African Americans today, especially those living in the urban, inner city who are primarily working and of the lower and middle class. We see that there is still modern-day slavery, as in the prison system and industry, and that our people are disproportionately represented in jails. We see that drugs that devastate us are allowed into our community. In fact, we are systematically targeted for alcohol and tobacco sales. But there are a lot of current forms of modern-day slavery, like the prison industry. It's an industry, a moneymaking venture. And that's modern-day slavery to people in African American communities. We know this, and it's important that practitioners know that this is how many of us think about it. That drugs are allowed into our community. It is not surprising that African American people feel abandoned, uncared for, disenfranchised by the social institutions that are "supposed" to help them. When you have a poor school, and you have unequal protection under the law, when you have a lack of basic services, like you don't have any banks in your neighborhood or groceries that have good prices, and you have more alcohol stores than grocery stores, and you have media that portrays you negatively, and only fast foods that are available to you, and unaffordable brand names that are targeted specifically toward your group. When all of this continues to happen, your relationship to these larger social institutions is going to be one of mistrust. You feel uncared for, unprotected at a basic level. For example, you know that if you call the police right now and live in Berkeley, they will probably come within a half hour. If you live in Oakland, they will come in four hours.

So, here comes the psychologist: well-meaning, a professional, who's part of a social institution, a school, or maybe the client is court-mandated. You're not going to be necessarily trusted. Practitioners need to know that. It has nothing to do with you as an individual; you're connected to a larger social institution that does not have a track record of building trust. Our families feel disrespected by contact with the system, intruded upon by institutions that are largely staffed by white people that don't understand or care for us. That's how many people in the community think. Here's an agency whose staff is all white, and all the kids getting treatment in the program are black. And then they're calling CPS (Children's Protective Services). If an African American client is testing you or untrusting, you might see that as a natural and healthy thing because these folks come from a group that has not been cared for. Providers of service also need to know that there's a real lack of safety in our communities, and that lack of safety is stressful for those of us who live there. You may feel some fear coming to that community. Imagine what it's like to live in a community where you're continually afraid. But it's more complex than that because you also have really good relationships with many of the people there (your neighbors), and there are times when the fear is not present. You have to be strong, creative, and adaptive to survive here.

Question: What kinds of problems are most commonly brought by African Americans into treatment?

Thompson: All the problems that other Americans have, African Americans have too. Depression. Anxiety. We all live in American society, and that can create stress and problems—too much time at work; not enough help and support. People get tired and cranky, drink, abuse their partners, etc. It is the same for African Americans, but on top of that, we have to deal with the effects of modern-day discrimination and racism. It's much subtler. Nobody's riding down the street burning a cross on your front lawn. That subtlety in some ways is harder to understand for the person who's experiencing it. Sometimes, a client doesn't realize it (the experience of racism, for example) until you ask the question, and then they can put it together. But it subtly makes it extremely stressful to African Americans. They bring it (stress) into therapy and they don't bring it in saying that's what it is. Some people call it extreme mundane environmental stress. It comes out as self-doubt, self-criticism; that's how it comes into the office. But it is really the effects of social and economic disenfranchisement. People come in with the problems that are most obvious to them: self-doubt, family problems, drug, alcohol, tobacco-related addictions (our community is targeted for these), and issues of group identity and belonging. A bit more about the last one; when you belong to a group that's really put down, it poses quite a challenge for you because you have a human need to belong, yet who wants to belong to a group that's seen so negatively? That's what you see with the early doll studies (Clark and Clark, 1947) with African American children, when they were choosing the white doll. The kids got, really early on, that there is something about that black group nobody seems to like. Children may say: "I think I'd rather belong to the group that people like." The only thing that can really buffer and save us from this brutality of discrimination is to belong to our own group and to have pride and a healthy sense that the people that you come from are good people. This is a dilemma that every African American person faces and can get addressed in therapy with a practitioner who is aware of it.

Question: What factors do you see as important in assessing African American clients?

Thompson: Formal testing and assessment of clients is not something I practice these days. African American clients have good reason to be suspicious of psychological testing. Historically, it has been used to track our children into special education classes and to justify stereotypes of lower intelligence. The instruments that have been traditionally used have not been culturally sensitive and therefore put our children at a disadvantage. There is also the issue of trust once again. Everyone who is assessed by a psychologist feels somewhat vulnerable. When you assess someone, you're in the position of judging them. If you are from a group of people who are incredibly vulnerable to rejection—who are incredibly sensitive to being misunderstood—trust is enormously important, and you must develop it before conducting an assessment. (See Chapter 3 for more information on how to work with African American clients.)

Question: Are there subpopulations in the community that you feel are particularly at risk?

Thompson: I think there are subpopulations that we need to pay particular attention to. Black men, for example. There have been books written about the black male as endangered, and understanding their position is a complex task having to do with the intersection of racism and sexism. In some ways they are accorded some amount of privilege for being male but at the same time are devalued because white society fears them—and fears them even more than black women. So, their maleness both hurts and helps them, and this can be very confusing both for them and for practitioners. Understanding the situation of African American women is important because there is the double burden of being both female and African American. Yet, at the same time, African American woman are elevated over black men, and you can imagine the conflicts that that causes in relationships and families. African American women are seen as less threatening (by the general society) and therefore viewed as objects of oppression in the same way white women are. So, we are subjected to the same things that make it harder for all women—the focus on beauty, lowered expectations around intelligence, etc.—but also higher mountains to climb as African Americans.

And then there is the gay/lesbian/bisexual/transgendered community. First, you're outcast in the wider culture and then you're outcast in your own African American culture. I get so angry about that and even tearful—that the GLBT community would be doubly rejected from within their own group, which should be more sensitive to such issues of exclusion. There needs to be more attention paid to what it is like being black and gay.

Finally, there are the children, who are the most voiceless. A significant number of African American children are born below the poverty line and for generations have remained impoverished—born into poverty and most likely to stay in poverty. There is this overgeneralization that all African American people are poor, and as a result, both the very poor and those who are economically higher up remain invisible. Another issue that impacts African American children greatly, as it does white children, is addiction to drugs among their parents. Addicted parents are unable to properly raise children because drugs rob you of your mind, your sense of social connection, and your ability to be responsible. Families with rampant addiction tend to be chaotic environments, difficult places to grow up, and addicted parents are incapable of passing on cultural knowledge and identity, a very significant loss for African American children.

Question: What suggestions do you have for developing rapport with African American clients, and is there a therapeutic style with which African American clients are most comfortable?

Thompson: Being direct is very well received by African Americans. I don't mean doing away with social niceties or being blunt, rude, or crude, but not beating around the bush. Directness is often appreciated. There is this culture of politeness that shows up among practitioners that is mistrusted by African American people. Being too nice, or too open, or too solicitous before you know somebody is perceived as inauthentic. Remember, we are as a people very sensitive to inauthenticity and dishonesty. Many therapists claim to create a safe environment for all clients. But therapists really don't have the power to do that and having such an attitude is likely to raise the suspicion of African American people. Saying "I'd like this to be a safe place, and I'll do my best to do that, but I don't know if I can do that for you" would be much more authentic and therefore more trust-inducing.

So, directness, authenticity, and honesty are vital because people who have been lied to have special antennae in relation to: "This doesn't sound right. Why are you being so nice to me when you don't even know me?" We have feelers. Nancy Boyd-Franklin talked about it as a vibe. African American people get your vibe, and it's really hard to hide. Being passionate and interactive are also important because our cultural style is to be both. We're a very passionate, exuberant, excitable people. So, if your style as a practitioner is flat in its affect or distant, passive, or minimally reactive with frequent silences, it is likely to be interpreted as something negative. And it is critical to be respectful of people's spiritual beliefs. Not all African Americans are religious. In fact, awful things have happened to many of us in the name of religion. But African Americans are still spiritual, and that is a powerful issue around which to connect.

I have found that the use of (what I have termed) "socially conscious self-disclosure" is very effective with African American people. Nondisclosure can be problematic with people who are from oppressed groups. If you don't disclose personal information, there is no way to place you in a context and, therefore, to know if you can be trusted. The therapist must be sure that the self-disclosure is done in the service of the client—that is, it is an attempt to create safety, connection, empathy—not because the therapist is insecure, needs to vent, or needs to be heard. If the therapist shares personal information in that spirit—to do so in a socially conscious way—it will be helpful with African American clients.

The African American people I work with, they know I'm African American by looking at me, but again, it's not just a skin color thing. They have to know how "black" I am. They really want to know where my consciousness is located. They don't come out and ask me. But I know it is important that I make disclosures to them so that they know that we share a worldview—that I know what they are talking about. For example, I have an African American client who's raising boys. It was very important for her to know that I, too, have a boy, and we are both attempting to raise black boys in a culture that is very brutal on black males. I didn't go on and talk about my son, but that little bit of information changed things. Most people feel greatly held by such connections. There's something very healing and soothing about knowing that somebody shares a problem with you. Another therapeutic tool I use with African American clients is something I call "deep cultural knowledge." By that I mean knowledge about my group that I have gotten from living in and being a part of the culture. For example, I use humor. There are certain things that I could probably say in a humorous way with African

Americans that would be shared—that if someone else did it, it would be insulting. All of the folk knowledge that I've picked up as part of my culture I refer to and ask questions about as a way of connecting with my clients in small but mutually meaningful ways. These things come up in talking about people's lives, so I may refer to them or ask where you heard or were taught that. Using cultural metaphors is also helpful. I use a lot of them. Metaphors about freedom, escape, liberation, our ancestors, spirit and spirituality. African American people love these metaphors because they just make sense to us in a very deep place. And, of course, my language style. I use black English to flavor my speech. There are just certain things that have to be said in a particular way.

I would encourage other African American practitioners to consider some of these approaches. Now, if you're not African American, you obviously can't use deep cultural knowledge, and that's a limit. I don't think that means you can't work with African American clients, but I think it's important to acknowledge the limits of what your experience is. And don't try to join with African American clients by acting black. When white people try to do the "slap me five, brotha" thing, it's a turn-off. It's likely to be experienced as inauthentic and phony. I've met a few white people who grew up in African American culture, and for them, such behavior is natural, so that's fine. But for most whites, such appropriation of our culture is considered an insult.

Finally, it's not a good idea to ask too many questions initially. Such questioning without sufficient trust and rapport will be viewed as interrogation. Too many questions too soon. We're talking about people with a history where trust and giving out information about oneself has been repeatedly violated. When I was a teenager, the Census person came to the house. My mother said, "Don't tell them anything," and my mother is a very warm, welcoming person. She's not particularly suspicious or paranoid. We, as African Americans, are raised not to tell strangers, especially white ones, anything about ourselves. The Census, for example, was just seen as white people coming in and trying to find out about us. But as therapists, we're taught to ask questions. So, how do you do that? The timing and pace of when you ask questions is critical. I would suggest that one wait before asking too many direct questions. Give the client time for them to tell you their story, time to check you out, and time to develop rapport. That's a style I think works better with African Americans.

Question: By way of ending and putting together some of the ideas you've shared, could you present a case?

Thompson: OK. Let me give you a shorter and then a longer example. I had an African American graduate student who doubted herself so much—doubted her intellectual capacities, in spite of the fact that she was a teaching assistant (TA) in her graduate program in a statistics course. If you are a TA for a statistics class, you're probably very good at math, right? She just couldn't shake the idea that she really wasn't good at math and had a nagging worry about her intelligence. But when you are viewed and portrayed as being from a group where you are "less than" others, "bad," or "lacking intelligence," it's no wonder that you show up in my office with: "I don't feel good about myself, and I can't figure out why." For this particular woman, who's African American, I believe both sexism and racism had her doubting her intelligence, yet she was the TA for one of the classes that everyone else is really anxious about. I think this is one of the subtle ways that racism affects our people. She would never have named that as racism, and I asked her quite frankly, "Do you think racism has anything to do with this?" which is one of my favorite questions. Most clients' immediate response is no, but after a few minutes, they reconsider and come back to the question. Eventually, they begin telling you all the ways that racism has affected them. Why was it so initially hard to identify? Because it is quite painful to think about and easier to push it out of consciousness. And you don't want to think that so much of your life is defined by it (racism).

I was working with a second woman who had a lot of social anxiety and came into therapy quite well versed in the language of social phobia. She said she knew they had medicine for it and asked if she could she get some of that. I don't prescribe medication but told her she could pursue that if she liked. In her work with me, I was particularly interested in how she came to think of herself as a social phobic. Using narrative therapy, I helped her deconstruct the messages she had gotten in life about who she was and how she had gotten to think of herself. So, we developed a metaphor for how she was feeling, using the language of escape, liberation, and freedom. We externalized her fear as imprisoning her. She had become a prisoner of it. Though it is normal for most people to feel a little awkward in new social situations, she was terrified of meeting people, especially about going back to school.

She wanted to go back to school but felt quite strongly that she didn't belong. Part of it was the fact she would be going to a largely white institution where she was going to be an ethnic minority. This scared her and stimulated a sense of not belonging. As we sorted out what this was about, we found hidden messages about poor black girls not going on for higher education, about her not having important things to contribute, and that no one would listen to her. This is another subtle way that racism shows itself in people's lives, and therapists can ask questions that can help uncover racism in this way.

So, we externalized the fear as the experience of feeling imprisoned—of living in a prison of fear. Before looking into how to escape from that prison, it was necessary for her to understand the interior of that prison, what it told her, how it spoke to her, how it kept her locked away. In terms of her breaking out, I asked, "Who might know about escaping to freedom?" In response, she said: "I wonder if our ancestors might know, since they tried to escape slavery." Then, she wondered how she might ask her ancestors. Would it be in a prayer, a meditation, or a reflective moment? I encouraged her to pursue the thought. She said, "I think I'll go to the ocean because we came from the other side of the ocean, and we were dropped off here," and added: "I like the ocean; I have this affinity to it. When I have a burden, I often go to the ocean and it helps me think, clear my mind." In her next session, she told me she had gone to the ocean and asked the ancestors about escaping.

And I asked, "What did they say?" sitting on the edge of my seat. She said that the answer came to her in the form of a poem. She shared the poem, and it was eloquent. It was about breaking free, cutting the shackles of fear, liberating her from social anxiety and fear. The poem connected her culturally and gave her both pride and courage.

Here's a young woman who came in talking about social phobia and medication, disconnected from the social context of her fears. She was able to connect the fear to a cultural background and through that connection deepen her own connection with who she was culturally.

SUMMARY

In sum, African Americans are the most widely dispersed ethnic group in the United States, both geographically and economically. Steady immigration from African countries has increased the linguistic and cultural diversity within the African American culture. However, core values still remain: kinship bonds, role flexibility, and religion. Dr. Thompson's interview provided historical context to the African American experience, as well as suggestions for helpers working with this population.

ACTIVITY

In small groups, identify and discuss 3–5 factors that are shaping African American experience and culture today. Compare and contrast this list to the list created by Black (1996).

KEY TERMS

African American, 316	pre-enslavement, 325	enslavement, 325
kinship bonds, 317	Middle Passage, 325	post-enslavement, 326

14

Working with Asian American Clients: An Interview with Dan Hocoy

LEARNING OBJECTIVES

14-1 Interpret the implications of census data for Asian Americans in America today.

14-2 Examine family and cultural values of Asian Americans.

14-3 Examine Dr. Hocoy's experience as an Asian psychologist and multicultural researcher.

▶ Demographics `14-1`

Asian Americans were the fastest-growing racial group in the United States from 1980 to 2000, with their population nearly doubling (179 percent) during that period. The 2010 Census (which divides the larger group into two subgroups) reported an Asian population of 14.6 million, or 4.8 percent of the general population, and a Native Hawaiian and other Pacific Islander population of 540,000, or 0.2 percent. This represents an increase of 43.3 percent and 35.0 percent, respectively, for the ten-year period. Projections into the future estimate a population increase from 5 percent of the United States total in 2010 to 9 percent by the year 2050.

Like the Latinos/as, Asians represent a diverse collection of ethnic groups with very different languages, cultures, and, in some cases, a long history of intergroup conflict and hostilities. Included in this collective are forty-three ethnic groups—twenty-eight in the *"Asian" category* and fifteen in the *"Pacific Islander" category*. Included in the former are individuals who identify themselves as Asian Indians, Chinese, Filipino, Korean, Japanese, and Vietnamese, and in the latter are individuals from Hawaii, Guam, and Samoa. With changes in the Immigration Act of 1965 and large-scale immigration from Southeast Asia and other parts of the Asian continent, relative percentages of Asian American subgroup sizes changed dramatically. According to the 1970 Census, Japanese were the most populous, followed by Chinese and Filipinos. By 1980, however, Japanese were ranked third, with Chinese moving to first and Filipinos to second. As of 2000, Chinese represent the largest Asian subgroup with 2.3 million, Filipinos at 1.9 million, Asian Indians at 1.7 million, Vietnamese at 1.1 million, Korean also at 1.1 million, and Japanese at 0.8 million. Native Hawaiians and Pacific Islanders make up only 5 percent of the Asian population in the United States. For more information regarding Asian American culture, please see Chapters 9 and 10.

Most Asian Americans come from recent immigrant families. During the 1990s, immigrants were, in fact, responsible for two-thirds of the growth of the overall Asian population. In 1998, for instance, 59 percent were foreign-born, with 74 percent arriving since 1980. Many Chinese and Japanese Americans, however, have been here for three or more generations, originally a source of cheap labor in the economic development of the Western United States. Their history was one of extensive suffering and racial discrimination. According to Pollard and O'Hare (1999):

> Legislation enacted in 1790 excluded Asians and other non-whites gaining citizenship by limiting citizenship to "free white residents." Because most Asians were foreign-born and not citizens, they could be legally kept from owning land or businesses, attending schools with whites, or living in white neighborhoods. Asian immigrants were not eligible for U.S. citizenship until 1952. The 1879 California constitution barred the hiring of Chinese workers, and the federal Chinese Exclusion Act of 1882 halted the entry of most Chinese until 1943.

The 1907 Gentlemen's Agreement and a 1917 law restricted immigration from Japan and a "barred zone" known as the Asian-Pacific Triangle. During World War II Americans of Japanese ancestry were interned in camps by Executive Order signed by Franklin D. Roosevelt. (pp. 5–6)

Recent Asian and Pacific Islander immigration has followed two streams. One came from countries such as China and Korea, which already have large populations in the United States. The majority of these were college-educated and entered under special employment provisions. The second stream came from Southeast Asia—Vietnam, Laos, and Cambodia—arriving after the Vietnam War to escape persecution in their home countries. Most were poor and uneducated.

As a group, Asian Americans and Pacific Islanders, 49 percent of the U.S. population, are concentrated in the western United States, with the largest urban populations located in Los Angeles and New York City. Sixty percent of the Chinese population reside in California and New York; two-thirds of the Filipinos and Japanese live in California and Hawaii. Koreans and Asian Indians tend to be more dispersed, with the largest concentrations in California, New York, Illinois, New Jersey, and Texas. Southeast Asians, on the other hand, can be found in unexpected pockets of population as a result of governmental resettlement policies. For example, in 1990, 40 percent of the Hmong population resided in Minnesota and Wisconsin (Pollard and O'Hare, 1999).

Unlike African Americans, Latinos/as, and Native Americans, Asian Americans have been quite successful economically and educationally, even in comparison with the white population. In 2002, the median income in an Asian household was $65,469, when it was $54,461 for white households and $38,039 for African American households. Asian Americans, in addition, account for 30 percent of minority businesses, although they account for only 13 percent of the non-white population. They also score high on business ownership rates (BORs) (businesses per 1,000 population), with Koreans and Asian Indians surpassing white BORs. Asians graduate from high school at the same rate as do whites—approximately 90 percent—but the former are more likely to complete two or more years of college. In 1990, 13 percent of the Asian and Pacific Islander population earned graduate and professional degrees in comparison to 9 percent of whites and three to four times the rate of other minorities.

Because of such statistics and a cultural tendency to defer and not compete openly with white Americans, Asian Americans have been described as a *"model minority,"* a veritable success story. Sue and Sue (1999), however, see this image as a myth based on incomplete data that serves to validate the erroneous belief that any ethnic group can succeed if only they work hard enough, stimulate inter-group conflict, and shortchange Asian communities from needed resources. According to Sue and Sue (1999), the following facts need to be understood. High median income does not take into consideration the number of wage earners, the level of poverty among certain Asian subgroups, or the discrepancy between education and income for Asian workers. Education in the Asian community is bimodal; that is, there are both highly educated and uneducated subpopulations. Asian towns in large urban areas represent ghettos with high unemployment, poverty, and widespread social problems. Underutilization of services does not necessarily mean a lack of problems, but it may in fact have alternative explanations, such as face-saving, shame, or the family's cultural tendency to keep personal information hidden from the outside world. In short, the belief in Asian success does not mean that there is any less racism or discrimination directed toward Asian Americas or that there are not serious problems within crowded urban enclaves. At a psychological level, "model minority" status refers to the lack of threat whites experience in relation to Asian Americans. Such an attitude has eroded somewhat, however, with increased economic competition from Japan and other Pacific Rim countries and a growing number of Asian American students competing successfully for college and university slots.

▶ Family and Cultural Values   14-2

Lee (1996) offers the following description of traditional Asian families:

> ... in traditional Asian families, the family unit—rather than the individual—is highly valued. The individual is seen as the product of all the generations of his or her family. The concept is reinforced by rituals and customs such as ancestor worship, family celebrations, funeral rites, and genealogy records. Because of this continuum, individuals' personal action reflects not only on themselves but also on their extended family and ancestors ... Obligations and shame are mechanisms that traditionally help reinforce societal expectations and proper behavior. An individual is expected to function in his or her clearly defined roles and positions in the family hierarchy, based on age, gender, and social class. There is an emphasis on harmonious interpersonal relationships, interdependence, and mutual obligations or loyalty for achieving a state of psychological homeostasis or peaceful coexistence with family or other fellow beings. (pp. 230–231)

Family and gender roles and expectations are highly structured. Fathers are the breadwinners, protectors, and ultimate authorities. Mothers oversee the home, bear and care for children, and are under the authority of their fathers, husbands, in-laws, and, at times, even sons. Male children are highly prized, and the strongest bond within the family is between mother and son. Children are expected to be respectful and obedient and are usually raised by an extended family. Older daughters are expected to play a caretaking function with younger siblings.

Traditional Asian values differ dramatically from those of white, middle-class American culture. Immigration brings the strong possibility of cultural conflict within the family. Lee (1996) differentiates five Asian American family types that differ in relation to cultural conflict:

- "Traditional" families are largely untouched by assimilation and acculturation, retain cultural ways, limit their contact with the white world, and tend to live in ethnic enclaves.
- "Culture conflict" families are typified by traditional parents and acculturated, Americanized children who experience intergenerational conflict over appropriate behavior and values, exhibit major role confusion, and lack agreed-upon family structures.
- "Bicultural" families tend to include acculturated parents, born either in the United States or in Asia and exposed to Western ways. They are professional, middle-class, bilingual, and bicultural. Family structures tend to be a blending of family styles but with regular contact with traditional family members.
- "Americanized" families have taken on the ways of the majority culture, with ties to traditional Asian culture fading and little interest in connection to ethnic identity.
- "Interracial" families represent marriage with a non-Asian partner where family styles from the two cultures have been successfully integrated or there is significant value and style conflict.

Sue and Sue (1999) similarly identify five potential value conflicts that may arise between Asian American clients and Western trained counselors:

- Asian clients value a collective and group focus that emphasizes interdependence, and Western counselors adopt a focus on individualism and independent action.
- Asians tend to be most comfortable with hierarchical relationships in comparison with a Western emphasis on equality in relationships.
- Asian cultures see the restraint of emotion as a sign of human maturity, and the Western counselor is likely to see emotional expressiveness as healthy.
- Traditional Asian clients will expect the counselor to provide solutions, but the Western counselor will encourage finding one's own solutions through introspection.
- Mental illness and emotional problems are seen within the Asian context as shameful and indicative of family failure in contrast with Western counseling, which views mental and physical illness similarly.

As we shall learn from our guest expert, Dan Hocoy, Asian Americans—when they do seek professional helping services outside of their community—tend to present with a variety of problems, including value conflicts with parents and family, difficulties regarding identity issues, acculturation, extreme work ethics, and familial obligations.

▶ Our Interviewee   14-3

Dan Hocoy, Ph.D., received his degree in clinical psychology from Queen's University, Kingston, Ontario, Canada. His dissertation focused on the effects of apartheid and racism on black mental health in South Africa. He has also carried out research on racial identity and other cross-cultural topics throughout the world, including Chinese racial identity and the psychological impact of racism on Chinese in Canada. He is a member of the core faculty of the psychology department of the Pacific Graduate Institute, Carpinteria, California, and previously served as assistant professor in the PsyD (Doctor of Psychology) program at John F. Kennedy University, Orinda, California.

The Interview

Question: One of your areas of expertise is racial identity. Could you talk about some of your own experiences growing up Chinese?

Hocoy: Being Chinese has always been very central to my life, although I haven't always been conscious of it. That is to say, I didn't always recognize its influence. I went through various phases of racial identity development. At first, I felt embarrassed about being Chinese. My family was the only Chinese family on the block, and because we were struggling immigrants, I always associated being Chinese with being poor. There was a lot of ethnic self-hate in me at that time. There was also external discrimination. For instance, I was always picked on in school for being Chinese; kids would tease me about the way my eyes, hair, and nose looked. I got into a few fights in the schoolyard as a result. During this stage of my racial identity development, I always wanted to be white. This continued into high school. I wanted wavy, more combable hair. I wanted to be taller. I wanted a sharper nose. I always felt inferior. Chinese people were always ugly to me. At the time, I wasn't aware of the influences of having internalized Euro-American standards of beauty. I didn't think I was very attractive. At the height of my racial self-hate, my looks actually disgusted me. Not accepting my ethnicity pushed me toward greater degrees of conformity and assimilation. Yet, I never felt I fit into the dominant culture either. Not feeling comfortable in either culture, I found myself marginalized and caught in the middle.

In university, I moved into another phase of racial identity development. Initially, I still didn't like the fact that I was Chinese, but I began to challenge my negative self-feelings and attitudes toward my people. Fortunately, at this time, I had an opportunity to visit other cultures through international development work. It was in Africa that I observed the psychological effects of colonialism and Western domination. Witnessing black self-hatred helped me come to terms with my own racial self-hatred. This began a process of reclaiming my ethnicity, and eventually, I would study the impact of racism on black South Africans for my doctoral dissertation. I was attending a very Anglo-dominated graduate school, and it was an especially fertile environment in which to come to terms with my race. I realized that much of my perception of the world was based on a lack of acceptance of who I was. I grew increasingly uncomfortable with the feelings of self-hatred and was, in time, able to come to terms with them. I wrote my master's thesis on the topic of racism against the Chinese in Canada, and this was obviously motivated by a struggle for racial self-acceptance. In time, I developed a great interest in my heritage and started buying and reading books about the Chinese and, in a variety of ways, immersed myself in Chinese culture.

My training in psychology helped me process what was going on inside me, both in realizing the effects of my experiences as a person of color and in coming to terms with the self-hate. Today, I regard my Chinese identity as an asset both personally and professionally. As I became clearer about my own ethnic heritage, I also became aware of the cultural bias in psychology and the need to redress the systematic neglect of minorities in both research and therapy. That, in turn, spawned an interest in multicultural counseling. But the process of racial self-acceptance is an ongoing one, and I have yet to completely free myself from what Bob Marley called "the chains of mental slavery."

Question: Let's begin with some definitions. Who are the Asian Americans, and what characteristics do they share as a group?

Hocoy: First, I think it is important to understand that there is a large degree of diversity among Asian Americans and that they do not conveniently fit into one categorization or description. There are many shades of yellow, so to speak, and it is difficult to make global generalizations. Having said that, individual and subgroup differences are significant, and there do exist commonalities that Asian cultures share. When I talk about Asian Americans, I am referring to people with Mongolian and early Chinese ancestry. This includes the mainland Chinese, Japanese, Koreans, the Vietnamese, people from Hong Kong, Taiwan, Singapore, Malaysia, the Philippines, Laos, Thailand, and others from that region. I know this is not inclusive of all Asians, as it omits East Indians and others, for instance, but these are the groups with which I am most familiar.

With regard to Asian Americans, it is useful to realize that there are a number of factors—historical, psychological, and otherwise—that set them apart as a group in America. First of all, unlike any other minority group, there is a history of warfare between the United States and many of these Asian countries. You have the Japanese in World War II, the Korean War (in which the Chinese and North Koreans were both involved), the Vietnam War, and so on. So, for many Americans, there is a visceral resentment and distrust of all things Asian. This is reflected in U.S. culture and media, where Asians were and, at times still, are portrayed as the prototypical villains.

I think the lack of acceptance of Asians in U.S. culture at least partially stems from the fact that Asians possess such a different worldview. For instance, "East vs. West" is a common dimension of comparison and dichotomy. Individuals who have been socialized into traditional Asian cultures are likely to possess completely different worldviews with philosophies, values, and beliefs that are very disparate from Western ones. This major difference, I think, engenders much of the fear and misunderstanding about Asians. Another important factor is that much of Asian culture and society is based on the value of collectivism, which in recent years has been associated with Communism. Such ideas go against the familiar values and traditions of individualism and capitalism that are so basic to American culture and thus threaten many Americans.

The history and treatment of Asians in the United States have caused them to be very closed in terms of their interactions with other Americans. Asians have generally kept to themselves in very small enclaves. For instance, to this day, there are Chinatowns in most large urban areas, which from early times served as ghettos that ensured survival in the economic and political structure of the United States. Another trait Asians generally possess is a tendency to be less overtly militant and politically active than other racial groups. As a result, they have been an easy and frequent target for abuse and discrimination. Although, it should be acknowledged that Asians have historically made significant challenges to the status quo through equity legislation; this has primarily been through the judicial system. Generally, Asians have been less likely than other ethnic groups to engage in activism toward redress of public policy. Characteristically, this is very reflective of the Asian attitude of not wanting to disturb things. There's a saying among the Chinese: "If you don't know what to do, at least don't do anything." This is very different from the American maxim: "If you don't know what to do, at least do something." This tendency is probably also related to the cultural norm of not showing certain emotions in public. It is very important in many Asian cultures that certain social protocols are followed and that one conforms to the cultural script of not displaying emotions in public.

Recent research findings show that Asians, as a collective group, are more accepted in America than other ethnic minorities. This too seems to be culturally based, with Asians generally perceived as less threatening to the status quo or dominant culture. The Chinese, for example, have survived in America by not having competed economically with whites. Historically, they have always offered services that were lacking. For instance, when the Chinese were first brought to California, it was to provide services typically offered by women. California society at that time was predominantly male. Pioneer men had crossed the flatlands and over the Rockies looking for land and gold. Their womenfolk had, in general, remained behind. So, when the Chinese came to America, they took on what at that time was considered women's work. They cooked, cleaned, and did laundry for these pioneers. The Chinese also provided valuable labor for the expanding railway and picked grapes for the wine industry. These were services that were needed and desired by the dominant culture but were not in direct competition with those offered by whites. This tendency has generally held true to this day. Thus, in America, Asians have taken jobs that other Americans have just not wanted, especially those which are tedious and long in hours. Even now, many corner stores and restaurants are owned by Koreans, Chinese, and Japanese. These businesses involve excessive work and meager wages but offer a means of developing marketable skills and services without displacing and incurring the wrath of others in the economy.

Question: Could you next talk about the various names that Asian-American subgroups use to describe and identify themselves as well as protocols in addressing various individuals within Asian culture?

Hocoy: Again, I can speak most confidently about the Chinese. In terms of racial self-labeling, I think most Chinese regard themselves as Chinese, Chinese American, or just American. The name or self-reference that one uses is a useful source of information. Clinically, by asking clients what they consider themselves or what they would like to be called, you can get a sense of where they fall in terms of acculturation; namely, assimilation, integration, marginalization, or separation. If they identify themselves as Chinese, this says something very different about their cultural attachment, as opposed to referring to themselves as American. An integrationist would be more likely to say, "I'm Chinese American," whereas a separationist is more likely to self-label as Chinese. An assimilationist would typically use the term *American*, while someone marginalized would probably have difficulty identifying with any of these labels. It is thus quite useful for a provider to ask this question early on and to use it as an entree into these issues.

Personal names also vary somewhat from person to person. More recent immigrants and more traditional individuals use their Chinese name as their legal name. You have the person's family name, preceded by their Chinese first

name. Both would be phonetically translated into English for purposes of pro-
nunciation. Again, this kind of information is suggestive of a person's cultural
background and degree to which they had been acculturated. On the other hand,
a fifth-generation Chinese-American family would probably have an Anglicized
or transliterated family name, with a Christian first name in addition to a more
familiar Chinese first name that is used only in the home. This is my experience.
I was given a Chinese first name at birth, which is known to and used only by
family members. The Chinese practice of naming is similar to the Native tradition.
A person is named according to their character at birth, and it is believed that this
quality will define them throughout life. My Chinese name is Siao Kee, which
translates into "small wonder" to reflect my early curiosity about the world. Many
Asians are also given a European name for the sake of convenience in interacting
with the non-Asian world.

There are other aspects of naming that are important to know. Within Asian
cultures, great honor is given to authority and age, and this is manifest in a general
respect for people who are older than you. So, if there is someone in the room of
similar age or older than the therapist, it is important to address them formally and
with deference, as Mr. or Ms. or whatever is appropriate. If there were several people
present, the therapist should address the older person first. Conversely, an Asian
client may feel uncomfortable calling a therapist, especially an older one, anything
other than "Doctor," even if invited to do so. I, for instance, didn't call my supervisor
by his first name until the sixth year of graduate school, when I was about to defend
my dissertation. I didn't feel comfortable referring to him in such a familiar manner
until I was of similar academic status. It is also important to be aware that older
Asian clients, as a result of their traditional Asian worldview, expect to be treated
with a great deal of tolerance and patience by the therapist. Asian culture dictates
that elders be treated with an obvious tone of respect and deference, and such an
attitude is a necessity for facilitating rapport with older clients.

Question: These sound like some very useful and important suggestions. Let's
go back to a topic you alluded to earlier—the history of Asians in the United
States. Could you give a nutshell version of this history?

Hocoy: Of the Asians, the Chinese were the first immigrants in the United
States. Unlike other people of color who were either brought here forcibly,
such as African Americans, or already here and physically displaced, such as
Native Americans and some Latinos/as, they came voluntarily, as did the other
Asians. The history of Chinese in the United States dates back to the 1840s.
Many Chinese-American families have roots in California that go back many
generations to the time of the Gold Rush. They came mainly for a better life and
to escape harsh economic circumstances and a variety of social problems in their

native lands. Again, the early presence of Chinese made up for a lack of people willing to do what was considered women's work in California. They found work in areas which were sanctioned by the dominant culture. From these vocations came the core of the stereotypes of the Chinese laundry, the Chinese restaurant, hiring a Chinese cook, and so forth. They also were instrumental in building a national railroad system through both the United States and Canada. As I said, the Chinese were willing to take the jobs most Americans would not do. They were usually very dirty or involved high risk. There is a saying "not having a Chinaman's chance," which comes from this period. In the building of railroads, it was often necessary to dynamite the sides of a mountain. Chinese workers would be sent to set the dynamite, and often, it would go off prematurely or the mountain would collapse on them. Many Chinese died this way, and as a result, the phrase "a Chinaman's chance" was coined. I have also heard the phrase used to describe the already-exhausted mine areas, which were the only sites in which the Chinese were allowed to look for gold during the Rush.

There is a long history of racial discrimination against Asians in both legislation and public policy. In 1882, Congress passed the Chinese Exclusion Act, which prohibited Chinese immigration for ten years. It was renewed in 1892 and became permanent law in 1902. This resulted in great difficulties for the Chinese men already here. They were forbidden to bring their wives over, but what they could do was go back and father children, and these offspring were allowed to enter. The result was a very lonely existence: a culture of lonely, hardworking men, isolated from the dominant culture, who kept largely to themselves and lived lives of great hardship and misery. By 1943, immigration restrictions were loosened, and women were allowed to enter. They worked as dressmakers and in sweatshops in the growing Chinatowns, while men opened laundries and restaurants and, as had become typical, took jobs that were of interest to no one else.

And then there are the more recent reminders of discrimination against Asian Americans in the United States: the internment of Japanese during World War II; reactions to the influx of Southeast Asian refugees; reactions to Asian economic success in the United States; reactions to the emergence of Japan and the other "four tigers" as global economic forces; and in the 1990s, talk of quotas limiting the enrollment of Asian-American students in U.S. colleges, universities, and specialized professional programs.

There is anti-Asian sentiment intertwined throughout the history of this country, permeating all aspects of U.S. society—some more subtle than others. For instance, with the growing interest in Asian martial arts in the late 1960s, American television producers conceived of a storyline about a Chinese Shaolin priest set in the Old West. Chinese martial arts expert and actor, Bruce Lee, was initially chosen for the role of Cain in the television series *Kung Fu*. When the show was pilot-tested, the white audience felt quite strongly that Lee was just too Chinese for the part. A white actor, David Carradine, was chosen instead. Bruce Lee was a hero to many Asians in North America at the time, myself included. One can only imagine the racial affirmation that Lee could have provided for Asians if he had been chosen for the TV series.

Question: Let's change our focus somewhat and begin to look at issues related to help-seeking and treatment. First, could you talk about issues that influence the ways in which Asian Americans go about seeking help?

Hocoy: In general, we are talking about very closed and tightly knit communities. They are very insular and cohesive and distrustful of outsiders. Their survival has depended on it being this way. These enclaves or ghettos—the Koreatowns, Chinatowns, Japantowns—have learned to live on the fringes and construct for themselves self-sufficient alternative social and economic systems outside the dominant culture. As a result of this mentality, Asians can be very distrustful of white people. The Chinese call whites "ghost people" and consider their ways of life to be strange and sometimes inferior. There is clearly a sense of arrogance here. Both Japanese and Chinese mythologies contain beliefs that view themselves as highly advanced in terms of human evolution. My grandmother described it to me as there being a racial hierarchy according to color. White people reside below the Chinese because they are "pasty and ill looking" in appearance, whereas the Chinese have a touch of gold in their skin. Another example comes from the name China itself, which literally means Middle Kingdom; the early Chinese were pompous enough to believe that the world revolved around them. The Chinese do bring with them a rich cultural tradition outside of the United States and a long history of inventing everything from gunpowder to eyeglasses, from ice cream to the printing press. When these events were playing themselves out in the East, Europeans were still barbarians. This history engenders much pride among Chinese as well as arrogance and serves to support and justify their isolation.

In times of need, Asian Americans are more likely to turn to their immediate and extended family for assistance rather than to an outsider. There are, however, exceptions, like the family doctor, who may not be Chinese but who is someone the family has known for years and has learned to trust. With regard to psychological problems, Asian families may just live with the problem, preferring to work it out themselves rather than going outside for help. Psychological counseling, as a profession, is clearly not an integral part of Asian culture. So, if a client is Asian American, the therapist may have to initially describe and explain the purpose of therapy, the role of the counselor and client, and so on. It should not be assumed that the client understands the nature of therapy. Therapy is a foreign concept in Asian culture. Meditation and self-reflection are traditional ways to self-knowledge, while the writings and sayings of Confucius, Lao Tse, and other philosophers act as guides for human behavior. In addition, one finds extensive informal networks of support within the family and community which provide counseling and advice.

Another thing to be aware of regarding help-seeking is the fact that there may be a great degree of shame and stigma associated with someone leaving the community and seeking professional help. The airing and telling of private affairs to strangers are virtually unheard of; it is a concept foreign to the Asian worldview. Part of this has to do with a fear of not being understood culturally by Western counselors. So, building rapport is an important first step to therapy. It is important for therapists to convey—both explicitly and implicitly—a knowledge of Asian culture or at least a respect for it and an openness to learning more. It is also helpful to understand that given this general taboo, those who do seek out therapy are either very acculturated or desperate and have probably exhausted what resources they had within the culture and feel compelled to go outside.

Question: The discussion of help-seeking has led naturally to aspects of the Asian family and community. Could you talk more about family and community and how these shape what happens in therapy with an Asian American client?

Hocoy: To understand Asian culture, it's important to grasp the philosophical traditions and religious influences on the culture. One needs, for instance, to understand the role of Confucian ethics and the Buddhist "middle path" of moderation in life. Asians, in general, come from strong, interdependent family and community bonds; both are very self-contained and self-sufficient. Chinatown, for example, is a microcosm of the greater society in that it contains everything that is needed for life and sustenance. In terms of the family, an important value is the obedience of children. The flip side is respect for elders and their wisdom. These are Confucian values. In the home, there are many token gestures manifesting these attitudes. For instance, in my own family, my grandmother would always sit at the head of the table, even though she was demented in her later years. If there was a big decision to be made, her opinion would always be sought. It was obviously a token gesture, but what was more important was that it was a sign of respect. It's considered taboo to send relatives off to old-age homes once they get old, as is common among Anglo Americans. Doing so is almost unheard of and looked upon with disdain in Asian cultures.

Asian culture is heavily based on interdependence; thus, dependence is not necessarily regarded as a bad thing as it is in Western culture, which places prime value on independence. This interdependence is reflected in the Asian attitude toward family relationships. It is understood that children will be dependent upon their parents for caretaking and that these same parents will eventually become dependent upon their adult children in old age. Since the therapeutic situation is a relationship, this value will likely manifest itself in therapy in terms of the client's dependence on the therapist and in terms of the client's goals for life and treatment. It is particularly important to realize that these priorities may not have to do with achieving relational independence.

Much communication in the Asian family is indirect, wherein messages are not directly stated but instead must be inferred. There's a reticence to talk about personal issues openly. I think the fear is that someone may be embarrassed by what is said. In my own family, certain things are understood. For example, my mother says something without referring directly to it, but everyone knows what she's referring to. The therapist may see some of this reticence in therapy, especially in regard to subjects that are taboo or that the client finds sensitive. Sex might be such a topic.

The therapist may not initially get a very explicit account of the problem. Much may be implied, and clinicians must be attuned to subtle meanings and innuendoes. This is especially true with clients who are less acculturated. Again, this indirectness has to do with avoiding embarrassment. Clinicians need to be tactful and equally subtle in identifying the client's problems, being careful to validate the client's experiences, avoiding judgment or confrontation, and gradually honing in on the problem. In treatment, it may initially come down to talking in metaphors and indirectly about a topic in order to make the client feel comfortable enough to name and address it directly. This cultural tendency to imply meaning rather than to speak of it explicitly is very foreign to most Western therapists and counselors, whose training has focused on the spoken word and direct verbal communication. The therapist needs to recognize this difference as a cultural artifact rather than be frustrated by it.

Another Asian value that may result in different therapeutic goals for clients is tolerance for ambiguity and inconsistency in life. In Western psychotherapy, psychological integration is promoted through the achievement of clarity about one's life, consistency in various aspects of one's life, and the resulting decrease of cognitive dissonance. Among Asians, however, the ability to tolerate the ambiguities and contradictions in one's life is considered an aspect of maturity. Thus, striving for complete consistency in or understanding of one's life may not be considered as important nor a goal of therapy. In general, it is essential for Western counselors to realize that the paradigms and models upon which Western psychology is based are infused with Euro-American middle-class values and may have little application to other cultural groups.

A sense of balance and reciprocity is also very important in Asian cultures. Because the family is such a cohesive unit, individuals are brought up to think of family over self. This basic aspect of the Asian worldview is diametrically opposed to the Western emphasis on self-realization. For instance, research has shown that the concept of "self-esteem" does not exist in Japanese culture. This value difference between the two cultures often becomes a major problem for young Asian Americans who become caught in a conflict of values between generations. The older generation demands obedience and respect; the younger one has been more socialized to the American values of independence and individualism. The result is a conflict of cultures and the need for reconciling two very disparate cultural views and sorting out the confusion as to how to live in both worlds.

Another aspect of therapy with Asians relates to the tendency of Asian cultures to de-emphasize the self and a prescription against self-promotion. For instance, one is not supposed to accept a compliment without resistance. If I compliment my mother on her cooking and the preparation of a certain dish, she would never acknowledge that it was deserved. She would probably say instead: "Oh, no. There's not enough salt, and this is actually the worst I've ever made." The implication of this for the clinical setting is that affirmation of the client's self, which goes against cultural norms, may be difficult for him or her to model. A corollary to the lack of emphasis on the self is the avoidance of personal embarrassment. Consequently, direct confrontations and demands on the client to accept personal responsibility for personal difficulties or specific behavior may be problematic for the therapeutic relationship.

Question: What are some of the common problems that might bring Asian Americans into treatment?

Hocoy: Again, I want to emphasize the fact that many Asians in the United States today still retain traditional norms and values; most of the Asian population in America are immigrants. So, only a limited segment of the Asian American community will ever find their way into a therapist's office. Those who do are generally more acculturated and bicultural, often students, as well as those who are particularly desperate for help and have not been able to find it in the family or community. For students, intergenerational and cultural differences are commonly a source of difficulty. Young people who have grown up with Western norms often find themselves at odds with parents who have very different values and expectations of them. One such issue revolves around strong parental pressures on the young person to excel. This can become especially problematic when the parents of their non-Asian peers are saying to their children: "Just relax. Do what you want." In traditional Asian homes, discipline is strongly emphasized, as is the demand to be successful academically and otherwise. One symptom that may emerge is depression, resulting from feelings of failure and inadequacy, engendered by internalized, unrealistic family expectations. Also common is a conflict between independent needs and loyalty to family. Excessive guilt can also result from not completely conforming to family demands, as obedience to parents and loyalty are cardinal Confucian rules. In general, holding Western values as offspring of traditional Asian parents is inherently problematic.

A related problem has to do with identity confusion resulting from minority status and the impact of discrimination on personality development. Some young people have a hard time identifying with their Asian heritage because this identity is often disparaged in their non-Asian peer group. Strong pressures to assimilate to Western ways are also likely to be communicated, either explicitly or implicitly. A client might experience "a tyranny of shoulds," pulling in opposite directions. They should be doing this according to the peer group; they should be doing that according to their family. In addition, people may not possess a strong sense of themselves, of who they are, or of what they really want to do. Instead, they may feel caught between two worlds: one side saying, "You should be studying or practicing violin; you shouldn't be going out drinking"; and the other countering, "No, no, man. Come on out; you should be getting stoned and having lots of sex in college." It's a very difficult thing to bridge these different worlds. Feelings of being different because of one's ethnicity and not completely fitting in are often accompanied by feelings of alienation and loneliness as well as those of being misunderstood. It is a short psychological step from feeling different to feeling inferior—that there's something wrong with me; that I'm not worthy of love. And there's the depression that comes from wanting to be someone I'm not and will never be.

Many of these characteristics are subsumed in the literature under the title "mismatch syndrome," which speaks to the disparity in values between one's culture of origin and the dominant culture. Common symptoms of this mismatch are self-rejection and low self-esteem, depression, an emphasis on negativity, rigidity in thinking and problem solving, and even attempts to escape reality via addiction and suicide. Also inherent in the mismatch syndrome is active value conflict: traditional vs. modern gender role definition, an emphasis on family and community vs. self-interest, age status vs. youth emphasis, obedience and conformity vs. questioning authority and individualism. Self-restraint and formality may lead to a lack of social experience. People brought up in a culture that suppresses the open sharing of emotions may find themselves alienated and unable to make contact with their non-Asian peers, who depend on sharing emotions in order to move toward intimacy. Lack of emotional expression can also lead to the somatization of various ills. Insomnia is a particularly common way in which such problems are manifest.

Other typical problems for which Asian Americans may seek help include compulsive gambling, cross-cultural dating and marriage, overbearing parents, caring for aged parents and other family members, immigrant poverty, extreme work ethics, racial identity issues, and post-traumatic stress in those escaping war-torn countries of origin.

Question: In carrying out an assessment of a new Asian American client, what factors do you think are most important to attend to?

Hocoy: In working with Asian Americans, the first thing I would assess is where a client stands on the continuum of acculturation. It is useful to think of four modes of acculturation. *Integration* implies that the person equally embraces ethnic as well as dominant culture. An *assimilationist* tends to neglect his or her own culture in favor of fully adopting the ways of the dominant society. A *separatist* chooses to maintain ethnic ties and traditions—at the same time refusing to take on Western values/culture. Those who are *marginalized* are caught between cultures, unable to identify as Asian, yet at the same time uncomfortable in the Anglo world. It's vital to make an assessment of where each client stands in relation to these four possibilities and to then identify the social demands that are impinging on them. In my own work, I tend to promote and encourage the integration mode. Research strongly indicates that integration—or *biculturalism*, as it is sometimes called—brings with it the greatest likelihood of psychological well-being, with maximum flexibility, integration, and wholeness. Assimilation, with its rejection of cultural roots, is likely to bring up problems related to self-denial. Separation brings with it difficulties in navigating the dominant culture and can lead to isolation. Marginalization results in a lack of connection to any group and the possibility of serious mental health problems.

Equally important is assessing the nature of current demands upon the client, particularly from family. There may be serious difficulties both in the situation where (a) a family tends toward separation and is putting substantial pressure on one of its members to be more Asian, while the member has chosen a more assimilationist direction, and (b) a client wants to remain traditionally Asian and must function in an environment that demands conformity to mainstream values. It is the disparity between where a person chooses to be on the continuum and what the environment demands of them that is critical.

Other dimensions that I would assess include language dominance, degree of adaptive behavior, degree of identification with cultural heritage, attitudes toward that heritage and themselves (self-esteem), life history (particularly with regard to events of intercultural significance, like racism), and attitudes toward the dominant culture.

Question: You talked earlier about cultural differences and therapeutic style. What other suggestions might you have regarding establishing rapport and working therapeutically with Asian Americans?

Hocoy: I think something that is essential for non-Asian counselors to do prior to working with an Asian client is a thorough self-assessment of their own competence to work with this cultural group. They must possess sufficient understanding and knowledge about the culture as well as an awareness of what they are bringing to the therapeutic relationship—namely, the assumptions and values of Western psychotherapy, their own worldview, and personal experiences with biases and attitudes toward Asians. This is a critical first step.

As alluded to earlier, it may help to remember that the concept of counseling is foreign to traditional Asians. It's the counselor's responsibility to introduce them to the roles of the counselor and client and explain the process of therapy before any kind of rapport can be established. Counselors have to be perceived as knowledgeable about that client's cultural group right off. That's particularly important for Asians because they may be apprehensive about therapy. Fear of shame and distrust of non-Asians act as potential obstacles to building rapport. Thus, it is critical that the therapist demonstrates clearly that he or she respects and understands the cultural differences that exist and that these differences are not obstacles. At the same time, therapists must be very careful of stereotyping and of recognizing the kind of expectations they hold about Asian clients.

When treating Asian clients, it may be important for Western therapists to be more directive than they normally are with non-Asian clients and to be prepared when an Asian client exhibits what might be considered more than normal dependency in the therapeutic relationship. Western conceptions of psychological health emphasize client responsibility, openness, and personal exploration as well as self-reliance and self-determination in the therapeutic process. Clinical research, however, has found Asians to prefer a more directed and authoritative therapeutic style and to expect a certain degree of caretaking and direction. It is also important for the therapist to be nurturing and to have the therapeutic interaction reflect a familiar family atmosphere: directive regarding instructions, deferential to authority, but also nurturing.

For Asian Americans, few emotions are allowed and there is generally difficulty with public displays of feelings. Emotionally laden content may not be easily discussed or easily identified by the therapist. The therapist must realize that there may be substantial difficulty with trusting and establishing rapport, given the taboos related to going to non-Asians for help and expressing emotions in public. Similarly, interventions should reflect or be consistent with Asian norms. The alternatives offered should be equally subtle, indirect, and nonconfrontational. There's a risk of Asian clients dropping out early, so it's especially important to build rapport and trust and to intuit any problems and check them out early on. As the client can be rather nonverbal, the therapist may have to ask if there are problems or identify them rather than waiting for them to be reported.

Asians also tend to have a very different nonverbal communication system. Providers need to be aware of this because unlike the Western therapeutic focus on speaking, much of the communication in Asian cultures is nonverbal.

The meanings of facial expressions, gestures, eye contact, and various cultural symbols or metaphors are usually completely different from Western ones. Research has found Asians to be a "low-contact" culture; that is, more comfortable with little physical contact and larger interpersonal distances. Studies also indicate that clients from various cultural backgrounds feel most comfortable with therapists that show similar non-verbal behavior. This mirroring of the client's non-verbal communication happens on three levels: *proxemics*, which refers to physical distance and touch; *kinesics*, which refers to body and facial movement, gestures, and eye contact; and *paralinguistics*, which refers to the extra-verbal elements of speech, such as rate, tone, pauses, and so forth. It is absolutely essential that therapists pay special attention to the non-verbal dimension of therapy. Research has shown that appropriate non-verbal behavior conveys respect, honesty, interest, and genuineness.

With Asian Americans, the therapist may notice very subtle body gesturing and facial expressions. Large displays of emotion will rarely be seen, even if much is being felt and experienced. In many cultures, emotional states are rather transparent, easily read in the faces and body language of clients. With Asians (traditionally socialized), non-verbal communication is much more subtle. Sometimes, all one can discern is a very slight head nod as a sign of affirmation if a question is asked. There may also be a general reticence. Asians are brought up to be indirect and to avoid emotional expressiveness. You probably won't see much gregariousness or strong displays of emotion. Also, as suggested above, non-verbal cues may have different meanings than for non-Asians. For instance, giggling often means embarrassment rather than a sign of humor. This is particularly true for the Japanese. Irrespective of the particular message, it is vital not to assume a commonality between Asian and Western "non-verbals."

The therapist should not challenge or confront avoidance or resistance immediately or in any way single out the client for what might be experienced as criticism. One may eventually be able to address relevant issues through more indirect communication. It is, however, important to lead with regard to the direction of therapy and spell out expectations the clinician has of the client. This is different than being confrontational, which is likely to induce shame and guilt. Again, it's related to "saving face." The therapist can subtly bring up deficits and shortcomings in the person—but not directly. Asians do tend to be familiar with very direct advice giving—but as to how or where they might go or what they might do as opposed to direct commentary on their personality, faults, or shortcomings.

For example, if the therapist wants to tell the client the reason he or she doesn't have a very active social life is because of excessive negativity, it must be stated in a way that the Asian client can hear. With Westerners, a therapist can generally be more direct: "I've noticed something and want to give you feedback on it: It seems you're very critical of other people." With an Asian client, it is preferable to be more subtle. For example, the therapist might gently ask, "Do you think there is anything you contribute to the fact that your social life is not so good?" When the concern involves aspects of the client's personality or interpersonal style, it might be shameful, so it's important to be more subtle, indirect, implicit about it. At the same time, Asians tend to be quicker to listen to implicit messages than non-Asians. That's because of Asian cultural emphases on subtleties in meaning.

Finally, it is important to remember that Asian Americans often experience a sense of guilt or selfishness in pursuing their own interests in therapy as opposed to thinking of the family first. The whole act or exercise of going to therapy is an individualistic pursuit. A client may feel some guilt around it. There is also a sense of collective embarrassment to have to go outside the community. It is a capitulation saying, "My community cannot serve me." It may, in addition, be considered a sign of weakness to go outside the community. These are all issues Asian clients might bring with them to therapy.

Question: Finally, could you share with us a case that shows how these various themes that you have defined all come together?

Hocoy: When I worked as a university counselor, I'd very often work with Asian students feeling a lot of pressure to excel in school and having difficulty living in two cultures. Terrence is a good example. He was an engineering student who came to counseling because he was getting Bs, and there was a strong demand both from his family and from himself to get better—and even perfect—grades. Terrence revealed other difficulties as well. Because he focused almost exclusively on academics, he had developed few social skills and didn't have many friends. During his second year of university, these various factors came together to cause a depression. He found it difficult to concentrate in school and was increasingly losing interest because he was coming to the realization that there was more to life than just school. When his marks deteriorated, pressures from home increased. At the same time, he had difficulty forming the friendships he desired with non-Asians (his primary peer group).

It was obvious from his presentation that he wasn't clear what therapy was about. Nor was Terrence very psychologically-minded. He had a low awareness of his own emotions and had difficulty identifying them. He experienced an amorphous bundle of vague, uncomfortable feelings, and he couldn't dissect, label, or identify their source. He initially came in because of slumping marks, saying that he wanted to be able to get As and that he had problems with concentration. Through joint exploration, we discovered that he wanted to partake in more extracurricular activities. He also wanted to establish relationships with his non-Asian peers and had a romantic interest in a particular young woman (who was non-Asian). However, he knew his parents would not approve of his having a non-Asian girlfriend, nor the time he spent away from studying. It was the family's position that school was a time for study and that relationships and hobbies could come afterwards.

It became clear very early that much of his conflict was cultural in nature. He was caught between two worlds: unable to negotiate socially and establish relationships with non-Asians and, at the same time, unable to motivate himself to focus on his schoolwork. He also questioned the expectation that he had to date another Asian. Ultimately, what was at conflict were Asian values regarding the paramount importance of study and maintaining Asian cultural separation vs. the value of making friendships with non-Asian peers and spending more time in nonacademic pursuits. He did not feel a part of his non-Asian peers and was increasingly feeling unaccepted by his family because of his "failing" grades. In short, he was increasingly becoming marginalized.

We spent the initial sessions helping him discern his emotions; often, I had to make suggestions as to what he might be feeling. With time and effort, a bit more clarity emerged in what he was feeling. He had great difficulty separating his feelings from those of other people, whether it be his peers or his parents. His emotional boundaries were very blurred—not uncommon in individuals from collectivist cultures. He was eventually able to report feeling pressured by his family to pursue good grades at the expense of social activities and to date and marry someone Asian. These were accompanied by simultaneous feelings of guilt and resentment. He was eventually able to understand that he had internalized the pressure his family had placed on him vis-à-vis academic performance and began to sense that there could be a difference between the demands his family placed on him and what he wanted for himself. It became clearer to him why his studying had become difficult and why he was internally caught between the values of two cultures. He also came to recognize the disparity between the Asian values of academic success and cultural isolation and his desire for relationships with those in the dominant culture and activities outside of school.

I encouraged him to pursue an integrationist path—one that allowed him to maintain his cultural traditions and, at the same time, establish relations outside the Asian community. By this point, he had developed clarity that this is what he wanted to do but felt uncertain as to how to proceed.

I assured him that he could participate in the non-Asian world without compromising his heritage and that, in fact, he could have the best of both worlds. The issue with his parents actually worked itself out as his marks improved because he was able for the first time to pursue the things he wanted to do, including spending more time enjoying himself and establishing friendships with non-Asians.

SUMMARY

Dan Hocoy, a clinical psychologist and professor, was the interviewee for this chapter. His research focuses on the effects of apartheid and racism on black mental health in South Africa and he is core faculty of the psychology department of the Pacific Graduate Institute, Carpinteria, California. This interview contained several areas of importance regarding racial identity. Dr. Hocoy addressed definitions of Asian American culture, paying specific attention to subgroup names and protocols to identify various individuals in Asian culture. A highlight of this chapter is Dr. Hocoy's explanation of Asian American's migrating to the United States mainly for a better life. Another important aspect of Dr. Hocoy's interview is the shared example of a case which shows how Dr. Hocoy works with individuals.

ACTIVITY

Having read Dr. Hocoy's case example using Terrence, briefly describe how you felt about the direction Dr. Hocoy and Terrence's session went and explained how you might have acted differently or similarly.

KEY TERMS

"Asian" category, 337   "Pacific Islander" category, 337   "model minority," 338

15

Working with Arab and Muslim American Clients: An Interview with Marwan Dwairy

LEARNING OBJECTIVES

15-1 Interpret the implications of census data for Arab and Muslim Americans in America.

15-2 Explain the family and cultural values of Arab and Muslims.

15-3 Examine Dr. Dwairy's experience as a Palestinian-Arab psychologist, educator, and scholar.

▶ Demographics `15-1`

This chapter expands on the information provided in Chapter 5 regarding collective personalities of Arab and Muslim individuals and families. In the decade following 9/11, and stimulated by the attacks, U.S. involvement in wars in Iraq and Afghanistan, growing fears of terrorism, and longstanding prejudices against Arab and Muslim Americans quickly escalated into significant rates of racial hatred and hate crimes. The Arab American Anti-Discrimination Committee, for example, reported 700 violent acts against Arab Americans during the two months following 9/11. According to Bonnie and Hasan (2004), 53 percent of the Arab/Muslims they sampled reported incidents of discrimination, 47 percent having been the object of racism, and 46 percent having been called racist names. Such experiences weigh heavy on the psyche of Arab and/or Muslim Americans and represent, as we have seen throughout this text, real threats to mental health and well-being. These events represent the latest in a long history of evolving dynamics and changing identities within the Arab and/or Muslim communities in the United States. The first wave of Arab immigrants arrived between 1890 and 1920, and they were primarily Christian. They came from the area that is now Syria and Lebanon, primarily for economic reasons, and assimilated easily into American culture. According to Abudabbeh (1996), the second wave had very different characteristics:

> They were dominated by Palestinians, Egyptians, Syrians, and Iraqis, arrived with an "Arab identity" that was absent in the first wave of immigrants. With this crystallization of an Arab identity came also the practice of traditions and customs that affected either a hyphenated identity as "Arab Americans" or sometimes alienation from the majority of society. By the 1970s, the trend of easy assimilation began to change into a cultural separateness built on political ideology centered on the Arab-Israeli conflict and based on rejecting Western norms and customs. (p. 335)

A final peak of immigration occurred after the 1967 war between Israel and the Arab world and diminished dramatically after September 11, 2001. The last group to arrive in any significant numbers was Iraqis, escaping first from the Iraq-Iran War and then a decade later from the first Gulf War. This population exhibited particularly high levels of mental health problems and trauma. The tightening of immigration laws and legal statuses post-9/11—and again after the Gulf Wars—has made travel between the United States and their home countries impossible and has caused much distress for many Arab and/or Muslim families. The history of Arab and/or Muslims in America is especially complex because it reflects the ever-changing landscapes in relation to what is happening in both America and the Middle East. For example, as Abu-Baker (2006) points out, "differences in the ethnic and political conscience of each wave of immigrants reflects the change in the geopolitical map of the Arab World" (p. 33).

Similarly, as you shall learn from our interview with Marwan Dwairy, Arab and/or Muslim families often find themselves struggling with challenges of assimilation to their native, collective family patterns.

The 2010 U.S. Census data estimates 3.5 million Arab Americans: 80 percent are U.S. citizens while 37 percent are foreign-born. This population is about equally distributed between Christians and Muslims and emigrated primarily from the Middle East. As a collective, they share the Arabic language and descend from nomadic tribes from the Arabian Peninsula. Muslim Americans number 8.5 million, come from over 75 countries, and vary widely as to language, ethnicity, and national origin. In general, the combined Arab and/or Muslim American populations are younger (30 percent below 18 years old), more highly educated (40 percent have earned bachelor degrees), and earn more (over $50,000 yearly) than the average American. The vast majority resides in major cities (such as New York, Detroit, and Los Angeles) and is concentrated in 11 U.S. states.

Abu-Baker (2006) enumerates a number of difficulties and demands that Arab and/or Muslims regularly face in their adaptation to life in the United States. These include:

▶ Expectations that already settled immigrants will help bring over and settle relatives and friends
▶ Difficulties related to failing to develop language proficiency in English
▶ Problems of living in a non-Islamic country where religious requirements often clash with "the rhythm of American daily life"
▶ Work difficulties where individuals cannot find jobs in their professions, a resulting lessening of social status, and difficulties related to having to work in family businesses
▶ Differences in social interaction patterns between the collective and interdependent nature of Arab societies and families and the more individualistic values and interactive styles of mainstream America
▶ Increased tensions between spouses, tensions created by inhibitions on interfaith and intercultural relationships and marriages, and conflicts between parents and children over changing behaviors, values, and parenting practices

▶ Family and Cultural Values   15-2

As stated earlier, Arab Americans identify and practice in about equal numbers as Muslims and Christians. Abudabbeh (1996) offers the following overview of Islam:

> The essence of Islam, as preached by the Prophet Mohammed, was transmitted through the Qur'an, which is believed to be the literal word of God. In addition to the Qur'an, the laws of society were elaborated upon by adding the Prophet's own traditional sayings (*hadith*) and his practices (*sunna*). A

fourth dimension was also added, taking into account certain pre-Islamic traditions and also integrating other existing societal norms and customs. Except by implication, the Qur'an does not contain explicit doctrines or instructions; basically, it provides guidance. The *hadith* and *sunna*, however, contain some specific commands on issues such as marriage and the division of property. They also address daily habits as to how the believer should worship God and how all people should treat each other. (pp. 335–336)

There are five basic tenets, called the "Pillars of Islam," that define religious belief: *shahada* (oral testimony that "There is no God but Allah, and Mohammad is His prophet"); *Salah* (ritual prayer performed five times a day); *Diyam* (fasting during the holy month of Ramadan); *Zakah* (the giving of alms to the poor); and *haj* (pilgrimage to Mecca once in a lifetime). An additional prescription, **Jihad**, also exists. Although it has been often translated as "making war against the infidel," it is more broadly understood as the universal precept to be strong in one's efforts—intellectual, physical, spiritual—for the good of all. Dwairy (2006) adds the following distinction between religion and politics:

> Antagonism and hostility to the West is divorced from any true Islamic fundamental belief. On the contrary, Islam is very clear about the need to accept and respect other monotheistic religions, such as Christianity and Judaism. There are many verses in the Qur'an and in the Hadith that preach the advantages of diversity and the value of tolerance between nations. Extreme fundamentalist Muslim groups employ different interpretations of Islam (other than Qur'an or Sunna) to inflame antagonism against the West, an antagonism which had its roots in Western imperialism and unconditional support of the Israeli occupation, rather than in religious difference. (p. 17)

Although it is estimated that there are 14 million Arab Christians worldwide, they represent half the Arab population in the United States. The original split of Christianity into Eastern and Western branches occurred in the fifth century over the basic theological question of whether Christ was "spirit and body" or of "a single nature," which is referred to as "Monophyte." Middle-Eastern Christians, including Arabs, belonged to the Monophyte tradition, which in turn broke into various Eastern Orthodox ethnic sects. Most Christian Arabs merged into the American church system, at first especially Roman Catholic and Greek and Russian Eastern Orthodox, but today, very few ethnic Eastern parishes still exist.

Politically and culturally, Arab Christians identify very strongly with their Muslim brothers and sisters. They have also been in the forefront of Arab/Muslim politics. They were leaders in the early Arab nationalistic movement, actively opposed the negative and stereotyping of Arabs in the United States and the West, and have provided some of its most prominent spokespeople, such as Edward Said and Hanan Ashwawi.

In turning to Arab and/or Muslim American families, we must first acknowledge what will be the central theme in Dwairy's interview: the collective nature of the Arab and/or Muslim family and psyche. Elsewhere, Dwairy (2006) has written the following about the collective aspect of Arab Muslim society:

> Individuals in a collective society are dependent for their survival on their families; and families' cohesion, economy, status, and reputation are in turn dependent on individuals' behavior and achievements. Individual choices in life are collective matters, and therefore almost all major decisions in life are determined by the collective . . . In the collective, social norms and values determine the course of people's life rather than personal decisions, and therefore diversity within such a collective is very limited. People think, feel, and behave according to prior determined standards. Within the family, it is unusual to find diverse attitudes in social, religious, or political issues. All family members adopt and voice similar attitudes. (p. 24)

The Arab family has been described as patriarchal and authoritarian, hierarchical and extended. Although families have more recently tended—especially in the West—toward the establishment of individual households, allegiance to kin still remains strong. Men, women, and children are each given duties to perform in relation to each other and specific instructions on how to carry out these responsibilities. Men and women are expected to follow specific codes of family and honor, maintain the family, and rear the children. Communication within the family tends to be vertical rather than horizontal—top-down. Parents tend to "use anger and punishment and the children respond by crying, self-censorship, covering up, or deception" (Abudabbeh, 1996). Child-rearing techniques range from mild rebukes to threats, balanced by unconditional love and appreciation. This is especially true for sons. Boys and girls are treated differently, with an eye to instilling traditional sex role expectations in both. They are expected to maintain close family ties and discouraged from individualism and separation from parents and the family. They are expected to obey the authority of the father and family, as opposed to having and acting upon their own ideas. They spend more time with and are more emotionally attached to the mother, who often acts as a go-between in communication with the father. Abudabbeh (1996) points out that this style of parenting tends to encourage acting out and triangulation within the family. Of course, in many Arab and/or Muslim American families, these traditional patterns are challenged and often adjusted after immigration and over time in the United States. As we shall learn from Dwairy, respect and awareness for the collective nature of the Arab and/or Muslim family and psyche is critical to successful therapy.

▶ Our Interviewee 15-3

Marwan Dwairy, D.Sc, received his doctorate from the Faculty of Medicine at the Technion University, Israel, in 1989. He is associate professor of psychology at Oranim Academic College, supervises three of their areas of study (educational, medical, and developmental psychology), and has also taught internationally. He is also a licensed clinical psychologist. In 1978, he established the first psychological services center for Arabs in Nazareth, Israel. Professor Dwairy carries out cross-cultural research on identity, individuation, parenting, and mental health and has developed and standardized several psychological tests for Arab populations. Finally, he has published several books, including his most recent, *Counseling and Psychotherapy with Arabs and Muslims: A Culturally Sensitive Approach* (New York: Teachers College Press, Columbia University, 2006).

The Interview

Question: Can you first talk about your own ethnic background and how it has impacted and shaped your work?

Dwairy: I am a Palestinian-Arab citizen of Israel. This is the way I like to label my complex identity. Palestinians are the Arab peoples who live in Palestine and share national and cultural bonds with the Arab nations that live in different Arab countries in North Africa and Southeast Asia. My family is part of the 15 percent of Palestinians who remained in their homeland after the establishment of the State of Israel in 1948. As such, we became Israeli citizens. Unfortunately, the vast majority of Palestinian Arabs, including many members of my extended family, fled or were expelled from their homeland and then prevented from coming back to their homes in the area that became the State of Israel. They lost their properties and still continue to live as refugees outside their homeland. After several waves of Jewish immigration to Israel, Palestinian Arabs who became citizens of Israel in 1948 now constitute about 18 percent of its population. The vast majority are Muslims, followed by Christians, such as my family, also the Druze, who were diverted from Islam. I was raised in Nazareth, the biggest Arab town in Israel, among Muslims and Christians and studied in Israeli universities with Jewish students and teachers. Not surprisingly, national and cultural affiliation was a major lens through which I identified myself and those around me. Because of the conflict over statehood, nationality also became a major aspect of identity. Add to this mix the fact that Arabic culture is more collective and authoritarian, with the family or tribe holding priority over the individual. Within this political and cultural climate, the Western psychology that I was being exposed to in my education that tended to focus on the individual and to emphasize the self and self-actualization was both enlightening and fascinating to me.

After my graduation, I established the first Arab psychological center in Israel. It was in Nazareth. The most salient experience I remember about those early days was the fact that the people I saw in Nazareth were so different from those we learned about in theories of personality, psychopathology, and psychotherapy. The self or the ego as the core of the personality was either absent or enmeshed within a collective self or identity. Adults who one expected to be emotionally independent were still very dependent on their families. When I inquired about emotional experiences during therapy, I received moral answers such as, "It should not have been that way." When I argued against the irrational "musts" that Albert Ellis saw as problematic, I realized how important and rational these "musts" were in protecting the individual from rejection and punishment. Unconditional positive regard and Rogerian nondirective therapy seemed senseless to people who came looking for direct advice. This experience was both frustrating and threatening for a psychologist like myself who was trained to believe that these were the tools I needed to understand and help people who came to me suffering from psychological problems.

During the early years of my work, I tried to "educate" the people to fit the theories I learned and believed to be universal. I gave many lectures and wrote many articles to make people understand their life and stresses according to "my" theories.

It was a period of "fighting the wind" and took many years to free myself of the illusion that the theories I learned were universal and to realize that they just did not fit these people. With this realization, I started to study and understand the psychology of people in collective cultures. And it was amazing to realize that despite the hegemony of the Western individualistic values in the media and social science, the vast majority of the people on earth live and think collectively.

I would like to make one more important point here. Unlike many Western-oriented thinkers, I do not believe that collectivism is an immature stage of social development and that society should necessarily move on to become individualistic, liberal, and democratic. I prefer to look at individualism and collectivism as two legitimate ways of living, each fitted to a different political and economical situation. When the state takes responsibility for the needs of its citizens (jobs, security, education, health, etc.) and the economic system allows the individual to be economically independent, then individualism is a reasonable alternative. But when—as in many states in Asia, Africa, and South America—governments do not take such responsibility for their citizens, the individual family or individual tribe interdependence seems crucial and necessary. Within such systems, the family or tribe, rather than the state, provide for the people's needs. One should be aware that interdependent relationships are not a barrier to social and economic progress. It is simply an alternative way of living within which economy, science, culture, and prosperity can develop, as in Japan and many Asian and South American countries.

Question: How would you define Arab- and Muslim-Americans, and what characteristics do they share? (For how this question is answered within the literature, see Chapter 5.)

Dwairy: Arabs and Muslims immigrated to the United States in different waves and all from countries that tended toward collective lifestyles where the individual is expected to live by the shared norms, values, and interests. About half the Arab immigrants are Christians and half are Muslims. All speak Arabic. Regarding ethnicity, one can identify three separate Arab groups. First, there are those who came from Syria, Iraq, Lebanon, Palestine, and Jordan. This group tends to be more educated and includes the majority of Christian-Arab immigrants in the United States. Second are those who emigrated from North Africa, especially Egypt, Libya, Algeria, Tunisia, and Morocco. They are mostly Muslims and share many African traditions. Third are peoples who came from Saudi Arabia and the Persian Gulf countries; this group is mostly Muslim, too, and tends to be wealthier. Arab immigrants tend to be highly educated in comparison to the average American born in the United States.

Muslim, non-Arab immigrants number twice the population of Arab immigrants in the United States. Ethnically, they are quite diverse. They speak languages according to their countries of origin, such as Turkey, Pakistan, Iran, and Indonesia. This population includes Africans brought to the United States as Muslim slaves and other slaves who adopted Islam at a later date. Muslim, non-Arabs vary considerably in race and ethnicity. Some are Asian (as from Indonesia and Malaysia), Indian (as from Pakistan and Afghanistan), Middle Eastern (as from Turkey and Iran), and African (as from Uganda and Kenya).

Question: What historical experiences should providers be aware of in relation to Arab and Muslim American communities and clients?

Dwairy: Arabs and Muslims have historically viewed the West with great ambivalence and through the lenses of colonization of the Arab and Muslim world. The West—historically Europe and more recently America—is seen as the colonizer of lands and resources as well as an eternal hindrance to independence and national development. At the same time, it is considered powerful— even superior—because of its association with the scientific progress and technology that is so sought after in Arab and Muslim nations. This attitude is not based solely on the past but has been powerfully reinforced by the present invasions of Afghanistan and Iraq. This perception is based on the real facts of Western hegemony and also colored by the way Arabs and Muslims tend to explain their problems. Social and national problems are mainly attributed to Western colonialism and/or hegemony, and personal or familial problems are attributed to external factors, such as social circumstances, the state, or God's will. This tendency to external attribution is also a problem in the application of Western psychology that emphasizes self-responsibility *to* Arabs and Muslims.

This historical relationship is frequently brought into the therapeutic encounter between Arab and/or Muslim clients and Western providers. It may take the shape of unconscious transference in which the client views the Western therapist as superior and powerful and at the same time as associated with the oppressor who enjoys the fruits of the colonialism without taking responsibility for the suffering it has caused. Providers need to be aware of the existence of this psychology of oppression—to understand and acknowledge it. Therapists also must make special efforts to understand the collective experience of their Arab and/or Muslim clients and to show an awareness and empathy for the differences in their worldviews. This kind of joining is crucial in establishing genuine trust with these clients. Keep in mind that for non-Western people, the experience of the personal is not differentiated from the collective. Communicating personally within the collective experience is very helpful in breaking down many barriers during therapy.

Providers also need to pay attention to issues associated with immigration and to understand and explore the conflicts around leaving one's homeland and starting a new life in a foreign country. Complex mixtures of feeling love, commitment, disappointment, anger, and guilt upon leaving as well as admiration, frustration, and anger towards the United States and one's new home are not uncommon. Transitioning from a traditional to a Western culture is also problematic, as is dealing with the daily conflicts around assimilation or differentiation accompanying one's new lifestyle. The way each immigrant deals with these conflicts is different, and clients often need help in finding the best way for them and their family.

These conflicts typically exist between members of the family. Children are eager to become assimilated and adopt American values and norms, while their parents struggle to keep them tied to tradition and religion. Husbands become more quickly adapted to American life and spend much of the day at work and away from home, while their wives are expected to remain at home, as was the case in their homeland. But here they feel lonely without the larger family and the traditional company of other women. Because of these conflicts, many emotional and behavioral problems may emerge in the family.

Question: Can you next discuss some of the factors that influence the ways that members from Arab and Muslim communities seek mental health and helping services?

Dwairy: In order to understand the help-seeking behavior of Arabs and Muslims, we need to understand that they do not adopt the same dualism of the mind and body as Westerners do. Arabs and Muslims live their life holistically; therefore, most psychological distress is accompanied by somatic complaints. Western researchers tend to conceptualize this as somatization, implying a psychological distress that is expressed somatically. I disagree with this characterization because it is based on a clear-cut distinction between psychological and somatic processes, which is not the inner experience of most Eastern people.

Arabs and Muslims are not psychologically minded; rather, they give more attention to the body as the basis for living life. One of the famous proverbs in Arabic says *ala'ql alsaleem fi aljesm alsaleem* (healthy mind depends on healthy body). Within these cultures, bodily complaints draw more attention than emotional complaints and provoke sympathy and support. Psychological complaints are not viewed as deserving attention or help. Rather, the person is expected to tolerate them. The person who cannot do so both feels ashamed by their weakness and may be looked down upon by others because of it.

Due to the centrality of physical health and shame and when facing various distresses of life, Arabs and Muslims tend to seek help first from a physician and expect to receive medications to cure their bodily complains. As a by-product, it is assumed that the mind will be cured as well. Typically, they do not seek help from mental health professionals because they do not pay much attention to emotions nor believe that talking therapy is of any value. They also avoid psychiatrists because they are believed to be associated with madness.

Many Arabs and Muslims attribute psychological disorders to external entities such as the "evil eye" or "bad soul" that possess the body. That is why madness is called *Jinnoon* in Arabic. Again, this reflects their tendency to attribute their problems to external entities and avoid taking responsibility for the unaccepted behavior, thoughts, or feelings. These same people may seek help from religious healers (*Shekhes*) in order to undo the evil eye or to exhort the *Jin*. Believing in this system of cure, many patients find relief in such superstitious practices.

Because physicians and religious healers are the first sought out by Arab and Muslim clients, there is a real need for social workers, psychologists, and psychiatrists to develop cooperative relationships with them and seek appropriate referrals. Such cooperation is needed in order to legitimize clients seeking health from mental health clinicians as well as assuring that the full range of clients' spiritual, physical, social, and psychological needs get addressed.

Question: What do providers need to understand about the nature of Arab and Muslim American families and communities?

Dwairy: The first thing to understand is that Arab and/or Muslim American families can be located along a continuum of lifestyle and value systems; that is, individualistic vs. collective values. They tend to come from collective societies that prioritize the needs of the family and familial harmony over the self-actualization of its individuals. In such family systems, individuals are directed by collective norms, values, and expectations rather than the self and its needs. Typically, Arab and/or Muslim families do not immigrate with the desire to adopt the individualistic and liberal values of the West. Rather, they immigrate because of economic or political reasons. Very few Arab and/or Muslim families come to the United States ready to assimilate into the Western style of life. Younger students who come to the States to study tend to be more open and ready to assimilate and adopt Western values. After immigration, it is more typical for families, as they become aware of American culture, to commit and hold on to their traditional culture to avoid being lost in the new society. Some even become more traditional than they had been in their homeland. Putting on a head scarf (*hijab*) for women or growing beards for men and attending prayers in the mosque is not only a commitment to religious duties, but it is also a way to conserve their identities.

It is important that providers avoid making cultural judgments about their clients' collective lifestyle. Instead, I would recommend that they make every effort to be empathic and open—to learn and understand collective personality and the psycho-cultural rationale behind it and—adopt Rogerian empathy and unconditional positive regard to the collective culture as well as to the individual. A commitment to one's collective culture can also be considered a defense or coping strategy that immigrant families adopt in order to withstand the distresses of immigration. A therapist's neglect or disregard for collective culture is experienced as neglect or disregard of the person who possesses that collective self. Many therapists wrongly hold an attitude that "we are all in the end human beings regardless of race or culture." Such a pseudo-humanistic belief not only devalues culture but also rejects the core of the self and identity that is collective among Arabs and/or Muslims.

Arab and/or Muslim American families are divided not only by cultural considerations, but also live simultaneously in two worlds: the American world and the Arab and/or Muslim world. This is particularly true among women who spend most of the time at home connected to Arab and Muslim satellite channels that bring news and TV series from their homeland. They also frequently attend Arab and/or Muslim community centers where they talk about family and social issues. Many families spend much of their financial and emotional energy in an annual trip to visit the family of origin back home. Over the year, they save money and buy gifts to show their love and success.

The inner world of each family member is divided differently. Women are more attached to the culture back home and come into communication with U.S. culture mainly as consumers. Men tend to become assimilated to the U.S. business world and worry about their wives and daughters being influenced by Western permissive life and values. Children attending public schools are motivated to assimilate into American youth culture in order to be accepted by their peers and avoid looking or acting strangely. Arab and/or Muslim families are thus divided by and struggle with all of these issues.

Question: What are some of the common problems that might bring members of your community into treatment?

Dwairy: All psychological disorders are found among Arabs and/or Muslim people, but their clinical pictures may be different from what is described in Western psychopathology texts. For instance, depression, which is considered a mood disorder in the West, may appear among Arab and/or Muslims with only somatic complaints, such as pain or fatigue, but without any major depressive mood or sadness. Many problems and psychological symptoms can be understood as the result of bicultural conflicts within the family or as a consequence of the immigration process. Psychotic symptoms often appear mixed with symptoms of dissociation, where unaccepted drives are projected on an external entity such as "voices," bad *Jin*, or thoughts placed in one's head by Satan. Because Islam calls people to pray five times a day and follow strict rituals of prayer and ablution, anxiety and OCD (obsessive-compulsive disorder) symptoms are frequently colored by religious ideas related to purification and negative thought, called *Waswas*, associated with Satan. At that same time, many symptoms or states, considered abnormal in the West, are not considered as a problem among Arab and/or Muslims. For instance, what is called dependent personality disorder in the DSM-5 may be considered normal for Arab and/or Muslims, especially among women. Many sexual dysfunctions, such as premature ejaculation in men or sexual arousal problems of women, are not considered problems in need of treatment.

Because of the stresses of immigration, many couples cannot tolerate their marital problems. Therefore, some may seek marriage, couple, or family counseling to restore their marriages and family relations. Depression or anxiety among women may be associated with loneliness and homesickness, the burden of home and children, or dissatisfaction with their husband's absence. Emotional problems among youth are often associated with over-control by their parents. Based on research I conducted in eight Arab countries, authoritarian parenting is not associated with psychological disorders among Arab youth. This finding contradicts other findings in the West that link authoritarian parenting with youth dysfunction. My explanation of this contradiction is that authoritarian parenting may hurt the psychological well-being of children within a liberal and individualistic cultural atmosphere, such as in the West, but it does not seem to cause similar damage within a collectivistic, authoritarian culture such as exists within the Arab world. In the United States, immigrant parents continue to try to exert control over their children who are now being exposed to liberal climate and child-rearing of their peers. Many Arab and/or Muslim parents are confused and fearful of losing their control over their children—afraid of the "deviant" behavior they are seeing in their children. This may motivate some parents to seek help in counseling or therapy.

Question: In carrying out an assessment of an Arab or Muslim American client, what factors are most important to attend to?

Dwairy: Unlike general Western theories of psychopathology that attribute disorders to intra-psychic processes—such as conflicts, irrational or dysfunctional thoughts, or distortion of the self—the main distresses and conflicts of Arab and/or Muslim clients are associated with intrafamilial conflicts and problems in dealing with social expectations and norms. Before pursuing any intervention with such clients, the clinician must assess the balance between the conflicting parties; that is, the client and their family. Understanding this balance is crucial in helping the client fulfill their needs, become appropriately assertive, and assess in advance how best to bring about such a change given what the family can functionally tolerate. It is necessary to first ensure that the family will be able to absorb the changes and that the client can reach an acceptable level of individuation as well as possesses the strength to do so and face the pressure of the family. To accomplish this, I suggest—before any intervention—an assessment of three main factors: the client's level of individuation, ego strength, and the family's level of strictness.

Individuation concerns attitudes toward individualistic values that differ among Arab and/or Muslims. Some clients (such as students studying in the United States) have already developed relatively individuated, autonomous personalities and identities, while others (such as more traditional housewives) are more likely to have retained collective values and dependent personalities. What we must find out is to what extent and how the attitudes, motives, and values of each differ from those of their family. This can be done through questionnaires or an interview. In both, the client is asked to describe their attitudes, motives, and values concerning various life areas, such as gender roles, freedom of personal choice, and religion, and to compare these with where their family stands on each issue. From this, one can begin to assess where discrepancies exist.

Ego strength is imperative because self-fulfillment and assertiveness are not easily accepted in collective societies, such qualities are likely to generate conflicts within the family. Therapists need to make sure, before beginning any counseling, that the client has enough personal strength to withstand the conflicts that are likely to occur. Otherwise, the effort is likely to be counterproductive and perhaps even cause more oppression and distress.

Family strictness can be subjective since some families are just too strict and not ready to accept any change in their lifestyle, norms, and values, while others are more open to change. Readiness for change is an important factor in determining what goals can be set for the intervention. Within strict families, goals should be adaptive within the family structure and norms. In cases of extreme abuse, the client should receive support and protection, and if this cannot be accomplished, then temporarily move away from the family. With more flexible families, family therapy can be helpful in creating new familial structures so as to enable the client to have more freedom of choice within the family system. The more individuated and stronger the client and the more open and flexible the family, the more likely it will be to help the client fulfill herself. When the client possesses little individuation and lacks ego strength and the family is strict, such direct therapy should be avoided. Instead, interventions should help the client better adapt to the family system as it exists—through behavior therapy, relaxation training, and culturally sensitive indirect methods such as metaphor therapy, or what I call "culture-analysis."

Question: What do you mean by indirect interventions?

Dwairy: It refers to therapy that deals with intra-psychic conflicts without bringing unconscious content—that is, typically forbidden in collective family systems—to consciousness. Prematurely introducing such content is likely to create counterproductive confrontations between this kind of client and their family. In what I call indirect methods, such as art therapy and bibliotherapy, clients can begin to address their conflicts symbolically through colors and shapes or with the use of stories, tales, and myths. The use of such metaphors is particularly suited to Arabs and/or Muslims since the Arabic language and the Arab mind are especially attuned to metaphors. Typically, clients tend to describe their problems in the same manner, and this invites the therapist to also work in a metaphoric mode.

A phrase such as "my heart is burned," which expresses depression, may be utilized in repeated artwork or creative writing that allows change without bringing unconscious and forbidden content to consciousness. With such a client, the therapist may encourage her to draw, for instance, a picture of how she imagines her heart burning and then encourage her to be creative and develop another picture in a way that feels better to her. The client may work on changing the colors or removing some elements or adding some others to the picture. I find that such metaphoric work goes very deep, feels very real, and impacts psychological, body, and interpersonal experiences. Working on problems metaphorically and coming to metaphoric or imaginative solutions will also avoid counterproductive confrontation with the family but still have deep impact on the entire bio-psycho-social system. Another client who described his experience as a "boiling steam pot" and worked creatively on lowering the fire, adding water to cool it, moving it away from the fire, and opening a valve, felt better as a result of this work. He learned practical solutions by working with metaphoric ones. For example, he began to take daily walks for about an hour away from his family when he felt oppressed.

As to *culture-analysis*, it is a term I coined for work that precedes psychological analysis or in some cases avoids confrontations that may be generated in the family when forbidden content is brought to consciousness. In such therapy, instead of digging deep to reveal unconscious content, such as sexual or aggressive attitudes toward parents, therapists explore the client's belief system in order to reveal hidden values that may be useful in facilitating change. It is based on the assumption that every believe system or culture has many inner inconsistencies. Many times, this is reflected in contradictory proverbs. For instance, some proverbs in Arabic encourage the client to hurry and others to slow down; some suggest seeking help from people and others warn against it. Such opposing attitudes can be used and applied to facilitate therapeutic change. For instance, in Islam, one may find *Quraan* verses that call for strictness and fanaticism and others that call for diversity, tolerance, and respect for women. One of my religious, depressive clients attributed his negative experiences to his belief that God did not love him. He tried hard to fulfill all the religious obligations to please God—but with no success. I suggested that the basis of all religion is to appreciate the grace of God, even before fulfilling any formal obligation. In his religious belief system, this appreciation had been overlooked and forgotten. Once he realized this, he was able to think positively about all he had in his life and to minimize his bitterness over what he did not have. To apply culture-analysis, therapists must learn about their clients' culture but not necessarily become experts. Sometimes, therapists can consult religious or culture experts to find such alternative attitudes or references. Or they may ask their client to seek advice from religious leaders.

In culture-analysis, we work with the client's belief system in order to highlight new values and beliefs that can facilitate change. Sometimes this analysis is sufficient to bring relief, and at other times, it serves to "pave the road" to bringing out unconscious and formerly forbidden content that can be integrated in the client's consciousness. For instance, when one of my female clients became aware of values of equality between men and women in Islam, she became more aware of her own sexuality and felt more able to allow herself to challenge the strict attitudes toward sexuality of the world in which she lived.

Question: What suggestions do you have for developing rapport with members of your community, and are there therapeutic styles with which Arab and Muslim American clients are most comfortable?

Dwairy: The Arab and/or Muslim American family tends to be more authoritarian with clear power distances between its members. Typically, husbands and fathers are recognized as the authorities within the family while wives and children are expected to respect this structure. I generally have found that, in the United States, such authority is often eventually challenged among immigrant families, and as a result, husbands and fathers feel threatened with a loss of status and authority. I do not think it wise for therapy to challenge this threat. Rather, I suggest that therapists find ways to join with that authority. Joining means to respect it within certain boundaries. It clearly does not mean neglecting the experience or needs of other family members. But rather listening to these within a recognition and respect for the authoritarian structure of the Arab and/or Muslim families. Challenging the father or husband is likely to lead to the end of therapy and an escalating of conflicts within the family.

Joining with the familial authority may be best accomplished by inquiring about and listening to the concerns of the figures of authority and acknowledging their help. This may include appreciating the father's efforts in accompanying his wife or children in seeking help despite the stigma associated with it; by making him feel needed in the therapeutic process and that his support in crucial to the process; by listening to his experience of what has been going on in the family; and by expressing genuine desire to learn from him about how "his people think." Successfully joining with the familial authority is frequently the first step on the way to change. In most cases, I do not think that therapy can successfully proceed without it.

I typically interview parents and children together in our intake meeting. This allows the children to see me listening to their parents with respect without taking their side and allows their parents to see me talking with the children without judgment. After listening to the various perspectives of all sides, I next facilitate a discussion about how things are done in the family to better understand and assess their levels of individuation, ego strength, and family strictness. This assessment may continue in separate meetings with parents and children or husband and wife. Empathy and acceptance of the authoritarian structure of collective cultures and a readiness to understand and learn about the client's lifestyle as it currently exists is a crucial first step in building rapport and assessing the family's flexibility in order to plan an appropriate intervention.

Question: Lastly, could you present a typical case to give us a sense of how some of these various factors come together in treatment?

Dwairy: A married Arab Muslim woman, twenty-three years old, who lived in one of the Arab villages in Israel, had experienced a panic attack after one month of studying education at a university in a large Israeli city. This experience had been her first exposure to the freedom of student life. Her first attack occurred while she was sitting with other students in the cafeteria. Subsequent attacks had come in class, in the library, and other university settings. She was now afraid to go back to the university.

She came to my clinic with her husband, who was a high school teacher. I interviewed them together. She described in detail her experience of the panic attacks, her fears of returning to the university, and other concerns. The husband seemed reserved and wanted her to abandon her university work and rest up at home. I asked him to "help me understand her problem." He said he had not been supportive of her choice to go to college. He believed his wife should be home taking care of the house and children. He eventually submitted to her insistence that she stay in the university, but only after she promised to limit her time there and focus only on learning and not to spend time with other students, especially males. I encouraged him to explain to me his worries about his wife spending time with other students. For several minutes, he explained to me that such behavior was not accepted according to his family tradition and Islamic values. I was empathic and respectful of his values and expressed appreciation for his readiness to consider allowing her to stay in school in spite of his worries. He was touched by this and went on to explain how much he loves her and was ready to do "anything that might help her." At this point, he agreed to allow me to work with her on her panic disorder and discuss what was "best for her."

During our meetings, she told me she had been raised in a religious family. She was a good student and had wished since she was a child to study at the university. Her family had arranged a marriage for her when she became twenty-one years old. She could not refuse. Her new husband promised her he would not forbid her from studying at the university. She was happy to begin studying and become a part of the student social life.

This experience was quite new to her after spending most of her life in a traditional village with a religious family that allowed no experience with boys. The first panic attack occurred when she was sitting with male and female students and had skipped her class. It eventually became clear to me that she was experiencing conflict between her attraction to the social life of students and feeling fearful and guilty because of her husband and family's attitude about such behavior.

Based on her narrative, I learned that she continued to be emotionally dependent upon her family and did not have the ego strength to confront their very strict and traditional norms and values. Based on this assessment, I realized that helping her explore her need to spend time with boys and girls at the university would be counterproductive. She was trapped not only by her obligations to her husband and family, but also by her own traditional belief system. During her narrative, she had made several references to an Islamic religious maxim: "When a man and woman meet together, the Devil is the third party with them" (*Itha Igtama'a rajul wamra'a kan alshaytan thalethhuma*). Based on my model of culture-analysis, I decided to challenge this belief and brought to her attention another Islamic idea: "Doings are dependent on intentions" (*Inama ala'a'mal benneyat*), implying that it is not the meeting between a man and a woman that is sinful but rather their intentions. She did not respond well to this type of intervention. I decided instead to try a technique from metaphor therapy in which I asked her to describe her problem metaphorically. She said it is like "climbing a high tree," which she described as "scary and dangerous." I asked her how she might be able to make this experience less scary. She said she could be very careful, not go too high, and make use of climbing apparatuses, such as ropes and a safety net. I encouraged her to describe the scene and experience it in her imagination. I asked her to again imagine this metaphor and see if she could allow it to make her calm. Before ending that session, I asked her to think about what she learned from this metaphoric process. At the next session, she came wearing a scarf *hijab* on her head and told me she had made up her mind to change to a college in a nearby Arabic city. She said, "When I am within an Arab college with a scarf on my head and Qur'an in my bag, I feel safe and able to fulfill my wish to study and be together with Arab students."

This short description of a case exemplifies the process of joining with the family system—in this case, the husband—and how I avoided encouraging her to fulfill forbidden wishes in light of an assessment of her level of individuation, ego strength, and family strictness. Therapy that encourages acting upon forbidden needs and wishes is not productive with such clients. This became clear when the culture-analysis helped her to realize her own Islamic attitudes did not allow her to accept these forbidden needs. Metaphoric work brought forth a solution that acknowledged her Islamic values and at the same time allowed her to spend time with young men and women. Metaphor therapy helped her consider and find a solution she could live with.

SUMMARY

In sum, the attacks on 9/11 escalated racial hatred and hate crimes against Arab and Muslim Americans. With over half of the Arab and/or Muslims in America reporting incidents of discrimination, the need for culturally sensitive counselors to support this community is vital. Dr. Dwairy's recent publication provides insight regarding ways to work in that way with this population. The interview added to this and expanded on his experience as a member of this community.

ACTIVITY

30-Second Game: To prepare, write the Key Terms at the beginning of this chapter on small pieces of paper, fold the pieces of paper in half, and put them in a bowl. To play the game, divide the class into two teams. One team will send a representative to the front of the room where he or she will have 30 seconds to describe or explain for teammates as many of the terms in the bowl as possible without using the actual word or part of the word. The team will earn a point for each term guessed correctly within the 30-second period. Then, the other team will take a turn. Continue the rounds until all the terms in the bowl have been guessed.

KEY TERMS

Hijab, 368   Jihad, 361   Shahada, 361

Working with South Asian American Clients: An Interview with Sumana Kaipa

LEARNING OBJECTIVES

16-1 Interpret census data for South Asian Americans in America today.

16-2 Explain family and cultural values of South Asian Americans.

16-3 Examine Dr. Kaipa's experience as an Indian American psychologist, educator, and scholar.

The United States is a land of immigrants, but nowhere is the confusion that we experience as a nation around our own diversity more obvious than in the way we deal with issues of race and ethnicity in the U.S. Census process. Take, for example, the topic of this chapter's focus: working with South Asian American clients. Consider the following instructions in relation to a member of this group responding to the 2010 U.S. Census:

- To be counted as Indian → check "Asian Indian" box
- To be counted as Pakistani → check "Other Asian" box and write in "Pakistani"
- To be counted as Bangladeshi → check "Other Asian" box and write in "Bangladeshi"
- To be counted as Sri Lankan → check "Other Asian" box and write in "Sri Lankan"
- To be counted as Nepali → check "Other Asian" box and write in "Nepali"

NOTE: If you check the "Asian Indian" box and write in a response under the "Other Asian" box, your race will only be coded as "Other Asian."

As you shall soon learn from our guest interviewee Dr. Sumana Kaipa: "South Asian Americans are an incredibly diverse group," and so too are their myriad efforts at self-labeling and self-definition. So, for the purposes of this introduction, and because Dr. Kaipa's interview is particularly inclusive of the many subgroups within the category of "South Asian Americans," this brief introduction will focus only on South Asian Indians, with whom the reader is probably more familiar because they make up approximately 83 percent of the broader category of South Asian Americans.

▶ Demographics   16-1

According to the 2010 Census, South Asian Indians have become the second-largest Asian group in the United States after the Chinese, overtaking the Filipinos, who previously held that position. The South Asian Indian population grew from almost 1.7 million in 2000 (0.6 percent of the U.S. population) to over 2.8 million in 2010 (0.9 percent of the U.S. population): a staggering growth rate of 69.4 percent, making them one of the fastest-growing ethnic groups in the United States, second only to Hispanic Americans.

Geographically, early immigration centered South Indian Asian populations on the East Coast of the United States, especially in the states of New York and Florida. More recently, however, immigration trends have favored California as a destination, with significant populations in Chicago and Houston as well. A likely explanation for this shift is greater job and educational opportunities. But this depends somewhat on generation. Earlier generations took any jobs they could get, while more recent generations (and especially tech employees) emigrated to cities where there were large tech industries. Those of lower economic status tended to end up in cities where they had families with established businesses, such as liquor stores, and taxicabs.

These facts are reflected in economics statistics such as how South Asian Indians have continued to outpace most other ethnic groups socioeconomically. For example, 67 percent of all South Asian Indians have earned bachelor degrees or higher, compared to 44 percent for all other Asian American groups collectively. In addition, almost 40 percent have masters, doctorates, or professional degrees—five times the national average for all Americans. While Friedman (2006) attributes these statistics to a "brain drain," with the brightest and best in India emigrating to the United States for greater financial and job opportunities, more recent statistics seem to show that increasingly such people are staying in India because of the American outsourcing phenomenon.

By the beginning of the twentieth century, several thousand South Asian Indians, primarily male Sikhs from the Punjab region, had settled on the west coast of America, working in manual labor in the fields and construction. Many joined the Chinese in 1907 in building the Western Pacific Railroad in California and other railroad projects. Between 1910 and 1920, many turned to the agricultural opportunities that were becoming abundant in California. At about the same time, strong anti-immigrant sentiments grew. These in turn led to violence against South Asian Indians, much of it displaced from the large numbers of Chinese and Japanese workers already present, and in time, anti-immigration laws were passed in 1913, 1917, and 1923. The latter was of special significance because it included anti-miscegenation provisions that prevented Sikhs from marrying anyone who was not their same color. As a consequence, many intermarried with the Mexican or Mexican America populations, with a substantial hybrid Mexican-Sikhs community still in existence near Yuba City, California.

The Luce-Celler Act of Congress in 1946 restored naturalization rights for South Asian Indians in the United States. The first major wave of immigration occurred in 1965, and those who came were very different from their working-class predecessors. The majority lived in cities, were professionals, and were highly educated. There were those, however, who chose more rural areas of Georgia, Arkansas, and Texas to fill a need for rural doctors and educators. It is estimated that over 100,000 individuals and families entered the United States during the decade that followed. Of this population, almost 40 percent were students and visitors with exchange visas. The majority pursued graduate-level education, found jobs, and became permanent residents.

A second wave of immigrants followed. Often, they were relatives of the first wave, but they represented a far different demographic. Generally, without formal education, they tended to be merchants who ran small businesses or those who worked in them: restaurants, groceries, liquor stores, motels, and other small service providers. Members of this second wave generally found themselves drawn to ethnic enclaves in close proximity to other South Asian Indians, carrying on historic values and traditions, while members of the first wave and those who were better educated tended to become more acculturated, adopt nuclear family structures, and had greater professional freedom to live and seek jobs in non-urban or ethnic enclave areas. The smaller population numbers and isolation in suburbia made the passing on of culture and cultural values increasingly difficult, as their children were exposed to alien ways and mainstream American culture. For both, however, acculturation proved to be a major issue and challenge.

▶ Acculturation   16-2

For Asian Indian families in the United States, acculturation varied due to a variety of factors: education, class, caste, family size, economic support, connection to traditional culture, degree of religiosity, and migration history. Generally, however, it tended to increase with subsequent generations in America. Consider, for example, the following differences between first and second generations in their patterns of acculturation (http://en.wikipedia.org/wiki/Indian_American, 2011).

> First-generation Indian-Americans were acutely aware of readily apparent cultural differences. The family became a battlefield where modernity clashed with tradition, where Indian culture clashed with American culture, and where theory clashed with practice. American culture became the basis for interactions outside the home. Inside the home, first-generation Indian-Americans attempted to preserve their cultural and religious heritage and expected to live according to Indian cultural values. Women maintained the household (cooking, cleaning, childrearing, etc.) in addition to holding part-time or even full-time jobs. They were also the first generation of women to benefit from mandated education in America.

For second-generation Indian Americans, the sensation of being the in-betweens was particularly accentuated. Like their parents, the second-generation Indian American compartmentalized their lives. At home and within the local community component, they were governed by the compromised Indian lifestyle developed by their parents and the broader community. Conflicts typically arose from the cultural clash of American individualism versus Indian communitarianism. For example, a second-generation Indian American's desire to pursue an undergraduate degree in the fine arts would not be supported by the family. Career decisions were based on their impact on the family's financial well-being, not the individual's (http://en.wikipedia.org/wiki/Indian_American, 2011).

Family Organization and Values

Although India includes a wide range of cultures, Hindu values tend to be pervasive and define traditional family structures and communal life. According to Das and Kemp

(1997), an Indian family generally refers to a "large, flexible, and fluid entity encompassing several households ... that may be scattered over different geographical regions but composed of members who think of themselves as one." Hindu culture emphasizes the "sacredness of life" and the "dharma," which is the living of life according to certain prescribed rules of correct conduct and hierarchy within the family based on age, gender, birth order, and marital status. The dharma of each member is fixed and defined specifically by kinship ties, as well as that person's stage in the life cycle. The individual is expected to sacrifice personal desires when they conflict with one's dharma within the family. Failure to make the appropriate sacrifice is seen as bringing hardship, as well as shame and possibly ostracism, upon the entire family. Enormous attention is paid to attending to and fulfilling the dharma appropriate to a given time and place in one's life cycle. And complex rituals mark various life milestones, from birth into marriage, parenthood, loss of family members, and death. According to Almeida (2005):

> Indians believe in connectedness of all living things and in immortality maintained by reincarnation. This belief is reflected in the notion that when we die, the soul is born again into another human being or animal. Thus, patience and compassion toward all beings and the universe are essential human qualities. These values are embodied in the concepts of *karma* (destiny), *caste* (a hierarchy organization of human beings), and *dharma* (living life in accordance with the principles that order the universe), essential ideas for understanding the worldview of Asian Indian families, whether they are Hindu, Christian, Muslim, or Parsi. (p. 383)

South Asian Indian families generally adopt nuclear family structures in the United States, but it is not uncommon for extended family, especially grandparents, to visit or reside with the family for long periods. It is also typical for established families to encourage relatives in India to emigrate to America and provide them support until they have established themselves there. Families are very close-knit and feel strong obligations of responsibility to each other, especially in situations of financial need. As a consequence, one finds few South Asian Indians seeking public aid or assistance, with the exception of some elderly receiving disability benefits.

Traditionally, South Asian Indian parents arrange marriages and select partners for their children from within the larger ethnic enclave and with the consent of both families. Selecting a suitable mate is serious business. Potential partners are fully examined and vetted—in relation to education, family, and status—by family and close community friends before the two young people even meet. It is a strong cultural belief that similarities in traditions, social customs, and background make for the happiest and most stable marriages, and in turn create cultural continuity. Marrying outside the group was generally frowned upon, but with assimilation and acculturation, much of this has softened, with dating before marriage increasingly commonplace, as are interracial/intercultural marriages among the second and third generations.

Historically, gender roles were rigid, highly prescribed, and generally intolerant of women. Women were expected to marry early and produce sons. When families did educate their daughters, it was usually with the goal of making them more marketable as brides, as opposed to any commitment to their personal development. But such patterns have changed over time in India, just as they have in the United States. Beginning with those born in the 1950s, Indian women have gotten educations to prepare to support themselves as well as their families should they not marry, or to have a "fallback plan" should something happen to their marriages.

Finally, Almeida (2005) offers the following observations about the challenges of parenting among South Asian Indian parents:

> Parenting for most mainstream Americans is complex, given the current context of violence in schools and little to no support for mothers in the workforce. Added to these stressors for Indian parents is their desire to maintain traditional family patterns while upholding high expectations for their children. Lack of knowledge about developmental changes as they pertain to setting limits, for a child, differentiating between the positive and the harmful sources of information gathered from the Internet, music, TV, and the like, and the various ways in which children can socialize (sports for girls, sleepovers for all children) are among the many challenges they face. "Philosophical talks" are favored over behavioral consequences. Because of the collective psychology, single interventions such as time-out procedures, or rewards for positive behaviors, are not consistent with cultural or family values. (pp. 387–388)

A final concern for South Asian Indian families is the discrimination that has been on the rise over the last decade. While there is a long and persistent history of "Indophobia" in the United States that periodically emerges, two patterns are of more recent vintage. The first is the paranoia and racial discrimination directed against South Asian Indians, who have been blamed for the practice of U.S. companies outsourcing and offshoring white-collar labor to India. The second involves post–September 11, 2001 attacks on South Asian Indians who were mistaken targets for hate crimes against Muslims. In one example, a South Asian Indian man was killed in a Phoenix gas station by a white racist who claimed that the victim's turban made him think he was a Middle Easterner. More recently, another white supremacist killed six people in a 2012 Sikh temple shooting in Oak Creek, Wisconsin. It is little wonder that South Asian Indian parents fear for their children's safety whenever they are away from home. Chapter 4 explores racism and prejudice with regard to the South Asian American population in greater detail—providing examples of how South Asian American's are or were treated.

We shall now turn to our guest expert Sumana Kaipa, who will broaden our focus to include the full array of South Asian groups and explore in depth their cultural tendencies, mental health needs, and optimal ways of approaching them as clients.

▶ Our Interviewee   16-3

Sumana Kaipa earned a bachelor's degree from the University of California at Berkeley, a master of fine arts degree (poetry) from the Iowa Writers' Workshop, and a doctoral degree in psychology (PsyD) from the Wright Institute in Berkeley, California. Since 2004, she has provided individual, couples, family, and group psychotherapy to children, adolescents, and adults across the age spectrum. In her internship and postdoctoral training at the Kaiser Permanente Medical Centers, she specialized in the practice of neuropsychological assessment. Currently, Dr. Kaipa is the training director for the Wright Institute Assessment Service, where she teaches and supervises Wright Institute doctoral students in providing neuropsychological evaluations; and the Wright Institute Sanctuary Project, in which students provide psychodiagnostic evaluations for asylum seekers. Kaipa is also a writer and co-edited *Indivisible: An Anthology of South Asian American Poetry* (University of Arkansas Press, 2010).

The Interview

Question: First, could you begin by talking about your ethnic background and how it has led you to become a human service provider and impacted your work?

Kaipa: I am a 43-year-old female, who identifies as an Indian American and, in a larger sense, as a South Asian American. My family is from the state of Andhra Pradesh in India, and my parents immigrated to the United States in 1973, two years prior to my birth. My parents were part of a wave of educated Indian professionals who entered the country at a time of financial opportunities, and this perfect confluence largely yielded economic successes for this group. Yet, success in America came with overt and covert discrimination as well as the uncertainty of raising children in a new place, where the culture differed dramatically from their own. To a lesser degree, frictions between American and Indian values presented themselves in my childhood when I wished to dress and act more American than my parents would have liked. Or, conversely, when I wished to retain my Indian identity but at times felt ashamed to do so in the presence of American peers.

The differences only grew greater as I negotiated the struggles of early adulthood—determining my career path and finding a life partner. I did things that no "good Indian girl" was supposed to do. In college, I stopped taking pre-med courses and opted for a very impractical master's degree in creative writing. (I told my father I'd rather be a poet than a doctor, which I think might be almost every immigrant father's nightmare.) I lived in a bohemian alley of San Francisco without a clear path for financial success or independence and rejected attempts to be set up with suitable Indian partners.

As I think back on the struggles we faced together, I have tremendous empathy for my mother and father. They were hard-working immigrants who strongly believed in giving their children a better framework for success than they had been given. The trouble was, their idea of success was limited, constricting, and quite prescriptive. They wanted their daughter to "fit in" with the other second-generation Indian children, and this meant to be a professional (or at least married to one) with limitless earning capacity and a large home in a nice, suburban cul-de-sac. This wasn't my vision of achievement or comfort, so my response had been to make a radical departure from their expectations; it was the only way I felt I could "individuate." Furthermore, I think my parents and I were both confused about how acculturated to American norms I had become, and this was threatening to our relationship. I was keeping parts of myself that I thought would not conform to Indian values away from my parents for fear of rejection and disapproval. As a result, I felt I was living a fractured life.

My process of healing had much to do with coming to terms with aspects of my identity and integrating these parts in a way that was less compartmentalized, less secretive, and more whole. Though I know now that there were and are many other South Asian Americans going through the same process that I went through, I felt very alone at the time. I don't know what I would have done if I had not had my brother, who lent perspective to my parents' quirks and kept me sane in the process.

Though sometimes I regret having had to take such a difficult and anxiety-provoking journey in order to arrive at the place I am now; without it, I don't think I would have ever become a psychologist. It was my own experience that led me to feel that South Asian American providers were needed to lend understanding and support to this community, and it is my hope that more and diverse providers of South Asian American descent will build understanding of South Asian American clients and de-stigmatize mental health issues and seeking of services among this community. In my own journey of cross-cultural work, I've also discovered that being of the same cultural background as your client is not necessarily the only or most important factor in help and healing. As much as cultural and identity struggles are specific to the client, there is frequently the universal experiences of feeling different, alone, and rejected. An informed and open-minded human service provider, who seeks to understand a client's problems from the client's perspective, is in all likelihood more important than a culturally matched client-therapist relationship.

Question: How would you define South Asian Americans as a group, and what characteristics do they share?

Kaipa: First, I'd like to share that my particular ethnic identity (within the larger subcategory of South Asians) influences how I might present information about South Asians. I would like anyone who may be reading this interview to know that as an Indian, I represent one of the larger, dominant groups in South Asia. As such, I have more experiential knowledge and understanding of my subgroup in contrast to some of the others groups that are also South Asian. And although I am familiar with many of the cultural groups that are represented by the term "South Asian Americans," I am certain that I do not have the experiential knowledge of all peoples who comprise this group.

I give this caveat because *South Asian Americans* are an incredibly diverse group. Geographically, individuals who identify as South Asian typically come from the current countries of Bangladesh, Bhutan, India, the Maldives, Nepal, Pakistan, and Sri Lanka. But even this definition is up for dispute, as individuals from the present Afghanistan, Iran, Burma, and Bhutan are sometimes (and sometimes not) self-identified or identified by others as belonging to South Asia. Historically, some of these countries have had very fluid borders or were not considered separate countries until more recently, further complicating how individuals identify themselves. For instance, India, Pakistan, and Bangladesh were all considered part of one country until 1947, and some individuals and families may hold onto their identity with the former country, India, or with the region (Punjab) and not the country. Additionally, some groups, due to political or religious reasons, have immigrated to other parts of South Asia and have then become biculturally identified, such as the Tibetan population who now live in Nepal and India. Many of the countries of South Asia were at one time under the rule of European colonialism beginning in the 16th century and terminating in the 20th century, predominantly by the British, Dutch, Portuguese, and the French.

Among and within the countries in South Asia, there is extraordinary diversity with respect to religion, language, and customs. The region contains almost all the major religions of the world (as well as the various sects of these religions): Buddhism, Christianity, Hinduism, Islam, Jainism, Judaism, and Sikhism. Several of the countries of South Asia are strongly identified with a particular religion, and religious differences between countries or among individuals living within the countries can at times be a source of tension or conflict between members of different South Asian groups. One example is the tension between those of Hindu and Islamic faith in the region, and these differences and enmities sometimes persist even after immigrating. Another aspect of religious difference among some South Asian communities, such as Hindus, is that they subscribe to a caste system, in which a person's social position and status in a community is defined by birthright. Historically, caste has been an extremely oppressive tool that has kept many people poverty-stricken and socially ostracized. (When visiting India as a child, I remember that we were still not allowed to touch the lowest caste of people, who were known as "untouchables," nor were they allowed to enter my family's home. If my family had to interface an untouchable, the exchanges took place at the door.) Today, the caste system continues to persist, but its effect differs greatly depending upon the region and community in which it is practiced. In urban centers of India, for instance, people are likely to ascribe less importance to caste, and there are likely more opportunities for lower caste individuals to change their situation while in some rural areas where a community's views have not changed for many years, people of low caste status are likely to be treated very poorly and experience significant discrimination. Due to poor economic circumstances in South Asia that make it very hard, if not impossible, to immigrate, there are not many people from lower castes in the United States. There is no denying that caste is horrible, but its foreignness makes it an easy target to criticize by those who aren't familiar with how it operates. Though certainly not perfect, I think sexism in American society is a good analogy to discrimination based on caste. Like sexism, castism continues to persist, even as it improves, because it takes its power from both oppression from the dominant group as well as buy-in from members of all castes in order to give meaning to and perpetuate the system.

The most widely spoken languages are Hindi, Bengali, and Urdu, but many other languages are spoken throughout the region. In India alone, there are 16 major languages and over 200 additional dialects. Also, a number of people in South Asia (particularly those who are of a higher socioeconomic status or living in urban areas) are conversant or fluent in English, which became a key language in this region due to British colonialism. In some regions, language can be a very strong indicator of tribal identity (such as Pashto in Afghanistan), in other areas it may indicate a religious affiliation (such as Urdu in Pakistan and India), and for others, language may be an important part of familial lineage despite where the person or family may reside (identifying as Tamil despite living in the English and Hindi dominated city of Bombay). Another thing that might be important to know is that many people from South Asia speak multiple languages because they frequently need to know the more dominant languages of industry or commerce (English, Bengali, Urdu, and Hindi), may also need to know the language of a nearby area (where an entirely different language is spoken), and also wish to retain their family's traditional language.

Finally, the immigration path that various groups took before coming to the United States defines and shapes this population, too. The history of European colonialism in this area, particularly British colonization, led many South Asians to spread to different corners of the earth, especially in the late nineteenth and throughout the twentieth century, when many of the countries of South Asia were under British rule. Several groups first immigrated to the United Kingdom, Fiji, Kenya, Tanzania, South Africa, Guyana, Mauritius, and Trinidad and Tobago before coming to the United States. Where they went and under what circumstances they immigrated, how they acculturated to the places that they settled, and how they made their journey to the United States become an important part of their cultural identity. As an example, during British colonization, many Indians were taken as indentured servants to the Fiji Islands, and the descendants of these individuals who have retained some aspects of their Indian culture but have also, over several generations, acculturated to the Fijian way of life. In the late 1980s and early 1990s, some Fijian Indians fled Fiji due to political conflicts and settled in the United States. Thus, you have Indian-identified individuals living in the United States with very different cultural backgrounds, values, and immigration experiences.

After describing all the differences, one might wonder what similarities these disparate groups share. The countries that comprise South Asia did not have the boundaries that they now do, and their histories and ways of life were significantly intertwined, despite the diversity of people in this region. Colonialism, too, affected the collective history of the people of this area, and it also largely shaped the way the region was eventually divided. Though seemingly ephemeral, South Asians share similar ideas around the importance of family and community, especially over the value of the individual. As a result, many of these communities have emphasized family name, family pride, and family legacy as an important part of their identities. By and large, South Asian families have lived in extended family networks. Such a family structure can be very positive since it can provide strong community support and protect against isolation. Moreover, the elderly have a role in generational family life and are accorded respect.

South Asian family roles can sometimes be perceived as rigid with women having significant domestic and familial responsibilities without the respect and rights accorded to men. With increased education and work outside the home, women's roles have changed somewhat. There may also be differences between South Asian groups, and some families, regardless of region, may be more conservative or progressive in their views about women. Marriage and children continue to be central to South Asian family structure and because family reputation is important, many South Asian groups strongly discourage dating or premarital sex and still favor arranged marriages over choosing one's own partner. However, the nature of arranged marriages has changed over time, with some families introducing but not necessarily choosing ideal candidates and women having more of a voice in the arrangement. Nevertheless, women are often not held to the same standards as men with respect to marriage and coupling, in that men may be chastised but likely not ostracized for their sexual conduct (such as premarital sex) and can remarry after a divorce or death of a spouse without criticism from their families or community.

The identity of South Asian Americans takes on a different form as this group negotiates its identity on American soil. In that process, some of the differences between South Asian Americans are minimized, as minor geographical differences (such as coming from different states in the same country) and language differences become less important than sharing similar values and ideas about family and sharing similar interests in food, music, dance, and other cultural practices. Religion, however, appears to be a central facet of identity that persists, especially for the newly immigrated or those in the first generation, while caste, because it is of much less importance in the United States, does not play as large a role as it does in South Asia. Family continues to be a central focus of South Asian American life. More acculturated South Asian American families tend to live in nuclear family arrangements, though they tend to maintain extended family ties to a much greater degree than European Americans. South Asian American families tend not to allow dating and forbid premarital sex, and they focus on finding suitable partnerships for their children, even if such arrangements take place in a more Americanized way, through parental introductions and possibly even "dating" of acceptable matches. As in South Asia, parents also tend to encourage or even choose professions for their children as a way to secure their financial future and to ensure good reputations in the community. The extent to which this group maintains their cultural affiliation and follows the patterns that I've discussed here depends largely on the amount of time a family has spent in the United States, as well as how long it has been since the family lived in South Asia. In the case of Indians who lived outside of South Asia prior to immigrating to the United States, they are more likely to have also adopted the cultural values of the various countries in which they have lived. Most South Asian communities in the United States are located in California, Texas, Illinois, and New York; and those individuals growing up in areas with fewer South Asian Americans might not follow the same patterns as those in larger or more urban enclaves. In my experience, friends and family members who grew up outside of large South Asian communities reported feeling "different" and became more acculturated to dominant American norms and socialized with non-South Asians while those who had a large community of other South Asians around them were more confident about their cultural identity, even in the face of discrimination, and were more likely to socialize predominantly with other South Asians.

Question: Could you now talk about the various names that different South Asian American subgroups use to describe and identify themselves?

Kaipa: Not surprisingly, a group of individuals with a complex, multi-pronged identity don't agree on descriptions for themselves. Some individuals from this region might refer to the particular country or countries from where their families come, such as preferring to call themselves Pakistanis or Burmese. Individuals may also identify themselves by region, tribe, or caste, such as calling themselves "Telugu," "Pashto," or "Brahmin." More acculturated individuals, particularly those who have lived in the United States for a longer period of time or who were born in the United States, are likely to identify themselves with both their familial country of origin as well as "American"; i.e., "Pakistani American" or "Sri Lankan American." Some individuals might identify along religious lines, such as calling themselves "Muslim Americans" or "American Muslims." Some individuals reject the term *South Asian* altogether, finding it too broad or not wishing to be grouped with communities with which they do not wish to affiliate, such as Indians and Pakistanis wishing to distinguish themselves from one another due to political and religious animosities.

Acculturation plays a role in using the term South Asian, too. One reason for this might be that the more American-identified individuals become, the more likely they are to feel that they are treated similarly in the face of dominant American society, who may make erroneous assumptions about their identity based on the way that they look (such as believing Sikhs are the same as Muslims). Experience of discrimination or oppression by the dominant group may fuel a sense of solidarity among more acculturated South Asians, who then feel, regardless of their various self-identifications, that they are a part of a group of South Asian Americans.

Finally, if things weren't already confusing, individuals from this community aren't likely to be terribly uniform in their descriptions of themselves, calling themselves different things in different contexts or communities. For instance, I identify as (sometimes in this order and sometimes not) Telugu, Indian, Hindu, American, South Asian American, and Californian (and probably more things that I can't think of right now), and these identities become more or less prominent or important depending upon who I'm with and what their group affiliation or experience is. There are also subdivisions within these identities (i.e. different kinds of Telugu people or Californians), so you can see how it can get pretty complicated.

Question: Could you describe some of the shared history that South Asian Americans bring with them to the United States? Could you give us a nutshell version of historical events of which a provider should be aware?

Kaipa: Prior to 1965, the few South Asian immigrants who came to the United States did so for circumscribed educational opportunities (under a specified student visa) or were recruited as laborers, such as men who came to the United States in the late nineteenth century and early twentieth century to work in logging, mining, construction of railroads, and agriculture in the Pacific Northwest and California.

However, the bulk of South Asian immigration to the United States took place after the Immigration and Nationality Act of 1965, which loosened the restrictions placed on immigrants from non-European countries. This legislation was also instrumental in allowing families with United States citizenship or legal status to sponsor family members for permanent residency. While the initial group of immigrants that came in the late 1960s and throughout the 1970s was comprised of more educated professionals (e.g., doctors, engineers, scientists, etc.), the families that they sponsored frequently did not have the educational attainment and, as such, were employed in businesses such as the running of restaurants, hotels, and convenience stores. In contrast to the class of educated professionals, this latter group of less educated individuals have been more likely to live in a less nuclear, more extended family arrangement where they socialize exclusively with South Asians and frequently remain less acculturated to American culture.

Restrictions on immigration were reinstated in the early 1990s, when limits on the annual number of immigrants were once again instituted and reasons for immigration were more strictly limited to family reunification or the need for specific classes of workers. For instance, several Indians who came in the 1990s did so under work visas to fill the need for employees trained in informational technology, but some of these populations left the United States after being laid off and returned to their respective countries.

On the one hand, more recent immigrants have benefited from coming to the United States at a time when the South Asian American community is larger and, thus, they have more opportunities to socialize with others from their culture and maintain cultural ties. For example, South Asian Americans have the opportunity to take classes in order to learn their family language, classical dance, or music from their cultural tradition, have more exposure to food and popular media from their family's cultural background, and can practice in an established religious community (such as a mosque or temple). South Asian Americans are also a more visible community, appearing much more regularly in media, and there are now examples of successful South Asian American politicians, actors, writers, and scientists. The events of September 11, 2001, on the other hand, were a significant setback to South Asian Americans, many of whom experienced racial, ethnic, and religious discrimination; were victims of hate crimes associated with the anti-Muslim, anti-brown person backlash that resulted from the attacks; or experienced significant fear that they might be targeted or perceived as being anti-American.

Question: Let's switch our focus and begin to look at issues related to providing services to the South Asian American community. Could you talk about factors that influence how South Asian Americans go about seeking help when they have problems?

Kaipa: As a whole, it is not common for South Asian Americans to seek psychological help. As I mentioned before, South Asian Americans are generally communalist in nature and tend to emphasize the family and community rather than the individual. This arrangement can be supportive as it provides an infrastructure for tending to the welfare of all members of the community as well as a having a closely-knit social network for persons within the community. I remember that in Suketu Mehta's book, *Maximum City*, one of the women living in the slums of Bombay said she refused to move to a newly built development that had been constructed to alleviate the problems of slums because she feared that the strong social network of friends and families would be disrupted. Americans, myself included, tend to think of living in too-close-for-comfort situations as stifling and over-stimulating, but for this woman as for many, living in close proximity and with constant socialization is a huge protection against depression and other psychological issues. In my work as a psychologist, I have frequently found that the downside of the more individualistic culture is that elderly people lose relevance and purpose in the culture, and we have little resources or support networks to help care for people as they age. Many of the elderly Americans with whom I have worked are extremely isolated and have had few or no family or friends to turn to as they become infirm, struggle with cognitive problems, or mental health issues.

However, the family-centric orientation can also mean that an individual's behavior within the community reflects on the family or community as a whole. If the individual is succeeding, it can bring pride and respect to the family. But if the individual is suffering from problems, especially if they are not medical problems, this can become a cause of embarrassment or shame, and the family may deal with this issue by denying or hiding the problem from others. Additionally, when there is dysfunction in a family, such as abuse, the family may discourage or prevent help seeking for fear of the entire family or community being exposed or shamed. Because the family may not acknowledge problems, it may also lead to South Asian Americans to be unable to perceive or understand the psychological difficulties they or others around them are experiencing. The cultural belief that events and circumstances are preordained, or fated, may also make South Asian Americans more likely to believe that outside help cannot change their circumstances.

Another concern South Asian Americans may have is that service providers will not understand their values and their issues. For some, this may be partly a language issue, but for most, it is a question of cultural difference—a concern that Americans or Westerners might judge them without understanding their cultural differences. On several occasions, I have heard my mother or other family members relay horror stories in which children were removed from their parents by a child protection agency due to a cultural disconnect, such as a family co-sleeping rather than using a crib or continuing to [breast]feed their child when older than what is considered normal in American culture. Whether these stories are truth, myth, or something in the middle, they reflect a fear among South

Asian Americans that they can be easily misunderstood and that such misunderstandings can have terrifying consequences.

Acculturation is a key factor in whether individuals and families will seek help. Less acculturated South Asian Americans may be referred to therapy or to a psychiatrist through a primary physician who believes there is a mental health or stress-related issue. These individuals are usually unfamiliar with psychological diagnoses, the roles of mental health providers, what types of support or interventions are available, and how to negotiate getting help. More acculturated individuals will be more familiar with Western psychological concepts but may still feel nervous about seeking help, believing that their problems are not worthy of seeking outside help, feeling discomfort or fear in airing family problems, or worrying about being judged by providers who do not understand their particular issues.

Question: What are some of the common problems that South Asian American clients might bring to you as a counselor? Are any subgroups within the South Asian American community at particular risk for mental health problems?

Kaipa: Again, level of acculturation strongly affects the sorts of problems that South Asian Americans clients encounter. These individuals may be experiencing significant difficulties in adjusting to the demands of American culture (such as understanding how to find a job, an apartment, or other resources in the United States), difficulty negotiating situations due to poor English language skills, difficulty findings jobs or experiencing financial stresses as a result of caring for multiple families members (and supporting family who remained in the home country), feeling isolated from a community of family and friends, having witnessed or experienced political trauma in their country of origin or being displaced, domestic violence, and alcoholism abuse. It is also possible that the family may bring a loved one with more severe mental illness, such as a schizophrenia or psychosis, to the attention of a psychiatrist. Sexism and issues related to the historical treatment of women often make domestic violence a significant issue in the South Asian American community, and several organizations exist throughout the country to help women in abusive relationships.

Intergenerational misunderstandings and tensions are also likely to be a reason for family problems. Parents might complain, as my parents did, of their children not being compliant or becoming too Americanized in their values; children may complain that parents are too rigid or do not understand their experiences. In adolescence, these problems may manifest more for girls since families are more likely to impose strict restrictions on dating and/or socialization with non-South Asians, and the girls may feel that they cannot fit in with their peer group. Outside of family, South Asian American adolescents may also struggle to fit in with peers or feel stress related to being stereotyped.

Second-generation adults, especially young adults, are likely to seek help for problems related to identity and conflict with parents. They may either feel pressured by their family to make certain professional or partnership choices that don't feel right to them or, if they did not make the "right" choices (such as marrying interracially or interculturally), feel that that they have failed or disappointed their families. South Asian American families, because of the centrality of a heterosexual marriage and children, may have a lot of trouble understanding and accepting LGBT children, and these individuals may find it very difficult to go through the coming out process or to find a way to fit in with their families, given their sexual orientation

Even when conforming to their family's ideas of appropriate behavior or success, individuals may still experience stress and difficulties related to their parents or families lacking the ability to understand the cultural terrain that they must negotiate. A South Asian American young woman I saw briefly in therapy struggled with depression related to very high parental expectations about education and achievement. Her family could not understand how her depression affected her academic achievement or her future plans for law school. They also could not see how they might be contributing to the problem by holding her to very high standards, focusing on her failure to get good grades in her final year and trouble studying for the LSAT rather than encouraging her, and imposing restrictions on her behavior that did not exist for her male siblings.

Question: How do socioeconomic and class issues affect the psychological lives of South Asian Americans? Do class or other socioeconomic issues play any role in these various problems?

Kaipa: Socioeconomics and class definitely affect South Asians and their problems. Some groups, like my family, had the privilege of immigrating to the United States as professionals (who received a free or very cheap education in South Asia) at a time when America was in need of an immigrant work force, and they came voluntarily to find opportunity. It is likely that these individuals and their children may experience stress related to achievement and financial success, believing strongly in model minority stereotype and thinking that they have failed if they do not achieve as professionals.

But less-educated, poorer communities coming to the United States or individuals seeking refugee status may have felt pressure to move out of their existing circumstances or were displaced, thus coming involuntarily and with fewer resources or means to succeed in a new environment. Those with less education and fewer financial resources are less likely to be able to speak English well in contrast to highly educated counterparts, and these issues affect their ability to get higher-paying jobs as well as how they are perceived by the higher economic classes of South Asian Americans. Many of them find employment in family businesses, like running hotels (including single resident occupancy hotels) or liquor stores, with greater degree of stress related to the threat of being robbed, assaulted, or even killed. Thus, their stressors are more likely to be related to difficulty making ends meet as well as the threat of harm in the workplace.

Question: Next, let's talk about some of the factors that you see as important in assessing a South Asian American client. What kind of things would you look for? What kinds of information do you feel it is important to collect from a South Asian American client? What suggestions might you have for providers about developing rapport with South Asian American clients?

Kaipa: When working with South Asian American clients, I tend to want to know the exact nature of the client's cultural background (including what they consider to be their country of origin or countries they lived in before coming to the United States and what name they would give to themselves), their immigration history (when they arrived to the United States and whether they immigrated voluntarily or under significant duress, trauma, or financial hardship), religion and, if relevant, caste (as well as how important religion and/or caste is in their day-to-day lives), socioeconomic status (both the client's as well as their family status, how this may have changed in the immigration process), and generational status. I would also want to know if the client lives in an extended family and if family members strongly influence a client's decisions. Additionally, it is important to get a sense of whether the client and the client's family are more conservative with respect to family roles (such as gender), cultural and familial expectations, and adherence to religion. Though the client may not be forthright about domestic violence or substance abuse, a good assessment should also be mindful that these issues might be impacting the client or the client's family and could easily be overlooked.

It would also be useful to know what community and familial support systems are available for the client's problem. In some cases, individuals may be surrounded by family but do not feel that they can safely share their problems. Experiences of discrimination and oppression are also important things to know. Has the client experienced discrimination due to their ethnic or religious background? In Muslim South Asian Americans, I would ask about how the current climate in America of "Islamophobia" impacts them, especially the fear and lack of respect that they may feel in interactions with all non-Muslims. Is the client experiencing significant stress as a result of gender discrimination or gender roles? In the case of domestic violence, are there multiple perpetrators? All of these factors will give good information about the life experiences and common stressors affecting the client or clients with whom you are working. Providers should keep in mind that client's may not feel comfortable or be forthright with respect to all of these questions, and assessing discomfort and being flexible, patient, and gentle in how you approach these topics will likely go a long way toward putting the client at ease.

Given that assessing level of acculturation is very important, I also want to mention that some practitioners utilize acculturation measures in their work before planning interventions. Individuals rate themselves in terms of speaking South Asian languages or preferring South Asian food, music, cultural activities, friends, and values in contrast to speaking predominantly English and preferring American food, music, cultural activities, friends, and values. These measures can provide information about whether a person is highly identified with their culture of origin, highly acculturated to American norms and values, or some-where in-between and likely bicultural. They can serve as a good starting point for understanding what issues the client might be experiencing, and responses can be a springboard for other questions about their experience. For instance, if you find that the client is more identified with their culture of origin and is not highly acculturated to American norms, this may indicate that the client may or may not be familiar with therapy or counseling and it may be good to give education about therapy and other interventions to avoid any misunderstandings. How-ever, providers should be careful not to assume total understanding of the client based on acculturation scales, and it would be important to ask the client about any beliefs or values before assuming that they follow specific trends or patterns. As an example, with respect to behaviors, I would likely rate in the bicultural to more "American" range, but I am likely to place a greater emphasis on values that may be associated with those who are less acculturated, such teaching my daugh-ter my family's language and cultural stories and Indian classical dance and music.

Regarding building rapport, I think it is important for providers to strike a balance between being informed and being curious. Seeking consultation and learning about a client's cultural background are crucial steps to understanding the presenting issues. But it is also important to ask about the very specific and personal ways that client's experience family and culture—and whether or not the client thinks their concerns are cultural in nature. Individuals never perfectly follow patterns, and I think many people shut down if they feel providers have fixed or erroneous idea of who they are. Also, clients themselves might not be at a place where they are ready or comfortable to address issues of culture, and providers have to be mindful of this fact. Providers should be sensitive to match-ing clients to those of similar cultural background or to providers who speak the same language, if the client feels that this may facilitate an understanding of their issues. However, some South Asian American clients may feel more inhibited by seeing a provider of a similar background due to fear that this person might know their family or others in their community or, because of cultural similarity, judge them for the problems that they have.

Question: Do you feel that there are any therapeutic approaches that are better matched with certain South Asian American groups? Are there any subgroups within the South Asian American community that are at particular risk for mental health problems?

Kaipa: Given that South Asian Americans tend to have a better understanding of interfacing with the medical system, they may be more receptive to those therapies that appear to be more concrete, solution-oriented, and "medical" in nature, such as cognitive behavioral therapy. Also, psychodynamic therapies that focus on talking about family dynamics might cause clients to become very uncomfortable, as there may be a concern about airing the family's problems and, worse yet, to what they perceive to be a stranger. Taking psychiatric medication is a complicated subject, too. At times, it might feel less shameful, stigmatizing, and threatening to South Asian Americans since the problem can be externalized as a medical problem and doesn't involve talking with a stranger about personal things. South Asian American clients may also be likely to present with a more "tell-me-what-to-do" kind of attitude, which may lead providers to give advice rather than explore questions or seek more information. On the one hand, the advice-giving therapy relationship may be successful, but therapists may miss important family patterns or cultural information that would lead to be a better understanding of the problem and inform the best therapeutic intervention. In fact, providers should generally be mindful that South Asian American clients might downplay aspects of stress related to family and interpersonal dynamics. If possible, exploring all aspects of the system and cultural values and behaviors in which the clients live are an important part of working with this population. For example, in some cases, spiritually informed practices may be of paramount value to creating positive change.

Again, acculturation is a critical factor in how receptive clients will be to various styles of therapy and intervention. For instance, I think that more acculturated or assimilated groups of South Asians are likely to behave like dominant groups in the United States in that they might feel more comfortable sharing about difficult personal or family circumstances, are less likely to view the therapist as a "stranger," and may better understand the role of therapy. They may also adopt some of the dominant stigma about medication since they are less likely to frame it as helping with a "medical" issue. Nevertheless, in contrast to the dominant group, they may feel nervous about how their cultural or family experiences will be perceived by providers who may not be familiar with their cultural background, values, and responsibilities.

In my own experience, as a second-generation South Asian American, I felt I benefited most from a supportive talk-therapy environment in which I could discuss the different problems I was facing and how I was feeling about them. But I very much needed and appreciated having a therapist who was open and engaged about cultural and identity issues and who, though not from my cultural background, tried to put herself in my position to understand my struggles rather than being in a judging role in which solutions come from Western misinterpretations of situations or rigid ideas about "healthy" relationships or interpersonal dynamics. While I'd encourage providers to communicate their interest in being mindful of cultural issues as early as the first meeting with the client as well as periodic check-ins with their South Asian American clients about cultural comfort, misunderstandings, or misinterpretations; I also think that the therapist has to do the work to cultivate a sincere attitude of openness and self-reflectiveness about how one's own cultural ideas might help or hinder a client's progress.

Question: Last question. You've shared a lot of rich information with us. Could you finish by presenting a case that shows how it comes together in work with a client?

Kaipa: When I entered graduate school, I was confident that I would not see a South Asian American client until starting a private practice (with a focus on this population). But I've already had worked with several South Asian American clients. I think this is, in part, because I trained in hospital settings, and as I mentioned earlier, clients may be more likely to seek help in this context.

My first South Asian American clients sought therapy for couples counseling. The couple was in their early 40s and had two school-aged children. The wife, who I will call Rani, had at the age of 10 or 11 emigrated from the state of Punjab in Northern India to the United States with her family in the late 1980s. Her family was not college educated, and they first worked in hotels and liquor stores owned by extended family in order to make ends meet before gathering the resources to buy their own establishments. Rani attended middle school and high school in the United States, and she earned her associates' degree at a local community college. At the time that I saw them, Rani had been working part-time in an administrative role and spent the remainder of her time caring for the children and her in-laws. The town in which she was raised in central California had a sizeable Punjabi community and a local *gurdwara,* a Sikh temple, where her family worshipped, so outside of school, she was accustomed to socializing with mostly Punjabi Sikh families like her own. Though I do not know whether she considered her family traditional or conservative, they did arrange Rani's marriage when she was in her late teens or early 20s. Her husband, who I'll call Raj, was a recent immigrant to the United States, having come in his mid-20s after the marriage to Rani was arranged. He was not college educated. He was the full-time manager of a liquor store that the couple owned, and, as a result, he dealt with difficult, sometimes violent customers on a routine basis. According to family tradition, Raj invited his parents to live with them after they were married.

Rani initiated therapy and came to the intake appointment alone and, in her opinion, the major problems that she and Raj were experiencing were that Raj drank alcohol excessively and had a gambling problem. According to her, Raj had depleted their savings and caused significant financial and emotional strain in their relationship. Additionally, Rani's relationship to Raj's parents had taken a turn for the worst. She stated that they had gotten along well in the first few years of the relationship, but over the years, she felt that they expected her to serve and respect them without returning the respect, were very critical of her, and complained about her to other family members. In Rani's view, she felt that Raj's parents did not help with household chores even though they spent the most time at home while the couple worked, and, though they knew of the couple's financial struggles, they did not contribute to the household financially. Rani understood that the problems that she was struggling with were ones that needed to be addressed in couples counseling.

When Raj joined Rani in couples therapy the next time, he was very quiet and not very forthright about the troubles they were experiencing. It appeared to be Rani's goal to provide a "wake-up call" to Raj about how his drinking and gambling were becoming significant problems for the family. As I got to know the couple, it became clear that Rani was right about these issues, which Raj also acknowledged, but he was not yet ready to make significant changes in his behavior. Raj had a family history of alcohol abuse, and his brothers both drank excessively. Additionally, Raj's friends socialized by drinking excessively and gambling, so these behaviors were considered to be normal ways of "unwinding." Talking about the addictive behaviors took the form of "motivational interviewing" in that I felt that all that could be done was to seek information about how he felt his behaviors might be impacting him and his family. It was difficult for this discussion to take place in the context of couples therapy since Rani wished for the therapy to bring an immediate change to Raj's behavior. Additionally, I believe that she was hoping that if the recommendation came from outside (from providers at a medical institution), it would lend credence to the problem, and Raj would change his ways. It was as if she was hoping for a prescription from a doctor to cure Raj.

The other problems in the relationship as they described them were related to family expectations and family dynamics, particularly with Raj's parents. Rani's perspective was of in-laws who were demanding and ungrateful, but Raj saw the problem differently. He felt that Rani had a very negative, almost hostile attitude toward his parents, which made them feel very unwelcome in the home environment and contributed to their loss of respect for Rani. Thus, he felt he needed to stand up for his parents and did not always support her position in the home or try to help her. The focus on family dynamics was to explore the problem from both Rani and Raj's perspective with the goal of each of them understanding how the problem had developed as well as ways that they fueled rather than resolved the issue. I felt that the next step would have been to invite Raj's parents to be a part of family therapy in order to discuss how to increase understanding and respect among all family members in the household.

Already, you can probably see how some of the things I've discussed about South Asian Americans were very relevant to this case. There were differences in levels of acculturation between Rani and Raj, and this impacted many aspects of their day-to-day lives, including their beliefs and values. For instance, it was clear to me that Raj would never have sought outside services or even considered it to be an option had Rani not initiated the process, and Rani, being somewhere between first and second generation, was not only aware of counseling resources but felt empowered enough to seek help for their problems. Even still, her expectation was that the medical establishment "prescribe" what was needed for his problem, asking for more top-down and less exploratory intervention. Moreover, Raj's lack of interest in working with a counselor, as well as being in an early stage of change with respect to alcohol and gambling addiction, made engagement in the therapeutic process lopsided and of limited utility at times. It also appeared that addiction problems had a cultural component, as working in a liquor store with sometimes violent customers appeared to be a stressor common to more newly immigrated South Asians of lower socioeconomic status. Among South Asians, Punjabi men are commonly considered more alcoholic than other groups. I was not certain whether this was merely a stereotype, but I definitely got the impression that Raj socialized with men who considered it normal to drink excessive amounts of alcohol. Had I felt that Raj and Rani were open to the conversation and the relationship we had was more solid, I would further explored this issue.

A difference in acculturation and values was also at play with respect to family dynamics, as Raj and his parents were invested in the cultural idea that a son's parents should live with him, and they also likely believed that the role of the daughter-in-law was to care for her husband's family. While Rani appeared sympathetic to these roles as her own family might have held similar cultural beliefs, she also seemed to feel stressed by expectations that she be a financially contributing member of the family while also maintaining responsibility for her in-laws. Raj's perspective was also a very valuable and important one as he felt that it was important that his family be given respect and feel welcome in their household. It was my belief that including family in discussions around values, responsibilities, and respect would have likely been more fruitful than just talking with the couple alone about these issues, but it was highly likely that Raj's parents would have required a Punjabi-speaking therapist and would likely have felt that therapy was both unfamiliar and not a way that they might handle their problems.

Finally, I want to talk about my own work with this couple in terms of being a South Asian American therapist. On the one hand, I think I had a fairly good understanding of some of the cultural issues at play and knew what information to obtain from them in order to gain a more comprehensive understanding of the problems, but I think one issue that I've had in working with South Asian Americans, which I think also played out in the context of working with this couple, is how easy it can be to focus on characteristics that make South Asians similar and subsequently miss the subtle differences between groups that might help in building rapport and more thoroughly inform the work. I think this might happen less with my cross-cultural work, in which I'm acutely aware of what I don't know and that I can't speak for the issues of this group. I also think it is easy to feel that problems are unsolvable because issues feel more insurmountable if there are cultural values and beliefs that strongly determine worldviews and are difficult to change or reconcile with other beliefs. I definitely felt this way in my work with Raj and Rani.

SUMMARY

This chapter focused on the diverse group of South Asian Americans, with specific attention paid to South Asian Indians. This group of individuals have become the second-largest group in the United States and is considered one of the fastest growing ethnic groups. A highlight of this chapter was the interview with Dr. Sumana Kaipa, a psychologist who is currently the training director for the Wright Institute Assessment Service and the Wright Institute Sanctuary Project. Dr. Kaipa's interview focused on the full spectrum of South Asian groups and deeply explored their cultural tendencies, mental health needs, and optimal ways of approaching them as clients.

Regarding barriers to treatment, Dr. Kaipa mentioned that because the family may not acknowledge problems, South Asian Americans may be unable to perceive or understand the psychological difficulties they or others around them are experiencing. Some psychological difficulties Dr. Kaipa mentioned were issues adjusting to American culture, language barriers, financial issues as a result of caring for multiple family members, and being isolated from country of origin. When working with South Asian Americans, Dr. Kaipa explained that it is important to understand the exact nature of the client's cultural background, as well as the client religion and caste. Lastly, Dr. Kaipa mentioned that when building rapport, it is important to find a balance between being informed and being curious. She added that learning about a client's cultural background is an important step to understand presenting problems.

ACTIVITY

Given that South Asian Americans may be more receptive to those therapies that appear to be more concrete, solution-oriented, and "medical" in nature, such as cognitive behavioral therapy, identify and explore the following areas: (1) How would you build rapport with a South Asian American client? (2) How would your personal style of therapy be used in session? and (3) How might your cultural differences and/or similarities play a role in the therapeutic relationship?

KEY TERM

South Asian American, 385

Working with White Ethnic Clients: An Interview with the Author

LEARNING OBJECTIVES

17-1 Interpret the implications of census data for white ethnic Americans in America today.

17-2 Explain the cultural similarities of white ethnic Americans.

17-3 Examine the author's experience as a white ethnic psychologist, educator, and scholar.

▶ Demographics and Cultural Similarities `17-1`

Who are the *white ethnics?* Simply put, they are national immigrant groups of Eastern and Southern European descent that share a common experience of immigration to the United States. This question is answered in greater detail within Chapter 2 of this book. This group includes Italians, Poles, Greeks, Armenians, Jews, and various ethnic groups making up the Russian Republic (Czech, Lithuanian, Russian, Slovak, and Ukrainian). Because of historical similarities, the Irish are also included in this category. All brought with them long histories of oppression and racial hatred in their native lands, were met with suspicion and rejection as newly arrived immigrants, and, for a generation or two, were exploited as cheap labor.

The United States has experienced two major waves of immigration from Europe. The first, which occurred in the early nineteenth century, was made up of Northern and Western Europeans: Germans, English, Scandinavians, and French. According to Healey (1995), these groups shared characteristics with the **dominant culture** already in the United States. They were Protestants, came from developing and industrialized countries, and shared certain cultural values—such as the Protestant ethic of "hard work, success, and individualism," a belief in democratic governance, and levels of education and "occupational skill" that allowed them to compete in a modernized nation such as the United States. The second wave of Europeans, coming between the 1880s and 1920s, emigrated from Southern and Eastern Europe. These were the white ethnics. They were mainly Catholic and Jewish and came from rural, village-based cultures where the importance of family took precedence over individualism. As Healey (1995) suggests, they "came from backgrounds less consistent with the industrializing, capitalistic, individualistic Anglo-American culture" and, as a result, "faced more barriers and greater rejection than the Protestant immigrants from Northern and Western Europe" (p. 458).

In U.S. Census data, white ethnics are counted racially as "non-Hispanic whites." Respondents to the Census are allowed to self-identify as to "ancestry" (defined as national origin) but may choose to defer. Because of inexact interviewing methods, coupled with high levels of acculturation into "white" America, current white ethnic populations can only be estimated, not reported in exact numbers. The U.S. Bureau of the Census (2012), for example, reports the following estimates for certain white ethnic groups: Czech, 1,615,000; Greek, 1,390,000; Irish, 36,915,000; Italian, 18,085,000; Lithuanian, 727,000; Polish, 10,091,000; Russian, 3,163,000; Slovak, 801,000; and Ukrainian, 976,000. The Census does not report demographics for American Jews. They are considered a religious rather than an ethnic group and included in the census by national ancestry. Other sources, such as Singer and Seldin (1994), estimate the number of Jews in America at 5.5 million.

▶ Cultural Similarities   17-2

Today, there remain strong pockets of intact traditional culture within each of the white ethnic communities, although many descendants, as suggested previously, have taken the path of complete and irreversible assimilation. Because of their darker physical features and appearance, white ethnics were often viewed as non-white by Western Europeans and thus doubly rejected—both religiously and racially. In the United States, however, their skin color and physical features "paled" in comparison to the non-whites who were already here. As the economic and social circumstances of white ethnics improved, they increasingly identified themselves as "white" in order to distinguish themselves from the people of color with whom they competed for jobs and other economic resources. This dynamic is well-described by both Ignatiev (1995) in his book *How the Irish Became White* and Brodkin (1998) in her book *How Jews Became White Folks*.

This newfound identification with "whiteness" allowed white ethnic group members to assimilate more easily. As they did so, they took on the racial attitudes and prejudices of the dominant culture to which they aspired. Thus, white ethnics exist in a kind of psychological "demilitarized zone." Being white in America, they share the privilege of whiteness. But concurrently, as ethnic group members from cultures who have experienced long histories of oppression, they carry within them many of the internal dynamics that are similar to those of people of color. Human service providers working with these groups face the task of helping them integrate and deal with these two very different psychological realities—that of the oppressor and the oppressed.

As clients, white ethnics—especially those who have been in the United States for several generations—feel comfortable with European American providers. Some have assimilated so fully into majority culture, in fact, that they are culturally indistinguishable from other white clients. Most, however, still retain some cultural connection to the past, and in approaching these individuals, helping professionals should be aware of four important points:

- Although white ethnics may be seen and treated as white by society at large, they do not necessarily perceive or identify themselves as members of the majority. More typically, there is the sense that "I am not white; I am Irish (or Italian, or Jewish)." Nor may they identify culturally with the dominant Northern European worldview. Thus, it is important to be able to assess what a client's connection is to traditional ethnic culture and what traditional beliefs, values, and behaviors remain intact. If white ethnic clients do retain significant elements of traditional culture, providers must become familiar with the content of their culture.
- Such assessments should not be made merely on external characteristics. Like people of color, white ethnics differ widely on assimilation and acculturation. As suggested earlier, some have so fully assimilated and

intermarried that there is little, if any, cultural material remaining beyond surface artifacts like family names, food preferences, and the like. Others are still very traditional, although they may have for convenience taken on some of the outward trappings of majority culture. Only through careful interviewing can an accurate assessment be made. In this regard, it is important to realize that external markers of culture disappear more quickly than internal ones. Thus, cultural artifacts such as values and worldview, psychological temperament, and family dynamics are more resistant to change and disappear more slowly.

▶ The cultural identity of white ethnics may be conflicted in much the same manner as it is for people of color. This is true even for those who, at first glance, may appear highly assimilated. On a similar note, it is important to realize that even if an individual has been spared the direct experience of racial hatred and discrimination, its emotional consequences can be passed on from previous generations through family dynamics.

▶ The fact that white ethnics can assimilate so easily into American culture—thus seemingly escaping their collective past—creates a somewhat different identity picture. In comparison to people of color, who are constantly reminded of their ethnicity, white ethnics can bury their conflicts much deeper and further out of awareness. But again, as in the case of people of color, the rejection of such an important part of identity as one's ethnicity cannot help but cause deep inner conflicts that eventually affect behavior. Thus, it is not uncommon to find instances of identity rejection and self-hatred among white ethnics.

In the pages that follow, I "interview" myself about working with American Jewish clients as an in-depth example of clinical interventions with white ethnic clients. The interview is structured according to the question-and-answer format used in Chapters 9 through 16. Unfortunately, space does not allow an extensive treatment of each white ethnic group in the United States. I hope that this interview will give the reader a rich sense of the kind of clinical and cultural issues faced by white ethnics in general.

▶ Our Interviewee   17-3

Jerry Diller, Ph.D., is a licensed psychologist and member of the faculty of The Wright Institute, Berkeley. He has also taught at the California School of Professional Psychology, Wilson College, and Thomas Jefferson College. He has worked clinically with American Jews and done original research on Jewish identity for more than twenty-five years. He is the editor and author respectively of two books on the subject: *Ancient Roots and Modern Meanings* (1978) and *Freud's Jewish Identity* (1991).

The Interview

Question: Could you talk about your own ethnic background and how it has impacted you and your work?

Diller: As an American Jew, I am quite familiar with the personal struggles and conflicts around ethnic identity that many white ethnics face. I just have to go back into my own personal history. I remember my grandfather, a tailor and immigrant to America, arguing with his old cronies about Jewish politics and the future of the Jewish people. And I remember him ending those discussions with a deep sigh and the words: "Nu, what can I say, it's not easy being a Jew." My grandmother, for her part, was always pouring over the "English" newspapers and asking aloud, to no one in particular, whether this person in the headlines was a Jew or whether that event was "good for the Jewish people." For them, being Jewish was dangerous.

As a boy, I remember trying to tune out those comments. They made me uneasy, and I quickly learned to deflect them as nothing more than "Old World paranoia." I also remember my mother reassuring me that things were different in America and that this was a new start for the Jews. But that hopeful note was contradicted by other, more subtle messages. It was the closing years of World War II; my father was fighting in France, and as I would later learn, the majority of my grandmother's family was being killed in Poland.

Although I didn't realize it at the time, I internalized my family's fears. In response, I did whatever I could to assimilate and become a good American. In the process, I unconsciously rejected my Jewishness. As I grew into adolescence and young adulthood, my sense of identity as a Jew continued to recede, eventually becoming—or so I thought—totally irrelevant.

It was not until well into my thirties, a college professor with a family, that I began to gain a sense of just how alienated I had grown from my ethnic heritage. The discovery of how I truly felt about being Jewish—that is, what really lurked beneath my conscious sense of indifference—came quite unexpectedly. One morning, while walking across campus, I looked down at the bundle of books I was carrying for a course on ethnicity and saw on top a book entitled *The American Jew*. Without thinking, I reached down and turned it over so that the word *Jew* could not be seen. Seconds later, the gravity of what I had done hit me. My first reaction was utter shock and profound surprise that being Jewish was still an issue in my life, let alone the source of such negative feelings. The shock was followed by waves of anxiety and the haunting realization that being Jewish had always felt very dangerous to me. Finally, feelings of anger began to surface: anger at myself and anger at a world that would make a child hate who he was. The simple truth was that I was fearful, embarrassed, and ashamed of being Jewish and had learned to minimize, degrade, and discount it through indifference.

This experience propelled me into therapy to heal the inner rifts I had discovered. And I became so utterly fascinated by the process I was going through and what I found inside myself, I have been doing clinical work and research with Jews and Jewish identity ever since.

Question: Who are the Jews, and what characteristics do they share as a group?

Diller: Traditionally, Jews have been viewed as members of a religious community, sharing spiritual origins as well as a sense of peoplehood. But, in fact, they have become very diverse, and American Jewry is a microcosm of that diversity. All Jews share common roots in a religious tradition and lifestyle and a long history of anti-Semitism and oppression. But differences in geographic location over the last 2,000 years, acculturation into various host countries, modernization, and the extent of religious observance have created enormous diversity within the group. Jews range from ultra-religious to secular and atheistic. They reside everywhere, with the largest concentrations located in the United States and Israel. There are Jews who identify only on the basis of culture or politics or food preference. There are Jewish Buddhists, Jews by conversion, Jews of color, children of Jewish intermarriage, Jews who believe in Jesus Christ, Jews who were raised not knowing they were Jewish, and Jews who have not an inkling of what it means to be Jewish. It is probably most accurate to define Jews as an ethnic group made up of various ethnic subgroups. Some people hold that the only thing that has kept Jews together as a people is anti-Semitism.

Jean-Paul Sartre, for instance, once wrote: "If the Jews didn't exist, they would be created by anti-Semites." More traditionally based Jews see the commonality as spiritual and based in religious roots and observance. A traditional religious teaching, in fact, holds that all Jewish souls were formed during creation and were present at Mount Sinai for the giving of the Torah. As a psychologist, I see Jews as possessing a shared inner psychology and style which in general transcends all of the differences I have just described. Freud, himself a Jew, talked about the existence of an "inner identity" and a shared "psychological structure." I believe that each ethnic group has its own shared psychology. It is passed on within the family—like other cultural material, such as language and communication patterns—through socialization and shared historical experience. Much of it also remains at the level of the unconscious as I described earlier regarding my own experience as a Jew.

First, like all oppressed peoples, most Jews have experienced a long history of trauma and grief, which shapes family dynamics and individual behavior. Clients often exhibit repressed fears, anxieties, and traumas associated with being Jewish. Second, I see certain consistencies in psychological structure; for example, a highly developed conscience or superego, the use of rationalization and intellectualization as defenses, and a propensity toward sadness and pessimism. Third, most

Jews possess, I believe, a strong sense of morality, a strong utopian vision—that is, a desire to make the world a better place—and a spiritual urge toward wholeness and merging. Fourth, there is a shared worldview and style of thinking—one might call it "Talmudic"—that involves a careful consideration of alternatives, emphasis on rationality, rule following, and creative problem-solving. Fifth, there are a shared family structure and dynamics that I will describe later.

Question: Could you give us a nutshell version of Jewish history, especially as it has played itself out in the United States?

Diller: Jewish history is defined primarily by radical dislocations. A largely singular and insular ethnic people through Biblical times, the destruction of the Second Temple drove Jews from their homeland and dispersed them throughout the world. The Jews, as geographically splintered subgroups, experienced repeated migrations and resettlements. They existed at the whim of various host societies as anti-Semitism, based primarily on religious differences, ebbed and flowed in recurrent cycles. During their wanderings, each took on an identity of its own, accumulating a unique history, assimilating aspects of the cultures with whom it came into contact, and adapting traditional customs as necessary. Surprisingly, there remained substantial contact between various geographic subgroups. Two general population groups evolved: the Ashkenazim and the Sephardim. The former were Jews who were dispersed throughout Europe and shared a common tongue: Yiddish. The latter were Jews who originated in Spain and Portugal and were forced to migrate to Arab lands, Italy, Greece, and Turkey after the Spanish Inquisition of 1472.

A second watershed in Jewish history—of more recent vintage—occurred in relation to the European emancipation of the nineteenth century. This democratization of European society set the stage for widespread Jewish assimilation into gentile society as well as a disruption in traditional Jewish religiosity. Emancipation provided Jews an opportunity to escape the traditional lifestyle and to take on non-Jewish ways and habits. Newly modernized Jews also took this occasion to "reform" traditional religious beliefs and practices so that these would be more in keeping with their new lifestyles. The result was the creation of a variety of new Jewish subgroups (most notably Reform, Conservative, and Orthodox), differing both the extent of assimilation and modernization and the nature of the religious practices they adopted. These, in turn, existed side by side and often in tense conflict with those Jews who chose to ignore the lure of emancipation and stubbornly held to traditional lifestyle and religious observance. Many Jews rejected religion totally and became fully secular. The Holocaust and the establishment of the modern State of Israel represent two additional dislocations for the Jewish people.

Like the majority of American Jews, my own descent is Eastern and Central European in origin. My parents' families came from smaller villages in Galicia, located between Poland and the Ukraine. Most came to America to escape growing anti-Semitism and constricting economic conditions. Many wanted to forget the past and immerse themselves in American society and culture. Jewish identity became highly fragmented in America. With the exception of a relatively small group of Orthodox Jews who continue to practice a traditional Jewish lifestyle, most Jews have actively transformed themselves to better fit into American society.

Many have adjusted their religious practices to more closely parallel Christianity, attending services only once a week and on certain special holidays. Others have become predominantly secular, transforming their Jewishness into a set of ethical beliefs, a sense of peoplehood, the burden of 2,000 years of oppression, or merely cultural artifacts like Jewish food or rituals to be enjoyed on a "pick and choose" basis. Thus, for many, ethnic identity has been relegated to a peripheral or at most secondary position in their lives. There is, finally, a growing population of individuals of Jewish descent who today know nothing of their heritage and feel little connection to it. At present, intermarriage rates among Jews average around 50 percent, in some regions as high as 80 percent. It is nothing short of ironic that here in America, where Jews, like other white ethnics, have experienced more material and social success and have been more able to assimilate than ever before, there is a greater danger of disappearing as a group than ever before in history.

A cultural legacy of literacy, achievement orientation, and hard work combined with light-colored skin allowed Jews to quickly climb the socioeconomic ladder, primarily via professionalism and business. Like other white ethnic groups, most willingly took on the privilege of whiteness and its attendant racism while at the same time retaining a strong sense of social justice. Many, in fact, actively supported and identified with the plight of African Americans and their movement for civil rights. But the connection has not been mutual, and since the 1980s, Jewish-African American relations have reached an all-time low. In many ways, this tension epitomizes the psychological plight of Jewish and white ethnicity in America. Its essence is well-captured by Memmi (1965) when he described Jews as both the oppressor and oppressed at the same time. For many African Americans, Jews have become a symbol of white oppression and privilege. They are seen and experienced as very white.

Most Jews, on the other hand, perceive themselves not as white but as Jewish. Although certainly part of this has to do with the invisibility of white privilege, it is equally fed by the experience of feeling culturally different from America's Northern European majority, not to mention a collective history of oppression, continuing anti-Semitism (though it differs in intensity and pervasiveness from that which existed in Europe), and anti-Israel sentiment.

Question: Are there any things that are important to understand about the nature of family, community, and culture among American Jews that have relevance for human service providers?

Diller: It is critical, first of all, to realize that American Jews, like all white ethnic groups, have their own unique cultural values and worldview. Just as there is enormous diversity in cultural content across communities of color, so too do white ethnics differ culturally from each other and from mainstream Northern European culture. It is, in fact, compelling to assume that white ethnics possess the same cultural patterns and traits as majority whites, since they bear such a close physical resemblance. But this is just not the case, and white ethnic cultures, such as that of American Jews, are unique in their own structure and style.

Rosen and Weltman (1996) point to four central values that define and infuse Jewish culture (and much of what I am sharing is drawn from their work). These central values include:

▶ Centrality of the family
▶ Chosenness and suffering as a shared value
▶ Intellectual achievement and financial success
▶ Verbal expression of feelings

Jewish social existence is organized around these values, and the Jewish psyche is socialized to support and internalize them:

▶ Jewish tradition is highly family-centered. Unmarried men and women
   and childless couples are seen as incomplete; intermarriage and divorce
   are looked down upon and viewed as violations of family togetherness.
   Sex and family roles are fairly rigid and remain so throughout life within
   both the primary and extended family. High expectations are placed
   on children as well as adults, and socialization is accomplished through
   the threat of withdrawal of love and the engendering of guilt. The
   basic building block of Jewish life is, thus, the family as opposed to the
   individual, and there are strong pressures for family members to place
   the well-being of the family and the community before personal needs.
   Strong boundaries around the family protect Jewish ethnicity.

   Movement away from ethnicity is experienced and reacted to as
   rejection of the family. Within the family itself, relations are very close,
   often with unclear boundaries. Children are afforded higher status than
   in most other groups. They are expected to give their parents pleasure by
   way of their accomplishments and to remain within the family complex
   throughout life. Traditionally, the sexes tend to be segregated, yet there
   exists within the Jewish family very strong ties and conflicts between

fathers and daughters and mothers and sons. Owing to these complex interactions, Jewish men are often described as distant and dependent, and Jewish women as intrusive and controlling.

▶ Jews tend to view suffering as a basic part of life. Jewish history has so often been characterized by persecution and oppression that the expectation of suffering, attitudes of cynicism and pessimism, and even paranoia have become a central aspect of the family's ethos. Suffering also serves as a shared basis for group belonging, as does the experience of slavery for African Americans.

In other words, it is seen as an intrinsic part of Jewish history. Suffering is seen as something that is visited upon the Jew from outside as opposed to being a punishment for one's sins. Dwelling on suffering and life's negatives often has the consequence of eclipsing the experience of happiness and pleasure, and it is not uncommon for Jews to find it difficult to enjoy life without concurrently accomplishing something. Similarly, the focus on suffering is probably related to a high incidence of hypochondriasis among Jews. Such patterns are especially evident in families of Nazi Holocaust survivors in which parental suffering overwhelms and incapacitates children and where feelings of loss are too strong to talk about.

▶ Jews also place a high value on intellectual achievement and financial success. Historically, religious learning and scholarship were the primary sources of prestige and status in the Jewish world. A man learned, and all other aspects of family endeavor served to support that learning. As Jews assimilated into the gentile world, non-Jewish standards of success, including money, professional status, and secular educational accomplishment, grew increasingly important. The support of intellectual achievement within the family made success in these new secular activities easily transferable.

With assimilation, a growing conflict emerged between family and success. Especially for men, becoming successful meant less time available in the home for family activities and interaction. As an oppressed minority, Jews also tended to push harder to succeed and prove themselves equal to or better than majority group members.

Within the family itself, there is enormous pressure on children and spouses to achieve. In exchange for their special status and treatment, children are expected to perform, often at unrealistically high levels. The perfectionistic demands of the family can easily create a sense of failure irrespective of one's actual accomplishments. Such demands and their attendant sense of failure can also lead to competition among family members and the devaluing of each other to bolster self-esteem.

This cycle of unrealistic demands, failure, and mutual criticism leaves family members wounded emotionally and permanently poised against attack. Also related to success is the high value placed on helping others and taking care of one's own. Traditionally, success is viewed as carrying with it an obligation of charity and generosity. Doing good deeds and giving to those in need are considered highly meritorious.

▶ Verbal expression is highly prized in the Jewish world. The ability to articulate thoughts and feelings and a passion for ideas are encouraged and rewarded within the family. All members, including children, are expected to express themselves verbally, and it is not unusual for the intensity of interaction to escalate as passions rise. Jewish couples tend to deal with conflict openly and directly. They increasingly seek verbal resolution and understanding as arguments and disagreements intensify. Of course, external circumstances can do much to alter such family value patterns. For example, in the well-known silence of Holocaust survivors and their offspring, verbal expressiveness has been limited by the trauma of their experience.

The characteristics of heightened self-expression, achievement orientation, and adroit verbal skills often fuse in North American Jewish families to predispose its members to initiate verbal attacks when threatened. Aggressive language is used to express anger. Complaining, nagging, and criticism are means of controlling the behavior of others and at the same time venting frustration. Anger tends to be carefully controlled in the Jewish psyche and expressed only verbally or indirectly in action but seldom spilling over into overt violence. It is important to realize that inherent in these seemingly aggressive acts is a component of caring, which can make such interaction extremely confusing. Also relevant here, given Jews' long history as an oppressed people, is the possibility that some anger reactions may derive from a dynamic of identification with an oppressor.

Question: Let us switch our focus and begin to look at issues related to help giving and treatment. What factors influence how American Jews go about seeking help, and what kind of problems are they likely to present with?

Diller: Jews, like other white ethnics, exhibit unique patterns of help-seeking and attitudes and behaviors toward mental health issues. Generally, Jews tend to seek treatment earlier than other ethnic groups and to present with less severe neurotic symptoms. They tend to be more accepting of emotional symptoms and less so regarding symptoms of disordered thought. In general, they exhibit a low incidence of alcohol and drug problems. They are comfortable seeking mainstream professional treatment and prefer psychotherapy as opposed to shorter-term solutions. Families tend to seek help for aspects of their children's behavior, especially poor academic performance, lack of achievement, and problems in separation and leaving home. When marital therapy is sought, it is usually presented in terms of communication problems that classically translate into the husband being too distant and unaffectionate and the wife either sexually frigid or withholding. Problems with extended family, in-laws, and dealing with elderly parents are also frequent sources of difficulty. Counselors unfamiliar with Jewish culture may initially have problems dealing with a family's resistances to changing patterns of enmeshment, engaging distant Jewish men, dealing with demanding and assertive Jewish women, or misreading the use of verbal aggression.

It has been suggested that there is a strong relationship between Jews and psychotherapy. Jews are, in fact, overrepresented within the ranks of mental health practitioners and also as psychotherapy clients. There are various explanations for this connection. First, the roots of mental health treatment go back to Freud, who was himself a strongly identified cultural Jew. In Vienna, where Freud practiced, psychoanalysis was referred to as the "Jewish science." Ernest Jones, his primary biographer, described the psychoanalytic movement as "very Jewish" in nature. Freud was actually fearful that his work would be rejected because of anti-Semitism and actively recruited Carl Jung and his Swiss Christian followers to give it a more international flavor. Also, the growth of the mental health profession in the United States coincides quite closely with the assimilation and professionalization of Jews after World War II. Second, psychotherapy itself may be more familiar to those of Jewish descent. In my book *Freud's Jewish Identity* (Diller, 1991), I argue that certain aspects of Freud's theory—for example, the strong bonds between mother and son and father and daughter, tensions between same-sexed parents and child, repressed sexuality, strict incest taboos, and the inferiority of women—were modeled after his own experience of the Eastern European Jewish family. The emphasis in psychotherapy on verbalizing feelings, shared suffering, talking and insight as a means of resolution, and reliance on authoritative expertise also fit especially well with Jewish cultural patterns as described earlier.

Question: Could you talk more about issues of identity and group belonging as they affect members of the American Jewish community?

Diller: Jews, like other white ethnics, often report difficulties in group identity development. Some research findings might be helpful. In her research on Jewish identity and mental health, Klein (1980) found that of the 120 young Jewish adults from the San Francisco Bay Area tested, approximately 15 percent could be classified as positive identifiers, 15 percent as negative identifiers, and 70 percent as ambivalent identifiers. This means that 85 percent of the Jews tested voiced some inner conflict and discomfort with their ethnicity.

These numbers are rather shocking and indicative of the extent of identity problems that still exist among white ethnic populations. What such statistics seem to show is that ethnic identity conflicts are slow to disappear, even with significant reductions in hostility and intergroup hatred. Rather, they are passed on from generation to generation as part of family dynamics. It has also been found that self-awareness of ethnic identity increases with perceived anti-Semitism and racial hatred. American Jews, for example, report growing discomfort and vulnerability as Jews as Israel has been increasingly criticized for its role in the Middle East conflict.

Question: What factors do you see as important in assessing Jewish American clients?

Diller: As I said before, in general, Jews tend to seek psychological help when they experience difficulties in their lives, perhaps more so than any other ethnic group; however, this does not mean that they will present initially with problems related to ethnicity, even if those are central to what has brought them into treatment. Conflicts around ethnicity tend to be avoided and remain unconscious even if they are actively shaping one's life course. So, it is always useful to explore cultural and ethnic material—the role of Jewishness in one's family of origin, in growing up, in relationships, and in one's current life—when taking a personal history. Also, be prepared for some resistance in doing so. A common symptom of identity conflict is avoidance of ethnic material.

I would also like to say something about avoidance of ethnic material among providers. I do a lot of training of Jewish therapists about working with Jewish clients. What I find is that their own ethnic identities often dramatically shape how they work with their fellow Jews. If a therapist is conflicted around his or her own Jewishness, they will tend to avoid, distance, or manage discussions of the client's ethnicity in therapy. I remember back in the 1960s and 1970s, when there was a rebirth of interest in Jewish ethnicity and religiosity that paralleled the Power movements among people of color, many of the Jewish therapists I knew were reporting the same phenomenon. "The strangest thing has been happening in my therapy with Jewish clients. All of a sudden, they are talking about being Jewish." Jewish therapists, like therapists of any race or ethnicity, can also internalize negative stereotypes of members of their own group and unconsciously bring these into treatment.

Question: Are there any subpopulations among American Jews that you feel deserve special comment?

Diller: Yes. First, I would like to say something about survivors of the Nazi Holocaust and their families. The Holocaust is a critical issue to Jews, like slavery to African Americans, the Turkish genocide among Armenians, and the stealing of ancestral lands for Native Americans. It has been clearly shown that the trauma of the Holocaust crosses generations and is still very much evident psychologically in the children and grandchildren of survivors. Maria Yellow Horse Brave Heart's (1995) idea of unresolved trauma and historical grief, reviewed in Chapter 9, is very applicable here. Children raised by traumatized parents often become traumatized themselves. The unresolved grief is passed along, as is the sense of continual danger and loss. In Holocaust families, the separation of children is especially difficult because it is so evocative of previous loss. Going back to the question of assessment, it is always critical to ask American Jewish clients about family history, proximity to the Holocaust, and the experience of anti-Semitism in their own lives.

A second subpopulation that providers should be aware of is Israelis living in the U.S. Israelis represent a very different Jewish culture than American Jews. It is a Middle Eastern culture. It is a majority rather than a minority culture. It is a culture that has lived its entire history under the shadow of war. Secular Jews who live in Israel, which is the vast majority, identify themselves most prominently as Israelis, not as Jews. There is, in fact, a thread of "anti-Jewish" or identity conflict running through Israeli secular society. Anthropologist Stanley Diamond (1957), who studied the first *kibbutzim* (socialist communities) in Israel, sees the kibbutz structure as intentionally antithetical to Eastern European Jewish culture. Each value of Eastern European "ghetto" culture was turned upside down. The tight bond between parent and child was replaced by communal child-rearing, religion and materialism were rejected, physical labor was valued over book learning and intellectualism, and self-defense—rather than blindly submitting to the will of God—became the way of dealing with a hostile world. Tensions also exist between Israelis and Diaspora Jews (Jews living in the dispersion). Israel sees itself as a protector of world Jewry, as well as the proper and appropriate home—and only safe haven—for all Jews. U.S. Jews, in turn, feel that they ensure Israel's survival by influencing American economic and military support. They view this role as crucial to Israel's existence and as a justification for remaining in diaspora. U.S. Jews sometimes view Israelis as abrasive and haughty; Israelis, in turn, see U.S. Jews as soft and materialistic.

A central issue for Israelis living in the United States is their loyalty and responsibility to the State of Israel. All young adults are expected to serve in the army, and lack of service, for whatever reason, is looked upon with suspicion. Many Israelis experience feelings of guilt at residing outside of Israel. This is especially true during times of war or national threat. In order to deal with such feelings, the individual will often view their stay here as temporary, even if they have been here for twenty years and have no intention of going back. The downside of such a psychological strategy is the inability to mourn or grieve the loss associated with immigration. Attachments in the Israeli family are also very strong, and separating from parents, friends, and even the land is often a difficult and painful process.

Lastly, two Jewish subgroups—Jewish women and gays and lesbians—often feel less than comfortable with their treatment in traditional Jewish culture. Many women believe that their role in traditional Jewish culture is demeaning and second-class. This has led to a strong feminist voice in the Jewish world, especially in the United States. Jewish gays and lesbians, in turn, find their lifestyles unacceptable according to biblical law and thus find themselves alienated from their Jewishness.

Question: Can you make any suggestions for developing rapport with Jewish American clients?

Diller: Yes, several things. First, I find Jewish clients extremely verbal, cognitive, and desirous of discussing process in treatment. They prefer to be active collaborators in the therapeutic process and tend toward psychodynamic as opposed to behavioral forms of therapy. Any efforts you can make to reinforce these tendencies will be helpful. There is also high value placed on questioning and being verbally challenging in Jewish culture. This should not be routinely interpreted as aggression, although that may very well be present as well. I am reminded of an intermarried couple who sought treatment because of the wife's reaction to her Jewish mother-in-law. Having spent several years overcoming verbal abuse in her own family of origin, it was hard for her to tolerate and not react explosively as a result of interacting with her mother-in-law. She felt that she was once again being abused. We spent a significant amount of time looking at differences in cultural style and meaning between the world in which she was raised and the Jewish world she had recently entered. Therapy also involved encouraging the rather passive husband to be more supportive of his wife and to intervene in interactions with his mother.

Question: Finally, could you share some case material with us that shows how some of the various issues you have described in working with American-Jewish clients come together in treatment?

Diller: I would like to share with you some case material that has been excerpted from sessions of an ethnotherapy group with Jews run by Klein (1981). The term *ethnotherapy* was coined by Cobbs (1972) to describe a therapeutic group method developed to explore and change negative attitudes about one's own race and ethnicity. Members joined the group because of strong feelings of alienation from their Jewish roots. In order to more directly experience some of the specific inner conflicts they had internalized, group members were asked to participate in an exercise Klein called "I Am a Jew." Each took a turn (and as much time as needed) standing in front of the group and repeating the phase: "My name is . . . and I am a Jew." They keep repeating it until feelings, memories, or images begin to flow. Here are several examples:

▸ "My name is Beverly, and I am a Jew. I am a Jew. I am a Jew. The more I say it, the more nervous I get. I am a Jew. I am a Jew. It gives me the chills. It's not a strong word. It's too short, and I have to stand real tall. But it's not enough. It's as if someone is going to shake me. I realize that I've never let anyone insult me as a Jew. My trick is that I make it known from the beginning so they wouldn't dare make any anti-Semitic remarks in front of me. But I know deep down that I am really afraid. Afraid that someone is going to come in and destroy me."

▶ "My name is Marlene, and I am a Jew. I am a Jew. I am a Jew. I want to tell my father. I am a Jew. My father grew up in a wealthy home in New Jersey. He always felt self-righteous about it. Always felt better than my mother, and she was the Jewish one. She and my grandmother spoke Yiddish to each other. It was because of her that I grew up in a Jewish home, which my father never respected. As a child, I remember my mother cooking kippered herring, and my father complaining about the smell. I remember his comments. And I am ashamed of being a Jew. Especially with men. Dad, I am a Jew. And I am going to be a Jew if you like it or not. I am a Jew. Just like my mother. I am a Jew. I wouldn't care if I was Chinese. I just want to like what I am."

▶ "My name is George and, believe it or not, I am a Jew. I am a Jew. I am a Jew. Oy, am I a Jew. I am a dirty, #$%@& Jew. I am a Jew. I am a Commie pinko Jew. I am just beginning to get some of those feelings again. There was a lot about being a Jew in my childhood. I never felt that I was a good Jew. I can see myself having stones thrown at me as a kid because I was dressed in regular clothes. It was Easter, and all the Catholic kids were dressed in their best clothes. I was called a dirty Jew a lot. We fought the Italian kids a lot. That is just how it was. I want to keep saying it. I am a Jew. I am a Jew. (Very loudly) I am a Jew. Can you hear me out there?"

The experience is a very powerful one. Beverly was able to identify the basic terror she felt about being a Jew and the strategies she used to avoid anti-Semitic comments. Marlene was able to confront her father, acknowledge her shame about being Jewish and her attraction to anti-Semitic men, and bond more positively with her "Jewish" mother. And George was able to re-experience childhood conflicts and overcome longstanding feelings of alienation in order to assert his Jewishness before the group.

According to Klein (1980), such experiences and the opportunity to explore personal feelings about ethnic identity and belonging are highly therapeutic and "overwhelmingly positive." Her post-group research showed increases in self-esteem and ethnic identification and a decrease in social alienation. By way of summary, Klein (1981) suggests: "For minority group members group pride and self pride are inextricably bound. Struggling with and resolving conflicts in Jewish identity release tremendous energy formerly stifled by ambivalence and disaffiliation. This energy can be a potent source of self-acceptance and acceptance of one's own kind."

SUMMARY

In sum, this chapter identified the group titled white ethnics. This group has a unique position in America's history. Many of these individuals hold on to their cultural values but benefit from being white in America. Dr. Diller discusses this dynamic during his interview, as expands on ways to be more culturally sensitive when working with these clients.

ACTIVITY

Check Your Privilege: In small groups of for 3–5 students, identify and discuss your privileges (e.g., white, male, cisgender, able-bodied, middle upper class). Identify and discuss your disadvantages. Compare and contrast these differences within your group. Share how these privileges and disadvantages influence your well-being.

KEY TERMS

white ethnics, 402   dominant culture, 402

Working with American Male Clients: An Interview with Jon Davies

LEARNING OBJECTIVES

18-1 Interpret the implications of census data for American men.

18-2 Explain the history and narrative of men in America.

18-3 Examine Dr. Davies's experience as a counseling psychologist, educator, scholar, and Men's Center director.

▶ Demographics   18-1

Men have a profound effect on American society and make many positive contributions to our culture. However, there is strong evidence that men, as a group, are struggling and experiencing a health crisis. At the crux of this crisis is male behavior, which can be detrimental to themselves, others, and society at large. Men are more likely than women to engage in risk-taking behavior, abuse alcohol and other drugs, and commit suicide, and are less likely to engage in health-promoting behavior, such as maintaining a healthy diet, using sunscreen, or wearing seat belts (Courtenay, 1998, 2000). Despite all the issues they face, men are much less likely than women to seek help, and their life expectancy is four years less than that of women (National Center for Health Statistics, 2017).

Males make up 49.2 percent of the population of the United States (Spraggins, 2005). While more male than female babies are born each year (Howden and Meyer, 2011), by the 35- to 39-year-old age range, women begin to outnumber men. By age 65, women significantly outnumber men and, finally, by age 85, women outnumber men by 2.5 to 1. These numbers reflect men's limited life expectancy in comparison to women, which might be attributed to men's tendency to take risks, be aggressive, and avoid seeking help (Courtenay, 1998).

Men in the United States are a heterogeneous group of people who vary in terms of age, sexual orientation and identity, racial and/or ethnic background, socioeconomic background and/or status, and power. Men's racial and/or ethnic background in the United States mirrors the general population. General population estimates for the United States are White, 62 percent; Hispanic/Latino, 17 percent; African American, 12 percent; Asian American, 5 percent; and Native American, 0.7 percent (U.S. Census Bureau, 2013).

With regard to mental health, men are more likely than women to abuse alcohol and drugs, receive a dual diagnosis, and are almost four times more likely than females to commit suicide (Curtin, Warner, and Hedegaard, 2016). While most men are not violent, most acts of violence in the United States are committed by men, including 79 percent of hate crimes in the United States (Harlow, 2005). Approximately 20 percent of women and 1.7 percent of men will be raped in their lifetime, with the majority of perpetrators in most of these assaults being male (Breiding et al., 2014). Not only are men more likely to commit violence, but they are also more likely to be victims of violence—four times more likely to die from homicide than women (National Center for Health Statistics, 2017). Men are also more likely than women to commit intimate partner violence resulting in serious physical and emotional harm (Black, et al., 2011). Additionally, 94 percent of mass shootings in the United States have been committed by males (Blair, Martindale, and Nichols, 2014).

Although the majority of men do not break the law, men represent 93 percent of the adults incarcerated in state and federal institutions (Carson, Markman, Kaeble, Maruschak, and Alper, 2016). In comparison to their representation in the general population, men of color, particularly African American and Latino men, are overrepresented in the U.S. prison population.

Despite all these differences, most men engage in behavior to "prove" or enhance their manliness. The specific actions that they take may vary greatly across different groups of men. To prove one's masculinity, an inner-city youth might be tempted to join a gang, a suburban teenager may drive recklessly, a man in his forties might ignore his family responsibilities to spend more time working, and a male in his sixties might seek sexual performance–enhancing medication.

In order to increase men's life expectancy and reduce violence, particularly violence towards women, more effective ways to engage men in counseling must be implemented. To accomplish these goals, many psychologists have called for the development of counseling strategies that are congruent with the culture of men and masculinity (e.g., Brooks, 1998; Liu, 2005; O'Neil, 2008; Wester, 2008).

▶ Historical Background 18-2

For centuries, men in Europe and many other parts of the world have had significantly more power than women (Thornton and Young-DeMarco, 2001). From the beginning of U.S. history until the 1950s, men's primary role was to be the provider, responsible for hunting, farming, and/or producing income. Throughout history, women have demonstrated a willingness to do whatever tasks were needed; however, their primary role was taking care of household duties, including gathering, gardening, and raising children. Despite the changing times, the historic gender role differences and inequality between men and women continue in the United States.

Gender role socialization, men's physical strength and stature, and the role of being a provider gave men control over their families, power, and privilege in American society. Women did not gain the right to vote until 100 years ago. However, the last 80 years have seen a remarkable change in women's roles in our society. During World War II, many women entered the workforce, performing jobs traditionally held by men. As a group, women were highly successful in their work, demonstrating to employers (and themselves) that they were capable and valuable employees.

In the 1960s, women's ability to earn money and have access to birth control significantly changed their roles in society (Thornton and Young-DeMarco, 2001). No longer needing men for survival, and inspired by the Women's Rights Movement of the 1970s, women became increasingly independent as they grew more aware of the social, economic, and political inequalities that they were experiencing. During this time period, divorce rates increased, as did the number of women who were single heads of household. Women, therefore, experienced a rapid change in their gender roles.

Unlike women, men's role in society has been much slower to change. In fact, many men are currently struggling to understand what their role should be in society. While women continue to excel in many aspects of life, many men seem confused about if, how, and in what ways they should change.

Family and Cultural Values

Cultural values regarding manhood are first learned though interactions with one's family. The dominant view of masculinity in American culture is that a man should be an individual, independent of others. Emotionally, he should be stoic and in control of his feelings and his environment, while not allowing others to control him, as that will threaten his sense of being a man. He should also be aggressive and able to defend himself, strive to be successful, seek and initiate sexual experiences, and last of all, he should avoid any activity that could be perceived as feminine (Mahalik, Good, and Englar-Carlson, 2003; O'Neil, 2008). Compliance to these role expectations is strictly enforced; men who don't subscribe to traditional gender roles risk experiencing ridicule, shame, bullying, and even more serious forms of violence.

Some researchers believe that masculinity is largely a social construct, based more on what one's culture believes a man should be, as opposed to reflecting actual biological or genetic differences between genders (Courtenay, 2000; Pleck, 1995). Families and our culture communicate this construct to boys by teaching them how they are expected to behave. The messages that boys and men hear can be confusing and conflict with other messages that they receive. Boys are encouraged by health-care providers to take care of themselves, yet male athletes frequently receive the admiration of sports announcers and fans for playing while injured. Men are increasingly hearing a message from their romantic partners to be more vulnerable in expressing their feelings, yet many men can point to examples in which they were ridiculed for crying or criticized for expressing feelings that their partner did not want to hear. Boys and men also receive conflicting messages concerning what a man's role in his family should be, particularly with regard to being a father.

Over 23 million children, specifically boys, grow up without a biological father in the household (U.S. Census Bureau, 2010). This absence can have a profound effect on a child's identity as a male or female and one's feelings of self-worth. Conversely, there may be circumstances in which a father's absence creates a safer and more positive environment for a child.

There are several reasons for men's absence. The first is the high divorce rate and tendency for the children to reside with their mother. Also, many men adopt a view of masculinity that values their success as a provider more than being present for their children. Finally, there are some men who are unable or unwilling to meet the responsibilities of fatherhood due to mental illness, substance abuse, incarceration, and/or lack of a sense of responsibility.

Male Socialization and Role Expectations

A common belief about men is they are less emotional than women. However, research has shown that at birth, male babies are actually more emotionally expressive than female babies (Brody and Hall, 1993, Weinberg, Tronick, Cohn, and Olson, 1999).

Unfortunately, messages such as "Boys don't cry" quickly teaches boys that emotional expression is to be avoided. Anger often becomes the only acceptable emotion that boys and men can express (Pollack, 1998).

As early as three years old, boys begin hearing the message, "Don't be a mama's boy," meaning "Don't be dependent on your mother." Notwithstanding, what three-year-old child does not need his mother? Boys are frequently taught, through the use of shame, to avoid appearing weak and dependent; this early socialization often encourages premature separation from one's mother and contributes to men's lifelong reluctance to seek help (Pollack, 1998).

Many boys are reinforced for taking risks, being competitive, and aggressive and initiating sexual contact. Much time and energy in youth are spent "proving one's manhood"; thus, engaging in health-promoting behavior, such as routinely seeking health care, wearing seat belts, and using sunscreen, is seen as feminine and therefore discouraged. While what is considered manly may vary due to cultural or socioeconomic class differences, most boys experience some aspects of this socialization.

When boys leave home in late adolescence, many do so without societal permission to express emotion constructively or ask for help. These societal restrictions can interfere with young men's ability to navigate life transitions.

Gender Role Conflict and/or Gender Role Strain

Rigid adherence to masculine norms can result in an emotional condition known as men's gender role conflict (GRC) (O'Neal, 2008). In addition to harming one's well-being and human potential, GRC is harmful to everyone—boys and men, girls and women, transgendered people, and society at large. Extensive research has found a relationship between men's GRC and behavioral problems, including sexism, violence, homophobia, depression, substance abuse, and relationship issues. Gender role strain (GRS) is the state of tension that occurs from a gender role conflict (Pleck, 1995). GRS occurs when there is a discrepancy between a man's self-perception and his masculine ideal.

Male Power and Privilege. Men, as a group, have had considerable power in our society. The disparity of power between men and women is clearly visible in U.S. political history. As of 2018, there has not been a female president in the United States, and 80 percent of senators and representatives are male.

While men continue to have great power and privilege, this power is not equally experienced by all men. Collectively, white heterosexual men tend to have greater power and privilege than men of color or gay, bisexual, transgendered, and queer men, reflecting the racism and homophobia that exists in our society. Despite men's power and privilege overall, men, as individuals, are more apt to feel some level of inadequacy rather than great powerfulness.

Why don't most men feel powerful? Vandello and Bosson (2013) described the phenomenon of "precarious masculinity," which depicts men's struggles in achieving and maintaining social status. Proving to others and yourself that you are a man today does not guarantee that you will achieve manhood tomorrow. Some cultures conduct rites of passage signifying a boy's permanent transition into manhood. However, there are no widely accepted rites of passage for males in the United States. A man's perception of his own manhood may vary due to the available avenues he has for achieving status in our society. Men who come from marginalized groups—men of color, gay, bisexual, or transgender, as well as lower-class men—generally have fewer constructive options to achieve a strong sense of manhood.

While men continue to face significant problems and challenges, there is reason to feel cautiously optimistic about their future. In the last 30 years, there has been a growing amount of research conducted on men's issues, which includes an education in counseling strategies congruent with the culture of men. The American Psychological Association (APA) now has an entire division dedicated to examining and enhancing men's health, known as the Society for the Study of Men and Masculinities.

Despite these gains, more research and programming is needed in order to continue to design counselor training programs and educate society on the importance of addressing men's issues to create a safer society. On a positive note, training programs are slowly beginning to recognize the need for greater focus on counselor competence in addressing men's issues. Our society is starting to awaken to the vast amount of violence that men perpetrate, the necessity to address men's issues, and the importance of increasing men's involvement in violence prevention as more men participate in counseling and other therapeutic activities. Finally, with the help of the younger generation of men, males are slowly challenging some of the harmful masculine norms and are striving to find healthier ways of being men.

▶ Our Interviewee 18-3

Jon Davies is a licensed psychologist who earned his Ph.D. in counseling psychology from the University of Oregon. He has worked in multiple settings with a wide variety of clients, including low-income adults, prisoners, veterans, children and families, college students, and older white men. He is the cofounder of the University of Oregon Men's Center and the founder and current director of the McKenzie River Men's Center. Both centers are dedicated to helping men lead healthy lives and reducing male violence, particularly toward women. In addition, he is the cocreator of the Men's Center Approach (Davies, Shen-Miller, and Isacco, 2010) to working with college men to offer strategies to provide culturally congruent services to men.

Davies has shared his expertise through his supervision of master and doctoral student practicum students and interns and has provided training regarding counseling men for mental health and health-care professionals. He is active in Division 51 of the APA's Society for the Study of Men and Masculinities. In 2011, Division 51 selected him as Practitioner of the Year.

The Interview

Question: Can you begin by talking about your own gender background and how it has impacted your work?

Davies: My parents were both Euro-American, my father's family emigrated from Wales. My mother was of English and German heritage. Both my parents were born into lower income families. When my father became an ordained minister, our family became middle-class. However, after ten years as a minister, my father developed health issues and had to leave the ministry. As a result, our family lost our middle-class status and my parents worked for the rest of their lives in food service and/or janitorial positions.

My parents had a very non-traditional relationship. My mother was overtly the most dominant parent while my father was more nurturing, focusing on emotions and relationships. Ironically, I learned the traditional aspects of masculinity—stoicism, assertiveness, and taking charge—from my mother and learned about the importance of feelings, being warm, and relationships from my father. I struggled as an adolescent with what I perceived was my mother's controlling nature. In order to help me understand my mother, my father revealed to me that my mother had been a survivor of childhood sexual abuse and needed to be in control to feel safe.

My only sibling was my older brother. After graduating from college, he came out as a gay man. He worked for years as a counselor and mental health administrator. In his early forties, he contracted AIDS and died in 1991. His death had a profound effect on my life and piqued my interest in men's health. When I returned to college to work on my doctorate in Counseling Psychology, I had a supervisor who specialized in working with men. He encouraged me to learn more about men's issues. As I reflected upon his suggestion, I soon realized that I didn't even know what men's issues were! I later learned that, despite seeing myself as a non-traditional man, I had many issues that other men faced, such as a strong reluctance to seek help, difficulty crying and/or expressing deep emotion, and feeling conflicted about romantic intimacy. Through my own counseling and self-examination, I became aware that many aspects of my behavior were unconsciously being influenced by my beliefs about masculinity.

Through my work with children, families, and college students, I learned that sexual violence happens frequently and that men are responsible for over 95 percent of the sexual violence that occurs in the U.S. Being the son of a survivor of sexual violence, I decided to use my power and privilege as a male psychologist to reduce sexual violence. To accomplish this goal, I needed to step out of my familiar surroundings of my counseling office and venture into the campus community where men congregated to engage them in the prevention of sexual violence. Additionally, if men were not going to seek help to improve themselves, I needed to take the services to them.

Question: Can you discuss some of the factors that influence the ways men seek mental health services?

Davies: Men have a history of underutilizing medical and psychological care. One of the reasons for avoiding seeking help is the fear of appearing weak. Another reason is men's fear of being judged or misunderstood by the care provider. This is particularly true for men of color and men who identify as gay, bisexual, transgendered, or queer. Additionally, some men avoid seeking help because of the financial cost of services. They also may not be aware of the scope of services that are available to them. Since men are reluctant to seek help voluntarily, by the time they pursue services, they often have already exhausted all of their other coping strategies (Davies et al., 2001).

Some men only seek help when they are forced to come to counseling by a partner, family member, employer, or the legal system. While some counselors feel that being mandated to seek services is not an ideal source of motivation for help, many men who benefit from counseling would not have initially attended had they not been externally motivated. It is important, however, to address this issue to reduce the ambivalence and possible resistance that often accompanies mandatory counseling.

Question: What are the kinds of problems with which male clients might present?

Davies: Men will present with a variety of different issues. However, the problems that seriously motivate men include difficulty with a romantic relationship, problems at work, and sexual performance concerns—all issues that affect a man's self-worth. Given men's socialization to be stoic, issues of grief and loss are common in men who seek counseling. Experiencing depression and anxiety can additionally threaten one's sense of adequacy, resulting in a man feeling he should be able to cope with those feelings. Issues that often accompany men presenting problems are:

- Difficulty expressing emotions (alexithymia)
- Struggles with intimacy
- Social isolation
- Feeling shame for needing help
- Uncomfortableness being in a counseling relationship

Question: Do class and/or other socioeconomic issues play a role in these various problems?

Davies: Yes definitely. Money and wealth can bring a sense of power and status to one's life. Conversely, having limited resources can result in a sense of loss of control and power and, in extreme poverty, threaten one's survival. These circumstances can reduce one's feelings of manliness and hope in developing a more prosperous life. Not having socially acceptable ways to achieve success can lead to seeking power through ways that are harmful to oneself and one's society. In addition to wealth and status, being accepted into a group is an important human need; gang involvement is often motivated by a need to belong and gain greater status in one's community. How one defines masculinity is partially based on the norms of the peer group in which one is a member.

Question: In making an initial assessment, what kinds of information are important to collect from a male client?

Davies: Given men's uncomfortableness with formal therapy, it is important to conduct the assessment in a friendly, natural, and matter-of-fact manner. Here are some important questions to consider when assessing male clients.

- Is he taking care of himself (e.g. eating, sleeping, exercising, seeking routine medical care)?
- What is his social support system? Does he have people he can rely on? Is he able to access that support?
- What is his current romantic and/or sexual relationship status?
- How is he coping with stress? Does he routinely engage in positive stress reducing activities?
- What is his drug and/or alcohol use?
- What provides him meaning in his life?
- What are his strengths and growing edges?
- How congruent is the way he currently sees himself with the person he wants to become?
- How long does he plan to stay in counseling?
- Who are men he admires?
- What is his history of loss (e.g. job/career, status, esteem, loved ones, romantic relationships)?
- What is his depression level? Men's depression is often underdiagnosed by clinicians because their depression can appear as anger and/or irritability (Cochran and Rabinowitz, 1999).
- What is his risk for suicide? Given men's high rate of suicide, it is a crucial area to assess. Is he having current or recent suicidal ideation?

Has he made previous attempts? Does he have access to a means to kill himself?

▸ What is his risk for harming others? Is there a history of violence? Has he had current or recent thoughts of harming others? Does he have access to weapons?

(I have included only a partial list of considerations when conducting suicide or homicidal risk assessment. Seek consultation with your supervisor and follow your organization's and your profession's best practices for risk assessment).

Question: Are there subgroups of men that are particularly at risk?

Davies: In general, men who are marginalized by our society are at greater risk for self-harm or harm by others than able-bodied, white, heterosexual men. For example, men of color and/or men who identify as gay, bisexual, transgendered, or queer particularly struggle with a variety of issues. Men who are marginalized often feel they have less power, privilege, and status than white, heterosexual men. Men of color are more apt to experience the effects of racism and xenophobia. Gay, bisexual, transgendered, or queer men are at risk for experiencing homophobia. Both men of color and GBTQ men have greater risk of being ostracized and being a victim of violence. African American men are eight times more likely to die from homicide than white men (National Center for Health Statistics, 2017), with many of the victims between the ages of 15 and 24. These concerns are magnified for men who's sexual identity and/or orientation intersect with one's racial and/or ethnic identity, as in the case of men of color who identify as gay, bisexual, transgendered, or queer.

However, do not overlook the high suicide risk that single, older, white men experience due to their tendency to socially isolate themselves and engage in alcohol and/or substance abuse to mask their feelings of pain, loss, and hopelessness (Curtin, Warner, and Hedegaard, 2016).

Question: What suggestions do you have regarding building rapport with men?

Davies: Many people have been harmed by traditional masculinity resulting in some therapists having negative attitudes about working with men. It is important to reflect on your own attitudes about working with men and address any negative countertransference feelings you might have regarding working with them.

Spending time connecting socially prior to launching into a more professional discussion can help put male clients at ease. A friendly, accepting, and non-judgmental approach is often very helpful in developing rapport with male clients. Creating this atmosphere starts by placing magazines and art work in the waiting room that would be of interest to men. Displaying materials that portray a wide range of men including men of color and gay, bisexual, and/or transgendered men can help create a welcoming and inclusive space. Since men may be fearful about seeking help, it is important for the counselor to reassure the client he made the right decision to seek counseling.

Some beginning female therapists may doubt their ability to provide effective counseling for men, but it is important to recognize that a significant number of men prefer to see female therapists. This can be particularly true for men who had difficult relationships with their father and/or father figures. Additionally, since many heterosexual males have concerns about relationships with women, female therapists can be seen as a valuable and trusted source of feedback about how to improve one's relationships with women.

Question: What else is important to know in working therapeutically with men?

Davies: Many men entering counseling fear being judged negatively and are uncomfortable being in a "one down" relationship with a more powerful therapist. Therefore, engaging with a counselor who expresses unconditional positive regard and a willingness to share power with the client can have a positive impact on the counseling relationship. One way to share power is involving men in any decisions about the counseling process. Additionally, intentionally using self-disclosure can often deepen the therapeutic relationship, equalize the power within the counseling relationship, and normalize the issues the client is facing.

Some men who struggle with talking about emotions may feel more comfortable with cognitive-behavioral techniques; however, I don't assume that all men prefer this approach. Gaining insight into the underlying motivation for one's behavior and more deeply understanding one's relationship patterns can be very helpful for men. An interpersonal process approach can help male clients understand their relationship patterns. Using positive psychology strategies of focusing on the client's strengths and positive coping strategies is both effective and increases men's comfort in the counseling process.

Research has shown that men are more apt to seek help when there is a chance to reciprocate or give back to the helper (Addis and Mahalik, 2003). If your male client seems to feel uncomfortable with the counseling process, a simple way of providing an opportunity to reciprocate would be to ask him to share his knowledge, opinions, and/or experiences about a topic you are genuinely interested in. For example, I like to hike, and if one of my male clients is telling me about an enjoyable hike he took, I might ask him some questions about the hike. Many male clients appreciate the recognition that they have something of value to offer the therapist.

Most men appreciate a counseling relationship in which they feel they can be themselves and the therapeutic bond feels like an extension of a natural relationship in the environment. I believe it is important to help men recognize that behaviors they engage in are motivated by a desire to prove one's masculinity. Often this motivational factor is out of the conscious awareness of the client. Asking a male client what he likes and dislikes about being a man can help reveal some of his struggles with gender role conflict. Asking clients what kind of person and/or man he wants to be in the future, what barriers keep him from becoming the person he wants to be, and what steps he needs take to reach his goals can be very helpful in assisting men become "unstuck" in making positive changes in their lives.

The majority of men value equality, justice, and being helpful to others. Providing men opportunities to serve their community can motivate them to act in ways that provide them personal, emotional, and spiritual fulfillment. Mental health organizations can enhance men's involvement in treatment by offering therapeutic opportunities in non-therapy settings such as workshops, retreats, and nature outings, which contribute to the heath of men (Davies, Shen-Miller, and Isacco, 2010). Other suggestions include:

▶ Be a positive role model for men by modeling vulnerability, self-care, interdependency, and emotional expression.
▶ Not assuming men share the same conceptualization of masculinity you hold.
▶ Assume any man may be a survivor of sexual and/or physical abuse or domestic violence.
▶ Assume a man may not be heterosexual.
▶ Assume men of color and gay, bisexual, transgender, or queer men may have concerns about your ability to understand and accept their diversity.
▶ Offer group experiences for men.
▶ In your group work, encourage multidirectional mentorship, where men of different ages and experience levels can learn from each other.

Question: Finally, could you present a case that brings together the different issues and dynamics about which you have been talking?

Davies: Allan, a heterosexual, white male in his early thirties, was experiencing a divorce. His female partner had left him and started a relationship with another man. She indicated she no longer felt attracted to nor needed by Allan and believed he had difficulty being intimate with others. Feeling anxious, depressed, inadequate, and alone, Allan realized for the first time that he needed help from others. Despite working in a helping profession, he had never sought counseling before. Instead, he coped with his feelings of pain and loss by overworking and the excessive use of alcohol and drugs and sought to validate his self-worth as a man by having sex with multiple partners. He developed a cynical view of romantic relationships, and love in general. Unable to express his feelings of grief, loss, anger, and frustration, he began experiencing periodic suicidal ideation. When he felt he had no other option but to seek help, he finally entered individual counseling for support. Later in treatment, he was referred to a men's group for ongoing validation and support.

Allan slowly began to rebuild his identity as a man, an identity that included seeking help and accepting that he cannot control the behavior and feelings of others. He began to realize that his ex-partner's decision to leave him was more of a reflection of her needs and issues rather than proof of his inadequacy as a man. He started to recognize, accept, and express his feelings. He reconnected with important parts of himself he had neglected, including his creative and spiritual sides. He developed a new group of friends who valued him as a person, participated in group sports and music activities, and eventually developed a long-term romantic relationship.

An important insight was Allan's recognition that he didn't need to use drugs, alcohol, or sex to mask his pain and prove his masculinity. He significantly reduced his drug and alcohol use and eventually quit all together. He replaced his alcohol and drug use with healthy behaviors and activities such as running, joining a softball team, and routinely playing guitar with friends; these activities gave him a renewed sense of esteem and social connection. Developing the endurance to run long distances further enhanced his feelings of personal adequacy. Accepting he needed a strong sense of purpose in his life, he began engaging in meaningful activities and developed friendships with people who shared his interests. His suicidal ideation subsided. He developed a new image of manhood. He grew more comfortable with the fact he needed others and needed to be needed.

As a young man, he had relied upon his independence as a way of enhancing his sense of being a man. Through this painful experience he learned that a healthy man is not fully independent but rather lives interdependently with others. He reconnected with his family and challenged himself to grow in his career by creating opportunities to teach part-time at a community college and eventually becoming a supervisor.

When asked about what he learned from coping with his divorce he said, "There are painful events that happen in life that one can't fully control, only endure. However, you don't have to endure them alone."

Not every counseling experience with men results in as many positive outcomes as Allan experienced; however, providing counseling services that are congruent with the culture of men can increase the likelihood that men will engage in services and open them to the many potential benefits that counseling offers.

SUMMARY

This chapter revolves around the topic of men's effect on American culture with an interview from Jon Davies. Dr. Davies is a licensed psychologist and the cofounder of the University of Oregon's Men's Center and is the founder and current director of the McKenzie River Men's Center. In his interview, which focused on men's health, Dr. Davies discussed factors that influence the way men seek mental health services, the kinds of problems that men present with, and important aspects of working with men. Dr. Davies mentioned that one of the main reasons men avoid seeking help is the fear of appearing weak. But when men do seek help, their issues tend to involve difficulty expressing emotions, issues with social isolation, struggles with intimacy and sexual performance, and difficulty asking for help. When helping men, Dr. Davies suggests reflecting on your own attitudes and biases regarding men. It is important to acknowledge men's fears of being judged, the power dynamics within the relationship, and the client's desire to prove oneself.

ACTIVITY

Review this chapter's section on cultural style, values, and worldview. Think back to your most profound relationships with men in your life. In a brief paragraph, describe your definition of masculinity based on your previous relationships with men. Answer the question: What is a man?

Working with Deaf Clients: An Interview with Valentino Vasquez and Johanna Larson

LEARNING OBJECTIVE

19-1 Examine the struggles that some Deaf clients face throughout their daily lives.

This chapter was written by Shoshana D. Kerewsky, PsyD, HS-BCP. Additionally, the University of Oregon's Accessible Education Center provided sign language interpretation for this interview.

▶ Our Interviewees   19-1

Valentino Vasquez, MA, is a third-generation Latino who was born deaf in a Spanish-speaking extended family. His wife is deaf and their two children are hearing. As a child, he attended a deaf and hard-of-hearing program within a mainstream public school and attended Gallaudet University for several years. He teaches *American Sign Language (ASL)* and *Deaf Culture* courses in the Communication Disorders and Sciences program at the University of Oregon. He is involved with organizations supporting the Deaf community, both on-campus and off.

Johanna Larson, MS, is a native ASL speaker whose second language is English. She is the eldest hearing daughter of profoundly deaf parents in an extended Northern European American family with many other deaf members. Her father became deaf from spinal meningitis at age 3. Her parents met at Gallaudet University. She teaches basic linguistic principles of ASL, as well as Deaf Culture and Community Studies in the Communication Disorders and Sciences program at the University of Oregon.

The Interview

Question: Would you give a brief overview of "Deaf Culture," including your participation and relationship to Deaf culture?

Vasquez: This really relates to language as well as identity, including values, perceptions, and beliefs, as well as social customs. In Deaf culture, the language is ASL—using a manual communication as opposed to a spoken language communication. I participate in Deaf culture through the Oregon Association of the Deaf, Oregon Registry of Interpreters for the Deaf, and socializing with members of the Deaf community. Sometimes Jo and I will host Deaf events, such as performers or speakers. We reach out to the Deaf community and invite them to attend these events, and that becomes part of our Deaf community and therefore our Deaf culture.

One example of Deaf culture would be social customs. For example, when an event is over, people often notice that Deaf people stay well after closing hours. The lights will go off and people will say, "You all need to leave," and Deaf people tend to stay, whereas hearing people will leave on time. Deaf people often will go out of the building, but then we'll stand outside under the street lights and continue the conversations. It'll whittle down until the last person is there. That's a really big part of Deaf culture.

I'm involved with the Deaf community here in Oregon with a few organizations that support the Deaf, for example, the Oregon Association for the Deaf (OAD) and the Oregon Registry of Interpreters for the Deaf (ORID). Here on campus at the University of Oregon, I'm involved with the Disability

Studies Advisory Board, which advises and suggests courses that can be used for a Disability Studies minor. The ASL sequence and the ASL culture course is part of that minor.

Question: How do you see Deaf culture as similar to, or different from, an ethnic culture?

Vasquez: There are obviously some similarities with ethnic cultures, such as language. Another aspect of ethnicity is appearance, such as skin color and that sort of thing, but often it's really just the language aspect, and then that goes into culture, whether that be literature, sports, music, values, perceptions, beliefs, etc. The only real difference is the spoken language and the manual language of sign.

Question: What are some ways that Deaf culture interacts with your ethnic culture? How did your family communicate with you when you were a child?

Vasquez: Mostly it was gesturing with my Spanish-speaking family. My parents did know fingerspelling and some Signed Exact English. It depends on people's educational background as well as whether they have a hearing family or a deaf family. My parents both tend to use "Spanglish," going back and forth with a mix of Spanish and English, but in my signing, I don't tend to do that. I do use gestures to communicate Spanish language, but I use a different language—I use ASL when communicating English concepts. For example, the sign for "present" in Spanish sign would be equivalent to "spanking" in English. In my signing, there's not really anything with a Spanish influence. There are deaf families from Mexico where the parents and the kids are deaf, and when they come here to America, they do have some accents in their signing, but I don't.

Question: What should human services providers and counselors know about working with a deaf person or his or her family? What kinds of concerns and needs might a deaf person bring to a human services provider?

Vasquez: It's very important for them to know that one deaf person is not representative of all deaf people. They're all individualized—their background in their family, their educational background, their upbringing, the various external factors that affect who they become and how they grow up. What's really important to be aware of is the deaf person may not solely use ASL, maybe they don't fully identify as 100% Deaf, or there may be a balance. They could feel that they are bilingual and/or bicultural. They could be hearing-dominated biculturally, which means they are deaf and they use ASL, but they're comfortable socializing with the hearing community as well as with the Deaf community, but they tend to socialize with more hearing people because that's their comfort zone for various reasons. Whereas there are some deaf people who are dominant bicultural deaf, who tend to socialize more with other deaf people and less with hearing people. Some people have a balance and can go between the various cultures, deaf and hearing. There are a variety of people who have various psychological experiences and other factors that have influenced their lives.

Human service providers also should be aware of interpreting needs. There needs to be an interpreter, and the interpreter has to be a good fit for that deaf person's language needs. If the deaf person is an ASL-dominant user, versus an English-dominant user, it's important to be sure the interpreter can provide the appropriate language for that particular deaf person. The deaf person's background and upbringing may also matter—whether they were born into a deaf family or a hearing family and whether they went to a Deaf school or a mainstream hearing school.

Larson: It's important for people in all service fields to remember the power dynamic, especially if there is an interpreter involved in the meeting. Simple things, like speaking directly to the deaf person as opposed to through the interpreter and not speaking *about* the deaf person, but rather *to* and *with* the deaf individual.

And then there is terminology. We have been using the term *Deaf* with a capital D, *deaf* and *hard-of-hearing* rather than *hearing impaired* or *exhibiting a loss of hearing*, with the exception of those who lose their hearing later in life. The latter is not a cultural difference, but a physiological difference. Those who identify as a culturally Deaf person, predominantly use ASL, those politically and socially active in the Deaf world would call themselves *big D* or *capital D Deaf*. Those who have hearing loss, for whatever reason, and don't identify as a member of the Deaf culture, but as a member of the hearing culture who has experienced some audiological hearing loss would be *small d deaf*.

Vasquez: The *National Association for the Deaf (NAD)* and the American Sign Language Teachers Association (ASLTA) have talked about using different signs to differentiate between *big D* and *small d* deaf. There is no standardized ASL that makes this differentiation yet. For people who are culturally Deaf, they're talking about changing the sign from "deaf," a gesture from the ear to the mouth to a gesture from a pointer finger at the eye to the "5 handshape" [the technical term for a particular ASL hand position]. People who are culturally *big D* Deaf use that sign because deaf people rely on their eyes to communicate. They use their eyes for life, for behaving, for everything. They are always visual. They're in an eye-centric world, so pointing to your eye and going to the 5 handshape represents using your eyes and hands. People who are *little d* deaf tend to sign "deaf" with a "d" from the ear to the mouth to show their hearing and then going to the mouth for speaking. That's been a topic for discussion lately, to develop this new sign for *Deaf* to show it's our language and our culture. It's an interesting discussion about having two different signs.

Larson: The old sign is going from the ear and closing.

Interpreters follow a code of professional conduct or code of ethics that I think people need to be aware of. First of all, you want to make sure you have a qualified interpreter, and that is defined in a variety of ways in different states, so make sure, if at all possible, that the deaf individual or client can meet with the interpreter for a few moments beforehand to make sure they can establish effective communication. The most important standard is confidentiality. The role of the interpreter is as a conduit of information between all parties at the table. An interpreter should not interject or offer any opinion, counseling, or advice. There are many other rules, but those are the two primary ones that all people should feel confident in, provided they have a qualified interpreter. Depending on the event or situation, my strongest suggestion would be to use a qualified agency so the human services provider and the client don't need to go over the ethical considerations of the interpreter's role in depth.

Vasquez: The Oregon Registry of Interpreters for the Deaf (ORID) has a lot of focus on educating people about interpreting and the need for Certified Deaf Interpreters [who are Deaf or hard-of-hearing] to help facilitate communication between a Deaf person and other parties, and a hearing, qualified interpreter. Sometimes there will be two interpreters—one is a Certified Deaf Interpreter (CDI) standing on the platform at an event, and then off-screen is a hearing interpreter. There are other times where there's one interpreter who is hearing, so it goes back and forth between having a CDI or not. If a qualified hearing interpreter goes to a meeting and decides that communication is not effective, then it's helpful for them to be able to pull in a CDI.

It depends on what the person wants to share, especially, as Jo mentioned, talking about power dynamics or the client's coping skills in various situations, whether it be with their family, within their community, or their place of employment or school. They might be analyzing their self-identity: *Who am I? Am I okay? Are people looking at me funny? Am I different?* Struggling with other people's perceptions plus marriage and relationship issues can be difficult.

Larson: It depends where the Deaf person is, what services are already provided, and the awareness of the community. Ninety percent of deaf children are born to hearing parents so it's often a catch-up game in terms of language options. One of the things human services providers may see in a variety of settings around the country, though not everywhere, will be more isolated deaf individuals who don't have strong community ties because the Deaf-supportive community is so dispersed.

Larson: It took many, many years for us to have ASL accepted as a language option for the university's undergraduate second language requirement, which used to be entitled the "foreign language requirement." Now we have a two-year sequence and some ancillary coursework, including American Deaf Culture. Our Communication Disorders and Sciences program trains professionals in speech-language pathology and audiology. This is a better fit than previously, when they would take ASL through a linguistics class, for example. I believe that didn't work well in terms of the professional educating children and adults in ASL. The first professionals that most hearing parents of deaf children go to are in the audiology or speech-language pathology field. I have always hoped that this shift in ASL training might change things for the better.

Question: What resources or activities would you suggest for a human services provider to learn more about Deaf culture and clients?

Vasquez: It varies from state to state. The top two priorities would be to have a statewide commission for the deaf and hard-of-hearing as well as statewide services that could provide various resources and networking opportunities. Contacting them would be very beneficial. In addition, having state agencies for the deaf.

Some of these resources can be brought back to people who work in the human services or counseling community. Just being able to connect with them and ask people for resources and maybe meet some Deaf people to talk about interpreting issues that might arise. Maybe having someone come to their place of employment and give a presentation, pass out some paperwork, provide some resources that people can read that would help human services providers more clearly understand the state agency, the commission for the deaf and hard-of-hearing, or the state organization for the Deaf.

Larson: In addition to the state, there are often county and city resources available. It would behoove everybody to know what their resources are so if they need to hire an interpreter, it's not a mad scramble at the last moment. They also should verify that there's money in the budget because all human service agencies that receive federal funds are required to pay for the interpreter, which sometimes puts the onus on the Deaf person, though it shouldn't. As is true for many other cultures and communities; if people, especially undergraduates, can go to events where they're in the minority to learn what that feels like and watch how Deaf people interact, even one time, that will really help to make services more accessible. They'll think about how they apply that to their own services. And, of course, taking any coursework in American Sign Language and/or American Deaf culture, and working as a professional with Deaf clients!

Vasquez: There are a lot of articles available to counseling and human service providers working with the Deaf and hard-of-hearing population. I encourage professionals to read and collect that information.

Larson: My biggest plug is to make sure that coursework at post-secondary institutions always include something about deafness and Deaf culture from a knowledgeable professional. Don't lump deafness and Deaf culture under general Disability Studies—there are more factors involved in that.

Vasquez: Gallaudet University and National Technical Institute for the Deaf have research, readings, articles, publications, and other resources for the Deaf and hard-of-hearing population. They offer undergraduate and graduate programs in counseling and human services fields as well.

SUMMARY

This chapter includes an interview with Mr. Vasquez and Ms. Larson focusing on their experience as members of the Deaf community. They both give insight to how human services providers can improve the quality of their services with intentionality and curiosity. They both suggest counselors know their resources and seek literature regarding the Deaf and hard-of-hearing population.

ACTIVITY

As a large group, ask how many students know a deaf person. What can they say about them: their age, how they communicate, how their speech sounds, occupation, hobbies, special equipment they use, etc.

In small groups, identify and discuss the three most impactful ways your life would change if you suddenly lost your hearing (e.g., through illness or an accident).

KEY TERMS

| American Sign Language (ASL), 434 | Deaf, 436 Deaf Culture, 434 | National Association for the Deaf (NAD), 436 |

20

Closing Thoughts

LEARNING OBJECTIVES

20-1 Determine ways to gain more knowledge about cultural diversity.

You began your odyssey into the world of cross-cultural service delivery with an anecdote about Asian students who refused to avail themselves of mental health services at a college counseling center because its hospital-like setting reminded them of death. Such cultural "disconnects," which are still far too common in the human services, did not occur because of any lack of clinical expertise or caring. Quite the contrary, the staff of the counseling center where it happened boasts many skilled and dedicated clinicians. Rather, it occurred because of a lack of basic attention to the cultural dimensions of the world of their clients. In Chapter 5, the concept of a *paradigm* was introduced, referring to the worldview or perception of reality that a science or a practitioner learned to adopt. It was suggested that paradigms shape perceptions as well as what one sees and does not see. The counseling center's staff shared paradigm did not allow them to see the cultural messages about death and avoidance that were so immediately obvious to the Asian students.

But paradigms can change and broaden, and that is what pursing cultural competence is all about. To reiterate the model found in Cross et al. (1989), which is presented in Chapter 2, cultural competence involves five skills:

▶ Awareness and acceptance of cultural differences
▶ Self-awareness of one's own culture and cultural blind spots
▶ Understanding and working with the dynamics of cultural difference
▶ Gaining knowledge of the client's culture
▶ Adapting skills to cultural contexts

Hopefully, through your reading and study of this text, you have begun to see and acknowledge the importance of culture in working with clients. You should by now have gained a good basic understanding of concepts such as cultural competence, racism, prejudice, privilege, and culture (discussed in Chapters 1, 2, 4, and 5); a sense of how to get started (Chapter 3); insights into the psychological world of people of color (Chapters 6–10); introductory information on working with clients from various communities of color, as well as white ethnics (Chapters 11–17); and a sense of how men (Chapter 18) and deaf individuals (Chapter 19) experience the world and how to best work with them. It is likely that you have been emotionally as well as intellectually affected by this material, have had some personal attitudes and beliefs challenged, and have become at least a bit more culturally open and less ethnocentric. And although knowledge is no substitute for experience, you should have at least a beginning sense of whether working with culturally diverse clients is suited to your interests and temperament. If not, that is very important information to have. The rigor and demands of cross-cultural service delivery are not for everyone, and such work should be a matter of choice, not a matter of happenstance or default. In any case, you will find that what you have learned from this text will make you a better clinician, no matter who your clientele. After all, each client has his or her unique cultural background, which must be respected and viewed as the starting point for effective service delivery.

If you find yourself excited by the prospect of cross-cultural work and intend to pursue it further, I applaud your intentions. But remember what was said in Chapter 2 about becoming culturally competent—it is no simple task, and it cannot be accomplished by reading a book or two, taking a seminar, or working with a few culturally diverse clients. It is instead a long-term, maybe lifelong, process—one that never really seems to end. It is as much about learning about one's own internal processes as it is about gaining external cultural knowledge. It is also cumulative and based on actual clinical work with diverse populations. Yet when first encountering clients from a cultural group with whom one has never worked, it often seems like "starting from scratch." Finally, moving toward cultural competence is highly developmental and growth-producing. You will likely be as changed by it as are your clients—perhaps even more so. As suggested in Chapter 2: "This book is only a beginning. What happens next—what additional cultural learning experiences you seek and the extent to which you seriously engage in providing services cross-culturally—is up to you" (p. 17).

So, where do we go next? The following sections contain suggestions that you might find useful for further preparation, as a means of gaining support (because such work can be isolating), and in helping to allay some of the natural anxiety that you may experience in contemplating or actually beginning cross-cultural counseling.

▶ Gaining More Knowledge   20-1

It is necessary to broaden and update your education about cultural diversity continually. The more you can learn about the general topics of racism, culture, diversity, cultural competence, and cross-cultural service delivery, as well as specific knowledge about individual groups and their cultures, the more comfortable and conversant you will become. Again, this book is only a foundation upon which to build. Since the late 1980s, there has been an explosion of good material in this area and a dramatic increase in excellent training opportunities. You should take advantage of these whenever possible.

Continuing education implies several kinds of knowledge. First, it means keeping current on racial and ethnic politics. The world of race and ethnic relations is an ever-changing kaleidoscope. History is not static, and once you have been sensitized to the existence of race-related phenomena, it is hard to avoid the realization that racial and ethnic tensions are a central theme in our society. Witness, for example, the dramatic increase in hate crimes against Arab, Muslim, and Sikh communities in the United States since September 11, 2001. According to the U.S. Justice Department, more than 170 investigations of hate crimes were undertaken in the first month after the attacks. Muslim civil rights groups estimate the numbers of such hate crimes in excess of 1,000 and see this figure as very conservative, given the fact that most incidents are never reported. A Western European socialist journal, *Committee for Workers International* (Committee for Workers International, 2001), documents some of the most extreme reactions:

> A Sikh gas station attendant is murdered for wearing a turban in the Midwest. A Somalian is stabbed to death in Minneapolis. A Muslim man with an Arab name is found stabbed to death in Seattle. A man is murdered in Fresno, California, for looking Middle Eastern. A Salvadoran man screams for help in Spanish as a gang of five white youngsters beat him for being "bin Laden's next of kin." A Nicaraguan woman is assaulted in Los Angeles for her Turkish features. A mob attacks two Afghan teenagers in Prince William County, near Washington, DC. An angry mob of 300 "patriots" marches through a Chicago neighborhood chanting anti-Arab slogans and threatening local mosques with fiery destruction. A mosque in Central Kentucky is reduced to ashes by a fire bomb. Businesses with Arab or Muslim owners are threatened in New York, Detroit, San Francisco, Portland, Chicago, etc. Some are firebombed, others have windows broken or their storefronts decorated with the Neanderthal poetry of hate. (p. 2)

Such events have a dramatic impact on all culturally diverse clients, not just those who are Arab or Muslim. They create an atmosphere of fear and danger that cannot help but bring back past memories of experiences of racial hatred. Clients will bring such reactions into sessions with them, and it is critical they be acknowledged and processed.

Or consider the growing demand among African Americans for reparations from the U.S. government for slavery and its aftermath of racism. Chapter 10 describes reparations as part of the healing process following mass violence, such as in South Africa and its Truth and Reconciliation Commission. It also points out the sad state of efforts to gain reparations for slavery in the United States. Robinson (1999) calls it the "debt that America owes." African American scholars estimate the cost of unpaid wages during slavery and lost resources because of racism to be at least $4 trillion. Precedents for such reparations have been paid to Japanese Americans for incarceration and loss of property during World War II, Native Americans for lost land rights, and to European Jews for forced labor. And since 1989, retired Congressman John Conyers (D-MI) had been introducing a bill, HR 40 (nicknamed "40 Acres and a Mule" after Civil War general William Tecumseh Sherman's proposal of what each freed slave be given by way of compensation), to study the concept of reparations to black Americans. Although Conyers's bill never passed and will never garner enough congressional support to do so, it is still a very real issue in the African American community and for many African American clients. Reparations for slavery and racism are not merely about money. Rather, they are symbolic of much more: the acknowledgment of a historic injustice, a means of healing the past and "leveling the playing field," a step toward reconciliation between black and white America, and a matter of ethnic identity and pride.

Second, it means being aware that cross-cultural counseling and service delivery is a relatively young discipline in the helping services and, therefore, particularly prone to changing ideas, theories, and new research. State-of-the-art knowledge changes much more quickly than in established disciplines, and this calls for a much closer scrutiny of the emerging literature. The following topics will emerge as particularly important in the near future for providers of cross-cultural services:

- *Ethical guidelines for cross-cultural work.* Although there have increasingly been efforts to enumerate behavioral standards for cross-cultural service delivery in all the helping professions, these efforts have focused primarily on defining the skills necessary for culturally sensitive practice. You learned about three examples in Chapter 2. The thrust of such work is based on the idea that it is unethical to offer services to culturally diverse clients without cultural competence. What is still lacking, however, are more substantive discussions of the specifics of appropriate and inappropriate behaviors by practitioners in the cross-cultural setting.
- *Current definitions of general ethical standards.* These are typically based on the Northern European worldview and value systems, are often culture-bound, and lead to conflicts between practitioner expectations and the client's culturally prescribed behavior and style. Raising such issues is also at times experienced as an assault on the very heart of one's profession. Two good examples are professional boundaries and the confidentiality of personal information. Neither of these professional values is necessarily subscribed to nor given the same degree of importance among non-mainstream cultures.
- *Models of racial and ethnic identity development.* Increasingly, researchers are realizing the great value of assessing and matching the level of racial and ethnic identity development (see Chapter 9) of both providers and clients. In the future, such models will become more sophisticated and more fully enumerated for various ethnic and racial groups, as well as for mainstream white subgroups. In addition, there will be more detailed work on the consequences of matching providers and clients who are at different levels of development.
- *Countertransference in cross-cultural service delivery.* There has been, over time, a growing awareness of the impact of countertransference in cross-cultural work. *Countertransference* is a psychoanalytic term that broadly refers to the personal attitudes and issues that color and shape a provider's reaction to individual clients. Becoming aware of one's own "baggage," especially around ethnicity, has increasingly been acknowledged as critical in the development of cultural competence.

Future work will explore the impact of a provider's racial attitude (beliefs and stereotypes) toward a client's racial or ethnic group, ethnic identity and personal experience with "difference," awareness of the communal dimension of a client's culture, and awareness of privilege and the power dimension of the therapeutic relationship. Please review Deborah Ronay's section on "Talking about Race and Ethnicity with Clients," which appears at the end of Chapter 3.

▸ *Bicultural clients and interethnic group relations.* To a large extent, cross-cultural work has been defined in a binary fashion (i.e., in relation to the interaction of whites and non-whites). There has been and will continue to be increased interest and research in working with clients from bicultural and multicultural backgrounds and different cultural identities within the same person (see Pamela Hays's work on the ADDRESSING Framework in Chapter 3). Similarly, there has been growing attention paid to the relationships among cultures of color.

▸ *Transpersonal and spiritual dimensions of culture.* Unlike mainstream European culture, cultures of color and certain white ethnic cultures tend to place higher value on the transpersonal or spiritual dimensions of reality. This can be seen, for example, in the differing ways that healing and mental health are defined. In conventional Western medicine, dysfunction is defined primarily in physical and psychological terms. The body and mind are seen as separate, and transpersonal experiences tend to be pathologized. Traditional cultures tend to be more holistic and view spiritual dimensions of healing as critical. As mainstream society becomes more interested in religion, spirituality, and other forms of non-rational experience, more attention will be paid to traditional healers and the transpersonal beliefs and worldviews of cultures of color.

Third, familiarize yourself with all forms of diversity. Although this book focuses on issues of racial and ethnic diversity, it is critical to be aware of the impact of differences in age, ableism and disability, class, gender and sexual preference, language, and religiosity on human behavior. Each characteristic has been a source of bias and discrimination in our society, and although all share certain commonalities vis-à-vis the internal psychology of oppression, each has its own dynamics and characteristics. All represent sources of enormous variation and diversity within racial and ethnic groups. For example, age is defined, valued, and ascribed a very different role across cultures. In general, the elderly are revered, listened to, respected, and afforded high status among communities of color and white ethnic groups; quite the opposite occurs in Northern European culture, where youth is emphasized and aging is dreaded. It is suggested that you consider taking a separate course or reading a well-written text on each of the forms of diversity to familiarize yourself with their unique psychologies and how they interact with culture. In the "Selected Bibliography on Diversity," you will find a list of suggested readings in relation to each form of diversity. Again, in this regard, you are referred to Hays's work as described in Chapter 3.

Learning About Client Cultures

It is critical to prepare for work with clients from a particular ethnic group by doing research on that group's culture, history, and health care issues. This can include not only academic and professional reading and web searches, but also novels, biographies, social histories, and travel accounts, as well as movies, videos, theater, art exhibits, lectures, and so forth.

A valuable supplement to such cognitive learning is various degrees of immersion in the client's culture. This can range from attending celebrations, cultural events, and political rallies; eating regularly at ethnic restaurants; and patronizing community businesses to more sustained contact such as volunteering in the community, learning the language in programs in the community, and traveling to countries of the client's origin. One graduate program with which I was associated valued cross-cultural training to such an extent that it required its students' first field placement to be in a setting serving clients who were culturally different from themselves. As a learning strategy, students were responsible for gaining entry into these settings on their own.

This provided valuable—although sometimes frustrating—insights into cross-cultural interactions and cultural variation in organizational dynamics. Such cultural encounters and the cultural knowledge they impart are seen as so important that Coleman and Gates (1999) have added it as a sixth skill component of cultural competency in their extension of the model by Cross et al. (1989).

Finding Support for Cross-Cultural Work

It is also a useful idea to find a "cultural consultant," a professional who is indigenous to the community with whom you will be working to consult on a regular basis. As a beginner to cross-cultural work, you will find it particularly helpful to discuss all cases, especially early in your training, with someone who is knowledgeable about the workings of the client's culture. With more experience and comfort, one might feel the need for consultation only in more difficult or problematic cases. Agencies should also establish ongoing consulting relationships with indigenous cultural experts from all groups that they serve.

One might also consider establishing a peer study and/or supervision group with other providers who are involved in cross-cultural service delivery. Regular meetings can involve discussing shared readings, presenting cases, having guest experts, and the like. Such a group can provide opportunities to share resources and knowledge, receive supervision and support when helpful, and remain focused on the cultural dimensions of cross-cultural service delivery.

A final suggestion is to join local ethnic provider groups and networks. Often, providers who work extensively with a specific population join together as a means of sharing information and resources, advocating for the needs and rights of clients, and keeping knowledgeable on current research and trends in providing services to the population of interest. Active participation in such a group is an excellent way to learn more about a client population, connect with other providers who might serve as valuable resources, and demonstrate interest and commitment to cross-cultural service delivery as a career focus.

SUMMARY

The case of the Asian students who refused to seek services at a university because it reminded them of a hospital and a place of death, with which this book begins, is reviewed along with the model by Cross et al. (1989) of cultural competency skills for professional helpers. Readers are asked to review what they have learned and whether they feel ready or interested in pursuing further learning toward cultural competency. For those who wish to continue, suggestions are offered for gaining more knowledge (keeping current with racial and ethnic politics and emerging and changing ideas about cross-cultural service delivery); becoming more familiar with all forms of diversity; learning from immersion in client cultures; and developing support systems to facilitate further skill development and guidance. I sincerely hope that reading this text has been a satisfying, enlightening, and growth-producing experience for you.

ACTIVITIES

1. *Review of learning experiences.* Review in your mind the most important learning experiences you had during the course in which you are enrolled. Describe each briefly in regard to what happened, how you felt as a result of the experience, and what you learned. You might find it interesting and informative to categorize each learning experience in relation to the professional skill development models reviewed in Chapter 2. What would you say is the single most important concept you learned during the course and from this textbook?
2. *Enjoy a career fantasy.* Project where you might be ten years into the future. Envision a hypothetical work situation that incorporates all the fantasies you have about the kind of helping services work you would like to be doing in ten years. What kind of agency or setting are you in? What kind of tasks are you involved in? Who is your client population? What kinds of cross-cultural work are you doing? What levels of cultural knowledge and skill have you developed over the past ten years? What experiences in the interim have contributed to your growth in cross-cultural skills? How are you feeling about your cultural competency?

Glossary

Acculturation A form of assimilation wherein an ethnic group or individual takes on the cultural ways of another group (usually that of mainstream culture), often at the expense of traditional cultural ways.

Acculturative stress Stress and emotional distress and, at times, trauma caused by acculturation.

ADDRESSING framework A theory, developed by Pamela Hays, that summaries various aspects of cultural identity that may affect a client's behavior. The acronym stands for the following: **A**ge and generational influence; **D**evelopmental disabilities; **D**isabilities acquired later in life; **R**eligion and spiritual orientation; **E**thnic and racial identity; **S**ocioeconomic status; **S**exual orientation; **I**ndigenous heritage; **N**ational origin; and **G**ender.

African American An ethnic group of Americans with total or partial ancestry from any of the black racial groups of Africa. The term typically refers to descendants of enslaved black people who are from the United States.

Alloplastic An approach to personal change that involves altering the external environment to fit the needs of the individual.

Ambivalent ethnic identification An inner sense of group belonging in which positive ethnic experiences coexist alongside negative and rejecting ones, leading to a vacillation between positive and negative identification. Also referred to as *internalized racism*, *internalized oppression*, and *racial self-hatred*.

American Sign Language (ASL) A natural language that serves as the predominant sign language of Deaf communities in the United States and most of Anglophone Canada.

Anti-racist A member of the dominant culture who works to reduce his or her own internalized racism and becomes a cultural ally.

Apology A formal statement of regret that includes acknowledgment of the facts, acceptance of responsibility, expression of sincere regret, and promise to not repeat the offense. An aspect of reparations.

Arab and/or Muslim Americans A diverse array of Americans of Arab and/or Muslim descent who speak Arabic, tend toward a collective lifestyle, and originally resided in the Middle East, Africa, and Southern Asia.

Asian Americans A diverse array of Americans of Asian and Pacific Islander descent representing forty-three distinct Asian and Pacific Islander ethnic groups including individuals who identify themselves as Asian Indians, Chinese, Filipino, Korean, Japanese, and Vietnamese.

Assimilation A process whereby a previously distinct ethnic group merges socially into another group—usually a dominant or mainstream society. Forms of assimilation include acculturation, structural assimilation, marital assimilation, and identificational assimilation.

Authoritarian personality A psychological theory of prejudice derived from the work of Adorno et al. (1950) that views prejudice and racism as one of various characteristics of a global bigoted personality type.

Autoplastic An approach to personal change that involves adapting the self to the external environment.

Axiology A dimension of culture that describes the interpersonal values that a cultural group teaches.

Bicultural families Families in which individual members descend from two or more cultures or racial groups. They can be formed either by parents from different cultures or through adoption.

Biculturalism The belief that it is possible to live and function effectively in two cultures (also referred to as integration).

#BlackLivesMatter A global network in which an ideological and political intervention where black lives are systematically and, often, intentionally targeted for demise.

Capitalism An economic system in which private entities own the factors of production.

Chicano/a Developed by Mexican Americans who found themselves no longer from Mexico but also not clearly from the United States. It tended to be taken on by the young, coming out of the streets, and spoken with a sense of pride and assertiveness.

Collective personality The personality structure and dynamics of individuals who live in collective social systems and families; tend to be motivated by group rather than personal goals, contextually rather than dispositionally oriented, and are emotionally other-focused rather than ego-focused.

Collective treatment models As opposed to one-to-one or individualistic treatment models, collective treatment models actively depend on interactions with other group members for therapeutic outcomes.

Colonization The act of a more powerful nation or people taking control of the land and resources of a less powerful and often indigenous people and using them for its own benefit.

Communities of color Collectives of non-whites who share certain physical (racial), cultural, language, or geographic origins and/or features.

Community Psychology A systems approach to psychological intervention that focuses on addressing issues of social injustice and power differentials in society, community development and empowerment, and client strengths, as opposed to symptomatology.

Complex trauma An emotional state experienced by people who are exposed to repeated and prolonged trauma. A DSM category of anxiety disorders.

Concept of self A dimension of culture that refers to whether group members experience themselves as separate beings (individual self) or as part of a greater collective (extended self).

Concept of time A dimension of culture that describes how time is experienced within a cultural group.

Conflictive attitude Held by individuals who, although they would not support outright racism or discrimination, oppose efforts to ameliorate the effects of discrimination, such as affirmative action.

Constriction and numbing In association with trauma for when an individual experiences a psychic deadening or dissociation from reality.

Countertransference A psychoanalytic term that refers to a therapist's unconscious personal reactions to aspects of the client.

Cross-cultural Referring to diverse cultural backgrounds.

Cross-cultural service delivery The provision of human services in a situation where provider and client come from diverse cultural backgrounds.

Culture Differences in language, values, personality and family patterns, worldviews, sense of time and space, and rules of interaction between individual groups. Comprises traditional ideas and related values, is learned, shared, and transmitted from one generation to the next, and organizes life and helps individuals interpret their existence.

Cultural ally A white person who actively works to eliminate racism.

Culture analysis Work that precedes psychological analysis or in some cases avoids confrontations that may be generated in the family when forbidden content is brought to consciousness.

Cultural blindness An attempt to avoid bias by ignoring racial and cultural differences yet adopting a mainstream approach to service delivery.

Cultural case formulation A framework, included in the DSM-5, to be used in assessing and diagnosing of culturally diverse clients. It highlights areas of functioning where cultural character-istics may alter appropriate diagnosis, assessment, and treatment planning.

Cultural competence The ability to provide services cross-culturally in an effective manner.

Cultural destructiveness Policies and practices which are actively destructive of communities and individuals of color.

Cultural diversity The array of differences that exist among groups of peoples

with definable and unique cultural backgrounds.

Cultural incapacity Policies and practices unintentionally promoting cultural and racial bias.

Cultural myopia Viewing the world exclusively from the perspective of one's cultural paradigm.

Cultural pre-competence Having failed at attempts toward greater cultural competence due to limited vision of what is necessary by holding a false sense of accomplishment or overwhelmed by failure; showing a tendency to depend on tokenism and overestimate the impact of isolation of people of color.

Cultural proficiency Exhibiting basic cultural competence while advocating for multiculturalism.

Cultural racism The belief that the cultural ways of one group are superior to those of another.

Culturally diverse Individuals (e.g., providers or clients) who come from culturally different, diverse, or distinct backgrounds. Used synonymously with the term *cross-cultural*.

Culturally specific knowledge Being aware of and knowledgeable about the specific content of a client's culture(s).

Culture The conscious and unconscious content that a group learns, shares, and transmits from generation to generation that organizes life and helps interpret existence.

Deaf Lacking the power of hearing or having impaired hearing.

Deaf Culture The set of social beliefs, behaviors, art, literary traditions, history, values, and shared institutions of com-munities that are influenced by deafness and which uses sign language as the main means of communication.

Deficit theories Theories within the social sciences that purport to explain differences among racial and ethnic groups on the basis of cultural rather than genetic deficiencies.

Disconnection In association with trauma, when an individual experiences a shattering of the self, its attachment to others, and the meaning of human experience.

Disorders of dehumanization Emotional experiences and disorders that diminish an individual's experience of themselves as fully human. Such dehumanization is believed to be the core experience underlying psychological trauma.

Dominant culture A culture that is able, through economic or political power, to impose its values, language, and ways of behaving on a subordinate culture(s).

Dominative attitudes The belief that majority group members should be allowed to dominate those who are culturally diverse.

Emic Viewing a culture through a perspective that is indigenous to it.

Empowerment A helping strategy that involves supporting, encouraging, and giving clients skills to become their own advocates.

Enslavement The institution of slavery.

Epistemology A dimension of culture that describes a cultural group's preferred way of gaining knowledge and learning about the world.

Ethnic conflict Repeating cycles of violence between two groups, whereby acts of retribution by one side are answered with acts of violence by the other. Ethnic conflicts tend to spiral and are characterized by tunnel vision, historical grievances being perceived as if they were current, double victimization, lack of empathy for the other, and group chauvinism.

Ethnic group Any distinguishable group of people whose members share a common culture and see themselves as separate and different from the majority culture.

Ethnic identity or identification The aspect of personal identity that contributes to one's self-image as a member of an ethnic group, and the nature of one's sense of belonging to an ethnic group—how one thinks, feels, and acts in relation to one's ethnic group membership.

Ethnic psychology Psychological dynamics that are peculiar to the experiences of people of color and other oppressed ethnic groups. See also the discussion of ethnic-specific "psychologies" in Chapter 5.

Ethnicity The fact or state of belonging to a social group that has a common national or cultural tradition.

Ethnocentrism Assessing, interpreting, and judging culturally diverse behavior in relation to one's own cultural standards. Such behaviors are acceptable to the extent that they are similar to one's own cultural ways.

Ethnorelativism Assessing, interpreting, and judging culturally diverse behavior within its own cultural context. Such behaviors are neither good nor bad—only different.

Ethnotherapy A therapeutic group method developed to explore and change negative attitudes about one's own race and ethnicity.

Ethos A dimension of culture that refers to the basic values, assumptions, and beliefs that are held within a cultural group and that guide social interactions.

Etic Viewing a culture through a perspective that is external to it.

Extended self Ego development typical of ethnic group members who conceive of themselves not as individuals, but as part of a broader collective.

Externalization A narrative therapy technique that helps the client expose, name, and define the problem and map out its effects on the client.

Familismo The importance of the family, both nuclear and extended, in the Latino culture.

Felt experience of living Growing up, developing, and maturing in each culture yields a phenomenologically different experience; that is, the quality of life differs in tone, mood, and intensity.

Forgiveness An internal process of healing within the victim, whereby she or he is able to disconnect from self-destructive defenses and reactions, such as anger and guilt, brought to bear interpsychically in reaction to a traumatic event so as to move on toward a healthy lifestyle.

Frustration-aggression-displacement theory A psychological theory of prejudice that holds that racial hatred derives from frustration, which leads to aggression, which in turn is displaced onto more vulnerable ethnic or racial group targets.

Gender role conflict (GRC) A psychological state in which restrictive definitions of masculinity limit one's well-being and human potential.

Genocide The extermination and/or massive death of such magnitude that a group ceases to continue as a distinct culture and collectivity. A distinction is made between complete and partial genocide.

Globalization of mental health The contention in Watters (2010) that there has been a growing trend toward globalization and the exporting of Western concepts of mental health and their associated treatment modalities, including the use of psychotropic medications, especially in relation to Third World countries.

Grandparent A parent of one's father or mother; a grandmother or grandfather.

Group-specific and person-specific meanings Information about a client that a therapist gathers and uses to construct hypotheses, based on knowledge of the client's ethnic group versus the client's individual experience.

Hijab A head covering worn in public by some Muslim women.

Hispanic A term adopted by the federal government in the early 1970s for census and administrative purposes in order to create a single category for all the people whose origins are in Latin America.

Historic trauma response Brave Heart's description of psychopathology among Native Americans and other ethnic groups who have experienced trauma repeatedly across generations and have also lost their traditions of grieving.

Historical trauma and unresolved grief The damage that ethnic and racial communities may suffer from psychological violence that is passed on from generation to generation.

Human service providers Professional helpers (e.g., counselors, therapists, psychologists, and social workers) who provide social and emotional advice, resources, and education to those in need, most often on a one-to-one basis.

Hyperarousal In association with trauma, the internal biology of self-preservation on permanent alert.

Iatrogenesis Sickness or pathology that results from medical or psychological intervention and treatment.

Identity An inner sense of self that reflects a stable perception of who a person is individually and socially.

Immigrant A person who leaves one country to settle permanently in another.

Immigration The movement of people into a country or region to which they are not native in order to settle there. Immigration is done for many reasons, including temperature, breeding, economics, politics, family reunification, natural disaster, poverty, or the wish to change one's surroundings voluntarily.

Implicit bias Negative cognitive racial attitudes and attributions that are held unconsciously that can serve as powerful detectors of racial biases.

Indian Time A term this group has evolved to describe its "looser" sense of time.

Individual racism The beliefs, attitudes, and actions of individuals that support or perpetuate racism.

Individualism The prominent mode of Western psychology wherein the individual person, rather than one's group or family membership, is the focus of treatment.

Individualistic Cultures The cultures that stress the needs of the individual over the needs of the group as a whole; people are seen as independent and autonomous; social behavior tends to be dictated by the attitudes and preferences of individuals.

Institution Refers to societal networks that covertly or overtly control the allocation of resources to individuals and social groups.

Institutional racism The manipulation of social institutions to give preferences and advantages to whites, and at the same time restrict the choices, rights, mobility, and access of people of color.

Integrative attitudes Characteristically pragmatic in the approach to race relations. Individuals tend to have a sense of their own identity as whites and at the same time favor interracial contact and harmony, believing racism can be eradicated through goodwill and rationality.

Internationally displaced people (IDP) A term that refers to "refugees" who are displaced within their own country.

Intrusion When traumatized people relive the event as if it were recurring in the present.

Istighaba Involves expressing authentic feelings away from the family and social observation.

Jihad The Islamic spiritual struggle to be strong in one's efforts—intellectually, physically, and spiritually—for the good of all.

Just Therapy A Community Psychology approach to mental health treatment developed and implemented by the Family Center in Wellington, New Zealand.

Justice An inner sense of fairness that requires retribution for wrongs done to oneself, other individuals, or groups, including one's people. After a violation, justice tends to be experienced when there is physical or psychic retribution, the perpetrator is seen to suffer, and it is perceived that the perpetrator has learned a moral lesson.

Kinship bonds Complex kinship networks of blood and nonrelated individuals.

Latinas/os A diverse array of Americans who descend from ethnic heritages that share Spanish as a primary language, Roman Catholicism as a religion, and various cultural values.

Learning styles Preferred modes and styles of learning in which children from diverse cultural groups internalize, become proficient at, and become increasingly more comfortable with various learning styles as they are socialized. Individual learning styles are culturally informed.

Locus of control A dimension of worldview that reflects whether individuals feel in control of their own fate (internal control) or feel controlled externally by environmental forces (external control).

Locus of responsibility A dimension of worldview that reflects whether individuals believe they are responsible for their fate (internal responsibility) or cannot be held responsible because there are more powerful forces at work in their lives (external responsibility).

Logic In reference to culture, a dimension that describes the kind of reasoning and intellectual processes that a cultural group adopts.

Machismo A Spanish term in reference to the sense of responsibility a man feels to care for and protect his family and those around him.

Marianismo A Spanish term in reference to women having a tendency toward self-sacrifice and focusing on the needs of others for the benefit of the family as well as to acquiesce to their husband's role as the head of the family.

#MeToo A vehicle for women to share their abuse stories, including sexual violence.

Mestizo A mixture of Spanish and Indian backgrounds.

Microaggressions Unconsciously delivered racial slights, subtle snubs, dismissive looks, gestures, and tones. They are pervasive and automatic in daily conversations and interactions and frequently are glossed over as innocent and innocuous.

Microassaults Verbal and nonverbal attacks intended with varying degrees of conscious awareness to hurt a person of color through name-calling, avoidance, or other forms of discriminatory behavior and insensitivity.

Microinsults Communications that convey rudeness and demean a person's racial heritage of identity.

Microinvalidations Communications that exclude, negate, or nullify psychological thoughts, feelings, or experiential reality of people of color.

Middle Passage The ways in which African Americans were physically brought to America; the brutal transition from pre-enslavement to being enslaved.

Mismatch Syndrome The disparity in values between one's culture of origin and the dominant culture.

Model minority A term used to describe Asian Americans due to a cultural tendency to defer and not compete openly with white Americans.

Mosayara A Muslim and/or Arab term which involves hiding your real feelings and instead reacting in socially acceptable ways.

Multicultural ethical awareness The implication that commitment itself is not enough but must be accompanied by the requisite knowledge about cultural differences and how they may affect the expression of and solution of ethical problems.

Multicultural ethical commitment Requiring a strong desire to understand how culture is relevant to the identification and resolution of ethical problems. It demands a moral disposition and emotional responsiveness that moves psychologists to explore cultural differences and creatively apply the APA Ethics Code to each cultural context.

Multicultural ethical decision-making Includes creating a goodness of fit between the cultural context and the psychologist's work setting and goals;

and engaging in a process of co-learning that ensures the fit.

Multiracial People composed of or representing a variety of races.

Narrative therapy An approach to psycho-therapy introduced by Michael White that focuses on the harmful effects of social injustices and seeks to help clients reconstruct the self-limiting stories they tell themselves about who they are.

National Association of the Deaf (NAD) the nation's premier civil rights organization of, by, and for deaf and hard-of-hearing individuals in the United States of America.

Native Americans A diverse array of Americans descended from tribes indigenous to North America, including both American Indians and Native Alaskans.

Negative ethnic identification An inner sense of group belonging typified by primarily negative ethnic experiences, which are rejected or disowned, thus remaining unintegrated into a coherent sense of self. Also referred to as *internalized racism, internalized oppression*, and *racial self-hatred*.

Non-Hispanic whites A U.S. Census racial category that refers to Caucasians or whites.

Ontology A dimension of culture that describes how a cultural group views the nature of reality.

Pacific Islander A diverse array of individuals from Hawaii, Guam, and Samoa.

Paradigm A set of assumptions and beliefs about how the world works that structures a person's perception and understanding of reality. Personal paradigms of reality are largely shaped by the culture in which one is raised.

Parental child A child who has been given responsibilities or a parental role before he or she is emotionally prepared to fill it.

Passing The colloquial term for light-skinned, minority individuals who hide their ethnicity, often to gain the privilege of appearing white.

People of color A collective reference to groups of color in the United States, including African Americans, Asian Americans, Latinos/as, and Native Americans. Used synonymously with the term *non-white*.

Personalismo An interpersonal attitude that acknowledges the basic worth and dignity of all individuals and attributes to them a sense of self-worth—serves as a powerful social lubricant in Latino/a culture.

Pillars of Islam The five basic religious rules all Muslims should follow. These include the profession of faith, daily prayers, alms, fasting during Ramadan, and making a pilgrimage to Mecca, the Holy Land.

Positive ethnic identification An inner sense of group belonging that is typified by primarily positive ethnic experiences, which are integrated into a coherent sense of self.

Post-enslavement A period of reconstruc-tion that showed newly freed Africans' talents, forgiving spirit, and intelligence to become part of American culture and contribute to businesses and industry.

Post-traumatic stress disorder (PTSD) A mental disorder listed in the DSM-5 that involves an extreme internal reaction to a traumatic experience and includes symptoms of hyperarousal, intrusion of thoughts and memories, constriction of affect and other response systems, and social disconnection.

Power The capacity to produce desired effects on others.

Powerlessness The inability to influence others.

Precarious masculinity Depicts a man's struggles in how to achieve and maintain social status (prestige or dominance).

Predatory lending practices Making loans to individuals, usually poor or ethnic, who cannot possibly afford them and who eventually will face foreclosure and the loss of their homes.

Pre-enslavement A time when African Americans lived in many different cultural groups across the continent of Africa; a time before enslavement.

Preferred story A term from Narrative therapy that states alternative storylines are overshadowed by the problem story. Usually, they represent values, hopes, and preferred ways of being that the problem story has managed to overshadow and is kept hidden from the client and his or her family.

Prejudice An antipathy or negative feeling, either expressed or not expressed, based on a faulty and inflexible generalization that places a group of people at some disadvantage that is not merited by their actions.

Problem story A term from Narrative therapy that implies that pathology and personal problems result from the negative stories they tell themselves, which in turn leads to the experience of low personal agency, negative identity conclusions, and low self-worth.

Psychobehavioral modality A dimension of culture that refers to the mode of activity most preferred within a cultural group.

Race Biological group differences that derive from an isolated inbreeding population with a distinctive genetic heritage.

Racial classification ability The first step in the process of the development of racial identity; involves the child learning to apply ethnic labels accurately to members of diverse groups.

Racial evaluation The third step in the process of developing racial identity; involves the creation of an internal evaluation of one's racial group.

Racial identification The second step in the process of developing racial identity; involves learning to apply the newly gained concept of race to oneself.

Racial identity The aspect of personal identity that contributes to one's self-image as a person of color. Evolves in relation to the sequential acquisition of three learning processes. *See also* racial classification ability, racial identification, and racial evaluation.

Racial identity development The series of predictable stages that people of color go through as they struggle to make sense of their relationship to their own cultural group, as well as to the oppression of mainstream culture. A parallel process has been suggested for whites.

Racism The systematic subordination of members of targeted racial groups who have relatively little social power by members of the agent racial group who have relatively more social power.

Rankism The persistent abuse and discrimination based on a power differential in rank or hierarchy.

Reactive attitudes Involves a rather militant stand against racism. Categorically, these individuals tend to identify with people of color, may feel guilty about being white, and may romanticize the racial drama in addition to being very sensitive to situations involving discrimination and reacting strongly to the inequities that exist in society.

Reconciliation As it relates to cultural groups, efforts to bring about peaceful and nonviolent relationships between ethnic groups previously in conflict, as well as between perpetrators and victims.

Redlining The practice of banks and other financial institutions refusing to provide loans and other financial services to individuals in poor and ethnic neighborhoods.

Refugee A person who, owing to well-founded fear of being persecuted for reasons of race, religion, nationality, membership of a particular social group or political opinion, is outside the country of his nationality.

Reparations Acts of compensation offered to victims in an effort to restore what has been lost. An aspect of the restorative justice model.

Restitution The return of property, things, and even human remains to their rightful owners. An aspect of reparations.

Restorative justice Justice defined by restoring the social order. It seeks to repair social connections and establish peace between parties, rather than focus on punishment of the offenders, through truth-telling, public acknowledgment, and reparations to the victims.

Retributive justice Justice defined by retribution and punishment of the offender.

Self-regulation of prejudice When a low-prejudiced person has a negatively implicit evaluation of an outgroup member.

Shahada The Muslim profession of faith ('there is no god but Allah, and Muhammad is the messenger of Allah'), one of the Five Pillars of Islam.

Simpatico The Latino culture's emphasis on interdependence and cooperation.

Social Identity Theory This theory by psychologist Henri Tajfel maintains that individuals have a natural propensity to strive towards a positive self-image, and social identity is enhanced by categorizing people into in-groups and out-groups.

Social Science Statement A summary of research findings by 32 psychologists arguing that segregated schools were harmful to both black and white children and presented as evidence in the case of *Brown v. Board of Education of Topeka*, decided in 1952 by the Supreme Court of the United States. It is believed to be responsible for the decision that separate but equal segregation of schools was unconstitutional, and that desegregation of U.S. public students was mandated.

South Asian Americans Individuals who identify as South Asian typically come from the current countries of Bangladesh, Bhutan, India, the Maldives, Nepal, Pakistan, and Sri Lanka.

Stereotype An undifferentiated, simplistic attribution that involves a judgment of habits, traits, abilities, or expectations assigned as a characteristic of all members of a group.

Transference A psychoanalytic term that refers to the client's unconscious personal reactions to aspects of the therapist.

Trauma An extraordinary psychological experience, caused by a threat to one's life or bodily safety or a personal encounter with violence and death that overwhelms ordinary human functioning.

Tree of Life Exercise A collective, narrative therapy approach developed for the treatment of vulnerable children in South Africa.

Ubuntu An African concept or value, called forth by Nelson Mandela in an effort to reinstate justice to people in South Africa after the end of apartheid, that emphasizes the interconnection of all people and beings.

Vicarious traumatization Trauma caused by being in close emotional contact with a traumatized individual. Also known as *secondary traumatization.*

White Individuals whose cultural origins are Northern European. Also refers to majority and mainstream group members, as well as majority providers and clients.

White ethnics National immigrant groups of Eastern and Southern European descent who share a common experience of immigration to the United States and a history of oppression. Included in this designation are Italians, Poles, Greeks, Armenians, Jews, Irish, and various

ethnic groups making up the Russian Republic (e.g., Czech, Lithuanian, Russian, Slovak, and Ukrainian).

White identity development The series of predictable stages that whites and white ethnics go through as they struggle to make sense out of their own whiteness and their relationship to communities of color.

White privilege The benefits that are given to white Americans of European descent automatically on the basis of their skin color.

Witnessing An approach to trauma treatment that emphasizes the importance of the therapist acknowledging, believing, and understanding the unspeakable aspects of the client's experience.

Worldview A term referring to the meta-dimensions along which all cultures can differ. They include Psychobehavioral Modality, Axiology, Ethos, Epistemology, Logic, Ontology, Concept of Time, and Concept of Self.

References

Aboud, F. (1987). "The development of ethnic self-identification and attitudes." In J. S. Phinney and M. J. Rotheram (Eds.), *Children's ethnic socialization: Pluralism and development* (pp. 32–55). Newbury Park, Calif.: SAGE.

Aboud, F. (1988). *Children and prejudice.* Oxford, U.K.: Blackwell.

Aboud, F., and Doyle, A. B. (1993). "The early development of ethnic identity and attitudes." In M. E. Bernal and G. P. Knight (Eds.), *Ethnic identity: 1. Formation and transmission among Hispanics and other minorities* (pp. 46–59). Albany: State University of New York Press.

Abu-Baker, K. (2006). "Arab/Muslim families in the United States." In M. Dwairy, *Counseling and psychotherapy with Arabs and Muslims: A culturally sensitive approach* (pp. 29–46). New York: Teachers College Press, Columbia University.

Abudabbeh, N. (1996). "Arab families." In M. McGoldrick, J. Giordan, and J. K. Pearce (Eds.), *Ethnicity and family therapy* (pp. 333–346). New York: Guilford

Adames, H. Y., and Chavez-Dueñas, N. Y. (2016). *Cultural foundations and interventions in Latino/a mental health: History, theory, and within group differences.* New York: Routledge.

Addis, M. E., & Mahalik, J. R. (2003). Men, masculinity, and the contexts of help seeking. *American psychologist, 58*(1), 5.

Adorno, T. W., Frenkel-Brunswik, E., Levinson, D. J., and Sanford, R. N. (1950). *The authoritarian personality.* New York: Harper & Row.

Allen, Jon G. (2001). *Traumatic relationships and serious mental disorders.* New York: John Wiley & Sons, Ltd.

Allen, G. E., Garriott, P. O., Reyes, C. J., and Hsieh, C. (2013). "Racial identity, phenotype, and self-esteem among biracial Polynesian/white individuals." *Family Relations, 62*(1), 82–91.

Allen, Q. (2016). "Tell your own story: Manhood, masculinity and racial socialization among Black fathers and their sons." *Ethnic and Racial Studies, 39*(10), 1831–1848. doi:10.1080/01419870.2015.1110608

Allison, B. N., and Bencomo, A. (2015). "Hispanic families and their culture: Implications for FCS educators." *Journal of Family & Consumer Sciences, 107*(2), 56–61.

Almeida, R. (2005). "Asian Indian families: An overview." In M. McGoldrick and J. Giordan (Eds.), *Ethnicity and family therapy* (pp. 377–394). New York: Guilford.

Allport, G. W. (1954). *The nature of prejudice.* New York: Doubleday.

American Psychiatric Association. (2013). *Diagnostic and statistical manual of mental disorders (DSM-5).* Washington, D.C.: American Psychiatric Association.

American Psychological Association. (1979). "Membership register." In *Diagnostic and statistical manual of mental disorders.* Washington, D.C.: American Psychological Association.

American Psychological Association. (2002). *Ethical principles of psychologists and code of conduct.* Washington, D.C.: American Psychological Association.

American Psychological Association. (2003). *Guidelines on multicultural education, training, research, practice, and organizational change for psychologists*. Washington, D.C.: American Psychological Association.

American Psychological Association. (2017). "Ethics code." In *Diagnostic and statistical manual of mental disorders*. Washington, D.C.: American Psychological Association.

Anderson, J. A., and Adams, M. (1992). "Acknowledging the learning styles of diverse student populations: Implications for instructional design." In L. L. B. Borders and N. Van Note Chism (Eds.), *Teaching for diversity* (pp. 5–18). San Francisco: Jossey-Bass.

Arendt, H. (1964). *Eichmann in Jerusalem: A report on the banality of evil*. New York: Penguin.

Arredondo, P., Toporek, R., Brown, S. P., Jones, J., Locke, D. C., Sanchez, J., and Stadler, H. (1996). "Operationalization of the multicultural counseling competencies." *Journal of Multicultural Counseling and Development*, 3(January), 42–78.

Arredondo, P. (1996). "Multicultural counseling competencies as tools to address oppression and racism." *Journal of Counseling & Development*, 77(1), 102–108.

Atkinson, D. R. (2003). *Counseling American minorities: A cross-cultural perspective* (6th ed.). Boston: McGraw-Hill.

Atkinson, D. R., Brown, M. T., Casas, J. M., and Zane, N. W. S. (1996). "Achieving ethnic parity in counseling psychology." *The Counseling Psychologist*, 24(2), 230–258.

Atkinson, D. R., Casas, J. M., and Wampold, B. (1981). "The categorization of ethnic stereotypes by university counselors."

Hispanic Journal of Behavioral Sciences, 3, 75–82.

Atkinson, D. R., Morten, G., and Sue, D. W. (1993). "Defining populations and terms." *Counseling American Minorities: A cross-cultural perspective (4th ed.)*. Dubuque, Ia.: William C. Brown.

Atkinson, D. R., Whitely, S., and Gin, R. H. (1990). "Asian-American acculturation and preferences for help providers." *Journal of College Student Development*, 31 (March), 155–161.

Austin, J. T., and Austin, J. A. (2018). Initial Exploration of Therapeutic Presence Pedagogy in Counselor Education. *International Journal for the Advancement of Counselling*. doi:10.1007/s10447-018-9339-x

Austin, G. A., Prendergast, M. L., and Lee, H. (1989). "Substance abuse among Asian American youth." *Prevention Research Update No. 5* (pp. 1–13), Portland, OR: Northwest Regional Educational Laboratory.

Barden, S. M., Sherrell, R. S., and Matthews, J. J. (2017). "A National Survey on Multicultural Competence for Professional Counselors: A Replication Study." *Journal of Counseling & Development*, 95(2), 203–212.

Baruth, L. G., and Manning, M. L. (2016). *Multicultural counseling and psychotherapy: A lifespan approach*. New York: Routledge.

Bay Area Association of Black Psychologists. (1972). "Position statement on use of IQ and ability tests." In R. L. Jones (Ed.), *Black psychology* (pp. 92–94). New York: Harper & Row.

Beker, J., Isralowitz, R., and Singer, M. (2014). *Adolescent substance abuse: A guide to prevention and treatment*. New York: Routledge.

Bell, H., Limberg, D., Jacobson, L.,
and Super, J. T. (2014). "Enhancing
self-awareness through creative expe-
riential-learning play-based activities."
Journal of Creativity In Mental Health,
9(3), 399–414. doi:10.1080/15401383.
2014.897926

Bell, L. A. (1997). "Theoretical foundations for social justice education." In M.
Adams, L. A. Bell, and P. Griffin (Eds.),
Teaching for diversity and social justice
(pp. 3–15). New York: Routledge.

Bennett, M. B. (1993). "Towards ethnorelativism: A developmental model of intercultural sensitivity." In R. M. Paige (Ed.),
Education for the intercultural experience
(pp. 1–51). Yarmouth, Me.: Intercultural
Press.

Bernal, M., and Castro, F. (1994). "Are clinical psychologists prepared for service and
research with ethnic minorities?" *American Psychologist*, *49*, 797–805.

Bernard, B. (1991, April). *Moving toward a
"just and vital culture": Multiculturalism
in our schools*. Portland, Ore.: Northwest
Regional Educational Laboratory.

Bernstein, R. (2013). US Census Bureau
projections show a slower growing, older,
more diverse nation a half century from
now. *Retrieved February*, *15*, 2013.

Berry, J. W. (2017). Theories and
models of acculturation. *The
Oxford Handbook of Acculturation and Health*, *15*. doi:10.1093/
oxfordhb/9780190215217.001.0001

Black, L. (1996). "Families of African
origin: An overview." In M. McGoldrick,
J. Giordan, and J. K. Pearce (Eds.),
Ethnicity and family therapy (pp. 57–65).
New York: Guilford.

Black, M. C., Basile, K. C., Breiding, M. J.,
Smith, S. G., Walters, M. L., Merrick,
M. T., & Stevens, M. R. (2011). The
national intimate partner and sexual
violence survey: 2010 summary report.
*Atlanta, GA: National Center for Injury
Prevention and Control, Centers for
Disease Control and Prevention*, *19*, 39–40.

Blair, J. P., Martaindale, M. H., & Nichols, T.
(2014). Active shooter events from 2000
to 2012. *FBI Law Enforcement Bulletin*, *7*.

Bollin, G. G., and Finkel, J. (1995). "White
racial identity as a barrier to understanding diversity: A study of preservice teachers." *Equity and Excellence in Education*,
28(1), 25–30.

Bonnie, M., and Hasan, N. T. (2004). "Arab
American persons' reported experiences
of discrimination and mental health:
The mediating role of personal control."
Journal of Counseling Psychology, *51*(4),
418–426.

Boyd, N. (1977). "Perceptions of black
families in therapy." Unpublished
doctoral dissertation, Teacher's College,
Columbia University, New York.

Boyd, N. (1982). "Family therapy with
black families." In E. E. Jones and S. J.
Korchin (Eds.), *Minority mental health*
(pp. 227–249). New York: Praeger.

Bowlby, J. (1951). *Maternal care and mental
health*. Monograph. Geneva: World
Health Organization.

Bowlby, J. (1953). *Child care and the growth
of love*. London: Penguin.

Bowlby, J. (1969). *Attachment and loss.
Vol. 1. Loss*. New York: Basic Books.

Bowlby, J. (1980). *Loss: Sadness and depression. Attachment and loss: Vol. 3* (International psychoanalytical library no.109).
London: Hogarth Press.

Braginsky, B., and Braginsky, D. (1974).
Methods of madness: A critique.
New York: Holt, Rinehart, & Winston.

Brammer, R. (2012). *Diversity in counseling*.
Belmont, Calif.: Brooks/Cole.

Brave Heart, M. Y. H. (1995). "The return to the sacred path: Healing from historical trauma and historical unresolved grief among the Lakota." Unpublished doctoral dissertation, Smith College School of Social Work, Northampton, Mass.

Brave Heart, M. Y. H. (2004). "The historic trauma response among Natives and its relationship to substance abuse." In E. Nebelkof and M. Phillips, *Healing and mental health for Native Americans: Speaking in red.* Walnut Creek, Calif.: Alta Mira Press.

Breiding, M. J. (2014). Prevalence and characteristics of sexual violence, stalking, and intimate partner violence victimization—National Intimate Partner and Sexual Violence Survey, United States, 2011. *Morbidity and mortality weekly report. Surveillance summaries (Washington, DC: 2002), 63*(8), 1.

Brendtro, L. K., and Longhurst, J. E. (2005). "The resilient brain." *Reclaiming Children and Youth, 14*(1), 52–60.

Brittian, A. S., Kim, S. Y., Armenta, B. E., Lee, R. M., Umaña-Taylor, A. J., Schwartz, S. J., . . ., Castillo, L. G. (2015). "Do dimensions of ethnic identity mediate the association between perceived ethnic group discrimination and depressive symptoms?" *Cultural Diversity and Ethnic Minority Psychology, 21*(1), 41.

Brodkin, K. (1998). *How Jews became white folks and what that says about race in America.* Piscataway, N.J.: Rutgers.

Brody, L. R., & Hall, J. (1993). Gender and emotion. In M. Lewis & J. Haviland (Eds.), Handbook of emotions (pp. 447–461). New York: Guilford Press.

Brooks, M. (1998). "Men's views on male hormonal contraception—a survey of the views of attenders at a fitness centre in Bristol, UK." *British Journal of Family Planning, 24*(1), 7–17.

Broverman, I. K., Broverman, D. M., Clarkson, F. E., Rosenkrantz, P. S., and Vogel, S. R. (1970). "Sex-role stereotypes and clinical judgments of mental health." *Journal of Consulting and Clinical Psychology, 34*(1), 1–7.

Brown, M. T., and Landrum-Brown, J. (1995). "Counselor supervision: Cross-cultural perspectives." In J. P. Ponterotto, J. M. Casas, L. A. Suzuki, and C. M. Alexander (Eds.), *Handbook of multicultural counseling* (pp. 263–287). Thousand Oaks, Calif.: SAGE.

Budhwani, H., Hearld, K. R., and Chavez-Yenter, D. (2015). "Generalized Anxiety Disorder in racial and ethnic minorities: A case of nativity and contextual factors." *Journal of Affective Disorders, 175:* 275–280. doi:10.1016/j.jad.2015.01.035

Burroughs, M. (1968). *What shall I tell my children who are black?* Chicago: M.A.A.H. Press.

Burton, M., Boyle, S., Harris, C, and Kagan, C. (2007). "Community psychology in Britain." In S. Reich, M, Riemer, I. Prilleltensky, and M. Montero (Eds.), *International community psychology: History and theories* (pp. 219–237). New York: Springer.

Cabral, R. R., and Smith, T. B. (2011). "Racial/ethnic matching of clients and therapists in mental health services: a meta-analytic review of preferences, perceptions, and outcomes." *Journal of Counseling Psychology, 58*(4):537–554. doi: 10.1037/a0025266

Cardinal, M. (1984). *The words to say it.* London: Picador.

Carr, P. B., Dweck, C. S., and Pauker, K. (2012). "Prejudiced behavior without prejudice? Beliefs about the malleability of prejudice affect interracial interactions." *Journal of Personality and Social Psychology, 103*(3), 452–471. doi:10.1037/a0028849

Carrasquillo, A. L. (1991). *Hispanic children and youth in the United States.* New York: Garland.

Carrillo, C. (1982). "Changing norms of Hispanic families: Implications for treatment." In E. E. Jones and S. J. Korchin (Eds.), *Minority mental health* (pp. 250–266). New York: Praeger.

Carson, E. A., Markman, J., Kaeble, D., Maruschak, L., & Alper, M. (2016). Retrieved from https://www.bjs.gov/content/pub/ascii/p15.txt

Casas, J. M., and Pytluk, S. D. (1995). "Hispanic identity development: Implications for research and practice." In J. P. Ponterotto, J. M. Casas, L. A. Suzuki, and C. M. Alexander (Eds.), *Handbook of multicultural counseling* (pp. 155–180). Thousand Oaks, Calif.: SAGE.

Center for the Empowerment of Refugees and Immigrants. Website: http://cerieastbay.org/web3/index.php

Chao, R. C. L., and Zhang, Y. S. D. (2017). "Going through cultural barriers in counseling." In Anderson, S. K., and Middleton, V. A. (Eds.), *Explorations in diversity: Examining the complexities of privilege, discrimination, and oppression* (pp. 45–48). Oxford, U.K.: Oxford University Press.

Chu, J., Leino, A., Pflum, S., and Sue, S. (2016). "A model for the theoretical basis of cultural competency to guide psychotherapy." *Professional Psychology: Research and Practice, 47*(1), 18–29. doi:10.1037/pro0000055

Churchill, W. (1994). *Indians are us? Culture and genocide in Native North America.* Monroe, Mass.: Common Courage Press.

Clark, C. (1972). "Black studies or the study of black people." In R. L. Jones (Ed.), *Black psychology* (pp. 3–17). New York: Harper & Row.

Clark, K., and Clark, M. (1947). "Racial identification and preference in Negro children." In T. H. Newcomb and E. L. Hartley (Eds.), *Readings in social psychology* (pp. 169–178). New York: Henry Holt.

Clark, K. B. (1963). *Prejudice and your child.* Boston: Beacon Press.

Clark, K. B., Chein, I., and Cook, S. W. (2004). "The effects of segregation and the consequences of desegregation: A (September 1952) Social Science Statement in the *Brown v. Board of Education of Topeka* Supreme Court case." *American Psychologist, 59* (September), 495–501.

Cobb, C. L., Xie, D., Meca, A., and Schwartz, S. J. (2017). "Acculturation, discrimination, and depression among unauthorized Latinos/as in the United States." *Cultural Diversity and Ethnic Minority Psychology, 23*(2), 258.

Cobbs, P. (1972). "Ethnotherapy in groups." In L. Solomon and B. Berzon (Eds.), *New perspectives on encounter groups* (pp. 383–403). San Francisco: Jossey-Bass.

Cochran, S. V., & Rabinowitz, F. E. (1999). *Men and depression: Clinical and empirical perspectives.* Elsevier.

Cohen, J. A., Mannarino, A. P., and Deblinger, E. (2006). *Treating trauma and traumatic grief in children and adolescents.* Guilford Publications.

Colby, S. L., and Ortman, J. M. (2015). "Projection of the size and composition of the US population: 2014 to 2060." *US Census Bureau, 9.*

Coleman, D., and Gates, H. (1999). "Seven elements of cultural competency." In *The way of cultural competency: A conceptual framework*. Madison, Wisc.: Mental Health Center of Dane County.

Collett, J., and Serrano, B. (1992). "Stirring it up: The inclusive classroom." In L. L. B. Borders and N. Van Note Chism (Eds.), *Teaching for diversity* (pp. 35–48). San Francisco: Jossey-Bass.

Comas-Díaz, L. (2016). "Racial trauma recovery: A race-informed therapeutic approach to racial wounds." In A. N. Alvarez, C. T. H. Liang, and H. A. Neville (Eds.), *Cultural, racial, and ethnic psychology book series. The cost of racism for people of color: Contextualizing experiences of discrimination* (pp. 249–272). Washington, D.C.: American Psychological Association.

Committee for Workers International. (November 2001). *Hate crimes on the rise. Justice: The papers of the U.S.-Section of CWI.*

Constantine, M. G., and Sue, D. W. (2007). "Perceptions of racial microaggressions among Black supervisees in cross-racial dyads." *Journal of Counseling Psychology*, 54, 142–153.

Cook, A., Spinazzola, J., Ford, J., Lanktree, C., Blaustein, M., Cloitre, M., . . ., Mallah, K. (2017). "Complex trauma in children and adolescents." *Psychiatric Annals*, 35(5), 390–398.

Cook, D. T. (2005). "The dichotomous child in and of commercial culture." *Childhood*, 12(2), 155–159.

Cook, V. (2016). *Second language learning and language teaching*. New York: Routledge.

Costello, R. M. (1977). "Construction and cross-validation of an MMPI Black-White scale." *Journal of Personality Assessment, 41*, 515–519.

Council for Standards in Human Service Education. (2009). *National Standards for Master's Degree in Human Services*. Website: https://www.nationalhuman services.org/ethical-standards.

Courtenay, W. H. (1998). College men's health: An overview and a call to action. *Journal of American college health*, 46(6), 279–290.

Courtenay, W. H. (2000). Constructions of masculinity and their influence on men's well-being: a theory of gender and health. *Social science & medicine*, 50(10), 1385–1401.

Cross, T. L. (1988). "Services to minority populations: What does it mean to be a culturally competent professional?" *Focal Point*. Portland, OR: Research and Training Center, Portland State University.

Cross, T. L., Bazron, B. J., Dennis, K. W., and Isaacs, M. R. (1989). *Towards a culturally competent system of care*. Washington, D.C.: Georgetown University Child Development Center.

Cross, W. E. (1971). "The Negro-to-black conversion experience: Toward a psychology of black liberation." *Black World, 20*(9), 13–27.

Cross, W. E. (1995). "The psychology of Nigrescence: Revising the Cross model." In J. P. Ponterotto, J. M. Casas, L. A. Suzuki, and C. M. Alexander (Eds.), *Handbook of multicultural counseling* (pp. 93–122). Thousand Oaks, Calif.: SAGE.

Cunningham, J. K., Solomon, T. A., and Muramoto, M. L. (2016). "Alcohol use among Native Americans compared to whites: Examining the veracity of the 'Native American elevated alcohol consumption' belief." *Drug & Alcohol Dependence, 160*, 65–75.

Curry, N. E., and Johnson, C. N. (1990). *Beyond self-esteem: Developing a genuine sense of human value.* Washington, D.C.: National Association for the Education of Young Children.

Curtin, S. C., Warner, M., & Hedegaard, H. (2016). *Increase in suicide in the United States,* 1999–2014.

Daly, A., Jennings, J., Beckett, J. O., and Leashore, B. R. (1995). "Effective coping strategies of African Americans." *Social Work, 40,* 240–248.

Dana, R. H. (1988). "Culturally diverse groups and MMPI interpretation." *Professional Psychology, 19*(5), 490–495.

D'Andrea, M. (1992). "The violence of our silence." *Guideposts, 35*(4), 31.

D'Andrea, M., and Daniels, J. (1995). "Promoting multiculturalism and organizational change in the counseling profession: A case study." In J. P. Ponterotto, J. M. Casas, L. A. Suzuki, and C. M. Alexander (Eds.), *Handbook of multicultural counseling* (pp. 17–33). Thousand Oaks, Calif.: SAGE.

Das, A. K. and Kemp, S. F. (1997). "Between two worlds: Counseling South Asian Americans." *Journal of Multicultural Counseling and Development, 25*(1), 23–33.

Davies, J. A., Shen-Miller, D. S., and Isacco, A. (2010). "The men's center approach to addressing the health crisis of college men." *Professional Psychology: Research and Practice, 41*(4), 347.

Delgado, R., and Stefancic, J. (2017). *Critical race theory: An introduction.* New York: NYU Press.

Desmond, M., and Emirbayer, M. (2016). *Race in America.* New York: W.W. Norton.

DeVoe, E. R., and Ross, A. (2012). "The parenting cycle of deployment." *Military Medicine, 177*(2), 184–190.

Diamond, L. (1987). "Class formation in the swollen African state." *The Journal of Modern African Studies, 25*(4), 567–596.

Diamond, S. (2017). *In search of the primitive: A critique of civilization.* New York: Taylor & Francis.

Diller, J. V. (Ed.). (1978). *Ancient roots and modern meanings: A contemporary reader in Jewish identity.* New York: Bloch.

Diller, J. V. (1991). *Freud's Jewish identity: A case study in the impact of ethnicity.* Cranbury, N.J.: Fairleigh Dickinson University Press.

Diller, J. V. (1997). "Informal interviews about self-esteem and racism with people of color raised outside of the United States." Unpublished notes, Conference on Race and Ethnicity in Higher Education, Orlando, FL.

Diller, J. V. (2011). *Cultural diversity: A primer for human services* (4th ed.). Belmont, Calif.: Brooks/Cole.

Dillon, F. R., Odera, L., Fons-Scheyd, A., Sheu, H. B., Ebersole, R. C., and Spanierman, L. B. (2016). "A dyadic study of multicultural counseling competence." *Journal of Counseling Psychology, 63*(1), 57.

Draguns, J. G. (1981). "Counseling across cultures: Common themes and distinct approaches." *Counseling Across Cultures,* 3–21.

Duran, E., and Duran, B. (1995). *Native American postcolonial psychology.* Albany: State University of New York Press.

Dwairy, M. (2006). *Counseling and psychotherapy with Arabs and Muslims: A culturally sensitive approach.* New York: Teachers College Press, Columbia University.

Ehlers, C. L., Gizer, I. R., Gilder, D. A., and Yehuda, R. (2013). "Lifetime history of traumatic events in an American

Indian community sample: heritability and relation to substance dependence, affective disorder, conduct disorder and PTSD." *Journal of Psychiatric Research, 47*(2), 155–161.

Epstein, H. (1998). *Children of the Holocaust.* New York: Penguin Putnam.

Erikson, E. (1968). *Identity, youth, and crisis.* New York: Norton.

Erskine, R. G. (2015). *Relational patterns, therapeutic presence: Concepts and practice of integrative psychotherapy.* London: Karnac Books.

Falicov, C. J. (1986). "Cross-cultural marriages." In N. Jacobson and A. Gurman (Eds.), *Clinical handbook of marital therapy* (pp. 429–450). New York: Guilford.

Fisher, C. B. (2009). *Decoding the ethics code: A practical guide for psychologists* (pp. 87–89). Thousand Oaks, Calif.: SAGE Publishing.

Fisher, C. B., Hoagwood, K., Boyce, C., Duster, T., Frank, D. A., Grisso, T., . . ., Trimble, J. E. (2002). "Research ethics for mental health science involving ethnic minority children and youths." *American Psychologist, 57*(12), 1024.

Fisher, C. B., and Ragsdale, K. (2009). "A goodness-of-fit ethics for multicultural research." *The Handbook of Ethical Research with Ethnocultural Populations and Communities,* 3–26.

Fleming, C. M. (1992). "American Indians and Alaska natives: Changing societies past and present." In M. A. Orlandi (Ed.), *Cultural competence for evaluators: A guide for alcohol and other drug abuse prevention practitioners working with ethnic/racial communities* (pp. 147–171). Rockville, Md.: U.S. Department of Health and Human Services.

Fogelman, E. (1991). "Mourning without graves." In A. Medene (Ed.), *Storms and rainbows: The many faces of death* (pp. 25–43). Washington, D.C.: Lewis Press.

Fowers, B. J., and Davidov, B. J. (2006). "The virtue of multiculturalism: Personal transformation, character, and openness to the other." *American Psychologist, 61*(6), 581.

Freedman, D. G. (2003). "Ethnic differences in babies." In *The manner born: Birth rites in cross-cultural perspective* (p. 221). New York: AltaMira Press.

Friedman, T. L. (2006). *The world is flat: A brief history of the twenty-first century.* New York: Farrar, Straus, and Giroux.

Fuller, R. W. (2003). *Somebodies and nobodies: Overcoming the abuse of rank.* Gabriola, BC: New Society Publishers.

Gallimore, R., Boggs, J., and Jordan, C. (1974). *Culture, behavior, and education: A study of Hawaiian-Americans.* Beverly Hills, Calif.: SAGE.

Garcia Coll, C. T. (1990). "Development outcome of minority infants: A process-oriented look into our beginnings." *Child Development, 61,* 270–289.

Garcia-Preto, N. (1996). "Latino families: An overview." In M. McGoldrick, J. Giordan, and J. K. Pearce (Eds.), *Ethnicity and family therapy* (pp. 141–154). New York: Guilford.

Garlow, S. J., Purselle, D., and Heninger, M. (2005). "Ethnic differences in patterns of suicide across the life cycle." *American Journal of Psychiatry, 162*(2), 319–323.

Gaw, A. C. (1993). *Culture, ethnicity, and mental illness.* Washington, D.C.: American Psychiatric Press.

Geller, S. M. (2017). *A practical guide to cultivating therapeutic presence.* Washington, D.C.: American Psychological Association.

Geller, S. M., and Greenberg, L. S. (2012) *Therapeutic presence: A mindful approach to effective therapy.* Washington, D.C.: American Psychological Society.

Geller, S. M., Greenberg, L. S., and Watson, J. C. (2010). "Therapist and client perceptions of therapeutic presence: The development of a measure." *Psychotherapy Research, 20*(5), 599–610.

Geller, S. M., and Porges, S. W. (2014). "Therapeutic presence: Neurophysiological mechanisms mediating feeling safe in therapeutic relationships." *Journal of Psychotherapy Integration, 24*(3), 178.

Gil, E., and Drewes, A. A. (Eds.). (2015). *Cultural issues in play therapy.* Guilford Publications.

Gobodo-Madikezela, P. (2000). "On trauma and forgiveness." In F. Reid and D. Hoffman. *Long night's journey into day* [documentary], Facilitator Guide, San Francisco: California Newsreel, p. 19.

Gobodo-Madikizela, P. (2003, January 10). "The roots of Afrikaner rage," *The New York Times,* p. A23.

Gobodo-Madikizela, P. (2004). *A human being died that night: A South African Woman Confronts the Legacy of Apartheid.* Boston: Houghton Mifflin Harcourt.

Goodman, M. E. (1952). *Race awareness in young children.* London: Collier.

Gordon, M. (1964). *Assimilation in American life.* New York: Oxford University Press.

Graff, T. S. (2016). *The effect of immigration on identity: A study of Israeli immigrants in the United States of America.* Doctoral dissertation, Berkeley, Calif.: The Wright Institute.

Graham, J. R. (1987). *The MMPI: A practical guide* (2d ed.). New York: Oxford University Press.

Grant, D., and Haynes, D. (1995). "A developmental framework for cultural competence training with children." *Social Work in Education, 17,* 171–182.

Graybill, L. (1999). "South Africa's Truth and Reconciliation Commission: Ethical and theological perspectives." In J. Rosenthal (Ed.), *Ethics and international affairs* (2d ed., pp. 370–400). Washington, D.C.: Georgetown University Press.

Gready, P. (2010). *The era of transitional justice: The aftermath of the truth and reconciliation commission in South Africa and beyond.* New York: Routledge.

Grieger, I., and Ponterotto, J. G. (1995). "A framework for assessment in multicultural counseling." In J. P. Ponterotto, J. M. Casas, L. A. Suzuki, and C. M. Alexander (Eds.), *Handbook of multicultural counseling* (pp. 357–374). Thousand Oaks, Calif.: SAGE.

Grier, W. H., and Cobbs, P. M. (1992). *Black rage: Two black psychiatrists reveal the full dimensions of the inner conflicts and the desperation of black life in the United States.* New York: Basic Books.

Group for the Advancement of Psychiatry Committee on Cultural Psychiatry. (1984). *Suicide and ethnicity in the United States.* Series No. 128. New York: Brunner/Mazel.

Hacker, A. (1992). *Two nations: Black and white, separate, hostile, unequal.* New York: Ballantine.

Hale-Benson, J. (1986). *Black children: Their roots, culture, and learning styles.* Baltimore, MD.: Johns Hopkins University Press.

Han, M., and Pong, H. (2015). "Mental health help-seeking behaviors among Asian American community college students: The effect of stigma, cultural barriers, and acculturation." *Journal of College Student Development*, *56*(1), 1–14.

Hardiman, R., and Jackson, B. W. (1992). "Racial identity development: Understanding racial dynamics in college classrooms and on campus." In M. Adams (Ed.), *Promoting diversity in college classrooms: Innovative responses for the curriculum, faculty, and institutions* (pp. 21–37). San Francisco: Jossey-Bass.

Hardy, K. V., and Laszloffy, T. A. (1995). "The cultural genogram: Key to training culturally competent family therapists." *Journal of Marital and Family Therapy*, *21*(3), 227–237.

Harlow, C. W. (2005). *Hate crime reported by victims and police*. Washington, DC: US Department of Justice, Office of Justice Programs, Bureau of Justice Statistics.

Hauser, S. T., and Kasendorf, E. (1983). *Black and white identity formation*. Halabar, Fla.: Kreiger.

Hayner, P. (2000). "The truth and reconciliation commission." In F. Reid and D. Hoffman. *Long night's journey into day* [documentary], Facilitator Guide, San Francisco: California Newsreel, p. 10.

Hays, P. A. (2008). *Addressing cultural complexities in practice: Assessment, diagnosis, and therapy*. 2d ed. Washington, D.C.: American Psychological Association.

Hays, P. A. (2012). *Connecting across cultures: The helper's toolkit*. Thousand Oaks, Calif.: SAGE Publications.

Healey, J. F. (1995). *Race, ethnicity, gender, and class: The sociology of group conflict and change*. Thousand Oaks, Calif.: Forge Press.

Hearld, K. R., Budhwani, H., and Chavez-Yenter, D. (2015). "Panic attacks in minority Americans: The effects of alcohol abuse, tobacco smoking, and discrimination." *Journal of Affective Disorders*, *174*, 106–112. doi:10.1016/j.jad.2014.11.041

Helms, J. E. (1985). "Cultural identity in the treatment process." In P. Pedersen (Ed.), *Handbook of cross-cultural counseling and therapy*. Westport, Conn.: Greenwood Press.

Helms, J. E. (1990). "An overview of black racial identity theory." In J. E. Helms (Ed.), *Black and white racial identity: Theory, research, and practice* (pp. 9–32). Westport, Conn.: Greenwood Press.

Helms, J. E. (1993). "I also said, 'White racial identity influences white researchers.'" *The Counseling Psychologist*, *21*(2), 240–243.

Helms, J. E. (1995). "An update of Helms's white and people of racial identity models." In J. P. Ponterotto, J. M. Casas, L. A Suzuki, and C. M. Alexander (Eds.), *Handbook of multicultural counseling* (pp. 181–198). Thousand Oaks, Calif.: SAGE.

Henretty, J. R., Currier, J. M., Berman, J. S., and Levitt, H. M. (2014). The impact of counselor self-disclosure on clients: A meta-analytic review of experimental and quasi-experimental research. *Journal of Counseling Psychology*, *61*(2), 191.

Herman, J. (1997). *Trauma and recovery: The aftermath of violence—from domestic abuse to political terror*. New York: Basic Books.

Herman, J. L. (1997). *Trauma and recovery: The aftermath of violence: From domestic abuse to political terror* (rev. ed.). New York: Basic Books.

Hill, R. (1972). *The strengths of black families*. New York: National Urban League.

Hill, R. B. (2003). *The strengths of black families*. Lanham, Md.: University Press of America.

Hilliard, A. G. (1995). *The maroon within us: Selected essays on African American community socialization*. Baltimore: Black Classic Press.

Hines, P. M., and Boyd-Franklin, N. (1982). "Black families." In M. McGoldrick, J. K. Pearce, and J. Giordano (Eds.), *Ethnicity and family therapy* (pp. 84–107). New York: Guilford.

Ho, D. R. (1994). "Asian American perspectives." In J. U. Gordon (Ed.), *Managing multiculturalism in substance abuse services* (pp. 72–98). Thousand Oaks, Calif.: SAGE.

Ho, D. Y. (1987). Fatherhood in Chinese culture. In M. E. Lamb (Ed.), *The father's role: Cross-cultural perspectives* (pp. 227–245). New York: Routledge.

Ho, M. K. (1992). *Minority children and adolescents in therapy*. Newbury Park, Calif.: SAGE.

Ho, M. K., Rasheed, J. M., and Rasheed, M. N. (2003). *Family therapy with ethnic minorities*. Newbury Park, Calif.: SAGE.

Hollingshead, A. B., and Redlich, F. C. (1958). *Social class and mental illness*. New York: Wiley.

Holtzman, W. H., Diaz-Guerrero, R., and Swartz, J. D. (1975). *Personality: Development in two cultures*. Austin: University of Texas Press.

Hook, J. N., Farrell, J. E., Davis, D. E., DeBlaere, C., Van Tongeren, D. R., and Utsey, S. O. (2016). "Cultural humility and racial microaggressions in counseling." *Journal of Counseling Psychology, 63*(3), 269.

Howden, L., & Meyer, J. (2011). Census Briefs: Age and Sex Composition 2010. *Hyattsville, MD*.

Hoyt, C., Jr. (2012). "The pedagogy of the meaning of racism: Reconciling a discordant discourse. Social work." Retrieved from https://academic.oup .com/sw/article-abstract/57/3/225 /1888507?redirectedFrom=fulltext (PDF, 193KB).

Hsu, F. (1949). "Suppression vs. repression: A limited psychological interpretation of four cultures." *Psychiatry, 12,* 223–242.

Huey Jr, S. J., Tilley, J. L., Jones, E. O., and Smith, C. A. (2014). "The contribution of cultural competence to evidence-based care for ethnically diverse populations." *Annual Review of Clinical Psychology, 10,* 305–338.

Ignatiev, N. (1995). *How the Irish became white*. New York: Routledge.

Ikram, U. Z., Snijder, M. B., Fassaert, T. L., Schene, A. H., Kunst, A. E., and Stronks, K. (2015). "The contribution of perceived ethnic discrimination to the prevalence of depression." *European Journal of Public Health, 25*(2), 243–248. doi:10.1093/ eurpub/cku180

Imel, Z. E., Baldwin, S., Atkins, D. C., Owen, J., Baardseth, T., and Wampold, B. E. (2011). "Racial/ethnic disparities in therapist effectiveness: A conceptualization and initial study of cultural competence." *Journal of Counseling Psychology, 58*(3), 290.

Institute for the Healing of Memories. (2004). "Journey to healing and wholeness" [conference report]. Robben Island, Cape Town, South Africa: Institute for the Healing of Memories.

Internal Displacement Monitoring Center (IDMC). (2012). Global IDP statistics. www.internal-displacement .org. Accessed on March 27, 2018.

Jacobs, J. H. (1977). "Black/white interracial families: Marital process and identity development in young children."

Unpublished doctoral dissertation, the Wright Institute, Berkeley, Calif.

Jacobs, J. H. (1992). "Identity development in biracial children." In M. P. P. Root (Ed.), *Racially mixed people in America* (pp. 190–206). Newbury Park, Calif.: SAGE.

Jang, Y., Chiriboga, D. A., Herrera, J. R., Martinez Tyson, D., and Schonfeld, L. (2011). "Attitudes toward mental health services in Hispanic older adults: The role of misconceptions and personal beliefs." *Community Mental Health Journal*, *47*(2), 164–170. doi:10.1007/s10597-009-9274-8

Jensen, A. R. (1972). *Genetics and education.* New York: Harper and Row.

Jewell, D. P. (1965). "A case of a 'psychotic' Navaho Indian male." *Human Organization*, *11*(1), 32–36.

Jones, A., and Seagull, A. A. (1983). "Dimensions of the relationship between the black client and the white therapist: A theoretical overview." In D. R. Atkinson, G. Morten, and D. W. Sue (Eds.), *Counseling American minorities: A cross-cultural perspective* (2d ed., pp. 156–166). Dubuque, IA: William C. Brown.

Jones, C. P. (2000). "Levels of racism: A theoretic framework and a gardener's tale." *American Journal of Public Health*, *90*(8), 1212.

Jones, E. E., and Korchin, S. J. (1982). "Minority mental health: Perspectives." In E. E. Jones and S. J. Korchin (Eds.), *Minority mental health* (pp. 3–36). New York: Praeger.

Jones, J. M. (1972). *Prejudice and racism.* Reading, Mass.: Addison-Wesley.

Jones, J. M. (2008). "Racism on the down low: Subtle, implicit, and real." *Communique: Special section on psychology and racism: Ten years after the mini-convention*, American Psychological Association Convention, xxv–xxxi.

Jones, J. M., Kawena Begay, K., Nakagawa, Y., Cevasco, M., and Sit, J. (2016). "Multicultural counseling competence training: Adding value with multicultural consultation." *Journal of Educational & Psychological Consultation*, *26*(3), 241–265.

Jones, R. L. (1972). *Black psychology.* New York: Harper & Row.

Jung, C. G. (1934). "On the present situation of psychotherapy." In *The collected works of C. G. Jung* (1953–1979) (Vol. 10, pp. 157–173). Princeton, N.J.: Princeton University Press.

Kagen, S., and Madsen, M. (1972). "Experimental analysis of cooperation and competition of Anglo-American and Mexican-American children." *Developmental Psychology*, *6*, 49–59.

Kardiner, A., and Ovesey, L. (1951). *The mark of oppression.* Cleveland, OH: World Press.

Kendall, D. (2002). *The power of good deeds: Privileged women and the social reproduction of the upper class.* New York: Rowman & Littlefield Publishers.

Kerwin, C, and Ponterotto, J. G. (1995). "Biracial identity development: Theory and research." In J. P. Ponterotto, J. M. Casas, L. A. Suzuki, and C. M. Alexander (Eds.), *Handbook of multicultural counseling* (pp. 199–217). Thousand Oaks, Calif.: SAGE.

Keyes, Swan (2007). "Doing the white thing." *Turning Wheel Magazine* (Spring).

Kich, G. K. (1992). "The development process of asserting a biracial, bicultural identity." In M. P. P. Root (Ed.), *Racially mixed people in America* (pp. 304–317). Newbury Park, Calif.: SAGE.

Kim, K. H., and Zabelina, D. (2015). "Cultural bias in assessment: Can creativity assessment help?" *International Journal of Critical Pedagogy*, 6(2).

Kim, U., and Berry, J. W. (1993). *Indigenous psychologies*. Newbury Park, Calif.: SAGE.

Kinniburgh, K. J., Blaustein, M., Spinazzola, J., and Van der Kolk, B. A. (2017). "Attachment, self-regulation, and competency: A comprehensive intervention framework for children with complex trauma." *Psychiatric Annals*, 35(5), 424–430.

Kirmayer, L. J., Narasiah, L., Munoz, M., Rashid, M., Ryder, A. G., Guzder, J., . . ., Pottie, K. (2011). "Common mental health problems in immigrants and refugees: general approach in primary care." *Canadian Medical Association Journal*, 183(12), E959–E967.

Kivel, P. (1996). *Uprooting racism: How white people can work for racial justice*. Gabriola Island, BC: New Society Publishers.

Klein, G. (2002). *Reading into racism: Bias in children's literature and learning materials*. New York: Routledge.

Klein, J. (1980). *Jewish identity and self-esteem: Healing wounds through ethnotherapy*. New York: Institute on Pluralism and Group Identity.

Klein, J. (1981). *Ethnotherapy with Jews: Discussion Guide for Videotape Presentation*. New York: American Jewish Committee, Institute of Human Relations.

Kohout, J., and Pion, G. (1990). "Participation of ethnic minorities in psychology: Where do we stand today?" In G. Stricker, E. Davis-Russell, E. Bourg, E. Duran, W. R. Hammond, J. McHolland, . . ., B. E. Vaughn (Eds.), *Towards ethnic diversification in psychology education and training* (pp. 105–111). Washington, D.C.: American Psychological Association.

Kohout, J., and Wicherski, M. (1993). *Characteristics of graduate departments of psychology: 1991–1992*. Washington, D.C.: American Psychological Association.

Kramer, M., Rosen, B., and Willis, E. (1972). "Definitions and distributions of mental disorders in a racist society." In C. V. Willie, B. Kramer, and B. Brown (Eds.), *Racism and mental health* (pp. 353–360). Pittsburgh: University of Pittsburgh Press.

Kroeber, A. L. (1948). *Anthropology: Race, language, culture, psychology, prehistory*. London: Harrap.

Kunjufu, J. (1984). *Countering the conspiracy to destroy black boys*. Chicago: Afro-Am Publishing.

Kupers, T. A. (1999). *Prison madness: The mental health crisis behind bars and what we must do about it*. San Francisco: Jossey-Bass.

Landau, J. (1982). "Therapy with families in cultural transition." In M. McGoldrick, J. K. Pearce, and J. Giordano (Eds.), *Ethnicity and family therapy* (pp. 552–572). New York: Guilford.

Larsen, J. (1976). "Dysfunction in the evangelical family: Treatment considerations." Paper presented at the meeting of the American Association of Marriage and Family Therapists, Philadelphia.

Laszloffy, T. (2008). "Therapy with mixed-race families." In M. McGoldrick, *Revisioning family therapy: Race, culture, and gender in clinical practice* (pp. 275–285). New York: Guilford Press.

Laszloffy, T. A., and Hardy, K. V. (2000). "Uncommon strategies for a common problem: Addressing racism in family therapy." *Family Process*, 39(1), 34–51.

Lee, C. C., and Armstrong, K. L. (1995). "Indigenous models of mental health intervention: Lessons from traditional healers." In J. P. Ponterotto, J. M., Casas, L. A. Suzuki, and C. M. Alexander (Eds.), *Handbook of multicultural counseling* (pp. 441–456). Thousand Oaks, Calif.: SAGE.

Lee, E. (1996). "Asian American families: An overview." In M. McGoldrick, J. Giordan, and J. K. Pearce (Eds.), *Ethnicity and family therapy* (pp. 227–248). New York: Guilford.

Legters, L. H. (1988). "The American genocide." *Policy Studies Journal, 16*(4), 768–777.

Levitt, H. M., Minami, T., Greenspan, S. B., Puckett, J. A., Henretty, J. R., Reich, C. M., and Berman, J. S. (2016). "How therapist self-disclosure relates to alliance and outcomes: A naturalistic study." *Counselling Psychology Quarterly, 29*(1), 7–28.

Lewin, K. (1948). *Resolving social conflicts: Selected papers on group dynamics.* New York: Harper & Row.

Lewis, J. A., Dana, R. Q., Blevins, G. A. (2018). *Substance abuse counseling.* Pacific Grove, CA: Brooks Cole.

Lewis-Fernández, R., Aggarwal, N. K., Lam, P. C., Galfalvy, H., Weiss, M. G., Kirmayer, L. J., . . ., Boiler, M. (2017). "Feasibility, acceptability and clinical utility of the Cultural Formulation Interview: mixed-methods results from the DSM-5 international field trial." *British Journal of Psychiatry*, bjp–bp.

Lifton, R. (1986). *The Nazi doctors: Medical killing and the psychology of genocide.* New York: Basic Books.

Lige, Q. M., Peteet, B. J., and Brown, C. M. (2017). "Racial identity, self-esteem, and the impostor phenomenon among African American college students." *Journal of Black Psychology, 43*(4), 345–357.

Littleton, Brian P., (2016). "African American men's health: Regulating race-related stress through cognitive flexibility." *Dissertations.* 2478. http://scholarworks.wmich.edu /dissertations/2478

Liu, W. M. 24 Feb 2005 "The study of men and masculinity as an important multicultural competency consideration." *Journal of Clinical Psychology, 61*(6), 2005, 685–697.

Lorenzo-Blanco, E. I., Schwartz, S. J., Unger, J. B., Zamboanga, B. L., Des Rosiers, S. E., Baezconde-Garbanati, L., . . ., Pattarroyo, M. (2016). "Alcohol use among recent immigrant Latino/a youth: acculturation, gender, and the Theory of Reasoned Action." *Ethnicity & Health, 21*(6), 609-627.

Lu F., Lim R., and Mezzich, J. (1995). "Issues in the assessment and diagnosis of culturally diverse individuals." In J. Oldham and M. Riba (Eds.), *American Psychiatric Press Review of Psychiatry*, Vol. 14. Washington, D.C.: American Psychiatric Press.

Lum, D. (1982). *Social work practice and people of color: A process-stage approach.* Monterey, Calif.: Brooks/Cole.

Lum, R. G. (1982). "Mental health attitudes and opinions of Chinese." In E. E. Jones and S. J. Korchin (Eds.), *Minority mental health* (pp. 165–189). New York: Praeger.

Luskin, F. (1999). "Training materials." https://learningtoforgive.com.

Luskin, F. (2002). *Forgive for good.* New York: HarperCollins.

Mahalik, J. R., Good, G. E., & Englar-Carlson, M. (2003). Masculinity scripts, presenting concerns, and help seeking: Implications for practice and training. *Professional Psychology: Research and Practice, 34*(2), 123.

Manson, S., and Trimble, J. (1982). "American Indians and Alaska Native communities: Past efforts, future inquiries." In L. Snowden (Ed.), *Reaching* the underserved: Mental health needs of neglected populations (pp. 143–163). Beverly Hills, Calif.: SAGE.

Marin, G. (1992). "Issues in the measurement of acculturation among Hispanics." In K. F. Geisinger (Ed.), Psychological testing of Hispanics (pp. 235–252). Washington, D.C.: American Psychological Association.

Marshall, L. M. (2002). Cultural diversity in our schools. Belmont, Calif.: Wadsworth.

Martin, P., and Midgley, E. (2010). Immigration in America 2010. Population Bulletin Update. www.prb.org/

Mayer, J. C. (2012). "Toward an explanation of ethnocentrism versus ethnorelativism based upon reference group orientation" (pp. 29–39). Race relations and cultural differences: Educational and interpersonal perspectives. New York: Routledge.

McDougall, W. (1977). Is America safe for democracy? New York: Ayer.

McDowell, T., Knudson-Martin, C., and Bermudez, J. M. (2017). Socioculturally-attuned family therapy: Guidelines for equitable theory and practice. New York: Routledge.

McIntosh, P. (1989). "White privilege: Unpacking the invisible knapsack." Peace & Freedom, July/August, 10–12.

McWilliams, N. (2004). Psychoanalytic psychotherapy: A practitioner's guide. New York: Guilford.

Meadow, A. (1982). "Psychopathology, psychotherapy, and the Mexican-American patient." In E. E. Jones and S. J. Korchin (Eds.), Minority mental health (pp. 331–361). New York: Praeger.

Meierhenrich, J. (2014). Genocide: A reader. New York: Oxford University Press.

Melamed, D., and North, M. S. (2010). "The future in inequality." Social Psychology Quarterly, 73(4), 346–347. doi:10.1177/0190272510389008

Melton, M. L. (2018). "Ally, activist, advocate: Addressing role complexities for the multiculturally competent psychologist." Professional Psychology: Research and Practice, 49(1), 83–89. doi:10.1037/pro0000175

Memmi, A. (1965). Dominated man: Notes towards a portrait. Boston: Beacon Press.

Memmi, A. (1966). The liberation of the Jew. New York: Grossman.

Menashe, A., and Atzaba-Poria, N. (2016). "Parent–child interaction: Does parental language matter?" British Journal of Developmental Psychology, 34(4), 518–537.

Midgett, A., and Doumas, D. M. (2016). "Evaluation of service-learning-infused courses with refugee families." Journal of Multicultural Counseling and Development, 44(2), 118–134. doi:10.1002/jmcd.12041

Milgrim, S. (1974). Obedience to authority: An experimental view. New York: Harper & Row.

Minow, M. (2000). "The hope of healing: What can truth commissions do?" In R. I. Rotberg and D. Thompson (Eds.), Truth v. justice: The morality of truth commissions (pp. 235–260). Princeton, N.J.: Princeton University Press.

Minuchin, S. (1974). Families and family therapy. Cambridge, Mass.: Harvard University Press.

Minuchin, S., Montalvo, B., Guerney, G., Rosman, B., and Schumer, F. (1967). Families of the slums. New York: Basic Books.

Moon, D. G. (2018). "Changing men's health: Leading the future." World Journal of Men's Health, 36(1), 1–3.

Moynihan, D. P. (1965, March). The Negro family: The case for national action. Washington, D.C.: Office of Policy

Planning and Research, U.S. Department of Labor.

Myers, H. F. (1982). "Stress, ethnicity, and social class: A model for research with black populations." In E. E. Jones and S. J. Korchin (Eds.), *Minority mental health* (pp. 118–148). New York: Praeger.

Myers, H. F., Wyatt, G. E., Ullman, J. B., Loeb, T. B., Chin, D., Prause, N., . . ., Liu, H. (2015). "Cumulative burden of lifetime adversities: Trauma and mental health in low-SES African Americans and Latino/as." *Psychological Trauma: Theory, Research, Practice, and Policy, 7*(3), 243.

National Association for the Advancement of Colored People (NAACP). (2018), "Criminal Justice Fact Sheet." http://www .naacp.org/criminal-justice-fact-sheet/

National Center for Health Statistics (US. (2017). Health, United States, 2016: with chartbook on long-term trends in health.

Ncube, N., and Denborough, D. (2006). "The Tree of Life project: Using narrative ideas in work with vulnerable children in South Africa." *International Journal of Narrative Therapy and Community Work,* 2006#1. Videotape. Adelaide, Australia: Dulwich Center.

Neighbors, H. W., Trierweiler, S. J., Ford, B. C., and Muroff, J. R. (2003). "Racial differences in DSM diagnosis using a semi-structured instrument: The importance of clinical judgment in the diagnosis of African Americans." *Journal of Health and Social Behavior*, 237–256.

Nelson, G. and Prilleltensky, I. (2005). *Community psychology: In pursuit of liberation and well-being.* New York: Palgrave Macmillan.

Nobles, W. W. (1972). "African philosophy: Foundations for black psychology."

In R. L. Jones (Ed.), *Black psychology* (pp. 18–32). New York: Harper & Row.

Norton, D. G. (1983). "Black families' life patterns, the development of self and cognitive development of black children." In G. J. Powell, J. Yamamoto, A. Romero, and A. Morales (Eds.), *The psychosocial development of minority children* (pp. 181–193). New York: Brunner/Mazel.

Obasi, E. M., and Leong, F. T. (2009). "Psychological distress, acculturation, and mental health-seeking attitudes among people of African descent in the United States: A preliminary investigation." *Journal of Counseling Psychology, 56*(2), 227.

Obgu, J. U. (1978). *Minority education and caste: The American system in cross-cultural perspective.* New York: Academic Press.

Oetting, E. R., and Beauvais, F. (1990). "Orthogonal cultural identity theory. The cultural identification in minority adolescents." *International Journal of Addiction, 25,* 655–685.

Omar, D. (1996). "Introduction by Minister of Justice, Truth, and Reconciliation Commission." http://www.justice.gov .za/trc/legal/justice.htm.

O'Neil, J. M. (2008). "Summarizing 25 years of research on men's gender role conflict using the Gender Role Conflict Scale: New research paradigms and clinical implications." *The Counseling Psychologist, 36*(3), 358–445.

Painter, D., and Blanche, M. T. (2004). "Critical psychology in South Africa: Looking back and looking ahead." *South African Journal of Psychology, 34*(4), 520–543.

Paniagua, F. A. (2013). *Assessing and treating culturally diverse clients: A practical guide.* Thousand Oaks, Calif.: SAGE Publications.

Parham, T. (1992). "The white researcher in multicultural counseling revisited—Discussions and suggestions." Paper presented at the annual meeting of the American Psychological Association, Washington, D.C.

Pauker, K., Apfelbaum, E. P., and Spitzer, B. (2015). "When societal norms and social identity collide: The race talk dilemma for racial minority children." *Social Psychological and Personality Science, 6*(8), 887–895.

Pearl, A., and Reismann, F. (1965). *New careers for the poor: Nonprofessionals in human service.* New York: Free Press.

Pedersen, P. B., Lonner, W. J., Draguns, J. G., Trimble, J. E., and Scharron-del Rio, M. R. (Eds.). (2015). *Counseling across cultures.* Thousand Oaks, Calif.: SAGE.

Perry, T. L. (2014). "Race, color, and the adoption of biracial children." *J. Gender Race & Just., 17,* 73.

Perry, S. P., Murphy, M. C., and Dovidio, J. F. (2015). "Modern prejudice: Subtle, but unconscious? The role of Bias Awareness in Whites' perceptions of personal and others' biases." *Journal of Experimental Social Psychology,* 6164–61 78. doi:10.1016/j.jesp.2015.06.007

Peskin, H. (2009). "'Man is a wolf to man': Disorders of dehumanization in psychotherapy." A paper presented at The Wright Institute and Survivors International, March 7, 2009, Berkeley, Calif.

Pinderhughes, E. (1982). "Afro-American families and the victim system." In M. McGoldrick, J. K. Pearce, and J. Giordano (Eds.), *Ethnicity and family therapy* (pp. 108–122). New York: Guilford.

Pinderhughes, E. (1989). *Understanding race, ethnicity, and power: The key to efficacy in clinical practice.* New York: Free Press.

Pleck, J. H. (1995). The gender role strain paradigm: An update.

Pollack, M. E. (1987). A model of plan inference that distinguishes between the beliefs of actors and observers. In *Reasoning About Actions & Plans* (pp. 279–295).

Pollard, K. M., and O'Hare, W. P. (1999). "America's racial and ethnic minorities." *Population Bulletin, 54,* 3–47.

Ponterotto, J. G. (1988). "Racial consciousness development among white counselor trainees: A stage model." *Journal of Multicultural Counseling and Development, 16,* 146–156.

Ponterotto, J. P., Casas, J. M., Suzuki, L. A., and Alexander, C. M. (Eds.). (1995). *Handbook of multicultural counseling.* Thousand Oaks, Calif.: SAGE.

Ponterotto, J. G., Gretchen, D., and Chauhan, R. V. (2001). "Cultural identity and multicultural assessment: Quantitative and qualitative tools for the clinician." In L. A. Suzuki, J. G. Ponterotto, and P. J. Meller (Eds.), *Handbook of multicultural assessment: Clinical, psychological, and educational applications* (pp. 67–99). San Francisco: Jossey-Bass.

Poteat, V. P., and Anderson, C. J. (2012). "Developmental changes in sexual prejudice from early to late adolescence: The effects of gender, race, and ideology on different patterns of change." *Developmental Psychology, 48*(5), 1403–1415. doi:10.1037/a0026906

Pottie, K., Greenaway, C., Feightner, J., Welch, V., Swinkels, H., Rashid, M., . . ., Hassan, G. (2011). "Evidence-based clinical guidelines for immigrants and refugees." *Canadian Medical Association Journal, 183*(12), E824–E925.

Poussaint, A. F. (1972). *Why blacks kill blacks.* New York: Emerson Hall.

Powell, B., Hamilton, L., Manago, B., and Cheng, S. (2016). "Implications of changing family forms for children." *Annual Review of Sociology, 42,* 301–322.

Powell, G. J. (1973). "The self-concept in white and black children." In C. V. Willie, B. Kramer, and B. Brown (Eds.), *Racism and mental health* (pp. 299–318). Pittsburgh: University of Pittsburgh Press.

Prilleltensky, I. (1997). "Values, assumptions, and practices: Assessing the moral implications of psychological discourse and action." *American Psychologist, 52*(5), 517.

Reynolds, C. R., and Kaiser, S. M. (1990). "Test bias in psychological assessment." In T. B. Gutkin and C. R. Reynolds (Eds.), *The handbook of school psychology* (pp. 487–525). New York: Wiley.

Reynolds, C., and Suzuki, L. (2003). "Bias in Psychological Assessment An Empirical Review and Recommendations." In *The handbook of psychology, assessment psychology* (10th ed., pp. 82–113). Wiley.

Ricci-Cabello, Ricci-Cabello, I., Ruiz-Pérez, I., Labry-Lima, D., Olry, A., and Márquez-Calderón, S. (2010). "Do social inequalities exist in terms of the prevention, diagnosis, treatment, control and monitoring of diabetes? A systematic review." *Health & Social Care in the Community, 18*(6), 572–587.

Richardson, B. L., Macon, T. A., Mustafaa, F. N., Bogan, E. D., Cole-Lewis, Y., and Chavous, T. M. (2015). "Associations of racial discrimination and parental discrimination coping messages with African American adolescent racial identity." *Journal of Youth and Adolescence, 44*(6), 1301–1317.

Ridley, C. R., Liddle, M. C., Hill, C. L., and Li, L. C. (2001). "Ethical decision making in multicultural counseling." *Handbook of Multicultural Counseling,* 165–188.

Robinson, R. (1999). *The debt: What America Qwes to Blacks.* New York: Dutton.

Robinson-Wood, T. (2016). *The convergence of race, ethnicity, and gender: Multiple identities in counseling.* Thousand Oaks, Calif.: SAGE Publications.

Ronay, D. (2009). "White therapists addressing racism with white clients: A theoretical analysis and integrative treatment model." Doctoral dissertation, The Wright Institute, Berkeley, Calif.

Root, M. P. P. (1992). "Reconstructing the impact of trauma on personality." In L. S. Brown and M. Ballou (Eds.), *Personality and psychopathology: Feminist reappraisals* (pp. 229–265). New York: Guilford Press.

Root, M. P. (2001). "Reconstructing race, rethinking ethnicity." In A. Bellack and M. Hersen (Eds.), *Comprehensive clinical psychology: Sociocultural and individual differences* 10, 141–160. New York: Elsevier.

Rosen, E. J., and Weltman, S. F. (1996). "Jewish families: An overview." In M. McGoldrick, J. Giordan, and J. K. Pearce (Eds.), *Ethnicity and family therapy* (pp. 611–630). New York: Guilford.

Rosenberg, M. (1979). *Conceiving the self.* New York: Basic Books.

Rosenhan, D. L. (1975). "On being sane in insane places." In D. L. Rosenhan and P. London (Eds.), *Theory and research in abnormal psychology* (pp. 254–270). New York: Holt, Rinehart, & Winston.

Rosenthal, D. (1976). *Experimenter effects in behavioral research.* New York: Halsted Press.

Rosenthal, R., and Jacobson, L. (1968). *Pygmalion in the classroom: Teacher expectations and pupils' intellectual development.* New York: Holt, Rinehart, & Winston.

Rowe, W., Behrens, J. T., and Leach, M. M. (1995). "Racial/ethnic identity and social consciousness: Looking back and looking forward." In J. P. Ponterotto, J. M. Casas, L. A. Suzuki, and C. M. Alexander (Eds.), *Handbook of multicultural counseling* (pp. 218–235). Thousand Oaks, Calif.: SAGE.

Russo, N. R., Olmedo, E. L., Stapp, J., and Fulcher, R. (1981). "Women and minorities in psychology." *American Psychologist, 36*, 1315–1363.

Rutland, A., Killen, M., and Abrams, D. (2010). "A new social-cognitive developmental perspective on prejudice: The interplay between morality and group identity." *Perspectives on Psychological Science, 5*(3), 279–291. doi:10.1177/1745691610369468

Saeki, C, and Borow, H. (1985). "Counseling and psychotherapy: East and West." In P. B. Pedersen (Ed.), *Handbook of cross-cultural counseling and therapy*. Westport, Conn.: Greenwood Press.

Samuels, G. M. (2010). "Building kinship and community: Relational processes of bicultural identity among adult multiracial adoptees." *Family Process, 49*(1), 26–42. doi:10.1111/j.1545-5300.2010.01306.x

Sangalang, C. C., and Vang, C. (2017). "Intergenerational Trauma in Refugee Families: A Systematic Review." *Journal of Immigrant and Minority Health, 19*(3), 745–754.

Scanzoni, J. N. (1971). *The black family in modern society*. Chicago: University of Chicago Press.

Scarr, S. (1993). "Biological and cultural diversity: The legacy of Darwin for development." *Child Development, 64*, 1333–1353.

Seifer, R., Sameroff, A., Barrett, L., and Krafchuk, E. (1994). "Infant temperament measured by multiple observations and mother report." *Child Development, 65*, 1478–1490.

Shavelson, L., and Setterberg, F (2008). "Under the dragon–California's new culture." In *The Iranian therapist and her Cambodian clients* (pp. 100–104). Berkeley, Calif.: Heyday Books.

Singer, D., and Seldin, R. (1994). *American Jewish yearbook, 1994*. New York: American Jewish Committee.

Smail, D. (2002). "Psychology and power: Understanding human action." *Journal of Critical Psychology, Counselling and Psychotherapy, 2*(1), 1–10.

Snowden, L., and Todman, P. A. (1982). "The psychological assessment of blacks: New and needed developments." In E. E. Jones and S. J. Korchin (Eds.), *Minority mental health* (pp. 227–249). New York: Praeger.

Spenser, M. B., and Markstrom-Adams, C. (1990). "Identity processes among racial and ethnic minority children in America." *Child Development, 61*, 290–310.

Spraggins, R. E. (2005). *We the people: Women and men in the United States*. US Department of Commerce, Economics and Statistics Administration, US Census Bureau.

Stack, C. (1975). *All our kin: Strategies for survival in a black community*. New York: Harper & Row.

Staub, E. (2006). "Reconciliation after genocide, mass killing, or intractable conflict: Understanding the roots of violence, psychological recovery, and steps toward a general theory." *Political Psychology, 27*(6), 867–894.

Stonequist, E. V. (1961). *The marginal man: A study in personality and culture conflict*. New York: Russell & Russell.

Straker, G. (1999). "An interview with Gillian Straker on the Truth and Justice

Commission in South Africa." *Psychoanalytic Dialogues, 9*(2): 245–274.

Sue, D. W., Arredondo, A., and McDavis, R. J. (1992). "Multicultural counseling competencies and standards: A call to the profession." *Journal of Counseling and Development, 70,* 477–486.

Sue, D. W., Capodilupo, C. M., Torino, G. C., Bucceri, J. M., Holder, A. M. B., Nadal, K. L., and Esquilin, M. (2007). "Racial microaggressions in everyday life: Implications for clinical practice." *American Psychologist, 62*(4), 271–286.

Sue, S., and McKinney, H. (1975). "Asian Americans in the community mental health care system." *American Journal of Orthopsychiatry, 45,* 111–118.

Sue, S., McKinney, H., Allen, D., and Hall, J. (1974). "Delivery of community health services to black and white clients." *Journal of Consulting Psychology, 42,* 794–801.

Sue, D. W., and Sue, D. (1990). *Counseling the culturally different: Theory and practice.* 2nd ed. Oxford, U.K.: John Wiley & Sons.

Sue, D. W., and Sue, D. (1999). *Counseling the culturally different: Theory and practice.* 4th ed. New York: Wiley.

Sue, D. W., and Sue, D. (2012). *Counseling the culturally diverse: Theory and practice.* 6th ed. Hoboken, N.J.: John Wiley & Sons.

Sue, D. W., and Sue, D. (2015). *Counseling the culturally diverse: Theory and practice.* 7th ed. Hoboken, N.J.: John Wiley & Sons.

Sue, D., Sue, D. W., Sue, S., and Sue, D. M. (2015). *Understanding abnormal behavior.* Boston: Cengage Learning.

Sue, S., and Zane, N. (1987). "The role of culture and cultural techniques in psychotherapy: A critique and reformulation." *American Psychologist, 42,* 37–45.

Sutton, C. F., T., and Broken Nose, M. A. (1996). "American Indian families:

An overview." In M. McGoldrick, J. Giordan, and J. K. Pearce (Eds.), *Ethnicity and family therapy* (pp. 31–44). New York: Guilford.

Suzuki, L. A., and Kugler, J. F. (1995). "Intellectual and personality assessment: Multicultural perspectives." In J. P. Ponterotto, J. M. Casas, L. A. Suzuki, and C. M. Alexander (Eds.), *Handbook of multicultural counseling* (pp. 493–515). Thousand Oaks, Calif.: SAGE.

Swan, K. L., Schottelkorb, A. A., and Lancaster, S. (2015). "Relationship conditions and multicultural competence for counselors of children and adolescents." *Journal of Counseling & Development, 93*(4), 481–490.

Syed, M., and McLean, K. C. (2018). "The future of identity development research: Reflections, tensions, and challenges." In K. C. McLean and M. Syed (Eds.), *The Oxford handbook of identity development* (pp. 562–573). New York: Oxford University Press.

Tabak, L. (2011). "A thematic analysis of participant experience in the healing of memories collective, subclinical trauma treatment." Doctoral dissertation, Wright Institute, Berkeley, Calif.

Takaki, R. (1993). *A different mirror: A history of multicultural America.* Boston: Little, Brown.

Tatum, B. D. (1992). "Talking about race, learning about racism: The application of racial identity developmental theory in the classroom." *Harvard Education Review, 62*(1).

Tatum, B. D. (2017). *Why are all the Black kids sitting together in the cafeteria?: And other conversations about race.* New York: Basic Books.

Thomas, A. J., and Blackmon, S. M. (2014). "The influence of the Trayvon Martin shooting on racial socialization practices of African American parents." *Journal of Black Psychology, 41*(1), 75–89. doi:10.1177/0095798414563610

Thompson, C. (1949). "The Thompson modification of the Thematic Apperception Test." *Journal of Projective Techniques, 13,* 469–478.

Thompson, V. (2005). "What is a multicultural ally?" Curricular material developed for Multicultural Awareness course. Berkeley, Calif.: The Wright Institute.

Thornton, A., & Young-DeMarco, L. (2001). Four decades of trends in attitudes toward family issues in the United States: The 1960s through the 1990s. *Journal of marriage and family, 63*(4), 1009–1037.

Toch, H. (2017). *Violent men: An inquiry into the psychology of violence.* Washington, D.C.: American Psychological Association.

Tong, B. R. (2005). "On the confusion of psychopathology with culture: Iatrogenesis in the treatment of Chinese Americans." *The iatrogenics handbook: a critical look at research and practice in the helping professions, 355.*

Torrey, E. F. (1986). *Witch doctors and psychiatrists: The common roots of psychotherapy and its future.* New York: Harper & Row.

Totton, N. (2016). Power in the therapeutic relationship. In R. Tweedy (Ed.), *The Political Self: Understanding the Social Context for Mental Illness* (p. 29). London: Karnac Books.

Trawick-Smith, J. (2013). *Early childhood development: A multicultural perspective.* New York: Pearson Higher Ed.

Trawick-Smith, J. W., and Lisi, P. (1994). "Infusing multicultural perspectives in an early childhood development course: Effect on the knowledge and attitudes of in-service teachers." *Journal of Early Childhood Teacher Education, 15,* 8–12.

Trimble, J. E., and Fisher, C. B. (Eds.). (2006). *The handbook of ethical research with ethnocultural populations and communities.* Thousand Oaks, Calif.: SAGE.

Turner, E. A., and Richardson, J. (2016). Racial trauma is real: The impact of police shootings on African Americans. *Psychology Benefits Blog of the American Psychological Association.*

Turner, J. R. (1985). "Differential treatment and ethnicity." Unpublished notes. Berkeley, Calif.: The Wright Institute.

Tuval-Mashiach, R., Freedman, S., Bargai, N., Boker, R., Hadar, H., and Shalev, A. Y. (2004). "Coping with trauma: Narrative and cognitive perspectives." *Psychiatry, 67,* 280–293.

Umaña-Taylor, A. J., Quintana, S. M., Lee, R. M., Cross, W. E., Rivas-Drake, D., Schwartz, S. J., . . ., Seaton, E. (2014). "Ethnic and racial identity during adolescence and into young adulthood: An integrated conceptualization." *Child Development, 85*(1), 21–39.

U.S. Bureau of the Census. (2000). *Profile of selected social characteristics 2000.* Washington, D.C.: Government Printing Office.

U.S. Bureau of the Census. (2010). *Overview of race and Hispanic origin: 2010. Census briefs,* issued by Humes, K.R., Jones, N.A., and Ramirez, R.R. Website: www.census.gov/prod/cen2010/briefs/c2010br-02.pdf

U.S. Bureau of the Census. (2012). *About race.* Retrieved from https://www.census.gov/topics/population/race/about.html.

U.S. Department of Health and Human Services, Office of Minority Health. (2017). "Profile. Black/African American."

https://www.minorityhealth.hhs.gov /omh/browse.aspx?lvl=3&lvlid=61

Utsey, S. O., Ponterotto, J. G., Reynolds, A. L., and Cancelli, A. A. (2000). "Racial discrimination, coping, life satisfaction, and self-esteem among African Americans." *Journal of Counseling & Development*, *78*(1), 72–80.

Valentine, C. A. (1971). "Deficit, difference, and bicultural models of Afro-American behavior." *Harvard Educational Review*, *41*, 135–157.

Vandello, J. A., & Bosson, J. K. (2013). Hard won and easily lost: A review and synthesis of theory and research on precarious manhood. *Psychology of Men & Masculinity*, *14*(2), 101.

van der Kolk, B. A. (2003). "The Neurobiology of Childhood Trauma and Abuse." *Child and Adolescent Clinics of North America*, *12*, 293–317.

van der Kolk, B. A., Pelcovitz, D., Roth, S., Mandel, F., McFarlane, A. C., and Herman, J. (1996). "Dissociation, somatization, and affect dysregulation: The complexity of adaptation to trauma." *American Journal of Psychiatry*, *153* (supplement), 83–93.

van der Kolk, B. A., van der Hart, O., and Marmar, C. (1996). "Dissociation and information processing and PTSD." In B. A. van der Kolk, A. C. MacFarlane, and L. Weisaeth (Eds.), *Traumatic stress: The effects of overwhelming experience in mind, body, and society* (pp. 303–327). New York: Guildford Press.

Vandiver, B. J., Cross Jr, W. E., Worrell, F. C., and Fhagen-Smith, P. E. (2002). "Validating the Cross Racial Identity Scale." *Journal of Counseling Psychology*, *49*(1), 71.

Verissimo, A. D. O., and Grella, C. E. (2017). "Influence of gender and race/ ethnicity on perceived barriers to help-seeking for alcohol or drug problems." *Journal of Substance Abuse Treatment*, *75*, 54–61.

Villatoro, A. P., Mays, V. M., Ponce, N. A., and Aneshensel, C. S. (2017). "Perceived need for mental health care: The intersection of race, ethnicity, gender, and socioeconomic status." *Society and Mental Health*, doi:10.1177/2156869317718889.

Vontress, C. E. (1981). "Racial and ethnic barriers in counseling." In P. B. Pedersen, J. G. Draguns, W. L. Lonner, and J. E. Trimble (Eds.), *Counseling across cultures* (rev. ed., pp. 87–107). Honolulu: University of Hawaii Press.

Waldegrave, C. T. (1989). "Weaving threads of meaning and distinguishing preferable patterns." In *Plenary Papers, First Australia & New Zealand Family Therapy Conference*, Christchurch, New Zealand.

Walker, A. (November 7, 2008). "An open letter to Barack Obama." https://www.theroot.com/an-open -letter-to-barack-obama-1790900340.

Wampold, B., Casas, J. M., and Atkinson, D. R. (1982). "Ethnic bias in counseling: An information-processing approach." *Journal of Counseling Psychology*, *28*, 489–503.

Waterman, J., and Walker, E. (2009). *Helping at-risk students: A group counseling approach for grades 6–9*. New York: Guilford Press.

Watters, E. (2010). *Crazy like us: The globalization of the American psyche*. New York: Free Press.

Wechsler, H., Solomon, L., and Kramer, B. (1970). *Social psychology and mental health*. New York: Holt, Rinehart, & Winston.

Weinberg, M. K., Tronick, E. Z., Cohn, J. F., & Olson, K. L. (1999). Gender differences in emotional expressivity and self-regulation during early infancy. *Developmental psychology, 35*(1), 175.

Weinstein, G., and Mellen, D. (1997). "Anti-Semitism curriculum design." In M. Adams, L. A. Bell, and P. Griffin (Eds.), *Teaching for diversity and social justice* (pp. 170–197). New York: Routledge.

Weisman, K., Johnson, M. V., and Shutts, K. (2015). "Young children's automatic encoding of social categories." *Developmental Science, 18*(6), 1036–1043.

Weiss, T. G. (2018). *Humanitarian challenges and intervention*. New York: Routledge.

Weissmark, M. S. (2004). *Justice matters: Legacies of the Holocaust and World War II*. New York: Oxford University Press.

Wester, S. R. (2008). "Thinking complexly about men, gender role conflict, and counseling psychology." *The Counseling Psychologist, 36*(3), 462–468.

White, J. (1972). "Toward a Black psychology." *Black Psychology, 4*, 5–16.

White, J. (1980). "Towards a black psychology." In R. Jones (Ed.), *Black psychology* (pp. 43–50). New York: Harper & Row.

Wigren, J. (1994). "Narrative completion in the treatment of trauma." *Psychotherapy*, 31, 415–423.

Wijeyesinghe, C. L., Griffin, P., and Love, B. (1997). "Racism curriculum design." In M. Adams, L. A. Bell, and P. Griffin (Eds.), *Teaching for diversity and social justice* (pp. 82–109). New York: Routledge.

Williams, J. E., and Morland, J. K. (1976). *Race, color, and the young child*. Chapel Hill: University of North Carolina Press.

Wilson, K. (2003). "Therapeutic landscapes and First Nations peoples: An exploration of culture, health and place." *Health & Place, 9*(2), 83–93.

Wolkind, S., and Rutter, M. (1985). *Sociocultural factors in child and adolescent psychiatry*. Boston: Blackwell Scientific.

Wright, M. A. (1998). *I'm chocolate, you're vanilla: Raising healthy black and biracial children in a race-conscious world*. San Francisco: Jossey-Bass.

Wylie, R. C. (1961). *The self-concept*. Lincoln: University of Nebraska Press.

Yamamoto, J., and Acosta, F. X. (1982). "Treatment of Asian-Americans and Hispanic-Americans: Similarities and differences." *Journal of the Academy of Psychoanalysis*, 10, 585–607.

Yamamoto, J., James, O., and Palley, N. (1968). "Cultural problems in psychiatric therapy." *Archives of General Psychiatry, 19*, 45–49.

Yehuda, R. (1999). *Risk factors for posttraumatic stress disorder*. Washington, D.C.: American Psychiatric Press.

Yip, T. (2014). "Ethnic identity in everyday life: The influence of identity development status." *Child Development, 85*(1), 205–219.

York, S. (2016). *Roots and wings: Affirming culture and preventing bias in early childhood*. St. Paul, Minn.: Redleaf Press.

Zimmermann, K. A. (2015). "American culture: Traditions and customs of the United States." *Live Science*.

Index

A

Aboud, F., 149, 150
Abrams, D., 63
Abu-Baker, K., 360
Abudabbeh, N., 359, 360–361, 362
Academic performance and learning styles, 155–156
Acceptance of differences, 22–23
Acculturation
  community breakdown and, 218–219
  immigration and, 217–218
  modes of, 352
  overview, 214–215
  South Asian Americans and, 380–382, 387–388, 392, 395, 396, 399
  stress related to, 219–221, 231–232
  views of, 215–217
  youth substance use and abuse and, 225, 228–229
Acculturative stress, 215, 231
Achievement orientation in Jewish culture, 409
Acupuncture, CERI, 264
Adames, H. Y., 278
Adams, M., 156
Adaptation of skills to accommodate differences, 22, 25, 113–114
Addis, M. E., 429
ADDRESSING Framework
  as clinical tool, 43–48
  for making culturally sensitive diagnoses, 49–52, 117
  overview, 9, 43
Adolescents. *See also* Children
  academic performance and learning styles, 155–156
  African Americans, 228
  Asian American, 227
  bicultural, 139–140
  CERI services for, 265–266
  complex trauma treatment for, 159–165
  Latino/a, 226
  Native American, 227
  racial identity in, 153–155
Adoption
  bicultural, 140–141
  of Native children, 306
Adorno, T. W., 63, 252
Advocacy, CERI, 264
Afary, Mona, 261–262, 267

African Americans, 315–335
  anger in patients with mental health issues, 205
  assessment of, 330
  bias in service delivery to, 178–179
  common problems of clients among, 329–330
  community issues among, 328–329
  demographics, 316
  establishing rapport, 331–333
  family and cultural values, 316–317, 328–329
  family therapy with, 25
  help-seeking behavior, 327–328
  history and, 324–327
  institutional racism and, 66
  parenting for self-esteem, 130–131
  preparing children for racism, 131–134
  racial identity formation in children, 147, 150–151
  relationships with Jewish Americans, 409
  reparations for, 251, 443
  risk factors among, 330–331
  Thompson on, 322–333
  youth substance abuse, 228, 230
Agency cultural competence, assessment of, 19–21, 69–71
Alexander, C. M., 81, 100
Alexithymia, 426
Allison, B. N., 218
Alloplastic orientation, 108
Allport, G. W., 62–63
Almanzan, Roberto
  on assessment, 288–289
  on career and diversity training, 280–281
  on common problems of clients, 286–287
  on establishing rapport, 289
  ethnic background and impact on work, 278–280
  on generational issues, 287–288
  on help-seeking behavior, 282, 285–286
  on Latinos/as, 281–283
  on risk factors, 290–291
  on socioeconomic and class issues, 287
  on therapeutic approaches, 290
Almeida, R., 381, 382
Alper, M., 420
Ambivalent ethnic identification, 207–208
American Counseling Association professional code, 25
American Indians. *See* Native Americans
"Americanized" families, Asian American, 340

American Psychological Association
guidelines of, 30–31
membership in, 179
American Sign Language (ASL), 434, 436
Ancient Roots and Modern Meanings, 405
Anderson, C. J., 63
Anderson, J. A., 156
Anti-racist, White therapists as, 54
Apartheid in South Africa, 72–75
Apfelbaum, E. P., 149
Apologies, 249–250
Arab and Muslim Americans, 359–376
assessment of, 370–371
authoritarian parenting, 369–370
collective personality of, 111–112, 362
common problems of clients among, 369–370
demographics, 359–360
Dwairy on, 365–376
establishing rapport, 373–374
family and cultural values, 360–362, 368–369
help-seeking behavior, 367
shared history of, 365–366
therapeutic approaches, 373–374
Arendt, H., 252
Armenta, B. E., 207
Armstrong, K. L., 183
Arredondo, A., 25, 31
Arredondo, P., 29
Asian Americans, 336–357. *See also* South Asian
Americans
assessment of, 352
common problems of clients among, 350–351
concept of helping and, 187–188
cupping by Vietnamese parents, 24
demographics, 337–339
experience of, 60
family and cultural values, 339–341, 348–350
family therapy with, 127
health care and, 3–4
help-seeking behavior of, 347–348
history and, 345–347
Hocoy on, 341–357
mental health treatment and, 184
psychological representation of, 186–187
substance abuse among youth, 227, 228–230
therapeutic approaches, 352–355
"Asian" category, 337
ASL (American Sign Language), 434, 436
Assessment
ADDRESSING framework for, 43–48
of African Americans, 330
of agency cultural competence, 19–21, 69–71
of Arab and Muslim Americans, 370–371
of Asian Americans, 352
bias in, 188–191

of culturally diverse clients, 46–48
of Jewish Americans, 414
of Latinos/as, 288–289
male clients, American, 427–428
of Native Americans, 308–310
of South Asian Americans, 394–396
for trauma, 224
Assimilation
defined, 214
of Native Americans, 298–299, 301, 305
of White ethnics, 404
Atkins, D. C., 18
Atkinson, D. R., 12, 106, 107, 179, 180, 185, 208,
210, 212, 213
Atrocities, 233–273. *See also* Genocide
defined, 234
denial of, 235, 236, 299
Holocaust, 239, 251–257
Lakota Sioux, 239–241
refugees, immigrants and, 257–268
in South Africa, 242–251
victims of, 235
Attitudes, effect on behavior of, 177–179, 202
Austin, G. A., 229
Austin, J. A., 42
Austin, J. T., 42
Authoritarian parenting, 369–370
Authoritarian personality theory, 63
Autonomy attitude status, 83
Autoplastic orientation, 108
Avoidant racial attitude type, 80
Awareness of differences
client's worldview, 27
cultural competence and, 22–23
development of, in children, 149–153
Axiology, 98

B
Baardseth, T., 18
Baldwin, S., 18
"Banality of evil," 252
Barden, S. M., 21
Bargai, N., 112
Barrett, L., 149
Baruth, L. G., 41, 116
Basic cultural competence of agencies, 20, 21
Basile, K. C., 420
Bazron, B. J., 18, 19, 20, 21, 23, 441, 446
Beauvais, F., 216
Beckett, J. O., 221
Behavior, effect of attitudes on, 177–179, 202
Behrens, J. T., 80, 81, 82, 92
"Being-becoming" dimension of culture, 102–103
Beker, J., 225–226
Bell, H., 23, 24

Bell, L. A., 85
Bencomo, A., 218
Bennett, M. B., 17
Berman, J. S., 107
Bermudez, J. M., 217
Bernal, M., 179
Bernard, B., 225–226, 227, 228
Bernstein, R., 420
Berry, J. W., 106, 215, 216
Beyond the Whiteness of White: White Mother Raising Black Sons (Lazar), 324
Bias in service delivery, 174–203
    assessment, 188–191
    attitudes toward mental health, 184
    case study, 175
    conceptualization of ethnic populations, 185–191
    cultural aspects of, 184, 202–203
    diagnosis, 191
    dissatisfaction among providers, 180–181
    effect of attitudes on behavior, 177–179
    globalization of treatment modalities, 194–195
    microaggressions in therapeutic relationship, 198–202, 203
    paraprofessionals, 182
    provider-related, 179–182, 202
    under-representation of ethnic providers, 179–180
    variations in psychopathology, 184, 191–192
Bicultural children and families, 134–141
Bicultural clients, 445
"Bicultural" families, Asian American, 340
Bilateral, cross-cultural work as, 55
Birthrates and population change, 6, 12
Black, L., 316
#BlackLivesMatter, 2–3
Black, M. C., 420
Black psychology, 115
Black Rage (Grier and Cobbs), 205
Blacks, African Americans
Black-White Scale, 190
Blair, J. P., 420
Blaustein, M., 159
Blevins, G. A., 229
Bodywork, CERI, 264
Bogan, E. D., 152
Boggs, J., 156
Boker, R., 112
Bollin, G. G., 82
Bonnie, M., 359
Borow, H., 109
Bosson, J. K., 424
Bowlby, J., 162
Boyd, N., 317, 319
Boyd-Franklin, N., 316, 317, 319

Braginsky, B., 109
Braginsky, D., 109
Brammer, R., 42
Brave Heart, M. Y. H., 222, 223, 239, 240–241, 269, 415
Breiding, M. J., 420
Brendtro, L. K., 163
Brittian, A. S., 207
Brodkin, K., 404
Brody, L. R., 422
Broken Nose, M. A., 296, 297, 298
Broverman, D. M., 177
Broverman, I. K., 177
Brown, C. M., 219
Brown, M. T., 98–99, 100, 102, 110, 179, 180, 277
Brown, S. P., 29
Bucceri, J. M., 64, 198, 200
Budhwani, H., 184
Buffer zone, creating, 128–130
Burroughs, Margaret, 128
Bystanders, impact of Truth and Reconciliation Commission on, 245–246

C
Cabral, R. R., 179, 180
Cambodia, refugees from, 261, 262–263
Cancelli, A. A., 221
Capodilupo, C. M., 64, 198, 200
Cardinal, M., 244
Carr, P. B., 63
Carrasquillo, A. L., 276
Carson, E. A., 420
Casas, J. M., 81, 100, 179, 180, 216
Case studies
    African American client, 333–335
    Arab Muslim in Israel, 374–376
    Asian American client, 355–356
    bias in service delivery, 175
    CERI services, 264–265, 266–267, 268
    Community Psychology, 123–126
    complex trauma in child, 163–165
    cross-cultural miscommunication, 104–105
    institutional racism, 69–71
    Jewish American client, 416–417
    Latino/a client, 291–292
    male clients, 430–431
    Native American client, 312–313
    school-based social justice intervention program, 169–171
    South Asian American client, 397–400
Caste system, 385–386
Castillo, L. G., 207
Castro, F., 179
Categorical thinking, 61
Celebration: Certificates and Song, 167

Center for Empowering Refugees and Immigrants
(CERI)
   adult services offered by, 263–264
   case studies, 264–265, 266–267, 268
   Community Psychology and, 262
   innovations in trauma treatment at, 267
   overview, 257, 261–262
Center for the Empowerment of Refugees and
Immigrants (CERI)
   youth services offered by, 265–266
Cerea flexibilitas, 175, 176
CERI. *See* Center for Empowering Refugees and
Immigrants (CERI)
Cevasco, M., 13
Change in helping process, 108–109
Chao, R. C. L., 108
Chavez-Dueñas, N. Y., 278
Chavez-Yenter, D., 184
Chavous, T. M., 152
Chein, Isidor, 147, 171
Chicanos/as, 284
Children, 146–173. *See also* Adolescents
   African American, 330
   bicultural, 138–140
   complex trauma treatment for, 159–165
   cross-culturally adopted, 140–141
   developmental issues in, 148–150
   effect of school segregation on, 147–148
   of Holocaust survivors and Nazis, 251–257
   minority, population of, 12
   narrative therapy with, 165–167
   racial identity development in, 147
   refugee and displaced, 259
   school-based social justice intervention program
     for, 167–171
   treatment of, 157–158
   Tree of Life exercise with, 165–167
Chin, D., 221
Chiriboga, D. A., 192
Chu, J., 19
Churchill, W., 295
"Civilized" culture, 115
Clark, C., 115
Clark, K., 150, 172, 180
Clark, K. B., 147, 171
Clark, Kenneth, 129
Clark, M., 150, 172
Clarkson, F. E., 177
Classrooms
   identity development in, 84–85
   talking about race and ethnicity in, 15–17
Clinical counseling, CERI, 264
Cloitre, M., 159
Closeness/distance, parental, 130–131
Cobb, C. L., 217

Cobbs, P., 416
Cobbs, Price, 205
Cochran, S. V., 427
Cohen, J. A., 159, 163
Cohn, J. F., 422
Colby, S. L., 12
Cole-Lewis, Y., 152
Coleman, D., 446
Collaborative, cross-cultural work as, 39
Collateral social focus, 102
Collective group experience in trauma treatment,
267
Collective personality, 111–112
Collective treatment models, 111–113, 112–113
Collectivist culture
   definitions of mental health and, 109–111
   Dwairy on, 362, 365, 368
   Hocoy on, 343–344
Collett, J., 156
Colonization, 8
The Color of Fear, 278
Comas-Díaz, L., 221
Commitment, sustained, to cultural competence, 18
Communication
   cross-cultural, 104–105
   nonverbal, mirroring of, 354
   verbal, in helping process, 107–108
Communities of color. *See also* African Americans;
   Arab and Muslim Americans; Asian Amer-
   icans; Latinos/as; Native Americans; South
   Asian Americans
   acceptance of bicultural relationships in, 136
   defined, 7
Community breakdown and acculturation,
218–219
Community facilities, underuse of, 4
Community Psychology
   case study, 123–126
   CERI and, 262
   ethnic parenting, 127
   overview, 122–123
Complex trauma, 148
Complex trauma in children and adolescents,
159–165
Conflictive racial attitude type, 81
Conscious institutional racism, 68–69
Constantine, M. G., 64
Contact attitude status, 82
Continuing education, 442–446
Control, locus of, 109
Conyers, John, 251, 443
Cook, A., 159
Cook, D. T., 159
Cook, S. W., 147, 171
Costello, R. M., 190

Council for Standards in Human Service Education (CSHSE) cultural competency requirements, 29–30

Countertransference, 177, 444

Couples, bicultural, 135–137

Courtenay, W. H., 420

Crazy Like Us: The Globalization of the American Psyche (Watters), 194

Criminal justice system, racism in, 71–72, 328

Critical psychology in South Africa, 74

Critical race theory (CRT), 46

Cross, T. L., 18, 19, 20, 21, 23, 24, 31, 34, 441, 446

Cross, W. E., 84, 208, 209–210, 211, 216, 231

Cross-cultural service delivery. *See also* Bias in service delivery; Cultural competence; Culturally diverse clients
    assessment, 8, 46–48
    characteristics of, 38–39
    choosing to provide, 441–442
    conceptualization of, 39–41
    conflicting models of, 113–116
    finding support for, 446–447
    model and assumptions of, 18–19
    overview, 3–5
    power in, 41–42
    preparation for, 44–46

CRT (critical race theory), 46

CSHSE (Council for Standards in Human Service Education) cultural competency requirements, 29–30

Cullors, Patrisse, 2

Cultural allies, 85–86

Cultural blindness of agencies, 20–21

Cultural competence, 11–35. *See also* Model of cultural competence
    in agencies, continuum of, 19–21
    author experience of, 17–18
    with children, 157–158
    demographics and, 12–13
    fear and pain of moving toward, 14–17
    importance of, 13–14
    in individual practitioners, skill areas, 21–25
    model of, 18–19
    overview, 4–6
    professional standards, 25–33
    skills of, 441
    training programs and ethical standards, 29–30

Cultural consultants, 446

Cultural destructiveness of agencies, 19–20

Cultural diversity, defined, 6. *See also* Culturally diverse clients

Cultural identity, 40

Cultural incapacity of agencies, 20

Culturally diverse clients, 37–57. *See also* Cross-cultural service delivery
    ADDRESSING framework, 43–48
    assessment, 46–48
    dangers to, 5
    diagnosis of, 49–52
    establishing rapport and first sessions, 49–52
    overview, 6–7, 38–39, 55–56, 96
    talking about race and ethnicity with, 53–55

Culturally diverse parents and families, 120–145
    bicultural, 134–141
    Community Psychology, 122–123
    parenting, 128–131

Cultural myopia, 9

Cultural pre-competence of agencies, 20, 21

Cultural proficiency of agencies, 20, 21

Cultural racism, 60, 76–77, 106

Culture, 94–119. *See also* Family and cultural values
    bias in service delivery related to, 184, 202–203
    case study, 104–105
    defined, 2, 7, 95–96
    dimensions of, 98–99
    as paradigm, 95–96, 100–101, 115, 441
    "primitive" *vs.* "civilized," 115
    racial group/race compared to, 96–98
    theories of helping and, 106

Culture-analysis approach, 371, 372

"Culture conflict" families, Asian American, 340

Cupping, 24

Curandera/curandero, 285

Currier, J. M., 107

Curry, N. E., 129

Curtin, S. C., 420

D

Daly, A., 221

Dana, R. H., 190

Dana, R. Q., 229

D'Andrea, M., 180, 181

Daniels, J., 181

Darwin, Charles, 185

Das, A. K., 380

Davies, Jon
    on assessment, 427–428
    on common problems of male clients, 426
    establishing rapport, 428–429
    gender background and impact on work, 425–426
    on seeking mental health services by male clients, 426
    on socioeconomic and class issues of male clients, 427
    subgroups of men at risk, 428
    therapeutic approaches, 429–430

Davis, D. E., 108

Deaf clients
    interpreting needs and concerns, 435–438
    overview of Deaf culture, 434–435
    resources or activities, 438–439
Deaf culture
    comparison with ethnic culture, 435
    interaction with ethnic culture, 435
    overview of, 434–435
DeBlaere, C., 108
Deblinger, E., 159, 163
Deficit theories, 185
Dehumanization, disorders of, 237–238
Delgado, R., 46
Demographics
    African American population, 316
    Arab and Muslim American population, 359–360
    Asian American population, 337–339
    changing pattern of, 8, 12–13
    Latino/a population, 275
    male clients, American, 420–421
    Native American population, 295–296
    South Asian American population, 378–380
    White ethnic population, 403
Denborough, D., 112, 165
Denial
    of atrocities, 235, 236, 299
    of feelings and beliefs about race and ethnicity, 60
    of institutional racism, 68–69
    of skin color, 147
    of White privilege, 78–80
Dennis, K. W., 18, 19, 20, 21, 23, 441, 446
Dependence, perpetuation of, 5
Dependent racial attitude type, 80
De Rossi, Cristina, 95
Desmond, M., 97–98
Destructive tendency of Western culture, 115–116
Developmental issues in adolescents
    academic performance and learning styles, 155–156
    racial identity, 153–155
Developmental issues in children
    academic performance and learning styles, 155–156
    complex trauma, 159–165
    overview, 171–172
    racial awareness, 149–153
    temperament at birth, 149
    treatment and, 157–165
Diagnosis
    bias in, 191
    culturally sensitive, 49–52
    effect of attitudes on, 178
Diamond, L., 115
Diamond, S., 115
Diamond, Stanley, 415

Difference. *See also* Awareness of differences
    acceptance of, 22–23
    in cross-cultural work, 41
    dynamics of, 22, 23–24
A Different Mirror (Takaki), 59
Diller, Jerry
    on assessment, 414
    ethnic background and impact on work, 406–407
    on family and cultural values, 410–412
    on help-seeking behavior and common problems of clients, 412–413
    on history of Jewish Americans, 408–409
    on Holocaust survivors and families, 414–415
    on identity and group belonging issues, 413–414
    on Israelis living in U.S., 415
    on Jewish Americans, 406–418
Diller, J. V., 113, 115, 208, 231
Dillon, F. R., 45
Dimensions of culture, 98–99
Disciplinary style, 130
Discrimination. *See also* Racism; Segregation
    Asian Americans and, 341, 343, 346–347
    defined, 60
    preparing children for racism, 131–134
    service delivery, 4–5
    South Asian Indians and, 382
Disintegration attitude status, 82
Dissonant racial attitude type, 80
Diversity, forms of, 445–446
"Doing-oriented" dimension of culture, 102–103
Dominant culture, 403
Dominative racial attitude type, 80–81
Doubling, 252
Doumas, D. M., 27
Dovidio, J. F., 62, 63
Doyle, A. B., 150
Draguns, J. G., 38, 106, 107
Drewes, A. A., 147
Drug and alcohol use
    acculturation and, 225, 228–229
    African American youth and, 228, 230
    Asian Americans and, 227, 228–230
    cultural meaning of recovery, 229, 230–231
    Latinos/as and, 226, 228–230
    Native Americans and, 227, 310, 313
    overview, 224–225
    trauma and, 223
DSM-5, culturally sensitive diagnoses with, 49–52
Duran, B., 106, 110, 114, 115, 116, 222, 230, 241, 269
Duran, E., 106, 110, 114, 115, 116, 222, 230, 241, 269
Dwairy, Marwan
    on Arab and Muslim Americans, 365–376
    on assessment, 370–371
    on collectivist culture, 111–112, 362, 365

Dwairy, Marwan (*Continued*)
   on common problems of clients, 369–370
   on establishing rapport, 373–374
   ethnic background and impact on work,
      363–365
   on family and cultural values, 368–369
   on help-seeking behavior, 367
   on history of Arab and Muslim Americans,
      365–366
   on religion and politics, 361
   on therapeutic approaches, 373–374
Dweck, C. S., 63

E
Ebersole, R. C., 45
Ego, 103
Ego strength, 371
Ehlers, C. L., 241
Emic approaches to cross-cultural work, 106, 115
Emirbayer, M., 97–98
Emotional expression, male, 422–423
Empathy toward targets of racism, 60
Empowerment. *See also* Center for Empowering
      Refugees and Immigrants (CERI)
   defined, 5
   working with children and, 157, 158
Encounter stage of racial identity development, 209
Englar-Carlson, M., 422
Enslavement period, 325
Epistemology, 98
Epstein, H., 222
Erikson, E., 154, 155
Erskine, R. G., 42
Esquilin, M., 64, 198, 200
Ethical standards, 29–30, 444
Ethnic conflict, 242–251. *See also* Genocide
Ethnic groups/ethnicity
   assumptions about, 7–8
   bias in conceptualization of, 185–191
   defined, 7, 40–41, 96
   demographics, 12–13
   talking about with clients, 53–55
Ethnic identity
   defined, 206
   differences in, 2
   dynamics of, 206–208
   models of development, 444
   process of, 8
Ethnic provider groups, 447
Ethnic separatism, 130
Ethnocentrism, 17, 18, 60, 98
Ethnorelativism, 17
Ethnotherapy, 416
Ethos, 98
Etic approaches to cross-cultural work, 106

Experiential, cross-cultural work as, 38–39
"Experiential communality," 103
Exposure stage of identity development, 84
Extended families
   in African American culture, 317
   in Native American culture, 297–298, 305
Extended self, 110

F
Faculty of color, 180
Falicov, C. J., 137–138, 143
"Falling out" disease, 194
Family, definitions of, 25, 157
Family and cultural values
   African Americans, 316–317, 328–329
   Arab and Muslim Americans, 360–362,
      368–369
   Asian Americans, 339–341, 348–350
   Jewish Americans, 410–412
   Latino/a population, 276–278, 281–283
   male clients, American, 422
   Native Americans, 296–299, 305–307
   South Asian Americans, 380–382, 387–388
Farrell, J. E., 108
Feightner, J., 262
Felt experience of living, 99
Fhagen-Smith, P. E., 211
Finkel, J., 82
First sessions with clients, 49–52
Fisher, C. B., 31, 33, 34
Fisher, Celia, 31
Fleming, C. M., 107, 156
Fogelman, E., 222
Fons-Scheyd, A., 45
Ford, B. C., 191
Ford, J., 159
Forest of Life, 166
Forgiveness within models of healing, 248–249
Forouzesh, Roya, 265
Frankel-Brunswik, E., 63, 252
Freedman, D. G., 149
Freedman, S., 112
Freewheeling, cross-cultural work as, 55
Freud, Sigmund, 177, 185, 235
Freud's Jewish Identity, 405
Friedman, T. L., 379
Frustration-aggression-displacement hypothesis, 63
Fulcher, R., 179
Fuller, R. W., 63

G
Gallimore, R., 156
Galton, Francis, Sir, 185
Garcia Coll, C. T., 149
Garcia-Preto, N., 276, 277

Garlow, S. J., 197
Garza, Alicia, 2
Gates, H., 446
Gaw, A. C., 191
Gay/lesbian/bisexual/transgendered community
    African American, 331
    Jewish, 416
    risk factors, 428
Geller, S. M., 42, 43
Gender role conflict (GRC), 423
Gender roles
    African Americans, 318–319
    Asian Americans, 339
    of dominant culture, 5
    expectations, 422–423
    Latinos/as, 276–277, 283
    male clients, 422–423
    South Asian Americans, 382
Gender role strain (GRS), 423
Gender stereotyping, 177–178
Genetic deficiency model, 185
Genocide
    in Cambodia, 262–263
    of Lakota Sioux, 239–241
    of Native Americans, 295
    in Nazi Germany, 251–257
Giacomo, Daniel, 254
Gil, E., 147
Gilder, D. A., 241
Gin, R. H., 107
Gizer, I. R., 241
Globalization of treatment modalities, 194–195
Goals, long-term, in helping process, 108
Gobodo-Madikizela, Pumla, 222, 234, 237, 246–247
Good, G. E., 422
Goodman, M. E., 150
Goodness-of-fit ethics, 31, 33
Gordon, M., 107, 214
Graduate training programs, 179
Graham, J. R., 190
Grandparent, 297
Grant, D., 149
Graybill, L., 112
GRC (gender role conflict), 423
Gready, P., 243, 244, 248, 249
Greenaway, C., 262
Greenberg, L. S., 43
Greenspan, S. B., 107
Grella, C. E., 229
Grief, unresolved, among Native Americans, 239–240
Grieger, I., 47, 48
Grier, William, 205
Griffin, P., 66, 77, 85, 91
Group for the Advancement of Psychiatry Committee on Cultural Psychiatry, 195

Group therapy for children, 167–171
GRS (gender role strain), 423
Guidelines on Multicultural Education, Training, Research, and Organizational Change for Psychologists (APA), 30–31
Guzder, J., 257–258, 259

H
Hacker, A., 320
Hadar, H., 112
Hale-Benson, J., 156
Hall, J., 422
Hall, Stanley G., 185
Han, M., 108, 110
Hardiman, R., 208
Hardy, K. V., 55
Harlow, C. W., 420
Hasan, N. T., 359
Hassan, G., 262
Hate crimes, 442–443
Hauser, S. T., 154, 155
Hayner, P., 242
Haynes, D., 149
Hays, Pamela, 9, 40, 43–48, 56, 117, 224
Healey, J. F., 214, 403
Health care services
    underutilization, 4
Hearld, K. R., 184
Hedegaard, H., 420
Helms, J. E., 82, 83, 84, 92, 208, 213, 231
Helping process. *See also* Cross-cultural service delivery
    key aspects of, 107–109
    racial identity development and, 212–213
    self-disclosure in, 107–108, 332
Heninger, M., 197
Henretty, J. R., 107
Herman, J., 113, 221, 223, 235, 236, 237, 244, 252, 267, 269
Herrera, J. R., 192
Hijab, 368, 375
Hill, R., 317, 318
Hilliard, A. G., 317
Hindu values, 381, 385
Hines, P. M., 316, 318, 319
Hispanic, defined, 275, 283
Historic trauma, 223, 239–241
Ho, D. R., 107, 108, 110
Ho, M. K., 100, 101, 102, 103, 127
Hocoy, Dan
    on Asian Americans, 342–357
    on assessment, 352
    on common problems of clients, 350–351
    ethnic background, 341–342
    on family and cultural values, 348–350

Hocoy, Dan (*Continued*)
  on help-seeking behavior, 347–348
  on history of Asian Americans, 345–347
  on therapeutic approaches, 352–355
Holder, A. M. B., 64, 198, 200
Hollingshead, A. B., 179
Holocaust survivors and families, 239, 251–257, 414–415
Homeopathy, CERI, 264
Hook, J. N., 108
Horton, Robert, 90
Howden, L., 420
How Jews Became White Folks (Brodkin), 404
How the Irish Became White (Ignatiev), 404
Hoyt, C., Jr., 59
Hsu, F., 192
Huey S. J., Jr., 106
Human service providers
  challenges faced, 3–4
  underutilization, 4

I

Iatrogenesis, 187
Identity. *See also* Ethnic identity; Racial identity; Racial identity development
  in bicultural children, 134, 135
  cognitive preparation for racism and, 132–133
  cultural, 40
  defined, 206
IDPs (internally displaced people), 257–258
Ignatiev, N., 404
Imel, Z. E., 18
Immersion/emersion attitude status, 83
Immersion-Emersion stage of racial identity development, 210
Immersion in cultural experiences, 446
Immigration. *See also* Acculturation; Assimilation
  of Arab and Muslim Americans, 359–360
  of Asian Americans, 337
  of Latinos/as, 275, 284, 287
  mental health issues and, 290
  population change and, 12, 13, 259–260
  of South Asian Americans, 378–379, 385, 388, 389–390
  traumatized refugee and immigrant populations, 257–268
  of White ethnics, 403
Immigration Act of 1965, 337
Implicit bias, 64–65
Impostor phenomenon, 219
Indian Americans. *See* South Asian Americans
Indian time, 297
Individualist culture, 102, 111
Individual racism, 61–65
Individual treatment models, 112–113

Individuation, 370
I Never Promised You a Rose Garden, 322
In-group behavior, 61
Insidious trauma, 224
Institute for the Healing of Memories, 117, 247–248, 270
Institution, defined, 66
Institutional racism
  case studies, 69–71
  consciousness, intent, and denial, 68–69
  defined, 60
  determining, 67–68
  implications for providers, 75–76
  overview, 66–67
Integration stage of identity development, 85
Integrative racial attitude type, 81
Intended institutional racism, 68–69
Interethnic group relations, 445
Internalization-Commitment stage of racial identity development, 210
Internalization stage of racial identity development, 210
Internally displaced people (IDPs), 257–258
"Interracial" families, Asian American, 340
Isaacs, M. R., 18, 19, 20, 21, 23, 441, 446
Israelis living in U.S., 415
Isralowitz, R., 225–226
Istighaba, 111

J

Jackson, B. W., 208
Jacobs, J. H., 135, 139, 141, 143
Jacobson, L., 23, 24, 177
James, O., 179
Jang, Y., 192
Japanese Americans, internment of, 251
Jennings, J., 221
Jensen, A. R., 185
Jewell, D. P., 175
Jewish Americans, 405–418
  assessment of, 414
  characteristics of, 407–408
  emancipation and culture of, 115–116
  establishing rapport, 416
  family and cultural values, 410–412
  help-seeking behavior and common problems of clients among, 413–414
  history and, 408–409
  Holocaust survivors and families, 239, 251–257, 414–415
  identity and group belonging issues, 413–414
  PTSD in, 223
  therapeutic approaches, 416
Jihad, 361
Johnson, C. N., 129

Jones, A., 178
Jones, C. P., 60
Jones, E. E., 185, 186, 191, 193, 197
Jones, E. O., 106
Jones, J., 29
Jones, J. M., 13, 116
Jones, J. M., 64, 67
Jordan, C., 156
Jung, C. G., 185
Justice
    in Just Therapy model, 124–125
Justice, search for, 253–257
Just Therapy model, 117, 123–126

K
Kagen, S., 156
Kaeble, D., 420
Kaipa, Sumana
    on assessment, 394–396
    on common problems of clients, 392–393
    ethnic background and impact on work, 383–384
    on help-seeking behavior, 390–392
    on history of South Asian Americans, 389–390
    on socioeconomic and class issues, 393–394
    on South Asian Americans, 384–401
    on therapeutic approaches, 396–397
Kardiner, A., 150
Kasendorf, E., 154, 155
Kawena Begay, K., 13
Kemp, S. F., 380–381
Kendall, D., 79–80
Kerwin, C., 134–135, 138–139
Keyes, Swan, 86
Kibbutzim (socialist communities), 415
Kich, G. K., 138
Killen, M., 63
Kim, K. H., 189
Kim, S. Y., 207
Kim, U., 106
Kinesics, 354
Kinship bonds, 317–318
    in African American families, 317–318
    in Native American culture, 297–298, 305, 307
Kirmayer, L. J., 257–258, 259
Kivel, P., 299, 320
Klein, J., 207, 209, 231, 413, 416, 417
Knowledge of client culture, 22, 24–25, 446
Knudson-Martin, C., 217
Kohout, J., 179, 180
Korchin, S. J., 185, 186, 191, 193, 197
Krafchuk, E., 149
Kramer, B., 178
Kramer, M., 179
Kroeber, A. L., 46
Kugler, J. F., 188

Kunjufu, J., 108
Kupers, Terry A., 71–72

L
Labor market, demographics of, 13, 260
Labry-Lima, D., 191
Lakota Sioux, 239–241
Landau, J., 217
Landrum-Brown, J., 98–99, 100, 102, 110, 277
Lanktree, C., 159
Lapsley, Michael, 112, 247, 248, 270
Larson, Johanna
    on interpreting needs and concerns, 435–438
    resources or activities, 438–439
    on terminology used, 436
Laszloffy, T., 141–142, 143
Laszloffy, T. A., 55
Latinos/as, 275–293
    Almanzan on, 281–283
    assessment, 288–289
    common problems of clients among, 286–287
    demographics, 275–276
    establishing rapport, 289
    family and cultural values, 276–278
    generational issues among, 287–288
    help-seeking behavior, 282, 285–286
    history and, 284–285
    immigrants and acculturation, 217–218
    risk factors among, 290–291
    socioeconomic and class issues in, 287
    subgroups of, 283–284
    therapeutic approaches, 290, 291–292
    youth and substance abuse, 226, 228–230
Lawson, Jack
    on alcoholism and dependency, 310
    on common problems of clients, 307
    on establishing rapport, 310–311
    ethnic background and impact on work, 299–300
    on family and cultural values, 305–307
    on help-seeking behavior, 305
    on history of Native Americans, 303–305
    on Native Americans, 300–302
    on socioeconomic and class issues, 307–308
    on therapeutic approaches, 311–312
Lazar, Jane, 324
Leach, M. M., 80, 81, 82, 92
Learning styles and academic performance, 155–156
Leashore, B. R., 221
Lee, C. C., 183
Lee, E., 339, 340
Lee, H., 229
Lee, R. M., 207, 209

Legters, L. H., 239
Leino, A., 19
Leong, F. T., 50
Levinson, D. J., 63, 252
Levitt, H. M., 107
Lewin, K., 132, 215, 218–219
Lewis, J. A., 229
Lifton, R., 252
Lige, Q. M., 219
Limberg, D., 23, 24
Lim R., 49
Lisi, P., 151
Littleton, Brian P., 220
Liu, H., 221
Locke, D. C., 29
Locus of control, 109
Locus of responsibility, 109
Loeb, T. B., 221
Loewald, Hans, 238
Logic, 98–99
Longhurst, J. E., 163
Lonner, W. J., 38, 107
Love, B., 66, 77, 85, 91
Loyalty binds, racialized, 142
Lu, F., 49
Lum, D., 192
Luskin, F., 248–249

M
Machismo, 283
Macon, T. A., 152
Madsen, M., 156
Mahalik, J. R., 422, 429
Majority/minority population, 12
Male clients, American. *See also* Gender roles;
    Women
  assessment, 427–428
  case study, 430–431
  on common problems of, 426
  demographics, 420–421
  establishing rapport, 428–429
  family and cultural values, 422
  gender role conflict/gender role strain,
      423–424
  historical background, 421
  power and privilege, 423–424
  role expectations, 423
  on seeking mental health services, 426
  socialization, 422–423
  socioeconomic and class issues of, 427
  subgroups at risk, 428
  therapeutic approaches, 429–430
Mallah, K., 159
Malleable, cross-cultural work, 39
Mannarino, A. P., 159, 163

Manning, M. L., 41, 116
Manson, S., 101
Marianismo, 283
Marin, G., 216, 217
Markman, J., 420
Markstrom-Adams, C., 151, 152
Marmar, C., 159
Márquez-Calderón, S., 191
Marriages, cross-cultural, 137–138
Martaindale, M. H., 420
Martin, P., 259
Martin, Trayvon, 2
Martinez Tyson, D., 192
Maruschak, L., 420
Matthews, J. J., 21
Maximum City (Mehta), 391
Mayer, J. C., 17
McDavis, R. J., 25
McDougall, W., 185
McDowell, T., 217
McIntosh, P., 78
McKinney, H., 49
McWilliams, N., 223
Meadow, A., 194
Meca, A., 217
Mehta, Suketu, 391
Meierhenrich, J., 252, 253
Melamed, D., 63
Mellen, D., 62
Melton, M. L., 85
Memmi, A., 136, 409
Men. *See also* Gender roles; Male clients, American
    African American, 330–331
  PTSD in Native American, 241–242
Mental health issues, 204–232. *See also* Psycholog-
    ical trauma
  assimilation and acculturation, 214–219
  cultural definitions of, 109–111
  drug and alcohol use, 224–230
  Latino/a population, 290–291
  male client population, 426
  racial identity and group belonging, 206–211
  stress, 219–221
Merrick, M. T., 420
Mestizos, 275, 283
#MeToo, 3
Meyer, J., 420
Mexican Americans, hallucinatory experiences of,
    194
Mezzich, J., 49
Microaggressions, racial, 64–65, 198–202, 203
Microassaults, 198
Microinsults, 198
Microinvalidations, 198
Middle Passage, 325

Midgett, A., 27
Midgley, E., 259, 260
Milgram, S., 252
Minami, T., 107
Mindell, Arnold, 90
Minnesota Multiphasic Personality Inventory
  (MMPI), 189–190
Minow, M., 235–236, 249, 250
Minuchin, S., 318, 319
Mismatch syndrome, 351
MMPI (Minnesota Multiphasic Personality Inven-
  tory), 189–190
MMPI-2, 190
Moaveni, Mahtab, 167–171
Model minority, 338
Model of cultural competence
  assessing agency cultural competence, 19–21
  defining professional standards, 25–26
  enforcing professional standards, 30–33
  individual skill areas, 21–25
  overview of, 18–19
  training programs and ethical standards, 29–30
Models of racial identity development, 208–211,
  212, 444
modus operandi, 105
Mono-cultural work, cross-cultural work compared
  to, 38–39
Morland, J. K., 150, 151, 152, 153, 172
Morten, G., 106, 185, 208, 210, 212, 213
Mosayara, 111
Moynihan, Daniel Patrick, 318
Multicultural ethical awareness, 31, 32–33
Multicultural ethical commitment, 31, 32
Multicultural ethical competence, 31, 32–33
Multicultural ethical decision making, 31, 33
Multiracial individuals, 134
Munoz, M., 257–258, 259
Muroff, J. R., 191
Murphy, M. C., 62, 63
Muslim Americans. *See* Arab and Muslim Americans
Mustafaa, F. N., 152
Myers, H. F., 219–220, 221

N
NAD (National Association for the Deaf), 436
Nadal, K. L., 64, 198, 200
Nakagawa, Y., 13
Naming, in Chinese culture, 345
Narasiah, L., 257–258, 259
Narrative therapy with children, 165–167
National Association for the Deaf (NAD), 436
National Institutes of Mental Health (NI H), 182
Native Americans, 295–314
  assessment of, 308–310
  case study of bias in service delivery, 175

common problems of clients among, 307
demographics, 295–296
establishing rapport, 310–311
family and cultural values, 296–299, 305–307
help-seeking behavior, 305
historic trauma and unresolved grief among,
  239–240
history and, 303–305
Lawson on, 300–302
PTSD in males of, 241–242
socioeconomic and class issues, 307–308
subgroups of, 310
substance abuse among youth, 227
therapeutic approaches, 127, 311–312
Nature and environment dimension of culture, 101,
  298–299
Nazis, children of Nazis, and reconciliation,
  251–256
Ncube, N., 112, 165
Negative ethnic identification, 207, 208
Neighbors, H. W., 191
Nelson, G., 122
New Careers for the Poor (Pearl and Reisman),
  182
Newton, P., 150
New Zealand, Just Therapy model in, 123–126
Nichols, T., 420
Nobles, W. W., 103
Noninterference in Native American culture,
  296–297
Nonverbal communication, mirroring of, 354
North, M. S., 63
Norton, D. G., 128, 129

O
OAD (Oregon Association for the Deaf), 434
Obama, Barack, 2, 97, 121–122, 142
Obasi, E. M., 50
Obgu, J. U., 155
Odera, L., 45
Oetting, E. R., 216
O'Hare, W. P., 295, 316, 337
Olmedo, E. L., 179
Olry, A., 191
Olson, K. L., 422
Omar, Dullah, 243
Ontology, 99
Oppression, family structure of Native Americans
  and, 306
Oregon Association for the Deaf (OAD), 434
Oregon Registry of Interpreters for the Deaf
  (ORID), 434
Oregon State Alcohol and Drug Office, 299
Oregon State Prison System, 299
Oregon Youth Authority, 299

ORID (Oregon Registry of Interpreters for the Deaf), 434
Ortman, J. M., 12
Out-group behavior, 61
Ovesey, L., 150
Owen, J., 18

P
"Pacific Islander" category, 337
Palley, N., 179
Paniagua, F. A., 48
Paradigm, culture as, 95–96, 100–101, 115, 441
Paralinguistics, 354
Paraprofessionals, use of, 182, 187
Parenting
    buffer zone, creating, 128–130
    overview, 128
    preparation for racism, 131–134
    for self-esteem, 130–131
Parham, T., 181
Pauker, K., 63, 149
Pearl, Arthur, 182
Pech, Sandra, 268
Pedersen, P. B., 38, 107
Peer study/supervision groups, 446
People/clients of color, defined, 7
People relations dimension of culture, 102
Perceptions, distortion of, 62
Perpetrators, impact of Truth and Reconciliation Commission on, 246–247
Perry, S. P., 62, 63
Personalismo, 277
Peskin, Harvey, 237–239, 269
Peteet, B. J., 219
Pflum, S., 19
Pinderhughes, E., 41, 47, 48
Pinderhughes, Elaine, 319
Pion, G., 180
Pleck, J. H., 422, 423
Pollack, M. E., 423
Pollard, K. M., 295, 316, 337
Pong, H., 108, 110
Ponterotto, J. G., 47, 48, 134–135, 138–139, 221
Ponterroto, J. P., 81, 100
Porges, S. W., 43
Positive ethnic identification, 207, 208
Post-enslavement period, 326–327
Post-traumatic stress disorder (PTSD)
    atrocities and, 235, 236
    in Holocaust survivors, 252
    in Native American males, 241–242
    symptoms of, 221
    trauma experience and, 236
Poteat, V. P., 63
Pottie, K., 257–258, 259, 262
Poussaint, A. F., 131–132, 134, 143

Powell, G. J., 151
Power
    in cross-cultural work, 41–42
    male, 423–424
    White privilege, 79–80, 328
Powerlessness, 41
Prause, N., 221
Pre-encounter stage of racial identity development, 209
Pre-enslavement period, 325
Pre-exposure stage of identity development, 84
Prejudice
    defined, 60
    experience of, 86–87
    psychological theories of, 62–64
    traits and tendencies supporting, 61–62
Prendergast, M. L., 229
Prilleltensky, I., 122
Primer, 3
"Primitive" culture, 115
Prison system, racism in, 71–72
Problem stories, 169–171
Professional standards, cultural competence
    defining, 25–29
    enforcing, 30–33
    training programs and ethical standards, 29–30
Proshansky, H., 150
Providers
    bias in service delivery related to, 179–182, 202
    dissatisfaction among, 180–181
    under-representation of ethnic, 179–180
Proxemics, 354
Pseudoindependence attitude status, 83
Psychobehavioral modality, 98, 100
Psychological dynamics of cross-cultural work, 39–40
Psychological trauma. *See also* Atrocities; Mental health issues
    alternative view of, 236–239
    basic dilemma, 235
    in children and adolescents, 159–165
    in Holocaust survivors and families, 414–415
    in immigrants, 257, 259–260
    in people of color, 221–224
    in refugees, 257–259, 261–268
    as stress, 232
Psychopathology, cultural variations in, 184, 191–192
PTSD. *See* Post-traumatic stress disorder (PTSD)
    in Jewish population, 223
    symptoms, 221
Puckett, J. A., 107
Purselle, D., 197
Pytluk, S. D., 216

Q

Quality of life, 99–100
Quintana, S. M., 209

R

Rabinowitz, F. E., 427
Racial acceptance, 152, 153
Racial classification ability, 150, 151, 153
Racial conditioning/training, 88
Racial evaluation, 150, 151–152, 153
Racial groups/race
    assumptions about, 7–8
    concept of, problems with, 96–97
    culture compared to, 96–98
    defined, 7, 41
    talking about with clients, 53–55
    White attitude types, 80–81, 82
Racial identity
    in adolescents, 153–155
    process of, 8
Racial identity development
    in bicultural children, 138–140, 141–142
    in children, 147, 149–153
    dimensions of change, 210
    helping process and, 212–213
    models of, 208–211, 212, 444
    in Whites, 82–84
Racial tensions, 2
Racial trauma, defined, 221
Racism
    avoid dealing with, 90–91
    cognitive preparation for, 132–134
    cultural, 76–77, 106
    defined, 60
    emotional preparation for, 131–132
    individual, 61–65
    institutional, 66–76
    levels of, 60
    microaggressions and implicit bias, 64–65
    parental attitude toward, 131
    resisting, 143
    self-awareness and, 59
    stress and, 329–330
Rankism, 63–64
Rapport, establishment of
    African American clients, 331–333
    Arab and Muslim clients, 373–374
    Asian American clients, 352–355
    Jewish American clients, 416
    Latino/a clients, 289
    male clients, 428–429
    Native American clients, 310–311
    overview, 49–52
    South Asian American clients, 394–396
Rasheed, J. M., 100, 101, 102, 103
Rasheed, M. N., 100, 101, 102, 103

Rashid, M., 257–258, 259, 262
Reactive racial attitude type, 81
Reconciliation between former enemies, 252,
    253–256
Recovery, cultural meaning of, 229, 230–231
Redlich, F. C., 179
Refugees and trauma, 257–259
Reich, C. M., 107
Reintegration attitude status, 82
Reisman, Frank, 182
Religion. *See also* Arab and Muslim Americans;
        Jewish Americans; Spirituality
    of African American population, 319–321
    of Arab population, 361
    of Asian American population, 348
    Islam, 360–361
    of Latino/a population, 275, 282–283
    in South Asia, 385
Reparations, 249–251, 443
Resilience, 157, 163
Responsibility, locus of, 109
Restitution, 249
Restorative justice, 243
Reynolds, A. L., 221
Reynolds, C., 188
Ricci-Cabello, I., 191
Richardson, B. L., 152
Richardson, J., 221
Rivas-Drake, D., 209
Robinson, R., 443
Robinson-Wood, T., 41, 209
Role flexibility within African American families,
    318–319
Ronay, Deborah, 53
Root, M. P. P., 224
Rorschach test, 190
Rosen, B., 179
Rosen, E. J., 410
Rosenberg, M., 151
Rosenhan, D. L., 176
Rosenkrantz, P. S., 177
Rosenthal, D., 177
Rosenthal, R., 177
Rowe, W., 80, 81, 82, 92
ROYA (Youth Services Program: Reviving Our
        Youths' Aspirations), 265–266
Ruiz-Pérez, I., 191
Russo, N. R., 179
Rutland, A., 63
Rutter, M., 156
Ryder, A. G., 257–258, 259

S

Saeki, C., 109
Sameroff, A., 149
Sanchez, J., 29

Sanford, R. N., 63, 252
Sangalang, C. C., 222
Sartre, Jean-Paul, 407
Scanzoni, J. N., 318
Scarr, S., 149
Scharron-del Rio, M. R., 38, 107
Schonfeld, L., 192
School-Based Social Justice Intervention Program, 167–171
Schwartz, S. J., 207, 209, 217
Seagull, A. A., 178
Seaton, E., 209
Secondary traumatization, 252
Segregation
    de jure and de facto, 68
    "Social Science Statement" on, 147–148, 171
Seifer, R., 149
Seldin, R., 403
Self, concept of, 99, 110
Self-assessment, cultural, 40
Self-awareness
    activities for, 35–36
    of cultural values and biases, 22, 23, 26
    Lawson on, 308–309
    of prejudice and racism, 59, 65
Self-disclosure in helping process, 107–108, 332
Self-esteem
    parenting for, 130–131
    racial awareness and, 150–151
Self-expression in Jewish culture, 412
Self-fulfilling prophecy, 177
Self-honesty, 18
Self-regulation of prejudice, 63
September 11, 2001, hate crimes since, 442–443
Serrano, B., 156
Setterberg, F., 262
Shafiezadeh, Hamid, 268
Shahada, 361
Shalev, A. Y., 112
Sharing and cooperation among Native
    Americans, 296
Shavelson, L., 262
Sherrell, R. S., 21
Sheu, H. B., 45
Shimmin, Rita, 90
Sikhs, 379, 389
Simpatico, 277
Simplicity in Just Therapy model, 124–125
Singer, D., 403
Singer, Joseph, 250
Singer, M., 225–226
Sit, J., 13
Skill areas of cultural competence, 21–25
Smail, D., 41
Smith, C. A., 106
Smith, S. G., 420

Smith, T. B., 179, 180
Smith, Tracy, 159–165
Snowden, L., 188, 190
Socialization, male clients, 422–423
"Social Science Statement," 147–148, 171
Social services, CERI, 264
Social trauma, defined, 222
Sociocultural issues, 2
Solomon, L., 178
South Africa
    Afrikaner rage in, 234
    institutional racism in, 72–75
    Truth and Reconciliation Commission of,
        242–251, 269–270
South Asian Americans, 378–401
    acculturation, 380–382
    assessment of, 394–396
    common problems of clients among, 392–393
    demographics, 378–380
    establishing rapport, 394–396
    family and cultural values, 380–382, 387–388
    help-seeking behavior, 390–392
    history and, 389–390
    Kaipa on, 384–401
    socioeconomic and class issues, 393–394
    therapeutic approaches, 396–397
Southern Poverty Law Center (SPLC), 2
Spanierman, L. B., 45
Spenser, M. B., 151, 152
Spinazzola, J., 159
Spirituality. *See also* Religion
    African Americans and, 321, 323
    as dimension of culture, 445
    in Just Therapy model, 124–125
Spitzer, B., 149
SPLC. *See* Southern Poverty Law Center (SPLC)
Spraggins, R. E., 420
Stack, C., 317
Stadler, H., 29
Stapp, J., 179
Staub, E., 238
Stefancic, J., 46
Stereotypes
    defined, 62
    of drug and alcohol use, 224–225
    gender, 177–178
    of Native Americans, 298–299, 304
Stevens, M. R., 420
Stonequist, E. V., 215
Storms of Life, 166–167
Straker, Gillian, 244–245
Stress. *See also* Psychological trauma
    acculturative, 215, 231–232
    experienced by people of color, 219–221
    racism and, 329–330
Strictness of families, 370, 371

Substance abuse and dependence
  ethnicity and, 224–230
  trauma and, 223
Substance Abuse Counseling (Lewis, Dana, and
  Blevins), 229
Sue, D., 25, 49, 104–105, 106, 107, 108, 109, 185,
  212, 213, 277, 278, 296, 338, 340
Sue, D. M., 49, 64
Sue, D. W., 25, 49, 64, 106, 185, 198, 200, 208, 210,
  212, 213, 277, 278, 296, 338, 340
Sue, S., 19, 49, 114, 215
Sue, S. W., 104–105, 106, 107, 108, 109
Suffering in Jewish culture, 410, 411
Suicide, rates of, across ethnic groups, 195–197
Super, J. T., 23, 24
Superego, 103
Support groups, CERI, 264
Sutton, C. E. T., 296, 297, 298
Suzuki, L., 188
Suzuki, L. A., 81, 100, 188
Swinkels, H., 262

T
Tabak, L., 112–113, 118
Tajfel's social identity theory, 63
Takaki, Ron, 59
Talking about race and ethnicity
  in classrooms, 15–17
  with culturally diverse clients, 53–55
TAT (Thematic Apperception Test), 189, 190–191
Tatum, B. D., 153–154, 155, 210
Temperament at birth, 149
Terminology, 6–7
Testing, cultural bias in, 188–191
Thematic Apperception Test (TAT), 189, 190–191
Theories
  deficit, of ethnic populations, 185
  of helping, as culture-bound, 106
  of prejudice, 63–64
Therapeutic approaches
  with African American clients, 331–333
  with Arab and Muslim American clients, 373–374
  with Asian American clients, 352–355
  with Jewish American clients, 416
  with Latino/a clients, 290, 291–292
  with male clients, 429–430
  with Native American clients, 311–312
  with South Asian American clients, 396–397
Therapeutic relationship, racial microaggressions in,
  198–202, 203
Thompson, V., 85
Thompson, Veronique
  on African Americans, 322–333
  on assessment, 330
  on common problems of clients, 329–330
  on community issues, 328–329

on establishing rapport, 331–333
ethnic background and impact on work, 321–322
on help-seeking behavior, 327–328
on history of African Americans, 324–327
on risk factors, 330–331
on therapeutic approaches, 331–333
Thornton, A., 421
Tilley, J. L., 106
Time, cultural conceptions of
  African American, 323
  Latino/as, 283
  Native American, 297
  overview, 99, 101–102
Todman, P. A., 188, 190
Tometi, Opal, 2
Tong, B. R., 186–187
Toporek, R., 29
Torino, G. C., 64, 198, 200
"Traditional" families, Asian American, 340
Traditional healing practices, 116, 182–184
Training programs, 29–30
Transpersonal dimensions of culture, 445
Trauma. See Atrocities; Psychological trauma
Trawick-Smith, J. W., 149, 151
Treatment issues. See also Therapeutic approaches
  psychological trauma, 236–239
  with trauma survivors, 223
Treatment issues with children
  complex trauma, 159–165
  narrative therapy, 165–167
  overview, 157–158
  school-based social justice intervention program,
    117, 167–171
  Tree of Life exercise, 165–167
Tree of Life exercise, 112, 117, 165–167
Trierweiler, S. J., 191
Trimble, J., 101
Trimble, J. E., 38, 107
Tronick, E. Z., 422
Trump, Donald, 2, 97
Turner, E. A., 221
Turner, J. R., 179, 186
Turtle Island, 101
Tuval-Mashiach, R., 112

U
Ullman, J. B., 221
Umaña-Taylor, A. J., 207, 209
Unconscious institutional racism, 68–69
U.N. Refugee Agency (UNHCR), 258
Untended institutional racism, 68–69
UNtraining, 90
U.S. Census classifications
  American Indians and Alaska Natives, 295
  Arab and Muslim Americans, 360
  Asian Americans, 337

U.S. Census classifications (*Continued*)
  Latinos/as, 275
  male (American), 420
  of race, 97, 134
  South Asian Americans, 378
  White ethnics, 403
Utsey, S. O., 108, 221

V

Valentine, C. A., 216
Values. *See* Family and cultural values
Vandello, J. A., 424
Van der Hart, O., 159
Van der Kolk, B. A., 159
Vandiver, B. J., 211
Vang, C., 222
Van Tongeren, D. R., 108
Vasquez, Valentino, 434–439
  on Deaf culture, 434–435
  Deaf culture and ethnic culture, comparison, 435
  on interaction of Deaf and ethnic culture, 435
  on interpreting needs and concerns, 435–438
  resources or activities, 438–439
Verbal expressiveness in helping process, 107–108
Verissimo, A. D. O., 229
Vicarious traumatization, 223–224, 252
Victims, impact of Truth and Reconciliation Commission on, 244–245
Villatoro, A. P., 49
Violence. *See* Atrocities; Psychological trauma
Vogel, S. R., 177
Vontress, C. E., 107

W

Waldegrave, Charles, 123
Walker, Alice, 121–122, 142
Walker, E., 167
Walters, M. L., 420
Wampold, B., 179
Wampold, B. E., 18
Warner, M., 420
Waterman, J., 167
Watson, J. C., 43
Watters, Ethan, 194–195, 202
Watts, Alan, 18
Wechsler, H., 178
Weinberg, M. K., 422
Weinstein, G., 62
Weinstein, Harvey, 3
Weiss, T. G., 257
Weissmark, Mona, 253–256, 270
Welch, V., 262
Weltman, S. F., 410
White, J., 115, 317
White ethnics, 403–418
  assimilation of, 214
  defined, 7, 403

demographics and cultural similarities, 403–405
Diller on, 405–418
melting pot concept and, 97
Whitely, S., 107
White privilege, 78–80, 328
Whites
  defined, 7
  obsession with time, 101–102
  racial consciousness among, 78–80
  as therapists, working with White clients, 53–54
Why Are All the Black Kids Sitting Together in the Cafeteria? (Tatum), 153
Wicherski, M., 179
Wigren, J., 112
Wijeyesinghe, C. L., 66, 77, 85, 91
Williams, J. E., 150, 151, 152, 153, 172
Willis, E., 179
Wilson, K., 110
Witness, therapeutic, in trauma treatment, 237–238
Wolkind, S., 156
Women. *See also* Gender roles; Male clients, American
  African American, 157
  bicultural, 139–140
  Jewish, 416
  refugee and displaced, 258–259
  socialization of, into dominant culture, 5
Work and activity dimension of culture, 102–103
Worldviews, 27, 98–100, 109
Worrell, F. C., 211
Wright, M. A., 130, 143
Wyatt, G. E., 221
Wylie, R. C., 129

X

Xie, D., 217

Y

Yamamoto, J., 179
Yehuda, R., 223, 241
Yip, T., 209
York, S., 150
Young-DeMarco, L., 421
Youth Services Program: Reviving Our Youths' Aspirations (ROYA), 265–266

Z

Zabelina, D., 189
Zane, N., 114, 215
Zane, N. W. S., 179, 180
Zangwill, Israel, 214
Zealot-defensive stage of identity development, 84–85
Zhang, Y. S. D., 108
Zimmerman, George, 2–3
Zimmermann, K. A., 95